Youth from Every Quarter

For P. D. Block
from his friend
Fritz Allis

Youth from Every Quarter

A BICENTENNIAL HISTORY OF
PHILLIPS ACADEMY, ANDOVER
BY FREDERICK S. ALLIS, JR.

Published by Phillips Academy, Andover
Distributed by the University Press of New England
Hanover, New Hampshire 1979

Endleaf. Students at a rally, 1956.

The University Press
of New England

Sponsoring Institutions
Brandeis University
Clark University
Dartmouth College
University of New Hampshire
University of Rhode Island
University of Vermont

Library of Congress Catalogue Card Number: 78-56168
International Standard Book Number: 0-87451-157-7
Printed in the United States of America

Library of Congress Cataloging in Publication data
will be found on the last printed page of this book.

The author and the Trustees of Phillips Academy are grateful
to the Class of 1928 for financial support that has made
possible the publication of this book.

For Laura and the girls

CONTENTS

ILLUSTRATIONS

PREFACE

THIS history of Phillips Academy is the first of four volumes to be published in connection with the 200th anniversary of the founding of the School and the 150th anniversary of the founding of Abbot Academy. There are good reasons for a number of publications, rather than one. When I was first asked to undertake the writing of the history of Phillips Academy, I was immediately concerned about the problem of including in one volume all the manifold activities of the School in recent years. When the Reverend William E. Park wrote his history for the Centennial of 1878, it was possible to cover the story in one account, for the institution had changed relatively little in its first century. When Claude M. Fuess wrote his excellent history of Andover—*An Old New England School*—in 1917, he tried to cover all the aspects of the School's past, and although he was generally successful, there were problems. For example, he had two separate chapters on athletics, including varsity athletics—"Some Baseball Stories" and "The Lure of the Game." By necessity these chapters had to be superficial, and, more important from my point of view, they were essentially digressions that interrupted the main story. The same was true of Dr. Fuess's treatment of alumni affairs. In one place, for example, there are two pages simply listing the names of important alumni who had graduated during a certain period in the School's history. (There is no record of the hurt feelings that such a list must have caused among those omitted, but the chances are that they were substantial.) Finally, when Phillips Academy merged with Abbot in 1973, it was clear that no one volume could include the history of both institutions.

As a result of these considerations, it was agreed to break the story of Phillips Academy into four parts, each dealing with one aspect of the past of the School. The history of Abbot Academy was a separate story in itself, and fortunately a highly qualified person was available to write it, my colleague Susan M. Lloyd, who was a member of the Abbot Faculty at the time of the merger and is now Instructor in History and Social Sciences at Phillips Academy. Her book, *A Singular School: Abbot Academy 1829–1973*, is in press. It was also decided to publish a separate volume on Andover athletics, especially varsity athletics; and again, fortunately, a highly qualified person, my colleague Fred H. Harrison, the most effective Director of Athletics in the history of the School and an Instructor in History and Social Sciences, agreed to undertake this study. His book will be published soon. Finally, during the twentieth century, the financial history of the School, including the work of various alumni organizations, has become so important and so complex as to deserve separate treatment. After Stanley King had retired as President of Amherst, he wrote two volumes on this aspect of Amherst's history—*"The Consecrated Eminence": The Story of the Campus and Buildings of Amherst College* (Amherst, Amherst College, 1952) and *A History of the Endowment of Amherst College* (Amherst, Amherst College, 1950). One might suppose that accounts of these subjects would be dull, but in fact King's are fascinating. Certainly the financial history of Phillips Academy is as rich as that of Amherst. Again it was fortunate that a highly qualified person, Roger M. Murray of the Class of 1928, Professor Emeritus at the Columbia University Business School, was willing to undertake this part of the story. His work should be published before too long. These decisions have allowed the present volume to concentrate on the story of Phillips Academy as an academic institution. It is concerned primarily with the Headmasters, Faculty, and undergraduates of the School—and to a lesser extent with the Trustees.

Just after I had begun work on the volume, I read a review of the history of a college in the course of which the reviewer remarked that at least the author had not divided his book into chapters according to the institution's various administrations, implying that this practice was beyond the historical pale. Whatever may be true of college presidents, the Headmasters of strong schools have nearly always been the most powerful single influence in the institution. It is hard to think of any famous American boarding school today without thinking at the same time of its Headmasters. In any event, I make no apology for my decision to center most of my chapters on the administrations of some very extraordinary men. Phillips Academy has always been noted for its great teachers, especially in the second century of its existence, and thus the Faculty deserves special treatment. One recognizes, nevertheless, that undergraduates are what the School is all about, and the book therefore includes a large number of passages from student letters and reminiscences, recording not only academic experiences, but also extracurricular activities. In the early days of the School the Trustees devoted themselves to matters that today would be in the province of the Headmaster and Faculty. One Trustee Committee reviewed discipline cases, for example, and another checked regularly on achievements of the students. With the founding of the Andover Theological Seminary in 1808, the Trustees, who were responsible for that institution as well as Phillips Academy, turned more and more of their attention to the Seminary, with the result that first the Headmaster alone and later the Headmaster and Faculty together assumed a large part of the running of the school. Since in the twentieth century the Trustees have more and more concerned themselves primarily with financial affairs, a large part of their activities rightfully belongs in Professor Murray's forthcoming study. To be sure, there were important exceptions, as in the part the Trustees played in choosing Headmasters, in dealing with the problem of the School's Secret Societies, and in bringing about coeducation. Yet for the most part they were engaged in drawing up the School budget, managing the endowment, and fund raising.

It was not long after I had begun working on the research for this book that I realized there had really been two Phillips Academies during the School's two-hundred-year existence. The first, which lasted for about a century, was essentially the creation of Eliphalet Pearson, the first "Preceptor." It was a rigid institution, concentrating on the study of the Classics, deeply concerned with inculcating in students the principles of Calvinist religion, and generally opposed to innovation. Almost everyone connected with the School during this first century subscribed wholeheartedly to the doctrine of the depravity of man. Samuel H. Taylor, Principal from 1837 to 1871, was almost a carbon copy of Pearson. There had been few modifications on Andover Hill during those hundred years. Parts I and II—"The Early Years" and "Interlude"—deal with this period. Part III, the remainder of the book, focuses on the changes introduced by Cecil Bancroft after 1873. A more flexible curriculum, less rigidity in the religious program, the development of a strong teaching Faculty who played a major part in the running of the School, and a program to house the students in dormitories owned and supervised by the School—these were some of the principal elements in the Bancroft formula. Bancroft's successors—Stearns, Fuess, and Kemper—all pretty much followed the course he had laid out. It was not until the late 1960's and early 1970's that revolutionary forces brought about a series of dramatic changes which made the School of today a very different place from what it was fifteen years ago.

Also when I first started working on this book, I was determined to relate developments at Phillips Academy to political, social, economic, and educational developments in New England in particular and in the country generally. I was convinced that too many so-called house histories were written as if the institution existed in a vacuum. As I proceeded, however, I found that realizing this aim was difficult, if not impossible, because Phillips Academy *had* existed in a vacuum—at least until well after World War II. A striking analogy that points up this situation comes from James S. Kunen, '66. He remembers that when the Great Northeast Power Blackout took place in the early 1960's, Phillips Academy, with its own power plant, continued unaffected. Only the absence of traffic lights on Main Street suggested that things were not perfectly normal. For Kunen this isolation from what was going on in the world of electric power was symbolic of the School's isolation from national events (see page 576). To be sure, the staff of the short-lived Teachers' Seminary in the 1830's were aware of new educational developments in the country, but they all left after a few years. To be sure, Cecil Bancroft sought the advice of school and college administrators in initiating his changes. Yet the evidence is overwhelming that when it came to setting educational policy, Phillips Academy "rolled its own" during most of its existence. The only clear-cut case of the School's adopting a program that another School had developed was Andover's joining the Washington Intern Program in the late 1960's —a program started by Exeter. As a result of all this, the story of Phillips Academy that I have attempted to tell concentrates almost exclusively on events that occurred on Andover Hill.

Too many institutional histories are long paeans of praise for the institution studied. For example, there is a short history of the Pullman Company that makes almost no mention of the great Pullman Strike of 1894— without question the most important event in the history of the company. When I first undertook this assignment, I insisted that I be allowed to tell the story warts and all. This was readily agreed to, but I need not have bothered. Never during the five years that I have been working on this volume has anyone tried to tell me what to write, or vetoed something I had written. This confidence in me has been one of the most heart-warming things about the experience. Headmaster Theodore R. Sizer, in particular, has invariably urged me to include even warts I was doubtful about; the only time I can remember his suggesting any change in this area was when he opined that in one place I had more warts than were necessary to make my point and that the result was overkill, a judgment I concurred with completely. I have not, however, criticized frivolously. For example, I think it is important to record the School's anti-Semitic and antiblack admissions policy during the first forty years of this century. On the other hand I see no point in recounting various pieces of Faculty gossip about colleagues, some of it salacious.

One of the pleasantest recollections I have is of the contributions made by all segments of the Andover family—particularly by alumni and undergraduates. Early on, I wrote over two hundred alumni asking for their reminiscences about Andover. The list was chosen arbitrarily: in many cases they were old friends, in others they were people who I knew could write well, in still others they represented unusual types of undergraduates. The alumni responded magnificently with over one hundred letters and tapes, many of them of the highest literary quality. A general appeal for reminiscences that was inserted in the *Andover Bulletin* elicited more. I have been troubled by the problem of attribution in dealing with these letters, and finally decided, except in a few cases, to have no specific attribution at all but simply to say, "As one alumnus remembers it," and the like. There are two main reasons for this decision. First, the thought of corresponding with each alumnus to get a release, and to make sure the quotation was just as he would have it, was appalling, especially as by that time my deadline was rapidly approaching. A more important reason is that throughout the book I have been concerned with the undergraduate body as a whole rather than with particular individuals, and the decision not to attribute was consistent with that policy. I wrote the alumni who had written me and explained my proposal. Almost all agreed to leave the matter up to me. In a few cases an alumnus specifically asked to have his name included and at the same time absolved me from any responsibility for the quotation. I have complied with these requests and have also provided specific attribution for a few communications that were not really letters of reminiscence but rather polished essays, well worth publishing in their own right. At tht end of this preface is a list of those who took the time and trouble to write me; to them all I shall always be grateful.

Any teacher welcomes an opportunity to demonstrate how able his students are, and one of my proudest satisfactions in writing this book has been the contributions made by former students. In 1970 I started a seminar in the history of Phillips Academy, for Seniors. The aim was to give the students a chance to work with archival documents—the raw material of history—and to produce papers that would be almost entirely their own creation. After the merger with Abbot, the history of that institution was included also. In the years since the course began, a substantial number of papers have been produced. Some have been disasters, but a high proportion have been true scholarly efforts, some well worth publication. By chance a few of these papers were on topics that I had not researched myself, and as source material for the book were invaluable. Full credit is given to the authors in the Notes, but I do want to salute with affection and admiration these students of mine who have contributed so importantly to the volume.

Throughout the book, in fact, I have been plagued with the problem of naming names. It soon became clear that any attempt to cite outstanding undergraduates at any particular time in the School's history would be unrealistic. I have made a very few exceptions in order to deal with special cases—for example, there is a short account of Humphrey Bogart's career at Andover. There are so many varying legends about his stay on the Hill that the record should be set straight. The problem of naming particular members of the Faculty was equally difficult. Until about 1960 I selected men who, I believed, were great teachers and presented them mainly through alumni reminiscences. Although I have no apologies to make about the ones chosen, I am sure that many alumni readers will regret the omission of a favorite teacher. Generally I have used as a yardstick the question, "Would the School have been the same if so-and-so had not been there?" The problem is compounded when it comes to dealing with teachers currently on the Faculty. I have adopted a flat policy of not naming any of them simply as teachers. Department heads, administrative officers, and people who have made important contributions to the School outside the classroom have occasionally been mentioned by name. Generally my policy with regard to names has been adopted in an effort to avoid hurt feelings, particularly among the present Faculty; but I am fully aware that in this area I cannot possibly win, and I fully expect my nose to be bloodied.

There are a few stylistic inconsistencies that should cause no problem. For example, the class designation " '35" sometimes appears as "PA '35" or "Class of 1935." Some repetition remains though much was deleted. I suppose that my repetition stems from some unconscious pedagogical urge to make sure that everybody gets the message. I am consoled by the thought that not many people will read the book from cover to cover, but will focus on the period they are most familiar with. In part because there is no bibliographical information of any kind in Dr. Fuess's history of Andover, I have annotated this volume very fully. This has meant citing every single source that I have used. To those who believe that a large number of notes is a vulgar display of would-be scholarship, my apologies.

Some friends believe that to include a long list of people who have helped in the preparation of a book is in bad taste. I do not agree. If someone has been kind enough to give me time, I would like to acknowledge it. In thanking all these good people, however, I want to make it clear that I absolve them completely from any mistakes of fact or interpretation that I may have made.

Three in particular have had a great deal to do with the preparation of the work for publication. Juliet Richardson Kellogg, Associate Archivist at Phillips Academy, has been co-worker and friend throughout the whole enterprise. She has searched the Archives indefatigably for material that I hoped was there, has read most of the chapters and made useful suggestions, has transcribed important material, and has preserved throughout this long haul a cheerfulness and an optimism that were contagious. Ruth Flick Quattlebaum, a trained researcher and the wife of Edwin G. Quattlebaum, III, '60, currently an Instructor in History and the Social Sciences at Phillips Academy, worked with the Stearns correspondence, read through and noted the entire run of close to one hundred years of *Phillipians*, did a similar job for the *Phillips Bulletin*, proved herself a true professional in hunting down pieces of information difficult to find, and finally read galley proofs with a sharp eye for both inaccuracies and stylistic infelicities. Her contribution to this volume has been substantial. Susan Lambiris, a student in my seminar in the Class of 1975, wrote an outstanding paper on the development of the Phillips Academy Curriculum. She then agreed to work as my research assistant during the following three summers. During that time she made a complete calendar of all the Bancroft correspondence and was turned loose on a variety of special topics, which she researched with rare thoroughness and imagination.

Also, Martha Larson of North Andover patiently worked her way through masses of Fuess and Kemper correspondence and spotted key documents. Her job was the more difficult because most of the official correspondence of these two gentlemen was pretty routine.

My editor and publisher, David Horne, of the University Press of New England in Hanover, New Hampshire, has been all that one could ask of an editor. Indeed I want to say quite frankly that I was by no means certain of this book's outcome until we got him aboard. He has combined editorial skill with respect for an author's independence in bringing order out of the manuscript.

Two ladies that are dear to the whole Phillips Academy community have generously helped. Marjorie Stearns, the daughter of Headmaster Alfred E. Stearns, not only turned over to the School some very important private papers of her father but also talked with me most candidly about him and about their life as a family. Abby Castle Kemper, the widow of John Kemper, let me use the transcript of her husband's interview on tape for the Columbia Oral History Project, read the Kemper chapter and made some very useful suggestions, and talked with me frankly and objectively about the School that she knows so well.

C. Lloyd Thomas, '15, the present owner of the old Phillips Mansion in North Andover and the great-great-great grandson of Samuel Phillips, Jr., generously allowed me to reproduce two Phillips portraits in his possession and also made available to me some pertinent Phillips Papers.

My colleague Susan McIntosh Lloyd, whose history of Abbot Academy, *A Singular School*, is in press, as noted above, has read most if not all of this volume and made many incisive suggestions. Even more important, perhaps, she was always willing to commiserate with me about the agonies of authorship. Anyone who wishes a full picture of life on Andover Hill over the years should read her book in conjunction with mine.

My friend Bartlett H. Hayes, Jr., '22, not only accomplished with élan the difficult task of compiling the index, but in the process read galley and page proof with a sharp eye and saved me from many errors. Since he has lived in Andover almost his entire life, he is a gold mine of information about the past of the School.

In addition, a number of other people have read all or part of this book in its early stages and made helpful comments. Headmaster Theodore R. Sizer read it all, in manuscript or galley, and contributed very important points. More significant was his continuing support for the project since its inception. My friend and colleague William H. Brown, '34, until recently Head of the English Department at Phillips Academy, read chapters that he was particularly familiar with as an undergraduate and a member of the Faculty and reassured me that from his point of view that was the way it was. Principal Stephen G. Kurtz and Dean Donald B. Cole, both of the Phillips Exeter Academy and the latter a former pupil of mine, read the early chapters when I was just getting under way and gave me the benefit of their wide experience as editors. Harriet Ropes Cabot graciously gave me permission to quote from some of the letters of her father, James

Hardy Ropes, President of the Board of Trustees at the end of Al Stearns's administration, and read over that part of the story. Three nonacademic members of the Phillips Academy staff—Frederic A. Stott, '36, Secretary of the Academy and Director of the Bicentennial Campaign; Ann Caldwell, his Associate in both these positions; and Susan McCaslin, Director of the Central Publications Office—all read parts of the book. I had more or less expected that they might view some of what I had said with alarm, but I received nothing but encouragement and helpful suggestions. Finally, two friends have read the book after it was in galley or page proof. Attorney Thomas D. Burns, '38, one of Boston's leading trial lawyers, checked my work for libel. He assured me that there was nothing libelous in it— in large part because one cannot libel dead persons—but hastened to add that this was no guarantee against my being sued. My colleague Robert E. Lane of the Classics and Russian Departments, has given my book the benefit of his professional skill as a proof-reader and has saved me from many stylistic and mechanical errors.

Susan Lloyd has made extensive use of interviews for her book on Abbot Academy. I have depended much more on written communications. But I have conducted some interviews and am grateful to those with whom I talked for giving me their time. In addition to Marjorie Stearns and Abby Kemper, the following people have talked with me: Roscoe E. Dake, Instructor Emeritus in Chemistry; John S. Barss, Instructor Emeritus in Physics, and his wife Helen; A. Graham Baldwin, School Minister Emeritus, and his wife Kay; Robert E. Maynard, Instructor Emeritus in Mathematics; Mrs. Alfred Castle, now over one hundred years old, whose memories of the old Andover are as sharp and clear as ever; and Richard Hoyer, first Superintendent of the Moncrieff Cochran Sanctuary, whose recollections of Thomas Cochran added greatly to my understanding of the man.

J. Earl Thompson, Jr., Professor of Church History at the Andover-Newton Theological Seminary and the leading authority on the history of the Andover Theological Seminary, generously let me pick his brains for one whole afternoon and in addition gave me copies of the admirable articles that he had written on that institution.

A number of people have also helped with the illustrations. Gordon G. Bensley, '43, currently Instructor in Art at Phillips Academy, had done a great deal of work on pictures of the School in connection with the production of the magnificent slide tape entitled "Here's Andover." He generously shared his findings with me, made a number of useful suggestions, read the section entitled "Explosion in the Arts" in Chapter 18, and did the actual photographing of many of the illustrations. Juliet Kellogg and Helen Eccles, Director of Public Information, worked hard to make available the large collection of photographs in their files. Laura R. Allis drew a handsome map of Phillips Academy in 1790. Andrew Rutherford, '71, has allowed me to use two of the cartoons from "A Cartoon History of

Phillips Academy," which he drew in place of a term paper in American History. Finally, Anne Parks, the School's Graphic Designer, made two very effective overlays for a map of the School that she had already drawn, so as to show the buildings constructed during the Cochran era and also those built as a result of the Andover Program. I am fortunate to have had such imaginative assistance in this area.

No one can ever write a book of this kind without massive help from libraries, and my experience is no exception. Barbara McDonnell and the entire staff of the Oliver Wendell Holmes Library at Phillips Academy have endured me—that is the only word—for the past five years with rare patience and good humor. Not only did they put themselves out to get me material, but they excused my many breaches of their procedures—forgetting to sign out books and the like. Nancy Jacobson and the staff of the Memorial Hall Library in the Town of Andover were also of great assistance on many occasions, particularly in helping me to find my way around in various microfilmed town records and local newspaper files. Malcolm Freiberg, Editor of Publications at the Massachusetts Historical Society, did a splendid editorial job on my chapter on the Phillips Academy Centennial, which was first given as a paper before the Society in somewhat abbreviated form and later published in one of the Society's publications. And others of the staff of the MHS were helpful in numerous ways. Harley Holden, Harvard Archivist, made it easy for me to locate Phillips and Bancroft material in the University's Archives, as well as pertinent letters of Charles W. Eliot. The staff of the Yale University Library pointed my way among the Park Family Papers and arranged for the Xeroxing of a number of them.

Finally, I cannot close without acknowledging the tremendous debt I owe my family—my wife, Laura Reasor Allis, and my two stepdaughters, Frances Meriwether Hughes and Laura Hayden Hughes. For years these ladies put up with a husband and father who was either surly or abstracted, and did so with extraordinary good humor. Here's a toast to all three.

Andover, Massachusetts   *F.S.A., Jr.*
August 1978

ALUMNI CONTRIBUTORS

To the Phillips Academy Alumni who contributed to the volume by recording Reminiscences of their Andover experience, either in writing or on tape, I wish to express my gratitude:

CLASS OF 1908
Sumner Smith

CLASS OF 1912
Samuel C. Vail

CLASS OF 1913
Robert W. Morse

CLASS OF 1914
Ludwig K. Moorehead

CLASS OF 1915
William A. Kirkland

CLASS OF 1919
George F. Sawyer

CLASS OF 1920
William M. Rosenbaum
Stewart Sanders
Morris Tyler

CLASS OF 1922
Henry F. Howe

CLASS OF 1923
H. Donald Harris

CLASS OF 1924
Gardner Brown
Nelson C. Haskell, Jr.
William T. Kelly, Jr.

CLASS OF 1925
Alvah C. Drake

CLASS OF 1926
Anthony D. Eastman

CLASS OF 1928
James R. Adriance
David A. Dudley
Herbert R. Elsas

CLASS OF 1929
Theodore M. Adams
Richard Jackson

CLASS OF 1930
Amory H. Bradford
Henry Ehrlich, II

CLASS OF 1931
John H. Batten, III
Henry P. Brightwell, Jr.
John L. Cooper
Willet L. Eccles (Hon.)

CLASS OF 1932
W. Gordon Fawcett

CLASS OF 1933
Theodore H. Gregg
Hugh Samson
Murvyn W. Vye, Jr.

CLASS OF 1934
Harlan Cleveland
Thomas Thacher
John W. Woolsey, Jr.

CLASS OF 1935
Richard G. Woodbridge, III

CLASS OF 1936
Louis P. Dolbeare

CLASS OF 1937
Morrison M. Bump

CLASS OF 1938
John P. Furman
John W. Leggett
J. Read Murphy

CLASS OF 1939
Elias Clark
Justin C. Williams

CLASS OF 1940
Prescott S. Bush, Jr.
H. James Caulkins
Stanley M. Cleveland
Robert C. McGiffert
Arleigh D. Richardson, III

CLASS OF 1941
C. Stuart Grover
Randolph C. Harrison, Jr.
William S. Moorhead

CLASS OF 1942
Robert A. Furman
David Chavchavadze

CLASS OF 1943
Richard R. Harshman
John U. Lemmon, III
Gael Mahony
Eugene E. Pantzer, III

CLASS OF 1944
John B. Snook

CLASS OF 1945
William L. Saltonstall
G. David Schine

CLASS OF 1946
Lawrence W. Barss

CLASS OF 1948
Russell T. Barnhart
Nicholas Z. Kafoglis
Robert D. Mehlman

CLASS OF 1949
Donald C. Goss

CLASS OF 1950
John Arnold
Emmanuel d'Amonville
H. Donald Harris, Jr.

CLASS OF 1951
John M. Taylor

CLASS OF 1952
Edward I. Selig

CLASS OF 1954
Leslie H. Blank, Jr.
Paul J. Keaney

CLASS OF 1955
Alan R. Blackmer, Jr.
Thomas H. Lawrence, III
Donald R. Oasis

CLASS OF 1957
Stephen F. Larrabee

CLASS OF 1958
David W. Childs, Jr.
George B. Pidot, Jr.

CLASS OF 1961
James S. Durston
Tom I. Evslin

CLASS OF 1963
Matthew W. Hall

CLASS OF 1964
Stephen B. Burbank
John P. Volk

CLASS OF 1965
Daniel Warren

CLASS OF 1966
Andrew D. Abbott
James S. Kunen
David W. Tresemer

CLASS OF 1967
Mark J. Logsdon

CLASS OF 1969
Lawrence N. Gelb

CLASS OF 1970
James W. Stover

CLASS OF 1972
Robert R. Soule

CLASS OF 1973
Richard L. Kauffman

INTRODUCTION

ANDOVER HILL on 21 April 1778 was not a prepossessing place. Since most of the inhabitants of the town's South Parish had preferred to settle in the lowlands near the Shawsheen River, the area was sparsely populated. It has been described as consisting of great stretches of rocky pasture dotted with clumps of birches, alders, scrub oaks, and berry bushes, with here and there a farmhouse or a tilled field against a background of dark forest. Part of the territory was marshy, and the meadows during rainy periods were flooded until they resembled shallow lakes. Through the center of this land ran the road from Andover village to Salem, flanked on the left by a low stone wall. On the corner of what is now Main and Phillips streets stood an old carpenter's shop, about thirty-five feet by twenty, made of unpainted boards and embellished by a chimney on one side. A short distance down Phillips Street was the old George Abbot house, a simple clapboard structure where Samuel Phillips, Jr., and his family were living. In the area in front of the present Bishop and Adams halls were two dilapidated, unoccupied buildings. The old Blunt Tavern, later called Berry House, was on the left side of Salem Street, just beyond the present Commons. For the rest, the Hill was wild, uncultivated country. Aside from the magnificent prospect that it afforded —the broad sweep to distant mountains in the west—there was nothing to suggest the changes that would take place in the next two hundred years.[1]

On that April day in 1778 there were gathered in the Abbot House on Phillips Street a group of devout citizens who were determined to embark on a new venture. Present were "Esquire" Samuel Phillips, who lived in the North Parish; his brother, Dr. John Phillips, of Exeter, New Hampshire; and his son, Samuel Phillips, Jr. The group had come together to legalize the establishment of "a public free School or Academy." They expressed "a painful anxiety" about "the prevalence of ignorance and vice, disorder and wickedness" and sought to found an institution that would combat these baneful tendencies. They wished their school to instruct youth "not only in English and Latin Grammar, Writing, Arithmetic, and those Sciences, wherein they are commonly taught; but more especially to learn them the GREAT END AND REAL BUSINESS OF LIVING." To make the purpose of their institution doubly clear, they added: "And, in order to prevent the smallest perversion of the true intent of this Foundation, it is again declared, that the *first* and *principal* object of this Institution is the promotion of true PIETY and VIRTUE." The document the Phillipses signed that day, known ever since as the Constitution of Phillips Academy, went on to spell out the details of administering their school, providing for the transfer of a substantial amount of property to a self-perpetuating Board of Trustees and containing a precise statement of the religious doctrines that those concerned with the school must subscribe to.[2] Though they probably did not realize the full significance of what they were doing, these sober citizens of Andover were making a commitment unique in the history of American secondary education. Certainly in their wildest dreams they could not have imagined what their institution would become in the next two hundred years.

On that April day, still at Valley Forge after the brutal winter, General George Washington wrote a long letter to his fellow Virginian John Bannister, a delegate to the Continental Congress. The General was discouraged about the army and the progress of the war. Patriotism was at a low ebb, as witnessed by the number of officers who were resigning their commissions. The British were "endeavoring to ensnare the people by specious allurements of Peace." If victory were finally to be won, the army deserved better treatment from the Continental Congress than it had received to date. General Washington was understandably bitter on this point:

> For without arrogance, or the smallest deviation from the truth, it may
> be said, that no history, now extant, can furnish an instance of an
> Army's suffering such uncommon hardships as ours have done, and
> bearing them with the same patience and Fortitude. To see Men
> without Cloathes to cover their nakedness, without Blankets to lay
> on, without Shoes, by which their Marches might be traced by the
> Blood from their feet, and almost as often without Provisions as with;
> Marching through frost and Snow, and at Christmas taking up their
> Winter Quarters within a day's March of the enemy, without a House
> or Hutt to cover them till they could be built and submitting to it
> without a murmur, is a mark of patience and obedience which in my
> opinion can scarce be parallel'd.[3]

From the testimony of General Washington there can be no question that April 1778 was indeed a time that tried men's souls. The future success of the American experiment, as announced to the world in the Declaration of Independence, hung in the balance.

In April 1778 what was soon to become the Commonwealth of Massachusetts was in a period of transition and confusion. With the British evacuation of Boston in March 1776, the focus of military activity had moved southward, and except for a few minor skirmishes New England was to see no more actual fighting. But the shifting of the revolutionary campaigns to the middle states by no means solved the many problems facing the people of Massachusetts. Foremost among those was the question of erecting a new state government to replace the now defunct British rule. As one memorial put it, with "the Dissolution of the power of Great Britain over these Colonies they have fallen into a state of nature."[4] For a while an attempt was made to adapt the old charter of 1691 to present needs, with the extralegal Provincial Congress acting as both legislative and executive, but this makeshift proved unsatisfactory. Clearly something better was needed if the future Bay State were to realize the aims and aspirations of the Revolution.

One thing about their proposed new government the people of Massachusetts agreed upon was that it should be based on a written constitution. Only if the liberties of the people could be spelled out in writing, it was generally believed, could adequate guarantees be secured. But the two outstanding questions remained unresolved: Who should draw up the constitution—the Provincial Congress or a special convention? And should the finished draft be ratified by the people at large? In 1776 the Provincial Congress, in an effort to speed things up, announced that it would draw up a constitution and present it to the towns for ratification. Despite widespread opposition from those who wanted a special convention, the Congress went ahead with its plan and on 4 March 1778 submitted its handiwork to the voters. But the people of Massachusetts were not to be stampeded into accepting an imperfect instrument of government, they roundly defeated the proposal by a vote of 9,972 to 2,083. Among many objections to the document four contributed most to its defeat: the lack of a bill of rights, inadequate safeguards for property, the disfranchisement of Negroes, and the disproportionate amount of power given small towns. In Essex County delegates from a group of towns met at Ipswich in April under the leadership of Theophilus Parsons and drew up what came to be called the "Essex Result," an indictment of the proposed constitution on the ground that it contained no separation of powers, no independent judiciary, and no veto for the governor, and above all because it failed to provide sufficient qualifications for the "men of education and property" who should rightfully have a controlling interest in the new government. Perhaps even more important than the objections to specific parts of the constitution was the widely held belief that the task of erecting a new government was so important that no amount of time and effort should be spared in achieving the best political structure that human wisdom was capable of. Here was an opportunity, unique in the history of mankind, to wipe clean the slate of the past and construct a new government designed to promote the safety and happiness of all the people. It would be another two years before a special convention, under the leadership of John Adams, would produce a constitution that the voters of the state would ratify.[5]

In April 1778 the town of Andover, Massachusetts, was experiencing most of the same problems that the Revolution had visited on other New England towns. Founded in 1646, Andover had had a relatively uneventful history during the colonial period. It could, to be sure, boast of Anne Bradstreet, the finest poetic talent that Puritan New England produced, whose book of poems entitled *The Tenth Muse Lately Sprung Up in America* had been published in 1650. A more melancholy distinction came at the end of the seventeenth century, when the town became notorious for its part in the Salem witch hunt. For a few years Andover was caught up in the same hysteria that characterized Salem, and before sanity was restored two women and one man had been hanged for their supposed associations with the devil. The town had had its share of fighting in the Indian Wars. For example, one of its citizens, Jonathan Frye, had served as chaplain with Captain John Lovewell and had been killed in "Lovewell's Fight" in 1725. But from the historian's point of view there was little remarkable about the early history of the town.[6]

As the series of crises that were to lead to the Revolution developed, Andover could be counted among towns that steadfastly opposed what they believed to be usurpation of authority by the British, but the opposition was invariably conservative. Samuel Adams would find few sympathizers in Andover. Though the town opposed the Stamp Act, it refused to support the use of violence against that measure. Out of duty, it joined the boycott of British goods that followed the Townshend Acts and was properly outraged at the Boston Massacre. As war approached, though, feeling began to run much higher. In a letter to Eliphalet Pearson dated Andover, 10 March 1775, Jonathan French, pastor of the South Church, had this to say about the crisis with Great Britain:

> Pray, Sir, what do you think? Shall we come to blows or not? If we should, and you should want any Powder, I would have [you] apply to us, for *Andover* is become almost all Powder, and we only want a *Spark* to set us all in a *Flame*. Some of My Parishioners, can you believe it?, brought their Guns with them to Meeting the last Sabbath, lest upon a sudden Alarm they should lose the honor of being in the Front of Battle.[7]

The town had raised two companies of soldiers, and when the "Lexington Alarm" was sounded, these troops marched to battle—only to find that the British were already in retreat. Frustrated at missing the shot heard round the world, the Andover contingent proceeded to the patriot camp in Cambridge and later took part in the Battle of Bunker Hill, where four were killed and six wounded, and where a Negro slave, Salem Poor, the property of Andover's John Poor, distinguished himself by killing a British Lieutenant-Colonel. Though individual citizens of the town fought in later battles, and though the town faithfully provided its quota of men for the Revolutionary armies, Bunker Hill marked the last time that Andover troops fought as a unit.[8]

The town of Andover was to distinguish itself in a different kind of military activity during the Revolution: the production of gunpowder. One of General Washington's major complaints during the siege of Boston was the scarcity of powder, and any proposal to remedy this deficiency was more than welcome. A young citizen of Andover, Samuel Phillips, Jr., offered to build a powder mill in his home town. Immediately upon receiving the necessary encouragement for his project, Phillips returned to Andover and enlisted the help of neighbors in building a mill on the Shawsheen River. By May 1776 he was able to report that his enterprise was producing twelve hundred pounds of powder a week.[9]

Finally, on 12 June 1776, an Andover Town Meeting took the following action:

> The question being put—whether, should the Honorable Congress, for the safety of the Colonies, declare them independent of the kingdom of Great Britain, you will solemnly engage with your lives and fortunes to support them in the measure.—It passed in the affirmative, unanimously.[10]

Against this background—national, state, and local—the Phillipses founded their School. The times could hardly have been less auspicious. And yet the institution that in April 1778 was little more than a dream in the mind of Samuel Phillips, Jr., has survived and prospered for two hundred years. Today the school covers 450 acres and has 175 buildings, a faculty of over 160, and an undergraduate body of over 1100. This book will recount the story of how this remarkable development came about.

I. The Early Years

CHAPTER ONE

THE PHILLIPS FAMILY

THOSE WHO accuse private secondary schools of elitism can find support for their position from the fact that Phillips Academy was founded by members of a family that, since the first settlement of Massachusetts Bay in 1630, had been distinguished for leadership in the new colony. If the Puritans had possessed a *Who's Who* or a *Social Register*, many Phillipses would have been in both. One writer speaks of the family as "among the untitled nobility of New England, representing the best element of life there, not that which always dwells in the brightest glare of publicity, but that which directs and shapes the current of public opinion."[1] A large number of the family were college graduates—and in seventeenth- and eighteenth-century Massachusetts that meant Harvard. Many were active in town government, some in the government of the Province. To be sure, there were occasional black sheep;[2] but the Phillips batting average was generally high, and the branch of the family that founded Phillips Academy was outstanding in church, business, and government.

It all started when George Phillips, a graduate of Cambridge in 1613 and a Church of England vicar at Boxted, Essex, began to chafe at the straightjacket of conformity that was demanded of English clergymen in the first part of the seventeenth century.[3] One of Phillips' parishioners, John Maidstone, wrote to John Winthrop, his uncle, that the vicar was determined to go on "your intended voyage into the plantation" and recommended him highly to be company clergyman for the expedition. Winthrop must have been impressed with George, for it was agreed that he should go and that the "generalitie" should defray the transportation expenses of the Phillips family. On 29 March 1630 the emigrants set sail from Cowes, with Phillips and Winthrop aboard the *Arbella*, the flagship of the little fleet. On 5 April, while "rydinge before yarmouth" off the Isle of Wight waiting for favorable winds, Winthrop wrote his son: "Yesterday we kept a fast aboard our ship. . . . Mr. Phillips exercised with us the whole day, and gave very good content to all the company, as he doth in all his exercises, so as we have much cause to bless God for him." So it was that George became a kind of spiritual cruise director for the company.

No sooner had the expedition landed at Salem on 12 June than tragedy struck the Phillips family. As Cotton Mather puts it, "Here, quickly after his Landing, he lost the *Desire of his Eyes*, in the death of his *Desirable Consort*, who, though an only Child, had cheerfully left her *Parents* to serve the Lord Jesus Christ, with her Husband, in a Terrible Wilderness." Thus George Phillips was left to face the hardships of his new life with two small, motherless children. After reconnoitering the territory in the Boston area, the Puritans determined on three settlements—one at Boston itself, one at Dorchester, and one at Watertown. Later in the summer it was decided that George Phillips would be the minister at Watertown. To seal this arrangement, a covenant was drawn up, presumably by George, and signed by members of the Watertown community-to-be, in which they promised to give themselves wholly unto the Lord Jesus and to do him faithful service. Having got the affairs of the spirit squared away, it remained to arrange for more temporal things. George was to receive a house "att the publique charge" and an allowance of "3 hogsheads of meale, 1 hogshead of malte, 4 bushells of Indean corne, 1 bushell of oatemeale, halfe an hundred of salte fish; for apparell, and other provisions, XX £, or els to have XL £ given him in money per annum, to make his owne provisions if he chuse it the rather." Finally, George was granted thirty acres of land "upp Charles Ryver, on the south side, beginning att a creeke a lyttle higher than the first pynes, and soe upwards towards the ware." Considering these vague boundaries, one wonders if George ever found where his land actually was. By the end of the summer he was presumably settled in his Watertown house, but his troubles were not over. Sometime that fall his house burned down, and on 30 September Winthrop noted cryptically in his diary, "Mr. Phillips, the minister of Watertown, and others, had their hay burnt."[4] Yet finally things took a turn for the better. A new house was provided for him, and the next year he remarried. For the remaining fourteen years of his life he lived in Watertown, ministering to his flock and raising a family of nine children.

In many ways George Phillips was the most independent and unconventional of all the clan. The very first year of his ministry he stirred up a controversy by publicly declaring that "the churches of Rome were true churches," thereby adopting a live-and-let-live position toward Catholicism that would seem heretical to most Puritans. This caused such a row that eventually Governor Winthrop and other notables from Boston came to Watertown for an all-day debate on the subject. At the close of the meeting all those present except George and two others agreed that this opinion was in error—but there is no evidence that he ever changed his mind on the subject. It is, perhaps, testimony to the high esteem in which his congregation held him that they let the matter drop.

Another instance of George's independence can be seen in his insistence on following the true Congregational form of church organization. For him, "The ordination of a Pope, or Prelate, the presentation of a Patron, etc. give not the Minister a calling, nor are necessary at all to make a man a Minister. . . . But the people receiving a man . . . doe virtually and really give him all the just calling that he hath, which is a true Ministeriall calling." And George did not hesitate to put his theory into practice. When the church at Newtowne (Cambridge) invited neighboring churches to send delegates to assist at the installation of their minister, no one from Watertown showed up because "Master Phillips insisted that every church was competent to act alone." On another occasion, when the Watertown church installed a second pastor, the Reverend John Knowles, it did not follow the usual custom of inviting representatives from neighboring churches to attend. For a few years George Phillips seems to have been the only minister in the colony who held these independent views; later the Reverend John Cotton, likewise a strong Congregationalist, arrived and lent powerful support to the Phillips policy, until it became standard for all the Massachusetts churches.

Nor was George's independence limited to church matters. In 1632 Governor Winthrop and his assistants, who had been elected in England in 1629 to administer the colony's affairs, levied a tax of £60 on the colony to build a stockade. Watertown's share was to be £8; but George and a church elder named Richard Brown "assembled the people and delivered their opinions, that it was not safe to pay moneys after that sort, for fear of bringing themselves and posterity into bondage." Though George was unfamiliar with the phrase "no taxation without representation," that is what he was talking about. He and Brown were haled into court, where it was made clear to them that the General Court could indeed levy taxes, even though the failure of the colonial administration to hold elections since the company's arrival in Massachusetts gave the impression of arbitrary rule. Three months later George must have derived a good deal of satisfaction from the announcement that each town (including Watertown) was to choose two men to attend the next general court to "advise with" the governor about raising taxes and other matters of public policy. In a very real sense, George Phillips and Richard Brown had made an important contribution toward initiating representative government in Massachusetts.

But George's days in the Massachusetts Bay Colony were numbered. As Cotton Mather wrote, "He laboured under many Bodily Infirmities: But was especially liable unto the Cholick; the Extremity of one Fit whereof, was the *Wind* which carried him afore it, into the *Haven* of Eternal Rest." In another connection Mather wrote of him, "There was one *George* who was indeed among the first *Saints* of *New-England*! And that *Excellent Man of our Land* was Mr. *George Phillips*." Finally, the leading authority on George sums him up as follows: "It is clear that he was learned but modest, courageous, and courteous, independent in spirit but peaceable and tolerant; a worthy representative of the Puritan ministers who came to this colony to mould its thought and character through its early years."

The founders of Phillips Academy were descended from George's eldest son, Samuel. (Unfortunately for later historians, the eldest sons of the next four generations of Phillipses were also named Samuel.) The first Samuel was granted a double portion of his father's estate in George's will but was admonished by his father to let his mother have it during her lifetime.[5] This he apparently did; at any rate, when his mother died, she left Sam "all Latin, Greek, and Hebrew books now in the house." The congregation of George's Watertown church, in a show of affection for the deceased pastor, undertook to provide for Sam's education, and accordingly he was sent to Harvard, where he graduated in 1650. Evidence that the Watertown folk were carrying out their pledges is to be seen in the college records, where Deacon Stone "of watter towne" paid part of Sam's tuition by a "bush of appells"; another entry reads, "payd by Goodman Cloyes of watter towne by a lamb." He was also credited twice by "Allowance for his scollership," establishing a precedent of financial support for the education of indigent young men that was to be followed by later Phillipses at Harvard and was to become a basic policy of Phillips Academy. The year after graduation Sam became "teacher" of the church at Rowley, of which Ezekiel Rogers was pastor. When Rogers died in 1660, Sam became embroiled in an unfortunate wrangle with the widow over five pounds that the lady said was due her but had been paid to Phillips, who had done all the work of the church during Rogers' last illness. Mrs. Rogers was still full of fight when she died eighteen years later. In her will she stated that she was still due five pounds from Sam and added, "Therefore I would earnestly desire Mr. Samuell Phillips and Deacon Jewet that they would not ronge me in this particular, least it be a greefe to them at the apearinge of Jesus Christ." One Philip Nelson, who seems to have had a grudge against Sam, brought suit in the Ipswich Court and won a judgment, but Sam appealed to the General Court, which reversed the decision and admonished Nelson. Samuel remained in Rowley his entire life, finally becoming pastor in 1682 and dying in 1696. Cotton Mather had written an epitaph for George Phillips in which he called him "Vir Incomparabilis nisi SAMUELEM genuisset" (An incomparable man until Samuel was born), but it is hard to see how he justified the statement: Sam was certainly beloved by his congregation, but his main claim to fame was involvement in unpleasant lawsuits.[6]

The second Samuel Phillips is something of a mystery. All that is known of him is that he was born in 1657, died in 1722, had two wives, and "was instructed in the Goldsmith's Business, by the memorable Mr. Dummer of Boston and settled at Salem."[7] Apparently he was a very successful goldsmith; indeed it has been suggested that he was the founder of the family fortune. Whatever else he may have done, the second Samuel was able to send his eldest son to Harvard and may well have provided the capital for some of the son's successful investments later on.

The third Samuel,[8] whom I shall refer to as the Parson, reverted to the ministry with a vengeance. Throughout his life he was the prototype of the strict Calvinist New England clergyman—hardworking, shrewd, humorless, and dedicated. To encourage him to enter the ministry, his grandfather, the first Samuel, left him some property and half his library; and after being prepared for college by John Emerson, a relative of his mother's, he went to Harvard, where he was graduated in 1708. Like his grandfather before him, he was a scholarship student and apparently a very serious one, for he complained that other students, presumably the rowdy element, disturbed his meditations. For a year after graduation, the Parson kept school in what is now Essex and then turned to further theological study. At about this time some members of the Andover church who lived in the southern part of the town, unwilling to travel all the way to what is now North Andover for worship, broke away from the church there and established the South Parish, constructing a meeting house of their own. In 1710 the Parson began preaching at the South Church; a year later he received a unanimous call to become its pastor. The same year he married Hannah White of Haverhill and began a ministry that was to last just short of sixty years.

From the start the Parson proved a shrewd businessman, and as a result of careful investment of his own and his wife's inheritances, particularly in wild lands, it was not long before he was able to adopt a life style well above that of the average Puritan clergyman. Like many prosperous people of that time, for example, he owned slaves. But the Parson never let his relative affluence stand in the way of collecting the full salary due him from the church. Sometimes from the pulpit, sometimes in writing, he chided his congregation for not living up to their agreements for his support, and he became particularly cross when they failed to supply him with wood.[9] He was thrifty and economical in all that he did and is reported to have blown out the candle while engaged in family prayers, so as to save tallow. When his son, the fourth Samuel, was about to open a store in North Andover, he gave him the following advice:

> Be prudent but yet not over timorous and over Scrupulous in the article of Trusting, lest you stand in your own light. Some people are more honest p'haps than you think for, and it may be will pay sooner than you expect. Keep to your shop, if you expect that to keep you and be not out of the way when customers come.[10]

As time passed, the Parson became more and more of a power in the community. A story is told of a passing traveler who asked him, "Are you, sir, the parson who serves here?" to which the Parson replied, "I am, sir, the parson who *rules* here."[11] Throughout his life he preached the strictest form of Calvinism, and woe to the church member who strayed from the path. Church records indicate that the most common sins of the congregation were fornication and drunkenness,[12] and he was never slow to discipline sinners. Of particular concern to him was overindulgence in liquor at funerals. Another practice he deplored was "Swapping Horses, or other Creatures." Admittedly, an honest trade in animals could occasionally be condoned, "but for any one to make a Trade and Business of it, and spend their Time riding about, and visiting Taverns, on Purpose to tempt People to trade, and traffic with them, designing all the while, to over-reach them in the Bargain, and rather than fail, to speak falsely in the Matter, carries in it a very heinous Transgression." He was determined that good order should prevail during church services. After the earthquake of 1755, he rebuked his congregation for "sleeping away a great part of sermon-time,"

1. *The Reverend Samuel Phillips. Copy of a portrait attributed to John Greenwood, in the possession of the Trustees of Phillips Academy.*

but expressed the hope that since the "Glorious Lord of the Sabbath" had "given them *such a* shaking of late," they would reform. On another occasion he obtained a warrant for the arrest of a youth who, during church services, "sported and played, and by indecent Gestures and Wry faces, caused laughter and misbehavior in the Beholders, and thereby greatly disturbed the Congregation."[13] Perhaps one reason for the sleep and the horseplay during his sermons was that they were inordinately long. He used to turn the hourglass over at the start and usually was still going strong when all the sands had run out.

The unlovely side of Calvinism came through strong in a fearsome sermon the Parson preached after a member of his congregation had committed suicide. "His name," said the unforgiving minister, "as many think, had best be buried in oblivion," for "he yielded to the temptation of the enemy of souls, kept the devil's counsel concealed, nor did any person suspect that he was under the said temptation, until, being missed, he was found *hanging in his own barn.*" It was, said Samuel, "An occasion *quite new*, as well as *very awful*, such as, I think, has not occurred among us till now since I came into this place, and I pray God that we may never see the like again." To make his point the stronger, he had the sermon printed with a morbid title page, headed with skull and crossbones and bordered in black. A final act of unforgiveness occurred when the suicide's family was denied permission to bury him in the South Church graveyard, so that he had to be interred on a lonely farm under an oak tree.[14]

For close to sixty years the Parson labored for what he conceived to be the welfare of his flock. It was his proud boast that there were no unbaptized people in his parish. He never deviated from the strict Calvinism of his youth; George Whitefield and the Great Awakening were anathema to him. He dutifully made parish calls on all his congregation, riding horseback with his wife on a pillion behind him. Some idea of the awe in which he was held by the South Parish can be seen in his ceremonial walk to church each Sunday. He headed the family procession, with his Negro slave on his right hand, together with Madame Phillips, with her Negro slave on her left hand. Then followed the five children, arranged according to age. When the Phillipses arrived inside the church, the entire congregation stood until their pastor had mounted the pulpit and seated himself. When he died, in 1771, after a lifetime of almost perfect health, one eulogist said of him, "He was a Saint While he Lived and Dyed a Saint." Perhaps—it depends on one's definition. But there can be no argument about the statement from the same eulogist that "the graces of the holy Spirit in him Were very eminent and distinguishing."[15]

We now come to the generations that founded Phillips Academy. With the death of Parson Phillips in 1771, the tradition of producing eminent clergymen that had characterized the family from the start ran out. The emphasis now shifted to business and government, in both of which fields members of the family proved as able as their predecessors in the church. The Parson had three sons—Samuel (naturally), John, and William. The first two were true founders of Phillips Academy, while the third, though not in at the birth of the institution, soon became a generous benefactor and a Trustee, serving as President of the Board for two years in the 1790's. The Parson's three sons had one thing in common: they all married rich girls. Samuel married Elizabeth Barnard, the only surviving child of the wealthy Theodore Barnard; John married the widow Sarah Gilman, who had inherited a fortune of some eight thousand pounds from her first husband; and finally William, after having been apprenticed to the rich Boston merchant Edward Bromfield, followed the proverbial road to success by marrying the boss's daughter, Abigail. In a very real sense, therefore, the early endowment of Phillips Academy came from the Barnard, Gilman, and Bromfield fortunes.

The fourth Samuel,[16] whom I shall call the Squire, never entered the ministry, but he might as well have. Throughout his life he was an exemplar of the most rigid kind of Calvinism. His father the Parson was certainly not soft when it came to disciplining his flock. The son was, if anything, even more stern and severe. As one writer has put it, "Perhaps he had the temperament which, by hating vice too much, loves men too little."[17] Whether he was serving as town moderator, as magistrate, as representative to the General Court, as deacon of the church, as businessman, or as parent, he was a hard man—conservative, uncompromising, respected, but unloved. Perhaps some of his sternness can be attributed to the fact that of his seven children, only his son Samuel lived to maturity. It would be easy to see the hand of a punitive God in their fate. But for whatever reason, here was a man who set his face sternly against wickedness and had little of the milk of human kindness in him.

Born in 1715 and raised in the South Parish, the Squire, like his great-grandfather and father before him, was sent to Harvard as a scholarship student. Armed with the Hebrew Bible that every preceding Phillips had used at Harvard, he finally won a prestigious Hollis scholarship and graduated in 1734. After teaching school in Andover for a while, he returned to Harvard for a M.A., which he won in 1737, and seemed destined for the ministry. But for some reason he decided to go into trade, and in 1738 opened a store in the Andover North Parish. That same year he married Elizabeth Barnard, niece of the Reverend John Barnard, the North Parish Minister. Elizabeth is described as "a lady of rare vertues," one of the most attractive of which was her large inheritance. In the early 1750's the couple built a handsome mansion, still standing in what is now North Andover, but this did not in the least change the Squire's life style. He continued operating his store in his new house, just as he had in the old one. There are almost no records of the Squire's business activities among the Phillips Papers, but he must have done well, for he was soon one of the wealthiest men in Andover.

Throughout his life the Squire believed that a man of his position had a duty to serve the public, and his first opportunity to do so came in 1752, when he was appointed Justice of the Peace for Essex County. In this position he handled several cases of misbehavior that his father sent up to him and generally tried to keep his part of Essex County in line. For example, he issued a warrant against Phineas Parker of Andover "for having been a loiterer, misspending his time, not using any ordinary and daily lawful trade or business to get a living as the law directs, moreover by unlawfully travelling on the Lord's Day, he hath conducted himself contrary to the peace of our sovereign lord the king." Though there is no record of what happened to this eighteenth-century hobo, the presumption is that he was jailed.[18] Another case involved a complaint by Nathaniel Perley of Boxford against a Negro girl, Flora, who he said had been publishing "Lies and False Reports" about him. Flora's reports were "that he pull'd her coat up, that he had to do with her . . . by the old Shop and that he had

2. *Samuel Phillips, Esquire. Portrait by an unknown artist, in the possession of the Trustees of Phillips Academy.*

to do with her behind the Shop under an apple Tree, and that he had to do with her . . . in the Barn, meaning . . . that the Complainant committed the crime of Fornication with the said Flora at the severall Places aforesaid, and at diverse times." The Squire had Flora brought before him. She readily admitted to speaking the words charged but justified them "because she says they are true." Apparently this ended the matter. One can well imagine how the Squire would have abominated the whole episode.[19]

The Squire took his social position seriously and wanted it recognized. His son Sam was ranked at Harvard, as were all undergraduates, according to the social status of his father. The Squire did not believe that his son had been ranked high enough and protested to the President and Tutors. He was, he claimed, the senior Justice of the Peace and Quorum among the parents, and yet John Murray, whose father was less senior, had been placed ahead of Sam. The Harvard authorities agreed with the Squire, and the boy was placed ahead of Murray. The old man was wise enough to realize that his action put his son in a difficult position and advised him as follows:

> You are now in the most difficult situation, & the eyes of all, above and below you, will be upon you, & I wish it might be that you could be at home till the talk about change was a little over. Every word, action, and even your countenance, will be watched, particularly by those that envy you. Therefore keep as much retired as possible. . . . If Murray is uneasy and manifests it to you, say nothing to irritate him. . . . But by no means give the most distant hint of yielding your place.

One beneficial result of this contretemps was that a short while later the Harvard authorities decided to abandon the practice of ranking.[20]

One can gain insight into the character of Squire Phillips from other letters he wrote his son while the latter was at Harvard. These epistles are almost invariably moralistic, and if young Sam had followed all his father's instructions to the letter, he would have become the worst kind of prig. During his son's Freshman year the Squire wrote, "Beware of Bold Company. . . . Petition for such a Chamber and Chum as will be most advantageous for your studies next year. . . . Spread up your Bead as soon as you are up. Two mornings I found it very much like a pig's nest. Find some place for your Tea Kettle out of sight."[21] A year later he wrote, "Labour to maintain your good Character at College; Treat all Superiors with due respect; Shun all bad company; Be Intimate with *very* few. . . . Keep good hours, go to Bed in good Season and rise Early, you will find it much better, than setting up late, on all Accounts." The Squire was much disturbed when his son announced his intention of attending a dancing school. "I very much fear it will prove a Snare to you at College and am sure it will be no way for your Credit or Advantage when you leave College," he wrote.[22] On another occasion he saw dancing school as "a great Temptation to attend Balls and Assemblies, to lead you into Company and to be abroad at unseasonable hours, all of which I do detest and Abhor, as having the greatest tendency to Corrupt the Morals of young people."[23] In an undated letter he urged, "Don't go to Boston and Beware of all that come from Boston."[24] Finally, he counseled his son to avoid "Broad Laughs"—presumably the eighteenth-century equivalent of the "belly laugh." They have a disagreeable sound, he thought.[25] Despite the stern-parent posture in most of his letters, occasional hints of affection do appear; and it should be noted that he did not positively forbid young Sam to attend dancing school.

In the field of government the Squire did much more than serve as JP. In 1757 he was on a county commission to care for the exiled Acadians and charged the county six shillings a day for his work. From 1759 at least until 1775 he was regularly chosen as the town's representative to the General Court, where he tended to follow a conservative patriot line. He produced the town's resolutions in opposition to the Stamp Act and was instructed by his fellow citizens not to give his assent to any act that might signify "willingness . . . to submit to any internal taxes." In 1772 he was elected to the Province Council by the legislature and survived the purge of the radicals instituted by General Gage in 1774, again testimony to his relatively moderate position on the issues of the day. It has been said of the squire that he was not wholeheartedly behind the Revolution. Certainly the concept of revolution as a political policy must have run against his grain, but there is no evidence that he did not loyally support the cause once the die had been cast. He was in his sixties when the war started, and it seems clear that age and infirmity prevented him from playing a more active role in the conflict. When he was appointed to a committee to visit Washington about the military situation in 1778, he announced that "on Account of Lameness" it would be "dangerous for himself and unsafe for the Public" for him to serve. And a year later, when he was chided for not introducing a bill to limit "Balls, Concerts, Huskings, Bundling and other amusements," as he had promised to do, the chances are that the cause of his dereliction was physical.

By the spring of 1778, therefore, Squire Phillips had to all intents and purposes finished his public career. His business had proved highly successful and was to continue so. He still had another thirteen years to live. As a result, he had the time, the money, and the inclination to devote himself to a project that his son was enthusiastically working on—the founding of Phillips Academy.

The second founder, John Phillips of Exeter,[26] the younger brother of the Squire, should have been a carbon copy of his brother: he had the same family upbringing, the same training at Harvard, the same experience teaching school and studying for the ministry, the same success in business, and the same kind of marriage to a wealthy woman. Yet he never developed into the stern paragon of virtue that his brother did. He was less dogmatic, fonder of people, more willing to see another point of view, and generally more human. While a freshman at Harvard in the class of 1735, he invited his tutor "to step up to Swan's study and drink a glass of ale," an action that was certainly not in the Phillips tradition at Harvard.[27] Like his brother, he was a scholarship boy at Harvard; unlike his brother, he distinguished himself academically, winning the Hopkins Prize for excellence in his studies and delivering the Salutatory Oration at Commencement. After teaching school in Andover for a short while, he removed to Exeter, New Hampshire, where he continued to teach, both in a private Latin school of his own and in the town school.

A turning point in John's life occurred when he became associated with Sarah Gilman, widow of "Gentleman Nat." First he served as her clerk, then he proposed to her daughter Tabitha, who turned him down, and finally he went after the widow herself, although she was sixteen years his senior, and married her in 1743. With the Gilman fortune behind him, he embarked on a business career that eventually made him the wealthiest man in Exeter. The town at that time was mainly engaged in lumbering, and John saw the possibilities in trading lumber for food and other necessities that were in short supply. He traded in masts for the Royal Navy, speculated in New Hampshire wild lands, and later in his career became one of the area's leading bankers. Since he never had any children, he was able to devote his fortune to charitable purposes, particularly in his later years, and before he died he became one of the leading benefactors of his day.

Though he was traditionally an orthodox Calvinist, he was much more open-minded in religion than either his father or his brother. When a substantial number of the congregation of the First Church became dissatisfied with their minister, John Odlin, not so much on doctrinal grounds as on those of dullness, John Phillips joined a group that seceded and established the Second Church. A few years later that church called him to be its pastor, but he declined "because of the delicacy of his lungs," though it is more likely that he simply did not want the job. He was not personally enthusiastic about George Whitefield but did not object when some of his fellow parishioners supported him. Throughout the latter part of his life he was a trustee and leading benefactor of Dartmouth College, which was certainly more evangelical than Harvard, and the same interest is seen in his support of Princeton. His letters to his nephew, Samuel Phillips, Jr., about the choice of teachers for Phillips Academy said they should be orthodox, but he was willing to allow some latitude in religious belief.

Like his brother the Squire, John Phillips was soon active in affairs of government. In addition to a number of town offices, which he held almost

3. *Dr. John Phillips of Exeter. Portrait by Joseph Steward, in the possession of the Trustees of Dartmouth College and reproduced with their permission.*

continuously throughout his life, he served in the New Hampshire assembly and was a Justice of the Peace and a magistrate. While opposing various acts of the British Parliament, he drew back when colonial opposition threatened law and order generally. When the citizens of Exeter decided on a Cadet Corps and provided them with handsome scarlet and buff uniforms, the troops choose John as their commander, and Governor Wentworth commissioned him a colonel. So far his position seemed that of a moderate patriot, but when the actual fighting started, John Phillips could not accept it. Nor did his associations with the Tory Governor Wentworth make his life any easier. To avoid friction he retired temporarily from business and for the most part sat out the war. His attitude toward the Declaration of Independence is illuminating:

> I have just now seen the Declaration of Independency, and perhaps it will not be long before we shall experience whether we are able to support it—or whether the measures taken by the Government on both sides will not be ruinous. The Lord in mercy prevent it, and make us mutual blessings to and [not] destroyers of one another.

In the spring of 1778 John Phillips was no longer playing an active role in American politics. He had amassed a large fortune; he was dedicated to charitable enterprises, particularly in support of education; and he was generally in a position to lend assistance to his brother and his nephew in founding Phillips Academy.

In this latter endeavor, although Squire Phillips and his brother John both played important roles, the school was primarily the brainchild of the Squire's son, Samuel Phillips, Jr. His part in establishing the institution was so important that he deserves a separate chapter.

CHAPTER TWO

SAMUEL PHILLIPS, JR.

I N A seminal article a distinguished colonial historian has advanced the
thesis that in dealing with colonial educational history, one must think
of education "not only as formal pedagogy but as the entire process by
which a culture transmits itself across generations."[1] That definition
certainly applies to the education of Samuel Phillips, Jr., the founder of
Phillips Academy. He spent three years at Dummer School and four at
Harvard College and thus had as good a formal education as Massachusetts
had to offer in those days. Yet if one were to assume that the most important influences on him were his experiences at these two institutions of
learning, he would be greatly mistaken. One must consider as well the combined agencies of family, church, and town if we are to understand what
kind of man graduated at Cambridge in 1771 and went on to found a
school seven years later.

The town of Andover, into which Samuel Phillips, Jr., was born on 5
February 1752, had been undergoing profound changes beneath the sur-
face, particularly with respect to family structure. The old patriarchal family
unit that had produced a society of "stability and health" until well into
the eighteenth century was breaking down. Children married at a younger
age, increased mobility led many to settle in other towns, and the young
men who stayed on acquired title to land at an earlier age. All these changes
represented a threat to the authority of the patriarchs who had dominated
Andover social life for three generations, and challenge to their authority
in this area spilled over into challenges in others. The decline of the patriarchal unit may well have precipitated a questioning of the authority of the
church and later of royal authority over the colonies. Samuel Phillips, Jr.,
was born into a community where the basic educational institutions that had
served the town so well in the past to transmit culture across generations
were undergoing profound change.[2]

How much influence the changes in his native town had on young Sam
is impossible to say with precision. Certainly they could not have been apparent within his own family. Since Sam was the only one of his parents'

seven children to reach maturity,[3] it was hard for his father, Squire Phillips, to be a patriarch. If the familial changes occurring in Andover had an influence on Sam, it would have come from hearing his father express alarm at the breakdown of the old social patterns. Though during Sam's early years the town of Andover had a grammar school and various "out-skirt" schools, there is no evidence that he attended any of them.[4]

He was brought up virtually as an only child and is described as having "a frail constitution, which seemed unsuited to physical hardship" and as "growing up in comparative solitariness—his companions not only in the main his elders, but his revered parents, who were now approaching the meridian of life."[5] The picture one gets is of a lonely little boy, insulated from the world around him, perhaps vaguely aware of the profound social changes that were taking place beyond the small world of his home.

The two most important influences on the young Samuel were his family and the church—influences that in his case were very nearly one and the same. On both sides of his family, Sam came from a line of orthodox Cal-vinist ministers. His paternal grandfather, the Parson, must have been an awe-inspiring figure to a young boy, while his father, the Squire, though technically a business man, was a minister in all but name. Sam's mother, Elizabeth Barnard, did not need to yield to anyone in her dedication to strict Calvinist principles, and she could count among her forbears and con-temporaries the same kind of Puritan divines as could her husband the Squire. Her grandfather, the Reverend Thomas Barnard, was Andover's minister at the turn of the seventeenth century, while his son, John, her uncle, was his successor in the North Parish and served there until Sam was five years old. Two of her cousins were clergymen, while a third married one.[6] Though the Barnards were not as stern and awe-inspiring as the Phillipses, they were solidly orthodox, and it could not be expected that Elizabeth would challenge her husband when it came to choosing the right road to salvation. Sam's biographer speaks of him as inheriting from his mother "the fire which glowed in all these [his] virtues."[7] Perhaps. Cer-tainly the letters that she wrote him while he was at Dummer School and at Harvard are warm and full of concern for her son's material and spiri-tual welfare. Crudely written and full of misspellings, these epistles are half motherly injunctions on practical matters, half moral lectures. In one letter she urges her son to be careful of his clothes. "Dont wear them in the weat; if you weat your linen it will take off the Gloss."[8] In another she promises to send him a spread. There are no chickens to roast, but she may send a quarter of lamb, some cake and cheese, and some "Syder."[9] At Harvard there was the usual problem of student laundry. Elizabeth was after Sam to send back his "Dirte Linen—hope you will change your Linnen Twice a week and won clean Towel evere weak—you must not go so Dirte."[10] Yet it was her son's religious development that was most impor-tant to her: "Remember the one thing needfull and that is an Intrest in

Christ; we are told to seek and we shall find—that's a promis—But then—then we are not to seek in a cool, lasy, Formal manner—But with our hole hearts."[11] And again, "Leet him that stands take heed leest hee fall. Dont stand in your own strength. You know whear to go for Direction and Strength in evry time and kneed—oh—Be allways found in the way of your Duty—if your with God hee will be with you—But if you forsake him hee will forsake you. Search the Scriptures Dayly for in them ye have Eternal Life—without Knowleg the heart cannot be good. Dont mistake me, I did not say knowleg made the heart good. No, knowleg is won thing and Grace another. Above all labour for saving Grace."[12] Though the father might address him with sternness, the mother with warmth, the aims of the two were identical—the salvation of their son's soul.

Fortunately for the Squire and Elizabeth and for most New England parents who wished to train their children in the true faith, there was a ready-made discipline available to them—drill in the Westminster Assembly's *Shorter Catechism*. Normally the family undertook to teach this catechism to their children until about the age of eight, when the church took over for another eight years. At that time the young person was eligible for entry into the church. For the young children catechetical training consisted of little more than a parrot-like repetition of material learned by rote, but as the child matured, he was expected to understand the meaning of what he recited.[13] In view of his later devotion to the Westminster Catechism, it is safe to assume that young Sam received a full measure of this religious discipline from his father and mother and later from his church. If the aim of parents is to reproduce in their offspring likenesses of themselves, the Squire and his wife were supremely successful with young Sam. Throughout his life he never departed from the strict orthodox Calvinism in which he had been nurtured. From the example of his father he accepted as axiomatic the duty of public service. And during his entire career he labored unremittingly to conserve those qualities that he had learned from his parents and that he was later to insist constituted "the great end and real business of living."

In the summer of 1764 Sam was sent to Dummer School in neighboring South Byfield, presumably because it promised to be superior to the local grammar school. It had been founded a year earlier and was then under the forceful and eccentric leadership of Samuel Moody.[14] This extraordinary pedagogue, after graduating from Harvard and trying unsuccessfully to establish himself as a clergyman, had been called to Dummer to serve as its first master and soon had an institution going that was very different from the grammar schools of the day. An enthusiastic classicist, he spent little time teaching mathematics or science, but provision was made for the study of the French language and, over the violent protests of local bluenoses, dancing. The master's costume was bizarre enough; he wore a long green flannel gown and tasseled smoking cap. He thought enforced silence dur-

ing study hours was nonsense and permitted his charges to read their lessons aloud, talk with each other, and wander around the room during study
hall. Unlike most pedagogues of his day, he believed in encouraging students to do their best rather than in terrorizing them, and he boasted that
he had never used the rod during his entire career as a teacher.[15] On warm
days, when the tide was right, he used to take the entire school for a swim,
the older boys in the Parker River, the younger ones in a shallow swimming hole nearby. Though the boys must have gone to the local church on
Sundays, there is no evidence that Master Moody paid much attention to
religion during the school week, and unlike many contemporary schoolmasters he had a genuine affection for his boys and could not bring himself
to think of them as sinful. As a result of all this, his students worshiped
him, and he made an enviable record during his early years.[16]

The evidence is clear that young Sam was happy at Dummer. In a letter
to his parents he speaks of being "happily Attached to my very dear Master,"[17] and later at Harvard his father wrote him to associate himself with
Tutor Eliot and "you will find a Master Moody in him."[18] Other letters reveal a typical schoolboy concerned about his clothes, his trips home, and
other material matters. Requests for such items as "black Breeches, Blue
Coat Buttons, linen to mend my Pockets, Quils, some silk ferret to ty my
Hair with," and last but not least "money" appear regularly in Sam's
correspondence with his parents.[19] "My father forbad my pricking any
tunes in my singing Book. I should be exceeding glad if you would know
whether I may not get some Tunes pricked in it," he wrote on one occasion.[20] Apparently the tunes got pricked, for Sam is soon urging his parents to visit school and hear some "very Superior Singing."[21] There are
also among the Phillips Papers a few samples of the schoolboy's work at
Dummer—a sheet headed "Upon the sixth Conjugation of verbs in *aire*,"
indicating, perhaps, that Sam was availing himself of Master Moody's
French program. There is also a writing book in which the boy had written,
among other things, "Contentment is the most precious Jewel" and "Depart from Evil and do good" over and over again. Presumably to enable
Sam to return home for visits more easily, his parents gave him a horse,
which he kept at school, an animal he describes as "quiet" and "orderly."
And Master Moody approved, believing it "very necessary that I should
have a horse here, considering my health, and the heat of the season."[22]

Just before graduation he wrote his parents a long letter summarizing
his experiences at Dummer and looking to the future:

> Dummer's Sons begin to feal the Approach of Commencement;
> ardently and impatiently to wait the wished for Time, and yet with
> fear to dread it, when he must pass the fiery Tryal, and be weighed
> in the Scails. I hope no part thereof is rusty, and that any of us will
> not be found despicably wanting. The very Thought striks my das-
> tardly pusillanimous Soul with Fear. . . . I can scarce perform one

Period to my Master without a strange Palpitation. . . .

I hope I shall ever be thankful that it was my Fortune to fall
under the Tutelage of such a worthy Gentleman [Moody]. He has
almost every Thing requisite to constitute the Schollar, and the Gentleman. . . . He has one very valuable Quality in particular . . . in
telling People their Failings and Faults, without incurring their Displeasure. . . . he has been extreamly kind upon every Occasion; he
scarce ever denyd me a Request, I believe never a reasonable one; he
has treated me with all the Tenderness possible. . . . The Needy are
Witnesses to his very great Generosity. . . . but I am . . . dispairing
of ever recompensing him, except by Behaving in the best Manner
I am able.[23]

And he closed, characteristically, by giving precise specifications for a pair
of "Leather Breaches" he was anxious to buy. The letter is certainly a
typical schoolboy missive—the examination jitters, pride in the school's record (thirteen were going to Harvard), affection for his teacher, especially
with school days all but over, concern about clothes. All things considered,
young Sam could not have had a better preparation for college than he got
from Master Moody. And yet the Dummer years were in a sense atypical
ones when one considers Sam's life as a whole. In his letters home there is
no trace of the almost morbid concern with salvation that would occupy
him at Harvard. This period of his schooling was a cheerful, bright interlude in what, for the most part, was to be a somber life.

Harvard College, when young Sam Phillips entered it in the late summer
of 1767, was approaching the end of an era. President Edward Holyoke,
who had assumed office in 1737, had two more years to go before his death.
During his administration Harvard had prospered. The curriculum had
been overhauled, teaching strengthened, and the plant improved. When
Sam arrived, he would have found two new buildings in the yard—Hollis
Hall, in which he would live, and a new Harvard Hall, replacing the one
that had burned down in 1764. Moreover, the College was crowded; in
1761 ninety students had been forced to board in the town of Cambridge;
and Sam's own class of 1771 numbered sixty-three—the largest to date in
the history of the college. If Sam followed the normal procedure, his admission would have been determined by an examination in Greek and
Latin and testimony to his having a "good moral character." When President Holyoke died in 1769, he was succeeded by Samuel Locke, who would
head the College for the rest of Sam's stay in Cambridge, and be forced to
resign after three years on the job because he impregnated his maidservant.

Undergraduate life was anything but puritanical. A Loyalist lady wrote
of Harvard, "Here is a College indeed, but the Independency and Liberty
with which the Youths are brought up, and indulged, makes too many of
'em proficients in Vice." In 1759 the Overseers had repealed a law for-

bidding the drinking of punch, and from then on, undergraduate behavior, perhaps encouraged by the political fracases of the day, began to
degenerate, reaching a new low during the presidency of the unfortunate
Samuel Locke. Classes and chapel were cut with impunity, parties in Boston were popular, and the undergraduates became more and more insub-
ordinate. To control all this the College had instituted a series of punishments, mostly fines ranging from twopence for tardiness to twenty shillings
for breaking open doors and picking locks. Blasphemy, fornication, rob-
bery, forgery, or "Any other very atrocious crime" was punished by expulsion. And expulsion was not just a matter of packing one's bags and
leaving. The culprit was drummed out of the institution before all his classmates. The food was bad and constantly complained of, with the climax
coming in the great butter riot of 1764, precipitated by the serving of ran-
cid butter. Despite the relaxing of standards of behavior, academic excellence was still prized, and the long list of distinguished Harvard graduates
who were there in Sam's time indicates that one could still get a good education in Cambridge.[24]

While Sam was at college, he kept a journal intermittently, fragments of
which are preserved in the Phillips Papers. The outstanding characteristic
of this journal is the amount of space devoted to self-flagellation for presumed faults, morbid discussion of failings, and apprehension for the
future if sinful behavior is not corrected. "I am very much inclined to a
State of Indolence and Sloth," he wrote, "I am almost continually guilty of
shamefull Neglect." When alarmed by a severe thunderstorm, he wrote,
"may it be my constant care to be in Readiness, so that my last change may
not . . . prove awfull as it is to those who have not made their peace
with God."[25] On another occasion he reviled himself for sleeping in church
during the sermon.[26] He was constantly thinking of death and judgment;
when he heard his grandfather was sick, he wrote, "May I make it my
Business to be preparing for the Agonies of dissolving Nature."[27] On New
Year's eve, 1768, he reviewed the year just past and found little pleasing
in it: "My Sins are very great, for I have often sayd I will forsake my sinful Ways, but my Fruit has not Witness'd a Reformation. Oh that the Almighty would inspire me with Zeal in this World which if neglected must
occasion endless Horror." He was still at it on the last extant page of his
journal, written on 8 September 1770, where he comments again on his
failure to reform: "yet I immediately return'd as a Dog to his Vomit, and
as a Sow that has returned to her Wallowing in the Mire."

To judge by his journal one would suppose that young Sam did almost
nothing at Harvard for four years except worry about his soul, but this is
by no means the case. In March 1768, for example, he wrote his parents
an angry letter denouncing his Divinity Professor, Edward Wigglesworth,
who was relatively young and inexperienced and seemed to Sam completely unqualified for his position.[28] According to Sam, "A Large Number here

are very uneasy about our Divinity Professor. His Lectures are generally attended with a very indecent Noise of the Feet which yesterday . . . he took Occasion to denounce. He told them that if any would bring their Names to him and a Note from their Fathers that they did not desire they should be instructed in the Branch of Theology . . . he would lay it before the Overseers and try to get us excused." This, according to Sam, would be the equivalent of making the students "Publickly proclaimed ATHEISTS." Nor could the students get together and draw up a petition, for the College authorities had made them all promise that they would never enter into any "Combinations." As a result, "Should they inflict upon us the *tormenting* Punishments and like the Tyrants of Old order us to be torn in Pieces for their Amusement, we may not as a Body bring it to the Case in Hand; should the most despicable Person in the World be plac'd in the most Important Station (as this truly is) we must remain in Silence, without the least murmur, submit our Necks to the Yoke, rather than seek Redress or else violate their Commands and our own Solemn Engagements."[29] Despite Sam's outrage, this contretemps blew over without further trouble, and Wigglesworth went on to have a distinguished career at Harvard.

Yet the undergraduate attacks on their Divinity Professor were just a curtain-raiser for the most serious disturbances that occurred a few weeks later and are known in the Harvard records as "The Disorders of 1768."[30] The trouble arose when the tutors, in an effort to tighten up classroom discipline, decreed that no student could offer an excuse for not reciting unless he got his instructor's permission before class. This decree was met with defiance and violence by the undergraduates and before the affair was over, some undergraduates had threatened to transfer to Yale, two tutors had had their windows broken, the deputy sheriff of Middlesex County had been called in, and four ringleaders were fired. Sam Phillips played only a minor role in this fracas, and that primarily because his friend Stephen Peabody of Andover was one of the ringleaders who got expelled. Sam was one of fifty-five students examined by the President and Faculty in an effort to get at the truth. He readily named the ringleaders and reported that Peabody had threatened to bring down a mob from Andover to intimidate the officials. Other students reported that it was Sam's idea to have a class meeting to organize resistance and that when he heard about the tutor's windows being broken, he said he was glad of it.[31] Eventually the Overseers rescinded the Administration's decision to expel the ringleaders, much to President Holyoke's outrage, and the trouble died down. As might have been expected, Sam's father, the Squire, took a dim view of the whole business. He wrote Sam a stern letter ordering him to avoid combinations and under no circumstances to combat properly constituted authority.[32]

Sam recorded in his journal some new disorders later in the year, but did not participate in them. "On Wednesday night," he wrote, "Mr. Wigglesworth's and Mr. Scale's Effigies were hung on the Tree in Hollis Square with their Dying Speaches on their Breasts, and a Copy of each was posted on the Tree in Harvard Square. The Form of a Heart was taken out of his [the Governor's] picture in the Hall, in the Night. The Widow Wyth's Fowls were stolen, 6 Sheep killed, which must have been done by some inconsiderate Person, an Enemy to the Peace of Society. We have received good Treatment from the Governor since Commencement and we cant expect better from this."[33] Sam the Sophomore is more law-abiding than Sam the Freshman.

Despite the rising tide of trouble with Britain, undergraduate attitudes at Harvard during this period were "mainly apolitical."[34] Earlier writers would have us believe that once the trouble with Britain began, Sam became an instant patriot and threw himself wholeheartedly into the American cause.[35] His journal and letters do not bear this out. He does record a few of the political events of the period in his journal, but he invariably returns at once to the problem of his soul. On 18 June 1768 he wrote, "from the State of National Affairs we have reason to fear a Revolution, and justly may we expect it for we have sinn'd with a very high Hand." His account of the arrival of British troops that same year is purely factual, written without personal comment.[36] He records the vote of the Harvard undergraduates not to use "Tea of foreign Production" and adds, "there were some in each Class that dissented, and were very resolute; tho' it appears to me without any Reason. They did not act the part of Gentlemen. By all these things we can see what human Nature is. Is it not the working of Pride?"[37] In another entry he writes, "Last Monday Evening was observ'd here as the Anniversary of the Repeal of the Stamp Act, but the Fatigue I experienc'd therefore is Folly. I have misspent a vast deal of precious Time."[38] The best example of Sam's attitude toward political events is his account of the Boston Massacre: "Monday there were four mortally wounded at Boston by the Soldiers, several others very bad if not more dangerous. On Thursday they were buried in the presence of a large Number of People. Let this among others prove a Warning to me. Can I recollect that this Day Week they made as much Dependence on Life and with as good reason [as] I did?"[39] When the time came for Sam to serve the Revolutionary cause, he dedicated himself to it without reservation, but during his college years, like other Harvard undergraduates, he was not aroused by the political issues of the day.[40]

Other, less serious aspects of Sam's life at Harvard, as revealed in his letters and journals, included getting seasick on his first sailing expedition,[41] singing at Thanksgiving services in chapel "with Applause,"[42] and attending a memorable dinner with Colonel William Brattle. Sam describes this last occasion as follows:

Last Sabbath Morning in common Time Colonel Brattle came up to

College and went into the Kitchen among the Negroes, and there took his Seat. His Habit, which may be better conceived than describ'd I will give a short Description of. He had on a very remarkable Cap, such as I never saw before and I do not think there is such another, an Old Rusty, dirty, greasy, Red, Hatsthick Coat bound on with an old Belt, a Pair of miserable Shoes slip-shod. He invited Mr. Willard, one Master viz. Mr. Marvel [?] Mr. Hall Sr., my Chum, Saltonstall, Governor's Son, and me to dine with him. We all waited upon him and were entertained with the following Dellicacies (Viz) 1st. an Indian Pudding, 2ndly an uncommon Soop consisting of Cabbage, turnips, Carrots, Biscakes, Meat etc.etc.etc. 3rd some cold meat, 4th Neat's tongue, 5th Hog's Harslet, 6th a Rost'd Goose, 7th 2 Rost'd Ducks, 8th a Chicken Pye. We were tended by 3 Negroes, defended by 8 Swords with many other Instruments of War. Thus he.[43]

Little evidence remains of Sam's progress as a student. The Harvard Faculty Records indicate that he was given a Hebrew grammar, excused from Commons twice, fined once for absence, and was the recipient of the Hopkins Gift, in his case Montesqueri's *Rise and Fall of the Roman Republic*.[44] Among the Phillips Papers is an undated essay entitled *Obsequium Amicos, Veritas Odium parit*. Despite the Latin title, the theme is in English and deals with the problems of correcting the mistakes of one's friends. Sam's biographer speaks of a "salutatory oration" in Latin that Sam delivered on Commencement day, but the document is no longer among his papers.[45] In his senior year he led some of his classmates in the formation of what was called the "Speaking Club," later known as the "American Institute of 1770" and, later still, absorbed by the Hasty Pudding Club. Every two weeks the club met to hear one of its members declaim before his fellows, but there is no record of Sam's speaking, for all his zeal to found the organization.[46] It can hardly be said that Sam was a true leader at Harvard. But he was accepted and respected, and he could well be proud of his overall achievement.[47]

As commencement approached, a problem arose. The budding graduate wanted to invite a large group of friends, put them all up in Cambridge, entertain them properly, and have his father foot the bill. He was particularly anxious to invite the Foxcroft family, including Phoebe Foxcroft, who, although nine years his senior, was soon to become his wife. The old man seems to have been diffident about Sam's proposal. As a result he wrote his father a long letter arguing his case:

in any joyful event there seems to be great fitness in calling in our friends to rejoice with us ... . That this is a time to rejoice I think I may venture to say; for (*thro' the goodness of God*) I don't know how I could have made a more honorable egress, than I have a prospect of making, if we take into consideration the whole term of my residence. Many instances present themselves in Holy Writ, of eminent servants, who assembled their friends to partake with them in the happiness of any prosperity. . . . The cost, I know, will be great; but why is wealth given, but to be used in a lawful and proper way?"

And he signed the letter, "Duty and love, sir, if you please."[48] Unfortunately, there is no record of whether or not Sam had the kind of Commencement he wished. One hopes that the Squire loosened his purse strings and put on a fine show for the boy.

Fairly soon after his first arrival at Harvard young Sam began to be a regular visitor at the home of the Honorable Francis Foxcroft in Cambridge. It was quite natural that he should do this, for the Foxcrofts were related by marriage to the family of his uncle, William Phillips, then living in Boston. Besides, the Foxcrofts were attractive, upper-crust people and their home was very close to the Harvard Yard. Francis Foxcroft was a Harvard graduate (1712) who had throughout his life held a variety of judicial positions in the Province, the most important being that of Judge of the Court of Common Pleas for Middlesex County. He was a Harvard Overseer, whose devotion to his Alma Mater is attested by his laborious preparation of an alphabetical list of all Harvard men since the founding of the College, "in order for the more speedily finding the Names of our Worthy Ancestors." He was a pious man, evidenced by the fact that he never swore, even under "the most cruciating Paroxisms of the Gout." He and his wife Mehitabel had produced ten sons and five daughters, most of whom died in infancy.[49] But there was one, Phoebe, born 12 August 1743, who must have attracted the attention of young Sam early in the game, even though she was nine years his senior. It is difficult to tell just when the affair became serious, for most of the references to the Foxcrofts in the Phillips Papers for this period are undated. But the Squire and his wife Elizabeth often ask to be remembered to the Foxcrofts in letters to their son, and Sam, in an undated letter to his mother, urges his family to invite the Foxcrofts out for a visit. "Their Company is entertaining & improving and unless they come to Andover in the Fall Vacation I can't see them hereafter with a good Face," he writes.[50] Finally, in the letter to his father about celebrating Commencement, he includes the Foxcrofts among the desired guests, as noted above, and particularly mentions the need for inviting "some of the other sex." In view of later events, it is clear that young Sam was smitten.

Well he might have been. Phoebe has been described by Sam's biographer as "highly cultivated in mind and manners, the very centre of an attractive and courted circle, sprightly, ardent, sanguine."[51] A run of letters to her mother, written before her marriage, bears this out. Unlike the crude epistles that Sam's mother scrawled to him, Phoebe Foxcroft's letters are those of a well-educated woman. They reveal an affectionate daughter, well adjusted, with a good sense of humor and a shrewd business sense. Like her husband-to-be, she was a highly religious person, but there is none of the morbidity in her writing that is characteristic of his. She took family ties seriously, and her letters are full of concern for her parents and other relatives. She enjoyed sending her mother little presents: "I cou'd think of nothing so agreeable as what is contain'd in the Bottle I send by my Brother . . . and beg you wou'd when tasting it think of your good for nothing Daughter—who presents the Triffle." Or again: "I send you a Bottle of Snuff which is reckon'd here *very good* & a little Oatmeal."[52] Phoebe went frequently to Boston as a young girl to visit friends. Her letters written on these visits detail the prices of articles in Boston stores, express indignation at the mud in the Boston streets ("it seems impossible to stir"), request shopping money ("when I came from home I had not even a Copper at Command"),[53] describe a trip in 1768 ("to see the soldiers exercise"),[54] apologize for messy writing ("such a pen & Ink I never wrote with in all my Life"),[55] and are generally informal and sprightly.

The course of true love did not run smooth for Sam Phillips and Phoebe Foxcroft. What follows is undocumented family tradition, but there seems to be no reason to doubt at least the main outlines of the story. When Sam announced his intentions to his parents, they apparently raised strong objections—primarily because of the age difference but also because of what the Squire called a "disagreeable criticising Disposition" on the part of Phoebe. But Sam was, perhaps for the first time in his life, unwilling to accept parental dicta on such an important subject. He decided to enlist the help of his Uncle John Phillips, who, Sam might well believe, would be sympathetic to his problem, since John's first wife had been sixteen years his senior. In a long and passionate letter the young lover attempts to dispose of the various objections to the match. That Phoebe, as one of a large family, would bring no dowry was of little consequence, since the Squire had repeatedly said "he does not care whether I get one Copper with a Woman." Differences in ages, he insists, mean nothing when two people love one another. To blame unhappiness in marriage on such difference is to confuse cause and effect; it is like claiming that differences in stature produce marital misery. The attitude of the Squire his father was hardest to bear. He had already given Sam "the black Character of an undutiful Son, a Charge, my Uncle, I am forced in tears to tell you, has already harrow'd . . . I hope it did not give a Kind Father so much Pain to say it as it did his ungrateful Son to hear it." In closing, Sam begged "the Liberty of casting myself at your Feet, there to supplicate with that Importunity which is natural to one in the most melancholy Dilemma, that you would advice with my father, in that Way and in that Season, which your Wisdom and Tenderness shall direct, promising that a Sense of your Kindness shall swell the Obligation of your very Obliged Nephew."[56]

There is no evidence of what effect, if any, this impassioned appeal had on either Uncle John or the Squire. The chances are that the Squire, who must have heard all these arguments before, remained unshaken in his resolve. But something else did intervene to change the Squire's mind. According to Sam's biographer, who must have got his information directly from members of the family:

> It was with this bitter weight on his spirit, in other respects so glad, that he left the college. For a time, he struggled against the deep current of his feelings and judgment, if so be he could possibly ere long forget her, and she him; but in health his spirits were depressed, and in sickness his wounded heart was his worst malady. It was in the hour of deep solicitude for him, when there were but faint hopes of his life, that his parents, who had not been sensible, till his physician told them, how deeply he had suffered on account of their opposition, consented to yield.[57]

Whatever the truth of all this, Sam and Phoebe were finally married on 6 July 1773 and began a marriage that was to prove all the groom's predictions true and his father's false. The only relic of the wedding is a poem composed "In Celebration of the Nuptuals of Mr. Phillips and Miss

4. *Samuel Phillips, Jr. Portrait by John Johnston, in the possession of C. Lloyd Thomas of North Andover, Massachusetts, and reproduced with his permission.*

Foxcroft. Humbly presented to the Bride." A short sample will suffice:

> Before this day, which shines serently bright,
> Completes its Revolution; and Yon Clock
> That faithful Monitor, that counts the Time,
> Strikes Twelve to warn us of the Midnight hour;
> Will be enroll'd in Hymen's Sacred List
> The happiest Couple, and the worthiest too,
> That ever yet ador'd the Nuptial Torch . . .
>
> This is a Match, that sure was form'd in heaven,
> By God himself ordain'd for wisest Ends;
> Such noble hearts were made to blend in one,
> To share each other's Bliss, and live in Love![58]

Shortly after the wedding the happy couple moved to North Andover, where they lived with the Squire and Elizabeth for a time and then moved to a little house near by. In a letter to her mother, composed some three weeks after the wedding, Phoebe wrote: "I am happy if the continued Kindness of the most agreable Partner can effect it. . . . I am as yet treated

5. Phoebe Phillips. Portrait presumably by John Johnston, in the possession of C. Lloyd Thomas of North Andover, Massachusetts, and reproduced with his permission.

with all the Marks of Tenderness which I am conscious of deserving."[59] That Phoebe was assuming housewifely duties is seen in a later letter where she requests her mother to send the receipt for Metheglin, a fermented drink made of honey, and asks if the Foxcrofts would like any honey at 5/6 or possibly 5/3.[60] Since Francis Foxcroft died in 1768, Phoebe's mother was left pretty much alone in Cambridge, and the daughter's letters are full of concern for the old lady's health and happiness. Sometime in the late 1770's Mehitabel Foxcroft moved out to Andover to spend her last days with her daughter and son-in-law, and died there in 1782. Phoebe's life in North Andover must also have been cheered by the arrival of her niece, Martha Brandon, a cultivated and charming girl who married Samuel Osgood of North Andover in 1775, only to die tragically three years later.[61] But the most joyful event in Phoebe's life occurred on 18 October 1776, when her son John was born. Writing to her husband in Boston shortly after the birth, she says, "Mr. Osgood has just call'd to give me an opportunity of writing a Line to my Beloved, which I dismiss our little Son to embrace; he is now asleep in *his* little Box,, and well, except something of a Cold."[62] Or again, "I would be tedious to enter into the minutia relative to our little Boy. . . . I want you shou'd see him very much, but not more I dare say than you want to hold him to your Honest Heart."[63] Her husband responded in kind. He wrote of being "abstracted from every care other than a Solicitude for the Welfare and happyness of my Partner and our little Boy."[64] Sometime in 1777, when it had become clear that Phillips Academy was to be on Andover Hill and not in North Andover, the couple moved to a house on what is now Phillips Street, formerly belonging to George Abbot, and were living there in April 1778. By the time the school was founded, therefore, Samuel Phillips was happily married to a remarkably congenial and gifted wife, was the proud father of an infant son, and had cut loose from his parents to establish himself in Andover's South Parish.

It remains to speak of Sam's remarkably active public life during this period. He appears, after graduation from college, to have helped his father with the latter's store and to have engaged in various mercantile transactions with Samuel Abbot, a merchant in Boston who later moved to Andover, and with his uncle, William Phillips. In addition, he acquired several tracts of land that were farmed by hired hands under his supervision—so successfully that he gained the reputation of being one of the best farmers in the area.[65] Two years after graduation from college, at the age of twenty-one, he first entered public life when he was chosen to succeed his father as town clerk and town treasurer, positions he was to hold for many years, ably assisted by his wife, who copied most of the minutes for him and kept some of the treasurer's books as well. Early in 1774 he was made chairman of a committee to draft resolutions expressing the town's reaction to British policy. The committee came up with a resolve

that anyone using tea of foreign importation should incur the town's displeasure—no mean thing in those days. After the fighting started, he was
chosen to represent the town at the Provincial Congress that met at Watertown in July 1775, appropriately enough near the grave of his great-great-
great grandfather, George Phillips. The records of the Congress make it
clear that from the very beginning Sam Phillips was an extraordinarily able
and active member. The mere listing of his committee assignments is impressive: he was twice on a committee to confer with General Washington
about the war; he served on committees to countersign notes emitted by the
Continental Congress, to direct the mustering and paying of militia, to
superintend the delivery of powder to towns, to report on the condition of
the defense of Boston harbor, to bring in a bill to punish deserters, to see
what should be done with men "who enlist or are drafted into the army,
but have not marched," to confer with the Faculty of Harvard College respecting grants to the officers, to bring in a bill to encourage the manufacture of iron, and to draft a letter to Congress upon the subject of the em-
bargo. But it was not simply the multiplicity of legislative chores that distinguished him. He was an effective speaker before the Congress. One
writer says of him, "He was in the first grade of eminence; his speeches
were clear, concise, logical, direct, and nervous; but he made no effort to
amuse the fancy, and never sacrificed anything to mere rhetoric."[66] Yet he
did not limit his work to legislative matters. In 1775 he was put in charge
of moving the books from the Harvard Library to Andover for safe-keep-
ing—indeed, while at this task he missed hearing the guns on Bunker
Hill.[67] In short, whatever reservations he may have had about the coming
conflict while he was a student at Harvard, he had no doubts about the
justice of the patriot cause once the die had been cast for war. He wrote
his wife during this period: "But what Demands are so strong as my Country's; after that Duty is discharg'd, which he that does not regard is worse
than an Infidel."[68]

The best known contribution that Samuel Phillips made to the Revolutionary cause is, of course, the production of gunpowder for the Continental Army at the mill he established in Andover.[69] The desperate need
of the patriot forces for gunpowder is so well known as to need little
documentation. During almost all the siege of Boston General Washington
was placed in the cruel position of being unable to attack for want of gunpowder, and his temper was not improved by the constant criticism he received for not attacking, a criticism he was unable to answer openly for
fear the British would learn of his army's weakness in this respect. As he
wrote the Continental Congress, "To maintain a post within musket shot of
the enemy for six months together without ammunition . . . is more than
probably was ever attempted."[70] In an effort to correct this situation, the
Provincial Congress, late in 1775, took steps to establish two powder mills,
one in Sutton, the other in Stoughton, where it was thought that an old

powder mill could be reactivated. Early in January, however, Sam Phillips approached the legislature with an offer to build and operate a mill at Andover. This offer was immediately accepted by the Congress and in a few days Sam was off and running. Since neither Sam nor the Congress knew much about the manufacture of gunpowder, the first step was to call in some specialists. Sam accordingly wrote one Samuel Cunnabell at Bernardstown and all but drafted him for the job. Cunnabell, described as a person of "great Ingenuity," was enjoined "without *fail* to set off *immediately* for Watertown" and join Sam as soon as he got there. To make his point even clearer, Sam added, "It is of the [first] importance not only that this Business be accomplished, but accomplished with the greatest conceivable Expedition:—one hour's unnecessary delay may prove fatal. No particular Concerns of your own can possibly be consider'd as any Bar to your complying instantly with this Request. No previous Engagement to any private person can be view'd as of any weight when compar'd with this Call—in short every other Concern must give way to this—for on the Expedition of this undertaking may depend our Salvation."[71] For all his enthusiasm for the patriot cause, Sam made sure that the enterprise was founded on sound business principles. The following week he formalized an agreement with the Congress whereby it was to furnish him with saltpetre and sulphur at cost for a year and pay him a bounty of eightpence a pound for what he manufactured. In return Sam agreed to sell only to the government or its agents, publish all discoveries about powder manufacture that he should make, and keep a guard at his mill "to prevent any wicked and designing person from destroying the same."[72] Immediately after this agreement was reached, Sam rushed back to Andover and called a meeting of the townspeople to put the project before them. He had already purchased a mill-seat on the Shawsheen River, near where the Marland Mills were later established, and now he needed labor. According to tradition, he told his fellow-citizens: "I want your help, and will engage to pay you if the business pays; but if it fails, you must consent to lose your labor; the powder is needed for the common cause, and we must work together."[73] All that remained was to find out how to make gunpowder.

There is nothing in the record to indicate that Samuel Cunnabell, for all his "great Ingenuity," contributed anything to the new project. Fortunately for Sam, however, his old Dummer classmate and Harvard friend, Eliphalet Pearson, was living in Andover at the time. Pearson was a scholar of the first rank and had at least some knowledge of chemistry, which was more than most of the others connected with the enterprise had. To Pearson was assigned the task of developing the proper formula for making powder, and he went to work with a will. Among the Pearson Papers are several documents containing specific instructions on the manufacture of powder and collected from a wide variety of sources. One Levi Shephard of Northampton had written a long description to Major Joseph Hawley, a representative at Watertown, and this had found its way to Andover. There was a long report of the Committee or Congress which had been asked to investigate the matter, and a similar article from a Pennsylvania newspaper. There were also passages from Neumann's *Chemistry* and Macquer's *Chemistry*.[74] Pearson, who was teaching the town school at the time, turned his classroom into a laboratory for experiments, and on several occasions his pupils arrived only to be greeted by a cluttered classroom and a sleepy master muttering, "No school today. No school today."[75] Eventually success crowned Pearson's endeavors and a more or less adequate formula for making powder was developed. The main problem was to get enough saltpetre. Pearson's authorities all had advice on how to scrape it off old cellar walls, how to distill it from earth impregnated with the chemical, and how to purify it. Yet even though the barns and outbuildings in the town were scoured, it was always difficult to maintain an adequate supply. While Pearson was solving the chemical problems, Sam was leading his fellow citizens in the construction of the mill itself. Just how all the problems were finally overcome is not clear, but by the spring of that same year the Phillips mill was turning out an estimated twelve hundred pounds of powder a week.

New difficulties with the enterprise continued to arise. First, there was a shortage of stoves, presumably needed to distill the saltpeter. Sam wrote the Commissary-General that he was "borrowing" one from the meeting house, without waiting for the approval of the legislature, so that work would not be delayed, and he wrote Timothy Pickering that the selectmen of Marblehead had agreed that he could use their stove in his mill. Just as things seemed to be going well, the foreman and his chief assistant were drafted into the army. Sam, moving quickly, got the Congress to defer the two men. There were still plenty of bugs in the manufacturing process itself, as is evidenced by complaints from various people, including General Washington himself, that the quality of Andover powder was substandard. Washington wrote General Heath that there must be "either roguery or gross Ignorance" among the powder manufacturers.[76] To correct this failing, Sam sent one Lemuel Cox, another "Person of singular Ingenuity" to Elbridge Gerry in Philadelphia to see if any new manufacturing techniques could be discovered to the south.[77] Apparently Cox was turned over to Robert Treat Paine; in any event Cox wrote him later that he had "deliver'd yr. Letter to Mr. Phillips which he receiv'd with the greatest pleasure & thanks; if anything more comes to yr. knowledge respecting Salt peter or powder making he would be much oblig'd for a Continuation of yr. kindness as he is determined to pursue all measures that may be any ways conducive to the salvation of American Liberties."[78]

Later on, two French specialists, Nicholas Fouquett and his son Mark, who had come to America "to propagate the art of making powder in these States" were ordered to Andover to help. Although the two foreigners came up with an ingenious method of "forming the Morter," Sam disagreed with some of their other suggestions, and it is doubtful whether, on balance, the enterprise benefited very much from the counsel of the two Frenchmen.[79] The whole project received a severe setback when, in June 1778, just after the founding of Phillips Academy, an explosion wrecked a good part of the mill and killed three men. Though the Congress absolved Sam from responsibility in this disaster, the effect of it on the town was chilling, and production fell off badly for some months afterward. Before the war was over, Sam's labor force had been augmented by some German prisoners captured at the time of Burgoyne's surrender, but again problems arose when the government proposed to recall them for use in a prisoner exchange. Sam protested this strongly. In addition to slowing down production, he said, the men would prefer to stay in Andover, where "some have married, had Children, taken the Oath of Allegiance, paid taxes, and become useful Members of Society."[80] Presumably the Congress relented and allowed the Germans to stay. The mill continued to produce powder for the rest of the war and on into the 1790's, when a second explosion convinced Sam that he had better concentrate on the manufacture of paper, an enterprise that had already been started. Even when allowances are made for the inferior quality of some of the Andover powder, however, there is no question that Sam made a signal contribution to the patriot cause in the production of this essential ingredient of war.

By April 1778, therefore, Samuel Phillips, Jr., had established himself as a man of business, head of a happy household, leader in the war effort, and a representative in the Massachusetts legislature. One might think that he had enough hay on his fork, but this proved not to be the case, for in the midst of these manifold responsibilities, during one of the darkest periods of the Revolution, he and his father and his uncle found time to establish a school.

CHAPTER THREE

THE FOUNDING OF PHILLIPS ACADEMY

O N E O F the most extraordinary things about Phillips Academy is the date of its founding. Only the most compelling of reasons could have led Samuel Phillips, Jr., to devote the time and energy necessary to establish a school in the dark days of 1778, when the cause of American freedom was still in the balance and when he himself was already committed to so many other activities. Changes were occurring in the New England society of his day, and he viewed them with deeply felt alarm. In a very real sense Phillips Academy was founded as a bulwark against change, an agency for maintaining the virtues of the past.

An understanding of colonial education cannot be obtained merely by a study of formal educational institutions. Agencies like the family, the church, and the community, as noted, generally played a much more important part in the development of the young than did schools and colleges.[1] The early settlers did not anticipate a transformation of the educational system they brought with them from England. "The basis of education lay secure within the traditions of an integrated, unified culture. The future might be uncertain, but the uncertainties were limited. Nothing disturbed the confident expectation that the world of the child's maturity would be the same as that of the parents' youth, and that the past would continue to be an effective guide to the future."[2] But as the eighteenth century wore on, the American colonists were in for a rude shock:

> By the end of the colonial period [the educational system] had been radically transformed. Education had been dislodged from its ancient position in the social order, wrenched loose from the automatic, instinctive workings of society, and cast as a matter for deliberation into the forefront of consciousness. Its functionings had become problematic and controversial. Many were transferred from informal to formal institutions, from agencies to whose major purpose they had been incidental to those, for the most part schools, to which they were primary. Schools and formal schooling had acquired a new importance. They had assumed cultural burdens they had not borne

before. Where there had been deeply ingrained habits, unquestioned tradition, automatic responses, security, and confidence there was now awareness, doubt, formality, will, and decision. The whole range of education had become an instrument of deliberate social purpose.[3]

For one like Samuel Phillips, Jr., dedicated to the preservation of the old concepts of family and church, these changes could only be alarming.

A recent study of Andover during the colonial period shows that the town was changing also. Seventeenth-century Andover, once the trauma of transplantation passed, had developed into a stable community dominated by the patriarchal family. By the middle of the eighteenth century, however, the old patriarchal system was beginning to crumble. This transformation of one of the basic educational institutions of the land—for the family is certainly that—undoubtedly had repercussions in other fields as well. Though Andover remained orthodox during most of the eighteenth century, towns where Andoverians had settled welcomed with enthusiasm the revivalist movement known as the Great Awakening. Finally, the breakdown of paternal authority over sons may well have prepared the way for a similar breakdown in royal authority over the colonies. In short, by 1778 the basic societal institutions that had played such a large part in educating children in the broadest sense—the family, the church, and the political system—were all being challenged and in some cases were in disarray.[4]

There is clear evidence that Phillips was alarmed at the changes taking place around him. He felt keenly that the basic institutions of the society he knew were coming down around his ears. Though his was not a patriarchal family in the technical sense of the term, his father the Squire was certainly a patriarch, as we have seen. Even though his native town had thus far withstood the inroads of evangelical religion, the Reverend William Symmes, pastor from 1759 to 1807 of the First Parish, in what is now North Andover, was suspected of holding unorthodox beliefs, and waves of heresy were lapping at the town's boundaries. Sam's experiences at Harvard would not have been reassuring to a pious young man, and the widespread relaxing of moral standards that usually accompanies war would be a matter of serious concern to him and to his father. Finally, we should not underestimate the trauma that defiance of British authority must have brought to even such stout patriots as Sam. To defy the king, to be branded as a rebel could not have been accepted easily by one as conservative as Sam Phillips—indeed his Uncle John in Exeter could not bring himself to take such a step. There can be no question of Sam's concern for the future of the society he knew. In an undated letter that was probably written in 1776, he speaks of "the present degeneracy which has increased upon us with such rapidity." In the preamble he wrote to the School's Constitution, he speaks of "the prevalence of ignorance and vice, disorder and wickedness" and asserts "that YOUTH is the important period, on the improvement or neglect of which depend the most important consequences to individuals themselves and the community." He goes on to say, "A serious consideration of the premises, and an observation of the growing neglect of YOUTH, have excited in us a painful anxiety." From these statements it follows that Phillips Academy was founded not only to combat the revolutionary changes in New England society, but to keep the Revolution from going too far in effecting changes in American society generally. When he speaks of "painful anxiety" his words must be taken literally and his concern as genuine. His purpose to "learn them [youth] the GREAT END AND REAL BUSINESS OF LIVING" meant instruction in the old virtues that he feared would be abandoned in the uncertain days ahead.[5]

Even if one accepts this explanation, the question remains, why did he choose the type of school he did? Earlier writers have suggested a wide variety of possible influences on the young man, including Plato's Academy, the Spartan gymnasia, Milton, Locke, Benjamin Franklin, and the British dissenting clergyman Philip Doddridge. There are superficial similarities in one or another of Sam's early plans for a school to all of these. He must have been aware of the first two from his reading in college, and he does speak about following the "antients" in establishing a school. Both Phillips and Milton (in his *Essay on Education*, 1644) write of the need of having boarding students housed in comfortable quarters. Both Phillips and Locke (in his *Some Thoughts Concerning Education*, 1693) stress virtue as the primary aim of education. Both Phillips and Franklin questioned the emphasis on the classics and desired a more practical education, though Sam was talked out of this before the Phillips Academy Constitution reached its final form. The difficulty is that there is no hard evidence that Sam ever read these particular works, though he does make a general reference to Milton at one point. If one is to assume that the form of Phillips Academy was the result of something he had read, Dr. Doddridge is the most likely influence, for he and Isaac Watts were Sam's favorite clergymen, and he read their books over and over again. For example, when, just before his death, he left one thousand dollars to provide for the distribution of religious books among the citizens of Andover one stipulation was that Doddridge's *Address to the Master of a Family on Family Religion* should head the list. The case is strengthened by the fact that Doddridge had founded a dissenting academy in Northampton, England, in 1729 and had conducted it for twenty-two years. But this academy bore little resemblance to Phillips Academy. Its main purpose was to train dissenting ministers, and the whole establishment was run in a slipshod manner because Dr. Doddridge was busy with other matters. Finally, it is impossible to determine just when Sam became so enamoured of Doddridge; there is no mention of him in any of Sam's papers dated before 1778. In short, speculation on the influence of specific authors is a dubious business.[6] It seems much more likely that Phillips Academy was given the form that its Constitution prescribed as a result of Samuel Phillips' own experiences in life and as a result of many discussions with his family and friends.

One of the influences on the young man, either positive or negative, must have been the system of secondary education in the Massachusetts of his day. This system had had a long history.[7] No sooner had the Puritans arrived in Massachusetts than they started schools. But early in the game the General Court decided that education was too important a matter to be left up to the inclinations of different towns, and in 1642 the first important province-wide act was passed, placing responsibility on parents and masters of apprentices to see to it that young people were taught to read so as to be able to understand "the principles of religion and the capital laws of the country." The most famous of early Puritan educational measures was, of course, the "old deluder Satan" law of 1647, passed, apparently, in the belief that leaving education up to parents was too loose a policy to be effective. The act required every Massachusetts town with fifty families to appoint a schoolmaster to teach children to read and write, and every town of one hundred families to establish a grammar school to fit youth for college. Reinforced by supplementary statutes passed at later times, this law still reflected the basic policy of Massachusetts Bay toward education at the time Phillips Academy was founded.

Passing a law was one thing; enforcing it was another. Over the years, most towns eventually complied with the law, but there were always at any given time a substantial number that reneged. For this dereliction they could be haled into court and fined as much as twenty pounds. Though many towns were charged with violating the law, they proved most ingenious in advancing reasons for their noncompliance. Chelmsford, for example, insisted in 1710 that it would be unsafe for children to go to school in these times of Indian raids, where they might be "exposed to the snares of our Lurking Enemy." Generally speaking, most courts were lenient in dealing with delinquent towns, and as the population increased and the Indian danger receded, compliance steadily improved.

The schools were administered by the towns themselves. Aside from establishing general policy, the province set up no machinery to deal with education. At the start town meetings discussed school matters, but by the eighteenth century the practice had become fairly widespread of having special school committees, elected by the town, deal with the schools. Then, as now, membership on the town's school committee was considered a mark of distinction, and the committeemen tended to be persons of wealth, education, and importance in the town. Financing the town schools was difficult at best; indeed many of the towns who were delinquent under the 1647 school law insisted that they were too poor to support schools. In some towns land was set aside, the income from which was to be devoted to schools, but in few cases was this source of revenue adequate to the needs. In others tuition fees were charged. As time went on, more and more towns turned to taxation for support of their schools, and then as now the school budget took a healthy bite out of the town's total resources, it being estimated that in the average town about one third of the income went to school support.

Throughout the colonial period towns had great difficulty in attracting and holding schoolmasters. Indeed some of the delinquent towns claimed that the reason they had not established schools was their inability to find suitable masters. A majority of colonial schoolmasters were young Harvard graduates who taught school for a few years after graduation while they were deciding on their ultimate careers. Certainly, then as now, one could not get rich schoolmastering. The average annual salary probably ran about twenty pounds a year, though a few got as much as sixty. It is hardly surprising that the turnover was high and few men decided to devote their entire careers to teaching. An exception to this rule was the most famous of all New England colonial schoolmasters, Ezekiel Cheever, master of the Boston Latin School for thirty-eight years, who died in harness at the age of ninety-two without ever having missed a day of school.

Theoretically, according to Massachusetts law, towns of one hundred families were required to provide both elementary and secondary schools for the town's children. In actual practice these two were usually merged. Often there were at a particular time no boys who desired to prepare for college, and as a result the schoolmaster devoted himself to teaching reading and writing to the younger children. When a boy or two came along who wished to learn the classics, the teacher would make special arrangements for them. In towns where there were a sizable number of students heading for college each year, a more formal secondary school education could be developed, as in the Boston Latin School, and it was invariably heavily weighted with Latin and Greek. The student usually started with a beginner's Latin book called the "Accidence," probably first composed by the redoubtable Ezekiel Cheever himself. During the next seven years he would be put through a rigorous course of Latin authors, including Ovid, Cicero, Virgil, Horace, a Latin translation of Aesop's fables, and many others. Not only were the students trained to translate the classics: they were drilled in speaking and writing as well. Toward the end of their course they studied Greek, beginning with Homer, Hesiod, the New Testament, and other works. Many of the so-called grammar schools never achieved anything like this degree of training, but one must not forget the boys who were tutored individually by the town clergyman, many of whom achieved distinguished careers at college.

Though the General Court attempted to establish norms for education in the towns, there were always exceptions to the rule. Three towns— Ipswich, Roxbury, and Hadley—had schools that were technically independent of town government, run by the modern equivalent of a board of trustees. The history of all three is of a running battle with the town authorities, and in practice the schools themselves differed little from other grammar schools except in governance. During the eighteenth century, particularly in the larger towns, a number of truly private schools appeared. These institutions, which were advertised in the local newspapers, were run for profit by the teachers, and a wide variety of subjects were offered. Their curricula tended to be much more practical than those of the grammar schools—indeed many were really vocational schools, offering such subjects as navigation, surveying, shorthand, bookkeeping, fortification and gunnery, French, and fencing, as well as the more basic skills of reading, writing, spelling, and "cyphering."

Though the education of girls during the colonial period is poorly documented, there were a variety of schools that offered to teach young ladies the basic skills of dancing, cooking, sewing, embroidery, good manners, French, and literature. These private schools were usually run by a single master or mistress who often combined teaching with other work. For example, Mrs. Jane Day of Boston ran a boarding school for girls for some eight years and at the same time made women's dresses "in the newest Fashion." The towns, particularly Boston, had little control over these schools, though the masters or mistresses had to get licenses to run their institutions, and the costs of maintaining them were, of course, borne entirely by the parents who paid tuition fees. While these private institutions broadened the curricular offering of colonial schools and contributed colorful strands in the fabric of colonial education, they were mostly fly-by-night enterprises, and none survived very long.

At the time of the founding of Phillips Academy, therefore, the typical Massachusetts institution of secondary education was the town grammar school. Certainly by twentieth-century standards the schoolboy's lot was a hard one. Starting at about the age of seven, he would attend school six days a week for the next seven years. His schoolhouse was a rude one-room building, perhaps twenty feet by twenty feet, with a fireplace at one end as the only source of heat in winter. If he was lucky, the windows would have panes in them. He would sit on a hard oak bench hour after hour being drilled by a young Harvard graduate who served as master. Much of the master's time would be taken up teaching the three R's to students who had no college ambitions. A few of the older boys would be spending most of their time with classical authors. The day would be started with prayer and closed by having an older boy recite the Lord's Prayer in Latin, and occasionally the master would deliver himself of some remarks on Christian virtue, for he took seriously his responsibility for molding the character as well as the minds of his charges.[8] Superficially at least, the colonial grammar school seems unimpressive by today's standards; yet by and large it accomplished its main purpose, as the relatively high literacy rate in Massachusetts and the success in preparing boys for Harvard testify. Although Sam Phillips never attended a grammar school, at college he knew a wide variety of boys from different schools, including the better ones like Roxbury Latin and Boston Latin, and he must have been familiar with the school system of his day.

But what of the schools in Andover? Did they have something to distinguish them from those of other towns?[9] The answer seems to be that Andover schools had little if anything to make them different, and if they had any influence on Sam, it would have been to convince him that they would not help him accomplish his purpose. In the seventeenth century the Reverend Francis Dane and the Reverend John Woodbridge seem to have kept some kind of private school which prepared boys for Harvard. In 1678 the town evinced its interest in education by contributing twelve bushels of corn for "the new building of the college" at Cambridge. Three years later, however, the town was haled into court for not complying with the 1647 law about grammar schools. During the hearing, the Reverend Dane, a Cambridge graduate, testified as follows: "I thought it my duty to signify that for these thirty and two years I have taught any Schollers that they sent me to learne to write, and some in their grammar"—"grammar" here meaning the classics. Finally, in 1700, the town got around to complying with the 1647 law when it was voted at town meeting "that a convenient school-house be erected at the parting of the ways, by Joseph Wilson's, to be twenty feet long and sixteen feet wide." The town experienced the usual difficulties in obtaining a master; as the selectmen wrote the court, "we cannot compell gentellmen to come to us; and we do suppose they are Something afraid by the Reason we Doe Ly so exposed to our Indyen Eenemys." Despite these difficulties the selectmen persevered, and over the next sixty years they managed to procure some very promising teachers—all for a short time, to be sure—including Esquire and John Phillips, Philemon Robbins, Edward Wigglesworth, and Eliphalet Pearson.

Like many other towns, Andover was faced with the problem of where to locate its school, a problem made the more difficult because the town had already split into the north and south parishes. Some idea of the headaches this situation occasioned can be gained from the records of Philemon Robbins' teaching. He "began his school in the south end of Town and continued there 3 months, and then went behind the pond [presumably North Andover] in the first day of December and continued there until the 25th day of said December, and then Returned to the middle of the Town and was sent to the south end of the towne and continued there until the Last of January, and then was sent and continued in the middle of the town into the Last of February next, and then was sent behind the pond in the 3d day of March and to continue there fourteen nights and then the 16th March was returned to the middle of the towne, and continued there nine weeks." Obviously the town was trying to get as much mileage as possible out of poor Mr. Robbins, but this peripatetic arrangement could hardly have been conducive to the education of children. By the middle of the eighteenth century the town was beginning to build and staff "outskirt" or district schools, the center school presumably remaining as the grammar school. Though Andover probably did as well as most other towns in providing for the education of its children, there was certainly nothing innovative about the system that might have attracted Sam Phillips, and the testimony of his father, his uncle, and his friend Eliphalet Pearson, all of whom had taught in Andover, presumably convinced him that something new and different was needed if he were to accomplish his purpose.

Finally, there was Dummer School, where Samuel Phillips had gone. One might think that since he had been happy there and had the highest regard for Master Moody, he might well have wanted to model his school on Dummer. And in some respects he may have. Yet earlier writers on this subject dismiss offhand the possible influence of Dummer on Sam.[10] The legal form of Dummer, established under the will of Lieutenant-Governor William Dummer, certainly did not serve as a model. According to this document, two Boston ministers and Nathaniel Dummer of Newberry were appointed Trustees to see to it that the Lieutenant-Governor's property in Newberry was used to found a grammar school. The details of building a schoolhouse and appointing a master were entrusted to a committee consisting of the ministers of Newberry and five freeholders elected by the town. Finally, the removal of the master for sickness, senility, or "a profligate, wicked life" was entrusted to the Overseers of Harvard. In the early years of the school it seems clear that none of these bodies did much to administer the institution; once Master Moody had been appointed, they simply left matters up to him and to his brother Joseph, who was business manager. It was not until 1782, four years after the founding of Phillips Academy, that provision was made for a fifteen-man board of trustees to run the school. Even then, it was not until the resignation of Master Moody that the trustees began to take over. Certainly the organization of Dummer School could not have served as a model for Samuel Phillips.

In view of Sam's enthusiasm for Master Moody, one might suppose that he could not have wished to do better than adopt the educational policy of Dummer. Why he did not is related to the position of religion at Dummer. Though Samuel Moody had been trained for the ministry, I can find no evidence that he made religion a central part of his school. To be sure the boys must have gone to church on Sundays, but the impression one gets of Moody is of a man primarily dedicated to teaching boys the classics. And when he departed from strict classical discipline, it was to introduce French, dancing, and swimming. In their accounts of Moody neither of the Dummer School historians has a single mention of religious activity at the school. Moody's way was to encourage boys. About human nature he was constitutionally an optimist and the reverse of Esquire Phillips, who, by hating vice too much, loved men too little. He could not bring himself to believe that his pupils were depraved or sinful. Dummer School could not serve as a model for Phillips Academy because Master Moody was not concerned enough with "true piety" in the education of his boys.[11]

In conclusion it is apparent that Samuel Phillips was not influenced to any significant degree either by what he read or by what he saw around him in the schools of Massachusetts when he came to draw up the Constitution of Phillips Academy. He wanted an institution of which the main thrust would be toward the moral education of the students; at the beginning he thought of abandoning the traditional classical curriculum; and he conceived of a kind of work ethic that, he was convinced, would be good for the characters of young men. Even when some of these early concepts were modified, particularly with respect to the curriculum, Phillips Academy was *sui generis*, a new type of institution, the first of its kind in the history of American secondary education.

It is difficult to determine when any individual first began thinking about a project that later was brought to fruition. This difficulty is compounded in the case of Samuel Phillips, Jr., and his school, since two key documents in which he outlines his early thoughts about an institution of secondary education are both undated. Certainly a major influence on his thinking was his Dummer classmate and Harvard friend Eliphalet Pearson. Pearson taught in the Andover grammar school during at least a part of 1774; the following year he brought his future wife, Priscilla Holyoke, and her mother, the widow of President Edward Holyoke of Harvard, to Andover in the spring of 1775, after the fighting at Lexington and Concord; and he continued to live in Andover in close association with Samuel Phillips until the founding of Phillips Academy, resuming his position in the town grammar school during at least part of 1776. Pearson was a man of originality and drive, and it seems clear that he began early to ponder the problems of contemporary secondary education as he was witnessing them at first hand in the Andover grammar school. Since he and Sam lived in such close proximity, there was little need for written communication between them; thus there is no solid documentation of their relationship at this time. But the presumption is strong that the two discussed secondary education together and that out of these conversations, Phillips Academy, as established in its constitution, eventually took shape.[12]

The first document on the subject of secondary education is addressed simply "Dear Friend," but the "Friend" is almost certainly Eliphalet Pearson.[13] The letter is in reply to a request from Pearson for Sam's opinion on some "Rules & Regulations of the public school about which you [Pearson] have been so thoroughly engaged" and more generally how the proposed school might be advanced "to a greater Degree of Perfection." Unfortunately, Pearson's proposals are not to be found among either the Phillips or Pearson Papers, so that Sam's rather general comments on the "Rules & Regulations" do not mean very much. When he came to comment on how the school might be brought to a greater degree of perfection, however, Sam really opened up. Admitting that he found himself in "a Wilderness of Tho't thro' which I scarcely perceive a Ray to guide me safely to any particular Determination," he still could see little benefit that "the public or Individuals may receive from the Institution." Admitting that knowledge was a great blessing, Sam insisted that "the fear of the Lord is the Beginning of that Knowledge" and wondered if that were "the first rudiment" taught in Pearson's school. Youth, Sam was persuaded, was a happy, sweet time "to cast in the principal Seed, which is the plain and most Interesting Doctrine of the Gospel."

Sam then launched a bitter attack on the emphasis on the classics in most grammar schools:

> . . . our general Plan of Educating Youth, is injudicious, is unnatural, is absurd. As soon as an infant is capable of muttering English he is then put to his Accidence [Latin grammar]. . . . In our own Language we have Beauties that will engage the Attention of an Infant. . . . But in the Latin they look back to something, that has been dead, these hundred Years and never will exist again and if there was not a fragment of it remaining it would not exclude us from Heaven. In it they study Months without one new Idea, and yet it has a Great Tendency to make the little ignorant Scholar a pedant, if he can throw out one latin Word, tho he knows no more its significance than a Parrot.—Is it not unreasonable, that nearly six years as is commonly the case and those the innocentest part of Life, and most suitable to receive the best Impressions, should be spent chiefly in studying Heathen Writers ? Are Ovid and Horace and Virgil and Tully of such infinite Consequence, that they should consume our best Moments, until the Tenderness [?] of the Mind is gone and it is grown more unapt to that which is good and very prompt to Iniquity? [Why are these authors] almost the first Books put into the Hands of Christian Children? Why the first two were infamous Debauchees and one half they wrote is not fit to be read by Christians; and as for the last, if he liv'd in these Days he must be called an adept at blackguarding. But these authors still have the sweetest Stile, and are the most correct latin writers.—Be it so.—Must a Youth's mind be poisoned with unchristian, with pagan Sentiments, for the sake of reading correct Latin? As all our Latin Authors of Note were pagans, and wrote before the coming of our blessed Savior, and their Works all contain more or less of the foolish and stupid Religion of those Times, I think they ought not to be read untill a person is well established and settled in our wise and holy Religion. Virgil and Homer have always been admired, and read with Pleasure, and have been esteemed as the first poets that have wrote! but where is the christian that would not infinitely prefer Milton, Young and Thompson?

What is the result of this faulty system of education? ". . . . the greater part of the Youth that enter our College are unprincipled and immoral, and remain so until their very Subsistence obliges them to be otherwise, at least in Appearance. . . . What is the mighty Sum of Knowledge that our Youth in general have, when they enter our College? They are neither capable of writing, reading or speaking English: and in this miserable Condition many leave their Alma Mater. . . . yet english is the only Language which we meet with in every day Occurrences, and in which we are conversant all our lives." No wonder parents find the views of their children unreasonable and unaccountable, when the children "are permitted to attempt navigating for themselves, when they are as St. Paul was, without Sun, Moon and Stars, without compass and pole Star; and this world is not less dangerous than the adriatic Gulph where paul was shipwreckt."

> The whole success of your Seminary will depend, personally speaking, upon an Instructor who is willing to do this: and whose Willingness arises from an infinetly better principle than any Heathen Moralists ever could.—Purchase such a Man if he may be found at any Rate; his Industry will keep pace with the sun; and his Wishes will always be reasonable.—Give him a generous Latitude, he will not abuse it.—Every Evil that can be, will be remedied by him.—All his views will be to inspire his pupils with that Knowledge, which will most of all influence them, to remember their Creator in the Days of their Youth.

Sam closed his letter with more practical suggestions. The school would need "buildings and convenient Accommodations," the students "a simple Diet, proper Exercise and Neatness, which have a great Tendency to preserve the Health.—which cannot be attended to when the Scholars board in private Families and at a Distance." Then follow some comments on scholarship boys that are surprising in the light of the later history of Phillips Academy:

> With Regard to Charity Scholars: these Arguments following may have some Weight against planning for them in general.—There is no doubt a great Number of respectable wealthy Persons, would be glad to have their Children educated, and chearfully be at the Expense but they find so great Danger of their Morals being totally corrupted, that they are utterly deterred therefrom.—this great Difficulty being removed, there is Reason to suppose that a School would always be as full as Conveniency would admit of, and certainly the Happiness of such a Child is of as great Consequence, as that of a poor Child, their Opportunity of Doing good greater.—Their disinterestedness a great Argument in favor of their honest Intentions in following the professions of Minister; that they do it from principle, and not from a lucrative View; but Charity Scholars must pursue this: they

speak because they are hired to.—It is their living, say the Scoffers.
Ye have taken your Ministers and Teachers from among the lowest
of the people.—

If indeed this is Sam Phillips's earliest statement on secondary education, it is interesting to note that most of the points he makes failed of incorporation in the final Constitution of Phillips Academy. The presumption
is strong that Eliphalet Pearson, himself a poor boy and a classical scholar,
talked him out of his antipathy to the classics and to scholarship boys. Yet
Sam's reservations about the classics never completely died out. Writing to
Timothy Pickering in 1794 about the possibility of establishing an Agricultural Society in Massachusetts, he said, "If half the time which is spent
in the study of the greek language (except by those designed for the desk)
was appropriated to agricultural improvements, the advantage to our youth
both in entertainment and improvement woud be very great and the benefits to the public might be immense."[14]

Sometime after Sam's first letter was written, he prepared a second addressed to "Hon'd Sir," almost certainly his father.[15] The letter is headed
"Monday Morning 5 o'clock," suggesting that Sam had either burned a lot
of midnight oil on his effort or was getting off to an early start in the best
tradition of John Quincy Adams. As a whole, the document indicates that
Sam's thoughts on secondary education had become more conventional and
more practical. The long attack on the classics and the doubts about "charity scholars" are missing; in their place are a rationale for the founding of
a school and specific plans for its administration. The letter starts off with
a statement of the young man's reasons for believing that a new school is
needed:

> "Observations have been first made upon the various Irregularities
> which are daily appearing.—the very frequent Instances of the Decay
> of Virtue publick and private, the prevalence of publick and private
> Vice, and the amazing Change in the Tempers, Dispositions and
> Conduct of People in the Country in general, within these thirty
> Years. . . . From what Source does this Spring?" This trouble is
> owing to the neglect of good instruction. ". . . the Habits of Youth
> reign thro' Life. . . . by Age and Exercise they acquire further
> Strength. . . . how much depends upon *early* Instruction? What less
> than (in a great Degree) their Happiness or Misery in this Life and
> the next, the Comfort or Grief of their parents;—the Welfare or
> Disorder of the Community—the GLORY OR RUIN OF THE
> STATE. . . . When we . . . consider . . . how much 'tis neglected
> tis enough to alarm the Concern of the Rational and give Rise to a
> Fear of Events the most dreadful.

Sam went on to say that the local grammar school could not solve this
problem, primarily because the master was obliged to divide his time

among various parts of the town, with the result that he never had more
than a few weeks consecutively with any group of pupils. To hire enough
masters for all the different parts of the town would be prohibitively expensive. Thus nothing less than a boarding school would do, the type of institution employed with such success by the "Antients" in classical times.

> Let a Publick Building be erected for the Purpose, and the Children
> sent, supported and continued there for a certain Term, perhaps from
> seven to fourteen—To obtain a Consent to this, *only view the Advantages, hear Answers to Objections, see them weigh'd together
> and then judge*—If there is such Provision and the Children thus
> devoted, it is to be hoped that every Advantage necessary to obtain
> the great Ends in view would be provided.
>
> In the first Place one of the best of Men to take Command—One
> who shall be every Way as thoroughly qualify'd as is to [be]
> found,—who shall be dispos'd to proportion his Attention to the
> various Branches of Education, according to their Importance,—
> consequently will make it his first and chief Concern to see to the
> regulation of their MORALS most attentively and vigorously to guard
> against the first Dawning of depraved Nature; to be early, diligently
> painting in the purest simplicity the Deformity and Odiousness of
> VICE, the Comeliness and Amiableness of VIRTUE—who will
> spare no Pains to convince them of the indispensable Obligations
> they are under to abhor and avoid the former, and to love and practice the latter, not only from a view of their different Natures, but
> because it is the pleasure and Requirement of the SUPREAM . . .
> and in short the whole Course of his Education, *one continu'd Lecture
> upon all that's great and good*: . . .

There follows a long paragraph in which Sam extols the virtues of gardening for the young. Not only would such a program provide some of the
food for the school; it would teach the boys to respect labor: "as Indolence
and Extravagence are either of them a sure Road to Ruin,—and both together must soon end in Misery, there would be *indefatigable* Exertions
to guard against every Appearance of either, to inculcate the inconceivable
*Importance of INDUSTRY AND DILIGENCE, FRUGALITY AND
OECONOMY.*"

> From such an Institution, what a surprising Change might be reasonably expected!—Instead of the present apparent Degeneracy . . .
> what Blessings might we not immediately expect! . . . The Plan not
> only appears *extreamly* fair in Theory, but it has been practis'd with
> *almost incredible Success* among the Antients.—by Attention to this
> alone, they had better Men (according to their Notions of Goodness),
> better Members of Society, and better regulated States than we have
> with all our shining Privileges—If it wrought such Wonders then

among the Antients, *what may not be expected from it Joyn'd to the Advantages of the Christian Religion?*

And I have the satisfaction to say, that among the thirty in Town, chiefly the first for Sense and Influence, to whom I have propos'd it, I have not only not met with one dissentient, but have Recd *vastly higher Approbation* from every Individual of them than I could reasonably expect—

But, some might object, would not a boarding school be very expensive? Sam pooh-poohed this argument. If the parents would only send the money equivalent of the food that the boy would eat at home, that should cover almost all his expenses. The diet at the School was to be Spartan, the clothes were to be very plain, and in addition the parents would be saved the extras that a child living at home often received. But, a parent might say, that is not the whole story. I would lose the labor of my boy during his years at School. This would be a not inconsiderable sum. Sam admitted that there might be some loss here, but he asked the parent which he would rather have—some additional income or a son with "the fairest Prospect of Happiness in this Life and the next." Besides, Sam added, for most of the time he would be in the Phillips School, he would be too young to earn much money anyway.

We know that no small Charge will be necessary to establish such a Design—The Support of such a Man as the Place would demand and what is very encouraging (such an one we know of—who is admirably form'd for the Sphere, and would exert himself in the Cause— must be honorable,—upon the Principle that the Labourer is worthy of his Hire, and each according to the Difficulty and Importance of his. The Head of such a Society might rationally expect more than a Minister's Sallary, because his Duty would be much more arduous, and his Opportunity for Service much greater, for Reasons mention'd before—But must so glorious a Plan fail of it's Accomplishment only for the want of Interest, when there are so many, to whom it would be a Relief rather than otherwise to part with some of it— What have any in View by continual Addition of Wealth but the Addition of Happyness? Now, who would not gain inconceivably in this by sparing some of that for which he has no Occasion, and can't rationally ever expect to have, to establish a Design?

Though this "Monday Morning" document contains flights of fantasy and exaggerated hopes for the institution that Sam was anxious to found, he is facing up to more practical problems. The idea of having the students save themselves and the institution money by raising some of their food and at the same time gaining respect for hard work and healthy exercise is by no means far-fetched; similar programs have been tried in schools in the twentieth century. Though Sam's agricultural program eventually failed, he was getting down to earth, in both senses, when he proposed it. His concern for the loss to a parent of a son's labor is also a practical consideration. Though one may have reservations about Sam's arguments on this point, he is attempting to meet a real problem head on. Finally, evidence that his "design" is approaching implementation is suggested by the way he reminds his father that "you can't take it with you."

Whatever the actual dating of these two documents may be, other evidence makes it clear that by the end of 1776 the plan for a school was well on the way. The earliest documentation for this is a letter from Dr. John Phillips of Exeter to his nephew, dated 24 September 1776. In the course of this letter Uncle John had this to say:

> I rejoice that our judicious well-dispos'd friends so heartily agree with us on our present establishment, and that there is so good a prospect of procuring land in a part of the Town which so agreeably and remarkably strikes our minds. . . . I doubt not you will endeavor to secure the lands as soon as may be—and wish you would consult our friends respecting the best manner of holding lands to the use intended without *incumbrance*. I greatly desire a school may be forwarded, if the land can't *yet* be obtained; but leave the whole to your conduct.[16]

It is clear from this letter that a decision had definitely been reached to found some kind of school, that progress was being made in the selection of a site for the school, and that, though not expressly stated, John Phillips and his brother Samuel were ready to foot the bill. It was not long before acquisition of land for the school began. Apparently the Phillipses first considered an area in North Andover near the old Kittredge mansion but were forced to abandon the plan when they were unable to purchase a large enough tract.[17] It was then that they settled on what was to become Andover Hill. Early in 1777 two purchases were made, one from Solomon Wardwell, the other from Captain Joshua Holt, administrator of the estate of George Abbot, totaling about one hundred and ten acres and covering most of the land presently owned by the Academy west of Main Street and part of the Main Campus to the east. Early in 1778 another tract of about thirty-two acres of woodland was purchased from Nehemiah Abbot, extending the property of the future Academy further to the east. All these purchases were made in the name of Squire Phillips, acting for himself and his brother John. Included in the acquisitions were two buildings that particularly concern us—one, the former home of George Abbot located on what is now Phillips Street, at the southwest corner of the Old Campus; the other, a small joiner's shop that was soon moved to the present site of the Academy's Archaeology Building.[18] Sometime in the latter part of 1777 Sam Phillips, his wife Phoebe, and their infant son, John, moved from North Andover to the Abbot house so as to be near the soon-to-be established school, and it was in this building that the formal founding of Phillips Academy took place.

During the latter part of 1777 and early 1778 a few documents give us glimpses of further progress toward the actual opening of the school.[19] During this period what was to become the Constitution of Phillips Academy began to take shape. There exist among the Phillips Papers two drafts of that document, one of which is full of additions and corrections that make the edited copy correspond very closely to the final form. It is interesting to note that in what appears to be the earlier draft the original intention of the founders was to vest all the land and other property of the school in the person of Samuel Phillips, Jr., alone. Had they persevered in their original intention, Phillips Academy would have become a proprietary school, and it is doubtful if it ever could have been incorporated; certainly its later history would have been very different. Fortunately, as a result, one supposes, of legal counsel on the subject, the plan was changed to provide for a board of trustees. These early drafts indicate that some legal help must have been obtained. Since the Constitution is in the form of an indenture providing for the establishment of a trust, it would be necessary to employ the language of the law in much of it, and though some of the passion that characterized the early proposals of Sam Phillips remains, the document is lean and sparse when compared with Sam's first efforts. The decision to vest the trust in a board of trustees created problems, however. Should Sam's friend Eliphalet Pearson, who was early slated to be the first Preceptor, be a trustee? Objections were raised that in such matters as his own contract with the school there would be conflict of interest. But it was finally decided that the Preceptor's knowledge of the school and, presumably, his great devotion to it would more than outweigh these objections. There was also a problem about Uncle William of Boston, third brother to the Squire and to Uncle John of Exeter. Though he had been invited to become a trustee, no one could get an answer out of him, let alone a promise to contribute financially. Eliphalet Pearson went to Boston to try to track him down, but to no avail. Yet Uncle William must finally have come around, for he appears on the first Board. Finally, Samuel Phillips, Jr., was concerned about whether he should be a trustee. It might make too many Phillipses, he thought. Three would be enough. Primarily at the insistence of his Uncle John, he, too, was finally included.[20] We can get some idea of the young man's enthusiasm for his project from a letter he wrote to his Uncle John in March, 1778, in the course of which he says:

> To have the School open'd is what I am almost too impatient to see. . . . I am employing every hour I can get, upon the Articles of Indenture [the Constitution], with much Mortification that they are not in a better hand;—Almost every review affords the discovery of Room for amendment in some respects; but that it should be finish'd, or rather ended immediately is necessary; for if my Father pleases I

hope next Week, there will be a meeting of the Trust, and that before the expiration of this, the chief of the Gentlemen will have a
copy of the proposed Plan:—before they can act, the Instrument must
be sign'd—and for this Purpose shall send to Exeter next Week, perhaps Tuesday, if not on Monday; how Happy should we be, if it
should prove consistent *with your Enjoyment*, to prevent this, by
giving us the pleasure of your Company; but if you can't be present
at both this Meeting and that of the opening (perhaps a fortnight
afterwards) I must needs say I should *much* prefer the latter:—it
would be *extremely* desirable that *your own Eyes* should behold the
Commencement of an Institution that our hands have founded, which
I trust will be a powerful Means of bringing happiness to Mankind
and Glory to the great Redeemer, till the foundations of the Earth
shall be removed.[21]

At last the great day—21 April 1778—arrived. On that day Phillips
Academy can be said to have begun its legal existence. Uncle John had
come down from Exeter and the Squire from North Andover, and it is
quite possible that other future trustees like Eliphalet Pearson, Jonathan
French, and Nehemiah Abbot, all of whom lived in Andover, were present
in the unpretentious Abbot house on Phillips Street when the Deed of Gift
or Constitution of Phillips Academy was signed by John and Samuel Phillips. John Abbot and Hannah Holt were on hand to witness the signa-
tures—neighbors who, like all good witnesses, had no personal concern in
the transaction. If, as young Sam had suggested, the Constitution was not
"finish'd," it was at least "ended," and in its final form it is an impressive
document.[22] Since the full text of the Constitution is printed in the Appendix, only the high points will be dealt with here.

The Constitution starts with a preamble, unchanged in form from earlier
drafts, which sets forth in moving language the reasons for the founding
of the institution:

> A short reflection upon the grand design of the great PARENT OF
> THE UNIVERSE in the creation of mankind, and the improvements, of
> which the mind is capable, both in knowledge and virtue as well, as
> upon the prevalence of ignorance and vice, disorder and wickedness,
> and upon the direct tendency and certain issues of such a course of
> things, must occasion, in a thoughtful mind, an earnest solicitude to
> find the source of these evils and their remedy; and a small acquaint-
> ance with the qualities of young minds,—how susceptible and tena-
> cious they are of impressions, evidences that YOUTH is the important
> period, on the improvement or neglect of which depend the most
> important consequences to individuals themselves and the community.
>   A serious consideration of the premises, and an observation of
> the growing neglect of YOUTH, have excited in us a painful anxiety

for the event, and determined us to make, in the following Conveyance, a humble dedication to our HEAVENLY BENEFACTOR of the
ability, wherewith he has blessed us, to lay the foundation of a public
free SCHOOL or ACADEMY for the purpose of instructing Youth, not
only in English and Latin Grammar, Writing, Arithmetic, and those
Sciences, wherein they are commonly taught; but more especially to
learn them the GREAT END AND REAL BUSINESS OF LIVING.

Earnestly wishing that this Institution may grow and flourish;
that the advantages of it may be extensive and lasting; that its usefulness may be so manifest, as to lead the way to other establishments on the same principles; and that it may finally prove an eminent mean of advancing the Interest of the great REDEEMER, to His
patronage and blessing we humbly commit it.

As has been suggested, the purpose of the founders—and especially of

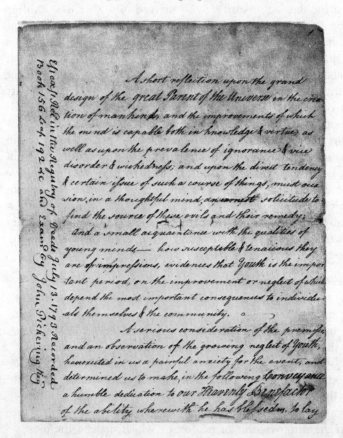

6. *The First Page of the Constitution of Phillips Academy, signed*
21 April 1778.

young Samuel Phillips—was to *conserve* the attitudes, the behavior patterns, and the beliefs of an older New England society, especially at a time when they saw them threatened on all sides. The old "knowledge and virtue" are to be pitted against the new "ignorance and vice, disorder and wickedness" that characterized Revolutionary America. The inculcation of knowledge could be accomplished by following the conventional curriculum of the classical grammar schools of the day; but it was the inculcation of "virtue" that clearly dominates the preamble—learning youth "the GREAT END AND REAL BUSINESS OF LIVING," which would certainly include training in the orthodox Calvinist faith, strict attention to proper behavior, and dedication to goodness. In stressing virtue in the Constitution Sam Phillips was following the example of almost all the Revolutionary leaders of the day. "We shall succeed if we are virtuous," wrote Samuel Adams. "Liberty without virtue would be no blessing to us," said Benjamin Rush.[23] Yet Sam's virtue was a concept that differed from those of other leaders of the day. When the patriots thought of virtue, they thought of it as civic rectitude—a quality that a republican form of government would help to foster. For Sam, virtue was theologically oriented—it was goodness in the eyes of the Lord.

After the preamble comes the Indenture or Deed of Gift, whereby Squire Phillips and John Phillips transfer to a board of twelve trustees the one hundred and forty odd acres already purchased on Andover Hill and an additional two hundred acres of land in the town of Jaffrey, New Hampshire, which the Squire had purchased as an investment for the school. In addition to the land conveyed, the two grantors transfer to the Trustees the sum of sixteen hundred and fourteen pounds, which John Phillips had promised to give the school almost a year earlier.[24] The lands were to be "let out on proper terms" and "the money put to interest on good security" entirely for the benefit of the "public FREE SCHOOL or ACADEMY in the south parish of the town of Andover."

With property matters attended to, the Constitution proceeds to the organization and character of the school itself—and first to the Trustees. Originally it was planned to have a Board of seven, but by the time the Constitution had been completed, the number had been increased to twelve. In addition to the four Phillipses—the three brothers and Sam, Jr.—the Board was to consist of four clergymen and four laymen. The four clergymen were the Reverend Jonathan French of Andover, the Reverend William Symmes of North Andover, the Reverend Elias Smith of Middleton, and the Reverend Josiah Stearns of Epping, New Hampshire. The four laymen were Oliver Wendell of Boston, John Lowell of Newburyport and Boston, Nehemiah Abbot of Andover, and Eliphalet Pearson of Andover, about to become the School's first Preceptor.[25] The Board was to be self-perpetuating and was to be governed by rules of procedure that were spelled out precisely in the Constitution. A major part were to be laymen—

an interesting requirement in view of Sam Phillips' concern with religious instruction—and a major part must not come from Andover, to avoid parochialism. This requirement had to be waived during the earlier history of the School, for six of the original Trustees did come from Andover and it was not until after the turn of the century that the requirement could be met. On the other hand, the North and South parishes of Andover were already fairly distinct communities, and there were never six Trustees from either parish alone. The Trustees were to meet at least once a year—more often in case of emergencies—and were to elect annually a President, Clerk, and Treasurer. The Clerk was to keep a record of all votes of the trustees, of those present at meetings, of all donations with the names of the benefactors and the purpose of the gift, and of all expenditures—the whole to be "open for the perusal of all men." The Treasurer was required to give bond "for the faithful discharge of his office," give receipts in duplicate for all donations, and comply with any other measures the trustees might take to ensure his accountability. The Trustees were also given broad powers to buy or sell any of the school's property if necessary to improve the School.

When it came to the choice of the Master, the Constitution was again most explicit. Apparently Squire Phillips and his brother John had already appointed Eliphalet Pearson as first Master, but from then on, the full Board was to have this responsibility. The Master himself had to be a "professor of the CHRISTIAN RELIGION, of exemplary manners, of good natural abilities and literary acquirements, of a good acquaintance with human nature, of a natural aptitude for instruction and government," and in the choice of a master his qualifications were to be considered without "preference of kindred or friend, place of birth, education, or residence." The master and assistants were to receive salaries, "of which there shall be no alteration, but in their favor"—a clause that the faculty of Phillips Academy had reason to bless Sam Phillips for in the days of depression in the 1930's. The Trustees were to "inquire into the conduct of the Master and Assistants" and to remove them if they were guilty of "misconduct, neglect of duty, or incapacity." Finally, to guard against any trustee orgies, it was stipulated that "decent, not extravagant entertainment" was to be provided at trustee meetings. Economy, it was thought, was to be ever viewed as an object worthy of the Trustees' particular attention.

There follows a section dealing with the students and the Master's relationship to them. The Master was to determine which students were to be admitted, subject to rules established by the Trustees, and also to make rules for the "internal management of the Seminary," but these rules could be examined, amended, or discontinued by the Trustees at their discretion. It was the Master's principal duty "to regulate the tempers, to enlarge the minds, and form the morals of the Youth, committed to his care." The subjects to be taught were English, Latin and Greek, Writing, Arithmetic,

Music, the Art of Speaking, practical Geometry, Logic, and any other liberal Arts and Sciences as the Trustees might direct. The Master was to concern himself with the health of the students, try to inculcate in them the habit of industry, and encourage them to perform some kind of manual labor like gardening. If there should be a profit from the gardening, it was to be applied to the purchase of books for the library or some other useful purpose.

Lest there be possible doubt about the main purpose of the institution, the Master's responsibility for the moral education of his charges is re-emphasized in a special passage very reminiscent of some of Sam's earlier writings on his ideas of what a School should be. Above all, "the Master's attention to the disposition of the *Minds* and *Morals* of the Youth was to exceed every other care. Since goodness without knowledge is weak and feeble, and knowledge without goodness dangerous, the two united are necessary to form the noblest character and lay the surest foundation of usefulness to mankind." The Master must, therefore, "guard against the earliest irregularities, delineate, in their natural colors, the deformity and odiousness of vice and the beauty and amiableness of virtue, to convince the students to abhor and avoid the former, and to love and practice the latter. He must explain to the students the great duties they owe to God, their country, their parents, their neighbour, and themselves" and furnish them "such maxims of conduct as may best enable them to pass through all with ease, reputation and comfort."

Almost all of the Constitution is admirably flexible, allowing ample opportunity for future change. The one major exception to this is the next passage, which attempts to define exactly the Calvinist creed that the students should be taught. Since many students, it was hoped, might enter the ministry, it was to be the duty of the Master not only to instruct them in the truth of Christianity but also "to inculcate upon them the great and important scripture doctrines of the existence of One true GOD, the FATHER, SON, and HOLY GHOST; of the fall of man, the depravity of human nature; the necessity of atonement, and of our being renewed in the spirit of our minds; the doctrines of repentance toward God and of faith toward our Lord Jesus Christ; of sanctification by the Holy Spirit, and of justification by the free grace of God, through the redemption, that is in Jesus Christ or in opposition to the erroneous and dangerous doctrine of justification by our own merit, (or a dependence on self righteousness) together with the other important doctrines and duties of the HOLY CHRISTIAN RELIGION." And to make sure these doctrines became firmly implanted in the student's minds, the Master was to employ frequent repetition, "urge and reurge," and continue from day to day to impress these instructions. Finally, as if the message were not already clear enough, the Master was to remember that "the design of this Institution can never be answered, without his persevering, incessant attention to this duty."[26]

From the vantage point of two hundred years, it seems unfortunate that Samuel Phillips, Jr.—for it must certainly have been he—should try to define as precisely as he did the religious beliefs that he wished "inculcated onto" his students. Indeed this is the only part of the Constitution that must be ignored today by Headmaster and faculty alike. Writing in 1917, Claude M. Fuess could say: "For nearly a century and a half Phillips Academy has been conducted with this Constitution as a guide, without the necessity for a single amendment or the revision of even a word."[27] Perhaps Alfred E. Stearns, Headmaster at the time Fuess wrote, could subscribe to the particulars of Calvinist doctrine that were written into the Constitution, but the same can certainly not be said of his successors. It is doubtful, for example, if there is a single member of the present (1978) Phillips Academy faculty who believes in the "depravity of human nature." Apparently Sam felt so strongly about the threat to the old Calvinist orthodoxy that he hoped to weld onto his School forever a particular set of dogmatic beliefs. Thus this section of the Constitution, where the wise flexibility that characterized the rest of the document was abandoned, has proved to be the only unworkable part today.

Two hundred years is a long time, and many things in America have undergone profound changes that Sam Phillips could not possibly have anticipated, especially in matters of religion. Yet it is interesting to note that this passage in the Constitution was criticized by contemporaries as well. There is a hint, for example, that Uncle John Phillips did not want to push the matter of religious orthodoxy too far. Writing to his nephew about teachers for the new school in January 1778, Uncle John said: "I am convinced of the need of Scholars being under the Tuition of Instructors who are of what we call Calvinist Principles. I would not employ any that neglected teaching the Assembly's *Catechism*—or if any part was objected to, should expect to know what part."[28] As one of the leading authorities on John Phillips says of this passage, "The latitude suggested in the last phrase is more important than the proposed restriction."[29] On the other hand, when Uncle John came to draw up the Constitution of the Phillips Exeter Academy, he included the passage, adding a few more dogmatic beliefs.

A more striking criticism of the passage was made by Timothy Pickering, writing in 1785. Sam Phillips had sent a copy of the Constitution to him and asked him to comment on it. Certainly Pickering can by no stretch of the imagination be called a radical, or even a liberal thinker. In the 1790's, at the time of the Alien and Sedition Acts, he and Sam were to see eye to eye on the need for repressive legislation against the Jeffersonian opposition. Yet in 1785 Pickering wrote:

> I am charmed with the leading thought in the institution,—that the master's attention to the *morals* and *dispositions* of the youth is *to exceed every other care*. But there is one article which I should wish

to see materially altered. And this alteration would, in my view, render it more conformable to the first and *principal* object of this institution,—'the promotion of true piety and virtue.' The article I refer to defines the *fundamental principles* of the Christian religion. Now, as Christians, and *serious* and *enlightened* Christians, have never yet been able to agree on what should be deemed the fundamental principles of their religion, I really wish it had not been attempted to define them in laying the foundation of this institution. To instance one point: All Christians believe in the existence of One True God; but multitudes of devout and well-informed Christians cannot admit of a plurality of persons in the Godhead, because it is a doctrine not merely beyond their reason, but inconsistent with their ideas of possible existence, and a doctrine which *they* do not find in the words of Christ or his Apostles. I am sure the institution originated in benevolent motives, and that it was intended to be a liberal one; yet the position above mentioned (to say nothing of some others) greatly narrows its foundation. If it be practable now to alter the article in question, the hint here given will be sufficient.[30]

A few weeks later Pickering came back with another letter on the same subject: "In stating the qualifications of the principal instructor, it is only required that he be a *Protestant professor of the Christian religion*, and of *exemplary manners*. And what more would you demand or wish for in the pupils committed to his charge? Establishments in matters of religion or government once made, and confirmed by the practice of some years, it is in the highest degree difficult to alter, whatever errors, absurdities, or follies may, in the progress of mankind in knowledge, be discovered." And Pickering went on to cite the Church of England, "every government in the world" and the Constitution of Pennsylvania as examples of what he was talking about.[31] Of course Pickering was right, and the Constitution of Phillips Academy would have been a prouder document had that passage been omitted. Yet this one failing should not detract from the extraordinarily flexible character of the charter as a whole.

The Constitution closes with some specific clauses on a variety of subjects. Only Protestants could serve as trustees or instructors in the School (a clause that has been quietly ignored since the Fuess administration). Election of officers was to be by ballot. And then came a clause that has proved to be one of the proudest hallmarks of Phillips Academy: "This Seminary shall be ever equally open to Youth, of requisite qualification, from every quarter," the only qualification being that they be able to read English well. Sam Phillips' early reservations about "Charity Scholars" had been overridden, probably by Eliphalet Pearson.

Despite the many places in the Constitution which clearly spell out the main aim of the institution as moral education, Samuel Phillips, Jr., apparently wanted to nail down that aim once again. Near the close of the document the following sentence appears: "And, in order to prevent the smallest perversion of the true intent of this Foundation, it is again declared, that the *first* and *principal* object of this Institution is the promotion of true PIETY and VIRTUE." The Founders made their position clear.

One week after the signing of the Constitution, on 28 April 1778, the first meeting of the Board of Trustees of Phillips School took place in Samuel Phillips' home. Eleven of the twelve Trustees were present, only the Reverend Josiah Stearns of Epping, New Hampshire, failing to make the meeting. The Board at once took up some procedural matters that had to be attended to before the School could open. Squire Phillips was elected President; the Reverend Jonathan French, Clerk; and Nehemiah Abbot, Treasurer—all three officers coming from Andover. The Founders—apparently not the full Board—then appointed Eliphalet Pearson the "*first* instructor," with the title of Preceptor, and the Board voted to call the institution "Phillips School." Because of Pearson's poor health, it was decided to limit the School to thirty pupils at the start, but a committee was appointed to enlarge that number if his health improved. It was then voted to have two three-week vacations during the School year, one to start late in April, the other late in October. The Board met again the following day and voted that the Preceptor should have the use of two properties belonging to the School and a salary of eighty pounds for the coming year, while an assistant, Mr. Joseph Mottey, a graduate of Dummer Academy and Dartmouth College, was appointed at a salary of twenty dollars for two months. In admitting students it was voted that preferences be given to those planning to study the classics, but if there were not enough of these, the balance of places could be filled with students wishing to study only the three R's. Bearish as they were on the subject of human nature, the Trustees then set up a procedure for the expulsion of students "so incorrigibly vicious" as to be "dangerous to the morals of the other Scholars or inconsistent with the good government of the Seminary." A committee of Trustees was appointed to pass judgment on these unfortunates, and the expulsion itself was to take place in the schoolhouse in the presence of the trustee committee, the Preceptor, and the students—a true drumming out of court. Nor could a student, once expelled, ever be readmitted. Then twenty-seven Andover families were licensed to keep students as boarders in their homes, with the added caveat that no public house should ever be thus licensed. The Treasurer, Nehemiah Abbot, was bonded in the sum of one thousand pounds and authorized to expend rents from property belonging to the school for the benefit of the institution. Finally a trustee committee was appointed to apply to the General Court for books "belonging to the estates of Absentees"—a euphemism for loyalists—for the use of the school. The Board then adjourned to meet again on the first Wednesday in October, presumably well satisfied with the start that they had made.[32]

To complete the story of the various additional steps that were taken to give the new institution its final legal form: lest there be any question about title to the property deeded to the Trustees by the Squire and John Phillips, Samuel Phillips, Jr., in July 1793, signed a release of all claims he might have against the estate of his father, by then deceased, and at the same time had the Constitution recorded at the registry of Deeds for Essex County in Salem.[33] Once it was determined that the school would actually be founded, it seems clear that all concerned agreed that the new institution should be incorporated under Massachusetts law as soon as possible. The purpose, as stated in the final Act of Incorporation, was as follows: "And, whereas the execution of the generous and important design of the grantors aforesaid, will be attended with very great embarrassments, unless by an act of incorporation, the Trustees . . . and their successors, shall be authorized to commence and prosecute actions at law, and transact such other matters in their corporate capacity as the interest of the said Academy shall require . . ."[34] At their meeting on 8 October 1778 the Trustees appointed a committee consisting of William Phillips, Oliver Wendell, John Lowell, and Samuel Phillips, Jr., to apply to the legislature for an act of incorporation and left the details to the discretion of the committee. At their next meeting, in April 1779, this committee was empowered to change the name of the institution from "Phillips School" to "Phillips Academy" and the title of the principal instructor from "Preceptor" to "Rector"—"provided it may be done without giving offence." It was also voted that, if possible, there should be a clause in the act of incorporation to the effect that the number of Trustees should not exceed thirteen, nor be less than eleven.[35] The trustee committee for the incorporation of the school had no precedent to follow, for this was the first secondary educational institution to be incorporated in New England.[36] The chances are, since the Founders and most of the Trustees were Harvard men, that they could realize the advantages of incorporation from their knowledge of the Harvard experience, but the fact remains that they had to blaze a new trail. That the committee was making progress can be seen from a letter that Sam Phillips wrote Uncle John in September 1780, in which he said, in explaining why he could not attend a trustee meeting at Dartmouth, "I am under a still further difficulty on account of an act of incorporation for Phillips School, which I am solicitous to get through this session, by reason of Mr. Lowell's being a member of the General Assembly, as well as for other reasons."[37] The act that finally passed on 4 October 1780 was the last act of the old Provincial legislature, and apparently it just squeaked through. Writing his uncle about its passage early the following year, Sam Phillips described some of the problems as follows: "I must not omit to give the reason for deviating from the determination of the Trustees, in settling the smallest number which the board must ever hereafter consist of;—at the latter stage of the bill, an objection which had been before made by an ingenious gentleman of law—(viz. Mr. Sedgwick of Sheffield) to that clause which enacted that the number should in no case be less than eleven, took more hold of Mr. Lowell, than ever before;—the apprehension was that it might produce a *dissolution* of the body, especially without some express provision to prevent it, which they said would be difficult and in fact there was not time to make, (for the loss of one hour, as things were circumstanced, would have protracted the bill, which was already exceptionable on account of its length)—My Uncle William was particularly consulted on this difficulty:—and on consideration thereof, he was of opinion, that the circumstances of the case, would justify the Committee to the Trustees, in making the alteration:—It has the approbation of my father and Mr. Pearson;—others of the Board I have not been able to consult."[38] From this vantage point it looks as if the General Court were wiser than the Trustees. Had the minimum number been set at eleven, and had two members of a

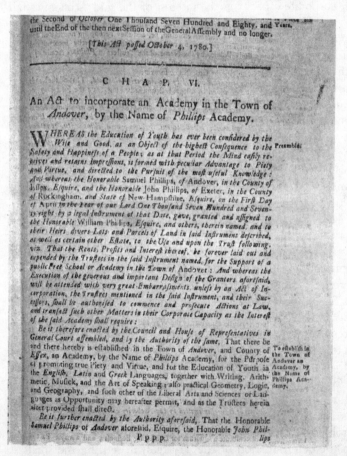

7. *The Act of Incorporation of Phillips Academy, passed 4 October 1780 and signed by John Hancock.*

board of twelve died suddenly, all kinds of legal complications might have developed.

In any event, the act finally went through, giving to the Trustees the status of a corporation that they thought was so important. The measure seems to have been drafted by Sam Phillips, Jr.—indeed the first part of the original in the Massachusetts Archives is in his handwriting. And it is no surprise to learn that he followed the Constitution very closely. The purposes of the institution, as stated in the preamble and the first clause, are taken almost verbatim from that document. The act established Phillips Academy, confirmed the Trustees in their position of authority over the school and in the possession of the property that the Founders had bequeathed to the institution. A new clause authorized the Trustees to use "one common seal" in conducting the business of the Academy and to "sue and be sued in all actions real, personal, and mixed, and prosecute and defend the same unto final judgment and execution, by the name of the Trustees of Phillips Academy." The clauses dealing with such powers of the Trustees in electing their officers, making rules for the school, and choosing their successors follow closely the Deed of Gift, though, as we have seen, the legislature changed the minimum number to seven. It was standard practice to limit the holdings of corporations; thus, while the Trustees could receive "by gift, grant, devise, bequest or otherwise" real and personal property, the annual income from real estate could not exceed five hundred pounds and the annual income from personal estate could not exceed two thousand pounds—"both sums to be valued in silver at the rate of six shillings and eight pence by the ounce"—a very necessary provision considering the depreciated state of paper money in the United States at this time. The Trustees were forbidden to receive any gift with conditions attached to it that would violate the design of the grantors, nor could they make any rules for the school contrary to the laws of the state. The final clause repeated, in essence, the provision for moving the Academy to another location, should two thirds of the Trustees believe it necessary. Apparently the earlier intention of changing the name of the master from "Preceptor" to "Rector" could not be accomplished "without giving offence."

It remained to procure a seal for the new institution, and here the Trustees were in luck, for two of their number, John Lowell and Oliver Wendell, were neighbors and close friends of the leading silversmith of the day, Paul Revere. At their meeting on 17 August 1781, the Trustees appointed these two gentlemen, together with Eliphalet Pearson, a committee to procure a seal for the Academy. In the meantime it was voted that "a cornelian seal, being a man's head, which is in the possession of the treasurer, be considered and used, as the seal of the Academy, untill another be adopted in its stead."[39] Apparently the committee went right to work, for the seal was ready the following spring. Claude Fuess authenticated the seal as the work of Revere on the basis of an entry in Revere's account book for 5 April 1782 which read: "John Lowell, Esq. To engrav'g Silv'r seal 36/ the Seal & mak'g 12/" for a total of two pounds eight shillings.[40] The standard authorities on Revere silver have also accepted the seal as his work.[41] Yet I have never been completely happy about this. The date, the subject, and the man in the entry are right, but it is possible that John Lowell ordered a seal for some other purpose than for the use of Phillips Academy. It was therefore a pleasure to discover among the Phillips Papers evidence that proved the seal to be Revere's work. Writing to his Uncle John on 2 May 1782, Sam Phillips said: ". . . am highly gratified to find that the seal has your approbation—Messrs. Wendell & Lowell procured it, and have not yet inform'd us of the cost—Mr. Revere of Boston cut it."[42]

Paul Revere certainly "cut" the seal, but who designed it? On this the record is silent, and one can only conjecture. That Sam Phillips had noth-

8. *The Seal of Phillips Academy, "cut" by Paul Revere.*

ing to do with it is strongly suggested by a statement in the same letter to Uncle John, where he writes, "I am unable to say what device would be most eligible for the P.E. Academy, not having attended to such matters, and am much pleased that you are so lucky in a Committee for this purpose." The most likely person to have designed the seal is Eliphalet Pearson, who, together with Lowell and Wendell, made up the trustee committee. He would have been the logical man to have suggested the Latin phrases on the seal, and he may well have designed the whole. On the appropriateness of the two main parts of the design—the beehive and the sun with rays—one cannot do better than quote Dr. Fuess's interpretation:

> The central feature—a beehive, with an adjacent flowering plant (species unknown), and bees flitting between the the two—is traditionally attributed to Judge Phillips, who deemed idleness to be the most insidious and demoralizing of the vices. It doubtless symbolizes a group of industrious scholars in his Academy engaged in emulating the example set for them in the hymn of Isaac Watts:
>
> > How doth the little busy bee
> > Improve each shining hour,
> > And gather honey all the day
> > From every opening flower!
>
> The unclouded sun above, with rays extending in every direction, may well represent the light of learning shining out from the newly established Phillips School. We are told by specialists in heraldry that these details show, in form and arrangement, no acquaintance with that highly technical art; but the idea which they conveyed was expressed with perfect clearness—at least to the Trustees and friends of Phillips Academy.[43]

When it comes to the mottoes on the seal, *Finis origine pendet* (the end depends on the beginning) and *Non Sibi* (not for self), again one can only conjecture who chose them, but as the leading classicist on the Board of Trustees, Eliphalet Pearson appears the most likely. Both Andover and Exeter classical authorities—Exeter's seal is very similar—agree that *Finis origine pendet* is a quote from the *Astronomica* of the Roman poet Manlius, and believe that originally its meaning was fatalistic.[44] It has also been suggested that it might have been chosen because it could be interpreted as a statement of the Calvinistic doctrine of preordination. More likely, since it was to apply to two schools, it was chosen to stress the importance of getting off to a good start in life and was considered similar to the English adages "Well begun is half done" or "As the Twig is Bent, so is the Tree Inclined." The second motto, *Non Sibi*, may well have been taken from the poet Lucan's *Pharsalia* in a line referring to Cato, in which the poet speaks of him as having been born not for self but for the entire world.

Whatever the source of *Non Sibi*, the message was certainly consonant with the altruistic principles of the Founders in establishing Phillips Academy.[45]

With an act of incorporation and a seal, the Academy's legal position was well established. The only changes in its corporate position that have proved necessary over the years were for the purpose of enlarging the limitation on the amount of property that the Trustees might hold. Aside from this relatively minor alteration, the Constitution, the Act of Incorporation, and the seal have served the Academy well for close to two hundred years.

CHAPTER FOUR

ELIPHALET PEARSON:

SETTING THE PATTERN

ON 30 April 1778 the long-awaited day arrived. The opening of Phillips School itself was certainly no portentous event. As one of the early historians has written, the School "fell into the world of that day as gently as a leaf falls from a tree in the forest, as a seed drops from the hand of the sower. No sound of trumpet nor roar of cannon heralded her birth. She was looked upon as a very little thing by the world of that day."[1] The educational facilities were far from impressive. An old carpenter's shop, about thirty-five feet by twenty, made of unpainted boards and embellished by a chimney on one side, had been acquired on the land purchased over a year before from Solomon Wardwell and had been moved to the corner of what is now Main and Phillips streets, on the site of the present Archaeology Building. Some rude benches had been installed, but little more in the way of furniture. It was in this building that Eliphalet Pearson met thirteen students, the first of thousands who would eventually attend Phillips Academy. When the Calvinist background of the founders is remembered, it is not surprising that they should have celebrated the occasion with a sermon—the Reverend Jonathan French preaching a splendid one to launch the new institution on its way.[2]

Phillips Academy has always been noted for its teachers, and its first master established that tradition firmly. Whatever one may think of Eliphalet Pearson—and in many ways he was an extraordinarily difficult person to deal with—he insisted from the start on the highest standards of academic excellence and left on the School a personal imprint that was to last many years. About four months younger than Sam Phillips, he was born on 11 June 1752 in Newbury, the eldest son of a respectable but poor farmer and miller, David Pearson. The newly established Dummer School was close by, and he attended as a day student, starting in 1765. Each day he walked four miles each way, carrying his lunch and books with him. His father had no intention of spoiling the boy and made him sign promissory notes for all the money expended for his education.[3] Tradition has it that Pearson and Sam Phillips became fast friends at Dummer School. In a small institution like Dummer, the two would certainly have known each other, but there is no documentation of an unusually close friendship, nor is there any for their presumed close relationship at Harvard. Pearson had been obliged to delay college for two years, presumably to save up enough money to go, and though he joined the Institute of 1770, of which Sam had been one of the founders, there is no record of their seeing much of each other. Pearson's college career was a distinguished one; his graduation-day debate with Theodore Parsons, "On the Legality of Enslaving the Africans," was considered so outstanding that it was ordered printed by the administration. Pearson, incidentally, supported slavery; anticipating the arguments of pre-Civil War Southerners, he summed up his case by saying:

> On the whole, since it is evident beyond all controversy, that the removal of these Africans from the state of brutality, wretchedness and misery in which they are at home so deeply involved, to this land of light, humanity and christian knowledge, is to them so great a blessing, however faulty any individuals may have been in point of unnecessary cruelty practiced in this business, yet, whether the general state of subordination here, which is a necessary consequence of such removal, be agreeable to the law of nature, can by no means longer remain a question.[4]

After graduation from Harvard in 1773, Pearson came to Andover—possibly at the suggestion of Sam Phillips—to teach in the town school for a short time, but he was soon back in Cambridge to pursue theological studies and to continue courting Priscilla Holyoke, daughter of the late President Holyoke, a lady twelve years his senior. With the start of the war in the spring of 1775 Pearson returned to Andover, bringing Priscilla and her mother with him, and resumed his teaching at the town grammar school. It was probably during this period that he first began to ponder the problems of secondary education, as Sam Phillips' long letter to him headed "Dear Friend" implies.[5] Just where he and the Holyokes lived in Andover in 1775–76 is not clear, but his manuscript diary for the first part of 1777 indicates that by that year he had stopped teaching school and was engaged in study, itinerant preaching, getting inoculated for the smallpox, and in doing various chores in his home.[6] The diary reveals a man dedicated to routine and order in his life, recording many minor details of his existence, with the amount of time spent on each. He even entered the amount of time spent in bed each night, and the early part of the diary is full of such entries as "Abed 9½ H." Pearson got plenty of sleep; the shortest entry is "Abed 7¾." In addition to sleeping, he regularly spent time reading, composing sermons, and visiting friends. An entry on

24 February reads "Dined at Mr. Phillips in company with 6 Indian Chiefs of the Oneida tribe & Rev.ᵈ Kirkland."[7] One would hardly know from his diary that there was a war on. On 6 January he writes, "Hear that 919 Hessians are taken at Trenton" and on the first of July, "News—Ticonderoga besieged—1100 of enemy this side lake." Aside from these two entries, however, the diary is silent on military and political affairs. When not busy at his desk reading such authors as Hume, Tillotson, and Stackhouse, he did a good bit of gardening. Apparently June 1777 was an unusually fine month for farmers, for Pearson rhapsodizes, "The finest season in the world. Pastures, fields of grass and Grain incomparable—This month a perfect contrast to the same of last year, in which there was not rain enough to lay the dust—A time of general health." Nor did Eliphalet neglect affairs of the heart. There are frequent entries about driving with "Miss Holyoke" to various places; on one occasion he broke down and spoke of driving with "Miss Prissy."

The most interesting part of the diary, however, records Pearson's experience with inoculation for smallpox, at a hospital in Brookline. He entered the hospital on 28 February and was inoculated by Dr. Rand at 11 o'clock. That night he took "a 4 grain Mercurial Pill" and "slept on straw." The next day he rose at 8 o'clock and "took a Red Pill Composed of Native Cinnabar and Cinnabar of Antimony." At 11 o'clock he breakfasted on milk and rice and learned at noon from Dr. Howard that he had "taken" the smallpox. That afternoon a nurse came, and he dined on hasty pudding and took some exercise. For the next three weeks he remained in the hospital, taking a variety of red pills, black pills, and mercurial pills, drinking vast quantities of tea, and eating vegetables and various kinds of pudding. In the course of his stay he experienced some mildly unpleasant symptoms—soreness under his arm, stiffness of the neck, nausea, backache, and upset stomach. Usually he "decamped" at about eleven o'clock at night and slept well, awaking feeling very "clever," but one night he was awakened by "extreme pain in neck, back, shoulders and arms" and on another he "sweat copiously." At one point he mentions that the "Number of Pock" had increased, at another that he put a plaster on his arm. Generally, he appears to have had a mild case, for in less than three weeks he writes of eating cake and drinking punch and walking to Cambridge, and on 20 March he was back in Andover.[8] Pearson's son Henry, in a biographical sketch of his father, says that in 1777 Eliphalet "was seized with a slow nervous fever, which confined him many months, and proved a heavy trial, leaving his eyes in so weak a state as to prevent his literary pursuits altogether."[9] This statement certainly cannot be referring to his smallpox inoculation, for his diary from March to August is full of references to reading, composing sermons, and preaching. The severe illness must have occurred in the fall of that year, after the close of the diary, and may well have been the reason why, at their first meeting, the trustees of Phillips

School limited the number of students to thirty "considering the present state of the preceptor's health."[10] In any event, 1777 appears to have been a difficult year for him, and he must have welcomed the opportunity to establish himself in a more secure position as preceptor of Phillips School.

We have already discussed the part that Pearson played in assisting his friend Sam Phillips in the manufacture of gunpowder and in planning for the future Phillips School; indeed, it is doubtful if either of these projects could have brought to successful fruition without Pearson's help. Now it was up to him to translate into action what the Constitution considered the "first and principal duty of the Master, to regulate the tempers, to enlarge the minds, and form the morals of the Youth, committed to his care." There was apparently little question among the founders that Pearson was the man to be the first preceptor. In his proposal to his father about founding a school, Sam Phillips, speaking of the importance of a master to a school, says, "such an one we know of—who is admirably form'd for the Sphere, and would exert himself in the Cause."[11] and must certainly have been referring to Pearson. At the first meeting the Founders, not the Trustees as a whole, appointed Pearson, suggesting that the matter had been settled beforehand. There is an undated proposal to Pearson to become Preceptor, with some notes of his added, which must have been written well before the first trustee meeting.[12] In any event, on 29 April, the day before school opened, Pearson and Nehemiah Abbot, as Treasurer, signed a contract whereby the former agreed to become Preceptor and "to the best of his abilities perform the duties of said office agreeable to the

9. *Eliphalet Pearson, First Preceptor of Phillips Academy. Portrait by Samuel F. B. Morse, in the possession of the Trustees of Phillips Academy.*

institution of the Founders and the rules established by the Trustees." In return Pearson was to receive the use of all the School lands in Andover, wood from the woodlot in Wilmington, and eighty pounds a year.[13] With these preliminaries settled, the next day Pearson went to work.

There is no record of what happened in the converted carpenter's shop during the first two years, but it can be assumed that the routine followed was very similar to that described by Pearson in a long report to the Trustees in April 1780.[14] The first part of this document is devoted to a description of a typical school day. At eight o'clock the students gathered for a short religious service; a chapter from the Old Testament was read, each student reading one verse, then a psalm was read and sung, and finally a prayer was delivered by the master. Then came recitations by the four classes: four boys repeated by rote two pages from the Greek grammar; thirty repeated a page or so from the Latin grammar; then the "accidence tribe" of fourteen recited from Cheever's *Accidence*, a book for beginners in Latin; then three students repeated pages from the English grammar. There were, in addition, several boys who did not fit into any one of these four classes and who recited individually. After the grammar recitations came translation from classical authors, and for this purpose the School was divided into twelve sections on the basis of ability and experience. Such classical authors as Corderius, Aesop (in Latin translation), Erasmus, Eutropius, Nepos, Ovid, Virgil, and the Greek testament were used. In addition to the classical scholars three pupils were studying arithmetic, one the Rule of Three, another in Fellowship, and the other in Practice.[15] These exercises continued until noon, when school was dismissed for one hour and a half for the midday meal. In the afternoon the first hour and a half was devoted to penmanship and the rest of the day to recitations similar to those conducted in the morning. The session closed with readings from Doddridge's *Family Expositor*, the singing of a hymn, and a prayer.

Pearson's report then took up the problems of a master trying to deal with students of differing abilities in a crowded classroom. First, there simply was not enough time in the day to hear recitations from twelve different groups, let alone the number of individuals who had to be treated separately:

> To hear an individual or a class or a succession of classes recite for 3 hours, in a calm and silent room where nothing, but the class, demands attention, would be a *pleasure*; But what must be the situation and feelings of an instructor, who must be *eye*, *ear*, and *voice*, not only to the *class* under his immediate examination, but to ten times as many more, at the same time? . . . Who is liable every minute and every line to be interrupted by some interrogation, request, or complaint—whose eye needs to be perpetually fixed upon the idle and dissipated? These and other considerations, gentlemen, together with the uneasiness, noise, and bustle of 60 scholars, crowded into a

small house, are circumstances, which render the business of this
school fatiguing and painful to a degree which a person, unexperienced in it, can but faintly conceive. I hope no one, gentlemen, will
think this to be merely picturesque. I speak of real *feeling* and *facts*.

Scarcely a minute passes in a day, in which I am not called upon,
tho' ever so much engaged, to explain some difficult passage, to correct some error of the type, to shew the etymology or derivation of
some word, to grant some request, to accept some excuse, to hear
some complaint, or to settle some contention or dispute; these things
are in addition to the uneasiness and pain I necessarily feel from the
too constant dissipation, thoughtlessness, and ill humor of numbers.

Things were bad enough on normal, routine days. Special exercises on
special days made matters even more difficult. On Mondays the students
were quizzed on the sermons they had heard the day before. On Saturdays
conduct records for the week were reviewed and punishments administered.
And there were special days for spelling matches and examinations. One
might think that the presence of an assistant would help, but in actual
practice all of the difficult problems had to be handled by the master himself. As a result he had no time for speculation or enjoyment or self-im-
provement. And since there was no time during the regular day to instruct
the students in singing, the master was obliged to do this before the evening meal. Finally, there were countless tasks to perform in the administration of the School—visiting with parents and reporting on student progress,
writing letters to those interested in coming to the School, meetings of
trustee committees, and the like. Pearson had other more specific complaints: training in speaking and singing had to be sacrificed because of
work in the School garden, a favorite enterprise of Sam Phillips but apparently anathema to Pearson; more books were needed to supply proper reading for students whose ages ranged from six to thirty; and he was concerned lest the manifold occupations of master and student alike prevent
adequate attention to the moral education that was supposedly the main
purpose of the School.

There were a few slight modifications to this stern regimen of classics
and religion. Pearson was an accomplished musician, singing bass and playing the cello with distinction,[16] and he worked hard to build a choir at the
School. That he had some success is evidenced by the trustee records, where
mention is made of visiting the School and hearing the boys sing anthems.[17]
Isaac Watts's *Hymns for Children*, one of Sam Phillips' favorite works,
provided additional pieces for the choir's repertoire. In 1783 the Trustees
voted to introduce Mason's *Self-Knowledge* into the School as "a classical
book," but this dreary tract could hardly have lightened the student fare.[18]
Since both Phillips and Pearson had studied French at Dummer School, it
was natural that they should attempt to introduce the subject at Phillips,
but though the Trustees passed several votes authorizing the appointment

of a French instructor—with the provision that the parents of those taking French bear the extra charge—there is no record of the subject actually having been taught during this period.[19] One can also get some idea of the student work from the Exhibition pieces that were prepared for the annual visits of the Trustees. Early in the 1780's a list of such pieces included dialogues between a Whig and a Tory, between Tullus and Coriolanus, between Aesop and a Frenchman, with a trialogue among Addison, Swift, and Mercury as a grand finale. The 1783 Exhibition included, among nineteen pieces, a "severe satire on the absurd doctrine of transubstantion [sic]," "Goliah's [sic] death," "A scene between St. Christopher and St. George, in presence of Pluto," "The lucky Spider," and "Interview between *Virgil* and *Horace* in the Elysian shades, to whom *Scaliger* the *Critic* is introduced by *Mercury*."[20] These performances must have been impressive, and the Trustees are recorded as being pleased with them, as well as with the students' proficiency in the classics. Yet one wonders if the Exhibitions were not a pretty artificial business, consisting primarily of demonstrations of rote memory. Timothy Pickering, in his critique on the Phillips Academy Constitution wondered about this: "But what avail examinations, if conducted in the usual way? I mean by previously instructing the scholars in those *particular lessons* to which the examinations are to be confined. If we would know what progress a boy has made in a dead or foreign language, does not common sense obviously show that his books should be

10. *Cartoon of Samuel Phillips, Jr., drawn by Andrew Rutherford of the Class of 1971, reproduced with his permission.*

opened at the discretion of the examiner and the boy then set to construe and parse? If we would discover his knowledge in geography, shall we hear him repeat certain articles which he purposely has been directed to commit to his memory? Or shall we not rather ask the solution of any problem, or description of any country, taken at discretion?" Pickering then went on to blast Harvard Commencements as a "farce."[21] Certainly Pearson was a thorough drillmaster, and the records of his boys at college indicate that they were admirably prepared, but the Exhibition programs had better be taken with a grain of salt as evidence of normal academic achievement at Phillips Academy in his day.

Unfortunately, we have only one detailed student account of what studying under Pearson was like, and that one must be qualified. It comes from the pen of Josiah Quincy, later Congressman, Mayor of Boston and President of Harvard. Quincy was the grandson of William Phillips of Boston, brother of the two Founders. His father had died just as the Revolution was beginning. As a result, he and his mother were forced to live with Grandfather Phillips, a crochety and disagreeable old gentleman. Partly to support the family enterprise in Andover, and partly to get the young boy out of his grandfather's house, he was sent to the Phillips School in May 1778, at the age of six. To force a boy that young to submit to the rigorous discipline of Eliphalet Pearson was not to make him love the School. In addition, his recollections were written when he was over seventy, after a long and busy life that must have caused some of his early memories to blur. Even when allowances are made for these circumstances, however, Quincy's portrait of Pearson and of Phillips School is hardly complimentary.

> The discipline of the Academy was severe, and to a child, as I was, disheartening. The Preceptor was distant and haughty in his manners. I have no recollection of his ever having shown any consideration for my childhood. Fear was the only impression I received from his treatment of myself and others. I was put at once into the first book of Cheever's Accidence, and obliged, with the rest of my classmates, to get by heart passages of a book which I could not, from my years, possibly understand. My memory was good, and I had been early initiated, by being drilled in the Assembly's Catechism, into the practice of repeating readily words the meaning of which I could not by any possibility conceive. I cannot imagine a more discouraging course of education than that to which I was subjected.
>
> The truth was, I was an incorrigible lover of sports of every kind. My heart was in ball and marbles. I needed and loved perpetual activity of body, and with these dispositions I was compelled to sit with four other boys on the same hard bench, daily, four hours in the morning and four in the afternoon, and study lessons which I could not understand. Severe as was my fate, the elasticity of my mind

cast off all recollection of it as soon as school hours were over, and I do not recollect, nor believe, that I ever made any complaint to my mother or any one else.

The chief variety in my studies was that afforded by reading lessons in the Bible, and in getting by heart Dr. Watts's Hymns for Children. My memory, though ready, was not tenacious, and the rule being that there should be no advance until the first book was conquered, I was kept in Cheever's Accidence I know not how long. All I know is, I must have gone over it twenty times before mastering it. I had been about four years tormented with studies not suited to my years before my interest in them commenced; but when I began upon Nepos, Caesar, and Virgil, my repugnance to my classics ceased, and the Preceptor gradually relaxed in the severity of his discipline, and I have no doubt, congratulated himself on its success as seen in the improvement he was compelled to acknowledge. During the latter part of my life in the Academy he was as indulgent as a temperament naturally intolerant and authoritative would permit.[22]

Fortunately for the young Quincy, he boarded with the Reverend Jonathan French, Clerk of the Trustees, and his wife, in the old manse opposite the South Church on what is now Central Street. The French family clearly did much to counteract the harsh discipline of the classroom. Quincy wrote:

The comfort of my life was the family where I boarded. Jonathan French, the minister of the parish, and his wife, were father and mother to me. They were both kind and affable, consulted my wants, and had consideration for my childhood. . . . He [French] took an interest in my progress, and occasionally assisted me in my studies. His wife was amiable and affectionate, but she had an increasing family, so that the care of the boys, my schoolfellows, six or eight in number, devolved on her maiden sister, Ruth Richards by name, who took care of our rooms, saw to our clothes, and had the general care of us. Aunt Ruthy was consequently an object of great importance to the boys, whose affections she found means to gain. We slept in one large chamber, in which were three or four beds, two boys occupying each. The family table was sufficient, but simple, the food being of the most common kind. Beef and pork were the standing dishes, with an ample supply of vegetables. As to bread, there being little or no intercourse with the South, rye and Indian bread was our only supply, and that not always thoroughly baked. The minister alone was indulged in white bread, as brown gave him heart-burn, and he could not preach upon it. Our time out of school was diminished by a lesson to be prepared for the next morning, and also by morning and evening prayers. On Sunday our time was filled up by morning and evening prayers and a commentary on some portion of Scripture, or by an exercise to be got by heart—either a hymn or a passage from the Bible. At meeting, both morning and afternoon, we carried our ink-bottles, and took down the heads and topics of the sermon, of which, at evening prayers, we were called upon to give such an account as we could. The Sabbath was anything but a day of rest to us. The old Puritan restrictions, though wearing away and greatly reduced, were still wearisome and irksome.[23]

In addition to these published recollections of his life as a student at Phillips School, Quincy recorded other experiences in letters to friends, one of which again throws light on Pearson's teaching methods. "I was called upon to give the principal parts of the Latin verb 'noceo.' Unfortunately I gave the 'c' a hard sound. I said, 'nokeo, nokere, noki.' The next thing I knew I was knocked."[24] On another occasion he wrote, "Pearson was a convert to thorough discipline, monitors kept an account of all of a student's failures, idleness, inattention, whispering, and like deviations from order, and at the end of the week were bestowed substantial rewards, for such self-indulgences, distributed upon the head and the hand, with no lack of strength or fidelity." According to Quincy, the boys started with Cheever's Accidence, then proceeded to Corderius, then Nepos, and finally to Virgil. Ward's Latin grammar, where all the rules were explained in Latin, was a standard accompaniment to the Roman authors read, and Gloucester's Greek grammar was the principal guide for that study. Quincy thought the study of Greek "slight and superficial": "a thorough ability to construe the four Gospels was all that was required of us to enter the College," and that was apparently all Pearson attempted. "Our preparation was limited enough," he thought, "but sufficient for the poverty and distracted state of the period."[25] On the other hand his opinion of Samuel Phillips, Jr., was highly laudatory:

I was a frequent visitor in his family, though never a member of it. My mother was daughter of his father's brother, always staid in his house, when she visited Andover, which brought me to be almost a daily inmate. I have heard his addresses to the school, as a trustee, to the College as an Overseer, and as a boy and man, my opportunities for personal intercourse with him have been many; and I can truly say that I have never met, through my whole life, with an individual in whom the spirit of Christianity and of good will to mankind were so naturally and beautifully blended with an indomitable energy and enterprise in active life. He was a leader in the Church, a leader in the State, the young loved and listened to him, the old consulted and deferred to his advice. I have traveled with him from Boston to Andover, alone, then a journey of the chief part of a day; his discourse, adapted to a boy, as I then was, full of sweetness and instructions; his love of the young was intense. He delighted in the poetry of Watts, which he seemed to have, all of it, by heart so readily and appositely he introduced it in conversation, accompanied by a never-ceasing flow of wise maxims, given not with an air of authority, but the natural outflowing of a good and kind heart. I cannot, in language, do justice to the interest and affection with which on these occasions he excited the young mind.[26]

Quincy tells an interesting story of his arriving at Phillips School and being seated next to a twenty-nine-year-old man whom he calls Cutts but who must have been James Anderson of Londonderry, New Hampshire. According to Quincy, Anderson had been a surgeon in the Revolutionary army, had become sensible of his educational deficiencies through contact with cultivated men in the service, and had resigned his commission for a try at remedying his lack of training. He attended Phillips for two years and then went on to graduate from Harvard. Quincy remembers him as a man of "wit and talent" who, after classes were over, associated on equal terms with the Preceptor and other gentlemen of the town. Though there have been students in their early twenties who have attended Phillips Academy since then, it says something either for the flexibility of the Pearson administration or of its desperate need for pupils that both the youngest and oldest students ever to attend the school were in the very first class.[27] One final Quincy story. Apparently Eliphalet Pearson decided, after many

11. Cartoon of Eliphalet Pearson, drawn by Andrew Rutherford of the Class of 1971, reproduced with his permission.

struggles with the young boy, that he could never go on to college and advised his mother to put him in a counting house. Fortunately, Mrs. Quincy was a lady of spirit who refused to take the advice. As a result, Quincy eventually went to Harvard and later, of course, served as its President.[28]

Pearson's prowess as a martinet became a tradition at Phillips Academy and was remembered long after he left there. On one occasion, after some undergraduate fracas, he appeared and shouted, "Let the one who had performed that outrage appear instantly before me." Apparently the guilty party stood up at once and confessed. On another occasion a miscreant who had been dressed down by Eliphalet was asked how he felt: "I pinched myself to know whether I was alive," was the answer. The only boy who ever had the last word with Pearson—at least the only recorded one—was a student who, wishing to see the Preceptor, knocked repeatedly at his door. When he was finally admitted, the master said, "Why do you rap so often? You never should rap but once at the door of a gentleman." To which the student replied, "I never do."[29]

Not all his students remembered Pearson as a harsh drillmaster. Writing to him in 1826 just before his death, Judge Samuel Putnam had this to say:

> The kindness which you extended towards me during the three years
> which I enjoyed at Andover will never be effaced from my mind:
> and my sense of gratitude for your indefatigable care and instruction
> has increased with my years. I love to dwell on that delightful period
> when the love of letters was impressed upon your pupils with the
> sound principles of morality and with the pleasing recollection I al-
> ways associate the venerable name of my Preceptor. Allow me to offer
> you this tribute of thankfulness. It is not the less sincere or strong
> because it has been delayed until my hair has been whitened by time.
> Accept it as a free will offering justly due and flowing from feelings
> unmixed with earthly hopes or considerations.[30]

To provide housing for the students, the trustees followed the only course available to them—placing them in private homes. This practice, never satisfactory, was a continual source of trouble for the School until it was finally abandoned over a century later. Each year at their annual meeting the Trustees voted on a list of names of those licensed to board students, and it is clear that they took this duty seriously. After finding that the families treated their charges in different ways, and desirous of providing a uniform set of procedures, in August 1781 they drew up a statement of "Regulations for Families boarding Scholars." The Trustees assumed that all families boarding scholars would hold family prayers in the morning and evening—indeed, failure to do so would be sufficient grounds for disqualifying a family from having students board. The Trustees expected the head of the family to see to it that the students attended both sessions. Decency and order were to be observed at meals, and no one should sit down until a blessing had been asked. The head of the family was to establish sensible study hours and not allow a student to be out of the house after nine o'clock. Rules for Sunday were very strict: the students were to attend both morning and afternoon services and spend the rest of the day in "reading the scriptures and in other religious exercises." Nor could they be absent from the house after sunset on Saturday or at any time on Sunday. At no time was there to be "fighting, striking, or quarreling" among the students. If a boy used "profane or obscene language," he was to be rebuked by the family head, and if he continued in this vile practice, he was to be reported to the Preceptor. The students were to go to bed at a reasonable hour, keep silent after retiring, and rise early in the morning for family prayers and "to wash their faces and hands, comb their heads, breakfast with decency, and seasonably attend the duties of the Academy." If a student was to be absent in the evening, he was to tell the head of the family where he was going, but above all he was to avoid "bad company" or go to any public house. To make sure all these rules were being obeyed, the Preceptor was expected to make regular visits to the homes where scholars boarded. Apparently the Trustees had some qualms about the strictness of their rules, for at the end it was stated that if any regulation proved to be "grievous or impracticable" they could be referred to the Trustee Committee of Exigencies. The regimen thus imposed on students and families alike makes it seem that the Trustees were bent on establishing Sam Adams's "Christian Sparta" on Andover Hill.[31]

As might be expected, most students during Pearson's term of office came from Massachusetts—many of them friends of the Phillips family. There was also a smattering of pupils from New Hampshire, but it was not until 1781 that any came from Maine, still technically part of Massachusetts. By 1785, the last year of Pearson's tenure, apparently because the reputation of the school had spread, the makeup of the undergraduate body really began to expand. That fall Louis Charles François Cougnacq, aged fifteen, listed as coming from Hispaniola, West Indies, arrived, to be joined by William Lee, aged twelve, from Halifax, Nova Scotia, and two Southerners, Henry Daingerfield, aged fourteen, from Spottsylvania County, Virginia, and Howell Lewis, aged thirteen, from Fredericksburg, Virginia. Despite this leavening, Bay Staters continued to dominate. Boston contributed members from some of the leading families of the city: in addition to Phillipses, there were Lloyds, Cabots, Lowells, Lathrops, Searses, Higginsons, and Gores, among others. Doubtless the parents of these boys knew and respected Samuel Phillips, Jr., himself, but they may also have been thankful for a school that might stand as a bulwark against the confusion and uncertainties of those troubled times. Among Pearson's students were a number who later distinguished themselves. John Thornton Kirkland, like Quincy, later became President of Harvard, and Benjamin Abbot became principal of the Phillips Exeter Academy. Another Abbot, John, became a professor and trustee of Bowdoin, while a third, Abiel, served as principal of Dummer Academy. William King became the first governor of Maine, and Charles Cutts was a United States senator. These first Andover boys also included an impressive number of representatives to Congress, judges, and members of the foreign service. Never again in the history of the School would so high a percentage of its students distinguish themselves in various kinds of public service.[32]

One gets a different insight into the first years of Phillips Academy from reading the records of the early trustee meetings. Throughout the Pearson administration the Trustees dutifully elected the same officers each year: President Squire Phillips; Clerk, Jonathan French; and Treasurer, Nehemiah Abbot. In 1781 the Reverend Josiah Stearns—the one Trustee who "cut" the first meeting—resigned, to be replaced later that year by the Reverend David Tappan of Newbury. As one authority has remarked, "Trustees [of academies] could never resist dividing themselves into groups, especially those of Phillips Academy, who found an extraordinary number of uses for committees."[33] Indeed in the early years almost every concern of the Board was entrusted to a committee, the classic example being a committee to furnish the School with wood, which consisted of one man, the Treasurer.[34] One of the first things the Trustees discovered was that the income from the Founders' munificence would not be enough to meet the costs of the school, and in the fall of 1778 it was voted to assess each student a share of the expenses for the Assistant and for wood and other incidentals above and beyond the income available.[35] At the end of the first year Uncle John and Uncle William Phillips were obliged to foot the bill of eighty pounds for Eliphalet Pearson's salary, and Uncle John later contributed another thirty-two pounds to settle the Treasurer's account.[36] Soon part of the Preceptor's salary had to be included in the student assessment, but the concept of helping appeared at the same time, when a committee was formed to exempt certain students from the charge.[37] It was one thing to assess, another to collect, and we soon find the Board demanding security from parents, a deposit of eighteen shillings for all entering students, and an inevitable committee to devise measures to deal with those delinquent in payment.[38] Whether a disciplinary or financial measure, fines of one shilling a day for absences from School were also initiated during this period.[39] Another committee was appointed to apply to the Massachusetts legislature for tax exemption for the School.[40] In short, during these early years the School lived pretty much a hand-to-mouth existence, fortunately protected from serious financial difficulties by the willingness of the Phillips brothers to bail the institution out when necessary.

Eliphalet Pearson was apparently as dictatorial in dealing with the Trustees as he was with his students. When it became clear that the School was a going concern, Pearson wanted a permanent contract to replace the annual ones that had been drawn up hitherto, and in May 1780 he drove a hard bargain with the Trustees. In return for acting as "principal Instructor" at the school, according to the Constitution and the rules established by the Trustees, Pearson was to have the use of practically all the land on the Hill and in Wilmington that the School owned—about one hundred and forty acres in all. In addition he was to receive annually four hundred Spanish milled dollars and "three hundred and ten ounces Troy weight of coined Silver of sterling alloy." In connection with these payments there was an interesting escalator clause, whereby the amount of money paid could be raised or lowered by reference to the cost of living in 1774. If the School were larger than thirty—which it then was—the Trustees were bound to give Pearson an Assistant. If they did not do so within a fortnight after the resignation of the previous Assistant, Pearson was to have the Assistant's salary added to his own until a new teacher was found. Pearson was authorized to build a house on his property, but if he should leave his position, the Trustees agreed to buy it back at a price agreed upon by three disinterested appraisers. In the meantime the Trustees agreed to take care of all repairs on the property that cost more than twelve ounces of silver annually. There were further clauses dealing with the upkeep of the property.[41] Apparently this generous contract did not entirely satisfy Pearson, for a few years later we find the Trustees appointing *another* committee to deal with the Preceptor's salary in the future.[42] One of the most hilarious themes running through the Trustee Records is the problem of Pearson's outhouses. A trustee committee had succeeded in erecting a "necessary and woodhouse" for the School itself, but apparently the problem of Pearson's outhouses was almost insoluble.[43] The term covered more than Chic Sale structures and must have included chicken coops, stables, and the like. Pearson never got around to building his house. At one point the Trustees voted to apply the proceeds from land sales to a house for the Preceptor, but at the same time they voted to shingle the house he was in.[44] When Pearson left for Harvard in 1786, the Trustees must certainly have regretted the departure of a distinguished schoolmaster, but they may well have heaved sighs of relief to be rid of such a tough negotiator in financial matters.

The Trustee Records also show the Board struggling with the administration of the School itself. Apparently Pearson's health improved rapidly, for by June 1778 the limitation of thirty students of the previous April was modified to forty-five, and in November of that year the number was raised again, to sixty.[45] All good schools have a School bell, and the Trustees were determined that Phillips should be no exception. First, a committee was appointed to procure a bell; then it was announced that a bell had been borrowed from a Mr. Hooper of Newburyport. Some disaster must have occurred, for another committee was appointed to fix the bell.[46] At about the same time, a Captain Wyer lent the School some globes. The committee appointed to thank these gentlemen for their loans reported that "thro' a multiplicity of public business they had omitted to execute their commission," and Squire Phillips was drafted to write the letter and apologize for the delay in expressing gratitude.[47] The Board also had great difficulty in acquiring books. A committee was appointed to prepare a list, and a general request for loans of books was circulated, but the problem remained, as evidenced by the fact that the Trustees took the trouble to vote thanks to John Lowell for the gift of two volumes of Enfield's *Speaker* and to Deacon Mason for the Works of John Newton.[48] The Board was also interested in beautifying the Hill: a committee was appointed to set out locust and fruit trees and later reported that fifty, a gift from Sam Phillips, Jr., had been planted; and the same group was charged with preparing a school garden.[49] A memorandum of Pearson's, written in 1779, suggests that at least some return in the way of produce from the school lands was being realized. According to this document, 29½ barrels of cider, 31 bushels of potatoes, 1 bushel of pears, and 14 bushels of oats had been produced on the school property, but whether the boys had any part in this is not clear.[50] The problem of getting assistants for the Preceptor was vexatious. Because of the relatively low pay, most of those appointed seem to have accepted positions only temporarily, while they were looking for something better, and during Pearson's eight years there were five different assistants. In the Phillips Papers is a letter from Sam Phillips, Jr., to one Jeremiah Smith of Peterborough, New Hampshire, offering him the Assistant's job. After outlining the general situation, Sam wrote: "The terms have varied with the Currency, but it has been our aim to make them as good as in any Country School around us"—which was not saying much. Young men interested in teaching "give this a preference to most," Sam thought, and added that in the company of the Reverend French and Preceptor Pearson "a Gentleman of Sentiment may spend his leisure hours with profit and pleasure."[51] Smith decided to give Phillips Academy a whirl, but like most of the others, he lasted but one year. That the students were testing the administration in various areas is to be seen in a trustee vote forbidding firearms to undergraduates without special permission,[52] and a pinch of nepotism was added to the record when Sam's son John, although only six years old, was allowed to enroll to be taught English. Considering all that Sam had done for the place, it would have been difficult not to waive the eight-year-old requirement recently voted.[53] One may smile at the Trustees' addiction to the committee system and at some of the problems they had to deal with, but the overall impression one gets is of a dedicated group of men whose devotion to the welfare of the School was deep and whose determination to make the new institution a success was steadfast.

In 1782 Samuel Phillips, Jr., finally got a house to live in that was appropriate to his standing as a leading citizen of both the town and the state.

In order to be near the new school, Sam, his wife Phoebe, and their infant son John had moved to the old Abbot House on Phillips Street in the latter part of 1777, and it was there that the early trustee meetings were held. Since plans for providing Eliphalet Pearson with adequate housing never seemed to materialize, and since, in 1780, he finally married Priscilla Holyoke,[54] Sam and his family turned the Abbot House over to the newlyweds and moved "to a little red house on the Woburn Road," later the residence of Sam's confidential clerk, Moses Abbot, and located on the right-hand side of what is now Hidden Road.[55] Early in 1782 the Trustees signed an agreement to exchange land belonging to Sam around the present bell tower for school property in front of what are now Bishop and Adams halls, and it was on this property that the famous Mansion House, one of the handsomest dwellings in Essex County, was erected. The frame, made of select New Hampshire timber, was raised as a community project. On the appointed day the town's stores and schools were closed and most of the community gathered on the Hill to assist in erecting the structure. After a prayer by Jonathan French, everyone pitched in with ropes and pikes, and amid much cheering from the spectators, the frame was hoisted into place. After the job was done, according to one authority, "festivity followed." The Mansion House immediately became a show place. With sixty-two windows, three stories, large square rooms with big fireplaces, fine paneling, and heavy doors with wrought iron hinges, the impressive edifice soon was known as "the largest and most elegant house ever built in town."[56] Sam Phillips and his wife were hospitable people, and hundreds of visitors were entertained in their home, with President George Washington only the most distinguished. In addition, the Judge and Phoebe regularly boarded a number of Academy students. Until it burned down in 1887, the Mansion House was a fitting complement to the Academy, first as the Phillipses' home and later as a public house where the Trustees held their meetings and enjoyed "decent, not extravagant entertainment." Of all the buildings destroyed by fire on Andover Hill—and there were a large number—this one represented the greatest loss to School and community.

By the time that Eliphalet Pearson left to go to Harvard, Phillips Academy was firmly established in a pattern that was to last for many years. Although the School was clearly beginning to be known outside the confines of Massachusetts, it appears that the dedication and hard work of the Trustees and the Preceptor were achieved pretty much in a vacuum. There is almost no reference to what was going on in the world outside in the early history of the School. A year after its founding, the convention to draw up the Constitution of Massachusetts met, and a year later the document—the first written constitution in the United States—was ratified by the people. Samuel Phillips, Jr., was a delegate to that convention and distinguished himself there, but he seems to have kept his manifold activities compartmentalized, for the School seems to have paid no attention to this striking development. There is no notice of a community celebration after Yorktown, no "free day" for the students after the signing of the Peace Treaty in 1783. The only way in which the outside world impinged upon the school was with the problem of currency, the depreciation of which made it difficult to set salaries. In 1781 Samuel Phillips, Jr., had been elected senator in the first legislature of the new Commonwealth; five years later he was chosen President of the Senate. In 1781 he had been appointed one of the justices for the Court of Common Pleas in Essex County, a position that required three or four months of work a year. Yet his interest in the School never flagged, and he always seemed able to find time to attend to countless academy matters as they came up.[57]

Anyone who thought that a man of Eliphalet Pearson's talents would be content to remain long as Preceptor of a school like Phillips Academy would have been naive. As one writer said of him,

> It is generally admitted that he was a consummate rhetorician, one of the keenest critics of his day, a finished and widely read classical scholar, noted for the accuracy and elegance of his Latin prose composition, a master of Hebrew, Syriac, and Coptic languages, possessed of a good knowledge of metaphysics, a very respectable chemist. . . . an able preacher . . . and a match for the best lawyers of his day. He was also a skillful mechanic, a most accomplished musician, publishing an important work on psalmody; he was a good bass singer and played well upon the violincello, once making one of these instruments with his own hands. He also projected a system of phonetics which he never published; speculated upon the origin of ideas; was a scientific agriculturist and, during his later years, proved himself to be one of the best farmers of his time. . . . For statistical work he had a passion. . . . His philanthropic work alone was enough to engage and fatigue a score of ordinary men. . . . Had he been able to confine his powerful mind to a single subject, he might have exhausted all the possibilities of any one department of thought.[58]

To be sure, some of these achievements must have been realized after he left Andover, but by 1786, the year of his departure, he was clearly a man of extraordinary promise. It is hardly surprising, therefore, that in October 1785 he was informed by President Willard of Harvard that he had been elected to succeed Stephen Sewall as Hancock Professor of Hebrew and the Oriental Languages at Harvard College, at a salary of two hundred and eighty pounds a year.[59] The offering was too flattering, from all points of view, for Pearson to refuse, and the following January he formally notified the Trustees of his resignation, announcing at the same time that he could continue as Preceptor for only two weeks.[60] The Trustees, as we shall see, were hard put to find a successor in such a short time. Pearson stayed long enough to see the School established in its new building on 30 January 1786, but his actual departure was something of an anticlimax. Writing to his wife about a month later, Sam Phillips said, "Your parting with Mr. Pearson will be, or has been, a grievous one, but perhaps the parting will not be a final one, and that all your good days are not over;—I was in hopes that he would have left Andover with a little ceremony, as his wife did—but did not think of the Circumstance of his being without a bed to lay on, for the last night."[61] Apparently, sadly, no one had seen fit to have the School and some of the Trustees bid Eliphalet a formal adieu. Considering his unlovely and unloved disposition, it is easy to understand why no one thought to do so, but some one should have offered him a bed for his last night in Andover as Preceptor.

Eliphalet Pearson left a substantial legacy to Andover: a stern insistence on academic excellence; an almost exclusive concentration on the study of the classical languages; a system of discipline based on fear; the dictatorship of the Preceptor in the management of the School; an interest in enabling indigent boys to get an Andover education; the housing of students in private homes; and a determination to inculcate in the students the old virtues of the Puritan religion. It would be nearly a century before anyone at Phillips Academy would attempt to change any of these educational concepts. Yet the parting with Pearson was *au revoir* rather than goodbye. He remained on the Board of Trustees until his death in 1826 and served as President of the Board from 1802 to 1821. And in about twenty years he was to return to Andover Hill to place on Phillips Academy and the community surrounding it the imprint of his powerful personality even more deeply.

CHAPTER FIVE

THE PASSING OF THE PHILLIPSES

T H E P E R I O D between the departure of Eliphalet Pearson and the arrival of John Adams—from 1786 to 1810—should be treated as a single unit. Though there were two Preceptors during this period—Ebenezer Pemberton and Mark Newman—neither left his mark on the Academy in any positive way, though both were well intentioned gentlemen who were popular with the students. During most of the period the Trustees made all the important decisions; and after the death of Judge Phillips, a specially appointed Select Committee rode herd on Mark Newman, coping with details of the administration which would have been left to the Preceptor had he been a stronger man. The basic set of principles and procedures established by Eliphalet Pearson went unchallenged during this period; rather, the question was whether they could be maintained. When Pearson resigned as Preceptor of Phillips Academy, he continued to hold his position on the Board of Trustees, and in 1802 was elected President. Until his death in that year Judge Samuel Phillips kept a watchful eye on his favorite enterprise, and after that his widow, Madam Phoebe Phillips, and his son, John Phillips, continued as watchdogs. John had served as Assistant at the School during 1795–96 and in 1801 was chosen a trustee; he was thereafter in a position to follow in his father's footsteps. Though he never achieved the distinction of his father, he worked faithfully for the welfare of the Academy.

By 1810, when John Adams arrived, the influence of the Phillipses was beginning to wane. Phoebe Phillips died in 1812, her son John in 1820. Though Eliphalet Pearson remained President of the Board until 1821, his major interest after 1808 was the newly founded Andover Theological Seminary, and the same was true in large measure of Phoebe and John Phillips. This period, therefore, saw the passing of the generation that had founded Phillips Academy. The question was: Could the school survive without the powerful support of this extraordinarily talented family?

Eliphalet Pearson's sudden resignation and departure from Andover put the Trustees on the spot. Not having been given enough time to find a replacement for Pearson, they had to adopt stop-gap measures. Since a meeting of the full Board could not be arranged in time, the Committee of Exigencies voted to empower Samuel Phillips, Jr., and Eliphalet Pearson, as a committee of two, to offer the position to Caleb Bingham, who was identified as "a schoolmaster in Boston," and if he should not accept, to try "Mr. Paine, butler of the college."[1] Mr. Bingham agreed to try his hand at Phillips Academy for a few months at least, but it soon became clear that he did not have the stamina to hold the position longer. In a letter to his wife Phoebe, Sam Phillips wrote, "Mr. Bingham had better attend the Academy, only as his health will permit, tho' it should be but half the time, than to overdo and render himself unable to attend at all."[2] So the search for a permanent replacement for Pearson continued. Writing to his wife on another occasion, Sam Phillips discussed various possibilities for a replacement, including Ebenezer Pemberton. Other possibilities were a clergyman from Newbury and two unidentified schoolteachers.[3] In the meantime, Caleb Bingham had resigned and John Abbot, 3d, had filled in.[4] Finally, in May 1786, the problem was resolved when Ebenezer Pemberton came to Andover and after two months' probation was appointed Preceptor.

Pemberton, the second Preceptor of Phillips Academy, was very different from Pearson.[5] Where Pearson had been hard-driving, rough, and fear-inspiring, Pemberton was gentle, well-mannered, and friendly. He was a native of Newport, Rhode Island, who had been sent at an early age to Boston to be educated by his uncle of the same name. Since Uncle Ebenezer had been a founder of the College of New Jersey, the boy was sent to Nassau Hall, where he became the Valedictorian of the Class of 1765. He tried his hand at both the ministry and the law before finally becoming a schoolmaster. First he read theology with the Reverend Samuel Hopkins in Newport but "could never be persuaded to preach." Finding that the ministry was not for him, he spent the next four years as a tutor at Princeton, where he had as pupils James Madison and Aaron Burr. Though he was a great success, as evidenced by testimonials from his students which he used to exhibit in his later years, he could see no future at Princeton, and in 1772 he left to read law with Judge William Livingston of New Jersey. It has been suggested that Pemberton acquired the courtly manners for which he became so famous while living with the Judge.[6] After completing his studies in the law, he returned to Newport, where he opened practice, only to find that the rough and tumble of colonial lawsuits was not to his liking. Uncle Ebenezer was distressed that his nephew did not enter the ministry and promised him a large library of books if he would do so, but by this time the young man had set his heart on schoolmastering. In 1778 he moved to Plainfield, Connecticut, where his mother was living, and opened an academy there, but soon left to teach school in Windham. He was occupied in this position when the call to Andover came, and after some preliminary negotiations, he accepted the Trustees' offer.

12. *Ebenezer Pemberton, Second Preceptor of Phillips Academy. From a portrait by an unknown artist, in the possession of the Trustees of Phillips Academy.*

In 1786 Phillips Academy was to acquire not only a Preceptor but also a building. Soon after the opening of School in 1778 it became clear that the old carpenter's shop could never serve as permanent quarters, and early in the 1780's the trustees began to plan for a new schoolhouse. By 1783 a committee had been formed to draw up specifications for the "new academy" and the following year a larger committee headed by the three Phillips brothers was empowered "to determine where the new academy should be placed, and carry the plan of it into execution as far, as they should be able to find the means therefor."[7] If there were going to be a problem about "means," it was a shrewd move to put the three Phillipses on the building committee, and it was they who footed the bill for construction, estimated at a little over three thousand dollars. It has been described as "a two-storey edifice of wood, with recitation rooms and a study on the lower floor, arranged for one hundred pupils, and a spacious hall for exhibitions and other public purposes on the second floor."[8] The new building was located in the southwest corner of what is now the Main Campus, approximately at the present site of the armillary sphere. Visitors to the New Academy were impressed; the Reverend William Bentley of Salem visited Andover in 1789 and had this to say:

It is an elegant building, situated upon an hill, in free air. In the front are enclosed two rooms, designed for private Schools, and a Library, etc. Between there [sic] you pass into the Academy. Between 40 or 50 youth were present under the Preceptor Mr. E. Pemberton, and the Sub P. a Mr. Abbot. The Preceptor is an amiable man and communicative. His abilities are admirable for his profession. Above unfinished, and fitted out for the religious Congregation, for which an house has been rebuilding, was the Hall, and Theater. It is arched with great success for the exhibitions of the youth of the academy.[9]

This building was to be the new home of Phillips Academy until it was destroyed by fire in 1818.

William Bentley's high opinion of Ebenezer Pemberton was held by many others. Josiah Quincy said of him, "Mild, gentle, conciliatory, and kind, inspiring affection and exciting neither fear nor awe . . . he made himself beloved and respected by his pupils."[10] To be sure, from Quincy's point of view anyone would have been an improvement over Eliphalet Pearson, but his tribute is obviously sincere nonetheless. For all his gentleness, Pemberton was able to maintain a strict discipline and was particularly interested in cultivating the manners of his charges. Here is a description of a chapel service under him:

At the hour appointed for morning prayers, every scholar was expected to be in his seat. Dr. Pemberton entered, the pupils rose and bowed to him, he returned the salutation, ascended to the desk, and

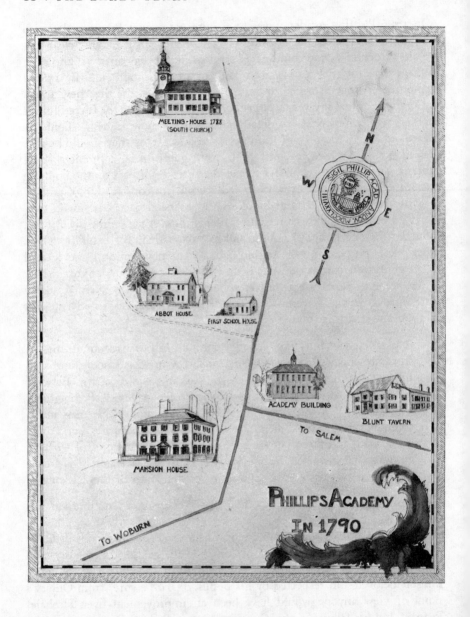

13. *Phillips Academy in 1790. Drawn by Laura R. Allis. Since no contemporary drawings of either the first schoolhouse or the first Academy Building exist, the representations of these have been based on written descriptions of the buildings.*

pronounced the invocation, after which the scholars read verses in
turn, from a chapter in the Bible, a method of conducting the school
devotions which has remained in use until the present time. But at
the close of school in the afternoon, each scholar withdrew separately,
bowed first to the principal, then to the assistant upon the other side
of the hall, and retired.[11]

Parents of boys who were trained under Pemberton were happy with the
results. Caleb Strong, later Governor of Massachusetts, sent his son Theodore to the Academy in the early 1790's and had this to report at the end
of the term: "My son's manners are much improved. He is a good deal
mended of the trick of moving his feet and his fingers."[12] But Pemberton
taught more than manners. He emphasized public speaking and elocution,
as well as drilling his students in the classics, and, at the request of the
Trustees he spent every Monday morning going over the material of the
services of the previous Sabbath.[13]

Even those who were unhappy at Phillips Academy during this period
approved of Pemberton. Robert Hallowell Gardiner, who spent a short
time at the school in 1793, had this to say about his Andover experience:

The following year I was . . . sent to Phillips Academy, Andover, of
which Mr. Pemberton, an excellent instructor, was master. The class
in which I was placed was large and soon after divided, and I was
put in the lower section, being told that it was because I was not acquainted with the grammar used in the school. I felt that injustice
had been done me and that I was fully equal to those in the upper
division. My section was put into Ovid's Metamorphoses, and we
were told that we might get as long a lesson as we chose. I studied
intensely, and when we were called up to recite, I had learnt three
or four times as much as any other in the section, and after being very
closely examined, and found to have learnt the whole perfectly, was
immediately transferred to the upper section. Mr. Pemberton, tho'
an excellent man himself, could neither change the habits of the
people or liberalize their minds. The great and universal want of
cleanliness was disgusting to boys brought up in respectable families,
and the extreme puritan bigotry of the people was very unfavorable
to the cause of religion. On Sunday we were required to commit to
memory one of Watts's hymns, to be repeated at school on Monday
morning. Four of us occupied a small chamber with a sanded floor,
without curtains or blinds, and fronting the south west. One Sunday
afternoon we left our chamber, intensely heated by the summer sun,
and went into the orchard to learn our hymns under the shade of
the trees. For thus desecrating the Sabbath, the old man, Timothy
Abbot, with whom we boarded, rated us as if we had been guilty of
felony, and threatened that if we ever again left the house on the

Sabbath before the sun was down, except to go to meeting, he would complain to the master and have us expelled from the school. Owing to the want of cleanliness in the place, the boys were seldom free from cutaneous diseases. This, united to coarse fare and salt provisions and heavy bread, seriously injured my health, for I had been accustomed to delicate treatment and great indulgence. When I came home, Dr. Jeffries was consulted and gave it as his opinion that I would not regain my health so long as I remained at Andover. I was accordingly taken home, retaining like most persons who had been educated there, a rooted dislike to the place. My brother-in-law, William Tudor, had been at the same school, and his aversion to the place was quite as strong as mine. After getting away from Andover, I avoided passing through the town for very many years, and when at length I drove through it with my family, I felt a sort of surprise that it had green fields and spreading trees like other places in the world.[14]

Even if some of the students were unhappy, Judge Phillips was enthusiastic about the condition of the school under Pemberton. Writing to his Uncle John in June 1787, he said:

> This Seminary is I believe in a more prosperous State than it has ever been;—the Preceptor is indefatigable,—The pupils bear to him that duty and respectful love, which is shown by well disposed children to an Affectionate Parent;—The Assistance [sic] follows the example of the head in attention and pains,—The number of the Scholars is 65, and I have a pleasing account of their application, improvements and deportment;—I hope to be able personally to observe it more than has heretofore been in my power.[15]

To be sure the numbers declined somewhat in the years immediately following, partly because of the scarcity of money and partly because there had been an unusually large graduating class, the members of which went on to college in 1788.[16] But there can be no doubt that the Trustees were more than satisfied with their choice of Pemberton as Preceptor. In the first place, they agreed to pay him £ 140 annually, which was more than most ministers made. Though they wanted to sign him up for life, they agreed that the Preceptor's contract could be terminated by either party on three months' notice. They also agreed that he could have one week off each winter term.[17] If material considerations were to determine whether Pemberton stayed on, it is hard to see how he could have asked for better treatment.

For all their enthusiasm, the Trustees continued to exercise broad supervision over the school and dealt with many matters that at a later time would be left to headmaster and faculty. To improve the morals of the students the Trustees voted to punish any "profanity or other scandalous immorality." For the first offense the student was to be rebuked by the Preceptor, for the second, a notice would be sent to the miscreant's parents, and for the third, notice would be sent to the Trustees.[18] To prevent students from incurring debts, no scholar under the age of twenty-one could purchase anything from another scholar "on trust," and to encourage regular habits in the use of money, each student was to keep a careful account of his expenses and show it to the Preceptor whenever asked to.[19] Later a trustee committee was appointed "to regulate the pocket expenses of the scholars."[20] Swimming was apparently a problem. First, the Trustees forbade any scholar from bathing in any millpond. Then, anticipating the buddy system of modern camps, they forbade any boy from swimming anywhere unless in the company of two pupils who could swim or else a man approved by the School administration.[21] The Trustees also saw fit to challenge what must have been an early example of what is known as the "schoolboy code." In 1791 they voted:

> that it shall be the duty of each scholar, when required, by the principal, the Assistant, or any of the Trustees to give evidence in any case of criminal misconduct in others, to declare the truth, the whole truth, and nothing but the truth. And in case any scholar shall be so lost to all sense of moral obligations, as to be guilty of either withholding evidence, or of giving false evidence, upon conviction thereof at any future time, while a member of the Academy, he shall be publicly and solemnly admonished before the whole Academy, and such of the Trustees as can attend the sad solemnity. And upon conviction of a second offense of this kind, he shall be expelled from the Academy.[22]

In addition to providing regulations for the scholars, the Trustees concerned themselves with a variety of administrative matters. The problem of holding Assistants remained as difficult as ever. In the course of Ebenezer Pemberton's term there were seven different Assistants, averaging about one year. Two of them, Abiel Abbot and John Thornton Kirkland, were later to achieve distinction as Principal of Dummer Academy and President of Harvard College, respectively.[23] Yet it remained abundantly clear that the position of Assistant could not hold an able man, and those who accepted appointment did so on a temporary basis while deciding what career to pursue eventually. From the start, the Board had been fastidious in choosing families where the scholars might board. Each year a committee reviewed the list and made recommendations for licenses. In 1791 it was voted that single ladies should not board more than two students and that no family could board more than six.[24] Vacations also presented problems, and their time and duration were altered frequently. In 1791, for example, the Board voted four—one of three weeks in October, one of one week in January, one of two weeks in April, and one of two weeks in July.[25] Schooling at Phillips Academy was to be considered a year-long commitment with occasional breaks, rather than our present nine months with a long summer vacation.

Apparently Ebenezer Pemberton was not nearly as interested in preparing his students for Exhibitions, as had been the case with Pearson. On several occasions during his tenure the Board voted to have the Exhibitions private but did allow the parents of the scholars to come.[26] Writing to his son John in 1792, Judge Phillips quoted Pemberton as saying the Exhibition would be "quite bare,"[27] and the following year he wrote, "The prospect is not flattering by any means from the exhibition; indeed Mr. Pemberton is so dull about it that he would not wish to have any."[28] As has been suggested, Eliphalet Pearson's Exhibitions were to a large degree pedagogical *tours de force*, and it may well be that Pemberton saw no educational value in putting his charges through an artificial exercise.

Changes in the make-up of the Board also showed that the old order was passing. Squire Phillips, who had been President since the School's inception, died in 1790 and was succeeded by his brother John Phillips of Exeter. He served until his death in 1795 and was succeeded by the third brother, William Phillips of Boston, who served two years. From 1796 to 1802 the President was Judge Phillips himself, who was succeeded at his death by Eliphalet Pearson. Though Pearson remained in the chair until 1821, after 1808 his major concern became the Andover Theological Seminary. To be sure, the next generation of Phillipses was well represented on the Board after 1800. William Phillips, son of William Phillips of Boston; John Phillips, son of Judge Samuel Phillips; and another John Phillips, a second cousin of the Judge all were elected to the Board in the 1790's and early 1800's, but though dedicated to the School, they did not have the drive of the previous generation, and they, too, became wrapped up in the affairs of the Theological Seminary.[29] Before they died, the three original brothers made further contributions to the welfare of the School. We have already seen how they divided among them the cost of the new Academy. In 1789 John Phillips of Exeter gave the Academy something over £7,000 for the purpose of "promoting the virtuous and pious education of youth (poor children of genius, and of serious disposition especially)." The trustees then passed a vote of thanks and added "their fervent wish and prayer, that the *Donor*, the distinguished *friend and patron* of science and religion, may live to behold, with increasing joy and satisfaction, the happy fruits of this, and of his other pious liberalities; and at a very remote period, his numerous acts of benevolence may receive that reward, which original and infinite goodness can bestow."[30] In 1794 William Phillips gave the school ten shares of stock in the Andover Bridge Company, also to help charity scholars—a gift the Trustees thought "calculated to promote knowledge, virtue, and piety, and diffuse their benefits to those, who, without such aids, might remain ignorant, and of course exposed to irreligion and vice."[31] Finally, when John Phillips of Exeter died, he left two thirds

of his estate to the Phillips Exeter Academy and one third to Phillips
Academy. Or at least he thought he had. But he had reckoned without his
widow Elizabeth, who announced to the Exeter trustees that she would not
accept their offer of one thousand dollars and an annuity of fifty dollars
for her right of dower in the estate. The Exeter Trustees went into a hud-
dle and came up with a more generous offer—fifty pounds, one cow, the
articles of furniture that she brought with her, an annuity of one hundred
pounds, and permission to use the Phillips house and garden for the rest
of her life. The Exeter Trustees added that the Andover Trustees must
agree to this offer, since they were interested in the estate. So the Andover
Trustees voted to support the offer and to pay one third of the cost. With
a flourish of generosity, they added "one other cow."[32]

Phillips Academy can be justly proud of its contacts with George Washington. Not only did he stop there briefly in 1789; he also sent some of
his kinfolk to the School. In 1789, after his inauguration and sufficient
time to get the various departments of government operating smoothly,
President Washington determined to make a tour of the eastern states. He
wanted to see the country and meet some of the people, and he hoped also
that his visit would serve to strengthen eastern support for the new federal government. After visiting Boston, he proceeded north to Portsmouth
and then headed back. He spent the night of November 4 in Haverhill
and the next morning set out for Lexington. On the way, he stopped for
an hour or so in Andover. His account of his Andover experience appears
in his diary:

> *Thursday, 5th.* About sunrise I set out, crossing the Merrimack River
> at the town, over to the township of Bradford, and in nine miles
> came to Abbot's tavern, in Andover, where we breakfasted, and met
> with much attention from Mr. Phillips, President of the Senate of
> Massachusetts, who accompanied us through Bellariki to Lexington,
> where I dined, and viewed the spot on which the first blood was spilt
> in the dispute with Great Britain, on the 19th of April, 1775. Here
> I parted with Mr. Phillips and proceeded on to Watertown. . . .
> The country from Haverhill to Andover is good, and well cultivated.
> In and about the latter (which stands high) it is beautiful . . .[33]

This is, I believe, the only contemporary account in writing that covers
Washington's visit to Andover. The rest is tradition, and like all traditions
concerning Washington must be taken with a fistful of salt. The tradition
that he spent an hour or so in the Mansion House with the Phillipses and
some of their neighbors seems accurate. After Washington left, Phoebe
Phillips put a ribbon across the chair he had sat in, and then changed it to
a black crepe after his death. This chair still exists and is at Phillips Academy, being on loan from the Andover Theological Seminary.[34] The story
that Washington reviewed townspeople and Phillips Academy students on

the training field that is now the area around the Bell Tower could have happened. People who claim to remember him seated on his horse may be wrong, for most of his tour of the Eastern States was done by carriage.[35] Finally, the story of the little girl who mended Washington's glove at Abbot's Tavern is probably apocryphal. According to the story, when she had finished the mending, the President gave her a kiss, after which she refused to wash her face for a week.[36] Whatever the truth of these tangential traditions, the fact remains that President Washington did spend some time on Andover Hill in 1789.

The second contact that President Washington had with Phillips Academy came as a result of his interest in obtaining a good education for two great nephews, Augustine and Bushrod Washington, sons of Colonel William Augustine Washington. Apparently dissatisfied with educational opportunities for boys in Virginia, the Colonel turned to his uncle for help. President Washington went to work on this project and late in 1794 wrote his nephew a letter with some preliminary information on educational

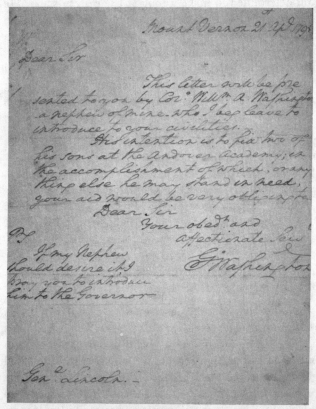

14. *Letter from President George Washington to General Benjamin Lincoln about the possibility of the former's great-nephews' coming to Andover. In the Phillips Academy Archives.*

opportunities. Much would depend, the President thought, on how far eastward the Colonel was willing to have the boys go. "There are two or three private Academies in the State of Massachusetts that are spoken very favorably of, the College in that State is also in good repute; but neither in that nor at Yale College in Connecticut, do they admit boys until they are qualified by a previous course of education."[37] In March the President was forwarding to his nephew letters from Senator George Cabot of Massachusetts and from Judge Samuel Phillips, both giving descriptions of Phillips Academy. It was now up to Colonel Washington, the President thought, to make his own decision.[38] In April the Colonel decided to head north with his two boys and two other distinguished young men from the Old Dominion, Cassius Lee and Francis Lightfoot Lee, sons of the patriot Richard Henry Lee. The President had given his nephew letters of introduction to prominent people in New York and Boston, and one in particular to General Benjamin Lincoln, one of the President's old comrades in arms.[39] Apparently there was some difficulty in enrolling the boys at Phillips Academy. Senator Cabot wrote the President that they would "probably" be admitted, but added that if they were not, he was sure they could go to Exeter, "an establishment in all respects similar and enjoys the equal patronage of Judge Phillips."[40] At about the same time Charles Lee, guardian of the Lee boys, wrote to Judge Phillips about the course of study he wished the boys to pursue and then added:

> My principal inducement in sending these lads so far from Virginia and their friends is that they may be brought up in the purest principles of religion, morality, and virtue, may clearly learn to take care of themselves and on themselves to depend for their well-being and happiness; and from the manners and habits of your state bring hither a portion of its industry, frugality, perseverance, and republican virtue.[41]

Whatever the difficulties about admitting the four boys, they were overcome, and by summer the four young Virginians were settled in Andover, the Washingtons boarding at the home of the Reverend Jonathan French, the Lees with Judge Phillips and his wife. It must have been a difficult adjustment for the four boys, for they were the only scholars entering that year who came from outside New England.[42]

Unfortunately, the sojourn of the Washington and Lee boys on Andover Hill was not a particularly happy one. Judge Phillips must have gained some insight into the Washington boys from a letter that their grandmother wrote him in which she spoke of Bushrod as having "a very sprightly disposition, or as it is generally termed wild, yet very innocently so." She hastened to add that "their young minds are both humane and accommodating" and expressed confidence that they would conduct themselves well.[43] After the boys had been at Phillips Academy for about a year, their father, William Augustine Washington, wrote Samuel Phillips expressing his regrets at not writing earlier—"my old and Cruel companion the Gout has confined me to my Room and Bed for about five weeks"—reporting that the boys were happy with Mr. French, and requesting Judge Phillips to "inspect into their conduct and give them your friendly advise."[44] There were also difficulties about sending money from Virginia to Massachusetts to pay for the boys' expenses. Finally Colonel Washington was obliged to enlist the help of his uncle the President to arrange for the transfer of the necessary funds.[45] As if Judge Phillips were not having enough trouble with young Virginians, in the fall of 1796 Cassius Lee was in trouble and with the advice of the school authorities was attempting to enroll in some other—presumably less exacting school.[46] By the summer of 1797 it was clear that the Washington boys must leave. Writing in June, Colonel Washington spoke of "the idle conduct of my Son Bushrod, and how illy he improves his time" and accepted Judge Phillips' suggestion that they return to Virginia. He asked the Judge to find a private tutor for the boys and also passage to the southward.[47] In reply, Samuel Phillips wrote that young Bushrod's progress had been much less than hoped for; he agreed that the boys should return to Virginia, that he wanted to wait for cooler weather because of Augustine's health. The boy had all the symptoms of tuberculosis.[48] Finally, in September, arrangements were made to have the boys travel to Virginia from Salem on the Schooner *Sewall*, Captain Silver, Master.[49]

Augustine Washington's disturbing symptoms were indeed of tuberculosis. In the following year he died, and Cassius Lee, who had managed to get admitted to the College of New Jersey, died in the same year of the same disease. Bushrod Washington, for all his "idle Conduct," managed to enter Harvard, though he never graduated. Francis Lightfoot Lee not only entered Harvard but graduated in 1802 and got a Master's degree in 1806. When allowances are made for the sickness of two of the four scholars from Virginia, Phillips Academy's record with them is acceptable, and it is impressive to think that the reputation of the School and of Samuel Phillips should have reached as far afield as the Old Dominion.

It should be noted that in their dealings with Phillips Academy the Washington family depended on Samuel Phillips and later on his son John Phillips for reports on the progress of their boys and for advice and counsel on how to deal with various problems that the young men presented. At no time did they correspond with the Principal of the School.[50] It was natural for the Phillipses to pay special attention to the members of such a distinguished family, but there was another reason. In the fall of 1793 Ebenezer Pemberton had tendered his resignation, and the replacement the Trustees finally decided on, Mark Newman, was young, inexperienced, and weak. Phillips took over many of the tasks that a principal might normally be expected to perform, and after his death a Select Committee of the Trustees supervised closely everything that Mark Newman did.

Pemberton's resignation came as a shock to the Trustees, all the more because there is ample evidence that they were more than satisfied with his work. The reason that Pemberton gave for his resignation was "that the cares and labors of that office are incompatible with a due attention to his health."[51] The Trustees were sympathetic and did all they could to induce Pemberton to stay. They offered to reduce the size of the school from 60 to 50, to have members of the senior class help teach the younger boys, to set regular times for the admission of new students so that they would not come dribbling in throughout the year, and to give the Principal a leave of absence to regain his health. When Pemberton refused to continue even with these concessions, the Trustees asked him what would induce him to stay. He wanted to have a permanent second assistant, to teach senior classes in his own home, particularly in winter so as to avoid a "disagreeable" stove in the Academy building, and generally to turn a major part of the routine work of the School over to the Assistants. The Trustees understandably objected to these proposals. They had no funds to hire a second assistant and they were unwilling to turn the School over to young and inexperienced teachers.[52] They whole matter was referred to the Committee on Exigencies, who, in December 1793, voted regretfully to accept the Pemberton resignation. They also voted "to make known to Mr. Pemberton their grateful sense of the ability, attention, and fidelity, with which he has discharged the duties of his office, at the same time to express their best wishes, that his health may be restored and confirmed, and that his usefulness to mankind may be long continued." They also voted to continue Pemberton's salary for the rest of the year, to let him stay in his house, and to permit him to take firewood from the Academy lands.[53]

At the same time, there are puzzling aspects to the Pemberton resignation. His health could not have been really poor, for in the next few months he moved to Billerica, where he opened a School of his own and continued to conduct it until 1810.[54] It has been suggested by one authority that Pemberton left Andover because he had displeased Judge Phillips by conducting a love affair of which the Judge did not approve.[55] Part of this claim is based on a letter that John Phillips wrote his mother in 1796 in which he said, "It seems as if Mr. Pemberton were determined to injure our family and the Academy as much as possible. I suppose that he has now thoughts of making his office at Billerica hereditary."[56] Yet this statement was penned over two years after Pemberton had left Andover and is much more easily explained as resentment against the success that Pemberton Academy was having in Billerica. When one remembers the long jeremiad that Eliphalet Pearson wrote about the difficulties of the position of Preceptor,[57] it seems much more likely that Pemberton left Andover because he preferred schoolmastering in an institution that he himself could control. Finally, the fact that Pemberton's successor, Mark Newman, went to Billerica in 1795 to spend the Sabbath with Mr. Pemberton would indicate that there were still friendly relations between the two institutions.[58] Pemberton remained in Billerica until 1810, when he moved to Boston at the request of a group of gentlemen in that city. He continued to teach in Boston for fifteen years, after which he retired on an annuity raised by his former pupils.[59] The chances are that had Pemberton remained at Phillips Academy and been given full control of it, the school would have developed into a very different kind of institution, for he would have opposed the sternness and rigidity of both curriculum and religious observance. As it was, he left Andover before he could impress upon it his own pedagogical principles.

The Pemberton resignation placed the Trustees in a quandary. They were unable to find an experienced master to head the school as Pemberton had done, and finally had to make do with Mark Newman. This young man—he was only twenty-two when appointed—had gone to the Phillips Exeter Academy and had graduated from Dartmouth in 1793. Throughout his early years he had as a patron Uncle John Phillips of Exeter, who had watched his progress through the Academy, urged him to go to Dartmouth, and then recommended him to the Andover Board. He was first appointed Assistant, immediately upon his graduation from college. And when Ebenezer Pemberton resigned, he was, *faute de mieux*, a candidate for the Principalship. Nor were his chances hurt by the fact that he and John Phillips had become close friends, which gave him pretty much the run of the Mansion House. Finally, in 1795 he married Sarah Phillips, a sister of the first Mayor of Boston and a second cousin once removed of the Judge, and this certainly did his chances no harm.[60] There are almost no Newman letters in the Phillips Academy Archives, but three, written in 1793 and 1794 to John Phillips at Harvard, reflect a good deal about the character of the writer. The first reads as follows:

> Last evening I attempted to write a few lines and was interrupted. Your mama's desire with my own inclination induces me to make a second attempt. The evening is far spent and imagination dull.
>
> However, I can probably form an idea of your happiness while puzzling your pate with the dry problems of Euclid and loading your memory with the dialects of Homer. You are wishing and expecting happier days. Don't be too confident, lest the object at which you are grasping should prove a delusive Shadow.
>
> Let us, like rational beings, enjoy the present, and lay aside anxiety concerning the events of Tomorrow.
>
> I enjoy as much happiness as I ought to expect, considering the disturbed nature of this ocean of life—In addition to the happiness which Miss Sally communicates, we have another young lady in the

15. *Mark Newman, Third Preceptor of Phillips Academy. From a portrait by an unknown artist, in the possession of the Trustees of Phillips Academy.*

family, viz. Miss H [?] Foxcroft who is by no means devoid of merit
—Your Honored Parents are well—In walking the fields of science
that you may crop the best of every flower is the sincere wish of your
friend and humble servant, Mark Newman.[61]

Another letter describing life in Judge Phillips' Mansion House, where
Newman was staying, closes as follows:

The boys occupy the next room. Jonathan engrosses the most attention,
for the scholars have formed a singing Society, admitted him, and
he is almost incessantly sounding—The kitchen folks are well except
Becky— . . . Hope for a line soon—Mr. Pemberton well—in an
unsettled state at present.[62]

And finally some advice sent to John Phillips at Harvard:

Am sorry that you do not enjoy more, my friend, in your present
situation—It is of infinite consequence to our own happiness to culti-
vate a disposition to enjoy in every situation—There can be no state
in life, entirely free from inconveniences of some kind and in some
degree—And from such position of things we are taught an important
lesson—to acquiesce and be contented—Don't entertain the idea,
that when you shall be free from College, you will consequently be
free from trouble—This life is a state of trial, which would cease to
be the case, were all our wishes gratified—Let us then discharge
present duty and expect complete happiness only beyond the grave.
Physician heal thyself. Be kind enough to write by your Papa and say
how you like my morality.[63]

These three passages reveal a young, light-hearted man whose attitude toward life was a far cry from the stern Calvinistic tenets of the school. They
bear out a statement that Wendell Phillips, Newman's nephew, made
about him: "most men thought Newman too easy and contented in his
mood."[64] That the Trustees had qualms about him is indicated by the fact
that after Pemberton's resignation they offered Abiel Abbot 4 pounds a
month as Assistant and Newman only 3, and that they offered Abbot the
Principalship at 120 pounds a year, but Newman only 50 for six months
of probation.[65] Since Abbot declined the Trustee offer, there was nothing
but to turn to Newman, and he took over his duties in 1794. But though he
held the title of Principal for over fifteen years, the Trustees, fearful of his
easy-going qualities, kept a close watch over him so that he was more
Principal in name than in fact.[66]

During the period from the appointment of Mark Newman as Principal
and the death of Samuel Phillips, the School's Trustees busied themselves
with a variety of matters. One matter that presented difficulties was how
best to make use of various tracts of land in New Hampshire and Maine
which the Academy had been given by Uncle John Phillips and others. In

a few cases land had been sold for nonpayment of taxes and had to be redeemed, and for all the real estate some kind of orderly procedure for sale had to be developed. Though the Trustees struggled manfully with these problems and appointed various of their number to act as agents for the sale of the property, little was realized during this period.[67] Perhaps the most valuable resources the Commonwealth of Massachusetts possessed after the Revolution were the large tracts of wild land in the District of Maine. In an effort to realize something on this property, the state appointed a Committee for the Sale of Eastern Lands, and Samuel Phillips was named chairman. After an attempt to conduct a lottery for the sale of some of these lands had failed, the Committee turned to private sales with more success.[68] In the 1790's the General Court started the practice of giving lands in Maine to various Massachusetts educational institutions, in an effort to promote their development. The program was a popular one, for the state could subsidize education without having to raise any money in taxes for that purpose. By 1796 seven Massachusetts academies had received grants of land, but some of the older, like Phillips Academy and Dummer Academy, had been passed over.[69] One reason for this may well have been the opposition to academies voiced by Governor Samuel Adams:

> It may be justly apprehended that multiplying them [the academies] may have a tendency to injure the ancient and beneficial mode of Education in Town Grammar Schools. The particular advantage of such schools is that the poor and rich may derive equal benefit from them, but none except the more wealthy, generally speaking, can avail themselves of the benefits of the Academies.[70]

The old patriot was holding fast to the doctrines he had espoused in the period of the Revolution, when he believed special institutions for the wealthy would weaken the new fabric of government. But the Governor's opposition did not prevail for long. In 1797 a state committee chaired by Nathan Dane, who had served on a committee of the old Congress of the Confederation in the 1780's to deal with the land of the Northwest Territory, came up with a general policy for the granting of lands to Academies. First, the committee believed, no land should be granted to any academy unless it already had three thousand dollars worth of endowment, and second, in an effort to provide for geographical distribution, new academies were to be chartered only when they had a population of 30,000 to 40,000 to draw on.[71] Since Phillips Academy could certainly meet the first requirement and probably the second as well, it was in 1797 granted one half a township of land in Maine. The Trustees could select the half township they wanted, and Phillips Academy chose one half of the present town of Greenwood, in the southwestern part of Maine. One of the stipulations of the grant was that there be reservations for church and school, and the Trustees proceeded to reserve three hundred-acre lots, one for the church, one for the minister, and one for the school.[72] The sale of wild lands was difficult unless some improvements were made, and to achieve this the Trustees considered building roads and mills in the half township.[73] Time would show that even with improvements the sale of Maine land would be slow, particularly when there was so much competition from Western New York and the Ohio country, and it would be some years before the Trustees could realize much on their investment.

In addition to dealing with the school's investments, the Trustees were busy with other matters. With the death of John Phillips of Exeter, the resignation of the Reverend William Symmes—"chiefly on account of the increasing failure of the sense of hearing"—and an already existing vacancy, the Trustees chose Samuel Abbot, a wealthy Boston merchant moved to Andover; Jacob Abbot, an Andover businessman; and Dr. Jedidiah Morse, a clergyman who was also known as "the father of American geography."[74] A minor wrangle occurred when Treasurer Nehemiah Abbot demanded payment for all the work he had done, especially since the Reverend Jonathan French was being paid as clerk. Eventually the Trustees gave Abbot $400 for past services, at which point he resigned, to be succeeded by Judge Oliver Wendell.[75] A committee was appointed to make improvements on the Academy Building, especially on the stove, which seems to have smoked incessantly. Before they were through, the stove had been repaired, new seats had been acquired, and an additional aisle was provided in the schoolroom. Improvements were also made on the stone walls on either side of what is now Main Street.[76] From the very start of the School the Trustees had been concerned about increasing the holdings of the library, and in 1796 they voted $200 for new books. They also expressed the hope that some book on the defense of Christianity, along the lines of Mason's *Self-Knowledge*, might be introduced into the curriculum.[77]

In dealing more directly with teachers and boys, the Trustees gave the Mark Newman regime a boost by voting an expression of their gratification "at the regularity and decency" that Newman, Assistant Samuel Stearns, and Writing Master Abiel Holbrook were showing in the conduct of their duties.[78] They raised Newman's salary to 150 pounds a year. He still found it difficult to make ends meet, so the Trustees each year voted him an extra 100 dollars "in consideration of the advanced prices of the necessaries of life."[79] In an effort to regularize the admission of students, it was voted to admit them only at the start of a term, and only if they agreed to stay six months.[80] In dealing with Uncle John Phillips' grant for charity scholars, the Trustees voted that scholars on that foundation must sign a pledge to repay the money to the School if they did not enter the ministry.[81] Instruction in music presented problems. A certain Mr. Johnson had apparently been training a choir in the old carpenter's shop that was the first Academy Building. The presumption is that this activity had been developed by the boys themselves. In any event, the Trustees voted that

Johnson could continue no longer as singing instructor, that no improvements were to be made to the carpenter's shop, but that the boys could continue to sing there if *they* made improvements, such as replacing broken window panes. Yet the Trustees were not opposed to music as such: in 1798 they voted to purchase six "Massachusetts Compilers," collections of hymns and songs, for the use of the students, and they were willing to introduce a course in music if the parents of the boys concerned paid extra.[82] A puzzling vote empowered the Committee on Exigencies "to declare a vacancy in the Academy, if they think it expedient, in consequence of the disorder prevalent, at present, in Andover." The Committee did think it expedient and voted a one-month vacation in February and March 1796. Because of this, however, they canceled the usual April vacation.[83] Apparently the undergraduates were no better than they should have been, for we find the Trustees appointing a special committee "for the reformation of idle boys belonging to the Academy."[84] And in 1800 a mysterious vote was passed prohibiting the scholars "from exercising themselves in any wheel, called a federal balloon, fandango, or by any other name"[85] In the spring of 1798, when it appeared highly likely that the United States would go to war with France, the Trustees showed that they were good Federalists by passing the following votes:

> Whereas the military exercise is manly, healthful, and useful, and may be especially advantageous at this juncture, considering the present aspect of our public affairs—Voted, that it be recommended to the Students of the Academy, to form themselves into a company for the purpose of acquiring a knowledge of the art military; to practice at such times, as will not interfere with their Academic duties, or as the Preceptor shall approve. 2nd—Voted, that the Trustees will have no objection to the students admitting into their company a convenient number of the youth of the Town of good moral character and decent behavior; provided it be agreeable to the Students. Whereas strict discipline is necessary to military improvement 3rdly Voted, that it be recommended to those, who shall compose the company, to form such regulations, as shall produce such discipline —and it is expected that all the members of the company will, for their own reputation and the success of the design, pay strict attention to the regulations, which shall be adopted by the majority.[86]

There is nothing in the record to show that the undergraduates ever put these recommendations into practice. They may not have been as enthusiastic about a war with France as the Trustees; they may simply not have had enough time for military drill. In less than a year, President John Adams would send a commission to treat with the French and the war scare would be all but over. Finally, during this period, the Academy had a new experience in dealing with a Trustee son, when Samuel Finley Breese

Morse, son of Dr. Jedidiah Morse, applied for admission.[87] He first enrolled in Mr. Foster's elementary school in Andover, the main purpose of which was to prepare boys for Phillips. He finally entered the Academy, and despite bouts of homesickness—he may have run away from school a couple of times—he finally finished and entered Yale.[88] The activities of the Trustees at the turn of the century covered a broad range and indicate the same deep concern for the welfare of the Academy that had characterized earlier boards.

In the last years of his life Judge Samuel Phillips continued to exhibit an extraordinary capacity for work of all kinds. As his biographer wrote, "he preferred to live fast rather than long."[89] Whether it was his business concerns, his duties in the state government, dangers to the United States as a nation, his close attention to everything affecting the welfare of Phillips Academy, or his devotion to his wife and his sons, he somehow found time to deal with all these with wisdom and charity and selflessness. Fortunately for him his business affairs could, to a large extent, be handled by others. This was true of his two stores—one in Andover and the other in Methuen—and of his paper mill. For the rest, he invested mainly in land, both in Andover and in Maine. When he died, his estate was estimated at just under $150,000, which in those times made him a very wealthy man indeed.[90]

His public career became, if anything, more distinguished and more demanding in his last years. He continued to serve as judge in the Court of Common Pleas for Essex County until 1800, when he resigned because his health would not permit him to attend every session, as his conscience required him to do. In the first election under the new Massachusetts Constitution, he was elected Senator from Essex County, and with one exception, was chosen each year until 1801. The one exception came in 1787 when he was a member of a three-man commission sent to work out amnesty arrangements with the Shays's rebels. In writing about this chapter in his career, he said, "I apprehend that to quiet, conciliate and compose the minds of the people at large is one of the greatest objects now before us and perhaps the most difficult to be effected. The raising of more men, especially if it must be accomplished by draft . . . will militate in a powerful manner against the attainment of this object."[91] Despite his sensible position on dealing with the residual problems of the rebellion, he could not win over all the people; before he had finished his work, one man had been indicted for calling Judge Phillips a Tory.[92] The following year he was returned again to the Senate, where he was elected President, a position he continued to hold until just before his death. He was such a fair presiding officer and had so little of political partisanship about him that people of all shades of political opinion voted for him, and the office seemed to be his for life. At that time all members of the Massachusetts Senate were automatically Overseers of Harvard College. Each spring the

Overseers would ride out to Cambridge to give the Senior Class its final examination, after which Judge Phillips would deliver a formal address. Generally speaking, the Judge was anything but showy; his carriage, however, was an exception, and the spectators used to remark on how the Phillips carriage was the most elegant and costly of them all, with its harness decorations done by Paul Revere.[93] Though his main interest was Harvard, he was also a Trustee of Dartmouth, having accepted the position out of courtesy to Uncle John, but he was unable to attend many meetings.

When the 1798 crisis with France developed, the Judge took his place solidly behind President John Adams. In May of that year he chaired a committee of the town of Andover formed to prepare an address to the President. The document praised Adams for standing up to the French and concluded: "no hope of safety is left for us without our own united virtuous exertion." And the townspeople must have been gratified to receive a very flattering thank-you letter from the President himself.[94] That the judge was taking the whole crisis very seriously can be seen in a letter he wrote his son John, in the course of which he said, "No time ought to be lost in providing yourself and me with arms and accoutrements complete; the prospect of our needing them increases. It would not be very surprising to me, if we should be called on to use them, much sooner than is generally expected. Don't enter into any further pecuniary engagements, where they can be avoided;— . . . Don't go to Boston, unless in cases of urgent necessity;—and not in the vicinity of any infected place, on any account."[95] The following year the Judge wrote Timothy Pickering alarming news:

> I have just been informed that a person in female habit came to a tavern kept by a Captain Butterfield in Dunstable on monday last, who said she came from Philadelphia in the Stage to Worcester, and from thence with a horse and chaise to Dunstable. At this place she pretended to have business with a brother at Pelham (who probably is not to be found), a town adjoining Dracutt—but before she left the tavern, she enquired for Colonel Varnum of Dracutt, the Representative in Congress—and not being able to hire a horse and chaise, she set out on foot toward Dracutt—said she should be back at Butterfield's the next day, was to be at Worcester by Wednesday night—and must set out in the stage from thence on Thursday morning for Philadelphia—I am told she was well dressed, appeared to be about 30 yrs. old—and to be well supplied with money. If my information be correct, I have strong suspicion that this traveller was a man in disguise.

And he urged Pickering to watch for the lady's arrival in Philadelphia.[96] With the election of 1800 approaching, there was reason for alarm, the Judge wrote Pickering, and he deplored the growth of what he called the Anti-Federalists. One of the problems was the weakness of the Federalist press. In an effort to get better circulation of newspapers he wrote a long letter to Jedidiah Morse with suggestions for improvement.[97] And shortly after the election, he wrote Eliphalet Pearson of the necessity of "improving the federal newspapers to undeceive the deluded and awaken the *drowsy* nominal Feds." He continued:

> If the Friends of the Constitution could be aroused to exertions nearly equal to those of its enemies, our hopes might revive. I am sensible this is an Herculean task; but unless this can be done, our case appears to me desperate, without a miraculous interposition of Providence; and the moral character of this people affords no grounds to expect this. . . . I hope you will be able to excite the pretious [sic] few, who are awake to our danger, to join you in one more exertion to save our Country.[98]

Finally, in July 1801, the Judge sent a new standard to his son John, who had recently been appointed to the command of a Company of Light Infantry in the militia. "It is confidently hoped," the Judge wrote," that this Standard will never be tarnished by any unsoldierlike conduct of any member of the company; that it will be readily unfurled, at the proper command, when the safety of our Country, or the preservation of our Governments shall require it. . . . That the day when this dernier resort shall become necessary may be far, very far distant, must be the fervent prayer of every good man; and may it be ever remembered that one of the most effectual means of attaining this object, is to be completely prepared at all points and at all times to meet any invader."[99] Samuel Phillips' political views at the end of his life were those of a High Federalist. Had he lived, he might easily have worked with the Essex Junto. But when it is remembered that the Jeffersonians were soon to take over Massachusetts, it is perhaps fortunate that the Judge died when he did and did not have to suffer the humiliation of a Jeffersonian victory.

One might think that with all these heavy public responsibilities Phillips would have had to neglect his family, but nothing could be further from the truth. He was a most affectionate husband and father and always found time to write his wife and son when duty separated him from them. When he first entered the Massachusetts Senate, he used to work in Boston during the week and then ride out to Andover on horseback for the Sabbath. As time wore on, this schedule became more and more difficult for him to maintain physically. He admitted that he sometimes fell asleep on horseback while riding out to Andover and often missed his way in the darkness. The climax came in the winter of 1794 when he fell from his horse and broke his leg. Fortunately, he had a riding companion and was near the home of his friend Dr. Brooks of Medford. The Doctor's Negro servant went in a sleigh to the scene of the accident and tenderly brought Judge Phillips back to the house. When some one remarked on the particular care that the Negro was showing, he replied, "I'd like to do anything *for him*; he *always touches his hat to me when he goes by here.*" Fortunately, the fracture was not a severe one, and the combined ministrations of his wife Phoebe and his cousin Sally Phillips soon had him at work again, even though on crutches. But the accident did convince him that he must modify the killing schedule that he had been trying to maintain.[1]

Judge Phillips' correspondence with his wife during this period follows the pattern set at the start of their marriage. The letters contain very little about practical affairs, either public or private, but are rather devoted to affectionate concern for his family and morbid introspection. In commenting on the death of a friend, he wrote, "he had been unwell for a day or two; took a pill when he went to bed,—his wife awoke in the night and found him dead by her side. What a warning to the living to be *always ready.*"[2] On another occasion he wrote, "I daily feel more and more and more my unhappiness and am ready to think sometimes, the world will be glad when they are rid of me;—if I have been so useless in the prime of life, what can be expected when declining and that so fast."[3] Finally, "the clock has struck 12, I will wish you an uninterrupted continuance of refreshing slumber till the return of morn and then all the health, content and chearfulness you can wish."[4] The Judge took his duties as a parent seriously and regularly wrote his son John long letters admonishing him to lead a good life. In a letter written just before his son's twenty-first birthday in 1797, he urges him to spend the day in serious recollection, meditation, humiliation, thanksgiving, and prayer, and documents the whole with quotations from Scripture. If John had carried out half the suggestions made in the letter, he would have had no time for anything else on his birthday.[5]

On 1 January 1800 the Judge awoke at 3:00 in the morning and "the activity of my mind having banished sleep from my eyes, I arose and betook myself to such exercises as are proper for the season"—in this particular case penning another long letter to his son.[6] The following year another New Year's letter was begun, but the Judge was beginning to fail badly and did not get it finished until the following December. Wistfully he wrote at the end of the letter, "it is very doubtful whether I shall ever be able to write you again on any subject of moment."[7] None of the family had fully recovered from the death of a younger son, Samuel. The boy had shown a great deal of promise at Phillips Academy and was a particular favorite of Mark Newman's. In February 1796 "he was seized with the fatal fever which deprived him of reason, and finished his temporal existence."[8] For the Judge the boy's death was something to be accepted as the will of Almighty God. "We must be fully convinced that the best possible disposition *is now* made of our dear child; and should not this conviction produce entire resignation? Should we be willing to oppose and disappoint the purpose of *Infinite Wisdom*, if it was in our power? The very idea excites horror! Let us, then, in humble, filial submission, acknowledge that the *Supreme Ruler* has done perfectly right."[9]

Particularly from the twentieth century point of view, it is paradoxical that Judge Phillips could accomplish so much in the world and win the respect and affection of so many people at the same time that he was engaging in so savage a denunciation of his own failings.

For some years Samuel Phillips had suffered from a chronic asthma that continually sapped his strength. By 1801 his health had become so bad that his family and friends began to despair of his recovery. In May of that year the Reverend Jonathan French wrote to Eliphalet Pearson that the Judge was "raising blood" and expressed the fear that a proposed journey to Boston would be his last.[10] French had tried to dissuade him from going, but the call of duty was too strong.[11] In July the devoted minister was hoping that a conference of Boston doctors might examine the Judge in an effort to save "the most valuable man . . . in the commonwealth, if not in the United States."[12] In August it was finally decided that the Judge and his wife should take a trip to the Berkshires, in hope that the pure air there might help him. Eliphalet Pearson agreed to accompany them. For a while it seemed as if the ailing man were better. According to Pearson he was breathing "the purest air," drinking his bottle of claret each day according to the doctor's prescription, and generally having comfortable nights.[13] But the improvement was only temporary. Trouble with the horses forced the party to cut short the trip, and once returned to Andover, the old trouble returned. From then on, it was downhill, and on 10 February 1802 he died.

News of his death caused an outpouring of grief throughout Massachusetts. His funeral in Andover was an impressive ceremony. The procession consisted of, first, the pupils of Phillips Academy, then former pupils, then the Trustees, then the Trustees of Phillips Exeter, and finally "the Corpse." The pall was borne by the Governor of Massachusetts, three members of the Council, the President of the Senate, and the Speaker of the House of Representatives, and the procession closed with a large number of relatives and friends. At the service a select choir sang several anthems, one of which, "I Heard a Voice," had been composed expressly for the occasion. After a prayer delivered by Jonathan French, in tears, the Reverend David Tappan delivered the main address, followed by remarks by Governor Gilman of New Hampshire. There was no military escort at the funeral because, characteristically, Judge Phillips, a few days before his death, requested that there be none for fear the health of the escort might be endangered at that season of the year. There was another ceremony in Boston for which the members of the Legislature moved to "the old brick meeting-house" and heard prayers and an address by the chaplains of the Senate and House. At two o'clock all the bells in town were tolled and continued until four, when "minute guns were discharged by Captain Johonnot's company."[14] Those who participated in these ceremonies must have realized that a great man had died. It is not surprising that a neighbor could speak of him as "governour from Essex County."[15] Though there were many tributes to him at the time of his death, the finest one came from Josiah Quincy many years later: "I have never met, through my whole life, with an individual in whom the spirit of Christianity and of good-will to mankind were so naturally and beautifully blended with an indomitable energy and enterprise in active life."

It was appropriate that the last two acts of Judge Phillips were in keeping with the beliefs and purposes of his life. In December he signed an instrument bequeathing to the Trustees of Phillips Academy the sum of one thousand dollars, most of the income from which was to be used to provide religious books like Doddridge's *Family Religion*, Watts's *Divine Songs*, and the Westminster Cathechism to citizens of Andover, especially those who were about to be married. In January the Judge expanded this program by bequeathing to the Trustees the sum of four thousand dollars, most of the income from which was to be devoted "partly for rendering those females who may be employed as instructors in the several District Schools, within the aforesaid Town of Andover, better qualified for the discharge of their delicate and important trust; and partly for extending the term of their instruction in such districts within the said town . . . may stand in most need of additional aid . . ." and if there was ever any surplus it was to be used to provide religious books for "the inhabitants of new towns and plantations." In closing the Judge stressed "that the principal object of this donation, is the preservation of the essential and distinguishing doctrines of the Gospel, as professed by our pious ancestors, the first settlers of New England, and of such writings as are consentaneous thereto; above all, it is ardently hoped and expencted, that in their selection of books for the distribution aforesaid, all possible care will be taken . . . to guard against the dissemination of the least particle of Infidelity or Modern Philosophy; and also against the dispersion of such theological treatises or speculations, as tend to undermine the fundamental principles of the Gospel plan of salvation, or to reduce the Christian religion to a system of mere morality; without which guard there will be great reason to fear that the object of this donation will be totally frustrated."[16] As he lay dying, Samuel Phillips's faith was just as strong—and just as rigid—as it had been throughout his entire life. Because he spelled out the conditions of his donation in such detail, the Trustees of Phillips Academy have found it difficult to live within the terms of the grants. As time passed and the world changed, it became impossible to adhere to the letter of the Judge's text. For one thing, Doddridge's *Family Religion* went out of print. With the development of the public school system in the town of Andover, the Judge's grant to the female instructors in the District Schools presented additional problems. In the early twentieth century, the Trustees asked the Supreme Judicial Court for a ruling on the matter. The Court appointed

Alden P. White of Salem as Master, and after the usual delay he came up with a sensible solution—namely, that 60 percent of the money for female instructors should go to the public library in Andover and 40 percent to the public library in North Andover. The Master also seized on the phrase "and other pious books" as authority for expanding the kind of religious book that might be distributed. Recently the two donations have been merged, and the income from the combined fund divided as follows: one fifth for books to be distributed in Andover, until recently by the ministers of the town; one fifth to the libraries, as explained above; and three fifths to the Massachusetts Bible Society. As a grace note to the 1906 settlement, the Trustees of Phillips Academy were granted 5 percent of the income for the administration of the grants—a tiny recompense for the vast amount of time and trouble that had been expended in order to carry out the last wishes of the founder of the School.[17]

Even though Samuel Phillips had died, his spirit and influence continued strong in the School for many years. One way in which this influence was felt was in the appointment of a Select Committee to check on the operation of the school and to make sure that the great aims of the founders were being kept in view. Judge Phillips had requested appointment of this Committee just before he died, and in November 1802 the Trustees made his request a reality. The purpose of the Committee, as stated in the Trustee vote, was "to meet once in a quarter, or oftener, to enquire into the state of the Academy, the proficiency of the Scholars, and the conduct of the Instructors, *that the core of the Institution may be attended to.*"[18] The original Committee was composed of Eliphalet Pearson, Jonathan French, Samuel Abbot, Jedidiah Morse, and John Phillips. The first task that Committee set for itself was a thorough examination of the scholars at regular intervals. Their first examination plan, which was modified somewhat from year to year, was to devote twenty minutes to spelling, twenty minutes "to hear ten of the best readers," twenty minutes for arithmetic and writing, fifteen minutes for geography, fifteen minutes for English grammar, sixty minutes in the forenoon to Latin and Greek, another hour in the afternoon for Latin and Greek, twenty minutes on Beilby's *Evidence of Christianity*, twenty minutes on Mason's *Self-Knowledge*, and finally a general inquiry into the state of the Academy.[19] The Committee also voted to revive the study of Watts's hymns and the Westminister Catechism and promised to examine the students "in the History of the Birth, miracles, doctrines, sufferings, death, burial, resurrection, appearances, and ascension of the Savior." To give themselves plenty of time for all this examining, the committee also voted to spend three and a half hours in the morning and three and a half in the afternoon on the examinations.[20]

Another area of school life which the Committee addressed was the conduct of the scholars. The three areas that were particularly emphasized during this period were punctuality, spelling, and whispering. At each examination period the Committee would review the records of the students in these three areas, admonishing the sinful and praising the pure. In 1803, for example, three were admonished for tardiness, two for whispering, and two for spelling. A general review of the fifty-seven students then in school showed that 38 had no tardy mark, "31 by their silent attention to business, not being charged with a whisper since the last visitation of the Committee," and 6 had made no mistakes in spelling. Four paragons of virtue had no mark of any kind against their names.[21] At the next meeting one culprit who had been admonished by Preceptor Newman for whispering "and not having reformed, but being found upon the bills at this visitation highly charged for the same offence be consigned to the Reverend Mr. French to be seriously reproved for his continued delinquency."[22] Whispering clearly was difficult to control. At another meeting the Committee "with regret and disapprobation, have noticed the increased number of whispers on the part of a large number" and urged Preceptor Mark Newman to get on the stick and remedy the evil.[23] In December 1806 the Committee decided that some "farther provision" should be made to carry into effect "the great and principal object of the pious founders" of the School and asked some of their members to study the Academy Constitution to see what might be done, but the Committee ceased functioning before any report could be made.[24] One interesting insight into the life of the School which the Minutes of the Select Committee reveal is the number of students who were present for only part of each term. In 1807, for example, there were 64 boys present "during the course of the term" but only 32 present during the whole term.[25] This constant movement in and out of classes must have been a heavy burden for the instructors to bear. From 1802 to 1809 the Select Committee conscientiously performed its task according to its lights. One of the reasons for its existence had been to support Mark Newman in his difficult position as Principal. When it became clear that Newman would resign, the Committee became much less active, confident that a new Principal could manage the school without its help.

The undergraduate body in the first decade of the nineteenth century tended to follow the same patterns as those set in earlier years. Despite interest in boys coming from outside New England, the great majority continued to be from Massachusetts in particular and New England in general. The group that entered the school in 1806, for example, consisted of forty-eight students, forty-six of whom came from Massachusetts, one from the District of Maine, and one from New Hampshire.[26] As earlier, Harvard College was where most of the college-bound boys went. During Mark Newman's term as Principal, 198 went on to college, 150 of them to Harvard, 17 to Dartmouth, and 13 to Yale.[27] There was, however, more diversity in the student body as far as family position—social and financial—is concerned. The gift to the School of Uncle John Phillips to enable pious and indigent young men to study there attracted many applicants. Indeed all the extant letters about boys applying for admission during this period come from people hoping to get financial assistance from Uncle John's fund. A typical letter reads as follows:

> To whom it may concern.
> This certifies that the bearer Isaac P. Foster, who has been a member of my family for about two years, is a youth of regular habits, of an amiable disposition and is possessed of talents, which if cultivated promise usefulness to the World.—His pecuniary circumstances, his desire of knowledge and close application recommend him to every charitable assistance.
> Tyngsborough, July 26, 1809 Nathaniel Lawrence

The letters recommending boys for financial assistance were usually from clergymen, but in one case the Selectmen of Ashley recommended one Jonas Chamberlain, who was unable to earn his living by labor because of lameness but who had a good moral character and was a good English scholar.[28] The trustees had difficulty dealing with these applications—there were at this time no true entrance examinations—and they tried putting indigent boys on trial for a term as a means of determining the most deserving.[29] One thing is clear; even at this early date Phillips Academy had already become known as a school where poor boys could get help. Though the phrase in the Constitution about the Academy's being open to "Youth from every Quarter" might not have meant much as far as geographical distribution was concerned, a good start had been made toward admitting an undergraduate body that would have economic diversity.

One gets a charming picture of what life was like for the undergraduates from the letters of Henry B. Pearson, son of Eliphalet, who came to the Academy in 1804 at the age of nine. In December 1804 he reported, "The traveling was so bad last sunday that I could not go to meeting one part of the day" and added, "I will thank you to send me up a pair of shoes."[30] The following month he reported: "I was so unwell so as not to go to the Academy all day. I was sick at my stomach in the morning. I had a dizy head all day, was well the next day. I will thank you send me up a pair of corks as it is very slippery and the snow covers the ice and there is great danger of falling down. Mr. Newman says I may go into Virgil as soon as I understand my grammar. The most steady scholars in the Academy are in our class and are very studious."[31] Later that month he reported, "Mr. Newman says I am a very good boy in everything but writeing [sic] and says that I shall not go into Virgil if I do not write better. . . . There were 9 turned out of our class because they did not get their lesson well: John Washington, Bushrod Washington, Edward Brooks and John Bartlett."[32]

By March it was clear that Henry had been making progress: "We are now in the 5 Bucolick and go at most 20 lines a lesson. . . . I have wrote this term XIV chapters of Latin. . . . I am not on the spelling bill but once this term and have not been on the whispering once since I have been at the academy."[33] In April Henry reported a heavy rainstorm, from which many of the boys caught cold: "I have got one myself, which makes me sneeze very often. I have got to the 475 line of the 1st Book of Aneid. But I must forbear as I have but very little time."[34] By summer he reported that he was well into the 2nd Book of the Aenead "Where it tells how the Grecians made a large horse and carried it to Troy and filled it with Grecians and the Trojans carried it into their temple and the Grecians came out and destroyed or burnt all Troy."[35] Shortly after that he wrote that he had recited the first lesson in Greek Grammar but was unable to write more "as the recess is up and Mr. Newman has forbid writing a letter in the Academy time."[36] The next milestone was the "optative Mood in the passive voice in Greek."[37] Early in August Father Eliphalet wrote the boy a three-page letter filled with moralistic advice and commenting particularly on death: "On this sad event you do well in giving vent to your tears. Let it sink deeply into your heart. Meditate upon it; and bring death near to your view; and ask yourself, what preparation you have made for eternity."[38] A few days later Henry wrote back dutifully: "I sincerely wish that these deaths may awaken me to a sense of my sin and prepare me for judgment."[39] In September Henry could think of nothing to write his father about and so copied out two pages of translation of Virgil that he had been working on.[40] Shortly afterward he wrote to thank his parents for some socks that Samuel Farrar had brought: "I find them very comfortable in this cold as Jack Frost has come."[41] By the end of the year he was in the fourth chapter of the Greek Testament of John.[42] Unfortunately the letters stop at this point, but it is only fair to say that Henry did improve his handwriting tremendously; in 1806 he lettered a handsome declaration partly in old German script; and in 1809 he produced an elaborate and ornate penmanship drawing entitled "Vive Plume."[43] To be sure, Henry must have been a model student while he was at Phillips Academy, but even so his letters throw a good deal of light on what an undergraduate's life was like in the early years of the nineteenth century.

Another document from this period is "A List of the Curiosities in the Museum of Phillips Academy, Andover, with the Names of the Donors." The museum was begun in the 1790's but continued into the new century as well. Among its exhibits were "An Armadillo or Hog in armour, A Hogfish caught in the West India Seas, A Trinidad Grasshopper, A Beetlenut from China, Petrified Water, A Singular Fly, The wing and bill of an Albatross, Skin of a Rattlesnake, An Ostrich's Egg, A piece of the Rock on which our Forefathers first landed at Plymouth December 20th 1620, A Bat preserved, Lava of Vesuvius, A Chinese sandle, An Artificial Blackberry, Curious worms from Virginia . . ." The record is silent on where these curiosities were kept or what use if any was made of them in the education of the scholars. But the museum must have provided a colorful alternative to the drab routine of the school.[44]

In the years following the death of Samuel Phillips, the trustees busied themselves, for the most part, with routine matters. As usual there were problems with the plant. One of Ebenezar Pemberton's complaints about his job had been teaching in a room where the stove was forever smoking. It was still smoking in 1802, when the Trustees decided that this nuisance must be abated. Amos Blanchard was asked to buy a new stove and sell the old one, though the latter brought in only $7.37. Nor did this move settle the matter, for in 1807 two of "Mr. Pollack's patent stoves" were purchased. At the same time a student stove-tender was hired at one dollar a week, to be followed shortly by a student sweeper at fifty cents a week. A receptacle for ashes was built in the cellar of the Academy Building, and repairs were made on the school pump and trough.[45] The old joiner's shop that had served as the first schoolhouse was becoming an eyesore, and it was finally sold for thirty dollars. Concern for the trees on the Academy property was revealed when the Trustees voted that each tree "be dug around at least two feet from the roots." In the 1780's there was trouble, as noted, about Eliphalet Pearson's outhouses; in this period it was Mark Newman's hogpen that the Trustees had to worry about. In 1804 the Trustees purchased the old house on Salem Street occupied by a Captain Towne and repaired it so that scholars could board there. This was the present Hardy House; it was offered to Eliphalet Pearson when he returned to Andover in 1806. In addition to dealing with material things, the Trustees attempted to get Phillips boys excused from military service, took away the license to board students from one Jacob Shed for "neglecting to maintain family order in his house," set the salary of the new Treasurer, Samuel Farrar, at $120 a year, and tried to encourage music at the school.[46]

Most of these actions were routine and pedestrian. In one area, however, the Trustees tried to face up squarely to a problem that had existed in the Academy since its founding—the problem of the teaching assistants. A special committee was appointed to study this matter, and in 1808 they reported:

> That they find . . . that since the Academy was first opened, a period of thirty years, thirty Assistants, exclusively of writing Masters, have been employed;—that of the whole number, three only have been prevailed on to continue in office two years; two others about a year and a half each, most of them but one year, and several of them a shorter term. . . . With a few exceptions, these Assistants have been immediately transformed from Pupils into Instructors, most of them young and without experience. . . . Instantly connected with sixty young strangers; oppressed by a crowd of different occupations, and

hurried from one object of instruction to another without intermissions, not weeks only, but months are passed away, before the young Preceptor has learnt the characters or even the names of all his Pupils, and certainly before he has had leisure time to renew his acquaintance with Authors, or to refresh his mind with the principles of those Arts and Sciences, which he is now called to teach. . . . What then can in reason be expected of a young man, transiently caught and a few months detained in the Academy, who never finds his object for the hour, and thro' the day is longing for the hour, that will dismiss him to his professional pursuits? Were this view of the subject the result of reflections merely, your Committee would feel more hesitation in suggesting that a remedy is desirable. But the appeal is made to solid facts, to the experiences of every Preceptor in this and every other Institution, in which there has been a similar succession of unexperienced Instructors . . .

In view of this painful situation the Committee recommended the appointment of a second permanent instructor at a salary of $750. It was agreed that the two instructors would divide the work of the school more or less evenly, that each would have a classroom of his own, that one should teach Latin and the other Greek, and that every effort should be made to make the new position an attractive one.[47] The Trustees tried to put the committee's suggestions into effect. They voted, for example, that the second instructor should have the west room in the Academy Building. But to no avail. In 1808 they engaged the services of Mills Day, younger brother of President Jeremiah Day of Yale, to act as second instructor, but he, too, lasted but one year. It would be many years before Phillips Academy could attract outstanding men who would be willing to spend all their lives at Andover teaching boys.[48]

By 1810 it was clear that the School was in a perilous condition. The generation of the founders was passing; when William Phillips resigned from the Board in 1802 because of "age, ill health, and inability to attend the duties of the office," the last of the three brothers was gone.[49] Madam Phoebe Phillips, though a great source of strength, died in 1812. Colonel John Phillips, her son, died in 1820, leaving a wife and thirteen children in the family manse in North Andover. Though two Boston Phillipses would remain on the board for a few years longer, their interest and influence could never match those of the founders themselves. In 1809 there were three trustee meetings in a row in which there was no quorum.[50] In that same year only sixteen boys entered the Academy, the smallest number since its founding.[51] Finally, in that same year, Mark Newman submitted his resignation to the Trustees, "feeling the labours and responsibility of the office a burden which I cannot longer sustain, the state of my health requiring less care and more exercise."[52] The Trustees first chose Ebenezer Adams of Exeter to be Newman's successor, only to have him turn the offer down.[53] There followed a period of confusion, with Mark Newman agreeing to remain in nominal charge but with the teaching done by various theological students. Discipline weakened, order was difficult to maintain, and the future looked truly grim. At this point the Trustees learned that another Adams—John of Connecticut—had just resigned his position. Much to their relief John Adams accepted the Trustees' offer and by the fall of 1810 was in Andover prepared to take charge.

II. Interlude

THE YEARS between 1810 and 1870—including the terms of John Adams, Osgood Johnson, and Samuel H. Taylor as Principals—were a static period in the history of Phillips Academy. The School changed very little. Indeed the legacy of Eliphalet Pearson seemed, if anything, to have gained strength at the close of these sixty years. Pearson left the Academy a basic set of governing principles. They included a demanding insistence on academic excellence, an almost exclusive concentration on the classics, a system of discipline based on fear, the dictatorship of the Principal in carrying out School policy, a concern for indigent boys who needed help if they were to gain an education, a program for housing students in private homes, and, finally, a stern emphasis on moral education and religious training according to the old Calvinist tradition. Had Ebenezer Pemberton remained longer at the Academy, he might well have modified some of these principles—especially discipline based on fear. Mark Newman was too weak to combat the heritage, and, as we have seen, the Trustee Select Committee and the Trustees as a whole were de facto in charge during Newman's term as Principal. Osgood Johnson, who was Principal from 1833 to 1837, might have modified Pearson's system had he lived, even though he was not an innovator by nature, but his four-year term was too brief and too difficult for him to effect any changes. Thus the fifty-six years when Adams and Taylor were Principals set the tone for the period. Neither of them—and particularly Taylor—would have wanted to change the Pearson legacy if he could, and there is no question that Eliphalet Pearson would have thought Samuel H. Taylor an ideal Principal.

There were, of course, some changes. During the 1830's the Latin and English Commons were built to house some of the students, particularly those on scholarship. But there was no real supervision by the Faculty, and the experiment was a far cry from the modern dormitory with close Faculty guidance. In addition, a substantial number of the students continued to live in private homes, as they had done since the beginning of the School. One of the reasons why the Trustees made so few changes in policy was

their concern for the newly established Andover Theological Seminary.
The administration of this institution had been placed in the hands of the
Academy Trustees, and it soon came to dominate life on Andover Hill.
Another innovation, the Andover Teachers' Seminary, was also divorced
from the Academy, and though it had but a short life, it too demanded the
attention of the Trustees. In short, with such outside distractions it was
easy for the Trustees to turn the running of the School over to Adams and
Taylor, particularly as neither was about to embark on any radical educational program.

In his historical address given at the time of the Centennial of Phillips
Academy in 1878, the Reverend William E. Park stated: "We find it to
be a peculiar feature of the academy that the materials for its history become less ample as we approach the more recent period." The "more recent
period" that he was talking about is the same sixty years to which we have
been referring. The Phillips and Pearson papers provide ample documentation for the founding and early history of the School. When Dr. Cecil
Franklin Patch Bancroft took over in 1873, he kept all his correspondence
intact, and from then on, the materials from which a history of the School
might be written are once again ample. But for this sixty-year period there
are almost no letters from any one of the Principals and few other official
records aside from the Treasurer's accounts. Fortunately, the Trustees
Records are still intact, as well as some annual reports to the Trustees from
Dr. Taylor on the Classical School and James S. Eaton on the English Department. Fortunately, too, there is a fairly substantial collection of student
letters and alumni reminiscences, particularly for the Taylor period, which
can supplement the official material. The paucity of official records can be
explained, in part at least, by the static character of the School during this
period. Had there been more change and controversy, more documentary
material might well have been produced. After an introductory chapter on
the Andover Theological Seminary, there are two chapters dealing with
Phillips Academy during this period. Because of the nature of the source
material, these two chapters tend to be descriptive rather than analytical.

CHAPTER SIX

THE ANDOVER THEOLOGICAL SEMINARY

I N 1808 an event occurred that was to have a profound effect on the fortunes of Phillips Academy: the Andover Theological Seminary was founded.[1] It is not too much to say that the Seminary was the most important single influence on the School; but during its hundred years of existence, it set the intellectual and religious tone of Andover Hill as well. It soon eclipsed Phillips Academy in endowment, buildings, and reputation. A few years after its founding, it included two large brick dormitories—the present Foxcroft and Bartlet Halls—with a chapel and recitation building, the present Pearson Hall, located between them to make an impressive façade in the eastern part of the campus. In addition, a number of homes had been constructed for the Seminary professors, the most impressive being the present Phelps, Pease, and Stuart houses. By contrast Phillips Academy had one wooden classroom building and a modest house for its principal. Since the administration of the Seminary was made the responsibility of the Trustees of Phillips Academy, it soon began to demand a disproportionate amount of their time and energy, the School and its problems being forced to take a back seat. It would be a hundred years before the Trustees would be relieved of their Seminary responsibilities, free once more to devote all their time to the School.

The Andover Theological Seminary was the child of the religious ferment that characterized New England as the nineteenth century opened. The American Revolution had done more than bring about a separation from Great Britain. It had challenged and shaken many of the old New England institutions as well. The French Revolution provided additional liberal influences that threatened the old way of life further. Much to the horror of New England Federalists, the Jeffersonian Republicans made serious inroads into what had once been a Federalist stronghold. Similarly, in the field of religion the old Congregational Calvinist orthodoxy found itself besieged on all sides: on the one hand, Universalists and Unitarians were steadily gaining new adherents; on the other, Baptists and Methodists were vigorously recruiting new members from among the working classes of New England. Small wonder that the Reverend Leonard Woods, one of the founders of the Seminary, could write: "It is a day of alarm and danger. There is a flood of anti-Christian error and soul-destroying corruption coming in upon us, and threatening to sweep away every remnant of primitive truth and goodness. Faithful Christians [orthodox Calvinists] are few in number."[2]

The crowning blow to the orthodox came when Harvard went Unitarian. In 1803 David Tappan, the orthodox Hollis Professor of Divinity, died, and immediately the various shades of religious opinion in the Harvard community began jockeying to choose his successor, with "as much intrigue . . . as was ever practised in the Vatican." The most powerful personality in the contretemps that followed was Eliphalet Pearson, the first master of Phillips Academy, who, since 1786, had been Hancock Professor of Hebrew at Cambridge. The problem became complicated still further when Harvard's President Willard, another champion of orthodoxy, died in 1804. Appointed Acting President by the Corporation, Pearson determined to have an orthodox Calvinist chosen for the Hollis chair and himself chosen as President. In his campaign to keep Harvard uncontaminated by liberal doctrines, he was ably assisted by the Reverend Jedidiah Morse. But the conservatives simply did not have the votes. Much to Pearson's outrage, the Reverend Henry Ware of Hingham, a man with pronounced Unitarian leanings, was chosen Hollis Professor of Divinity, while the Reverend Samuel Webber, a man "without friends or enemies," was chosen President. Stating that he could no longer remain at Harvard under these circumstances, Pearson proceeded to resign both his professorship and his fellowship on the Corporation.[3] Throughout New England pious conservatives were horrified; the devil had clearly captured Harvard; the orthodox must close ranks if they were to succeed in stemming the liberal trend. And since there was no longer any hope that true Christian ministers could be trained at Harvard, a bastion of orthodoxy must be erected to preserve the ancient truths.

What was the nature of this challenge by the liberals to the old orthodoxy? In essence, the liberals insisted that the practice of religion should be an intellectual rather than an emotional experience. They were strongly opposed to revivalism and believed that the sermon should be a rational exposition of religious truth in which felicity of style and delivery were both important. Although they admitted that individual conversions often took place, they were opposed to making attested conversion a requisite of church membership. They "affirmed rather that the Christian life was a continuous rational process of self-dedication." Communion, they believed, should be available to all on an equal basis, since it was a "simple memorial" rather than a sacrament reserved for the elect. What alarmed the orthodox most was the humanistic beliefs of the liberals, who thought of man not as depraved and sinful but as a free agent who could work out his own salvation. And their confidence in man's potentialities was enhanced by the faith they held in the American political experiment that was being tried under the new Constitution. Although the Unitarians got their name from their supposed denial of the concept of the Trinity, they and other liberal groups actually made little of this doctrine until they were forced to define their position by the attacks of the orthodox. They were also more or less agreed on salvation for all, though they did not press this issue either. Finally, they were strong Congregationalists, believing in the right of each congregation to determine its own affairs and beliefs and opposing strongly any attempt to form Congregational churches into a larger organization with a fixed, absolute creed for all.[4]

These fresh winds of doctrine would have been anathema to all the Phillipses, and particularly to the late Lieutenant Governor, Samuel Phillips. In his school's constitution he spelled out the beliefs that the Master should hold: "The existence of One true God, the FATHER, SON, and HOLY GHOST; of the fall of man, the depravity of human nature; the necessity of an atonement, and of our being renewed in the spirit of our minds; the doctrines of repentance toward God and of faith toward our Lord Jesus Christ; of sanctification by the Holy Spirit, and of justification by the free grace of God, through the redemption, that is in Jesus Christ, (in opposition to the erroneous and dangerous doctrine of justification by our own merit, or a dependence on self righteousness,) together with the other important doctrines and duties of our HOLY CHRISTIAN RELIGION."[5] And he reiterated this position in the Second Donation that he gave just before his death: his purpose, he said, was "the preservation of the essential and distinguishing doctrines of the Gospel, as professed by our pious ancestors, the first settlers of New England . . . and to guard againt the dissemination of the least particle of Infidelity or Modern Philosophy . . . as tend to undermine the fundamental principles of the Gospel plan of salvation, or to reduce the Christian Religion to a system of mere morality."[6] In the coming struggle between the liberals and the orthodox, there would be no doubt where Phillips Academy and those connected with it would stand.

With Harvard lost to the liberals, with Boston churches abandoning the ancient truths, with the liberal contamination spreading throughout New England, something must be done to strengthen the orthodox position. And what better way could be devised than by establishing a seminary where pious young men could be taught the old truths and the old values to prepare them to carry the doctrines of orthodoxy all over the land. For all their conservatism in matters of dogma, these orthodox Calvinists were radical in trying to establish a theological seminary, for there was no institution in the entire country solely dedicated to training ministers. To be sure there were professors of divinity at Harvard, Yale, and Dartmouth who were supposed to supervise graduate students studying for the ministry, but the training was superficial at best. Timothy Dwight at Yale did try to meet the problem with a course of Sunday morning lectures for theology students. Most of the leading ministers, however, were prepared by individual clergymen, who would often take students into their family. This was not unlike the training that law students received by reading law with some distinguished attorney. A more or less standard practice in training these theologues was to have the student read widely under the supervision of the minister, be given a list of questions to answer which involved difficult theological points, discuss the answers to these questions, write sermons that would then be criticized for content, style, grammar, and other mechanics, and engage in long conversations with the teacher. One minister wrote, "I often hear them read, that uncouth habits, if they have contracted any, may be corrected." There must have been many a New England clergyman who trained students for the ministry in this way, but a few were outstanding. The Reverend Nathaniel Emmons, for example, who had a church in Franklin, Massachusetts, trained eighty-seven students during a long career, while the Reverend Joseph Bellamy, of Bethlehem, Connecticut, taught more than fifty. Both Emmons and Bellamy were extraordinarily effective teachers who were beloved by their students, but this apprenticeship system was hardly satisfactory if an army of orthodox stalwarts were going to be trained to combat the heresies of the day.[7]

Phillips Academy and those connected with it had been concerned about the training of ministers ever since its founding. Writing in 1778 the Reverend Jonathan French had suggested the establishment of a Theological Seminary in connection with the new Phillips School.[8] In the Academy's constitution appears the clause "And, whereas many of the Students in this Seminary may be devoted to the sacred work of the gospel ministry . . ."[9] Finally, in John Phillips' will he left one third of his estate to Phillips Academy "for the benefit more especially of Charity Scholars" who "may be assisted in the study of Divinity (if a Theological Professor is not employed) . . . under the direction of some eminent Calvinistic minister of the gospel, until such time as an able, pious, and orthodox Instructor shall . . . be supported . . . as a Professor of Divinity, by whom they may be taught the important principles and distinguishing tenets of our holy Christian Religion."[10] When Eliphalet Pearson resigned his various positions at Harvard, he was invited by the Phillips Academy Trustees, of whom he was at the time President, to return to Andover and live in the present Hardy House, which the trustees had acquired from one Captain Towne in 1804 and which they had just finished remodeling.[11] Pearson's intimate knowledge of the past of Phillips Academy, coupled with his determination to found a seminary to combat the liberal heresies, made him an ideal person to lead a campaign for the establishment of a theological institution. No sooner had he returned to Andover than it became clear that he would have important allies. The Reverend Jedidiah Morse of Charlestown, who, like Pearson, had strongly opposed the changes at

Harvard, was a tower of strength in the orthodox camp. Most widely known for his American geography, Morse had founded *The Panoplist*, a journal to champion Calvinist views, but he was also convinced that a seminary was essential to save the true faith. From the very beginning Morse lent his considerable talents to the project.[12] Samuel Farrar, Treasurer of Phillips Academy, was also to play an important role, particularly in drawing up many legal documents for the seminary. For all their enthusiasm for the proposed new institution, these three men would have been helpless had it not been for the support of three people of means who were in a position to provide the wherewithall for its foundation. The most generous single donor was Samuel Abbot, an inhabitant of Andover and a Trustee of Phillips Academy. He had been a successful merchant in Boston before the Revolution, but had returned to Andover at its outbreak. Since that time, through careful management and investment, he had increased his property substantially. Since he had no children, he originally had planned to leave his money to his wife's grandson, only to see him die. He then planned to leave his money to Harvard for the support of Divinity students, only to see the institution captured by the Unitarians. He was now in an ideal position to sponsor a new institution that could put his deeply held religious principles into practice. A cautious and simple man, he derived tremendous peace of mind once he had made the decision to help, and hoped the new institution would be "the means of saving millions of souls."[13] Two other generous benefactors—Madam Phoebe Phillips and her son John—were strong in their support of the new project, certainly in part because they must have known how enthusiastic Samuel Phillips would have been about it. Before the task was finished, they contributed about a hundred thousand dollars for buildings and endowment. In speaking of one of the buildings she gave, Phoebe said, "I hope a prayer will be offered for every hod of brick, and every bucket of mortar used in its erection."[14]

Yet a serious obstacle had arisen to complicate the work of the Andover group. At about the same time that its plans were maturing, Jedidiah Morse discovered that a rival group was planning to establish a seminary at Newburyport. To make matters more difficult, the Newburyport group were Hopkinsians—followers of Samuel Hopkins, a Connecticut clergyman who had made changes in the Westminster Catechism, which the Andover group considered the basic document of their beliefs. The Hopkinsians were by no means liberal; indeed their differences from the Westminister Calvinists were relatively few; but they felt as strongly about their beliefs as did the Andover group.[15] It soon became clear to far-sighted men like Morse and Pearson that to found two seminaries, each of which would compete for essentially the same support and the same clientele, would be a disaster. It would be hard enough to establish one strong institution; if two were attempted, the chances were excellent that both would fail. The leader of the Newburyport group was the Reverend Samuel Spring, a graduate of Princeton who had been chaplain on Arnold's famous march up the Kennebec River to Quebec. He had been pastor of the North Congregational Church in Newburyport since 1777 and had for some time had his heart set on a seminary. To support him in this venture he had enlisted the aid of William Bartlet, one of the shrewdest merchants of Newburyport, who had made a sizable fortune by being able to outguess his competitors. Another supporter was Moses Brown, like Bartlet a successful merchant, though on a much lesser scale. It is interesting to note that neither of these businessmen was a "professor" of religion—that is, neither had publicly announced his conversion. But both were devout Christians who saw in a seminary an important institution for the spreading of God's word. The third of the Newburyport benefactors was John Norris of Salem, who is described as "inclined to seek after wealth too earnestly, and to hold it too tenaciously." As he grew older, he became more and more concerned about his own spiritual state, ending one letter "I want holy love! O what don't I want of spiritual blessings!"[16] And so the two groups faced one another—each with its own precisely defined creed, each with its three benefactors, each determined to have its own kind of seminary.

Fortunately for the future of Andover Theological Seminary, there were strong and able men who insisted that some kind of compromise could be effected. Jedidiah Morse was the first to attempt it but before the job was done, Eliphalet Pearson and Leonard Woods had performed yeoman's service in bringing the two parties together. Dr. Spring was sure that if his group were to join the Andover one, they would lose their identity and be forced to accept the Andover creed. Eliphalet Pearson, ever one to be practical, suggested that it was extremely unlikely that the Massachusetts legislature would vote to incorporate an institution as conservative as the one the Newburyport group planned on. The rise in power of the Jeffersonians would mean that a charter would be blocked.[17] On the other hand, Phillips Academy was already incorporated, the legislature had just finished enlarging the power of the Trustees to hold property,[18] and there need be no further political problems. That was just the beginning. The Andover group, despairing of reaching an agreement, went ahead, establishing their seminary in 1807; but Pearson, Morse, and Woods refused to give up. They discovered that the opposition to the merger of Bartlet, Brown, and Norris was not nearly so strong as was Spring's. Accordingly, Leonard Woods called on the three laymen and found that they were willing to compromise. He then approached Dr. Spring. "You have trigged our wheels," the good doctor said, but the worst of the crisis had passed.[19] Before a final agreement was reached, Eliphalet Pearson had driven over to Newburyport thirty-six times—a distance of twenty miles each way—to do battle with the rival dialecticians. "Today I was occupied three hours in a metaphysical dispute with Dr. Spring," he wrote. And again, "I have just come from an interview with Dr. Spring, who spent two hours in examining me on the knottiest points of metaphysical theology."[20] Finally, Pearson's and Wood's patience was rewarded. Though Dr. Spring still had serious reservations about the merger—in part he thought it was illegal under the Phillips Academy charter[21]—he finally agreed not to oppose it further, and by 1808 it was possible to move ahead with more or less united support.

The documents establishing the Andover Theological Seminary were complicated enough. In the first place there was the Constitution of the Seminary, drawn up by the Andover group in 1807 and modeled more or less after the constitution of Phillips Academy, in which Samuel Abbot agreed to give $20,000 for a professorship and Phoebe and John Phillips agreed to give two buildings. This constitution also spelled out the courses that were to be taught and contained rules for the governance of the institution and a set of beliefs based on the Westminster Catechism that the professors were to subscribe to. In addition, the professors were required to declare themselves "in opposition, not only to Atheists and Infidels, but to Jews, Mahometans, Arians, Pelagians, Antinomians, Arminians, Socinians, Unitarians, and Universalists, and to all other heresies and errors, ancient and modern, which may be opposed to the gospel of CHRIST, or hazardous to the souls of men."

When the Newburyport group joined, they had prepared a number of "Associate Statutes," which would safeguard their interests in the new institution. Most important among them was the establishment of a Board of Visitors of three, one chosen by the Andover group, one by the Newburyport group, and a third who would be mutually acceptable. This Board was to have general supervision over the seminary, particularly in safeguarding the orthodoxy of the professors, and each new appointee must be approved by the Visitors. In addition, the Associate Statutes contained a long creed, drawn up by Dr. Spring and Leonard Woods, which differed in certain respects from the doctrines expressed in the Westminster Catechism. When they read over the Associate Statutes, the Andover group decided that they must expand their original constitution so as to make it congruous with them. Accordingly, they prepared for that purpose thirteen "Additional Statutes." The resulting set of documents was impressive, for length if for nothing else. The Constitution had thirty-four articles, the Associate Statutes twenty-eight, and these two, together with the Additional Statutes, cover thirty-seven large pages of type.[22] But the important thing was that, despite this verbiage, the two groups had finally reached a mutually agreeable settlement. To place a capstone on the compromise, a generous arrangement was reached in the appointment of the first two professors. Although he was an old Calvinist, Samuel Abbot agreed to appoint Leonard Woods, the Hopkinsian, Professor of Christian Theology, while William Bartlet, though a Hopkinsian, appointed Eliphalet Pearson, an old

Calvinist, Professor of Natural Theology. And when the Seminary opened, prayer was offered that the two professors might be "a lovely, happy pair."[23] The formal opening occurred on 28 September 1808 with everyone who had played a prominent part in attendance. Since Eliphalet Pearson had never been ordained, this matter was attended to, while Dr. Timothy Dwight of Yale preached the sermon. Jonathan French, Jedidiah Morse, Samuel Spring, Leonard Woods, and others officiated at the services, the music being supplied by the musical associations of Middlesex, Essex, and Suffolk counties, aided by "other respectable gentlemen, both of the clergy and the laity, who politely gave their assistance in the solemnities of the day."[24] Despite almost insuperable obstacles, it appeared that the Andover Theological Seminary was off to a good start.

The generosity of the founders changed the appearance of Andover Hill markedly. Before they were through, Phoebe and John Phillips contributed close to one hundred thousand dollars; William Bartlet gave thirty-five

Teachers Seminary (Stone Academy)   Samaritan House   Students Workshop

16. *The Andover Theological Seminary in the 1830's.*

thousand, as well as paying for five buildings; Samuel Abbot brought his total to over one hundred thousand dollars; the Norrises gave forty thousand; and Moses Brown, thirty-five thousand. When lesser gifts are added, the total comes to about four hundred and fifty thousand dollars given during the early years of the Seminary, a sum that completely eclipsed the modest endowment of Phillips Academy during this period.[25] Gradually the new buildings were erected along a general plan that, according to tradition, Eliphalet Pearson laid out by climbing a large oak tree then located in what is now the lawn in front of Samuel Phillips Hall. Colonel John Phillips made a special trip to Brown University to examine the college buildings there, and the first edifice, Phillips Hall, now Foxcroft Hall, was finished in 1809. In good time there followed Bartlet Chapel, now Pearson Hall, then located parallel to Phillips Hall. The third building to complete "Seminary Row" was Bartlet Hall, still in its original location and with its original name. In the area where Samuel Phillips Hall now stands,

Phillip's Hall   Chapel   Bartlett Hall

there was a wooden dining hall with quarters for the steward. Nor were the changes limited to seminary buildings proper. Through the generosity of William Bartlet three handsome residences for seminary professors were built along what is now Main Street. The present Phelps House was originally constructed for Professor Edward Griffin. Mr. Bartlet had given him a free hand in decorating the building but had mildly protested fancy wallpaper that cost a dollar a roll. Professor Griffin thereupon had the room redone with paper that cost twenty-five cents a roll, also billed to Mr. Bartlet.[26] A second house was the Stuart House, constructed in 1812 for Professor Moses Stuart. Finally, in 1816, what was then called Woods House, now Pease House, was built for Leonard Woods. At about the same time Mark Newman built the house that still bears his name, across the street from Stuart House. Finally, to complete the imposing row of buildings, Squire Samuel Farrar built a house on the site of the present Archaeological Building, which would be moved in the 1880's to its present location further down Phillips Street. In contrast, one house was provided for the staff of Phillips Academy—the present Hardy House, then occupied by Principal John Adams.[27]

Andover Hill was to be changed in more than material ways as a result of the founding of the Theological Seminary. For the most part, the early professors at the seminary were giants as theological scholars. Eliphalet Pearson resigned his position after one year, finding his teaching duties uncongenial, while Professor Edward Griffin soon found unworkable his plan of combining teaching at the Seminary with holding down the pulpit of the Park Street Church in Boston, and he too resigned. Leonard Woods, who had done so much to help found the Seminary, held his Professorship of Christian Theology for the remainder of his career. In 1820 he attacked the Unitarian position of William Ellery Channing in a book called *Letters to Unitarians*, which was immediately answered by Henry Ware, Hollis Professor of Divinity at Harvard. This inaugurated the so-called "Wood 'n Ware" controversy that lasted for four years and resulted in five large volumes of polemics.[28] Upon the resignation of Eliphalet Pearson, Dr. Samuel Spring set out to find a replacement for him. He asked Dr. Timothy Dwight of New Haven about a promising young man named Moses Stuart. "Mr. Stuart is well qualified for the office," said Dr. Dwight, "but we can't spare him." Dr. Spring replied, "We don't want a man that can be spared."[29] In due course Stuart accepted the position of Professor of Sacred Literature and like Leonard Woods was to spend the rest of his career in Andover. Like Woods, also, he engaged in battle with the Unitarians at Harvard, his *Letters to Channing* representing a powerful statement of the orthodox position. For all his patience in scholarly matters, he used to become enraged at the problems of a New England farmer.

> Bah! was there ever climate and soil like this! Manure the land as much as you will, it all leaches through this gravel, and very soon

not a trace of it can be seen. If you plant early, everything is liable to
be cut off by the late frosts of spring. If you plant late, your crop is
destroyed by the early frosts of autumn. If you escape these, the burning sun of summer scorches your crop, and it perishes by heat and
draught. If none of these evils overtake you, clouds of insects eat up
your crop, and what the caterpillar leaves the canker-worm devours.[30]

The last of what might be considered the first run of professors was Ebenezer Porter, Professor of Sacred Rhetoric, who lived in Phelps House. A
frail man whose work was continually limited by bad health, he nonetheless
made his mark teaching the students of the seminary how to deliver sermons.
In addition he produced a book entitled *Rhetorical Reader*, which soon became a standard text for would-be clergymen. In 1827, when the trustees
thought that the Seminary needed a president, he was chosen. It was at his
house that a group of the Seminary professors, with Squire Farrar, Mark
Newman, and others, used to meet to discuss the problems of the day and
how to meet them. Out of these discussions came a number of important
developments, including the American Education Society; the *Boston Recorder*, the first religious newspaper in America; the American Tract Society, to distribute religious materials; and the American Temperance Society, whose members pledged "entire abstinence from intoxicating liquors."
The achievements of the first faculty of the Seminary bore testimony to the
fact that the Trustees had chosen well.

As one might imagine, Eliphalet Pearson insisted from the beginning
that the new seminary be a place where high scholarship was honored and
scholarly works produced. To ensure the publication of scholarly endeavors,
he insisted that the Seminary should have a printing press of its own.
Though there had been a press in Andover as early as 1798, it was not
until 1813, under Pearson's prodding, that it was expanded and moved to
the second floor of an ugly old wooden building located on the site of the
present Cooley House, where Mark Newman had established a store. Timothy Flagg and Abraham J. Gould, who were the first printers, were men
after Pearson's own heart. Members of the South Church and definitely
"pious," they were in complete sympathy with the concept of making the
press the means of publishing and distributing orthodox religious materials.
Presumably as a result of Pearson's driving interest, the press early acquired
the first fonts of Greek and Hebrew type in America, and for years Harvard
had its Greek printing done at Andover. Moses Stuart took full advantage
of the opportunities the press offered. Though he did not know Hebrew
before he came to Andover, he soon learned the language and prepared a
Hebrew grammar for publication. Since no one in Andover—or probably
anywhere else in New England—knew how to set Hebrew type, Stuart
learned to set it himself, and in 1813 the first Hebrew grammar to be published in the United States appeared. In the 1820's, with the help of generous contributions, it became possible to purchase additional esoteric

types, until the press was able to print books in eleven Oriental languages as well as Hebrew. Stuart was indefatigable. As Oliver Wendell Holmes remembered him, he was "tall, lean, with strong, bold features, a keen, scholarly, accipitrine nose, thin, expressive lips, great solemnity and impressiveness of voice and manner . . . my early model of a classic orator. His air was Roman, his neck long and bare like Cicero's, and his *toga*— that is his broadcloth cloak—was carried on his arm whatever might have been the weather, with such a statue-like rigid grace that he might have been turned into marble as he stood, and looked noble by the side of the antiques of the Vatican."[31] Stuart suffered acutely from dyspepsia, and "when his malady interfered with his labors, his voice could be heard from his study, rising and falling in a wailing prayer for relief." Professor Stuart's example was contagious, and Andover graduates who went into missionary work produced grammars, lexicons, and in some cases alphabets in such esoteric languages as Mahratta, Tamil, Armeno-Turkish, Cherokee, and Choctaw. In 1832 the press moved to a new brick building situated in front of the present Adams and Bishop halls, where it remained for the next thirty years. Warren F. Draper, its last proprietor, estimated that in its first seventy years the press had published the equivalent of 233 octavo volumes of 500 pages each. More than one hundred titles were written by Andover professors, with a total circulation of 400,000. Nor did the press lack women authors. Harriet Beecher Stowe and Elizabeth Stuart Phelps, with others, produced books through the Andover press which reached a combined circulation of over a million. Finally, the press handled many assignments outside Andover, such as the publications of the American Tract Society, the Temperance *Herald*, and *Bibliotheca Sacra*. In many ways, it was the most outstanding achievement of the Andover Theological Seminary.[32]

As for the students—or "theologues" as they came to be called—the great majority were graduates of New England colleges. During the first twenty-five years only forty-two out of six hundred and seven were not. Yale and Dartmouth led the list, with Middlebury, Williams, Amherst, and other following in order. Not surprisingly, Harvard was barely represented. Fewer than two thirds of the students finished the full three-year course. In some cases this was due to a student's desire to study with one particular professor only, in others a desire to get married, poor health, or emotional exhaustion. Rooming conditions were Spartan at best. Addison Kingsbury wrote the following description of Phillips Hall in 1825, after leaving Boston in a coach with eleven passengers inside and four outside and spending three hours on the road:

> I have at last succeeded in obtaining a room in the fourth story, though with few or no accommodations. I expected the rooms were furnished. I accordingly brought no furniture with me and I find none here of consequence except a poor bed without any clothing. . . .

My tables are not fit to stand in your old kitchen, and as for chairs
I am now sitting upon one without any back writing to you . . ."[33]

When Bartlet Hall was built in 1821, it was more attractive. In the first
place, it had suites with a living room and fireplace and two bedrooms. A
student described his condition: "Here you will find my chum and myself
each bending over a comfortable writing desk laid upon two marble-
colored tables. You see our room ornamented with four pretty chairs, a
beautiful mahogony bureau, large mirror . . . All the rooms in this building are furnished alike. Nothing could add to our convenience if we had
a carpet. But this is of little consequence."[34] It might be pointed out that
tight-fisted Samuel Farrar, the Treasurer, was in charge of the furnishings
of Phillips Hall, while Mrs. Bartlet had chosen the furnishings for Bartlet
Hall. The students were responsible for their own wood and water, and if
one lived on the fourth floor of Phillips Hall, this could be a real chore.
Yet most of the students did not seem unhappy with their lot. Here is one
commentary written in 1819:

> "We are at present in a very small business, that is, reviewing Greek
> grammar. Besides this we have the Hebrew alphabet to learn. But I
> have quartos around me enough to frighten a very timid man out of
> his senses. Our living is quite as good as I expected. . . . That you
> may know how much a slave a man may be at Andover, if he will
> follow the rules adopted by the majority, I will give the order of the
> day." Then follows a detailed account of how every minute of the
> day is taken up by devotions, study, and eating. "Now, my dear
> Seraph, if you can tell me if this is consistent with those means to
> preserve health, which have been said to be so abundantly used here,
> I will confess that your discernment far exceeds mine. For my own
> part I expect to become an outlaw; for I will not be so confined. Few
> means are wanting to enable us to become great men; but the op-
> portunity to kill oneself with study is rather too good."

Generally speaking, life at the Seminary was a Spartan one. When a distinguished German scholar asked Professor Park, "How do you get along
without the opera and theatrer?" Park's reply was in the best Andover tradition: "You forget that we have the church and the sewing society."[35]

One of the most charming accounts of life at the Theological Seminary
in the early time is *Old Andover Days*, from the pen of Sarah Stuart Robbins, a daughter of Moses Stuart. Mrs. Robbins grew up on Andover Hill
during the 1820's and 1830's, and though her book was written when she
was an old woman, her memory is clear. The theologues, as she remembers
them, like most students of the time, had to fetch their own water and
wood from outside their dormitories, make their own beds, do their own
sweeping, and fill their own lamps. Nor was the "Commons" a place to
remember with pleasure. The food was of poor quality, and to make it

even less palatable the "tough meat and soggy vegetables" were eaten to the accompaniment of readings on religious subjects—Jonathan Edwards, eternal punishment, redemption through free grace, and the like. When funds ran low, molasses was substituted for meat, and Mrs. Robbins tells the story of a student who had to be bled by his doctor, only to find that the physician could get nothing but molasses from his veins. "The long tables, the blue and white dishes, the capacious water-pitchers, the dingy tumblers, the patched table-cloths, the piles of brown and white bread, the crackers, mush, and buckwheat, the poor joints and cheap vegetables" indicate that there was no danger of the Seminarians being tempted by the pleasures of the flesh. William Bartlet believed that the theologues should get plenty of exercise—as if their housekeeping chores were not enough— and as a result a grisly form of manual training was introduced whereby the students made *coffins* in a stone shell of a building that was later re-modeled into the present Stowe House. According to Mrs. Robbins the students were not very good carpenters: "There were pale, puzzled, weary faces, bending over corners that wouldn't fit, and over boards that were too long or too short, too narrow or too wide. There were failures to hit nails on the head; there was dulling of saws, breaking of hatchets, and rasping of files. . . . Each man was as solemn as if the coffin he was making were his own."[36]

The Puritan Sabbath, as Mrs. Robbins describes it, was a grim business, even by contemporary standards. Faculty children started the exercise with a three-hour session in the schoolhouse on Saturday morning, where they studied the Westminster Catechism and sang hymns. Saturday afternoon was free, but the minute the sun set, the Sabbath proper began; not to be home by sunset was a serious sin, and by nine o'clock all lights on the Hill were out. Sunday began with family prayers—and lengthy ones too— followed by a "Sunday hush," when everyone, particularly children, was to remain quiet, feeling "as if Satan in bodily shape was waiting near to gob-ble up any poor, unlucky sinner who should venture ever so little from the strait and narrow path." At nine o'clock came Sabbath school, taught by various theological students, after which the children were marched to chapel for the morning service. The chapel walls were dingy blue, the pews, gallery, and desk a yellow white. Candelabra held long thin tallow dips "which had a sacerdotal habit of dropping large, round, hot drops upon unsanctified heads." But there were plenty of Bibles and Watts hymn books. In winter footstoves were used, the passing of which provided a diversion during the service. Each professor had a pew: Dr. Ebenezer Porter, a chronic invalid, sat with a yellow bandana around his throat and a long dark coat hanging from his shoulders. Leonard Woods, the hand-somest member of the faculty, reputed among the children to be of the "Old School" because of his stern demeanor, made them feel as if they were "practical illustrations of original sin, native depravity, and free agents gone astray." Moses Stuart, with his long blue cloak, reflected by physical movement his opinion of the sermon: if it was poor, he would shrug, move about in his seat, and put on a long face; if it was good, he would rise in his seat at some particularly pertinent remarks, turn around to his students, and draw his red silk handkerchief across his mouth several times to show his approbation. Other pews contained Dr. James Murdoch, Principal John Adams of Phillips Academy, and Squire Samuel Farrar. At the close of the morning service there was a two-hour intermission, during which a cold dinner was eaten—one must not work on Sundays—and a pious book read. Then back to the chapel for more prayers and psalm-singing. The pleasantest part of the day was the family tea that followed, with toast, doughnuts, and preserves. Finally the children had another go at the Westminster Catechism until the sun finally dipped below the horizon, when at last they were free.[37]

The Sabbath was simply the most important religious day of Andover Hill. It by no means followed that weekdays could not be utilized for religious services as well, and in fact one was scheduled for each day of the week. On certain Monday nights there was a "Monthly Concert of Prayer for Foreign Missions." In the dimly lighted chapel, reports were read of missionary activities throughout the world. When Mrs. Robbins attended these meetings, the missionary movement was just starting, and she could not understand how the meager reports could inspire anyone in the audience to undertake missionary work. Yet they must have, as the Seminary's proud record in the field indicates. On Tuesday nights came the meetings of the Society of Inquiry, at which various theologues discussed matters of religious interest. On Wednesday nights came the "conference meeting," a prayer meeting at which professors and students discussed together the latter's moral needs. Thursday nights were made livelier by the "Porter Rhetorical." Students were given a chance to practice speaking—a debate, an oration, sometimes a poem. On Friday nights came the most bizarre meeting of all—the so-called "Jews' Meeting," held at the home of Professor Porter to pray for the conversion of the Jews. If the purpose of the meeting was bizarre, the surroundings were even more so. Presumably because of his chronic invalidism, Professor Porter's house was all but hermetically sealed—outside shutters closed, inside window shades drawn, and doors shut tight; it seemed to Mrs. Robbins like a "wooden tomb." Mrs. Porter arranged the meetings and ran them. She was a tiny little woman dressed in black, a tight lace cap with narrow black strings surrounding her face. All conversation, including whispering, was taboo. A few theologues conducted the meetings, which consisted of Bible readings, hymn singing, and an occasional reading of an appropriate newspaper clipping. Finally, on Saturday nights, came a "social prayer-meeting" with more prayers and hymn singing. When it is remembered that the theological students' days were full of classes and study, not to mention their housekeeping chores and coffin-making, it is clear that their theological regimen left no time for sinful thoughts.[38]

The high point of the year was the Seminary Anniversary, or Commencement, which came in September. At least two weeks before the event, the institution began to prepare for it. Faculty families searched the countryside for delicacies with which to regale the guests; the grounds were weeded and raked; every inch of space in every house was utilized for the accommodation of the guests, while the children were relegated to attics and haylofts. At last the great day arrived when the ceremonies would start. Mrs. Robbins remembered a time before the railroad had reached Andover, and as a result the journey to the Hill was a difficult one for many of the guests. Some, like the Reverend John Codman, would come "with his stout English horses, his stout English coach, his stout English coachman, his ruddy, cordial English self, and his noble little wife." William Bartlet came in "a large, old-fashioned stage-coach drawn by four horses," with as many of his grandchildren as the vehicle could carry. For many a poor country parson, however, "There were long, weary miles trodden by weary feet, rough roads driven over with a thin, hungry horse in the old one hoss shay, and rusty saddle-bags mended and packed with scanty, seedy wardrobes, always containing . . .the immaculate white cravat."

In the 1830's the Anniversary ceremonies followed a set pattern. On Monday nights came the meeting of the Porter Rhetorical Society, with graduates declaiming on such subjects as "The Power and Benevolence of God," "God Everywhere," and occasionally more secular pieces—"Edmund Burke" and "The Characteristics of English Philosophy." The following day Seminary graduates delivered sermons and addresses on religious topics —one year, for example, the leading speaker was President Mark Hopkins of Williams—he of the log. On Tuesday evenings came the meeting of the Society of Inquiry respecting Missions—presided over, on one occasion, by a graduate who was soon to go as a missionary to Eastern Africa, "that dark corner of the earth." In one class nine of the graduates had already been accepted by the American Board for missionary work. Wednesday was the big day, however. The Seminary Alumni met at 7:30 in the morning, and at 9:00 the Commencement exercises were held in the Bartlet Chapel, which was always packed with visitors. Indeed at some Commencements clergymen who had traveled a long way to come to Andover were unable to get in. The rest of the day, morning and afternoon, was devoted to hearing each graduate deliver what amounted to a short sermon—sometimes exegesis of a particular Biblical text, sometimes on a broader theme. Since the graduating class numbered in the thirties in those days, the audience got their money's worth. Then, after refreshment at faculty houses, the assemblage vanished as quickly as it had come. Nor were these exercises simply to demonstrate the competence of the graduates; particularly effective deliveries were often rewarded with attractive and important church positions.[39]

From some of the foregoing descriptions it is easy to imagine the three leading professors—Woods, Stuart, and Porter—as saintly, Christian men with a love for all mankind. Their treatment of Professor James Murdoch, however, shows that they could be vindictive, small-minded, and nasty when they believed their interests were being threatened. The story of the unfortunate James Murdoch begins when Moses Brown, one of the Associate Founders of the Seminary, determined to found a professorship of Church History, a subject that, according to the Constitution of the institution, had to be taught.[40] When the three professors heard of this, they moved heaven and earth to get the decision changed. Since Ebenezer Porter was in poor health and often missed classes—in 1817 he missed an entire term—it was thought that the new chair should be filled by a second professor of Sacred Rhetoric, who could share Porter's responsibilities with him. When Brown refused to change his plan without trustee approval, Woods wrote a compromise statement that provided for a professor who would share his time between Sacred Rhetoric and Church History. Eliphalet Pearson, as President of the Board, saw through this plan and did all he could to limit the new chair to Church History alone, but the Trustees waffled, and Woods's compromise was adopted. It then became a matter of choosing the new professor. Woods was dispatched to sound out James Murdoch, then Professor of Greek and Latin at the University of Vermont. Not only did the three professors admire his scholarship, but they believed, wrongly as it turned out, that he could easily be recruited to support their position. Murdoch, who has been described as "a dry little man with a large elastic brain and nerves like catgut" demurred.[41] He knew little of Sacred Rhetoric, he protested, and he added, "if I go to Andover I shall have no department of my own, and have a life of drudgery." Against his better judgment, he allowed himself to be persuaded and moved to Andover in 1819.

His worst fears were soon realized. During his first year the senior class sent a delegation to Woods to complain of Murdoch's poor teaching. When he asked his colleagues' advice, Murdoch was told to resign, and indeed he sent a letter of resignation to the Trustees. But Eliphalet Pearson smelled a rat. He suspected a faculty cabal whose purpose was to keep Church History from the curriculum. The cabal kept the pressure on. They claimed that Murdoch was an albatross around the neck of the Seminary and were horrified to discover that he drank brandy. Since they could not gain their objectives by themselves, they turned to Moses Brown, who wrote the Trustees that Murdoch was incompetent and ought to resign. When he refused, Brown demanded a trial before the Board of Visitors. Plans for this were under way when the Trustees got cold feet. There was a question whether the Board of Visitors had full legal authority to act in a case of this kind, and in addition Murdoch threatened to appeal to the Supreme Court of Massachusetts if they did. So the matter was patched up temporarily by defining Murdoch's position and responsibilities more precisely. For a while it looked as if things would be calmer on Zion's Hill, but it was merely the lull before the storm. Murdoch's colleagues spurned social relations with him, regularly voted down his proposals in faculty meeting, and generally made his life miserable. To get relief Murdoch turned to the students and began confiding to them the story of his difficulties. He stepped out of line when he told some students the details of a discussion in faculty meeting to choose the class valedictorian. Far from improving, the difficulty seemed to be getting steadily worse.

The final round in this fracas was precipitated by a decision to revise the curriculum of the Seminary in 1825. Woods, Stuart, and Porter were agreed that the first year should be devoted to the study of the Bible, the second to Theology, and the third to Sacred Rhetoric. They were also agreed that Church History should play a secondary role. This was not simply because they wanted more time for their own fields; they did not want the students exposed to the long line of heresies, church disagreements, and sectarian controversies, which would be presented in a course in history, before they had been thoroughly indoctrinated in the basics of Bible study and theology. The majority decided that Church History should be taught in the spring term of the senior year, admittedly a time when the seniors were restless in anticipation of getting pastoral positions after graduation. Despite an appeal to the Trustees—Eliphalet Pearson, his defender, had now died—Murdoch was forced to accept the proposed schedule, and his first spring term with the seniors fulfilled his worst apprehensions. The controversy almost tore the Seminary apart. By 1827 student behavior was getting so out of hand that the Trustees appointed a special committee to look into it. Furthermore, almost all the students signed a memorial demanding that Church History be given a prominent place in the curriculum, but their demand was ignored by faculty and trustees. Finally the special committee held hearings and on the basis of the testimony presented—particularly that of Woods, Stuart, and Porter—recommended that Murdoch should be dismissed. The only charge of substance was that he had neglected to give lectures in Sacred Rhetoric as he was scheduled to do, in 1826-7. The Board of Visitors upheld this one charge, as did the Massachusetts Supreme Judicial Court, to which Murdoch had made a last appeal. Forced to leave Andover, Murdoch went into semiretirement for the rest of his life in New Haven, where he engaged in various scholarly pursuits. It had taken his opponents nearly ten years to get him fired, but they had finally triumphed. He did, however, leave one legacy at Andover. Though never on an equal basis with the other disciplines, Church History became an integral part of the Seminary curriculum from that point on.

In the spring of 1823 a Southern clergyman visited the Seminary and was much impressed by what he found. He thought the buildings "finished with sufficient taste" and estimated the value of the plant at $500,000. He thought the Seminary needed more scholarships for indigent students and more books in the library for the professors, but generally the institution was "a noble one, even in its present state, and does the highest honour to its founders, and to the public spirit of the citizens of Massachusetts. In this particular they do certainly go beyond any others in the United States, and perhaps are not surpassed by any people in the world." Despite his general enthusiasm, he had reservations about the course of instruction. He took issue with Moses Stuart's insistence that the students be allowed unlimited freedom to read in the field of theology, including the works of atheists, free thinkers, and critics of the Christian religion. The visitor feared that this would simply lead to confusion among the students and result in their accepting the *ipse dixit* of the professor. He was disturbed, also, because the students could go forth to preach the gospel without a creed. He admitted that in 99 percent of the cases the creed was orthodox, but he thought that the graduates, like the professors, should be required to subscribe to a definite set of beliefs. The visitor was less than enthusiastic about what he called "pulpit eloquence." The New England tradition, he felt, had produced a dry analytical method of preaching. "*Feeling*, instead of being exemplified, is analyzed. The mixed emotions and complex motives of human beings are . . . taken to pieces, much in the way a chemist separates the different parts of a compound substance subjected to experiment." He doubted if speaking orations ever made a man eloquent and thought that too much emphasis was placed on physical movements in speaking and ornaments of style rather than on "the deep tone of powerful moral feeling, which moves the heart, which agitates and sways the passions as the trees of the forest are agitated by a mighty wind." In some areas he thought the students poorly prepared. For one thing, their minds were not sufficiently imbued with classical literature, and thus they lacked "maturity and delicacy of taste." More important, "There is a sad want of acquaintance with the literature and spirit of the age. Causes are continually at work to modify the state of public feeling, and change the face of society; and all the while students and professors are shut up in their halls or chambers, poring now over the writings of the fathers, and then over some obsolete metaphysical subtleties, ignorant of almost all that is going on in the literary world around them." After voicing these criticisms, the visitor hastened to add that Andover was so strong that it had nothing to fear from censure. And he closed on a note that is wistful in the light of what was to come. He believed that institutions like Andover would draw more closely the bonds of affection between North and South, since the professors had a "strong feeling of brotherly kindness towards southern people," and that the result would be a stronger union and the belief by all that the United States formed a common country.[42]

In the 1830's the Seminary became convulsed over the slavery question, and after prolonged discussion took a decided position in opposition to the abolitionists or immediatists.[43] As a result of this decision the institution and its professors came under bitter attack from the more radical elements in the antislavery movement. John Greenleaf Whittier, for example, could write in 1835, "Anti-slavery is going on well in spite of mobs, Andover Seminary, and *rum*." Yet the position of the professors was by no means in support of the institution of slavery; on the contrary they were sympathetic to the plight of the Negro slave in the United States and hoped that emancipation could be brought about gradually. They were interested, too, in the possibilities of colonization in Africa as a solution to the problem. But above all, they were concerned lest immersion in a highly emotional national issue should divert their students from their main purpose—preparing themselves to be Christian ministers of the gospel.

Student interest in the slavery question dated back to the founding of the undergraduate Society of Inquiry in 1811. At the start the Society discussed the problems of slavery in general, read accounts of the institution as it existed in the South, and wrote essays on their findings. In the 1820's interest was stepped up with the formation of the Committee on Colonization of the Society of Inquiry, which moved toward more direct action in support of their cause. The Committee became closely associated with the American Colonization Society, helped to distribute literature on the subject, and wrote a series of annual reports on their activities. During summer vacations some of the students worked as agents for the American Colonization Society, helping to spread their message, and in 1833 Andover students pledged $3,000 to emancipate and expatriate one hundred Kentucky slaves. In the same year, however, the colonization forces among the students were challenged by the formation of an Antislavery Society that believed in the necessity of immediate emancipation. Though small in numbers, they vigorously attacked the concept of colonization, believing it to be a program of expediency backed by people who simply wanted to remove the Negroes from American society. They were alarmed at what the slavery issue was doing to the country and believed that if the question were left to the politicians, serious sectional strife would result. All the more reason for Christian ministers to take up the question. They sought to advance their position through persuasion and peaceful discussion and hoped through these means to achieve a settlement of the difficult national problem. Until 1835 the professors at the Seminary did not interfere with these student movements. Though they were probably all supporters of colonization, they preferred to let the students engage in their activities without faculty control. As a result, by 1835 most of the students were colonizationists, with a small minority taking a stronger antislavery position.

All this was changed by the arrival in Andover of the famous British abolitionist George Thompson early in 1835. So powerful was his message that the Seminary students insisted that he speak at their chapel, a permission that was reluctantly given. A dialogue ensued between Thompson and various students in which the former showed himself extraordinarily skillful at answering questions on his position. So effective was his presentation that a local newspaper reported that "almost if not quite every Student in the Seminary, has become an Abolitionist." Although this was a gross exaggeration, for only about one fourth of the students supported the Abolitionist position, the faculty were dismayed and immediately called a meeting of the entire student body to discuss the dangers to the Seminary of continued controversy over slavery. Such controversy, the professors believed, would seriously split the institution, distract the students from their studies, jeopardize a student's chances of securing a position after graduation if he were identified with a radical position on slavery, and threaten the position of the Seminary as a broadly based orthodox institution by alienating individual churches and potential benefactors. It is an interesting commentary on the undergraduates of the day that they accepted the faculty recommendation almost unanimously and agreed to defer taking a position on the slavery question until after graduation. That was to remain the Seminary's policy right up to the Civil War.[44]

The Abolitionists continued to bring their message to Andover, in hope of enlisting at least some of the students in their cause. Such leaders as Garrison and Thompson, James G. Birney, Theodore Weld, and the Grimké sisters visited Andover to speak to large and interested audiences. Nor was their work without effect. At one time it was estimated that one third of the Seminary students supported their position, although they remained faithful to their agreement not to engage in active work in support of Abolition. To the professors this development was seriously diverting the students from their basic ministerial training. Moses Stuart wrote. "The baleful spirit . . . of the anti-slavery dispute, has nearly destroyed every thing of solid progress for the last six or seven weeks." To strengthen their position the Professors appealed to the Board of Trustees to give them authority over informal undergraduate societies, and though they probably had this power anyway, the Trustees passed a specific vote of authorization. From then on, whatever the opinions of individual students, the antislavery dispute gradually faded into the background.

If one accepts the desirability of sending American Protestants to faraway lands to convert the inhabitants to Christianity, the Missionary activities of graduates of the Andover Theological Seminary must remain one of the institution's proudest boasts.[45] As one writer has put it, "No more compelling is the call of the South to the waterfowl when summer wanes, than was the Macedonian call from heathendom to the dormitories and classrooms of Andover Hill." The original impetus for the movement came from Williams College, where, in 1808, a group of students under the leadership of Samuel J. Mills first drew up a "Constitution of a Society of Brethren" to be dedicated to work with the heathen. According to tradition, the Constitution was adopted under a haystack, where the founders had been driven by a sudden shower of rain. Though the original members scattered after graduation from Williams, the Society itself transferred to Andover, where in 1811, the students formed the "Society of Inquiry on the Subject of Missions." The year before, a group of these students had prevailed upon the Massachusetts Association of Congregational Churches to establish the American Board of Commissioners for Foreign Missions, and with the backing of this organization, financial and otherwise, it became possible to start actual missionary work. Shortly afterward, two Andover graduates, Adoniram Judson and Samuel Newell, with their wives, set sail from Salem in the *Caravan*, the flagship of a mighty fleet, to bring the gospel to the subcontinent of India. After the war of 1812 Andover men sailed to Ceylon, where the difficulties were so great at first that it was reported that "More missionaries died than there were natives baptized." In part because a native of Hawaii, Obookiah, had been at Andover off and on, a third mission was sent to the Sandwich Islands, while a fourth penetrated the Near East, finally making its headquarters at Beirut. In ten years twenty Andover men had gone to bring the Christian faith to heathen lands.

From these humble beginnings the missionary movement expanded steadily throughout the nineteenth century until it almost literally covered the globe. Spectacular progress was made in India, where, by the middle of the century, the missionaries had established central boarding schools and village schools, where new churches were built and more emphasis placed on preaching, and where a program for training native clergymen was undertaken. Fired by the example of Moses Stuart on Andover Hill, printing houses to publish books in the native languages were set up, issuing such works as a Marathi edition of the Bible, a Tamil-English dictionary, and translations, grammars, and commentaries in Turkish, Bulgarian, Armenian, and Chaldee. Similar publications were prepared for the Kanakas of Hawaii and the Cherokees of the southern United States. In the latter half of the century missionary activities were stepped up in China, with Andover graduates as usual playing a prominent part. Some of these had received medical training and made signal contributions to solving the problems of famine and disease in the land of the Manchus. William S. Ament was in Peking when the Boxer Rebellion took place. Despite the difficulties and dangers of that time he could write home, "I would rather ride a little donkey from village to village and sleep on bricks at night, with the privilege of testifying of the Grace of God and communicating a little hope to the dull lives of the people than anything else." One of the proudest accomplishments of the whole movement was the establishment of Doshisha College, a Christian institution in Japan that is still functioning effectively, founded by a Japanese graduate of Andover named Joseph

Neesima. In a very literal sense the influence of the missionaries was felt from "Greenland's icy mountains to India's coral strands."

There were drama and heartache and unbelievable obstacles in the careers of almost all these courageous men. William Goodell, for instance, a graduate of Phillips Academy in the Class of 1813 and of the Andover Theological Seminary in 1820, was born in a two-room farmhouse, the son of a poor farming family in Templeton, Massachusetts, and had never considered getting an education until a revival movement swept the town in the early 1800's.[46] As a result of this, he and his father determined to investigate the possibilities of a good education for the boy, who, accordingly, walked and hitched rides some sixty miles to Phillips Academy, where he conferred with Principal John Adams. The Principal explained that there were at the moment no places on the scholarship list, but urged the boy to return in the fall and hope for an opening. The following fall the boy strapped a trunk to his back containing all his wordly possesions and walked the whole sixty miles to Andover, arriving with an extremely sore back. Though there was still no place on the scholarship list, he managed to find lodging with a poor shoemaker and the following spring was overjoyed to hear that Lieutenant-Governor William Phillips had picked up the tab for those boys who had not yet been placed on the scholarship list. His expenses for his senior year were taken care of in a rather bizarre way. Solomon Goodell, a relative of the boy from Jamaica, Vermont, had written Principal Adams and asked if the boy were worth raising. Apparently receiving an affirmative answer, he sent a yoke of oxen to the school, with a note addressed to Principal Adams that read, "Sir, I send you a pair of fat oxen for William Goodell, in your school." From then on Goodell's financial problems seemed to diminish and he was able to graduate from Dartmouth College and the Seminary without serious interruption to his career.

Goodell's first interest in a missionary calling seems to have been aroused at the ordination of a group of the first five missionaries destined for India, which took place at the Tabernacle Church in Salem on February 6, 1812. Principal Adams had given permission to some of the older Phillips Academy students to attend if they wished, and Goodell and a classmate named Cummings set out for Salem on what was described as the coldest day of the winter. They managed to reach Salem without mishap and found the service an extraordinarily moving one. As he writes, "God was there, and in that great assembly there was, at times, a stillness 'like the stillness of God, when He ariseth in silence to bless the world.' At times the whole great assembly seemed moved as the trees of the wood are moved by a mighty wind. . . . the feelings of the audience, and especially our own, were wrought up to the highest pitch." Inspirational though the ordination was, there was still the journey home to be faced, and this ordeal very nearly ended Goodell's missionary career before it had started. "Long before we reached home, I had ceased to have any control over the muscles of locomotion, but staggered like a paralytic. Some theological students, who had also been at Salem, overtaking us, assisted in supporting me along. Being placed between two of them, and bearing my whole weight upon them, they, by taking turns, succeeded in carrying their load. Through a kind Providence we reached the house where I first boarded at Andover. The family immediately spread a bed for me on the floor, before the fire, and tried to make me comfortable; but I shook and shook, till it seemed as if my nerves and muscles would never again become quiet. It was certainly a wonder I did not become permanently paralyzed by this exposure, excitement and excessive fatigue." The seed planted on this occasion lay dormant for a while, but after graduation from college and the Seminary, Goodell began to consider seriously the career of a missionary.

Goodell first completed his preparation by attending some medical courses at Dartmouth and then for a short period traveled in the West for the American Board of Missions. In 1823 he and a newly acquired wife set sail for the Near East. They stopped first at Malta, which was a kind of headquarters for missionary work in the Mediterranean countries, then proceeded to Beirut, where he founded a mission. In a few years local warfare forced his return to Malta, where he spent some time working with the printing press there in the publication of tracts and translations. Finally, in 1831, he received the order from the American Board that was to determine the rest of his life's work. He was ordered to Constantinople, where he was to work principally with the Armenians, a position he was to hold for close to forty years. Though not strong physically, he seems to have had an ideal temperament for a missionary, exhibiting kindness, common sense, and patience. Nor was his career an easy one. Wars—especially the Crimean War—threatened his work, there was constant danger from disease, at times the Turkish authorities persecuted Christians, and on several occasions there were plots against his life. Yet he stuck to his guns, and after a career of fifty-two years in the Near East, interrupted by only one short return to the United States, he certainly deserves the title of founder of the American Board's work in Turkey. One of his proudest achievements was a translation of the Bible into Armeno-Turkish, a work in which he was assisted by some distinguished Turkish scholars. When he finally returned to this country in his early seventies, after that long and taxing career, it could certainly be said of him that he had fought the good fight.

On the occasion of the hundredth anniversary of the American Board in 1910, the record of graduates of the Andover Theological Seminary in the field of missions was reviewed. In the first ten years every missionary but one was trained on the Hill. In the first fifty years one hundred and twenty-five went abroad, and in the first century, two hundred and forty-eight.

During the course of the celebration some five hundred people journeyed to Andover, where, on the north side of Rabbit Pond, they unveiled a tablet that had been fixed to a large granite boulder. The tablet read:

> In the 'Missionary Woods' once extending to this spot the first missionary students of Andover Seminary walked and talked one hundred years ago, and on this secluded knoll met to pray. In memory of these men . . . whose consecrated purpose to carry the gospel to the heathen world led to the formation of the first American society for foreign missions. In recognition of the 248 missionaries trained in Andover Seminary and in gratitude to Almighty God, this stone is set up in the Centennial year of the American Board, 1910.

"New occasions teach new duties; Time makes ancient good uncouth," writes the poet. In this day the American people are much less certain about the validity of trying to impose their religious beliefs on the inhabitants of foreign lands than they were one hundred years ago. But even though one may challenge the basic assumptions of the Andover missionaries of the nineteenth century, one cannot help admiring their courage, their steadfastness, and their selflessness.

"The New England theology was constructed on the principle that there are certain truths which abide in the very nature of things and condition

17. The Andover Theological Seminary in 1886.

any system of doctrine. Since these truths do not change, an orthodox system of doctrine must not change." This statement by the historian of the Andover Theological Seminary explains why, as the nineteenth century wore on and liberal movements began to sweep through American religions, the institution found it more and more difficult to maintain its original position. From the very beginning the Seminary had been absolutist in the beliefs it required its professors to subscribe to. The Westminster Catechism and the Associate Creed both spelled out in absolutist terms the specifics of the true faith. To insure against possible backsliding by the professors, they were required publicly to acknowledge adherence to the creed every five years, and one of the main functions of the Board of Visitors was to act as a kind of watch and ward society to prevent contaminating doctrines from entering the institution. During the early years of Woods, Stuart, and Porter the Seminary managed to get along with only minor squabbles on doctrinal matters inside the institution. But that there was to be trouble ahead became clear in 1849 when the Reverend Daniel Dana, a Trustee, presented a "Remonstrance" to the Board. Dana, who was a theological reactionary, had been the one Trustee who refused to vote for the merger of the Hopkinsian group with the Andover group when the Seminary was first established, and now, over forty years later, he was convinced that his worst fears had been realized. He started what came to be called the "Andover Fuss." Dana said that he had been disturbed to discover, in examining Andover graduates as candidates for the ministry, that in many instances they had exhibited alarmingly unorthodox views. But his main guns were leveled at the newly appointed professor, Edwards A. Park, who, Dana believed, was a man of very dangerous tendencies. Since Park was to become the acknowledged champion of orthodoxy for the next thirty years, there was more than a touch of irony in Dana's charges. The Seminary, he feared, was becoming "an instrument of corrupting pure gospel truth, and of spreading destructive error through the churches and the community." Park's doctrines "would sweep away almost every doctrine of the Bible" and nullify "the cardinal and fundamental doctrine of natural depravity." That was it—"natural depravity." To think of human beings as potentially good was clearly subversive of the true faith.[47] Much to Dr. Dana's annoyance, the Trustees paid no attention to his Remonstrance, and as a result he published it, in 1853. Though the wider dissemination of his charges caused a flurry in orthodox religious circles, the general conclusion was that the good doctor was in an advanced stage of senility, and he resigned in a rage in 1856. The whole affair might well be considered a ludicrous footnote in the history of American religion were it not for the fact that it highlighted a situation pregnant with trouble for the future.

From 1850 until his retirement in 1881 the dominant figure at the Seminary was Edwards Amassa Park, the "last of the old guard" of New

England theology.[48] Essentially he was an apologist for the old faith, and though he was aware of the challenges of modern criticism, he never let them interfere with his championship of the past. His classroom lectures were masterly expositions of orthodox doctrine, but there was no opportunity for discussion, no thought of challenging the instructor's dicta. In addition to being an outstanding teacher, Park was a powerful preacher, handing down the word from the pulpit with such authority that his audience sat "so still that the buzzing of a fly would have boomed like a cannon." As time went on, Park became more and more set in his ways and less and less tolerant of anyone who crossed him. There were times when he refused to have anything to do with his colleagues on the Seminary faculty, boycotted faculty meetings, and generally behaved in a churlish and unlovely manner. Yet his influence remained undiminished until his retirement, and almost single-handedly he prevented liberal influences from reaching the Hill. One writer claimed that it was Park's "ambition to become the final exponent of New England theology. As a formal system it may almost be said that he did finish it—and it was buried with him."[49]

Yet the liberal influences were knocking at the door. In the last half of the nineteenth century major theological changes were taking place throughout the country. The trend was generally humanistic. Man's capacity for good was stressed, sin was merely human error, natural depravity was

18. The Faculty of the Andover Theological Seminary about 1890.
First Row: William Ladd Ropes, Egbert Coffin Smyth, and John Phelps Taylor. Second Row: Edward Young Hincks, William Jewett Tucker, Charles Cutler Torrey, and George Harris. Third Row: William Henry Ryder, John Wesley Churchill, and George Foot Moore.

drummed out of court, moral education was more important than dogma, the sacraments were slighted, and denominational differences were deemphasized. The prevailing mood was optimistic, humane, confident. Coupled with the changes in belief came a new concern for the "Social Gospel," a desire to improve the human condition, to reform existing abuses, to deal with specific evils in the world. Powerful as Edwards Amassa Park might be, he could not live forever, and once his influence in the Seminary was removed, the forces that he had combated so rigorously moved in.[50]

The group that came to be known as the "Andover Liberals" did not join the Seminary faculty at the same time.[51] As early as 1863 Egbert C. Smyth had been appointed Professor of Ecclesiastical History. Smyth was willing to accept the creed and made no attempt to challenge Park while the latter was on the faculty, but he insisted that no Christian doctrine could be understood apart from its history, and he introduced a fresh approach to a subject that had been hitherto neglected to a large extent. About the time of Park's retirement the liberal professors were strengthened by George Harris (later President of Amherst) in Christian Theology, William Jewett Tucker in Sacred Rhetoric, George F. Moore in Hebrew, Edward Y. Hincks in Theology, and John P. Gulliver in a professorship that said much about the coming changes in the Seminary—Relations of Christianity and Science. In 1884 this group established the *Andover Review*, a liberal theological quarterly that for the next ten years served as a means of disseminating the views of the Andover group to a wide audience. Indeed, a collection of articles from this quarterly, published separately under the title *Progressive Orthodoxy*, was a fresh statement of new viewpoints in Congregational theology. More important, perhaps, the group moved to revise the Seminary curriculum. They instituted a postgraduate program for students who wished to go beyond the required minimum; they broadened the undergraduate offerings to introduce such subjects as Biblical Archaeology and generally to give the students a wider experience in a variety of different courses; they introduced a modified elective system —the first of the Seminaries to do so—and, finally, Professor Tucker introduced a program of education in the field which enabled students to study at first hand some of the pressing social problems of the day. Interest in this last change led to the establishment of Andover House—now the South End House—in Boston, where theologues lived and worked with the poor of the city. The changes introduced in the 1880's and early 1890's at the Seminary soon made the atmosphere and training a far cry from what it had been since its founding in 1808.

Ironically, the changes that were bringing Andover up to date with the problems of the day contributed to the Seminary's undoing. The first sign of trouble came in 1880 when Professor Tucker, in acknowledging adherence to the creed, said he believed that "No confession so elaborate and with such intent may assume to be the final expression of the truth or an expression equally fitted in language or tone to all times." Two years later two professors resigned because they objected to subscribing to the creed every five years. There was further trouble when Newman Smyth, though approved by the Trustees, was turned down by the Board of Visitors. All of this, however, was mere preamble to the so-called "heresy" trial that started in 1886, when the Board of Visitors brought charges against Egbert Smyth, William Tucker, George Harris, Edward Hincks, and John Churchill on the ground that their teachings and writings were "not in harmony with sound doctrine as expressed in the Creed which the Founders and Donors of this institution made the unalterable condition of the gifts which were committed in sacred trust to this Board." The Board of Visitors acted in this instance without consulting the Phillips Academy Trustees, only one of whom, Dr. Wellman, was in sympathy with the action. One member of the Board of Visitors abstained in four of the five cases, but Egbert Smyth was singled out as guilty for suggesting that the Bible was not the only rule of faith, that no man has the power to repent without knowledge of God in Christ, and that there is probation after death for all men who do not decisively reject Christ during earthly life. Professor Smyth appealed to the Supreme Judicial Court of Massachusetts, which set aside the verdict against Smyth on the ground that the Trustees had not been allowed to participate in the case. A final attempt to revive the issue was made in 1892 by the Board of Visitors, but they finally decided to dismiss the case without passing on its merits. Though the liberals stuck to their guns throughout this whole controversy, it was harmful to the institution. Enrollment began to drop off despite the able group of teachers who were now in undisputed control. In addition, the Seminary began to suffer from its relatively isolated position, at one time considered one of its great advantages. With the growing emphasis on the social gospel and particularly on the problems of the city, many thought that an institution located in the heart of twentieth-century America would better serve the purposes of theological education. For whatever cause, the Seminary's existence at Andover was soon to end.

Throughout the nineteenth century the Andover Theological Seminary set the tone for life on Andover Hill. During the period Phillips Academy was a kind of poor relation, much less generously endowed with buildings and money. For most of this period the primary interest of the Trustees was the Seminary rather than the Academy. In the 1890's, for example, the Trustee Records contain one wistful note after another, written by the then clerk, Cecil Franklin Patch Bancroft: "No Academy business was transacted."[52] Finally, the rigid orthodoxy of the Seminary was transferred to the School as well. An article on the Phillips Exeter Academy which appeared in *Harper's* in 1877 stresses the point. After commenting on the relative liberality of John Phillips and some of the early Exeter Trustees, the author goes on to say:

The interpretation of the constitution was therefore likely to be less rigid than was the case at Andover; and as the establishment of a theological school at Andover served to confirm the religious element in the school there, so the freedom from such alliances at Exeter, and the affiliation which the school there had with Harvard University, tended to make the Exeter Academy less positively religious in its influence, and to concentrate the energies of the school upon its special work of preparing boys for admission to college. The strictness and careful conformity to theological standards which prevailed at Andover gave place in Exeter to a certain freedom of government and a regard for those principles and habits which we are wont to speak of as related to ethics, big and little, rather than to religion.[53]

While there were undoubtedly more similarities than differences between Andover and Exeter in the nineteenth century, the author's point is well taken, and it is probably not too much to say that the modern Andover could never have developed into the school that it is today had the Theological Seminary remained on the Hill in the twentieth century.

CHAPTER SEVEN

THE DAYS OF SAMUEL FARRAR

T HERE ARE often periods in the history of educational institutions when the titular head is not the dominant force in determining policy. The period from 1810 to 1840 was such a one in the history of Phillips Academy, when Samuel Farrar, the school treasurer, ran things rather than the Principals. Farrar was certainly a conservative—in most ways the epitome of the old New England Calvinism. Yet, paradoxically, it was he who conceived and executed the important innovations of this period. There have been few Principals in the history of the School who were more dedicated than Samuel Farrar, its treasurer from 1803 to 1840. Farrar was born on a farm in Lincoln, Massachusetts, on 13 December 1773, and spent much of his time during his youth working on the farm.[1] The most eventful episode during these early years occurred when he fell from the roof of the barn and broke his leg. Characteristically, "he made no sound, but crept along to the house, dragging his broken leg the best way he could." After secondary schooling at New Ipswich Academy in New Hampshire,[2] his family was able to send him to Harvard, where he graduated in 1797. By the merest chance, he came to Andover. Judge Samuel Phillips, Jr., had engaged a classmate of Farrar's, Daniel Appleton White of Salem, to be an assistant at Phillips Academy the following year. During the Commencement exercises, which the Judge attended as an Overseer, White gave a speech in which he questioned the orthodox doctrine of human depravity. After the ceremonies, the Judge suggested to White that if he would like to be released from his assistantship, the Judge would not object. White resigned, and when the Judge asked him to name some one to replace him, he chose Farrar.[3] Like most assistants during this period, Farrar spent only one year at Phillips Academy, but he must have impressed the Phillipses, for he became a member of their family. At this time, as in later years, he suffered from dyspepsia, and according to tradition Madam Phoebe Phillips took pains to see that he got a proper diet and generally looked after his health.[4] After a year Farrar returned to Cambridge, where he received an A.M. in 1800. He served as a tutor during the academic year 1800–01 and, determined to study law, spent the next year in Springfield, Massachusetts, in the law office of George Bliss.[5] He then returned to Andover early in 1802 to hang out his shingle and become a country lawyer.

Farrar arrived in Andover just as Judge Phillips was dying—indeed he witnessed the Judge's last bequest, made just a few days before his death.[6] It is clear that he must have been a great comfort to Phoebe Phillips in the years ahead, for he became once again a member of the family. The other Trustees also must have had confidence in him, for they elected him to the Board in November 1802.[7] The following year, when Oliver Wendell resigned as Treasurer of the Board, Farrar was chosen to succeed him, a position he would hold until 1840.[8] From the start, he was a dedicated and generous supporter of both Phillips Academy and the Andover Theological Seminary. In 1807 he offered to contribute three years' back salary—the munificent sum of $450.00—to a fund to be invested for the benefit of the school.[9] At the time of the founding of the Theological Seminary, when Madam Phoebe Phillips and her son John were having difficulty meeting their pledge to erect Phillips Hall, he came to their aid. His daughter remembers seeing in his account book entries that said simply "Ch----y" [charity] with no statement as to the object aided.[10] His legal acumen proved invaluable when the complicated negotiations leading to the founding of the Andover Theological Seminary were taking place; the original draft of the Associate Statutes was in his handwriting.[11] Madam Phoebe Phillips, near the end of her life, experienced financial difficulties, partly because of the drain placed on her resources by the cost of Phillips Hall and partly because of her son John's business reverses. Squire Farrar —as he was called—again helped. In 1812 he finished building a new house, located on the site of the present Archaeology Building. As soon as it was completed, he asked Madam Phillips to move in and spend her remaining days there. Even though she died that same year, it must have been a comfort to her to know that she was provided for.[12] Two years after her death, Samuel Farrar married Mrs. Phoebe Hooker, widow of the Reverend Asahel Hooker, and established his family in the new house, where he was to live for the next fifty years.

Squire Farrar had a precise lawyer's mind, and it offended him to discover legal inconsistencies in matters connected with the Academy and the Seminary. When he tangled with the Massachusetts General Court in 1815, however, he was forced to admit defeat. The matter started in 1807, at the time of the founding of the Seminary, when the Trustees petitioned the Massachusetts legislature to be allowed to hold more property than was specified in the original Act of Incorporation in 1780. The legislature obliged, with an act passed on 19 June 1807 which allowed the Trustees to hold additional property with an income of up to five thousand dollars.[13] Increased gifts to the Seminary soon made it clear, however, that the Trustees had not asked for enough, and in 1814 a trustee committee came back to the well with a new petition.[14] Once again the legislature obliged with "An Act in addition to an Act entitled 'An Act in addition to an Act entitled an Act to incorporate the trustees of Phillips Academy in Andover.'" This time the General Court enlarged the power of the Trustees to an amount of property the income from which should not exceed $20,000. They put a hooker at the end:

> provided that no student belonging to the said institution sustaining a fair moral character shall be deprived of any privileges of said institution or be subjected to the forfeiture of any aid which has been granted by the said institution for the purpose of enabling him to prosecute his studies or be denied the usual testimonial on closing his studies on the grounds that his interpretations of the scriptures differ from those which are contained or may hereafter be contained in the Articles of faith adopted by said institution.[15]

This clause struck hard at some of the basic provisions in the Constitution and Associate Statues of the Theological Seminary, and accordingly Squire Farrar and Trustee Samuel H. Walley, a Boston merchant, were appointed as a committee to petition the Massachusetts legislature for a repeal of the disputed clause. In their petition it was pointed out that the Constitution of the Seminary provided that none but Protestants should be admitted, while the Statutes of the Associate Foundation limited the students to Congregationalists and Presbyterians. This did not jibe with the disputed provision of the act, which "provides that all students indiscriminately, of whatever denomination or religious opinions, shall be entitled to the privileges of the said Institution." The petitioners therefore prayed that "this incompatibility may be removed by the repeal of that part of the said Act" so that the Trustees of Phillips Academy could manage their Seminary "with the freedom which is indulged to other similar institutions."[16] The request seemed reasonable, but at this time the Massachusetts legislature was reflecting more liberal trends in political and religious matters and was unsympathetic to the old Calvinism. After what a Boston newspaper called "a very eloquent and animated debate," the motion to repeal was lost, 126–90.[17] Although there is no record of any member of a bizarre religious sect coming to the Seminary as a result of the act, the Trustees—and particularly Samuel Farrar—had to accept what was, in part at least, a political decision on the part of the legislature.

After 1814 until his retirement in the 1840's Squire Farrar became more and more powerful in Phillips Academy and the community generally. What one writer has described as "his methodical habits, and his cautious and exact manner of doing business"[18] gained him the confidence of all he dealt with. As Treasurer of Phillips Academy he had charge of the funds of both the School and the Seminary, and he managed these funds with rare acumen. He believed that the best investments he could make would be in loans to local farmers and businessmen, and from all reports he had scarcely a single default during his entire term. Aside from his responsibility for school finances, Squire Farrar was a combined business manager and superintendant of buildings and grounds. He supervised the construction of the first buildings of the Theological Seminary and of the professors' houses. When the Academy building burned down in 1818, he saw to the construction of Bulfinch Hall. He was clerk of the works when Samaritan House was built and may well have designed Stowe House. Finally, he oversaw the construction of the Double Brick on Main Street. For most of these buildings the design was not his, but he had an itch to be his own architect, and before his career was over he was to make additional important contributions to the Academy plant. He was an enthusiastic tree planter and followed the policy established by Samuel Phillips of landscaping the Hill with plantings, particularly of elms. The present Elm Arch was laid out by him.

As if this were not enough, he took a leading part in the management of other local institutions. He was the first president of the Andover Bank

19. Samuel Farrar, Treasurer of Phillips Academy from 1803 to 1840. From a portrait by Joseph Eames on loan to the Trustees of Phillips Academy by the Trustees of the Andover-Newton Theological Seminary.

when it was established in 1826, and he remained so for thirty years. When a group of citizens met to consider the establishment of a female seminary, Abbot Academy, in Andover, the Squire took a leading part and loaned the new institution the money to construct the first building. He served on the Abbot Board of Trustees from its founding until 1851.[19] Other groups and individuals would call on him for help. In 1818 he was asked to help elect the "federal republican" ticket in Essex County.[20] In 1811 a Yale official asked his advice about "Rumford's cooking apparatus," apparently under consideration for adoption in New Haven.[21] Finally, as a change from business affairs, he was for many years librarian of the Theological Seminary. With all these manifold activities, it is not surprising that Squire Farrar became one of the most respected men in the community and that his opinion would not be opposed lightly.

During these years the Squire developed a life style that made him the talk of the town. Precision, discipline, and routine were the qualities he prized and built his life on. He was always an old-fashioned figure, dressed in black with a frilled shirt. His daily regimen was rigid, to put it mildly. Precisely at 6:09 (not 6:10) A.M. each morning family prayers were held—which meant that in the wintertime it was still dark. The Squire would stand by the table on which was placed the family Bible and lead the prayers with one hand resting on the back of his chair. Either before or after prayers he would spend some time in the woodhouse sawing wood, primarily for exercise, though this practice had to be abandoned as he grew older. After breakfast he would retire to his office chamber and read from his boyhood Bible, which had his favorite texts underlined, and afterward set out on the first of his daily walks, downtown to the bank. On all his walks he invariably followed the same route at precisely the same time, so that, it was said, people could set their clocks by him. He would return for dinner at 12:30 and walk back and forth in the south parlor of his house for a little while. Then up to his office room until time for his afternoon walk. It was said that on his walks he always carried a cane with an iron ferrule that he kept precisely nine inches off the ground. According to tradition it had touched the ground only twice in his lifetime. To vary the routine, on some days he went on a third walk before supper. During most of his career he took his evening meal by himself upstairs. It was always the same—bread and butter with a glass of water. But even the Squire could slip up occasionally. It was reported that his clock had run down *three* times in forty years. If variety is the spice of life, the Squire's was unseasoned. As one who knew him well wrote, when asked to give incidents from his life, "I think I never knew a life that had fewer."[22] From the foregoing it might seem that Farrar was no more than a very efficient treasurer and business manager, but he was much more. In the course of his career he was responsible for important *educational* innovations. Indeed, despite his extreme conservatism in other matters, he was the only innovator in what was otherwise a very static period in the history of Phillips Academy, as will be made clear.

John Adams, Principal from 1810 to 1833, was born in Canterbury, Connecticut, on 18 September 1772, the eldest of ten children of a successful farmer in that town. As a boy he had his full share of farm chores and was early given a good measure of responsibility. On one occasion, when he was nine, he was sent to Providence to market some butter, only to be cheated on the price by a kind-looking lady. Until his marriage he vowed that he would never trust a woman again. On another occasion, when fifteen, he drove a flock of his father's sheep ninety miles to Boston and never lost a head. "Take care of the ringleaders and the rest will follow of themselves" was his maxim in sheep-herding and one he applied later to schoolmastering. In 1791 his family sent him to Yale, where, in contrast to his later piety, he proved a very gay blade. He was reputed to be the best dancer in his class. He wore a powdered wig and queue, knee breeches, shoes with silver buckles, and a three-cornered hat. Nor did the subject of a speech he gave at commencement foreshadow his later life. It was entitled the "Benefits of Theatrical Establishments." After graduation he returned to Canterbury, to find his mother seriously sick with an eye infection. At her request he agreed to teach in the local schools so that he could nurse her properly, an arrangement that he maintained for three years. One of these summers his father, needing a hired hand, asked John if he would work for him, thinking that perhaps a Yale graduate would shun hard manual labor, but the young man accepted the job with a will. Just before his mother died, a charming young woman named Elizabeth Ripley came to visit in Canterbury; it was apparently love at first sight, and some months later the two were married. In 1801, after his mother's death, he was called to head Plainfield Academy, then in what was described as a "sickly condition." In two years Adams restored the School, but the stay in Plainfield had its tragic side; his eldest son, Gamaliel Ripley, died at the age of two, and it is from this event that the beginning of his piety can be dated. In 1803, because of the reputation of Plainfield, he was called to Colchester Academy, where he was equally successful at building up the School. Under his leadership its reputation reached well beyond Connecticut, and a number of Southern students attended. In 1810, however, he got into a dispute with the trustees over a matter of discipline. He insisted that in this area he must have a free hand, and when the trustees refused his request, he resigned. Thus, when he was called to Phillips Academy, he was an experienced schoolmaster of thirty-eight, with a growing family (there were eventually ten children) and a steadily growing concern for the moral education of his students.[23]

The new Principal was an imposing figure. He has been described as "erect, handsome, of good presence, the habitual sternness of his expres-

20. John Adams, Fourth Principal of Phillips Academy. From a portrait by an unknown artist, in the possession of the Trustees of Phillips Academy.

sion relieved by the humor which lurked in his full blue eyes." Another remembers him coming into church "with the prestige of one born to command . . . his great ivory headed cane coming in before him and ringing down with an emphasis not to be mistaken."[24]

The Principal was not the only Adams to make an impression on Andover Hill. His wife was one of the kindest women in the community, ever ready to nurse the sick and comfort the unfortunate, and her garden at the back of the present Hardy House, where they lived, was a delight to all beholders. With her ten children—"Mrs. Adam's children made a flight of steps which seemed to reach the stars," wrote one friend—one might think that she had enough young people in her house, but there were usually five or six Phillips Academy students boarding there as well. A pillar of strength in the running of the household was the family maid, Betsey Cleveland, who was almost a second mother to the family.[25] Principal Adams found the highly religious atmosphere on the Hill completely to his liking, and it was not long before he joined the group of Seminary professors who met regularly in Phelps House to discuss the founding of such organizations as the American Education Society, the American Tract Society, and the American Temperance Society. There is no evidence that he took a leading part in any of these movements, but he was apparently an accepted and respected member of the group.[26] In order to get away from his duties as Principal, Mr. Adams purchased some farm land near the school and used to drive over to it in his shay. There were two houses on the property that provided him with some income, and in addition, supervision of the estate gave him an outdoors interest that became his chief relaxation.[27] In short, it was not long after their arrival that the Adams family was firmly settled in the Andover community, accepted and respected by all.

As a schoolmaster Principal Adams was methodical and strict. Josiah Quincy the younger wrote of him:

> He was an excellent man with no distinguishing traits. He was very religious, but had no literary tastes. His classical attainments enabled him to fit boys for college, but went no further. He was particular in the observance of all religious exercises, both in the family and in the school, and did all he could to promote the moral and spiritual interests of his pupils.[28]

The following is a description of the daily routine of school as it was practiced in the 1820's:

> For morning prayers the scholars assembled in the academy, where two desks upon separate platforms were built for the principal and his assistant; the floor was an inclined plane; the desks of the scholars had movable lids; the monitors, all older boys, at the appointed time rapped down the lids, calling "Order!" Mr. Adams arose and pro-

nounced the invocation, a selection from the Scriptures was read with some of the notes from Scott's commentary, the hymn was given out, in the singing of which all were expected to unite, the music being led by a violin, a most impressive prayer was offered, and the discipline of the school attended to, after which there was a loud call for the "Class in Daboll's Arithmetic!" Mr. Adams and Mr. Clement heard classes upon their respective platforms; two other teachers, usually students from the seminary, heard recitations in the adjoining rooms; a writing and a music master each visited the school once a week . . . every Monday morning a class recited in Mason's Self-knowledge, and on Saturdays a parsing exercise was held, in which the grammatical antagonists were matched against each other very much in the style of an old-fashioned spelling bee . . . on the appointed day the principal solemnly ascended the step-ladder and wound up the school clock in the presence of the scholars, making some comment upon the motto inscribed upon the dial, "Youth is the seed time of life."[29]

It was not to be expected that a man as conservative as John Adams would plump for any radical change in curriculum. The only time during his term when the matter was discussed was in 1820 when a Trustee Committee composed of Adams and Josiah Quincy the elder recommended to the Board the study of twenty different subjects. Thirteen were Greek and Latin—grammar, Caesar, Virgil, and the like; two were English, though the course in English composition was to be held only once every three weeks; two were Mathematics: one, Geography; one, Declamation, to be held Wednesday evenings; and one, the study of religious texts like Mason's *Self-Knowledge*. For students who were advanced in the Classics, special programs for the study of more difficult classical authors could be set up at the discretion of the Principal. It was a regimen that Eliphalet Pearson, then President of the Board, must have supported heartily.[30]

In 1818 the Trustees approved the granting of the forerunner of the modern diploma. Every student of "fair character" who had passed all examinations on the prescribed course of study and paid all his bills was entitled to receive a certificate from the Principal, except that scholarship boys had either to pay the money lent to them or get permission from the Trustee Committee on Charity Scholars before receiving their certificates.[31] Aside from these relatively minor changes, the routine and curriculum of Phillips Academy remained unchanged while John Adams was Principal.

For all his benign and avuncular appearance, Adams was a strict disciplinarian who "ruled not a little by the ferule,"[32] and he was ably abetted in his use of corporal punishment by his Assistant, Jonathan Clement, who, unlike most previous assistants, remained at the Academy for ten years, from 1819 to 1829. A former student describes the disciplinary system as follows:

The doctrine of a cruel Jehovah, who had survived the purpose for which Judaism created him, naturally led to an imitation of his methods on the part of our preceptors. There were two of them, Adams and Clement. I am not quite sure if I spell the name of the latter correctly. If so, he notoriously belied it. It was an almost invariable rule with them that one or more boys should be called up on the platform to be feruled after morning prayers. The practice seemed to our tyrants to be a sweet accompaniment of devotion. I remember that Mr. Adams, who usually "led in prayer", had a peculiar way of blinking his eyes, so that about half the time they were closed as if he was in the presence of the Almighty, and during the other half he could catch some boy in a misdemeanor.

Moses Stuart, the son of the great theological professor, was always in mischief; and this was almost a foregone conclusion of the prayer: "And thine, three persons in one God, be all the glory forever and ever, amen.—Moses Stuart, come up and hold out your hand." While the hand and heart of Moses had become so callous that he took his punishment most philosophically, it was not so with all the rest of us. We often yelled with the pain and shed tears at the degradation.[33]

The most famous disciplinary case that occurred under the Adams regime was the beating that Oliver Wendell Holmes received at the hands of Jonathan Clement. Just what Holmes's offense was has never been determined, but the punishment was unforgettable:

I was subjected to the severest castigation known, I believe, in the annals of punishment in that institution, such as made a sensation among all the delicate females of the vicinity, and caused young men to utter violent threats, and was, in fact, almost the occasion of a riot. It was an unfortunate display of temper on the part of one of the instructors.[34]

A fellow student remembers Holmes's stocism:

What a noble boy he was! Clement would have stopped if he had only said he was sorry, but he wouldn't say it. There he stood, and let him welt him. He never flinched nor cried; but he has carried the memory of it through his life, all the same.[35]

This system of discipline, thoroughly documented, is at strange variance with a set of rules that Adams himself drew up for the government of a School. Among his maxims are: "Never *threaten*; . . . never reprove, never punish a child in the presence of others . . . Never punish a child who criminates himself rather than tell a falsehood; Never deceive a child."[36] In a statement he wrote on teaching, there is little of the stern disciplinarian.[37] Yet in practice it is clear that he was a firm believer in the "Spare the rod" principle.

"Mr. Adams was, by all his views, habits, and impulses, a *revival* man, and was never happier than when he saw a revival beginning and going forward. His favorite hymns were in that strain. He often conversed personally with individuals on the subject of personal piety."[38] All who knew John Adams agree that this was his major concern in life. As another puts it, "Never before was such a powerful religious influence exerted upon the school; the spirituality of the principal was like a strong and penetrating atmosphere. Mr. Adams held prayer meetings at his house for the benefit of pupils, and tried to present the claims of religion personally to every scholar; revivals in religion were frequent and lasting in their effect, nor has any previous administration been so powerful in stimulating pupils to become ministers of the gospel."[39] It should be remembered that the revival meetings and prayer groups were in addition to a full schedule of religious exercises which was a basic part of the school's program. At one of the revivals a group of boys began meeting in the attic of the present Bulfinch Hall in what they called "the Academy Loft prayer meeting." One who attended describes the quality of the gathering: "We held for a long time what might be called a boys' prayer meeting in the third story of the academy building, an unfinished loft and very retired. As I remember them they were excellent meetings. There were members of the seminary in those years who took great interest in us boys and encouraged any appearance of a religious awakening."[40] Not all the boys were enthusiastic, however. Josiah Quincy the younger had this reaction:

> During the six years I spent in Andover there were several revivals of religion. The master believed in their utility and did everything in his power to encourage them. We had prayer meetings before school, after school, and in recess, and a strong influence was exerted to make us attend them. . . . One summer's day, after a session of four hours, the master dismissed school in the usual form. No sooner had he done so than he added: "There will now be a prayer meeting: those who wish to lie down in everlasting burning may go; the rest will stay." It is probable that a good many boys wanted to get out of doors. Two of them only had the audacity to rise and leave the room [one was Quincy]. . . . But no sooner was the prayer meeting over than Mr. Adams sought me out, asked pardon for the dreadful alternative he had presented, and burst into a flood of tears. He said with deep emotion that he feared that I had committed the unpardonable sin and that he had been the cause. His sincerity and faith were most touching; and his manliness in confessing his error and asking pardon from his pupil makes the record of the occurrence an honor to his memory.[41]

The records of the Board of Trustees during the Adams years reveal the same static quality that characterized the School as a whole. For the most part the Board dealt with routine matters, and it was only some fortuitous event like the burning of the Academy Building in 1818 that would galvanize them into action. The standard annual meeting consisted of an opening prayer, the reading of the Constitution, the election of officers, the licensing of Andover townspeople to keep boarders, the choosing of boys to receive scholarships, and the approval of the Treasurer's Report. There were Committees appointed, especially a Select Committee to visit and inspect the Academy. Aside from these matters, the Board concerned itself with trivial matters, though some of these were from time to time delegated to the Committee of Exigencies. Concerned about the danger of fire, the Board ordered a fire engine, had the well checked, and authorized Samuel Farrar to purchase one hundred fire buckets, six ladders of three different lengths, six firehooks, and four lightening rods. Ironically, all this was done before the Academy fire and was not enough to save the building.[42] The Board was also exercised about the perennial problem of the School stoves and appointed committees to deal with the matter.[43] They cooperated with the Exeter Trustees in the erection of a proper tombstone for John Phillips.[44] They licensed one Andrew Seaton to take in boarders provided he did not get a liquor license, and removed the restriction that had previously limited single ladies to two boarders apiece.[45] The Trustees were most considerate to John Adams, voting him grants in addition to his salary and also allowing him time off for reasons of his health.[46] They were concerned with the scholarship students and developed the position of "scholar of the house," the holder of which could earn most of his expenses cleaning, ringing the bell, and tending to fires. They started paying this scholar $1.25 a day, later raised it to $2.00, and finally decided to give him free board instead of money.[47] They also found it necessary to raise the costs for regular students. What had been a five-dollar deposit on entrance now became an entrance fee, and tuition was raised to five dollars a quarter to protect the income from the funds for charity students. In 1817 the tuition was raised to six dollars a term.[48] Another way of saving money was to underpay assistants: in 1829 one Kinsman Atkinson, presumably a student at the Theological Seminary, was hired to teach the younger boys at ten cents an hour.[49] So that there would be no running up of charge accounts, no student was allowed to obtain credit at any Andover store.[50] Finally, in 1827 the Trustees passed a dreary motion that the Board would "dispense with the provision of wine or spirits for their entertainment at their meetings."[51]

Only when outside events impinged on the routine of the School did the Trustees take aggressive action. In 1812 it became clear that Madame Phoebe Phillips would no longer be able to maintain the Mansion House, and, not wishing the property to fall into unfriendly hands, they offered to buy it for $15,000. They drove a hard bargain, however, for they insisted that some money due the school from unpaid pledges of Samuel Phillips be subtracted from the purchase price. To sugar the pill they offered to let Madam Phillips or her son John live in Mr. Blanchard's house if they so desired.[52]

Early in 1818 a student wrote his family:

> With a trembling hand and aching heart I attempt the painfull task of disclosing to you the afflicting scenes of providence I have latly [sic] witnessed. PHILLIPS ACADEMY IS NO MORE! Those sacred walls, within which the seeds of knowledge and virtue have been sown in my tender mind, where pious instruction has been faithfully given for many years, where the sacred gospel trumpet has often sounded, where the impenitent have often been pierced to the heart by the pointed arrows of the Almighty . . . I say those sacred walls,

21. Bulfinch Hall, constructed in 1818.

together with all therein contained, excepting a few volumes of the
academic Library, lie in one undistinguished mass of ruin. The cry
of fire! that dreadful cry, which strikes terror through the stoutest
heart was heard one O'ck on Friday night. The ringing of the church
bell . . . alarmed me and those with whom I reside, and called us
forth from the sweet embrace of sleep, to behold the raging flames
rapidly devouring our beloved Academy, which in less than 20
minutes lay prostrate in ashes.[53]

One reason why the old academy building burned so fast was that it was
made of wood, and the Trustees moved promptly to replace the building
with something more permanent. After making temporary provision for
the continuation of the school—the Seniors would continue classes but the
younger boys could go home—a vote was taken to construct a new building on a line with those of the Theological Seminary. It would be made of
brick and slate. Within a month plans for the building—the present Bulfinch Hall—had been approved, a committee had been formed to raise
money for the project, and William Phillips had started the ball rolling
with a contribution of $2,000.[54] The fund-raising committee, consisting of
Eliphalet Pearson, Daniel Dana, and John Adams, prepared an effective
prospectus in which they pointed out that they could not invade funds
given for charity students or for the Theological Seminary and therefore
were dependent on the public to help them rebuild. They called attention
to the fact that "the oldest Academy in the United States" had graduated
over thirteen hundred students, three hundred of whom had gone to Harvard. And they appealed to the public not to let the institution die.[55] Their
appeal was not in vain. The new building was started that summer with
the redoubtable Samuel Farrar supervising construction at a salary of
$300.00,[56] and before the year was out, the School was able to move in.
The Trustees had shown that, whatever their conservatism about existing
routines, they could act with dispatch when the occasion demanded.

In 1814 Adams had the first school catalogue printed, after which it is
possible to learn much more about the students. Adams was able to increase
the size of the School markedly. In 1809, the year before he came, only
sixteen new boys had been admitted, and it looked as if the institution
were in serious trouble. But things soon began to improve. In 1813 thirty-
four new boys came, and in 1816 the number was increased to sixty-three.
In 1820 seventy-seven, a bumper crop, were admitted. Though this record
was not equaled again, for the rest of the decade there was no problem
about filling the school. It is always difficult to determine just why students
enter a particular institution. It is probable that the relative prosperity of
the postwar period, coupled with the appeal of the Seminary for ministers,
who sent their sons in much larger numbers, was responsible for the increase. Of course, not all the boys who entered remained to graduate, but

the size of the School as a whole remained stable during this period. The bumper year was 1820, when there were a total of 142 students, but the number was over one hundred for eight of those years and dropped below that figure only at the end of the Adams term. The college choices of the boys also shifted. Despite the "devil down at Harvard" the largest number went there until 1819, when there was a definite shift to Yale. Adams was a Yale man and must have urged his charges to go there. In addition, Eliphalet Pearson was in the background, and he could be counted on to dissuade boys from going to Cambridge. In the class that entered in 1822, for example, three went to Harvard and fifteen to Yale, while of the 1829 entrants not one went to Harvard. For the rest, a few boys each year went to Dartmouth, Brown, Williams, Bowdoin, Amherst, and a scattering of other institutions.

There is also an interesting shift in the careers the boys eventually followed. After 1813 there was a marked increase in the number going into the ministry. Of the group who entered in 1819, for example, twenty-eight became clergymen, while the 1808 group produced but two. Clearly the combined influence of the Seminary and the piety of John Adams was having its effect. A similar shift occurred in the direction of teaching, where there had been but a handful before 1815, but in 1820 there were sixteen. Throughout the period law and medicine were well represented, with merchants, bankers, politicians, and other occupations also present. The claim of Phillips Academy to be a national school, which is made with such pride today, could certainly not have been made during this period. Almost all the boys came from New England, and almost all the New Englanders came from Massachusetts. In 1811, Adams' first year, of thirty-seven admitted, thirty-five were from New England, with the two exceptions from South Carolina. In the bumper crop of 1820 only four out of seventy-seven came from outside New England. In short, it would be some years before the geographical distribution on which the School prides itself would become a reality.[57]

Josiah Quincy the younger, who graduated in 1817, gives this description of the undergraduate body of his day:

> In the Academy were two classes of scholars—those whose expenses were paid by their parents, and "charity boys", as they were called, who were supported by certain funds controlled by a society for supplying the ministry with pious young candidates. These were persons who, having reached manhood, had determined to enter the sacred profession. They had served out an apprenticeship at some trade or in farming, and were generally uncouth in their manner and behavior. We, who were the real boys, never liked their sanctimonious demeanor. We claimed that they were spies, and shrank from them with all the disgust which their imaginary calling could not fail to excite.[58]

Even Quincy, however, had to admit that a "charity scholar" named William Person was a fine boy.[59] Person was illegitimate; as he said of his origins, "They picked me up in a tan yard, and that was all they could find out about me. I was just a person." His chances for an early education were dashed when he was, in effect, kidnapped by a tanner in Providence and forced to work for him for some thirteen years. Finally released from his indentures, he walked the sixty miles from Providence to Andover, a friend having promised to support him at Phillips Academy. He was duly admitted and soon found himself at home in his new school. He thought the religious exercises "delightful", found that "the most pious" were Principal Adams' peculiar favorites, and wrote, "We have the most excellent preaching here, especially on Sunday evenings at the chapel—and their music, O Heavens! 'Tis enough to animate the stupid marble!" After this promising start Person's status was radically changed when his sponsor withdrew financial support, with the result that the boy was required to become the "scholar of the house" and earn his way through school ringing bells, sweeping, making fires, and locking up. His job was onerous, to say the least. "I rise early, breakfast by candle light, hie to the Academy and make a fire by sunrise," he wrote. In the cold winter of 1814 he was also obliged to cut wood for three fires. On one particularly cold day he found the temperature in the Academy Building zero and managed to raise it to 38 degrees. The next day, with all fires going strong, he could not raise the temperature to half that and was obliged to stay in the Academy all night to keep the fires up. But help was on the way. Even though Person did not feel he could promise unconditionally to enter the ministry, he was interested in the calling, and accordingly he was made a charity scholar supported by funds from the School and was thus able to finish his education. The story has a sad ending. Person entered Harvard and seemed headed for a brilliant career when he contracted consumption, brought on by years of deprivation and hard work, and died. Still, during his years at Andover, he can stand as a prototype of the "charity scholar" of the day.

One can get a different view of the life of a Phillips Academy undergraduate during this period from an examination of the account book of Horace James, who was at Andover during the mid 1830's, at the end of the Adams period. James was anything but a charity scholar, but he kept close account of what he did spend so that he could justify School costs to his father. From early entries it is clear that not all the boys sawed their own wood, as tradition has it. Horace bought a cord of wood for $5.00 and then paid somebody $1.50 for sawing it. While he was about it, he picked up basic supplies—writing paper 12½ cents; an inkstand, 12½ cents; ink, 12½ cents; a toothbrush, 12½ cents; quills, 30 cents; wafers and pencils, 6 cents; and a peck of apples, 16 cents. A good deal of Horace's money went for schoolbooks: Greek Lessons, 42 cents; Herodotus, 75 cents; Greek Reader, one dollar; Greek Grammar, 83 cents; Greek Lexicon, five dollars; *Pilgrim's Progress*, 37½ cents; and others. Occasionally he would purchase books presumably for pleasure, as with *The Last Days of Pompeii*, 50 cents; *Demonology and Witchcraft* 45 cents; and the *History of Alcohol*, 10 cents. There were personal expenses as well: an umbrella, $1.50; cutting hair, 12½ cents; lucifers, 6 cents; court "plaister," 6 cents; a hat, 60 cents; peaches, 12½ cents; riding, 33 cents; a lamp, 42½ cents; tamarinds, 12½ cents; suspenders, 25 cents; frogs, 8 cents; a tuning fork, 75 cents; and a "bass viol" [?], 50 cents. Horace's concerns were not limited to material things. In the course of his stay on Andover Hill he contributed to a number of worthy causes and attended some lectures: singing school, 10 cents; Society tax, 12½ cents; contribution, 12½ cents; subscription to missionary society, $1.50; Philomathean society, 50 cents; Lyceum lecture, 14 cents; phrenological lectures, 25 cents; seaman's friend society, 22 cents; Social Fraternity 50 cents; and fee of admittance to society, 10 cents. Apparently Horace had some trouble with his teeth while at Phillips Academy. In addition to buying several toothbrushes at 25 cents each, he bought toothpowder for 33 cents and went to the dentist, thus producing an ominous entry: filling teeth, $6.00. Horace lived in Medford and apparently went home for weekends fairly regularly, for there are numerous entries like stage fare $1.25, stage fare, 75 cents. Finally, Horace's father gave him money to pay his tuition and his room and board bills. At that time the tuition was $6.00 a term, but it is difficult to tell how much his boarding charge was per term because it is not clear what period was covered. One entry for board is $30.01, the presumption being that this was the charge per term. Fortunately for us, Horace was a scrupulous accountant, and it is possible to obtain a fresh picture of an Andover undergraduate in the mid 1830's.[60]

In May 1819 there arrived at Phillips Academy a ten-year-old from Providence named James A. Burrill, the son of Rhode Island United States Senator James Burrill, Jr. The Senator had written a long letter of introduction to Principal Adams, spelling out what schooling the boy had had in the past and concluding, "I confide my only son to your care and can give you no stronger proof of my high opinion of your talents and moral character."[61] The boy had been instructed to write home regularly, which he did, and a substantial number of his letters have been preserved. His first report stated that the Theological Seminary buildings "are handsome and make a fine figure." He said he had bought a quire of paper and a bunch of quills and needed more money. He closed, "We have 2 prayers 1 in the morning and one at night. Excuse the writing."[62] Apparently James was a bit homesick. He writes of going down to the post office every day to see if there was a letter from home, and he asks frequently about his friends in Providence. In June he reported that Principal Adams had told him that if he did not pay his entrance money, he could not stay, but this matter was satisfactorily settled. He was not the only homesick boy:

"There were 2 boys came here to school one of them being home sick ran away home and today his father brought him back."[63] By the end of June, James was clearly settled in:

> Mr. Adams says I am the best boy in my class. We study one hour and an half in the evening or morning just as you please and 8 hours in school besides; all the time we have is at night. When we go into school we have two prayers and sing; we have one prayer in the morning at 6 oclock and another in the evening at 9. I commonly get up at 5, dress and wash myself and study till prayers, then eat breakfast and study till 7 oclock, play till 8 and then go to school, come out at 12, eat dinner at ½ past twelve, go to school again at 2, come out again at 6, supper as soon as school is done. In the evening we go in to the water or take a walk. . . . I have been a little poisoned on my hands but I have got over it. There are a great many whortleberrys and blackberrys here. I could pick a quart in a few minutes.[64]

In July Senator Burrill received a letter from Principal Adams telling him that his son was very deficient in Latin grammar, but that "We are now labouring the point with him, to set this business right. We find him to be pleasant and teachable, but like most other boys, fond of play." And he went on to say that no French was taught at Phillips Academy.[65]

The following November, James wrote that he was determined to succeed at Andover. "I am glad that you reproved me for my faults, for now I know them, I will try to do better for the future. I am much pleased with my situation here, for I am placed here for my good."[66] During the winter term James began to get bored. "I wish you would send me the newspapers for I want some employment for the long Winter evenings, for though I study an hour and an half and I begin at 6 oclock, I have a great deal of time."[67] In December sickness struck the Adams family. "Mr. Adams has been ill ever since Saturday; he was in such pain last night that he took hold of the bedpost and broke it off short; his wife thinks he is dying."[68] The following months one of Principal Adams' sons became seriously ill: "his complaint is the throat distemper. He got it by taking off all his clothes and rolling in the snow." But there were also more cheerful things to report. One of James's friends had managed to acquire a tame racoon, and they were all having a great time playing with it. James had bought a copy of John Marshall's speech on the death of Washington and seemed dutifully impressed by it. The boys had worked up a kind of private language or code; James signed his letter in code for his parent's information:

> Tenut E Dvgg, jkk
> Agjhkjot Efebune
> Emlpuaq
> Nett.[69]

James also wrote enviously about a boy named Dexter "who has got a complete set of carpenter's instruments which cost 9 dollars" and added, "I wish you would get me a set of them."[70] In March, James was looking forward to the summer and asking his father to get him a little gun "and next summer you and I can go out to the farm and shoot birds."[71] In April something unpleasant happened. His father had sent him a fairly substantial amount of money, to be used among other things, to pay his board bill of seventy-two dollars. About this time forty dollars was stolen from the Andover postmaster, and since James had possessed a large amount of money, he was suspected of the theft. Principal Adams grilled him and said he was going to write the Senator to see if the money had really been sent to James. It was not his character that made Mr. Adams suspicious but simply the fact that he had had so much money.[72]

The Principal finally decided that the boy was innocent and could return to pleasanter things: "We have very good amusement when out of school by playing ball. I have got a cross gun and ball."[73] And there the correspondence stops, even though James stayed on at Phillips Academy for another two years and graduated in 1822. Four years later he took his degree at Brown and five years after that, he died.

Passages from a few other undergraduate letters during this period are worth including. Edward J. Lowell of Boston had come to Phillips Academy at the age of nine in 1813. In 1817 he wrote a charmingly boyish letter to his aunt, Mrs. R. R. Gardner, asking for various items. He said they had all had good fun coming up on the stage, but that he had forgotten various things. Since he was studying algebra he needed his algebra book, which he had left with his sister Susan. He had also forgotten his slate. He was unable to find his comb and thought that if his aunt could locate it, she might send it up. Also he needed money to pay his term bill. He was enjoying the pears and cake that he had brought up with him. And then the punchline: "How are the rabbits?"[74] Illness was apparently a constant problem at the School. In November 1829 a boy who signs his letter simply "Thomas" wrote his mother a long account of an epidemic. It was blamed on the Academy's being cold in the forenoon and hot in the afternoon. True to form, Mr. Adams was "likewise affected." One of Thomas' friends believed the reason for his illness was his "wearing a flannel waistcoat pretty well *impregnated with musk*." He asked his landlady for "an egg dropped in water for his supper," but had nightmares all that night. In the morning, the landlady gave him a Rochelle Powder, but all to no avail. Finally Dr. Underwood was called, who gave the boy an emetic (ipecac) "which operated five times." The Doctor was sure the boy would be better in the morning and left.[75] Finally, an account of a temperance lecture written by Horace James in 1835—he of account book fame:

I attended a Temperance lecture last evening in the meeting house by

Mr. Sargeant and another one this evening by Rev. Mr. Cheever of Salem. I think it is pretty well to go to Tem. lectures two evenings in succession. Mr. Sargeant lectured very powerfully and eloquently for more than two hours; it was *very* interesting. He spoke chiefly about the use of tobacco in all its forms, and cider, wine, beer, etc., things not usually prescribed by Tem. Societies. He enforced the principle that these ought not to be used any more than Rum, Brandy, etc. He said that in a quart of Sicily wine there is as much alcohol, as in a pint of brandy. He held up the use of tobacco in all its forms in a most ridiculous light, enough to excite the disgust of every one. Mrs. Brown did not like him at all. She loves her snuffbox too well. He said that the most thorough pledge he had ever heard of was among the Oneida tribe of Indians. They plege themselves to abstain from every thing that makes drunk come. Mr. Sargeant has a red face and looks a great deal like an old soaker himself.[76]

The Phillips Academy administration during the Adams years did not concern itself with the boys' free time. There was not much of it, to begin with, and as long as the boys behaved themselves, they were usually left on their own. It was not long before the undergraduates began filling the vacuum by founding various societies—some secret and some not—to provide a social life that the authorities were not interested in. The first of these student organizations was founded in 1813 and was named "The Society for Promoting Good Morals in Phillips Academy, Andover." As the name implies, the outfit was very pious. It held meetings to discuss moral questions and drew up a list of "Engagements," which the members were bound to follow—no swearing, strict keeping of the Sabbath, daily Bible reading, and the like. The organization continued until the late 1820's and then faded away, to be replaced later by the Society of Inquiry.[77] In 1817 a stronger society met for the first time—the Social Fraternity. Its purpose was "mutual improvement in the following branches of English literature, Viz. Composition, Criticism, Declamations and Extemporaneous Debates." Membership was limited to the Senior Class, and an elaborate set of rules was adopted. To ensure regular attendance, members who were late or absent were fined. At the start the organization was secret, with a certain amount of mumbo-jumbo connected with it. The initiation procedure has been described as follows: "One of the members, perhaps 'Master of Ceremonies', dressed in a black robe, a black cap, and a black mask, conducted the candidate before the society, and addressed to him, in sepulchral tones, a few verses, which described in very strong language the fate awaiting him if he revealed the secrets of the society." The writer of this passage adds that he could remember no secrets to be preserved. This group had debates and compositions on subjects like slavery, and attempted to get some Latin, Greek, and English poetry written, but without much success. In order to stimulate interest, the members established a box, like a suggestion box, into which the boys could put questions, statements, and other expressions of opinion, but this procedure had to be abandoned because there were too many "scurrilous and indecent" communications. Occasionally a mock trial was held. One boy was accused and convicted of "pilfering apples," another for going out of town without Principal Adams' permission. Though the Social Fraternity was not to last beyond midcentury, while it was functioning it was a lively organization, and must have provided its members with welcome relief from the rigors of school life.[78]

Since only seniors could join the Social Fraternity, the younger boys determined to establish one of their own and in 1825 founded the Philomathean Society, the oldest student society currently extant at Phillips Academy. As with the Social Fraternity, the aim was mutual improvement in literary matters and, again like the Social Fraternity, the Society decided to build up a library. An early list of the books includes among others, Johnson's *Rambler, The Lady of the Lake*, a life of Franklin, a life of Patrick Henry, twelve volumes of the *Spectator*, Young's *Night Thoughts*, and Pope's *Essay on Man*. Great care was taken that the books be proper. All plays, for example, were considered dangerous. At one meeting it was voted that Campbell's *Journey* and Scott's *Guy Mannering* be burned as improper literature, though the members relented on the latter of these two and rescinded the vote at a later meeting.[79] Like the Social Fraternity, Philo had initiation ceremonies. Ray Palmer, one of the founders of the society, gives this description:

> The affair took place in the evening, and the end of the stage . . . was converted into a dark closet in which sat a personage so arrayed as to make, by the light of a very feeble lamp, a tolerable impersonization of Beelzebub. Into this presence the candidate was solemnly ushered, and found himself alone with this distinguished looking personage, who in awful and sepulchral tones addressed him in the following fashion:
> "If e'er these secrets thou reveal
> Let thunders on thy forehead peal;
> On thy vile bones thy flesh shall rot,
> and witches dire around thee trot."
> Nothing of what was coming was known to the wight who was to pass the ordeal; and the awe felt at the moment was very real, as was shown in one case by a student who, having some suspicion that there might be *some* humbug, courageously declared that, if there *were* any, *he* should treat it with contempt. This same person, when he found himself in the dimly lighted place, face to face with what seemed the Prince of darkness, actually got on his knees at the summons of his Princeship, whom he afterwards found to be none other than his own chum! This of course was nuts to the boys.[80]

Philo, in its early years, seemed to concentrate more on debates than on other literary exercises. Among the topics debated were "Do females possess minds as capable of improvement as males? (decided in the affirmative); "Are females as worthy of being introduced into society as males?" (decided in the negative); "Would the freedom of slaves be beneficial to our country?" (decided in the negative); "Is the condition of the monarch happier than that of the begger?"; "Ought persons stealing dead bodies for dissection be punished according to law?" (decided in the affirmative); and many others.[81] On several occasions during its early history, Philo appeared about to collapse, but the Society managed to hang on and eventually became a powerful influence in the School, supplanting the Social Fraternity and publishing a magazine of its own.

Considering Squire Farrar's extreme conservatism (as noted above), it is extraordinary that he took the lead in educational experiments. The period from 1820 to 1860 in the United States was one of ferment in the field of education. It saw a drive for universal public education, the brilliant work of Horace Mann and Henry Barnard, and a willingness to experiment with all sorts of new forms and concepts in education.[82] It would be easy to believe that Samuel Farrar and the Andover Board had been influenced by these new trends, but if they were, there is no record of it. Just where Farrar got his idea for a Teachers' Seminary combined with an English Department is impossible to say. But whatever the source his proposal was right in line with some of the most forward-looking thinking of the day in education. And there seems no doubt that he was the prime mover in the project. One authority speaks of the Teachers' Seminary as being established "largely through the influence of Samuel Farrar and William Phillips," who had given the money.[83] The Reverend Lyman Coleman, second Principal of the Seminary, wrote, "the Teachers' Seminary, according to the best of my knowledge and belief, was the conception and creation of Esquire Farrar."[84] It was natural that a practical man of affairs like the Squire should be interested in training boys for practical occupations like accounting and business. Though the institution eventually ended in failure, it might have succeeded had it been given more financial support by the Trustees; in any event it was a brave attempt to blaze new educational trails in the growing country.

In 1827 William Phillips, then President of the Board and long a generous benefactor of the School, died. When his will was read, it was found that he had left $15,000 to Phillips Academy. At a Trustee meeting that fall, Treasurer Farrar was authorized to invest the Phillips money, and the Board voted that because existing funds seemed sufficient to maintain the Classical School, the income from the new gift should be used to establish an "English Classical School," independent of Phillips Academy and with a separate building.[85] Since there was no money for the building, the question was referred to a committee. The next year the Trustees reiterated their support for an English School and authorized a committeee headed by Samuel Farrar to erect a building for that purpose, borrowing what was needed above and beyond the accrued income from the Phillips legacy.[86] The Squire needed no prodding. In this case he could be architect as well as clerk of the works. Claude Fuess describes what happened:

> Towards the close of John Adams's administration, in the spring of 1829, workmen were excavating a cellar on the northeast corner of Main Street and Chapel Avenue; and soon there rose an oblong, two-storied, massive edifice, with thick walls of rough gray stone, and a slanting roof, surmounted by a high wooden cupola or bell-tower, on which was perched an equally tall weather-vane. The architect was Squire Farrar, who, obsessed by a craving for simplicity, had created a style that was all his own, not Grecian or Gothic or colonial, but essentially "Farraresque." Bare, somber, and unrelieved by ornamentation, the building resembled a jail or tomb, and seemed to be at once the strongest and the ugliest structure ever produced by the hand of man.[87]

This Stone Academy, as it was called, was to play an important part in the life of the School until it, too, burned down, in 1864.

Even before the English School opened, the Trustees had shifted its focus. In 1830 they voted "that a leading and primary object in this [English] department be the education of Teachers for common and other schools and that instruction be also given to other persons in various branches of an English education."[88] Thus from the start the purpose of the School was ambivalent; it would train teachers, it would offer courses for nonclassical, noncollege-bound students, and later it would have classes of younger boys for the budding teachers to practice on. The interest in training teachers led to the appointment as Principal of the Reverend Samuel Read Hall, one of the leading exponents of teacher training in his day. Hall, who is credited with being the first teacher to use a blackboard, went to Kimball Union Academy but never got to college. In 1823 he established a kind of normal school in Concord, Vermont, and in 1829 he became nationally known when he published his *Lectures on School-Keeping*, the first teachers' manual printed in the United States. Hall had no use for the harsh discipline based on fear that characterized so many schools. "The great object is to prepare children to be happy," he thought, and for that reason the teacher should "adopt such a course as to render the school *pleasant*." In addition, his book was filled with practical suggestions —the usefulness of maps, globes, and visual aids, for example.[89] Hall was a prolific writer, and before he was through he had written an arithmetic book, a United States history, and several others for use in the schools. In arranging for Hall's salary, Squire Farrar devised a diabolical scheme that had a great deal to do with Hall's eventual resignation. The Principal was to receive no cash salary at all but was to have the use of the Stone Academy, the entrance fees and tuition money of the students, and the freedom to set those fees himself. In this way the Squire hoped to encourage the Principal to develop a thriving institution and at the same time save the Phillips Academy Trustees a lot of money.[90]

The first Seminary catalogue, published in 1831, the year the School opened, lists 80 students, over half of whom were from Andover. The purpose was "to educate Instructors of common and other Schools. Another object is to educate practical men, for all the departments of common life." Emphasis was placed from the start on instruction in the Natural Science, and the catalogue boasted of a fine set of apparatus, including a magic lantern with several hundred slides, an "Electrical Machine of a very superior kind," a chemical laboratory, "Pneumatic Apparatus," a telescope, and a cabinet of minerals. By 1832 the number had increased to 115, a course in civil engineering and surveying had been added, and a list of twenty-six subjects for the English Department (or "School") had been drawn up. The list shows no courses in Latin or Greek; it stresses mathematics and the sciences. By the middle of the decade the Teachers' class had been divided into three groups—Senior, Middle, and Junior—with the curriculum for each year spelled out more precisely. Up until 1838 the catalogues were printed as emanating from the Teachers' Seminary; in that year the title was changed to "English Department and Teachers' Seminary," indicating again the basic ambivalence of the institution. Tuition costs varied. At the start they were six dollars a term, then were raised slightly, and finally were changed to fifty cents a week. A Commons for meals was established on a farm that the boys were required to work on and thus helped to reduce the cost of their board, which averaged between $1.00 and $1.25 per week. As at Phillips Academy, attempts were made to help indigent students meet their tuition charges. By 1840 the catalogue had become more flowery: "The repeated calls from the South and West and from the public generally, for well educated teachers, have induced the Trustees from time to time to make large appropriations for increasing the advantages, and, at the same time, diminishing the expenses of the students in the Seminary." Yet the statement did no more than reemphasize in fancier language the hopes that the Trustees had for the institution.[91] Most of the Assistants at Phillips Academy during this period were a mediocre lot. By contrast the Seminary could boast several truly distinguished men. Alonzo Gray, teacher of chemistry and natural history, was a highly competent scientist who was interested in applying science to agricultural problems. William H. Wells, teacher of mathematics and English literature, later went on to become Superintendent of Schools in Chicago; and Lyman Coleman, the second Principal, taught at Amherst, Princeton, and Lafayette after leaving Andover. When the Seminary scheme was abandoned and these teachers forced to leave, the Phillips Academy community lost some very able men.

In 1832 there appeared in the *Annals of Education* an article on the Seminary which was highly favorable to it. The author had spent some time in Andover and had been impressed with what he saw:

> School books of a good character are selected, and the most improved methods of instruction adopted . . . much is accomplished by familiar lectures, giving the student ample opportunity for asking questions, suggesting doubts, etc. No attempts are made to hurry through a science for the sake of having gone through it. . . .
>
> In both departments of the school, there is nothing of that routine of mere memory work which is so often witnessed in our schools. . . .
>
> In both departments of the institution every branch is pursued . . . independently of every other. . . . In the higher departments, the exercises for every day of the week are written down plainly and minutely, and a monitor rings a bell at the arrival of the time for every new exercise. So exact is the order, and so accustomed to it have the students become, that, so far as discipline is concerned, it matters little whether the teachers are present or absent, provided the monitor performs his duty.
>
> The higher branches of the mathematics, geography, grammar, history, composition, drawing, philosophy . . . chemistry, political economy; indeed everything to which the attention of the pupil is called, is pursued . . . in the same rational and thorough manner, as spelling, reading, and arithmetic. Not only is everything rendered intelligible, but interesting; and the thinking powers of the pupils are called into useful activity. During my visit a course of chemical lectures was commenced by an assistant, which promised to be highly practical and useful. . . .
>
> But what rendered this Seminary most deeply interesting to me, was the conviction which I was unable to resist, that all its methods, and plans, and processes, were eminently adapted to the development and formation of character. As a place of instruction, it justly ranks high; and I do not believe it has been too highly appreciated. But as a place of education it has still higher claims. Knowledge of the best kind is successfully circulated by the best means; but the capacity and disposition to make the best use of Knowledge is regarded as of more importance.[92]

It is unlikely that the author of this article would have been able to say the same things about Phillips Academy had he visited it during his stay in Andover.

There were certainly some able students at the Teachers' Seminary—

for example, James S. Eaton, who later became head of the English Department at Phillips Academy. In 1837 Eaton decided to found a newspaper called *The Literary Recorder*, and until he graduated in 1838 it came
out fairly regularly. Whether it was ever printed is not clear; the only extant copies are in manuscript. In his first number he invited all kinds of
literary communications and then proceeded to an article defending the
Seminary students against various charges impugning their conduct. Generally the students were attacked for "their clownish habits, slovenly dress,
and indecent appearance," especially in comparison with the students of
Phillips Academy. It was also charged that when Seminary students paid
their bills to Squire Farrar, they kept their hats on. Eaton vigorously defended the Seminary students against these charges and added bitterly, "But
the Classical scholar is never guilty of such coarseness. *He* is in comparison,
a *gentleman.*" Furthermore, he added, if Seminary students did not have
to pay tuition and if they were helped by the charity fund, they might be
able to dress more like gentlemen. During its period of publication *The
Literary Recorder* carried a variety of articles—"The Revolutionary Soldier," a long poem entitled "The March of the American Army to Trenton," an account of a trip "down east," "Friendship and Tenderness of
Heart," and "Funeral Thoughts."[93] Not many letters from Seminary students have been preserved. One such is a communication from Davis Smith
to his mother in 1834. Davis had this to say about the School:

> I board in the commons. Mr. Hall told me that he thought it would
> be cheaper and that I should enjoy greater advantages than if I
> boarded myself. As I wish you to know all about my situation here I
> will tell you something about our diet. For breakfast and supper we
> have wheat bread with milk or molasses—of each one may choose.
> I take milk in the morning and molasses at night. For dinner we
> have rice and indian pudding, pork, fish, potatoes, beans, etc. My
> health is, and has been, very good. I enjoy myself very well. There
> are among the students many professing Christians and I should think
> the greatest part. We have a prayer meeting every Saturday night.
> There are generally several other meetings every week. My studies
> are at present Euclid's geometry, Grammar, Chemistry and Intellec-
> tual Philosophy. These studies do not take all my time; therefore I
> spend the remainder in reading on arithmetic and algebra.[94]

Despite the success that Samuel Hall and his corps of teachers had with
their students at the Teachers' Seminary, the institution was soon in
trouble financially. For one thing the number of students listed as enrolled
was misleading. Students training to be teachers were excused during the
winter terms of their second and third year to engage in practice teaching,
thus reducing the number substantially. In addition many students in the
General Department came for a term or two and then left. The catalogue

of 1840, for example, lists 154 students, but then indicates that only 90 were enrolled for the term during which the catalogue was printed. Samuel Hall became more and more unhappy about his lack of a guaranteed salary,[95] and it was often difficult to recompense the assistant teachers adequately. All through the 1830's, however, the Trustees worked hard to keep the institution viable. In 1834 they restated their position that the main aim of the Seminary was the education of teachers, and the following year they initiated a loan program for the students. To be eligible a boy must have a certificate from the Principal certifying his good moral character, must contract to go into teaching after graduation, and must sign a note, to be paid back a year after he left the School.[96] That same year the Trustees embarked on their most ambitious enterprise when they voted to conduct a drive for $40,000 for the Seminary. In February 1836 they published a circular announcing their intentions and inviting the interested public to a meeting in Boston. The meeting was held, and Samuel Farrar spoke on the subject of the Seminary, but the returns were disappointing and the problem remained.[97] In 1837 the Trustees introduced a department of Civil Engineering and voted one thousand dollars for equipment, but this did little more than spread the School more thinly among the various departments.[98] Despite the Trustees' insistence that the main purpose was the education of teachers, it was clear that the institution was going in too many directions, trying to serve too many different kinds of students.

In 1837 Samuel Hall, frustrated by the many problems of the institution and by his own unsatisfactory financial situation, resigned his position as Principal. He was succeeded by Lyman Coleman, a graduate of Yale and an ordained minister who was then head of the Burr Seminary in Manchester, Vermont. Coleman gave lip service to the idea of training teachers, but he was primarily interested in running an English High School. The statement that he wrote in the 1840 catalogue bears this out:

> The plan of this Institution, as here developed, is that of an English High School, occupying an intermediate grade between our common academic institutions and our colleges. The object of this system of instruction . . . is not to hurry the student through a superficial course, teaching a little of everything and nothing to any good purpose; but lead him to begin a *thorough* course of mental discipline, and to pursue it as far as circumstances will admit. To such as continue with us a sufficient length of time it offers essentially the advantages of a collegiate education in the several departments of English literature.

Although Coleman was an energetic and resourceful administrator, he arrived too late to save the institution. But the Trustees were slow to give up. In 1834 they published a circular for public distribution, with an attractive cut of the Andover campus, in the hope of attracting more students.[99] That same year they considered applying to the Massachusetts legislature for financial assistance for the Seminary, but finally gave up the idea as "inexpedient."[1] In 1841 they passed a resolution that they considered it "eminetly desirable that the English Department in Phillips Academy be sustained," and they advertised the institution in a Boston newspaper,[2] something they had never done for the Classical School. Finally, in 1842, came the mournful decision:

> That after the close of the present term in the English department the contracts with the Rev. Mr. Coleman and Mr. Gray should be closed for want of means to retain them.

Squire Farrar was authorized to "make the necessary communications . . . to the several members of the English School."[3]

The reasons for the failure of Squire Farrar's interesting experiment are not hard to find. First of all, the institution could never decide just where to focus its energies, witness the different names it was given—"Teachers' Seminary," "English Department," "English High School," and the like. Stimulating courses were introduced, but often without reference to any overall plan. The courses in agriculture, for example, though advanced for their day, had no direct bearing on teacher training. The Seminary got little support from Phillips Academy itself. Its students were generally looked down upon by boys from the Classical School, as James Eaton's article indicates. More important, "Uncle Sam" Taylor, who became Principal of Phillips Academy in 1837, was a dedicated classicist who had little interest in, or respect for, the English School. Later in life Lyman Coleman wrote:

> The high and deserved reputation of Phillips Academy, its overshadowing influence, its total lack of sympathy and cooperation, served to cast into shades and distance the Teachers' Seminary, and to give it the air of an abandoned orphan rather than a cherished part of the venerable institution.[4]

Finally, there is some reason to believe that Squire Farrar's interest in the project waned during its later years. In 1840 he had retired as Treasurer of the Board at the age of sixty-seven, and while he continued on the Board for another six years, he could never provide the driving support that he did at the project's inception. Furthermore, if he had had to choose between training teachers and balancing the Phillips Academy budget, there is no question what his decision would have been.

Yet the experiment was not all loss. The Seminary continued as the English Department of Phillips Academy for the rest of the century, and though its students were still treated as second-class citizens, it provided a wholesome alternative to the rigidly classical curriculum of Phillips Academy. Later in the century, as American education drew away from the classical and as the role of science in contemporary curricula became more important, the English Department would prove a useful vehicle for curricular change.

When Phillips Academy was founded, it was assumed that private fammilies would take care of the students' room and board. There had been talk of building a boarding house that would be run by the school, but nothing had ever come of it. Another of Squire Farrar's important innovations was to advance the idea that the School should provide dormitories and boarding facilities for at least some of the students. In 1830 the Trustees took the first step in this direction. They voted that "those of suitable age and character and standing who have commended themselves to their Instructors by orderly deportment and studious habits, may be permitted to study at their own rooms, such portions of each day, upon such conditions, and under such regulations as the Principal shall direct . . ." The motion went on to say that this would never excuse a boy from attending religious exercises and that abuse of the privilege would result in its being withdrawn.[5] Until this time the boys had had to study in Academy Hall in the main school building during times when they were not in class. Thus was

22. The English Commons, built in 1836.

initiated a policy that was for many years almost unique with Andover and Exeter—abolishing formal study halls and allowing the students to study on their own in their own rooms. The next logical step was to provide rooms in School houses where the boys might study. Again it was Squire Farrar who provided the leadership in what came to be known as the Latin and English Commons. Again Farrar was his own architect, and before he was through he had had erected six ugly tenements on what is now the north side of Phillips Street, and another six facing them in a line in front of what is now Draper Cottage. The first six were called the Latin Commons, the second six the English. The buildings were all identical wooden structures, clapboarded, and boxlike. On each of the three floors there were two suites consisting of a living room and two bedrooms. Plumbing consisted of one pump outside each row of tenements and a brick privy. The rooms were heated by stoves, with each student responsible for providing his own fuel and emptying his own ashes. Why the buildings were not all burnt down immediately is one of the great mysteries of the period. All the furniture for the rooms had to be provided by the students themselves, and as it was passed from hand to hand over the years, it resembled the contents of a junk shop. The Commons were designed primarily for scholarship boys, and the room rent was therefore one dollar a term.

23. Squire Samuel Farrar in his old age.

The construction of the Commons marks the first step in a policy that would eventually result in housing all Phillips Academy students in buildings owned and supervised by the School. The ownership was a fact in the 1830's, but the supervision certainly was not. In effect, under Squire Farrar's plan the boys were turned loose to fend for themselves. A half-hearted attempt was made to have the Commons inspected by a member of the faculty once a week, but these visitations were never taken seriously and could easily be anticipated by the boys. As a result they developed into a hardy, self-sufficient breed who had to learn how to run their own lives or perish. It was certainly no place for pampered weaklings.[6] It would be many years before Phillips Academy could provide adequate housing for its undergraduates, but the Commons at least established the principle that housing boys in its own buildings rather than in houses in the town was a proper policy for the school to follow.

Squire Farrar lived until 1864, when he died at the age of ninety-one, but for some years before that he had been sloughing off his manifold responsibilities. He resigned as Phillips Academy Treasurer in 1840 and as Trustee in 1846; in 1851 he left the Board of Abbot Academy, and in 1856 he resigned as President of the Andover Bank. In his later days he could look back on a career of extraordinary usefulness to Phillips Academy and the community. He it was who conceived the plan for the Teachers' Seminary; and although his project eventually ended in failure as far as the training of teachers was concerned, the goal was realized by the Phillips Academy English Department, which provided breadth to the curricular offerings of the School. He was probably instrumental in getting Trustee support for the decision to allow the students to study in their own rooms, thereby initiating a policy that has been a hallmark of Phillips Academy ever since. Finally, he started a program of lodging undergraduates in School-owned houses, which was eventually to become an axiomatic policy for the Academy. Although the first half of the nineteenth century was generally a sterile period in Phillips history, the innovations that were made came as the result of the imagination and drive of Samuel Farrar.

CHAPTER EIGHT

THE DICTATORSHIP OF

SAMUEL HARVEY TAYLOR

I N T H E early 1830's the Trustees appointed a committee to study the
condition of the School. The committee was not happy with what it
found and expressed its concern in a report signed by William B.
Bannister. A major cause of worry was admissions, which had dropped
from 82 to 28 in the course of six years. There were many causes, the committee believed—improvement in public education, increase in competing
private schools, the rising cost of education, and the economic condition of
the country. Furthermore, the Academy's required three-year course, with
the first year devoted to laborious drill, was unattractive to the public, both
for financial and for educational reasons. The relatively large number of
charity students at Phillips Academy was a financial handicap that could be
removed only by attracting more full-paying students. The committee did
not wish to reflect unfavorably on the Principal and Assistants, but the fact
remained that the students were transferring their dislike of the first-year
curriculum to their teachers. And this at a time when all sorts of exciting
changes were taking place in American education. Finally, it was expecting
too much to ask Principal Adams to change his way at the age of sixty with
twenty years of dedication to the old system. Though the committee made
no formal recommendation, the purport of their report was clear; Adams
had to go.[1] Just who it was that gave him the hard word is not recorded,
but by the fall of 1832 he knew he had to resign.

The old man took the blow hard, as well he might. There were no pensions for teachers in those days. Writing his son William after he had
received the bad news, he said:

> You are mistaken in supposing that I wish to continue in the Acade-
> my. The fact is that I cannot continue. I must resign my office as
> Principal, not because I think myself too aged, but because it is ex-
> pedient. If the Trustees, or any of their number feel that the best

interest of the Academy will be promoted by the introduction of a younger man, how can I make up my mind to remain?[2]

He added a Biblical quotation: "I have been young and now am old; yet have I not seen the righteous forsaken nor his seed begging bread." On 22 November 1832 Adams read a long letter of resignation to the Board of Trustees. It was a kind of *apologia* for his stewardship, a review of his achievements. It read, in part, as follows:

> Looking back upon the period of more than twenty-two years, I can say honestly and truly that I have been devoted heartily and exclusively to what I consider the best good of my pupils. Although I have neglected my own pecuniary interest I have not neglected them.
>
> I leave the Academy in a prosperous condition, containing . . . ninety scholars, all of whom are pursuing classical studies.
>
> I have admitted into the Academy one thousand one hundred and nineteen pupils. About one-half of this number have received a collegiate education. . . . During their stay at the Academy more than one hundred and fifty became hopefully pious [converted]. About two hundred, or nearly one in every five, have entered the ministry, and many have given themselves to the sacred cause of missions.
>
> I have loved my work and have devoted to it my all. How far I have been successful is left to the judgment of others. But, although my attachment to this school is strong, and the idea of separation from it is painful to me, yet the time has come when I judge it expedient to resign.[3]

The last years of John Adams' life were difficult at best. After selling his household furniture and arming himself with some letters of recommendation from some Seminary professors, he eventually went west to head a female seminary in Jacksonville, Illinois, and finally became the agent of the American Sunday-School Union in Illinois. He became a familiar figure in the state, driving around in his buggy and eventually organizing three hundred and twenty-two Sunday-Schools on the princely salary of four hundred dollars a year. In 1854 he must have been pleased when his *alma mater*, Yale, awarded him the degree of Doctor of Laws. Nine years later he was dead at the age of ninety-two.[4]

The Trustees had dismissed John Adams so that they might get a younger and more progressive Principal to replace him. Osgood Johnson, the man they selected, was certainly young—he was thirty years old when appointed, but there is nothing to indicate that he was more in tune with contemporary educational thinking than his predecessor. Certainly during his brief term of four years he made no attempt to change any of Adams' procedures, nor is there any indication that he would have done so had he lived longer. Johnson was a townie who had graduated from Phillips

Academy in 1823 and then gone to Dartmouth, where he won his degree *summa cum laude* in 1828. He tutored for a year at Dartmouth after graduation, got married, and accepted a call to return to his old school as an Assistant in 1829. His skill as a teacher combined with his outstanding scholarly attainments made him a natural choice when the Trustees were looking for a successor to Adams. Much to the new Principal's unhappiness he was treated to the same kind of salary arrangements that had been used with Samuel Hall of the Teachers' Seminary. According to this arrangement, the brainchild of Squire Farrar, the Principal would receive no salary but would support himself on the tuition income paid by the students. In Johnson's case, however, this arrangement lasted but a year. As a result of the Principal's protests, he was paid one thousand dollars a year and given his house rent free.[5] From that time on, the Principals of Phillips Academy have been paid regular salaries and have not been obliged to be business managers as well.

There seems to be no question that Johnson was an accomplished teacher. For one thing, he seldom brought any books to class, having memorized the texts that were to be studied.[6] His enthusiasm for his subject can also be seen in his practice of driving with his wife while she read classical works to him. A former pupil has this to say about his teaching methods:

> As a teacher, I never knew one more thorough, lucid, patient or inspiring. I never saw him disconcerted. He was always self-poised, awake to every emergency; and having full command of his varied and broad resources, he could meet every exigency incident to his responsible position with the most admirable tact and skill. . . . When he became Principal, he at once began the gradual elevation of scholarship, keeping it abreast, if not in advance, of the best Academies in the country.[7]

Johnson depended more on repartee, and occasionally sarcasm, to make his points than on fear, yet he appears to have been equally effective. His high standards led one pupil to characterize the Academy as "a grindstone for dull scythes."[8] The Principal was memorable in leading chapel services also. Another pupil was tremendously moved by these services:

> Every eye was fixed with respect upon Mr. Johnson as he entered the room. He ascended to the desk and pronounced a brief invocation, uniformly asking that our devotions might be performed as "seeing Him who is invisible." Then followed a few verses of Scripture, so read that a hidden radiance was made to flash out of its depths, as when a skillful lapidary holds before you a gem so adjusted that all its inner light beams upon your surprised vision. This prayer transported us into that unseen world where he seemed habitually himself to dwell, till he placed us before the great white throne in the very presence of the Most High.[9]

24. *Osgood Johnson, Fifth Principal of Phillips Academy. From a portrait by an unknown artist in the possession of the Trustees of Phillips Academy.*

A homesick boy went to his first chapel service and wrote: "But when I heard the familiar words of the New Testament read in turn by the scholars, when I heard the old hymns in old tunes, when I heard the clear, soft tones of the Principal, Mr. Oliver [sic] Johnson and listened to his tender and appropriate supplications as he led morning devotions, I felt that 'God was in that place,' that I was no longer an alien or alone."[10]

Johnson could be rigid on occasions. Two boys with limited funds who knew that they must finish Phillips Academy in two years decided to try to skip a year by extra study and then an examination, a practice that had apparently been allowed on occasion. The two really gave it all they had, rising at four in the morning and working till midnight. Finally they went to Johnson for their examination, only to have him say that he thought skipping classes was a bad idea and he would not, therefore, examine them. Since they had no money for a third year, they were both obliged to leave.[11]

The most interesting event of Osgood Johnson's administration was the so-called "Anti-Slavery Rebellion."[12] It was the only occasion before the Civil War when a national issue forcibly influenced the School. With the founding of William Lloyd Garrison's *Liberator* in 1831, the strength of abolitionism began to increase markedly in New England. Most people still accepted the constitutional guarantee of slavery as a basic property right or else supported the idea of colonization—sending the slaves back to Africa. Garrison and his followers refused to accept the constitutional guarantees of slavery and believed that colonization was far too slow a policy to deal with what they thought was a national sin. They embarked on a crusade to win New England over to the principle of immediate abolition. When in the summer of 1835 Garrison and George Thompson, a member of Parliament who was a brilliant antislavery orator, came to Andover, they were unable to get permission to speak at the Seminary or the South Church. They finally secured the Methodist church in the town and there they delivered a series of fiery attacks on the institution of slavery. At the end of one of the meetings every light in the methodist Chapel was blown out and a mob attempted to seize Thompson. The students present were able to forestall this attempt armed with staves. For the rest of the night they protected the house in which Thompson was staying and beat off a second attack. The mob is described as made up of Irish who were working on the Andover-Wilmington railroad.[13]

As we have seen, the professors at the Theological Seminary were opposed to the abolition movement, primarily because they were afraid that interest in the antislavery cause would divert the students from their regular course of study. Though, at the start, both theologues and Academy boys attended the lectures, the Professors were able to extract from the theologues a promise not to form an antislavery society on the Hill and to postpone the whole question until after their graduation.[14] Not so with the Academy students. About one hundred petitioned Osgood Johnson twice for permission to form an antislavery society and were turned down both times. A crisis developed when one Sherlock Bristol delivered an impassioned attack on slavery at one of the Wednesday afternoon speaking contests. When he had finished, a theologue who was acting as Assistant said to him, "in contemptuous and bitter tones," "There! Bristol! *You have done it! Sold Yourself! Sold yourself And for a NIGGER!*"[15] The next morning at chapel Johnson rebuked Bristol and wound up by expelling him from the Academy. When the boy asked for permission to reply, it was denied. Excitement throughout the School was intense.

Since the antislavery students could not find a place at the School to meet, they went in a body to Indian Ridge and held a meeting that was interrupted at one point by a thunderstorm. During the meeting they drew up a long manifesto, stating their grievances and asking for redress. They pointed out that all but two of them were twenty-one years of age and thus entitled to the basic rights of citizenship. They deplored the recently passed rule that no student could join any society in the town without the permission of the Principal, which was obviously aimed at the town's antislavery society, which some thirty of the Academy students had joined. They reviewed their repeated attempts to get permission from Johnson to form an antislavery society and insisted that the only way to attack this national sin was to work together through an organization. They explained that when it became clear that Johnson would never grant their request, they decided to petition him for an honorable dismissal from the School. At first Johnson seemed willing to do this, but eventually he reneged, and as a result the signers of the manifesto had no choice but to resign and take their chances. It seems clear that Johnson did not have a free hand in dealing with the boys. On one occasion he told them, "I am bound in chains of iron,"[16] a reference, presmuably, to the influence being put on him by the Seminary professors. Moses Stuart, in particular, seems to have taken an active role in quashing the antislavery movement at the Academy. It would be difficult, after winning the theologues over to neutrality on this issue, to have an antislavery society spring up in the Academy. On one occasion Stuart is reported to have asked a boy why he was involved in antislavery. "Because of my conscience," the boy replied. "Where did you get your conscience?" asked Stuart. "By hearing you preach two years," was the sharp rejoinder.[17] In any event something over forty students left the Academy over this issue, none of them receiving honorable dismissals. One of the number, Ephraim Adams, records that his father said nothing about his return and the reasons for it and the following morning suggested that he start haying. He was later able to get admitted to Dartmouth, which was sympathetic to the antislavery movement.[18] Another boy returned to the School, and when asked why he had, replied, "The fact is, that when one gets ten miles out of town, things look different."[19] The whole episode is an unhappy one in the history of Phillips Academy. One may accept the

Seminary professors' desire to concentrate on the training of professionals
and their concern lest outside issues distract their students. But the same
reasoning hardly applies to a group of fully grown men at Phillips Academy who were headed for many different walks of life. One suspects that if
Osgood Johnson had been given a free hand, he would have followed a
different policy and that it was the "chains of iron" in which he was bound
by the professors that led him to adopt the policy he followed.

Osgood Johnson's term as Principal was tragically short. He had always
been frail physically and was handicapped by a club foot. Shortly after his
accession he developed tuberculosis, which grew progressively worse. He
thought of resigning in the fall of 1836, but his students begged him not
to, and as he grew weaker they used to carry him to his carriage or sleigh
in their arms and bring him to the recitation room, where he would occupy
his regular seat while an assistant conducted the class. His wife was a tower
of strength in their home in Samaritan House. "All that winter she had
washed and dressed him and lifted him as she would a child." One of his
last acts was to send fifty dollars to the Foreign Missionary Society without
any signature.[20] The end came on 9 May 1837, with burial in the Chapel
cemetery, where a monument to him was later erected. Johnson was certainly a great teacher and one of the foremost classical scholars in the country. Had he lived, he might have had a profound influence on Phillips
Academy. As it was, he helped maintain the school's tradition of scholarly
excellence. As one of his pupils wrote:

> I have never met the man, I have never read of the man, who taught
> Pagan literature with so much of the Christian head and the Christian
> heart. I venerate his memory. As his strength went and his days in
> the classroom were shorter, and his voice feebler, there was a tone,
> there was a power to that reading of the Scriptures, those remarks,
> those prayers, that private conference. The pupils who were under
> his charge will never forget the man in that respect.[21]

One of the last acts of Osgood Johnson was to recommend that Samuel
Harvey Taylor be chosen as his successor. And Taylor was certainly a
promising candidate. Born in Londonderry, New Hampshire, in 1807, he
was, from an early age, given the management of the family farm because
of the frequent absences of his father. He apparently intended to spend
his life farming when a fall from a wagon so limited him physically that
he determined on a scholarly life. After two years of cramming at Pinker-
ton Academy, he entered Dartmouth, where he graduated with high
honors. He had now determined on the ministry as his life's work and
entered the Andover Theological Seminary right after graduation. Osgood
Johnson spotted him early as a promising Assistant, and Taylor taught at
Phillips Academy for one year. He refused to stay longer, despite the urging of both Johnson and his pupils, preferring to return to Dartmouth as

25. Samuel Harvey Taylor, Sixth Principal of Phillips Academy.

a tutor. When the Andover Trustees, following Johnson's advice, offered him one thousand dollars and a house to return as Principal, he found the offer too tempting to refuse, especially as he was about to be married to Caroline Persis Parker. In 1837 he and his new wife moved into the Double-Brick on Main Street to begin a career as Principal that was to last thirty-four years. That same year he completed his studies at the Seminary and was graduated. As far as academic training went, he seemed admirably prepared for his job.[22]

Samuel Harvey Taylor, Principal of Phillips Academy from 1838 to 1871, was an extremely controversial figure in his day. It has been suggested that he was the American equivalent of Dr. Arnold of Rugby, though such comparison fails to do justice to either man.[23] Professor George Herbert Palmer of Harvard thought him a "humbug."[24] His reputation has probably suffered with the passage of time, for his extreme conservatism and his rigidity in teaching and disciplinary methods are completely foreign to today's educational beliefs. "Uncle Sam," as he was called, ran the School with an iron hand; there was never any question about who was in charge. A former pupil wrote, "If I have ever seen anywhere any semblance of despotism and absolute monarchy, it was Phillips Academy under Dr. Taylor."[25] In a very real sense Uncle Sam was a throwback to Eliphalet Pearson, and the two would have got along famously. Taylor would have been completely happy with Pearson's emphasis on scholastic excellence, almost exclusive devotion to the classics, a system of discipline based on fear, and dedication to the inculcation of conservative Calvinist doctrine. He had a deep-seated distrust of change, and Phillips Academy in 1871, the year he died, was almost identical with the School in 1838. As is almost always the case with "tough" teachers, his students never forgot him, whether they liked him or detested him. Whatever judgment may finally be made of this difficult gentleman, there is no question that during his term as Principal he *was* Phillips Academy.

Considering the reputation of Uncle Sam, it is interesting to note that he was not always like that. A pupil who studied under him while he was Assistant to Johnson wrote of him:

> I remember well "Uncle Sam's" first appearance as a sub-teacher in the old brick acad. He blushed like a girl, and we boys had to be very careful not to frighten him, which we could easily do by only an abrupt question.[26]

Soon after this the iron entered his soul, and we hear no more about blushing. In the last analysis Samuel Taylor made his reputation as a great teacher of the classics, and in so doing he developed a pedagogical method all his own. It will be instructive to examine a book that he published in 1861, entitled *Method of Classical Study: Illustrated by Questions*.[27] As the title implies, Taylor insisted that the best drill a student could receive in the classroom was to have the teacher fire one specific question after another at the students. If every single possible point about a given word or grammatical construction were covered, the pupil would then get a complete grasp of the material. Here, for example, are some questions to be used with a class starting Virgil's *Aenead*:

> When was Virgil born? Where? Was it in Italy or Gaul at that time? At what time was his birthplace first included in Italy? What was that part of the country called before? Who were the consuls at Rome the year he was born? Was he older or younger than Augustus? How much? How much older than Horace?[28]

And so on for several pages. His grammatical questions were, if anything, even more searching:

> Where is the caesural pause in the third line? From what Greek word does *vi* come? Origin of the *v*? Is *vis* actually defective in any case? What case is used very rarely? What relation does the ablative *vi* express? By what principle in the ablative?[29]

Any boy who could survive one of Uncle Sam's barrage of questions would have to know his material.

Though Phillips Academy undergraduates of the day had sharply differing points of view about Uncle Sam as a disciplinarian, almost all respected and admired him as a classroom teacher. A few of the really able students almost worshipped him, while even the dullards had to admit that he was effective. One former pupil wrote:

> As I write of him, I seem to feel that I must be precise, unflinching, bold, or I shall hear his voice as of old in the recitation-room saying right in the middle of an ugly sentence of Sallust, without a conjunction to cling to, "You may sit down, sir; you don't understand it." . . . With him it was better to be wholly wrong than half right and half wrong. He knew the one meant some kind of attempt at work, the other none at all. . . . I never entered his recitation room without trepidation, nor left it without relief. And for an hour before the bell struck I felt the coming excitement of a recitation before him. It amounted to an almost personal combat, developing the strong and crushing the weak. . . . If you carried any trophies away, you were sure of the applause of the class; but *his* approbation could only be guessed at. He did not deal in praise and flattery. . . . I have known him keep a scholar on his feet half an hour on a few lines of Homer, with such a running fire of questions as seemed impossible to stand under, and when the whole class scarcely breathed for fear of a single mistake of their champion. . . . [His method] strengthened the strong and overwhelmed the dunces. But for what purpose

are dunces sent to school if not to find out they are dunces? . . .
He was a natural leader; he would have made an admirable soldier
or president where there was work to be done. But he was content to
make ladders for others to climb.[30]

Another student remembers the Principal's rages:

Dr. Taylor . . . enjoyed an occasional display of "Jupiter Tonans."
We had a wholesome awe of him, and watched his big face for the
presage of a tempest. Sometimes he was quiet as a lamb, but anon . . .
he would seize the reins and crack his magesterial whip most un-
mercifully. . . . One day . . . the line "Forsan et haec meminisse
iuvabit" was translated with a slight mistake, *et* being translated *and*
instead of *also*. Uncle Sam roused up at once. "Sufficient, the next."
The next did no better. Down went man after man. . . . Meanwhile
Dr. Taylor grew more and more wrathful. His face became red and
swollen, his eyes flashed with pent-up indignation. . . . My time
came, and I began unconsciously with that fatal *and*. "Sufficient," he
shouted. "*Et* means *also*," I exclaimed indignantly, for he had not
allowed me to finish the sentence. "Sit down," he roared like a bull
of Bashan. But my words had drawn the lightning, and in a moment
the sunshine came.[31]

After a particularly bad pronunciation by a new boy Uncle Sam reacted as
follows:

Dr. Taylor had a way of covering his face with his hands—or rather
fists—to hide his emotions. At this juncture both fists went to his
face, and we students sat and watched while the evident struggle
went on. His face assumed all colors; he rolled around in his chair.
His cheeks enlarged and contracted like a bellows, and those two
fists played their part most vigorously. Was it rage or amazement? . . .
Slowly Dr. Taylor came to his ordinary self. At last one hand was
lowered, and then the mystery was solved. A broad radiant smile, such
as only Dr. Taylor's face could wear, suffused it from ear to ear.[32]

A member of the class of 1863 had similar feelings about him:

I well remember the feeling of awe with which one entered the *green*
room, with its statuary, standing on brackets on the wall. There was
the bust of Homer—and other celebrities—Greek and Roman of
ancient times, but the object that impressed us most on entering this
room was the august presence of "Uncle Sam" himself.
    The room was furnished with settees, and we were assigned our
places alphabetically. Uncle Sam . . . shuffled the cards on which
our names were written, then taking the top card, looking through
his gold rimmed spectacles, and with his stentorian voice, announced

the name of the boy that was to recite; with fear and trembling the student arose, and I doubt if anyone, during our Senior year, overcame the feeling altogether so that he could recite at ease. I am sure that *I never did* . . . It was studying the Greek and Latin languages with a microscope and we failed to get a very broad idea of the Greek and Latin literature. . . . I never think of Uncle Sam without feelings of respect and love. . . . He was not a man of persuasion, but a man of command, and he insisted on the performance of what he said, even when he was in the wrong, as sometimes he was, like other men. I think he considered it beneath his dignity to acknowledge the wrong; at least I never knew of his admitting an error.[33]

Some different aspects of the School's academic procedure are revealed in the following recollection:

In Senior year "Uncle Sam" heard two recitations a day—one immediately after prayers in the morning—the other at 3:15 p.m. (Evening Prayers at 4:30). Wednesday afternoons, however, were devoted to declamations and compositions—and Saturday afternoons to recreation. Greek was our only study for one week (10 recitations). By the end of the week we were well saturated with Greek. The next week we had Latin and so on alternate weeks except that for the last six weeks of a term we had Mathematics the latter part of the week (four recitations) reciting in divisions to the assistant teachers. The instruction in the classical department was confined to Latin, Greek and Mathematics, at least for the Senior year. A little ancient geography—consisting chiefly of committing to memory names of the countries, gulfs, rivers, etc. about the Mediterranean—was included in connection with the regular Greek and Latin recitations.

Dr. Taylor was very sharp and decisive in his style of conducting recitations, tolerating no hesitation or inadequate preparation on the part of the pupil. It is fair to say, however, that he failed to ask a tenth part of the questions included in his famous "Method of Classical Study". . . . A few pet quotations involving some fine points of the formation of words or constructions were soon anticipated (with the help, perhaps, of some annotated interleaved editions bequeathed by former classes) and thereafter it was plain sailing for the average pupil. Dr. Taylor had a habit of calling on a pupil to recite an entire Grammar lesson in Greek or Latin including a review lesson. . . . As he called up by cards it happened that (in a class of fifty) some were not called up during the entire year, while others were called up several times. After the "shuffling of cards" it happened that I was one of the unfortunate ones very often called up, with the words (uttered with a peculiarly gruff voice and prolonged tone) "Nolen: Grammar."[34]

An illustration of Uncle Sam's stubbornness in refusing to admit mistakes is the case of a boy named Smythe who insisted that his name be pronounced with a long *y*:

> Uncle Sam, probably *thoughtlessly*, called upon Smythe to recite and called his name Smith. We had no Smith in the class, so there could be no doubt whom Uncle Sam meant. Smythe did not rise and Uncle Sam, instead of admitting the error, and calling him by his proper name, *persisted* in calling him Smith. But Smythe paid no attention to the call. Finally Uncle Sam said, "Smith will *leave the room*", which Smythe inconsistently did. Afterwards he and Uncle Sam had it out. Smythe *insisted* that Uncle Sam knew his name, and he refused to answer to any name but his proper name. Things looked serious for a while, and we did not know but Smythe would be obliged to leave the Academy for disobedience.[35]

Unfortunately the narrator of this story never tells how the impasse was finally resolved, if it ever was, but the presumption is that Smythe was not expelled.

Finally, a thoughtful analysis of Dr. Taylor's teaching by a pupil who went on to become a college president:

> I have sat under five great teachers. The first, and among the greatest, was Samuel Harvey Taylor. His greatness did not lie in his knowledge of the ancient classics, nor indeed apparently in his wide and deep knowledge of any subject. It lay in a good knowledge of the texts of Cicero and Virgil, Xenophon and Homer; but it lay far more in a logical method of teaching the paragraphs and verses of these authors. He saw details; he understood principles; he knew relations. These knowledges were bound together by a consistent and vigorous system of logic. His constant question was "Why". He cared for the fact, but he cared far less for the fact than for its significance. His was a scientific method applied to the teaching of languages. Paradigms, conjunctions, prepositions, were only the scaffolding for building up the structure of reason. . . . No waste of time, no waste of words were suffered. I have known Uncle Sam to reprimand a student who in answer to the question replied, "It is in the dative case" with "Dative sufficient" or he might sit a man down with "Too many words, Smith".
>
> In this mood was to be found, it must be confessed, an element of fear. Everybody in the classroom feared Uncle Sam. He did not often, if ever, use the Beelzebub's tool for a teacher—sarcasm, but he could crush by a word or phrase. . . . The cause of this fear was the desire for accuracy on the part of the teacher. The young mind is given to intellectual looseness and to looseness in expression. . . .

Dr. Taylor struck deep and hard into such weaknesses. A translation was to be right.[36]

It was one thing to sit at the feet of Uncle Sam Taylor and receive what he had to offer, quite another to be in a class taught by one of the Assistants. Throughout the period of Uncle Sam's principalship the Assistants were generally an inferior lot, partly because the low salaries paid them could not attract able men and partly because Uncle Sam gave them no share in the running of the School. He never held a faculty meeting, for example. One gets the feeling that Uncle Sam was not particularly interested in his subordinates. His own classes during senior year would whip the boys into shape for college, and what happened before that was of secondary importance. On one occasion, as we shall see, the Assistants tried to go over Uncle Sam's head to the Trustees, but very little came of it. Here is a description of a class conducted by what must have been one of the weakest Assistants of the lot. But the fact that he could be hired is clear indication of the quality of the subordinate teachers during this period.

The Academy was under thorough discipline in my day, but when the students had a chance for sport they were not slow to use it. We had a teacher who could not manage a class. The boys soon discovered it, and acted accordingly. One day the high-water mark was reached. A large portion of the class appeared in the most grotesque array imaginable. All sorts of garments, but especially collars of the most fantastic and exuberant description. Scarcely had the exercises begun, when liberal quantities of buck-shot were thrown over the room. Then another and another discharge, until the recitation came to a halt. The instructor seemed in a daze. He paid no attention to the extraordinary sartorial appearance of the students, but expressed his wonder at the interruption. It was suggested that the shot came from outside, the windows being open. Mr. ---- sent a student out to examine. He soon reported that he had seen a figure disappearing around the corner of a building. But the fusilade of shot continued until the recitation was suspended. It never appeared that Mr. ---- understood the real character of the show. He naturally left soon.[37]

The relatively insignificant position in the School held by the Assistants is borne out also by the fact that they are seldom mentioned in the letters of students of this time.

Samuel Harvey Taylor was not only the most powerful teacher at Phillips Academy. As Principal he was also the School's chief disciplinarian, and as might be expected he ran a very taut ship indeed. He wanted no nonsense about a student's being innocent until proved guilty; for him all were guilty until proved innocent. At times he would charge a boy with some offense even though he had no proof, in the hope of smoking out a malefactor. It seems well established that he employed a system of spies who reported to him regularly, and this was probably responsible for the student belief that he knew everything that was going on in the School. A pupil who admired Uncle Sam as a teacher had little use for his disciplinary system:

> He not only governed; he ruled; he was master. His method of ruling . . . was not unlike the atmosphere of his classroom. It was the method of fear; fear of the penalties of disobedience, fear of disapproval of his own judgment. He kept not a few boys in a kind of mortal terror . . . a terror which one now sees was ridiculous, both for the creator and for the victims. It may be well for some boys to be kept in terror, but I am sure that as a method of permanent academic government, it is not good for either growing souls or growing bodies. The doctrine of total depravity was taught in the neighboring theological seminary. Dr. Taylor apparently believed it as applied to boys. He seemed to think of boys as either little or big rascals until they proved themselves something else. . . . He held the peril of suspension or expulsion over not a few of us, and at times he used it in ways that now seem ridiculously cruel.
>
> The further I move away from the years of Uncle Sam the more heartily do I appreciate the worth of his teaching, and also with equal heartiness do I have an increasing detestation of the methods he used as Principal, in the formation of manhood among us young fellows.[38]

Not all students felt as bitterly about Uncle Sam's discipline as the previous writer. One who could see the humorous side recounts the return of Uncle Sam, whom he describes as "a large party with bow legs," from a year in Europe. All the School was at the railway station to greet him.

> As the train came to a full stop a shrill voice was heard to say. "Here he comes. I saw this end of the car go down." As luck would have it immediately afterwards Dr. Taylor stepped onto the platform from the door of the car and was greeted with yells of laughter, cheers and screams.[39]

On another occasion a boy was out of bounds during study hours, sitting on a stone wall.

> He happened to look down the road and saw Uncle Sam's head over the top of a slight hill approaching his resting place. He immediately tumbled over backwards and hid under a barberry bush, believing that he had not been seen. Uncle Sam walked slowly up the road, seated himself comfortably on the stone wall and began to eat barberries. The situation became so ludicrous that the boy burst out laughing, and Uncle Sam joined him in the laughter, and giving him

a very mild reprimand, sent him back with no other penalty for the violation of the rule. I think he would have sat there almost all day if the boy had not laughed.⁴⁰

This is about the only instance on record of Uncle Sam's having a sense of humor. On another occasion two boys were planning an unauthorized trip to the "Fem-Sem" (Abbot Academy) and ran into Uncle Sam:

> The evening was intensely dark, and there being no street lights, Dr. Taylor did not recognize the boys. He started after them very rapidly; as he accelerated his gait, theirs was accelerated at a greater rate; both parties broke into a run, but the Doctor was handicapped too heavily. When the boys reached the seminary they found the grounds so thoroughly patrolled that they had to give up their plan, and walked up the hill to a vacant lot next door to the house Dr. Taylor occupied. . . . In a few minutes Dr. Taylor's door opened and the boys tumbled backwards into the pasture lot and, lying flat on the ground, entered upon their watch. . . . Dr. Taylor walked slowly out of his yard, turned down the street and stopped under a tree, where he was completely invisible in the dense darkness. Here he stood over an hour to nab any boy that happened to pass or perhaps overhear a conversation. However the boys that evening were giving his house a wide berth, and after waiting an hour without accomplishing anything he went back into his house.⁴¹

An example of Dr. Taylor's unreasonableness in doling out punishment can be seen in the expulsion of a boy who later went on to become a bishop. Some of the boys had burned a shed back of the English Commons. The bishop had had nothing to do with it, but Uncle Sam wanted a victim, and the bishop had "a very stiff neck and backbone." The two simply did not get along together. As a result the bishop was expelled "after some words."⁴²

On occasion even Uncle Sam could be fooled. A boy had set fire to the grass around the Latin Common. Some workmen attempted to put it out and asked the undergraduates to help. But they were enjoying the fire and refused to do so—all, that is, except the boy who had started the fire and who was getting worried. The next morning Uncle Sam gave the School a lecture in which he reprimanded them for not helping put out the fire, and then added, "There was *one noble* young man who assisted in putting out the fire." This brought an "ear-splitting laugh" from the boys—"but Uncle Sam did not see where the laugh came in, and I do not know that he ever caught on."⁴³ But occasions like this were rare. For the most part the School stood in awe of Uncle Sam's almost superhuman ability to keep the undergraduates in line. One student wrote:

> There was nothing that he did not know. There was no wall so silent,

there was no bedroom so secret, there was no midnight so dark, there were no recesses of the mind so obscure, that the thought of any boy was not known to him; and oftentimes when we came up in the innocence of artless life, supposing that we had walked alone, there came that momentous sentence after morning prayers, when every boy awaited the words that should come next, "The following individuals are requested to remain."[44]

It is ironic that for all his ability as a disciplinarian the two most serious defiances of School authority should have occurred during Uncle Sam's regime. (The "Anti-Slavery Rebellion," involving a matter of principle outside the School, was really in a different category.) In 1846 occurred the "Catalogue Rebellion."[45] The senior class that year was particularly strong, with a number of self-willed and independent boys in it. When the time came to make preparations for commencement exercises, several of the leaders got into an altercation with Uncle Sam about the assignment of parts in the commencement proceedings and the form of the catalogue. The ringleader of the boys was William Stark, a grandson of General John Stark, the hero of Bennington during the Revolution. Stark has been described by a fellow student as being "a sort of Steerforth among us little fellows, full of music, poetry, impudence, and resolution."[46] When Stark (who thought he should be valedictorian) and his friends found Uncle Sam adamant on the matter of commencement procedures, they petitioned him for dismission from Phillips Academy.[47] Instead of granting their request, Uncle Sam expelled eight of the leaders, including Stark. When news of this reached the School "a fearful rumpus was created, a rebellion was at once inaugurated."[48] Uncle Sam was hissed in the Stone Academy and excitement among the undergraduates was intense. With the departure of the expelled boys, however, things began to quiet down and the School thought that was the end of the matter. But they reckoned without William Stark, who had no intention of letting the matter stop there. Before his departure from Andover he had obtained a copy of the 1846 catalogue that was to be distributed at commencement. He then traveled to Troy, New York, where he got a printer to publish a new set of catalogues that would include the names of those who had been expelled. He added a nice touch by listing himself as "Teacher of Sacred Music" with the rest of the faculty. He then returned with the copies of his new catalogue and by some extraordinary means managed to substitute them for Uncle Sam's catalogues on commencement day. As a final flourish he managed to persuade the band that was to have come out from Boston to play at commencement to remain in the Hub. When the commencement crowd became aware of the hoax and the absence of the band, there was consternation. But Uncle Sam rallied his forces and the ceremonies eventually proceeded more or less normally. A student of the time sums up the results by saying, "Uncle Sam had his way; but for a week Phillips Academy was in an uproar, and fierce rebellion prevailed."[49] Tricks like the one Stark played can be contagious, and the following fall there appeared an eight-page burlesque poem entitled *Phillipiad*. Although it left Uncle Sam pretty much alone, it attacked the Trustees and the school Treasurer, Samuel Fletcher. Of the Trustees it was written:

> Hold your temper, do not sneeze,
> Here's a board of twelve trustees,
> Hundred thousand dollars, cash,
> Given to them at a dash,
> Have increased for many years,
> Swelled by widow's toil and tears,
> Till it's reached a sum untold,
> Gloating o'er extorted gold.

Interestingly enough, the poem had high praise for Lyman Coleman, until recently head of the Teachers' Seminary, and for William H. Wells and Abner J. Phipps, two of the assistants. The doggerel was circulated widely in the school, but Uncle Sam, possibly making use of his spy system, discovered the authors and promptly expelled them. After this, things again returned to normal.[50]

The second rebellion under Uncle Sam occurred in 1867 and was a much more significant outbreak, particularly as far as the results were concerned.[51] It all happened innocently enough. "One glorious Saturday morning in early summer"[52] three boys decided to "cut" classes and go to Haggett's pond for a swim. They were all good students, and since their classes were simply reviewing old material, they did not think they would suffer as a result of their absence. When they returned, they found notes from Uncle Sam to report to his study. This they did and found the Principal in surly mood because of an attack of the gout that had crippled him for some days. Much to their consternation, they were informed by Uncle Sam that because of their action they should consider themselves expelled. That same day Archie Bush, captain of the baseball nine and a Civil War veteran, had gone with a friend to Boston to see a baseball game. These two were also caught and expelled by Uncle Sam. Student resentment at such a harsh penalty for a relatively minor offense was intense. After a mass meeting on the Old Campus, about half the class decided to commit a similar offense and, in effect, dare Dr. Taylor to expel them all. This group hired what one writer called "barges"[53] and proceeded to Lawrence in hope of attending a circus. Though there proved to be no circus in town, they stayed for supper and then returned to Andover, passing Uncle Sam's house and making a great deal of noise. If the boys thought that the Principal would not accept their challenge, they were sorely mistaken. Uncle Sam proceeded to fire the whole lot. One writer suggests that it was the Trustees of Phillips Academy who insisted on this mass expulsion and that

Uncle Sam would have preferred a lighter penalty.[54] In any event the Trustees voted to support the punishment,[55] and about half the class of 1867 never got their Andover diplomas.

The repercussions of this episode had a profound effect on Phillips Academy. Up until this time a majority of Andover graduates had always gone to Yale. The expelled group, since its members could not go to Yale as planned, decided on Harvard, only to discover that the Phillips Academy preparation did not qualify them for admission. Accordingly, many spent the rest of the summer with Harvard tutors cramming for the entrance exams, and most were admitted. Among them was Archie Bush, who proceeded to lead a series of Harvard baseball teams to victories over Yale during his entire college career. Uncle Sam was understandably outraged at this, for Harvard had not demanded a recommendation from him for the expelled boys. In his report to the Trustees for 1868 he pointed out that all the other colleges to which the expelled boys had gone had required them to write "a full and manly apology" to Phillips Academy for their dereliction. On receipt of this the Academy sent a statement to the effect that the boys had had good records, save for this one serious violation of the school rules.

> Harvard College, however, admitted those who applied, without any papers of any kind from us. As I considered such a course injurious, in its tendency, to our own school, as well as to others, I sought an interview with President Hill, during our last vacation, for the purpose of learning the facts in the case. . . . He treated the matter with great candor and courtesy. He said that there was a difference of opinion in the Faculty themselves, and that they had a sharp discussion in regard to the measure to be adopted, some of their number contending that the students had been sufficiently punished by their removal from the Academy here. He said also that he ought to have written here and learned more about the case, but that his mind was greatly distracted at that time. . . . He added, too, in the end, "I do not feel quite satisfied with our position."[56]

The most important result of the 1867 rebellion was to call attention to Andover's antiquated curriculum. In 1865 the four Assistants at the Academy had appealed to the Board of Trustees to give more time to mathematics. They pointed out that since math was taught only intermittently during the School year, it was "held in a certain degree of contempt." They pointed out that outstanding classical scholars with deficiencies in math often had leading roles at commencement exercises, while the reverse was never true. And they cited the testimony of math professors at Yale, Amherst, and Brown to the fact that Andover graduates were poorly prepared in that subject.[57] The case for more math certainly needed to be made, but one effect of the 1867 rebellion was to call attention to the fact that Phillips Academy's classical preparation was not sufficient for Harvard. As one student wrote:

> Now these matters [that Andover students were not prepared to enter Harvard] became quite widely known, not only in this vicinity, where they had more or less newspaper notoriety, but it must have been known more or less widely in the home towns of each of the boys, and the result was that Andover must have got quite a black eye, so to speak, because twenty five persons learned to one who knew it before that Andover could not fit boys for Harvard; consequently it must be a second rate preparatory school, compared with Boston Latin, Exeter, etc.[58]

All of this was a heavy cross for Uncle Sam to bear, and it undoubtedly saddened his last years. His son wrote of "the fearful strain on Father to take them back, both from his own impulse and external pressure."[59] The same student whom we have quoted before has this to say by way of conclusion:

> Another result was that it was the beginning of the end of the regime of Uncle Sam. It was the first big shake up which speedily led to great change at Andover, to new methods and to new men. I do not by any means assume that this episode was the sole cause of the change, because it was beginning to take place everywhere. The time was ripe for a change and it would have come anyway, sooner or later, for the old-fashioned type of school and the old-fashioned type of school master were soon destined to pass away, never to return, but this episode hastened the day for Andover.[60]

During most of Dr. Taylor's term as Principal the English Department of Phillips Academy occupied a subordinate position in the school. Uncle Sam himself was not interested in a nonclassical program and did little if anything to strengthen the department, and the boys in the classical section of the School, as noted, tended to look down on the English students as second-class citizens. The teachers in the department were underpaid, and the curriculum was disorganized. In 1857, for example, the following smorgasborg was offered as a "Course of Study":

> Reading, Writing, Orthography; Wells's Grammar; Morse's Geography; History of the United States (Lossing's or Wilson's); General History (Wilson's); Eaton's Arithmetic; Day's Algebra; Davies's Bourdon, Legendre, Surveying, Analytical Geometry and Descriptive Geometry; Bridge's Conic Sections; Olmstead's Natural Philosophy and Astronomy; Kendall's Uranography; Hitchcock's Book-keeping by Double Entry; Gray's Chemistry; Mineralogy and Geology; Wood's Botany; Hooker's Anatomy and Physiology; Paley's Natural

Theology; Evidences of Christianity; Rhetoric; Logic; Upham's Mental Philosophy; Wayland's Moral Science and Political Economy.[61]

And, it was added, any boy who wished could get instruction in sacred music without additional charge. There was no regular procedure for dividing the students into classes, nor had any clear-cut decision been made as to just what the department was trying to do. From 1847 to 1865, the Head of the English Department was James S. Eaton, a man who labored manfully to overcome the handicaps he was faced with. He had a back-breaking schedule, as his reports to the Trustees show:

> The classes to which I have given my attention during the past year, have been eight daily, reciting in Grammar with an analysis of poetry, Geography, Arithmetic, Algebra, Geometry, Trigonometry, Arithmetic, Surveying, Analytical Geometry, Philosophy, Book-Keeping by Single and Double Entry, Reading, Spelling, Writing, etc.—the classes varying from two to above thirty.
>
> Besides these duties I have had the oversight of the general school room, in which the younger members of the Eng. Dept. (And of the Classical Dept. in the Winter Term) have studied during school hours.[62]

As if this were not enough, Uncle Sam Taylor on one occasion tried to get him to take over the management of a School boarding house.[63] Eaton knew that things were not well with his department. He was one of the signers of the petition to the Trustees in 1865 urging more mathematics for the School. In another report to the Trustees he complained of the "wide range of subjects" being taught, the result being that there were only forty minutes per subject. Often a complicated scientific demonstration had to be interrupted because of lack of time. But the main problem, he felt, was in a lax admission policy, under which numbers of unqualified students were admitted.[64]

Eaton was underpaid during his whole career. Though he was head of a department, his salary was never more than half of Uncle Sam's. Fortunately, he was able to supplement his income by publishing some arithmetic books for School use, which became very popular. As for discipline, he was as different from Uncle Sam as night from day—invariably courteous, kind, and firm. When Uncle Sam went to Europe in 1856, Eaton took over the whole School and made a great hit with the students.[65] But when he died in 1865, worn out by his labors, he had succeeded in achieving few of the reforms that he desired for his department.

In 1866 the English Department received a tremendous boost when the banker George Peabody gave the school $25,000 to establish a chair in Mathematics and the Natural Sciences. Peabody knew of the School through some relatives who had attended and he was sympathetic with its aims.

"Cordially approving the general character and aims of the Academy and sympathizing with you in your efforts to give the Institution a higher and wider sphere" was the way he put it.[66] Peabody insisted that the income be used to pay the holder of the chair and for nothing else, for he wanted to be sure that the School engaged a top-flight teacher. The Trustees made an admirable choice when they appointed William B. Graves, an Amherst graduate who at the time was teaching Mathematics at his alma mater. Another of George Peabody's stipulations was that the holder of his chair would automatically be head of the English Department. Thus Graves moved in and soon had that part of the School thoroughly reorganized. First of all, he divided the students into three classes—Senior, Middle, and Junior—as had been done in the Classical Department for some years. Then he proceeded to draw up a precise course of study, term by term, for the three-year period. In the process he eliminated some of the more bizarre courses, like natural theology. Finally, he eliminated completely the idea that the English Department was to train teachers, a concept that had continued after the closing of the Teachers' Seminary.[67] When Graves left Phillips Academy in 1870, he had succeeded in putting the English Department on a much firmer footing, and he was to do much more when he returned to the School in 1881 under Dr. Bancroft.

In contrast to the changes that were beginning to be instituted in the English Department, the Classical Department under Uncle Sam held firm to the old ways. Dr. Taylor was ignorant of, or oblivious to, the educational innovations that were taking place in the country, especially as far as college admissions were concerned, and he remained supremely confident in the efficacy of his own program. His rigidity is illustrated in the annual reports he made to the Trustees—a series of arid and sterile documents. Most of the reports simply listed the number of students, outlined what teaching Uncle Sam himself had been doing, commented on the general deportment of the School, and reported on the number of "hopefully pious" who had been converted during the year. Occasionally a miscellaneous item or two would be added. In 1846 he mentioned the "considerable insubordination" that had occurred during the Catalogue Rebellion and explained why the Exhibition had been so confused. In 1848 he reported that the Latin Commons privy had burnt, but added with pride that he had caught all ten of the perpetrators and expelled them. About the only educational matter that he ever reported was the problem of frequent change of Assistants. In 1867, for example, he wrote:

> I regret to be obliged to repeat what was contained in my report of last year, that the Academy suffered from so frequent a change of teachers. One of our teachers left at the close of the autumn term on account of inadequate salary; and his place has been supplied since by three different teachers. Another left at the close of the spring term

on account of the state of his health, and his place has been supplied by two teachers. Most of these supplies have been from the Theological Seminary, the person employed hearing a single recitation in the forenoon and in the afternoon. . . . these changes are not favorable to the school. . . . By a vote of the Board we are allowed to offer a salary of $800 a year for a new Teacher. This sum was recently offered to one of our former scholars . . . but another more lucrative position was offered him, and in consequence we failed to secure him. . . . It is becoming pretty evident that we cannot get the best class of Teachers from our Colleges for the salary which the Trustees propose.

The only curricular modification that Dr. Taylor mentions appears in his 1870 report, just before his death, when he announced that the lower classes in the Classical Department were to have a class in English.[68] An examination of the school catalogues for Uncle Sam's period shows that the curriculum of the Classical Department remained unchanged throughout Dr. Taylor's tenure, aside from a few new courses in mathematics which presumably had been added as a result of the petition of the Assistants in 1865. By the time Dr. Taylor died in 1871 it was clear that reform was long overdue; it would fall to his successor to bring Phillips Academy up to date.

One can obtain some insight into the quality and effectiveness of the Academy's educational procedures during the Taylor years from a series of reports on the School made by the Trustee Examining Committees. The theme running through these documents is summarized in one of them, where the Committee reports: "The Committee would not, therefore, at the present time, recommend any particular change; but would recommend that the course which has been pursued during a few past years, with so much success, be for the present continued."[69] Nearly all the reports are very high in their praise for the abilities and accomplishments of the students, and when criticism is made, it is almost invariably on minor points. In 1843 the Committee thought the pronunciation could be improved in the classics and suggested that this would help the students' ability to handle the English language as well.[70] Two years later they were particularly impressed with the students in uranology in the English Department.[71] Early in the 1850's the Committee expressed some concern that there was not enough time given to mathematics, but they were delighted with the performance of the pupils in that subject and they made no strong recommendation that mathematics be given more time.[72] In the mid-1850's the Committee believed that too many students were being admitted to the English Department, many without adequate preparation, and recommended tightening admissions requirements. There were too many scholars, they thought, who were "too dull or too young for this place."[73] Throughout the whole period there are occasional references to the frequent turnover of teachers, but the Committee was unable to see how the Trustees could do anything about this—or about providing more mathematics—without "expenditures beyond the means of the Board."[74] The Committee was as pleased with the program at the end of the period as at the beginning. If changes were needed at Phillips Academy, they would not come from this group.

The records of the Board of Trustees during this period indicate that the Board was carrying out its duties in a pedestrian way. From time to time they bought new equipment for the School—"philosophical apparatus," a Galvanic battery, a melodeon, and some apparatus for gymnastic exercises.[75] They received gratefully the telegraph set that Samuel F. B. Morse had given to the School, which had been set up to connect the Academy building with the Principal's house. They authorized the planting of more trees and the painting of School buildings. They approved having a teacher live in the Latin and the English Commons to ride herd on the students there.[76] The most serious problem they had to face came in 1864, when the Stone Academy was completely destroyed by fire. Though it was never proved, it was generally believed that the fire had been set by a disgruntled student who had recently been expelled. In this case the Alumni got the jump on the Trustees and offered to raise the money for a new building before the Trustees had done anything about it. Eventually some $21,000 was raised, but since this sum proved insufficient, the Treasurer was authorized to borrow up to $20,000 more, thus creating a debt that was an embarrassment to the School for years.[77] The new building, constructed where Samaritan House now stands, was a huge, ugly structure, designed by a Mr. Cummings, but it had ample space for the School's activities and a large meeting hall on the third floor. It would serve as the main academy building until the construction of Samuel Phillips Hall in 1924. The Taylor period was a lean one as far as gifts were concerned. Aside from George Peabody's generous benefaction, the pickings were slim. In 1854 the senior class established a Students' Educational Fund of $100, and in 1867 James G. Clarke gave $1000 for a scholarship, but that was about it.[78] Without more funds the School could not pay adequate salaries or keep the plant in shape, yet the Board made no attempt to raise money. Since the new main building was large enough to provide for all the classroom needs, what is now Bulfinch Hall was vacant, and the Trustees voted to turn it into a gymnasium, the first action of a Phillips Academy Board to provide for the nonacademic needs of the undergraduate body.[79] All in all, however, the Board was anything but dynamic during this period.

An analysis of the undergraduate body during the Taylor years reveals some interesting changes. In 1842 Phillips Academy had 108 students; in 1843, with the addition of the Teachers' Seminary as the English Department, the number jumped to 283. Though the numbers fell off at the end of the decade, the 1850's saw a remarkable period of growth, the high point being reached in 1855 with 396 students. Enrollment remained over 300 during most of the remainder of Dr. Taylor's administration, though it dropped again in the late 60's. In terms of size it was a new School; yet no adequate provision was made to increase the faculty. In 1855, for example, there were only four Assistants and Uncle Sam to teach 396 boys. In addition to increasing in numbers, the undergraduate body became more diversified geographically. In the class of 1842 there was one boy from Iowa, with 72 from Massachusetts and 22 from New Hampshire. By 1855, with 222 from Massachusetts, the Midwest and South were beginning to be represented: 2 from Louisiana, 7 from Ohio, 5 from Illinois, 1 from Florida, 1 from Missouri, 1 from Michigan, 1 from Wisconsin, 1 from Arkansas, and 1 from the Oregon territory. This trend continued for the rest of Dr. Taylor's term. In 1868 there were 12 from Ohio, 13 from Illinois, and 4 from Missouri, with California, Montana territory, and Kansas also represented.[80] It is impossible to account for these changes in size and geographical distribution with precision. The increase in population of the Midwest, together with the construction of a railroad network connecting it with the East, must have been important factors. It is clear that the reputation of the School in general and Uncle Sam in particular had been steadily growing. Not only was Uncle Sam known as a great teacher; he was famous for whipping recalcitrant young men into shape, and there is reason to believe that many boys were sent to Phillips Academy by distracted parents who wanted them shaped up. One way in which the reputation of the School must have been expanded was through Andover boys in college who would recommend the academy for younger sons of classmates. As far as college choice is concerned, Yale was clearly in the lead. As one alumnus wrote:

> There was a deeply rutted road to Yale, and it was the only road in sight, though there were a few trails to some of the smaller colleges, which were very small indeed at this time. There was no record of anyone ever graduating from Andover and going to Yale with Uncle Sam's recommendation who failed to get in.[81]

A partial breakdown of the Class of 1858 shows that 20 went to Yale, 10 to Williams, and the rest to a smattering of other colleges. In 1863 21 went to Yale, 8 to Brown, 5 to Harvard, and the rest scattered. In 1868, after the Rebellion of 1867, Yale still had the largest number with 25, but Amherst and Harvard each had 12. During Uncle Sam's years, the tradition of Phillips for being a Yale feeder became firmly established and was to last well into the twentieth century. Partial returns on the occupations of graduates indicate a preference for the professions. In the Class of 1858 there were 6 lawyers, 12 ministers, 9 teachers, and 6 businessmen, with a broad scattering among such positions as editor, dentist, author, and the like. The Class of 1868 showed much the same pattern, except that the number of businessmen, teachers, lawyers, and doctors increased markedly. One graduate reported that he was a fish-dealer. Another reflection of the times is in the falling off of the number of ministers. In general the under-graduates during Uncle Sam's years increased in number, became more widely distributed geographically, and, toward the end, became less theologically oriented.[82]

In the 1840's at Phillips Academy was a boarding house on Phillips Street known as the "Academic Commons." It was designed to board students training to be ministers or teachers and, if there was room, other "sober minded youths." A superintendent was in charge and each member of the organization was required to work two hours a day on the Commons farm to help pay for his board. A system of student monitors was established to supervise the dining room and the neighboring Commons rooms. The purpose, it was explained, was as follows:

> It shall be the duty of all to live together as a band of brothers, act upon Christian principles, avoid levity, jesting, low language, and everything *inconsistent with the character of young gentlemen* who are looking forward to future usefulness in Church and State."[83]

At the end of the decade the Academic Commons was given up, partly because the superintendent could not meet expenses and partly, one suspects, because too many undergraduates disliked the extreme piety of its rules. In its place eating clubs were established, which would provide boarding facilities for at least part of the students for the rest of the century. These institutions were student-managed, a so-called caterer being responsible for the purchase of food and collection of money. Decisions on menu were determined by majority votes of the boarders. As the caterer of the Union Club wrote, "If it was voted to have meat twice a day, then meat was served twice a day. If the majority voted to have griddle cakes every morning, then the club had griddle cakes every morning." A Miss Gould did the cooking for the Union Club members and was paid 37½¢ a head per week. The caterer was very proud of the fact that he was able to provide meals for $1.40 per week when other clubs went as high as $2.00. The secret of his success, he said, was "care and judgment in the buying. It was my custom to visit the farmers and contract for butter and other supplies, buying at a price lower than the ruling prices maintained by the retail merchants."[84] An energetic member of the Class of 1865 wrote out the menu of his club for a whole week for his family:

Sunday	Chocolate Toast	Breakfast
	Cold Cornbeef Apple Pie	Dinner
	Tea Cake	Supper
Monday	Corn Cake Coffee	Breakfast
	Roast Beef & Potatoes	Dinner
	Tea	Supper
Tuesday	Milk Toast Coffee	Breakfast
	Beefsteak and Potatoes	Dinner
	Apple Sauce	Supper
Wednesday	Hot Rolls Coffee	Breakfast
	Beans	Dinner
	Tea	Supper
Thursday	Toast Chocolate	Breakfast
	Boiled dish, Corn, beans, turnips	Dinner
	Tea	Supper
Friday	Hash Coffee	Breakfast
	Fried Fish	Dinner
	Tea	Supper
Saturday	Biscuit Coffee	Breakfast
	Beefsteak, Tomatoes	Dinner
	Tea, applesauce	Supper

Bread and butter *always* every meal.
Potatoes for *dinner*.
Milk Breakfast and Supper except when we
   have chocolate.
Pudding twice per week and Pie three times
   per week.[85]

Interestingly enough, Uncle Sam Taylor left the boys to their own devices in the matter of the eating clubs. And they seem to have done surprisingly well in their management of them. Still, then as today, there was a great deal of complaint about the food. A student in 1849 wrote: "Our board grows worse and worse. I can hardly manage to eat anything. They have in reality nothing that is fit to eat. If you would board here a short time you would see something worse than anything you can conceive of in the shape of board."[86] This opinion was echoed by many others.

What did the students do when they were not eating or sleeping or studying? Since the administration made no provision for an athletic program or any extracurricular activities, the boys had to develop their own. Among the most popular form of outside activity were the student societies. The Social Fraternity disappeared in the 1840's, but, partly as a result of its demise, the Philomathean Society entered its golden years. Not only were the usual debates and declamations held; in 1854 the society founded *The Mirror of the Philomathean Society*, a literary venture that would continue to be published under one name or another until the end of the century. The magazine contained short essays and poems, the first number dealing with such topics as "Imagination," "True Happiness," "The Safeguards of the Republic," "The Garden of Cosmos—An Allegory," and the like. For the most part the magazine was serious and published with care. *The Mirror* was not by any means the only publication on the Hill, however. Perhaps inspired by the example of William Stark and his fake catalogue of 1846, a plethora of mock publications appeared in the 1850's and 60's, presumably to the great amusement of the undergraduates. In 1857 the first number of the *Phillipian* appeared—there would not be another until 1878. It contained among other things a spoof called "The Two Gentlemen of Andover" with S. H. Taylor playing the part of Valentine. Mock Exhibition programs appeared almost every year in the 1860's, complete with names like "F-lat B-rained Sears," giving orations on such topics as "The Quality of Blood's Tobacco." Handbills advertised "Phillips' Great Bare Show" and "Sam Taylor's Educated Gorillas." In 1866 the School was listed on the cover of a program as "Phillips Insane Asylum." Occasionally more ambitious students would get out four-page newspapers. In 1861 *The Plaindealer* had a take-off on Uncle Sam's classroom procedure: "Uncle next took out his spelling book, and called upon Newhall. 'Spell dog.' 'Dog, d-o-g, dog.' Uncle—'We cannot waste our time by saying dog, I asked you to spell *dog*, and I wish you to be more specific and scholarly. Now can you spell dog?' 'D-o-g.' 'Correct.' " In 1863 *The Scalpel* had a take-off on Uncle Sam's trip to Europe. This piece depicted the Principal as drinking tun after tun of beer in Germany, obtaining Dante's gold-bowed specs in Italy so that he could detect "total depravity in the hearts of innocent youth," and in Jerusalem finding Judas Iscariot's old brown straw hat. In 1859 *Trumpet* pronounced that the M.A.

after James S. Eaton's name meant "Master of Asses" and commented that during the sixteen years that he had been head of the English Department "he has always figured conspicuously in everybody's business but his own." To add to the fun most of these newspapers contained a series of false advertisements.[87] Despite the generally low quality of the fugitive sheets, it must have taken a great deal of energy, not to say money, to get them out, and one can be sure that the undergraduates of that day enjoyed them immensely. Uncle Sam apparently never paid any attention to them; as long as undergraduates obeyed the rules, he was content to leave them alone.

About mid-century the Theological Seminary turned Stowe House, where the theologues had previously been making coffins and other items, into a gymnasium. Phillips Academy students were allowed to use it by paying one dollar.[88] As one student described the new set-up:

> There is apparatus there for the development of every part of the body. It is a favorite resort of the students, and will undoubtedly add years to the lives of many students here. I spend the hour from 4 to 5 in the afternoon there in leaping, running, jumping, swinging, etc. I possess as yet little skill but make up in my zeal my want in that respect.[89]

In addition to this facility for letting off steam, the boys engaged in informal baseball and football games, usually played between different classes, while in the winter bobsledding was a favorite attraction, the boys watering the ruts so that they would become icy and make the sled go faster.[90] But the most popular recreation was walking around the Andover countryside—down to the Shawsheen River, over to Indian Ridge, up to Holt's Hill. And in the summer there would be a chance for a swim. Many of the boys commented on the beauty of the country around Andover. One wrote:

> Andover now is in a very flourishing condition, all is covered with green. The birds add novelty to the seen [sic] by singing their merry notes, all is beautiful and sublime. I can say now that we go a-sailing on the pond and get Lilies and other beautiful flowers.[91]

Another boy said, "I have just returned from a walk over Indian Ridge and the Shawshine. . . . those places are verily the *most* beautiful places I ever was in." He goes on, "My windows are open, and frequent perfumes fill the air from a neighboring grove of cherry and apple trees . . . and a number of beautiful Hum-birds are busy beneath my window, delicately sipping honey from the blossoms with long and slender bills, their rapid wings evolving soft melodious music."[92] On the other hand Andover in December was something else again. Writing in that month a new boy said, "I thought it was the lonesomest and most dreary looking place that ever was and my opinion has not altered but little since."[93]

A perceptive recollection of Phillips Academy comes from a farm boy who lived about eight miles away on the Merrimack River. In the fall of 1870 he came to Andover to have an interview with Dr. Taylor but was not accepted. He therefore went to the bookstore and bought Uncle Sam's *Method of Classical Study*, returned to his farm and established a regimen whereby he did farm chores all day, went to bed right after supper, and then got up at two o'clock to study his Latin. His efforts were successful, and in the spring of the following year he was admitted. He and his father loaded the farm wagon with some dry wood and the few furnishings he had for his room and drove to Andover. His arrival he describes as follows:

> As we drew up before the first house of Latin Commons I saw with burning cheeks that our queer turnout aroused an amused curiosity in the group of nattily dressed boys, lounging about the door. As we carried my possessions up to my room, I caught glimpses of bright carpets and prettily furnished rooms.

But his initial embarrassment soon passed:

> I found myself fitted into a comfortable and happy place in a great school. I soon saw that a meagerly furnished room and ill-fitting clothes did not count; that in Phillips Academy a boy was rated for what he really was, for what he was honestly trying to make of himself.

Unlike some students, he remembered the Latin Commons with nothing but pleasure—getting water in pitchers from the pump and all. "We never knew we were uncomfortable," he thought. He ate at an eating club near by and remembered particularly the hassles over the menu. Mr. President . . . I move that applesauce be substituted for stewed prunes for supper tonight," said a boy on one occasion. A heated discussion followed, with the steward warning the boys that apples were very expensive at that time. Yet the motion carried. They got along very well, he thought, primarily because they knew nothing about balanced diets, calories, and vitamins. His Andover experience, he concluded, was invaluable. He got splendid classroom training, while "Unorganized play on the campus, life in Commons, and enthusiastic support of the literary societies were efficient educative forces" as well.[94]

Particular happenings also served to vary the monotony of school life. One morning, on the wall by the stairs leading up to "No. 9," Uncle Sam's classroom in the Stone Academy, some wag had written:

Uncle Sam, L.L.D. is
A long leged donkey

And undearneath that:

> If flesh is grass as some folks say
> Then Uncle Sam's a load of hay.

Dr. Taylor soon apprehended the culprit and was, characteristically, more outraged by the misspelling of "legged" than by the doggerel itself.[95]

Fires were a continuing hazard for the Academy. In January 1849 Number 3, Latin Commons caught fire in mid-morning. Since the boys were all in classes, it took some time to get the bucket brigade and the dilapidated fire engine to the scene, and as a result the building burnt to the ground. Both Uncle Sam and one of the students got their ears frozen for their trouble.[96] Later one of the English Commons buildings caught fire early in the morning. A boy rushed to Uncle Sam's house to get a key for the Academy building and ring the bell, while another was dispatched to ring the Seminary bell and rouse the theologues. On this occasion the School's fire engine with its hand-pump was brought to the well, but sucked it dry in a short space of time. Fortunately townies came with their engine and finally extinguished the blaze. Uncle Sam supervised things throughout, "full of encouragement and hot coffee," as one boy put it.[97] Though Dr. Taylor believed Christmas to be a pagan festival and held classes as usual that day, the Fourth of July was celebrated in the community, sometimes with an enthusiasm that caused Uncle Sam great pain:

> Although Mr. Taylor has expressly forbidden that any use should be made of "crackers" or powder in any shape, yet as early as 20 minutes past 12 o'clock Monday morning, the "Commons boys" began to fire off crackers and torpedoes, and to ring the Academy bell furiously. It seems Uncle had anticipated something of this sort and before the bell had struck a doz. strokes, he was at the porch of "Doubting Castle" [Academy Building] in high dudgeon: the way of the egress being blocked up, the poor fellow who was "ringing his patriotism" jumped down the cellar stairs, Uncle just behind him, and dashed through a window and escaped. Uncle not liking to try the hazardous experiment retreated, and went up to "commons." He went into the house and silenced the "boys," but no sooner had he left the building than the rascals began to blaze away again. Hearing a tremendous racket in Sanford's room . . . he went up and kicked open the door while the "victims" in the room supposing it was one of the students, threw a lighted bunch of crackers at him: they soon found out their mistake, however, for Uncle immediately seized Sanford by the collar and ordered him to leave school as quick as possible; (upon reflection he was induced to revoke this decision.) For more than an hour Uncle strove ineffectually to quiet the disturbance, and when it became comparatively

still and Uncle had retired from the ground, then the bell began to
ring again, and the crackers and small cannon to blaze away, which
called the poor man up again, and from that time until morning
there was no sleep for Uncle, nor was he seen during the day, so it
was supposed that the unusual amount of exercise he had taken had
completely prostrated him . . .[98]

Occasionally an event in the town could arouse student interest. Here is
an undergraduate reaction to a temperance meeting in the village:

For the 5th of July they got in town a grand temperance celebration
of some 12 or 15 hundred children, had a speech in the Old South
from Rev. Mr. Hanks[?] of Lowell and then a collation in the grove
back of the Female Academy. I doubt not they were fine, though I
did not go near either of them. There were many temperance celebrations in this State on that day. Now the temperance cause is
spreading like wild-fire and among the lowest drunkards who are
taking the cause into their own hands and no one has a title to do
anything unless he has recently been a confirmed drunkard. It is
hardly an exaggeration to say that a poor, miserable, ragged, dirty,
drunken sot without money, without friends, without credit will
stagger into one of these temperance meetings . . . and in half an hour
walk out a sober, well-dressed, industrious citizen, with money,
friends, and credit and everything to make him a good member of
society. I do not know how permanent these effects will be . . . but
one year more like the last six months . . . and you cannot find a
drunkard in New England. . . . now reformed drunkards from Boston
. . . go out into the country to lecture.[99]

It is reassuring to think that for all its piety Phillips Academy was unable
to convert all its students to the cause of temperance.

From the School's point of view the big event of the year was Commencement, or, as it was called at Andover, The Exhibition. The following
account of the Exhibition of 1865 is based on the letters of a one-year
senior who graduated that year. The festivities opened with a Class Supper
at the Mansion House the night before, where the class was served a
handsome collation consisting, among other items, of lobster salad, chicken
salad, four kinds of vegetables, five kinds of pie, fourteen kinds of des-
serts, including floating island and porcupine cake, and tea, chocolate, and
lemonade. During the supper several songs, written expressly for the
occasion, were sung, and the feast was concluded by what is described as
"the smoking of the Pipe of Peace." After supper a mysterious ritual billed
as the "Funeral Rites of Kühner" took place. Kühner was the author of
the Greek grammar used at Phillips Academy, and the class would now
have their chance to revenge themselves upon him. According to the print-

ed program, a procession was to be formed consisting of a band, a standard bearer with transparency, priests, the orator of the "Night," pall bearers carrying the last remains of the lamented Kühner, mourners, and, last, but not least, "Rabble." The march was to start in Ballardvale and after wandering all over town was to wind up in front of the new Academy building. There appropriate ceremonies would be conducted. The audience was requested to maintain perfect silence during these ceremonies "to insur a safe passage to the departed across the Styx." First came an oration, then the "Burning and Mystic Rites," during which a dirge was played, then a eulogy, and finally a song in honor of Kühner. After the Greek grammarian had been properly disposed of, a "Grand Concert" by Gilmore's band took place, with selections by Flotow, Verdi, and Wagner, and as the pièce de resistance a clarinet solo by "Herr Leibsch." It must have been a gay evening, and all the more so when contrasted with the monotonous routine that had characterized the rest of the year at Phillips Academy.

Parents who get fidgety toward the end of the present forty-five-minute Commencement Exercises at Phillips Academy should be thankful that their offspring did not graduate in 1865. The Exhibition exercises for that year included *twenty-four* separate acts—English orations, Latin orations, Greek orations, dialogues, colloquies, and the like. The idea, apparently, was to give practically every member of the classs a chance to show off before the admiring audience of parents and friends of the School. So that the long ordeal of speeches would not become unbearable, there were five musical interludes. The exercises closed with a prayer and a class hymn, which ended with the following sober sentiment:

> We pray that when this life is past,
> We all may meet in heaven at last,
> Where partings are unknown.

Members of the Class of 1865 at Andover were apparently great believers in autograph books. At any rate one of the traditions at Exhibition time was to exchange autographs, usually embellished with appropriate sentiments and sometimes with really beautiful pen and ink drawings. Here are a few samples:

> That you may remember your seat-mate whose number of "Flunks" you have greatly lessened.

> How tempus does fugit.

> May you ever stick to your friends as closely as you and I stuck to each other when Uncle chased us last winter.

> Act well your part, and at last may Angels wreathe for you a Crown of Immortality.

Together we have endured the tortures of Senior year at Phillips.
That your suffering here may be productive of success at Yale
is my earnest wish.[1]

All in all, an Exhibition, with the festivities that preceded it, made quite a
show and must have sent the boys off feeling more warmly about the
School than they had felt during the long grind that had led up to the
graduation.

In 1852 a student at Phillips Academy wrote his family and asked them
to send him some newspapers, "for," he said, "Andover is truly an isolated point, since many of the students were astounded the other day, to
hear that another revolution had broken out in France which fact proves
conclusively the isolated condition of this place."[2] Since the Revolution
of December 1851 in France had occurred approximately two months earlier, the boy had a point. Generally speaking, during Dr. Taylor's years,
both the School and to a lesser extent the town remained impervious to
what was going on in the rest of the world. Certainly this is true of Uncle
Sam himself. He had developed a regimen that he believed was good for
boys and he saw no reason to keep in touch with educational trends in the
rest of the country. There is no record that he communicated with other
educators; for example, he met with Gideon Lane Soule, Principal of Exeter during almost exactly the same period, only once.[3] One might think
that the Civil War would have had a profound effect on the Academy, but
that was hardly the case. To be sure, during the first year of the war the
Phillips boys organized a regiment called the Ellsworth Guards and
marched at various patriotic ceremonies in town, but the regiment seems
to have been disbanded shortly after 1861.

The one boy who reported on the group was most enthusiastic about it.
It was not expensive, he wrote his Mother, because the drillmaster and
uniforms, haversacks, flannels, and muskets were paid for by the state, the
town, and private individuals.

> Our drill takes the place of football and takes only holiday time so
> that we pursue our studies just the same as ever. Our company
> consists of 64 privates and 18 officers, all stout and robust, and as
> good soldiers as any of the volunteer companies now drilling. . . .
> Last Wednesday General Oliver reviewed us and gave us a first rate
> drill. . . . Such orders as these we have learnt: Column Halt! Front
> Face! Right Dress! By the Right Flank March! By the Left Flank
> Counter March! . . . A few weeks more drilling will put us in almost
> perfect order for service.[4]

The following year Uncle Sam reported to the Trustees that "The general
state of the country is not as favorable for study as in more quiet times,"
but he added that greater effort on the part of the teachers would "secure

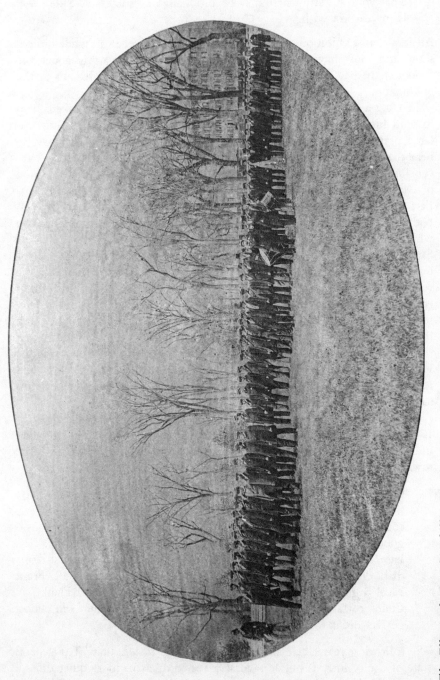

26. The Ellsworth Guards, Phillips Academy's Civil War Regiment.

the usual amount of study."[5] Clearly, Dr. Taylor planned no modification of the School's normal program because of the war. Looking back on the Civil War period, one alumnus wrote:

> The fact is that during the year [1862–63] that I was at Andover the war had very little effect on student life. We were absorbed in study (no athletics in those days) and Andover Hill was so remote from scenes of conflict that the roar of battles was like the sound of breakers on a far distant shore. . . . The surrender of Vicksburg occurred Saturday, July 4, 1863. When the news reached Andover, Tuesday, July 7th, bells were rung to celebrate the victory. The battle of Gettysburg, July 1, 2, and 3, 1863, made very little impression at the time.[6]

The one exception to this attitude was the Philomathean *Mirror*, which printed war stories, some of them brutal and realistic, throughout the period of the conflict. They even included one article that presented a strong case for the South. But the *Mirror* represented a relatively small number of students who liked to write, and the interest of its editors in the war does not counterbalance the lack of concern of most of the students— although none of this means that there were not hundreds of Andover graduates—and a few undergraduates as well—who fought bravely in the war. The conclusion is inescapable that during the Taylor years most Phillips Academy students lived in a vacuum, unaware of what was going on in the world around them, their isolation modified only by contacts with family and friends who lived outside the School.

Yet there were countervailing forces at work which would make the town of Andover and Phillips Academy less parochial. In 1836 the Andover-Wilmington Railroad was completed, making it possible for the first time to travel to Boston by rail. Now one could reach Andover without having to walk sixty miles or so, as a number of the earlier students had done. In 1845 the city of Lawrence was founded, and with it came a tremendous surge in the economic activity of the area. Symbolic of the changes to come was an episode that occurred during the fiftieth anniversary of the founding of the Theological Seminary. A speaker was delivering a eulogy on Moses Stuart when Trustee Alpheus Hardy entered the room and handed the presiding officer a paper that contained news of the successful laying of the Atlantic cable. When this news was given to the audience, they broke up the meeting, cheering and singing the Doxology.[7]

The insularity of the School and the town was punctured from time to time through association with distinguished people. In 1833 a then-unknown student at the Theological Seminary named Samuel Francis Smith had undertaken the translation of some German songs for Lowell Mason, famous for the hymns he had written. Smith found a German tune that he particularly liked, seized a scrap of wastepaper, and wrote down the words of "America" in almost the same form as they exist today. The song achieved almost immediate popularity, and the author became a national figure.[8] In November 1843 Daniel Webster came to Andover to give a political speech for the Whig Party at the behest of Moses Stuart. Two special trains came out from Boston, and the town organized a parade of between 4,000 and 6,000 persons. Heading the Phillips Academy contingent was Samuel H. Taylor, then a spry young man of thirty-six, before he had become the terror of his later years. He would surely support Webster, since they were both Dartmouth graduates. Webster had not been feeling well and his speech was not one of his best, but generally the affair went off very well, finishing with a collation in a "pavillion" near the South Church.[9]

In 1852 the Andover community was electrified when Professor Calvin Stowe was appointed to a position at the Theological Seminary and brought with him to Andover his wife, Harriet Beecher Stowe, who had just finished *Uncle Tom's Cabin*. Mrs. Stowe insisted on moving into the old coffin factory, later the Seminary gymnasium, and despite protests from the Seminary authorities that it would make a poor house, she had it remodeled most successfully. While at Andover, where the family remained until 1864, she continued to write, publishing *A Key to Uncle Tom's Cabin* (to prove that her information was accurate), *Dred, The Pearl of Orr's Island*, and *The Minister's Wooing*. Andover did not quite know what to make of Mrs. Stowe, for, like all Beechers, she had a mind of her own. She entertained informally, wandered around the campus with her dogs, and was suspected of going to the theater in Boston.

Finally, Elizabeth Stuart Phelps Ward, the daughter of Austin Phelps of the Theological Seminary and the granddaughter of Moses Stuart, began her career as an author in the later Taylor years. Though her books are difficult to read today, in her time she was a nationally known writer, and her first book, *Gates Ajar*, stressing the humanity of the Christian faith, sold thousands of copies. All these people called attention to Andover, and by doing so helped to shake the town and the school.

> Five days ago . . . Dr. Taylor appeared in his usual health, exhibited his wonted vigor in the exercises of his school, visited Boston and Cambridge in the afternoon; and, although he felt for a time a slight indisposition, he returned to his home with more than usual buoyancy of spirit. He rose on sabbath morning, prepared himself for his large Bible-class, but complained . . . of a stricture across his chest. He was importuned to omit the biblical exercise, and to remain at home; but for a biblical exercise like this he had been disciplining his mind and heart by long-continued toil; this was his most important study; this was his chief joy; and we have seen that to leave a duty unperformed was not his nature. He went forth like

a hero, carrying his New Testament through the deep and rapidly falling snow to this building, which had been erected under his care, and according to his plan. He loved the very edifice itself. His pupils were assembling to receive his Christian instruction; the bell was yet tolling; he stopped in the vestibule of his academy; his countenance changed; he fell; he said not a word; he neither sighed nor groaned, but ascended from the circle of his astonished and loving and weeping pupils to mingle with the angels of God. Bearing the sacred volume, he had passed through the storm; and then the door of his schoolroom proved to be "the gate of heaven." "And he was not; for God took him."[10]

So ended the long career of Samuel Harvey Taylor. It was characteristic of him that he should die in harness on his way to teach his students. Yet it is probably just as well that he died then, for, despite his many accomplishments, he had outlived his time.

III. The Modern Andover

DURING ITS two centuries of existence Phillips Academy has really been two schools. The first, from its founding in 1778 until the death of Samuel Harvey Taylor in 1871, was essentially an eighteenth-century institution, on which Eliphalet Pearson had imposed his imprimatur in no uncertain terms. Though there was some variation and some experiment during the first hundred years, the Academy in 1871 subscribed essentially to the basic principles that Pearson had insisted on from the start. In its second century it changed markedly. The School of fifteen years ago, let alone today, bears little resemblance to the first institution. The chief architect of the modern Andover—at least until ten years ago—was Cecil Franklin Patch Bancroft, the greatest headmaster of the Academy. He took an institution that was falling behind contemporary educational practices and concepts and brought it up to date. Perhaps his most important contribution was to change completely Pearson's concept that the Principal should be a dictator. Bancroft insisted that the faculty as a whole be given a share in administration, and before he was through the faculty meeting had become an important locus of power in running the school. Though Bancroft was a classicist by training and taught the classics, he refused to agree that they were the be-all and end-all of a school curriculum. In the course of his term as Principal, the curriculum was modified to include modern foreign languages, additional science courses, and four years of English. Pearson's School had depended on families in the town of Andover for the housing and boarding of the students. Bancroft embarked on a program that sought to have all Academy students live in School-owned dormitories, where they would be supervised by members of the faculty. Though Bancroft was a deeply religious man, he tried to modify the rigid emphasis on Calvinist beliefs and practices that had characterized the School's first one hundred years. He emphasized the humane and the loving in the Christian religion, rather than the stern and the punitive. At the same time that he was changing many of Eliphalet Pearson's original concepts, he held firm to two—an insistence on scholastic excellence and concern for poor boys (he hated the word "indigent"), both of which had characterized Phillips Academy from the very beginning.

Bancroft's concept of what the School should be served well until the 1960's. Indeed, one student of the early sixties has written that the School of his day was closer to 1910 than to 1975. Alfred E. Stearns, who succeeded Bancroft, in effect completed the original Bancroft plan, particularly by providing enough dormitories to house all the students and enough other buildings so that it could be a self-sufficient social unit. Claude M. Fuess, beset by depression and war, could do little more than attempt to preserve what had been accomplished. John M. Kemper, though he put through important tangential programs like School-Year Abroad, the Washington Interns, Outward Bound, and the study that led to the Advanced Placement Program, changed very little of Bancroft's original program.

It was not until the late 1960's, in the last years of the Kemper administration and the early years of the Sizer administration, that truly revolutionary changes in the School took place. The challenge to governmental authority in the conduct of the Viet-Nam War soon was transferred to a challenge to *all* authority, particularly that of schools and colleges. As a result, in the last ten years of the School's existence more changes have taken place than in the first one hundred and ninety years. This latter period saw the abolition of compulsory religious services (shades of Samuel Phillips), a revolutionary change in the curriculum with the introduction of term-contained courses, a fundamental change in the disciplinary system with the abolition of the "cut" system and the "sign-in" system in most areas, and, finally, coeducation.

Viewed against the School of the 1970's, Bancroft's reforms may seem mild. Yet at the time that he struggled to achieve them, they were forward-looking and wise, and the concepts that he insisted on served Phillips Academy well for over ninety years.

CHAPTER NINE

CECIL BANCROFT'S ACADEMIC REFORMS

CECIL FRANKLIN PATCH BANCROFT did not assume the Principalship of Phillips Academy directly upon the death of Uncle Sam Taylor. From 1871 to 1873 the institution was under the direction of Frederic W. Tilton, whose term served as a transitional period between the old School of Uncle Sam and the new School that Dr. Bancroft would develop. In some ways Tilton was like Ebenezer Pemberton, Principal in the 1790's. Both men were highly trained schoolmasters who started to introduce interesting changes. Both were sensitive human beings who found the harsh disciplinary system of Phillips Academy distasteful. Both men were unhappy with the rigid and oppressive insistence on conformity to the old Calvinist creed. And, finally, both men resigned supposedly for reasons of health but probably because they could not stand the pressures of the job. At least both were healthy enough to take up new teaching positions almost immediately after their resignations. The changes that Pemberton sought for Phillips Academy were never introduced during his lifetime; almost all of Tilton's proposed reforms, however, were soon put into effect by Dr. Bancroft. In short, Tilton was a man with the right ideas but without the emotional strength to put them successfully into practice.

Frederic W. Tilton was admirably trained for his position.[1] Born in Cambridge in 1839, he graduated from Harvard in 1862, studied for part of a year at the University of Göttingen in Germany, and after teaching for four years at the Highland Military Academy in Worcester was called to be Superintendent of Schools in Newport, Rhode Island. That he was a Harvard man would have made Uncle Sam turn over in his grave, but the Trustees liked him and went after him aggressively. At their meeting in May 1871 they voted unanimously to offer him the position, and when Tilton said he would accept "on condition that the Trustees approve of his views in regard to the administration of the Academy," they voted unanimously to approve them.[2] Unfortunately, the record is silent on just what those views were.

27. *Frederic William Tilton, Seventh Principal of Phillips Academy.*

With this matter taken care of, Tilton and his wife, the former Ellen Trowbridge, daughter of a Harvard professor, moved to the north side of the Double-Brick house on Main Street in the summer of 1871, and he prepared to take over his duties as Principal. He retained the staff that he had inherited from Uncle Sam. William G. Goldsmith, who had taken charge of the School after Dr. Taylor's death, continued as Head of the English Department, while George H. Taylor—Uncle Sam's son—and William W. Eaton remained as Assistants. In order to give Tilton a good send-off, the Trustees had voted to advertise the fact of his election as Principal in at least two newspapers.[3]

One of the most serious problems facing him was how to develop an academic program that would prepare Andover graduates for any good college in the country. In Uncle Sam Taylor's day, boys, as noted, could get into Yale simply on a Taylor recommendation. The boys who went to Harvard after the Rebellion of 1867, however, had found gaining admission a difficult task that required special tutoring. In 1871 President Charles W. Eliot had written the Andover Trustees about this problem. In addition there was the problem of providing an adequate course in mathematics, which had long been all but ignored in the Classical School. Principal Tilton made a start, at least, in dealing with these problems. To buck up the course in mathematics, he took it over himself and gave his students a very different kind of regimen. He and Assistant Eaton also worked with the seniors in the classics so that their preparation would be adequate for any college and not just Yale. At the end of his first year on the job Tilton could point with pride to the seventeen Phillips boys who had been admitted to Harvard and all the rest of the class to the college of their choice. A subtle change appeared in the catalogue; under Uncle Sam the classical students were to be prepared "for college"; now the statement read "for the best colleges."[4] Finally, Tilton introduced the study of modern languages into the curriculum of the English Department. With the backing of the Trustees he obtained the services of Professor Oscar Faulhaber, who had been conducting a small private school of his own in Andover, to teach French and German. There was, however, an extra charge of five dollars a term for boys taking these courses.[5]

Principal Tilton also took a different approach from that of Uncle Sam in dealing with his faculty. During the Taylor years the Principal dictated what was to be done in the School, whether the matter concerned curriculum or discipline. Tilton started having weekly faculty meetings at which disciplinary cases were discussed. To give the Assistants a share in the running of the School was obviously a great morale booster. The Principal also worked hard to appoint able men to the faculty. In his last year two distinguished men joined the School—Edward G. Coy, who was to be one of the School's great teachers until 1892, and John M. Tyler, who left after one year to go to Amherst, where he had a brilliant career as a teacher of biology.[6] Up until this time the Assistants, for the most part, had been men of mediocre ability who stayed but a short time. If the School could attract truly gifted teachers, Tilton believed, the whole atmosphere of the place would be changed. The Principal also moved to break the hammer-lock that the Theological Seminary had on the Sunday services. Twice each Sunday the boys were required to go to church to listen to long, involved sermons that they often did not understand. Tilton got the Trustees to vote that a Vesper service for the School alone be substituted for the afternoon Seminary service. According to the record the Seminary Professors approved this change, but if they did, they changed their minds, for it was not long before the permission to hold Vesper services was rescinded.[7] But this only paved the way for the establishment of such services under Dr. Bancroft.

It was in the field of discipline that Principal Tilton had his greatest difficulties. One alumnus wrote:

> I remember Mr. Tilton one day stating in the school that a certain number of boys would be expelled if another bonfire were started in the yard. I happened to be among those he named. Well a bonfire was started and yet we were not expelled. Such statements, of course, hurt his power over the boys. Doctor Taylor would not, probably, have made such a statement but if he had he would have carried it out and every boy knew that he would.

The same writer added: "Mr. Tilton did not have the force of character to succeed in disciplining the school along the line that Doctor Taylor followed."[8] As time went on, Tilton became more and more apprehensive about student outbreaks and is reported to have been out all night in hopes of forestalling them. At the Exhibition of 1872 a mock program entitled "The Pony Phaeton" lambasted the Principal harshly. "The depth of Misery—Tilly leading morning prayers" "Faculty Meeting: Tilly in the chair, George [Taylor] at the desk, Tommy [Thompson] drunk in the corner. . . Tilton—Well, I loike Wsgy bully. He gave me some gin onct; guess we'll keep him and kick some one on the list."

> Notice.
> All Old Clothes Dealers are hereby notified to fight shy of the Phillipian commons, as I want all the old clothes for myself. Donors please leave only shirts and pants, as I'm fond of them.
> F. W. Tilton.

Tilton and Eaton were billed as "The Great Egyptian Jugglers" in a bogus theatrical performance while Thompson and Starbuck were to juggle seven whiskey bottles previously emptied by the faculty.[9] All good clean fun, but with a bite to it.

Tilton did get the best of the students on one occasion. Fearing that some miscreant would steal the clapper to the chapel bell and thus prevent its being rung for church on Sunday, Tilton had a spare clapper made. Sure enough, one cold December Saturday night, the clapper vanished. Armed with his spare, however, the sexton simply replaced it and much to the discomfiture of the culprits, the bell pealed out as usual at the appointed time. Despite this victory it seems clear that the maintenance of discipline at Phillips Academy proved too difficult a job for a man with Tilton's temperament to handle successfully. And that must have been primarily responsible for his decision to resign "on account of his health being insufficient to a longer continuance of so onerous a trust."[10] So Frederic W. Tilton left Andover with his family in the summer of 1873 and returned to be Principal of a Newport high school. He remained there until 1890 and then retired to spend the rest of his life living in Cambridge and traveling. Despite his short stay and his weakness as a disciplinarian, Tilton moved purposely in the right direction while he was Principal, and he undoubtedly made it easier for Cecil Bancroft to continue where he had left off.

The man who came to Andover in the summer of 1873 to serve as the eighth Principal of Phillips Academy had an unusual background. Cecil Franklin Patch Bancroft was born in New Ipswich, New Hampshire, on 25 November 1839, the fifth child of what were to be eight in an old New England family that had for several previous generations lived in Groton, Massachusetts. Early in his life he was in effect adopted by a Mr. and Mrs. Patch of neighboring Ashby, Massachusetts, who named him for their son, who had recently died. His foster parents saw to it that he had a good education; after attending the public schools in Ashby, he was sent to Appleton Academy at New Ipswich, where he met John Wesley Churchill, who was to become a life-long friend. From Appleton he went on to Dartmouth, where he graduated in 1860, fourth in a class of sixty-five. He was a member of the Alpha Delta Phi fraternity, gave a commencement oration entitled "The Rhine," and was highly respected by his classmates. Like other undergraduates at that time, Bancroft taught school in the winter to help defray expenses, spending two seasons in Groton, Massachusetts. Upon graduation from Dartmouth, he returned to Appleton Academy, where he became Principal for four years, assisted by his sister, Susie F. Bancroft. During this period he became acquainted with one of his girl pupils, Frances A. Kittredge, whom he was later to marry. After four years at Appleton, he determined to enter the ministry and enrolled at Union Theological Seminary in New York City for a year, serving for part of this time as a member of the Christian Commission, a forerunner of the Red Cross, at the front lines in the waning days of the Civil War. The following year he entered Andover Theological Seminary, where he graduated in 1867, making his first contact with Phillips Academy by serving as an Assistant to Uncle Sam Taylor during part of his last year in Andover.[11]

After the Civil War a wealthy New York merchant, Christopher Rhinelander Robert, determined to found a "loyal, Christian, New England school" in the South, in an effort to help bind up the nation's wounds. He selected Lookout Mountain, Tennessee, as the site for his project, purchased from the federal government some hospital buildings that had been constructed during the war, and began looking for a Principal to run his institution for him. Knowing of Uncle Sam Taylor's reputation as a New England schoolmaster, he came to him for advice. As one of Bancroft's eulogists puts it, "the Lord, speaking thro' Dr. Samuel H. Taylor of young Bancroft who, David-like, was ruddy, and withal of a beautiful countenance, and goodly to look to, said, 'Arise, anoint him: for this is he.' "[12] Robert proceeded to anoint, Bancroft accepted, and there began what was to be a five-year experiment in bringing New England education to the South. On 1 May 1867, Bancroft was ordained at Mt. Vernon, New Hampshire. Five days later he was married to Frances Kittredge, and immediately the bride and groom set out for Tennessee. One who remembers them at that time describes the young couple as "young, handsome, genial, enthusiastic," being taken from Chattanooga "on a fresh May morning, up the winding, military road to the summit of Lookout Mountain."[13]

From all accounts the Bancrofts made an extraordinary record in a very difficult situation. It could not be expected that the recently defeated Southerners would welcome emissaries from that section of the country most identified in the public mind with the antislavery movement. The presence at the school of former slaves, not as pupils but as paid servants, served as a constant reminder of the basic change in Southern society. Nor did visits of Jefferson Davis and Robert Toombs to a nearby hotel make life any easier. Yet Bancroft and his wife proved to be masters of conciliation. As one pupil remembers it, "It was one thing for an orator of red blood in this climate in the days of Reconstruction to fire the Northern heart; it was altogether a different and more difficult thing for an orator from hated New England to speak words of wisdom and conciliation that won the respect of a Southern Consituency and at the same time maintaining unimpaired the respect of the Union. Dr. Bancroft did it." In addition to running the school, the new Principal preached regularly on Sundays. When an associate asked if this did not put too heavy a burden on him, he replied, "I like to preach Sunday to keep sweet thro' the week." A former pupil at Lookout Mountain remembers "when on Saturday afternoons we sauntered thro' inviting ravines, climbed the outstanding cliffs or gathered flowers from historic battlefields in the company of this bridegroom and bride, who were not only our teacher and matron, but our familiar friends." As long as Northern interest in Reconstruction remained strong, the school apparently prospered. White students, both boys and girls, came not only from the surrounding area, but from Georgia as well. In its five years of existence close to one thousand pupils attended. When in the early 1870's, however, Northern interest in Reconstruction began to wane and Southern leaders began to regain control of Southern society, difficulties developed. Former owners of the land on which the school was located brought suit against Robert and threatened to tie up the operation entirely. Robert himself transferred his main interest to the founding of what became Robert College in Constantinople. And finally, as one writer puts it, "local opposition to its [the school's] Yankee origin led him [Robert] soon to abandon the experiment."[14] In 1872 the institution closed its doors, and Bancroft was forced to leave what was for him "a romance of love, a romance of patriotism, and a romance of missions."[15]

Upon leaving Lookout Mountain, the Bancrofts, with their two children, Cecil and Frances, both of whom had been born in Tennessee, determined to spend a year in Europe. Part of the time was passed in travel and part at Halle, where Bancroft studied theology and the German educational system. In the early spring of 1873 he was in Rome apparently considering a position with "a mission station in Italy,"[16] when he received the offer to become Principal of Phillips Academy. The cablegram with the offer had been forwarded from Halle and pretty well mangled in transmission, so that it was not until he had returned to Germany and received further communication from the Trustees that he was able to determine the conditions of his appointment. His reply to the Trustees was characteristically modest:

> The work at Andover is so great, so conspicuous, and of such a quality that I could not regard myself as equal to it, nor for a moment think of undertaking it without a strong conviction that the Lord was preparing the way before me, and would not withhold the wisdom and strength necessary to the execution of this appointment.
>
> Dr. Wellman assures me of the unanimity and promptness of the action of the board. In such a momentous matter I value their judgment above my own.
>
> If I were equally certain of the cordial welcome and endorsement of the appointment, by the members of the Theological Faculty, and by the teachers to be associated with me in the Academy, I think I should give, in this, my unreserved acceptance.
>
> With a fair field and everything possible in my favor, I feel that I should imperil the interests of the Academy quite too much. Any individual disadvantage under which I should be put would seem to me decision against the acceptance of the trust. But of these things I cannot judge at this distance and with no opportunities of inquiry.
>
> I must therefore commit the question to the board of Trustees. If no better man in the meantime, willing to accept the position,

is found, and the Trustees still desire it I will do the best I can. I
wish the Trustees to recall the appointment, without the least hesitation as regards me personally, if the interests of the institution
can thereby be promoted. The question is one transcending personal
interests. . . . *Till I hear from you again I shall regard our engagement as binding upon me, but not binding upon you.* And may God
guide to the right decision.[17]

On receipt of this letter Dr. Seth Sweetser, President of the Board, wrote
Bancroft what must have been completely convincing assurance of the
Board's support, for on 17 May he telegraphed his acceptance of the position.[18] Thus it was that on the last day of July 1873 Bancroft with his
family moved into the Double-Brick on Main Street to start a career of
leadership that was to last close to thirty years.

The problems facing the new Principal were enough to daunt a man of
less heart. In the first place, people were always getting his initials wrong.[19]
The curriculum was antiquated, and Academy boys were having trouble
gaining admission to some colleges; the faculty was demoralized by rapid
turnovers, and between 1870 and 1875 every position was twice vacant
and twice filled; the discipline of the School, as a result of Tilton's lack
of firmness, was ragged at best; and the Academy's financial position was
perilous, with a sizable debt and an unbalanced budget. Cecil Bancroft
moved purposefully to deal with these problems directly, and after one
year had begun to make progress. In June 1874 he made his first report
to the Trustees, a most impressive document. After commenting on a
slight drop in enrollment which he believed due to the large number of
new teachers and the unsettling effects of Frederic Tilton's resignation,
he proceeded to the problem of discipline, where, he said, the new administration had had "considerable trial." Since he was ignorant of the
"familiar forms of disorder," he had had to do the best he could "in
much ignorance and inexperience." Still and all, there had been some
improvement over the immediately preceding years: the government had
not been resisted, and "the school sentiment has with remarkable unanimity sustained the authority of the Teachers." There were always trouble-
makers: "Some students have used strong drink, some left town to play
billiards, and a few kept company in Lawrence and elsewhere with lewd
women." As a result, twelve had been rusticated, four expelled, and five
suspended for a term. At the start, discipline was administered by the
Principal, but later in the year cases of misconduct were referred to the
Faculty as a whole, who voted the penalties. This became possible as new
teachers became accustomed to the School and their jobs. At the start, the
Principal added, he did not dare risk it.

As for the course of study, the new Principal proposed the addition of a fourth year for boys who would need it to gain college admission. In the new program there would be time for a more thorough drill in mathematics, courses in English for the Classical School could be included, and French and German could be available electives. There would still be boys who could complete the course in three years, but the fourth would create added flexibility. The new program was, however, still in the planning stage. During the summer the Principal and Assistants proposed to interview "various educated men, school officers and instructors, Presidents and Professors and hope to receive more light." Cecil Bancroft made six points in summary: not to fit specifically for any one college; not to invite boys to enter college from the Middle Year; not to curtail the course so that boys trying for Harvard would be "so heavily conditioned as to be practically excluded"; not to neglect students with good English instruction but no classics; not to forget that in the past the average stay of a student at Phillips Academy has been much less than three years; to provide a

28. Cecil Franklin Patch Bancroft, Eighth Principal of Phillips Academy.

course that will enable "men mature, in good health, with strong purpose and aptitude to study" to finish in three years. Another new feature of the proposed plan would be the introduction of written examinations, replacing the oral grillings that had been such a terror to undergraduates in the Taylor years. Biblical studies had been rearranged so as to occupy one half hour on Monday mornings. The Principal added candidly, "This was a compromise with the pupils for being required to attend church twice on the Sabbath." Furthermore, instruction was being given by the new teachers rather than by Seminary people. "This has secured better instruction, better work on the part of the boys, and made each teacher more specifically a *religious* teacher." As soon as possible, the Principal wanted to substitute one hour of Bible study for the "afternoon preaching service in the Chapel." "I see no good reason for not omitting that service altogether," he added. After listing some material needs of the school, Principal Bancroft summed up his concerns about the future of Phillips Academy:

> It is not enough that we have a history, not enough that we have an honorable fame; to live we must grow, comparing ourselves not with ourselves alone but also with our great rivals for the youth who are to be educated, many of whom surpass us already in numbers, endowments and equipment. Doing the advanced work now demanded renders it more important than ever that we have able and permanent teachers and keep up the numbers without which it is impossible to realize the best features of a great school. The increased expense of getting an education at Andover makes it necessary to render the school superior to the old order of things in educational merit.[20]

This first report has in it almost all the germs of Cecil Bancroft's long-range program: allowing the Faculty to participate in the running of the School; enlarging and modernizing the academic program so as to meet realistically the needs of the students, particularly with regard to college admission; determining to get advice from others outside the School and generally to involve the Faculty in educational movements at the state and national level; modifying the previous religious program, which was dominated by the Theological Seminary; and generally making Phillips Academy competitive with other preparatory schools in the nation. Seen in terms of the School's needs, the report is an extraordinary document.

Having been given a go-ahead by the Trustees for the introduction of a four-year program, Cecil Bancroft set out to draw the best plan possible. Nor did he intend to rely solely on the resources in Andover itself. He determined to get the advice of leading college presidents and other educators in the New England area and thus became the first Principal of Phillips Academy to go outside the School for advice on educational matters. To be sure, back in the 1780's Judge Samuel Phillips had asked Timothy Pickering to make suggestions on the School's constitution, but when he did so, the Judge paid no attention. From Eliphalet Pearson on, the Principals of Phillips Academy had run the School pretty much by themselves and made no attempt to confer with other educators on curricular matters. By contrast, Bancroft had the proposed four-year program printed up and sent to such people as President Charles W. Eliot of Harvard and President Noah Porter of Yale. Though Eliot's reply is no longer in the record, he and Bancroft corresponded regularly about college entrance requirements and other problems in what was certainly a fruitful exchange, and it can be assumed that he made some incisive comments on Bancroft's proposal. The response to the four-year course was generally favorable. President Porter of Yale thought it was a poor idea to print the titles of the books used and also the precise number of hours per week. He believed that the individual teacher should be given flexibility in these matters. He also thought that natural history might be better than physics and chemistry. But generally he praised the plan.[21] President William A. Stearns of Amherst, an Academy Trustee, was particularly pleased with the introduction of French and German. One of his Amherst professors thought that both should be required, but Stearns thought that would be too much.[22] President Robinson of Brown turned the plan over to two of his professors, who heartily approved it, suggesting only that the *Odyssey* be used instead of the *Iliad*.[23] Though few of the specific recommendations of these educators were adopted, their overall support for the program was encouraging, and in 1875 the new four-year course was published in the catalogue, including more mathematics, French or German, chemistry, and training in English composition once a week. It would be twenty years before Cecil Bancroft could get all the curricular changes he wanted for the Classical Department, but he had made a good start.

In July 1874 Bancroft was invited to address the University Convocation in Albany on "The Relations of the Colleges and the Secondary Schools." This was another first for Phillips Academy, as there is no record of any previous Principal speaking before a gathering of educators. Bancroft took his assignment seriously. After talking of the current revolution in education, he examined two forces at work in the country; one sought to extend the task of the secondary schools and have their graduates go directly to the university; the other sought to have the colleges reach down into the secondary school years and take over the last two years of their work. The first force, modeled on the German educational system with its gymnasia, was not, Bancroft believed, suited to conditions in the United States; the second force would dilute the work of both schools and colleges, to the disadvantage of both. More important was the tendency of the colleges to increase their requirements for admission. Harvard had done so by demanding another year of preparation from the schools, which had necessitated the development of four-year rather than the old three-year courses. This, said Bancroft, had produced "a feeling of suppressed revolt" among the schools. It would make a school "a mere appendage of another institution." It would mean that secondary school teachers would be no longer be free to teach as they thought best and would thereby tend to drive the best men from the schools. Preparation for college entrance examinations, with its precisely defined drill, destroyed the teacher's chance to teach as he wished and meant that, in effect, the colleges were dictating the content of school courses. What was the solution? The colleges must be willing to accept a certificate from a school stating a student's eligibility for admission and abandon the present examinations. Only by so doing could the morale and quality of secondary school teaching be maintained for the tremendous benefit of the students themselves and the country generally. The address was well conceived and well written; the theme that comes through loudest is Cecil Bancroft's concern for the welfare of secondary school teachers.[24]

Most heads of schools and colleges who are new on the job wish to make a name for themselves by revising the institution's curriculum. In many cases they push through a fairly comprehensive reform and then sit back and rest on their laurels for the remainder of their term of office. Bancroft did not follow this approach. His curricular reforms were instituted gradually and piecemeal and were continuing right up to the time of his death in 1901. In dealing with the Classical Department, his major aims were clear. Though a classicist himself, he agreed that too great an emphasis had been placed on Latin and Greek, and he sought to introduce French and German as well. He also believed that all members of the Classical Department should have more training in English, following the advice of President Eliot of Harvard, who had urged such a step.[25] Finally, he wanted to see a stronger science program at the School. It is not necessary to trace each step in the process by which these changes were instituted. The French program got under way in 1875 under Phillips Academy's first woman teacher, a Miss Courtis. "I had hoped," wrote the Principal, "that some friend of the woman's cause would have assisted in securing her an adequate salary." There was some difficulty introducing a female teacher at first, but she had done well, and he would be glad to retain her services.[26] The following year Bancroft reported that Professor Edward G. Coy was teaching nothing but Greek, realizing the first step in what he hoped could eventually become a standard policy whereby all teachers would instruct in but one subject.[27] As the quality of the program was stepped up, the need for books increased, and the Principal managed to divert $500 from the Phillips fund for that purpose.[28] By 1885 a great deal had been accomplished: the four-year program was well established, four years of English were required of all classical students, modern languages were required in the third year, and Bancroft could report to the Trustees that it was time to shift attention from instruction and the curriculum to buildings. Even though the shift was made, however, there continued to be curricular changes, and steady progress toward limiting teachers to one subject.[29] In 1893 six teachers had purely departmental work and three more approached it.[30] The policy made possible the specialization that led to superior teaching.

The best way of summarizing the curricular changes that Dr. Bancroft made in the Classical Department is to compare the curriculum of 1873, when he took over, with that of 1900, just before his death:

1873		1900
FIRST YEAR		FIRST YEAR
1st Term	Latin Grammar Arithmetic	(Full year courses)
2nd Term	Latin Grammar Caesar Arithmetic Latin Composition	Latin Algebra English Geometry Natural Science
3rd Term	Latin Grammar Nepos Latin Prosody Virgil Greek Grammar Method of Classical Study	
SECOND YEAR		SECOND YEAR
1st Term	Virgil Greek Grammar Anabasis Algebra History of Rome	
2nd Term	Cicero Virgil Anabasis Algebra History of Greece	Latin Greek French or German Algebra and Geometry English
3rd Term	Cicero Anabasis Geometry History of Greece	
THIRD YEAR		THIRD YEAR
1st Term	Virgil Anabasis Greek Syntax Homer' *Iliad* Latin Synonyms Greek Composition Geometry	

2nd Term Virgil
Cicero
Iliad
Latin and Greek Verse
Ancient Geography
Geometry
Review of Arithmetic

Latin
Greek
English
Algebra and Geometry
French or German

3rd Term *Iliad*
Translations from Greek
  into Latin and Latin into
  Greek
General Review

FOURTH YEAR
Electives from a long list
including the above and
Physics, Chemistry, three history
courses, Botany and
Mechanical Drawing[31]

While these changes were being made in the curriculum of the Classical Department, similar reforms were being introduced into the English Department curriculum. When Cecil Bancroft took over in 1873, the English Department was still an independent branch of the school, under the leadership of La Roy F. Griffin. When he left in 1875, Dr. Bancroft quietly suggested that his successor, George C. Merrill, be Peabody Instructor in the Natural Sciences but have no independent administrative control over the English Department. By eliminating the previous two-legged administrative system, the Principal gained overall supervision of the whole School, avoided duplication in procedural matters, and achieved uniform treatment of the students in the two departments. But the Principal left curricular matters in the hands of the Peabody Instructor, who continued to make separate reports to the Trustees. In 1881 Dr. Bancroft succeeded in persuading William B. Graves, who had been Peabody Instructor from 1866 to 1870, to return to that post, and for the remainder of the century the English Department prospered under his vigorous and enthusiastic leadership. Professor Graves frankly admitted that the nature of the science courses in his department was determined by college science courses and college requirements. In 1887, for example, Graves was busy preparing a new physics course that would meet a new one at Harvard, and the following year he reported that the Andover chemistry course was shaped by Harvard's "Chem. B."[32] As the requirements of scientific colleges like M.I.T., the Sheffield Scientific School at Yale, and the Lawrence Scientific School at Harvard grew stricter, pressure mounted to add a fourth year to the English Department program, and in 1884 this was done. It was also found that Latin was a useful subject in the scientific colleges, and accordingly at least one year of that subject was required after 1885.[33] This move did much to break down the barrier between the two departments and to remove the superciliousness with which the Classical students had regarded their English counterparts. As Professor Graves wrote, "The Introduction of Latin as a required subject has done much to give strength and steadiness to the Dept. It can not be said now that the 'English boys' have nothing to do."[34] As time went on, it became steadily clearer that the term "English Department" was a misnomer, and all the more so because the four-year English requirement in the Classical School was leading to the formation of an "English Department" there. Accordingly, in 1894 the name was changed to the much more appropriate "Scientific Department."[35]

In the Classical Department it was possible to conduct classes pretty much on the principle of Mark Hopkins and a log. A teacher, some pupils, and some books, and they were in business. In the Scientific Department, however, good laboratory equipment was essential if the boys were to be properly prepared for college. Thus in almost every report Professor Graves

29. *William Blair Graves, Head of the English Department under Principal Bancroft.*

tried to dun the Trustees for more money for better scientific equipment. In 1883 he wrote of the existing apparatus: "Purchased the year the Academy was dedicated, with scarcely any additions since, it is hardly worthy of the school."[36] The Trustees were sympathetic and each year granted from three to five hundred dollars for apparatus.[37] When Professor Graves went on a sabbatical in 1888, one of his main purposes was to purchase laboratory equipment in Europe, and it is clear that he overspent his grant in doing so.[38] Gradually the facilities for scientific study improved, as such items as a spectroscope, a polariscope, and a new gas machine—contributed by a parent—were added.[39] The trouble was that laboratory courses took a lot of time. In 1883 Professor Graves was complaining that he had to teach trigonometry, surveying, geometry, algebra, arithmetic, astronomy, physics, political economy and the Constitution of the United States, and insisting, reasonably enough, that he could not do justice to his science courses as a result.[40] In 1882 the sciences got a shot in the arm when the Trustees constructed a building to serve as a laboratory. It was a hideous brick, designed as part of a larger science building to come later.[41] The science people had to make do with this structure until 1891, when the rest of the building was completed to form the present Graves Hall. Professor Graves was ecstatic: "The completion of the Science Building marks an epoch in the history of the English Department. It restores to the Department something of the prestige which it had during the first ten years of its existence, when it possessed buildings and a faculty of its own. . . . it is clear that the new building, set apart for scientific work, will not only elevate the Dept

30. *An English Department Classroom in 1878.*

to its proper relative position, but will tend to make the school more attractive to students. In its architectural proportions, the arrangement of rooms and their equipment, little is left to be desired." The only fault that he could find was that the lavatory was not properly ventilated.[42] Thus by the end of the century the newly named Scientific Department was well staffed and well equipped to turn out well prepared students for the best scientific colleges in the country.

One educational reform that Dr. Bancroft insisted on from the start was the substitution of written for oral examinations. No copies of exams for the Classical Department during this period have been preserved, but a few for the English Department, prepared during the 1870's, reveal something about classroom procedures of the day. A German exam, for instance, included the following question:

> Translate and write in German script. Give that letter to the count; we have seen a comet.

French:

> What is the partitive article and to what does it answer in English?

Mental Philosophy:

> Define Consciousness, and state all that it presents to the mind.

Chemistry:

> Describe the process of making H_2SO_4 and give the reactions used.

Physics:

> Give the laws of vertical downward pressure in liquids.

English Literature:

> Write on the works of Fielding, Smollett, and Richardson.

Geography:

> What important rivers would you cross in going from Boston to Albany in a direct line? From Nashville to Chicago?

Grammar:

> Analyze according to model. Parse underlined words. "*An* axiom *is* a *truth assumed* as self-evident."

Rhetoric:

> Correct and tell which rule is violated. "I am obliged to remain as I have not enough money to proceed."

English History:

> Identify from the Cromwellian period: The Dutch War, Ireland, Foreign Policy, Religion, Long Parliament.

Trigonometry:

> The three sides of a triangle are 627, 718, and 1140. Find the angles and give the formula.

Arithmetic:

> If the bricks for a wall 30 ft. long, 24 ft. high and 1 ft. thick cost $72, when bricks are worth $5 per 1000, required the cost of bricks for a wall 128 ft. long, 37 ft. 6 in. high, and 16 in. thick, bricks worth $6 per 1000.

The questions indicate that being examined at Phillips Academy in the 1870's was pretty much a matter of rote memory. This was particularly true of the nonscientific and nonmathematical subjects, but even in algebra there are no word problems.[43] It would be many years before the students would be asked to think for themselves on examinations and not merely regurgitate what they had learned by heart.

The undergraduates followed the curricular changes of the Bancroft years with keen interest, at least if one is to judge by the School newspaper, the *Phillipian*, founded in 1878. The paper early noted the shift in emphasis to mathematics and the sciences and remarked that it was becoming fashionable to attack Greek and Latin while favoring modern languages and the sciences. The article went on to suggest, however, that those who attacked the classics were generally those with poor academic records, while the "brighties" stuck with Latin and Greek.[44] What was needed, the *Phillipian* thought, was a happy medium between the old rigidity and a system of free electives; they thought it should be possible to take modern languages instead of Latin and Greek and English history and literature for mathematics.[45] At the same time, the paper demanded more instructors, pointing out that the existing staff was working six hours a day when three were normal.[46] Some five years later it suggested that Greek and Latin were dying out as a monopoly and that modern languages were coming to be on a par with ancient ones. When, however, an attempt was made to have language tables at one of the boarding houses, the *Phillipian* pronounced them a "bore."[47] Since there was no hope of the administration's introducing such a course, the students themselves set up one in what was then called "phonography", or shorthand, much as students today arrange for courses in typing on a voluntary basis.[48] The two debating societies, Philo and Forum, debated such topics as the superiority of elective courses over prescribed ones and the superiority of a classical curriculum over a scientific one. When History Instructor Archibald Freeman decided to substitute a course in current events for one in medieval history, the *Phillipian* gave him a "Right On."[49] Nor were their articles limited to affairs on Andover Hill. In 1894 the paper published a full report on the work of the so-called "Committee of Ten" of the National Educational Association, under the chairmanship of President Charles W. Eliot of Harvard.[50] The chances are that no one in authority paid much attention to what the paper had to say about curricular matters, but at least the editors were attempting to make the undergraduate body aware of the educational trends of the day.

In achieving these curricular changes Cecil Bancroft, unlike previous Phillips Academy Principals, kept in touch with a wide variety of educators whom he used as a sounding board for his proposals. He had found the advice of college presidents useful when he established the four-year program for the Classical Department, and he determined to pursue the same line with later reforms. Exchanges of this kind can be a two-way street, and by the end of his career, Dr. Bancroft was probably the most sought-after secondary school man in the United States. He corresponded with President Eliot and Dean Briggs of Harvard on entrance requirements and the Andover program for the classics;[51] he wrote Albert C. Perkins, Principal of Exeter, about salaries.[52] President Franklin Carter of Williams, an Academy Trustee during most of Dr. Bancroft's term of office, unburdened himself frequently about a variety of matters—student smoking, the alarming competition from Amherst, language programs, and the need for moral tone in educational institutions.[53] Headmaster J. C. MacKenzie of Lawrenceville covered a wide range of topics—the pronunciation of Latin, football games between the two schools, and scholarships. "As I figure on your funds and running expenses I marvel that you do not increase your tuition," MacKenzie wrote. "I think it is a just principle that the rich should pay approximately what an education costs, and any income that comes to an institution in this way could be used to give additional help to the meritorious indigent student."[54] And he asked Dr. Bancroft to help him form the Headmasters' Association. Headmaster Richard M. Jones of Penn Charter thought the Headmasters' Association would be a waste of time.[55]

Nor was Bancroft content to pick only American brains. In the summer of 1878 he traveled in England and spent a good part of his time studying the great British schools—Eton, Harrow, Rugby, Winchester, Westminster, Christ's Hospital, and Charterhouse. He was convinced that the success of these schools rested on their "enormous endowments," which made the Headmasters "rank with Bishops in consideration and emolument." He also thought them progressive, with new buildings, new courses, new masters, and new prizes. Finally, he was impressed that the Chapel was the center of school life; "the Established Church, its ordinances, and creeds are recognized and honored and loved, and the religious life is represented and treated as exceeding in dignity and importance the intellectual life of the school."[56] The three things that Dr. Bancroft found impressive about the British schools—endowment, progressivism, and a meaningful religious program—were all things he had set his heart on for Phillips Academy, and thus his English summer must have served to urge him on all the more resolutely. In dealing with the school in general and the curriculum in particular, Cecil Bancroft was not content to depend on Andover resources; throughout his career he availed himself of a wide range of advice from other educators. And the result was just the kind of progressive program that he was looking for.

At the same time, Dr. Bancroft was no radical reformer. At the start of his administration he believed that the curriculum was too heavily weighted with the classics and that English, modern languages, and the sciences should be given more time and attention. But he had no intention of allowing the pendulum to swing too far in the other direction. In 1893 he gave an address before the International Congress of Education in Chicago on the question whether the time for languages should be further reduced to allow for more comprehensive science courses—a question that he answered with a resounding "No." According to Bancroft the increased amount of time accorded the sciences had benefited not only them but the languages as well. "It has been found possible to do in less time an equal amount of good work," he claimed. "The laboratory has not excluded the lexicon; on the other hand, the grammar and the lexicon have demanded for themselves a laboratory, and the languages have taken on methods as exact and scientific as botany, physics, and chemistry. It is now incumbent upon the sciences to make the most of the time already conceded, and to make a gain by an improved method equal to that which the languages have made." Furthermore, the schools should emphasize subjects that could be taught only in school, like the classics. Scientific studies could be pursued outside School much more easily. "Commerce and the arts are fostering the scientific studies" but cannot help cultural studies, at least directly. Thus the present balance between language and scientific studies was a healthy one, with the two programs being complementary rather than antagonistic. "Time given at the outset grudgingly is now accorded willingly, and the disparagement of the old education has given place to a grateful recognition of its coordinate value in the training of the coming generation." A classicist himself, Cecil Bancroft could not be expected to jettison the classics in contemporary curricula, but his defense of language was so conciliatory that it is hard to see how even the most commited scientist could object.[57]

It was all very well to devise a new curriculum for Phillips Academy, but without a strong faculty to teach the courses, curricular reform would

be meaningless. In building a faculty, Dr. Bancroft made his most important contribution to Phillips Academy and eliminated Eliphalet Pearson's
old concept of the dictatorship of the Principal in the running of the
school. Dr. Bancroft would surely have subscribed to the statement made
many years later by John Mason Kemper, Eleventh Headmaster of Phillips
Academy, who wrote:

> The policy of building a strong faculty at Andover . . . is remarkable
> also in that it so clearly accepts the premise that a teacher is not a
> hired hand, but a highly trained professional whose experience and
> judgment are vital assets to society, and for whom an adequate
> salary and satisfactory work conditions must be provided. It places
> the teacher in his school on a par with the lawyer in his firm or the
> doctor in his hospital. It is a way of persuading the teacher that
> others respect him and his calling.[58]

Dr. Bancroft clearly stated his policy on building a strong faculty when he
addressed the Boston Alumni Dinner in 1886. On that occasion he said:

> The second point has been the creation of a faculty. In the years
> from 1870 to '75, a period which will always be memorable in the
> history of the Academy . . . every place in the Academy, from the
> highest to the lowest, was twice vacant and twice filled. It was no-
> body's fault; it was everybody's misfortune. It would be a very
> strong school that could stand such a strain as that. To gather a
> faculty, able and stable, is not an easy task. It is one which has ab-
> sorbed the attention of the authorities, and the results are, to many of
> you, already measurably well known. We have aimed to get teachers
> who are both able and willing to remain with us, giving us not
> alone their 'prentice work, but also their highest and best professional
> work in the glory and pride of their teaching powers.[59]

Dr. Bancroft's aim to attract teachers who would spend their whole careers
at Andover was a new concept; before he became Principal, as we have
seen, the Assistants seldom stayed for more than a year or two. Dr. Bancroft's concern for his teachers never flagged throughout his entire career.
In 1891 he reported to the Trustees:

> The past year has been one of fidelity on the part of the teachers,
> some of whom are frequently approached with offers of attractive
> work elsewhere. It is very desirable to keep our tried teachers, even at
> great effort and cost. The teaching force is the strongest element
> in the school and must not be sacrificed.

Dr. Bancroft understood that good teachers would be more likely to stay
at Andover if they were given a share in the running of the School. In his

first report he announced to the Trustees that disciplinary cases were being handled by the Faculty as a whole, and he reported later that Faculty meetings were discussing a wide range of topics and were a useful institution in the administration of the School.[60] There are no full records of Faculty meetings before the 1890's, but the minutes of that decade indicate that the administrative role of the Faculty was significant. An important area of concern was the perennial problem of discipline. The usual student high jinks were landed on heavily: a group were dismissed "for holding carnival in their room after the Exeter game";[61] another boy was suspended for failure to conform to "requirements as to his return from New York City after the funeral of his aunt";[62] another was dismissed for sneaking out to attend what is described as "Grand Opera";[63] another theatrically minded youth got the same treatment for attending *Uncle Tom's Cabin.*[64] Drinking was always hit hard: one boy was fired for "taking liquor in Lawrence";[65] another for "taking intoxicating liquor on Washington's Birthday."[66] From the point of view of the Faculty mere conversation with members of the opposite sex was *ipso facto* evidence of complete depravity. One boy in 1900 "forfeited his school standing for conversing with unknown women upon the street";[67] another was dismissed for riding in Lawrence with an Abbot Academy senior, thereby contributing to her dismissal from her school;[68] and a third unfortunate was dismissed for "walking with a girl during church time" (presumably a time when the culprit thought nobody would catch him).[69] At times the Faculty resorted to unusual methods of preserving order: in 1898 it was voted "that in view of the recent disturbances near the Latin Commons and the cottages, certain selected members of the school be held as hostages for the good behavior of those houses."[70] Finally, the Faculty was death on plagiarism: in one instance a boy was called to account for a story in a school magazine that bore "resemblances to an Easter story in *The Ladies' Home Journal.*"[71] There is no evidence that the Faculty were any easier on the boys than Uncle Sam Taylor had been, though they were probably less arbitrary. Throughout this cops-and-robbers contest, however, they gradually began to draw up a disciplinary code differentiating among various types of crimes, and by the end of the decade they had the matter well in hand.

One of the most extraordinary evidences of faculty participation in running the School is to be seen in their relationship to Principal Bancroft. In 1892, for example, the Faculty voted that in their judgment the School needed a Recorder, and requested the Principal to "secure the appointment of such an officer and to define his duties." Later, after Dr. Bancroft had obediently complied with this request, his report on the matter to the Faculty was "accepted and adopted."[72] On another occasion the minutes read: "All present. Dr. Bancroft tardy."[73] On at least three occasions Cecil Bancroft was elected a member of Faculty committees to deal with such matters as the Dramatic Club, prize debates, and commencement entertainment.[74] On the other hand, one reads occasionally of a boy's case being left to the Principal; and on another occasion the Faculty, after directing the Registrar to assign the teaching of supplemental reading equitably among the whole Faculty, added the note, "the Principal excepted."[75] Toward the end of the 1890's one begins to read of committees appointed by the chair, rather than elected, as in the past, and there are other signs that whatever the latitude allowed the faculty at an earlier time, the Principal was beginning to reassert himself. Even so, there is no question that the Faculty, by 1900, had been given a large amount of power in dealing with School affairs, and that the Principal was *primus inter pares* rather than a dictator of the old type. This development is all the more remarkable when it is remembered that in the Constitution of Phillip's Academy, all the power to run the School is lodged in the Principal.[76]

The Faculty also moved into two areas of School life that had hitherto been neglected by the authorities—athletics and health. When the new Main Building was occupied in 1866, Bulfinch Hall—the old Brick Academy—became available as a gymnasium, and from time to time the Trustees voted small sums of money to buy equipment for the building. Mere gymnastic exercises could not serve, however, as a permanent solution for the athletic interests of the undergraduates, and in the 1870's they began fielding baseball teams that played outside games, the first with Exeter being played in 1878. The score of this first Andover-Exeter contest was Exeter 11, Andover 1. During those early years the teams were supported by undergraduate contributions, and the entire interscholastic program was run by the boys themselves. Since athletic activities were, in the long run, of great importance for the School, it was just a matter of time before the authorities would want to control and regulate them, and in the 1890's the Faculty moved in with apparent relish. First of all, they took an active interest in what sports were to be played. In 1892 they voted a list of events for track meets, including among other more familiar ones, "pole leaping" and a "two mile safety bicycle race."[77] When interest in tennis appeared, it was voted: "that the Tennis Association give an account of itself and its proposed plans."[78] The Faculty disapproved of "public boxing contests in school tournaments" and abolished them.[79] In those days it was the practice of undergraduates to hire "professional trainers"—that is, coaches—a system the Faculty apparently disliked. In any event, several votes were passed urging that trainers be eliminated.

The Faculty could come to the defense of an Andover team when occasion demanded it. In 1893, when a certain Exeter baseball player was apparently suspected of being a ringer, the Faculty voted that if his name "be certified in the list of players upon the Exeter nine, the protest of our management against his name be endorsed and supported."[80] They also concerned themselves with such practical matters as hours of practice, im

244 : THE MODERN ANDOVER

proved athletic facilities, umpiring football games and the like. They made various rules governing training tables, including the cost of the board, and wound up with a magnificent vote to the effect that "the use of ale at the training table be discouraged." The word "discouraged" was later crossed out and "prohibited" substituted.[81] What had started as a completely unregulated undergraduate activity was gradually taken over by the Faculty, the logical outcome being the appointment of Alfred E. Stearns as Director of Athletics in 1897. In this area it was the Faculty rather than the Principal who made policy.

In several of his reports to the Trustees Dr. Bancroft had expressed his concern about student health and the inadequate facilities for dealing with sickness. Several boys had died of disease—for example, consumption—while students at Andover, and the School had no program for dealing with such cases.[82] A sick student simply stayed in his room until he got better; if he were sick enough, he could call on a town doctor for treatment; but aside from physical examinations for athletic teams, the individual student was pretty much on his own in this area. One of the most persistent problems the Faculty had to face was boys they called "Chronic Invalids" and whom they apparently suspected of malingering. They finally drew up a list of the students with the largest number of absences through illness, labeled them "Chronic Invalids," and voted not to excuse their absences in the future without a doctor's certificate.[83] On occasion the Faculty would vote to have a boy withdraw until his health improved, but they refused to allow a boy to change his room because of a lame knee. The area in which the faculty evidently considered themselves most competent, medically speaking, was eyes. There were numerous boys excused from a course in supplementary reading for "weak eyes." Since an even larger number of petitions to drop supplementary reading were turned down, one suspects the trouble to have been the course, not the eyes. The Clerk of the Faculty was a most precise man in these matters: after the Faculty had voted to excuse a boy from a course, the clerk added: "(on account of eyes—one eye)."[84] Whatever one may think of particular policies developed by the Faculty during the 1890's, there is no dispute that here is a lively group of men, clearly dedicated to the School, and, more important, having a large share in the administration of it. Though it is unwise to be dogmatic, it seems clear that sharing the running of the School was of first importance in attracting great teachers to Andover and, what is more, keeping them there after they had come. Dr. Bancroft's policy of respecting his Faculty and treating them decently earned rich dividends.

Another piece of evidence that shows how teaching positions at Phillips Academy were valued in the profession is provided by a folder of applications for the position of Professor of Greek, which became vacant in 1894 when Clifford H. Moore, a distinguished scholar who would later be Pro-

fessor of Classics at Harvard, left to go to the University of Chicago. There
are twenty-three applications in Dr. Bancroft's files, and there may have
been more than that; but the impressive thing is not the number of applicants but their quality and training. Five were Ph.D.'s and two of them
from Johns Hopkins, then perhaps the leading graduate school in the
country. Several more had done graduate work in foreign universities—
Leipzig, Athens, and the like. Among the younger applicants was a Magna
Cum Laude from Harvard and a Salutatorian at Yale, while others had
had a college teaching experience at Amherst and Princeton or had taught
at strong secondary schools. Finally a professor of Greek at the University
of Utah—then still a territory—had had the unpleasant experience of losing his position when the territorial legislature abolished his job because of
lack of funds.[85] Some of these applicants may have hoped to improve their
financial position; the School paid as high as $2000, which was about the
average being paid professors in the large universities during this period.
Yet if many must have been attracted by more than salary, it would have
been because at Andover a teacher had a chance to teach and study with
freedom and, in addition, to participate in the running of the School. On
the other side of the coin, teachers who voluntarily left Andover during
the Bancroft years in most cases had been called to positions of greater importance in the field of education. A partial list would include John M.
Tyler, who left to be Professor of Biology at Amherst; H. C. Bierworth,
who, like Moore, became a language professor at Harvard; M. Clement
Gile, who became a professor at Colorado College; and Walter R. Newton,
who became a professor at Rutgers. Finally, Edward G. Coy and David Y.
Comstock left in 1892 to found the Hotchkiss School and thereby established the tradition of Andover faculty members being called to head other
secondary schools.[86] In short, both the quality of the applicants for positions and the important posts that members of the Faculty left the School
to hold testify to the high reputation of Phillips Academy teachers.

A high percentage of Dr. Bancroft's faculty appointees not only gave
the School their " 'prentice years" but remained at Phillips Academy for
their entire careers. The list is impressive:[87]

Matthew S. McCurdy	1874–1921
Georgte T. Eaton	1880–1930
Charles E. Stone	1890–1937
Charles H. Forbes	1891–1933
Archibald Freeman	1892–1937
Allen R. Benner	1892–1938
James C. Graham	1892–1937
John L. Phillips	1894–1938
Frederick E. Newton	1895–1939
Alfred E. Stearns	1897–1933

Some of these teachers were truly great; others were no more than competent; but the group as a whole constituted a force for stability and excellence in the School for the first third of this century. It is appropriate to mention briefly the work of some whose teaching was limited to the Bancroft administration. One of the foremost among them was Edward G. Coy, Instructor in and later Professor of Greek. A graduate of Yale in 1869, he came to Andover the same year as Dr. Bancroft, having taught for a few years at Williston Academy. Coy has been described as stiff and unbending in his attitude toward his students, but he was a highly competent scholar, and the boys, who called him "Eddie Greek," found his classes inspiring.[88] They also appreciated the frequent cuts that he gave.[89] In 1884 he was given a sabbatical and spent his time studying archaeology and philosophy at the University of Berlin and traveling in Italy and Greece.[90] His correspondence with Dr. Bancroft shows him to have been a stickler for precision in School administrative matters. At times he could be a prickly person for the Principal to handle. When he came to Andover,

31. *Edward Gustin Coy, Professor of Greek under Principal Bancroft.*

his contract read that he was to teach eighteen hours a week; as the School grew, it became necessary to increase the teaching loads, with some of the faculty teaching as many as twenty-six hours a week. Coy refused to budge, however, and insisted that the terms of his contract be honored.[91] When Dr. Bancroft went to Europe in the winter and spring of 1889, Coy, David Comstock, and William B. Graves became a 'Triumvirate' in the running of the School, with Coy technically top man. In his report to the Trustees that June he complained about not having been given proper authority for the job and went on to make sharp criticisms: "Our 'service' is wretched:

32. *David Young Comstock, Professor of Latin under Principal Bancroft.*

our grounds are unkempt, our outbuildings are neglected, and even the school-rooms, at certain seasons of the year, are positively unfit for the reception of visitors for four days a week." He went on to suggest that the "supposed night policeman" for the Hill should be fired.

He was also disturbed about undergraduate drinking: "Thus while it is true that drunkenness in its coarser and more beastly forms has been less and less among us, yet the habit of intemperance seems to have increased, and that, too, among boys from families of culture, refinement and high social position."[92] Coy was a scholarly man who wrote a short history of Phillips Academy for the *New Englander Magazine* and served in the Greek section of President Eliot's Committee of Ten. In 1892 he left Andover, as noted, to become the first headmaster of the newly founded Hotchkiss School. Since Comstock went with him, many thought that Phillips Academy could never recover from the loss of these two distinguished teachers, but there is reason to believe that Dr. Bancroft may not have been too unhappy about their departure. As Headmaster J. C. MacKenzie of the Lawrenceville School wrote: "I am not sure that I ought to sympathize with you in your recent losses. If I were in your place I should be glad to have a body of men about me wholly of my own choosing."[93]

Mention has already been made of the work of William B. Graves in the English Department during this period. The third member of the Triumvirate was David Y. Comstock, Professor of Latin, who maintained the strict discipline in teaching that subject which has characterized most Academy Latin teachers until recent years. One of his pupils wrote of him:

> Anyone who was taught Latin by Mr. Comstock may well be grateful
> that his boyhood's lot was cast in Phillips Academy in that great
> teacher's day. A thorough foundation of grammar, the requirement
> of exactness, the demand for promptness of thought, insistence on
> rigorous clearness of distinctions—all these admirable qualities of
> drill in what was then the center and marrow of a boy's education,
> were present in his teaching in the fullest measure. To many of us,
> the lively, almost fierce excitement of Commy's classroom was a
> stimulus that has left a deep influence on our whole life.[94]

A graduate of Amherst in the Class of 1873, he came to Phillips the following year, the second of Dr. Bancroft's administration. He was not merely a teacher; he edited a volume of the *Aenead* for use in the schools and was a strong right arm to the Principal in many Academy problems. His colleague, Matthew S. McCurdy, wrote at the time of his death:

> We sat at the same table at the old Mansion House for nearly two
> years. We "inspected" the old Latin and English commons together
> for many years; and at the request of the Principal put in a good
> many evenings looking up the origin of campus fires, horn-blowing,

out-of-town trips, and other things that occupied the attention of some of the boys of forty years ago. . . . He was a most delightful companion, quick at repartee, quick to see and make good use of any amusing situation, and an adept in getting harmless fun out of the follies and foibles of other people and yet always sympathetic and helpful, generous and kind, not only to his immediate friends but to all with whom he came in contact. . . . He had a quick temper which he usually kept in control; a slight vein of suspicion which some-times led him to misjudge the motives of others; a stronger one of sarcasm which he occasionally used rather too freely, and was ex-tremely sensitive to the opinions of others as to his methods and attitudes.[95]

Reading between the lines suggests that David Comstock was a difficult per-son to deal with, and when he left Andover to go with Edward Coy to Hotchkiss, Dr. Bancroft may not have regretted his departure all that much.

Finally, there was John Wesley Churchill, Professor of Elocution and an old friend of Cecil Bancroft. The two had prepared for college together at Appleton Academy, and while Churchill went to Harvard and Bancroft to Dartmouth, they joined forces again at the Andover Theological Seminary. Churchill was not, strictly speaking, a Phillips Academy instructor in the usual sense, for he also taught at the Theological Seminary, at Abbot Academy, and at numerous colleges, where he would offer a course for a term or so. In addition he was in great demand as a preacher and traveled widely over New England to meet preaching engagements. Even though he gave only a small part of his time to Phillips Academy, however, he was a strong influence in the School. Until he came to Andover in 1866, the Wednesday afternoon elocution exercises had been pretty feeble affairs, often taught by some disinterested theologue. From then on, with patience and enthusiasm for his work, Professor Churchill made the art of speaking an important part of a Phillips Academy education. He drilled the boys for the annual Exhibitions and saw the quality of speaking at these perfor-mances improve steadily year by year. His ability and his reputation were such that when Matthew Arnold came to the United States for a lecture tour, he turned to Churchill for instruction in speaking. Perhaps his most important contribution to the Academy, however, was as a staunch sup-porter and friend of Cecil Bancroft. There was probably no one on the Faculty on whom the Principal depended more. Thus, while his role in instruction at the School was relatively minor, he more than made up for that by his capacity for friendship and his support for useful causes.[96]

One reason why Cecil Bancroft was able to attract good teachers to Phil-lips Academy and, for the most part, hold them there, was that he under-stood what teaching was all about. Speaking before the Massachusetts Clas-sical and High School Teachers' Association in 1894, he made a powerful statement about new teaching methods as opposed to the old. Today, he thought, instruction was based on educational theory rather than tradition. "We have come to understand . . . that learning lessons is not education. . . . The valedictorians of the olden time were the men who got more A plusses than their fellows. We hold that accumulated information is not education. An encyclopedia is not literature. Accomplishments are no longer accepted as education. Today, teachers have studied the mind, its capacities and limitations, and have based upon a living and growing psychology the order and method of a new education. There is a nobler conception of what truth is, and how it comes into our lives, and how we can set others on its quest. There is a growing interest among teachers of all grades for a careful observation and understanding of mental phenomena, a careful study of the evolution of the mind and heart of the child." And he continued:

> The seriousness of life is the great motive. Our appeal is to something larger than the rod or a medal. We are somewhat beyond bribing or frightening children into learning. The order, the industry, the constancy, the hopefulness of *scholarship* rest on ethical theory. Our best teachers are trying to live the *intellectual* life indeed, but do not stop there. . . . they are caught by the enthusiasm of humanity and they come to their pupils to work with them in a true sympathy. . . . The magnificient emphasis which our generation lays upon sacrifice and service has created the new Sociology and it is changing the face of education. The old methods of governing and of teaching give way before the new spirit of mutual helpfulness. . . . Sympathy is not new in teaching, but as a habit, an attitude, a principle it was almost lost out of the magisterial school-master of the not long-ago. . . . The use of the library, the laboratory, and of extra-school material of various kinds, is one of the methods very much in vogue at present. To send pupils straight to the sources, to teach them how to accumulate material and how to conduct a genuine investigation has proved less difficult, more attractive, and more profitable than we used to think. Some years ago I often saw in school programmes in Southern States "The Dictionary" as one of the prescribed subjects of instruction. . . . The only way to learn to use a dictionary, an encyclopedia, a library, an arboretum is to use it. The laboratory physics is as much superior to text-book physics as drawing is to looking at pictures. A Kodak is more than a tool or a toy.

The good Doctor closed by deploring the growth of special classes for students and special treatment for particular individuals. The whole address has an extraordinarily modern ring to it and is striking evidence that Cecil Bancroft was one of the most thoughtful educators of his day. No wonder that his Faculty was happy to follow his leadership in educational matters.[97]

Impressive evidence that at least some of the Faculty had accepted Dr. Bancroft's philosophy of teaching can be seen in a letter written to him by Charles H. Forbes, destined to be one of the Academy's great teachers and Acting Headmaster in 1933. After teaching at Andover for two years, Forbes wrote:

> Andover suits me, and I think I have something to give to Phillips. . . . The school-master of the book-and-rule type has absolutely no attraction for me, but I would like to continue the effort to become an *educator* of boys. Would prefer to have my pupils remember me as something more than a mechanical pile-driver of facts—useful as such engines may be. It would also be pleasing if they left the recitation-room with minds somewhat better than mimeographic reproductions of the books they have used.[98]

By the end of his term as Principal, Cecil Bancroft had made tremendous strides in building a strong Faculty and in introducing the kind of pedagogy he wanted. Not all his teachers would be as sensitive as Charles Forbes to new teaching methods; there would still be "pile-drivers of facts" at Phillips Academy. And the road had not been easy. In his report to the Trustees in 1893, the Principal used the expression "sometimes I despair" in connection with meeting the problems that had to be overcome if Phillips Academy were to be the School he hoped for. On the other hand he must have been heartened by letters like the one from George Herbert Palmer, Professor of Greek at Harvard and an Andover alumnus, in 1888:

> I find a curious impression current in the community that Phillips reached the height of its prosperity and teaching power under Uncle Sam, and that now it is doing as well as could be expected when deprived of that mighty influence. In my judgment the Andover of today is enormously better than any other Andover that ever was known; and if I am asked to say anything at the Dinner, I shall be very apt to say this—civilly of course, but with no undue reverence for the Uncle Sam legend, which I believe rests on no solid foundations. Educationally and morally I believe him to have been a humbug.[99]

Seen from the perspective of the 1970's, there can be no question that Cecil Bancroft did more to modernize the curriculum and establish the tradition of a strong Faculty than anyone else in the history of the School.

CHAPTER TEN

THE CENTENNIAL

I N 1876 Cecil Bancroft reported to the Trustees, "It is a question, not of the life or death of the school, but of its being of a first- or of a second-class grade." And well he might make such a statement. While he was beginning to make progress in curricular reform and in building a strong Faculty, material considerations were a heavy burden. The debt on the Main Academy building remained unpaid; even the interest on that debt could not be met, with the result that it increased each year. The school budget was not balanced, which led to deficit financing. Enrollment had been falling off, and the reputation of Phillips Academy was low in comparison with that of its competitors. Clearly some dramatic move was essential to reverse these trends and to restore the School to the position it had once enjoyed. Fortunately for Dr. Bancroft, Phillips Academy would be one hundred years old in 1878. Here was a heaven-sent opportunity to strengthen the institution, and the Principal was determined to make the most of it. Dr. Bancroft had been in Andover less than one year when he began to think about the School's coming centennial in 1878. He wanted to call attention to Phillips Academy's proud record in education, to rally the alumni in support of the institution, to conduct a drive to increase the endowment, and generally to start Andover on its second century with renewed vitality. As early as June 1874 the Trustees voted to refer the Centennial and what to do about it to the President of the Board and the Principal. The following year a committee of the Trustees was appointed for the same purpose, with power to enlist the support of a committee of the alumni and with the recommendation that they invite the aid of Professor John Lord Taylor, then President of the Faculty of the Theological Seminary and the author of the biography of Samuel Phillips.[1] Placing Professor Taylor on the Centennial team provided an unexpected dividend when, the following year, he presented the School with one hundred dollars to establish "the Taylor Centennial Fund," with the provision that the money was to be invested for the next one hundred years or until it had increased one-thousand fold, at which time the Trustees could use it "ac-

cording to their best wisdom" for the benefit of "Your Grand Old School."[2]
In the meantime the Trustees got a taste of what the Centennial celebration might involve when they voted one hundred dollars to hire a tent for
the Semi-Centennial of the Philomathean Society in 1875.[3] What might be
called a curtain-raiser for the School's festivities to come took place on
Memorial Day 1876 as part of the National Centennial of that year, when
a Centennial tree was planted with appropriate ceremonies. After introductory remarks by Dr. Bancroft, there followed a poem, an oration, and an
ode, the latter apparently sung by those present, all three efforts the productions of members of the Senior Class. The ceremonies were then appropriately closed with a prayer by the venerable Edwards A. Park, Professor
at the Theological Seminary.[4]

Thus far, plans for the Centennial had consisted mainly of talk. In 1877
the pace was stepped up. At their June meeting the Trustee committee reported that they had engaged speakers for the Centennial celebration, including Dr. Oliver Wendell Holmes as poet. The Board then proceeded to
appoint a Central Committee consisting of the Reverend Edward G. Porter
of Lexington, the Reverend Francis H. Johnson of Andover, and Dr.
Bancroft. The Reverend Porter was an old hand at Centennials, having
been in charge of the celebration in the town of Lexington in 1875, but
the records indicate that Dr. Bancroft did the lion's share of the work.
Bancroft, who had a highly developed sense of town-gown relations, urged
the Trustees to include the Town of Andover in the celebration. Accordingly, at their December meeting in Boston the Board voted "That the
Trustees respectfully invite the Town of Andover to participate in the celebration of the Centennial of the Academy."[5] The response to this invitation
was one of the most remarkable features of the Centennial. At the annual
town meeting on 4 March 1878, Article 17 in the warrant read: "To see
what action the town will take on the following communication from
C. F. P. Bancroft, Clerk of the Trustees of Phillips Academy"—namely,
the invitation. It was voted "that the town gratefully accept the invitation
tendered and that a Committee of three be nominated by the chair to retire
and report a Committee to represent the town and cooperate with the Committee of the Trustees of Phillips Academy in their arrangements for the
proposed Centennial Celebration." After due deliberation, the Committee
of Three reported back to the meeting with nominees for the larger committee, which included the selectmen, the town clerk, the trustees of the
Punchard Free School, the school committee, the trustees of the Memorial
Hall Library, and eleven citizens at large.[6] Nor did the town stop there.
When the committee met to organize on 13 April 1878, it soon became
clear that, as the chronicler of the Centennial put it, the members "con-
strued the word 'participate' to mean the rendering of efficient and material
aid." The Honorable Marcus Morton, Chief Justice of the Massachusetts
Supreme Judicial Court, was elected chairman, E. Kendall Jenkins, the

town clerk, secretary; and fifteen subcommittees were appointed to deal with such matters as Reception and Entertainment, Tents and Tables, Press and Advertisement, Police, Decorations, Procession, Railway Accommodations, Carriages, Dinner, and Music. The finance committee embarked on a drive to raise twenty-five hundred dollars, which, it was hoped, would be sufficient to cover all the expenses of the celebration, and had succeeded in collecting something over two thousand by the time the festivities began in June. Two hundred and forty-two donors contributed to this fund in amounts ranging from ten cents to one hundred dollars.[7] Certainly the response of the town to the Academy's invitation to "participate" must have been heart-warming for Cecil Bancroft and his fellow-workers.

In the meantime, things began to move forward on the Hill. On 5 March 1878 a Centennial Fund Concert was held in the Academy Hall, featuring the Phillips Academy Glee Club singing college favorites, Miss E. D. Goodridge playing Schubert and Mendelssohn on the piano, Miss L. F. Kimball singing "Queen of the Night" and "Waiting," Mr. E. Wallner on the violin, and Mr. F. Allen blowing "Farewell from the Mountain" and "Long, Long Ago" on the trombone. Tickets were thirty-five cents but there is no record in the accounts of the Treasurer as to how much money was raised.[8] On 21 April 1878 the hundredth anniversary of the signing of the Phillips Academy Constitution, Mrs. Bancroft electrified the community by giving birth to her fourth child, a son. The undergraduates were so taken with this coincidence that they petitioned Dr. Bancroft to name the boy "Phillips," which he proceeded to do.[9] Attempts were also made to publicize the coming Centennial in the press. The previous fall a very solid article on Phillips Academy and other "classical" schools had appeared in *Harper's*,[10] and early in 1878 the Boston *Daily Advertiser* published three articles on the School, its future, and the Phillips family. A similar account appeared in *The Congregationalist* early in May.[11] Although interest in the Centennial would be limited primarily to members of the Andover family, at least some of the general public would be made aware of the School and its record.

Yet it was to its own alumni that Phillips Academy must turn if it was to achieve the aims of the Centennial. Early in 1878 the Central Trustee Committee sent a circular to leading granduates inviting them to become members of a Committee of Fifty to work for the success of the Centennial. According to this circular, the aims of the Centennial were to collect records of the Academy's past, enlarge its library, add to its collection of portraits, publish a catalogue of officers and students for the entire century, increase funds and equipment, and hold "a large home gathering" of alumni at Andover on June 5 and 6. Each member of the Committee of Fifty, chosen so as to provide for wide age and geographical representation, was to be responsible for developing interest in the program in his area and in his age group.[12] The Committee finally met in Boston on 1 May 1878, with the Honorable George O. Shattuck, the chairman and John C. Phillips, secretary. This Committee appointed a series of subcommittees, many of them paralleling those of the Town of Andover, to deal with specific subjects. Of particular importance for the future of the School were two: one on Endowments and Scholarships, under the chairmanship of Alpheus H. Hardy, a Trustee, and another on Alumni Association under W. A. Mowry of Providence.[13] The Committee on Endowments and Scholarships must have moved very rapidly, for well before the celebration they had prepared and distributed a statement on the School's financial difficulties. After calling attention to the debt on the Academy Building of $29,700, the committee went on to point out that the entire resources of the School amounted to $111,532, and $59,312 of that amount was earmarked for special purposes, leaving a mere $52,220 for general expenses. In 1877 the income on the unrestricted funds totaled $3,154, which, when added to the income from tuition, gave the School $12,734 for general operating expenses. Salaries alone amounted to $10,630, which left $2,104 for all other purposes. The committee was careful to point out that Phillips Academy should not be confused with the Andover Theological Seminary, which was relatively strong financially, even though the two institutions were under the same Board of Trustees. Finally, the committee listed the Academy's needs: to pay off the outstanding debt, to provide for salaries adequate to attract and hold good teachers, to cover the additional expenses attendant upon the establishment of a fourth year and new departments, and to maintain the policy, initiated by the founders, of never turning away a deserving boy because he could not pay the School's charges. For these high-minded purposes the committee asked the alumni to raise $100,000.[14]

Next came the problem of invitations. Certainly all the alumni received them, for a printed invitation dated 13 May 1878 went out from the Central Committee to all "Sons of Phillips," presumably accompanied by the statement of the Committee on Endowments and Scholarship. For special guests an engraved invitation was prepared over the signature of Professor John Wesley Churchill, who was to preside at the Centennial dinner, and who, with the exception of Dr. Bancroft, worked harder for the celebration than anyone else. Professor Churchill and his Invitation Committee shot high when it came to special guests. They invited the President of the United States and Mrs. Rutherford B. Hayes; the Governor, Chief Justice, and other leaders of the Commonwealth of Massachusetts; the Mayor of Boston; the Presidents of all New England colleges and some outside New England; the Principals of all the leading New England preparatory schools; the Trustees and Faculty of the Phillips Exeter Academy; the United States Commissioner of Education and the Japanese and Chinese Commissioners of Education; the Superintendent of the Boston School System; past donors to Phillips Academy and the Andover Theological Seminary; and finally all the members of the Phillips family whom they

could locate.[15] In addition, Professor Churchill asked a substantial number
of them to make ten-minute speeches after the dinner on themes that he
would present in the form of toasts, and he asked them for suggestions. It
is testimony to the flexibility of the orators of the day that most of those
approached said they would talk on anything Churchill wanted them to.
For example, President Charles W. Eliot of Harvard wrote, "If he [the
presiding officer] can conveniently send me a day or two beforehand my
text, I will govern myself accordingly." And Eliot went on to say that he
had no *amour propre* about precedence, simply because Harvard was the
oldest institution, and that since the poet and orator of the day were both
Harvard men, he thought other colleges ought to have the "chief seats" at
the dinner. When Churchill suggested the theme of "stability and progress" in education, Eliot wrote back that that was "perfectly agreeable" to
him, and added, with a possible swipe at Andover's close associations with
Yale in the past, "It seems to me that Harvard contributes its fair share to
this celebration."[16] Gustavus V. Fox, who had spent two years at Andover
in the late 1830's and had been Assistant Secretary of the Navy in Lincoln's cabinet, wrote, "Sailors very often cause anxiety to their friends
when called upon to speak in public but never for want of brevity."[17]
Trustee Alpheus Hardy agreed to make a financial report, but as for speaking, he wrote, "my tongue is coated with silence."[18] Though there is no
record of any reply from President Hayes,[19] the response to Professor
Churchill's invitations was generally heart-warming, and it soon became
clear that the gathering in June would be a very distinguished assemblage
indeed.

As far as the material preparations for the Centennial are concerned, the
record is silent, but the amount of work that went into them must have
been prodigious. There were buildings to be decorated, caterers to be hired,
transportation to be provided, lodgings to be arranged, undergraduates to
be drilled, programs to be printed, tents to be rented, musicians to be
engaged, processions to be organized, and order to be brought out of
potential chaos. As the event proved, all these things were successfully accomplished. At last the great day came, and it was clear that both School
and town had done themselves proud. A reporter for the Boston *Daily
Advertiser* described the scene as follows:

> Andover is beautiful now. Every tree is rich with green leaves; nature
> is luxurient; the streets are lined with flags and streamers on both
> sides; houses are decorated; red, white and blue drapery is twined
> about the columns and ornaments the porticoes. In some houses every
> window has its flag. Great exertions have been made by the people
> to make the town appear worthy of the occasion, and they have
> succeeded admirably. Abbott [sic] Academy honored the day of its
> sister institution by decorations, and in the evening the trees were

light with Chinese lanterns. Historical spots were conspicuously
noted. Where the first academy stood was erected a sign reading
"The Old Joiner's Shop. First Academy Building stood here in 1778."
Upon the porticoes of the house standing in the same yard [Farrar
House] was fastened a picture of Judge Phillips, the founder of the
academy, draped with the national colors. Farther up the hill, on the
other side, was another conspicuous sign: "Site of the Second
Academy Building. Built 1786; Burned 1818," and on the street
corner below was a third, which read: "Site of the Old Stone Academy.
Built 1832. Burnt in 1864." The Mansion house on the hill bore a
device, "Phillips Mansion, built 1782." The town hall, the railroad
station and other prominent places were ornamented, some of them
very gaily with streamers and inscriptions of welcome. The academy
building itself was richly adorned with flags, festoons, and streamers
of red, white and blue down its whole front. Altogether, the town
was wonderfully brilliant and attractive.[20]

33. The Academy Building, decorated for the Centennial.

The Boston and Maine Railroad decided to take advantage of the great day to do a little promotion of its own. As the Lawrence *American* described it, "The Boston & Maine depot was finely decorated by Supt. Richardson, with flags, bunting and shields; immediately over the ticket óffice was the motto: 'Welcome to the 100th Anniversary of the School of our Fathers,' and another motto read: " 'Boston & Main R.R., now the connecting link between the east and west; originated in Andover in 1833.' "[21] Across from the Mansion House, in the area where the Memorial Tower is now located, two large tents had been set up—one, accommodating thirty-five hundred, for the exercises on Wednesday evening and Thursday morning, the other accommodating fifteen hundred, for the dinner on Thursday. Finally, the weather was, by all accounts, gorgeous. When James Russell Lowell wrote, "What is so rare as a day in June! Then if ever come perfect days", he might well have been describing these two days on Andover Hill in 1878. It is hard to see how all those who had worked so faithfully could have provided a more fitting setting for the ceremonies to come, and the beautiful weather seemed to indicate that the Good Lord himself was smiling on their endeavors.

The Phillips Academy Centennial took place in the last years of what might be called the Age of Oratory in American life. When people wanted to celebrate something, they invited speakers to come to talk to them. And the speeches were expected to be exhaustive, if not exhausting. An orator who was worth his salt would never be satisfied with some half-hour statement; he was expected, literally, to go on for hours. Daniel Webster had set the fashion for this kind of oratory—some of his Congressional speeches actually lasted several days. Another leading orator was Edward Everett, who spoke for two hours at the dedication of the Gettysburg cemetery, at which Abraham Lincoln spoke but a few minutes. Those in charge of the Centennial clearly saw no reason to depart from the established practice. To be sure, there were a few musical interludes; to be sure, different kinds of people gave different kinds of speeches: but the fact remains that those who attended the exercises from start to finish would have listened to *fifteen hours* of speeches of one kind or another.[22]

The honor of opening the exercises was given to the Phillips Academy undergraduates; indeed, this was almost the only formal part they had in the two-day proceedings. At 3:00 p.m. what is described as a "great audience," "composed largely of graduates of the school and personal friends of the speakers," assembled in the Academy Hall on the top floor of the main Academy Building.[23] The occasion was the twelfth annual competition for the Warren F. Draper prizes in declamation, established by Mr. Draper, proprietor of the Andover Press, to improve the quality of public speaking by professional men. In this contest the students recited not compositions of their own but selections from the writings of famous authors, which they had memorized. The Centennial competition featured such selections as Wendell Phillips' "John Brown at Harper's Ferry," Carl Schurz's "Sumner's Battle-Flag Resolution," John Ruskin's "The Right Use of Wealth," and John Anthony Froude's "Luther at the Diet of Worms."[24] The boys, all of whom had been drilled by Professor John Wesley Churchill, apparently performed magnificently. One reporter wrote, "The speaking was of unusual excellence, and would compare, much to the credit of the Andover students, with the rhetorical exhibitions in the colleges."[25] Just before the announcement of the judge's decisions, Principal Bancroft rose to announce that he had been given a check by Mr. Draper to endow the prizes in perpetuity, the first of many windfalls that the Centennial would bring. The Right Reverend Thomas M. Clark, D.D., LL.D., Bishop of Rhode Island, then announced the winners, but, as is customary with judges, he had to make a speech first. He complimented the contestants on the excellence of their performances, stressed the difficulty the judges had had in reaching their decisions, and suggested to the students that "when Phillips celebrated her next centennial, their faces might adorn her walls, their writings find a place in her library, and *their voices be echoed by the phonograph through their halls.*"[26] He then announced that the first prize had been awarded to Burton M. Firman of Andover for his recitation of George William Curtis's "Fanaticism", second prize to Roland B. Whitridge of Boston for "The Pilot's Story" by William Dean Howells, and third prize to Francis Johnson Phelps of Andover for Wendell Phillips' "Toussaint L'Ouverture." The local boys certainly made good.

After the ovations came the presentation to the School of seven portraits: three were of former Principals—Pemberton, Johnson, and Tilton; one of James Eaton, late head of the School's English Department; one of Lieutenant S. H. Thompson, the fiancé of Elizabeth Stuart Phelps, who had been killed at Antietam; and two of alumni, Samuel Williston of the Class of 1815 and Horatio Hackett of the Class of 1826. Each presentation was accompanied by a speech, some of them quite lengthy.[27]

After the presentation of the portraits occurred a charming interlude that came as a surprise to the audience, since there was no mention of it in the program. Professor John Wesley Churchill mounted the platform and asked Dr. Bancroft if he (Churchill) and Edward G. Coy, Professor of Greek, might conduct a brief exercise. After gaining the good Doctor's permission, Professor Churchill then proceeded, "on behalf of the teachers and pupils of our sister institution, Abbot Academy," to present to the School a handsome banner with the accompanying sentiment: "To 'Phillips.' A birthday greeting with proud congratulations from 'Abbot.' May the coming centuries of the academy, and the years of its members, show how grand an ending hangs upon that true beginning,—*Non sibi.*" "The banner," writes the chronicler of the Centennial, "which is of silk, finished with gold fringe and tassels, hangs from a staff tipped with a small gilt eagle. The face, which is white, bordered with light blue, displays in colors the device of the Phillips Academy seal with its mottoes; the reverse is scarlet, and shows in gold letters the inscription: 'ABBOT ACADEMY TO PHILLIPS ACADEMY. 1778–1878.' Professor Coy then accepted the gift on behalf of the Faculty and Students and pledged to the ladies of Abbot "the honor of ideal knighthood,—a brave and generous loyalty." The undergraduates present then showed their appreciation of the gift by giving one of their favorite cheers: "P-h-i-l-l-i-p-s, rah, rah, rah" (repeated three times).[28]

At the conclusion of the Wednesday afternoon exercises the assemblage adjourned for supper. One wonders where they all ate. The School would give all the guests dinner the following day but had made no provision for a meal on Wednesday night. Some of the more illustrious presumably were guests at the homes of the administration and faculty; others presumably ate at the Mansion House, then a public inn; still others may have dined with hosts in the town. In any event the guests did not have much time to pleasure themselves with food, for at 7:30 that evening "a still larger audience than that of the afternoon" assembled in the greater of the two tents. The chronicler of the Centennial describes the event:

> The scene and its surroundings was one not easily forgotten. Outside the great tent Chinese lanterns were hung from the boughs of all the trees, while the interior was pleasantly illuminated by lamps and locomotive headlights. But high above these the great moon rolled in its splendor, and flooded everything with its mellow light. Pouring through the leaves of the overhanging elms, it penetrated the canvas walls, leaving them frescoed with masses of swaying foliage, and establishing an unexpected harmony between their otherwise bald expanse and the palms that graced the speakers' desk. Later in the evening the wind arose, and the sound of waving branches was mingled with the voice of the orator, while the canvas ceiling waved in great undulations overhead. It was not hard to be convinced that the old elms, and even the winds, were taking part in the general gladness. To quote the words of another, 'It seemed like a coronation, as indeed it was, of grand old memories of noble men, who, being dead, yet speak.'[29]

When it is added that the interior of the tent was decorated with "bunting, streamers, and flags of different nations," it is easy to see why the occasion could be described as "a brilliant spectacle."[30]

Promptly at seven-thirty the evening exercises began, with some numbers from the Lawrence, Massachusetts, Madrigal Club, S. A. Ellis, Conductor. There followed a prayer by the Reverend Ray Palmer, D.D. Dr. Palmer was to be featured twice that evening; later on the assemblage sang his hymn "My faith looks up to Thee / Thou Lamb of Calvary." It then became Principal Bancroft's turn for an address of welcome. The good Doc-

34. The Centennial Tents.

tor delivered a warm and sentimental speech, reviewing the School's great traditions, reminding his audience of their associations with the School itself and the beautiful Andover countryside, and closing with a welcome from the Trustees, the Faculty, the students, the Town of Andover, and finally from Alma Mater "to nestle again in the old arms and feel again the throbbing of the old heart." The Reverend William Adams, D.D., LL.D., the son of Principal John Adams, responded for the Alumni. He reminisced about his days at Phillips Academy, paid tribute to the courage of the Founders, and suggested that those identified with the Kingdom of Christ were the real heroes of this country rather than wealthy men who lived lives of "self-indulgence, luxury, and ostentation." Then came the *pièce de résistance* of the evening—an address entitled "The Earlier Annals of Phillips Academy" by the Reverend William E. Park, the son of Professor Edwards Park of the Theological Seminary. The Reverend Park had done his homework. If the audience wanted to hear about the early history of the School, he would tell them about it, and he did just that for close to two hours. He spent most of his time on the Phillipses and the founding of the Academy and gave substantial credit to Eliphalet Pearson for determining the kind of school it would be. The paper was scholarly, solid, unrelieved by humor or light touch; it was in the best Andover tradition.[31] By the time the Reverend Park finished, it was close to ten o'clock; the audience, which had had two and one half hours of speechifying, must have looked apprehensively at the next item on the program, which read "Reminiscences by Senior Alumni." Apparently the old boys never got a chance to reminisce, for Dr. Adams, as presiding officer, firmly announced that ten o'clock was "the orthodox time for retiring on Andover Hill"[32] and the ceremonies were closed with some more madrigals, the singing of the hymn "He leadeth me! Oh, blessed thought!", written by Professor J. H. Gilmore, and a benediction by the Reverend Enoch Stanford. The evening had hardly been one of light entertainment; it was a dignified and sober occasion; but the exercises undoubtedly symbolized, for those present, the seriousness of purpose which had characterized the spirit of Phillips Academy since its founding.[33]

At the close of the Wednesday evening exercises, the hospitable citizens of the Town of Andover took over. According to the record, ninety-three families opened their homes to guests and managed to provide lodgings for 297 visitors. In addition, the Reception and Entertainment Committee added, "a large number were received and entertained by friends of which the committee could render no account."[34] One wonders if there has ever been such an outstanding example of happy town-gown relations in the annals of American education. The town's hospitality was strictly a bed-and-breakfast affair, however, for those in charge of the Centennial had scheduled the first event for eight-thirty the following morning. At that time a large number of Phillips Academy alumni met in Academy Hall to

form an alumni association. At the start some spoilsport called attention
to the fact that there already was an alumni organization in existence, but
since it was moribund, those attending voted to merge the old with the
new. A simple constitution, presented by the Honorable Robert R. Bishop,
was adopted, and the Honorable George O. Shattuck of Boston was elected
President. In what was apparently an effort to share the wealth, the new
organization elected *twenty-eight* vice-presidents. Plans were made to hold
biennial meetings in Boston and quinquennial meetings in Andover. By the
end of the day it was reported that the new association had signed up
three hundred members, and all concerned were most sanguine about its
future. But it would be many years before anything like the present alumni
organization would come into being.[35]

"All the morning birds sang together for joy. . . . The wind was northwest, worthy of Andover and of 'the day we celebrate.' To your tent again,
O Phillips! It has three thousand sittings, and before noon hundreds standing in the aisles." With these words the reporter for *The Congregationalist*
introduced his account of the exercises of Thursday morning.[36] Every Boston & Maine train that day brought additional guests, come to Andover to
do Phillips honor. Promptly at nine-thirty the celebration was opened with
more music from the Lawrence Madrigal Club, which earned its pay during these two days. Then followed a prayer by the Reverend Jonathan
Stearns, a grandson of one of the first trustees of the Academy and a member of a family with many Andover connections. At this point Dr. William
Adams, who had presided the evening before, rose to introduce the orator
of the day, the Reverend Alexander McKenzie of Cambridge.

If the three thousand people who had come to Andover that morning
were looking forward to hearing an oration in the best style of Webster
and Everett, they certainly got their money's worth. The Reverend Mc-
Kenzie spoke for one hour and a half without a note of any kind, inter-
spersing his remarks with snatches of poetry and quotations from pertinent
authors. His theme was the great story of Phillips Academy, but in the
process of developing that theme he went back to the schools of the Druids
in ancient Britain and retold the story of the Puritan migration to New
England. Where the Reverend Park's account of the previous evening had
been sober and scholarly, Reverend McKenzie's was ornate and rhetorical.
It was not so much *what* he said as the manner of his saying it that was
impressive, while with the Reverend Park the reverse was true. Midway in
the course of his oratorical *tour de force* McKenzie was interrupted by the
arrival of Governor Alexander H. Rice of Massachusetts with his staff, accompanied by the Boston Cadet Band, which played "Hail to the Chief" as
His Excellency entered the building.[37] Such an interruption might have flustered a less experienced speaker, but the Reverend McKenzie never turned
a hair and resumed his rhetorical flights once the Governor was seated. According to several reports,[38] one of the most impressive parts of the Mc-

Kenzie oration was his calling of the roll of Phillips Academy's graduates:

> Call the roll. The response will come from all the land, from its towns and tents: from lands beyond the seas; from lands within the seas. . . . It will come from men who in the ministry of mercy heal the sick and restore the dying, who defend the common life and prolong its days. . . . The reply will come from the temples where justice sits with even scales, and law presides over property and industry. . . .
>
> Call the roll. The reply will come from among the merchants of the world, whose enterprise sustains society, whose ships penetrate to all climes, whose roads bind continents. . . . It will come from the council hall of the nation, and the village; from the school and college, and every seat of high learning; from the scholar's study and the poet's retreat. . . . from the broad fields where they are gathering the great harvests that they may give us bread and feed the world; from the soldier's camp and ship, where arms protect peace, and liberty rests serene and secure in the guardianship of the patriot's sword.
>
> Call the roll of the sons of Phillips, and from all places where good men are found, thousands of voices shall make reply, "Here;" and from the realms above us, where they rest from their labors, and their works do follow them, shall come the voice clear as the victor's trumpet, "Here"—"O mother dear! your wisdom taught us, your prudence defended us, your spirit inspired us, your courage ennobled us, and we are doing what you gave us will and might to do." Mother and sons, with the ancestral piety, standing between the centuries, in one glad voice shall raise the sons of the fathers, *Non nobis, Domine.*

The Centennial orator concluded his address with a stirring defense of the importance of a good religious education—an education that could be given at schools like Phillips Academy but that could not, under the United States Constitution, be given in the public schools. Nor did he forget to put in a plug for the Centennial Fund Drive. All in all it was a masterful performance. The peroration went as follows:

> Let the call upon us be loud, bold, unceasing. We are ready. Phillips is a hundred years old, yet stands erect, fronting another century, and answering the summons with a bold Ha, Ha! With free men freely furnished for their work, a free spirit in a free school, the centuries may ask what they will. . . .
>
> The grass withers. The tree falls. It is the word that remains. Learning will treasure and employ the trust we commit to her. The great forces whose seat is here, whose sphere is in the hearts and lives of men, will never lose their might or lack their opportunity. Men go. Institutions remain. . . .

Boys will come in unbroken procession and kneel before Samuel
Phillips. Out of the olden time, in the vigor of today, living hands
shall be laid upon their heads, and this prayer shall crown them:
"The angel which redeemed me bless the lads; and let my name be
named upon them, and the name of my fathers."

> "How sweet a thing it is to wear a crown,
> Within whose circuit is Elysium,
> And all that poets feign of bliss and joy."

How grand a thing it is to wear a crown within whose circuit is that
which seers have seen and sung; which patriots have longed for;
which wise men have wished for; which holy men have prayed for;
which good men have found and proved, and have bequeathed and
shall bequeath! The crown of a true knowing, wherein man towers
above himself, and is in league with the unseen and eternal! It is the
knowledge of the sailor, who looks up and down, and marks his path
across the trackless main. It is the knowledge of the scholar, who
makes all times his servitors, and all men, and forces the universe to
yield up its secret wealth. It is the knowledge of the man who finds
the invisible, secures the immortal, and commits his life to the change-
less Providence and the everlasting Redemption. The knowledge
which enshrines itself in duty and affection; which in a true childhood
waits to be taught and to be used; and in a real allegiance follows
Him whose banner over us is love; of which He said who knew all
things, and for whom all things are: 'This is eternal life.'[39]

Another round of madrigals and then Dr. Adams rose to introduce the
Poet of the Day, Dr. Oliver Wendell Holmes. By chance Adams had been
present at the Academy Exhibition of 1825, when young Holmes, a member of the Senior Class, had read a poem. "Well do I remember his ruddy
countenance, his plaited frill, his attractive manners, and the wave of surprise and delight which passed over the audience as with lips already 'wet
with Castilian dews' he charmed them by all the recital of his verse." Now,
fifty-three years later, the poet was again to recite to an Andover audience.[40]

More than just an occasional poet, to judge by his complete works, Oliver
Wendell Holmes did, however, rise, personally and poetically, to many and
disparate occasions. He soberly turned out a "Song for a Temperance Dinner to which Ladies were Invited;" he became grave at "The Dedication of the Pittsfield Cemetery, September 9, 1850;" and he cleaned his
pen "For the Meeting of the National Sanitary Association."

A loyal Harvard alumnus, the good doctor wrote much crimson verse:
"A Song for the Centennial Celebration of Harvard College, 1836,"
"Hymn for the Celebration at the Laying of the Corner-Stone of Harvard
Memorial Hall, Cambridge, October 6, 1870," "Hymn for the Dedication

of Memorial Hall, at Cambridge, June 23, 1874," and two sonnets, "Harvard."

Is it any wonder, then, that the centennial celebration of Phillips Academy brought forth the person and the poetry of Dr. Holmes? At the age of sixty-nine, Oliver Wendell Holmes wrote, in strict iambic pentameter, three hundred and fifty-four lines of rhyming couplets entitled "The School Boy." And that, poetically, was another occasion.

The day was bright and sunny, with Nature in tune with Man, as Holmes surveyed *alma mater*:

> What need of idle fancy to adorn
> Our mother's birthplace on her birthday morn?
> Hers are the blossoms of eternal spring,
> From these green boughs her new-fledged birds take wing,
> These echoes hear their earliest carols sung,
> In this old nest the brood is ever young.

The reminiscences that follow are intensely personal, and somewhat nostalgic:

> When first I sought the academic town.
> My cheek was bare of adolescent down

And yet, the vision is clear, not clouded with the mist of fifty years:

> The morning came; I reached the classic hall;
> A clock-face eyed me, staring from the wall;
> Beneath its hands a printed line I read:
> YOUTH IS LIFE'S SEED-TIME: so the clock face said.

Students, the class-room, masters, all are recalled with clarity and wit:

> Uneasy lie the heads of all that rule
> His most of all whose kingdom is a school.

A favorite master, nameless but immortalized, comes to life in the mantle of *non sibi*:

> His was the charm magnetic, the bright look
> That sheds its sunshine on the dreariest book;
> A loving soul to every task he brought
> That sweetly mingled with the lore he taught;
> Sprung from a saintly race that never could
> From youth to age be anything but good,
> His few brief years in holiest labors spent,
> Earth lost too soon the treasure that heaven had lent.[41]

Holmes then turns to *ubi sunt*, and with an echo of François Villon, he asks

Where now that time remote, its griefs, its joys,
Where are its gray-haired men, its bright-haired boys?

. . . .

Still in the waters of the dark Shawshine
Do the young bathers splash and think they're clean?

. . . .

Are there still truant feet that stray beyond
These circling bounds to Pomp's or Haggett's Pond?

The only figure from Andover's past who is specifically named is
Eliphalet Pearson, who made such a strong impression upon Holmes that
fifty some years later he could recall "the great Eliphalet,"

(I can see him now;
Big name, big frame, big voice, and beetling brow).

As he surveys the passing of the years, the many changes which have
taken place since he was, himself, a school boy, Dr. Holmes remarks how
easily one adjusts to change. The train, anesthesia, the archeological discoveries of Schliemann, astronomical advances, all these delight the mind.
He pauses, though, in his admiration of "that wicked phonograph! hark!
how it swears! / Turn it again and make it say its prayers!"

After apologising, surely with his tongue in cheek, that "too light my
strain" has been for the distinguished company,[42] Holmes ends "The
School Boy" with a mighty paean to Phillips Academy:

Darker and deeper though the shadows fall
From the gray towers on Doubting Castle's wall,
Though Pope and Pagan re-array their hosts,
And her new armor youthful Science boasts,
Truth, for whose altar rose this holy shrine,
Shall fly for refuge to these bowers of thine.

Oliver Wendell Holmes at Andover, on that day in 1878, was certainly
not the poet that Matthew Arnold was in Rugby chapel. "The School Boy"
is a highly parochial poem, as indeed befits the occasion for which it was
written. It is also intensely personal, filled not only with recurring portraits
of the author, but also with esoteric references and jokes. Accustomed as
we are, perhaps, to the sometimes wicked wit of Dr. Holmes, "The School
Boy" falls somewhat drily upon the ear, especially in the last sections.
Schools change with time, perhaps more quickly now than in the nineteenth century; yet one feels, in reading "The School Boy," that an elderly
Dr. Holmes is reviving an Andover no longer vital in 1878. Indeed,
Holmes, perhaps unwittingly, gives us a telling self-portrait:

If some tired wanderer, resting from his flight,

> Amid the gay young choristers alight,
> These gather round him, mark his faded plumes
> That faintly still the far-off grove perfumes,
> And listen, wondering if some feeble note
> Yet lingers, quavering in his weary throat.[43]

At the close of the morning exercises at twelve-thirty, the Centennial guests formed into a procession under the direction of General William Cogswell. First came the Boston Cadet Band, then the Academy undergraduates, then the Trustees, then Governor Rice with his staff, and finally the alumni and special guests, arranged in order of seniority. The procession marched down Main Street to the Academy Building, crossed to the Elm Arch, and marched down that to the dinner tent that had been erected next to the great tent where the morning exercises had taken place. At various points along the way the undergraduates stopped to cheer. The parade was an impressively long one; the head of it had disappeared over the brow of the hill before the rear got started. One striking sight during the procession was President Charles W. Eliot of Harvard and President Noah Porter of Yale walking arm in arm.[44] In the meantime the caterer, A. W. Tufts of Boston, had been busy preparing the banquet. Unfortunately, there is no record of the menu, but there was general agreement that the repast was excellent, one observer remarking particularly on the virtues of the dessert. Just before the guests entered, Tufts or his deputy explained to the waiters their duties, and added, "If you don't do just as I tell you, I won't hire one of you again at the next Centennial."[45] Approximately fifteen hundred people sat down to dinner that day. The guests had been given badges of different colors to determine where they should sit.[46] The special guests sat on a platform at one side, the alumni in the center, and at the two ends the ladies and undergraduates. Again the citizens of the Town of Andover had an opportunity to show real hospitality. Apparently there were more visitors that had tickets to the dinner than there were places; to remedy this situation a substantial number of "townies" graciously gave up their tickets—and their dinners—so that the guests might be seated. Throughout the meal the Boston Cadet Band played appropriate music, while at intervals throughout the afternoon a chorus of male voices under the direction of B. J. Lang favored the assemblage with a variety of numbers, "A Soldier's Farewell" and Mendelssohn's "Rhine-Wine Song" being especially well received.[47] This banquet and the speeches that followed were the climax to the celebration. When Dr. Bancroft looked around him at the distinguished men who were in attendance, he must have felt proud for the School.

By two-thirty the dinner was over and what the Boston *Daily Advertiser* called "the treat of intangible things" began,—and continued for over four hours. There were twenty-nine separate speeches, some of considerable length, and several other gentlemen were called on but had been obliged to leave. Both limitations of space and the patience of the reader demand that only a few of the high spots of the afternoon be touched upon.[48] Professor John Wesley Churchill presided with his characteristic grace and skill, even though it took him two pages in the record to explain why he did not wish to take time from the other speakers. With each introduction, Churchill proposed a toast, to which the speaker responded. For example, the first toast was "The Commonwealth of Massachusetts. On the rock of popular education the infant settlement was founded; on this it has ever rested." To this Governor Rice responded with some complimentary remarks about

35. Professor John Wesley Churchill, Toastmaster at the Centennial Dinner.

Phillips Academy and shortly thereafter departed as he had arrived, accompanied by the Boston Cadet Band. Trustee Alpheus Hardy, who had written earlier that "his tongue would be coated with silence" that afternoon, managed a most encouraging report on the fund drive. He announced that $50,000 of the desired $100,000 had already been subscribed, $25,000 being given by John C. Phillips. At this point the Reverend E. G. Porter rose and led the audience in three cheers for Mr. Phillips. Mr. Hardy then suggested that it would be "splendid" if the remaining $50,000 were subscribed before the afternoon was out, but this dream failed to materialize. After Phillips Brooks, the great preacher, had spoken as the representative of the Phillips family, there occurred a rather bizarre interlude. General Henry K. Oliver—he had made some unscheduled remarks at the portrait presentation the day before—read what he called a *Carmen Macaronicum*, or burlesque poem, described by one reporter present as "a curious metrical compound of Latin and English, with a few Greek words thrown in for spice." The opening line will be more than sufficient to illustrate what the old General was up to: "Fer, Dave, mihi, pens et inkum." To make sure that the audience would not miss a single joke, the General had had his *chef-d'oeuvre* printed up beforehand and distributed to the audience. The evidence is not clear as to what extent the General had his audience in the aisles, but the reaction of the reporters present was restrained, to say the least.[49] After the General had finished, Professor Churchill asked the Boston Cadet Band to play "Federal Street", the words to which General Oliver had written as a young man. This the band did "in a beautiful and effective manner."

Then President Charles W. Eliot of Harvard rose to respond to the toast "Harvard University. . . . the union of stability and progress." Eliot was at this time well along in his reform of the Harvard curriculum through the introduction of the elective system, and his performance at the Centennial made it clear why he was destined to be a great college president. He accepted the theme of "stability and progress" and illustrated it by remarking: "We see with regret that the elms which our ancestors planted in the college yard are getting feeble, and that our grandchildren will hardly walk under their lofty arches; but we set out young oaks, rock maples, and beeches, that our descendants may nevertheless enjoy a pleasant shade." Commenting on the Phillips family he said:

> What a curious mixture of conservatism and radicalism the Phillips family in the generations which founded this academy exhibited! Strenuous sticklers for social rank, yet making powder with which to fight his sacred majesty the king; evidently believing in the sufficiency through all generations of their own theology and political creeds, yet fostering learning and education, two forces which inevitably incline the children to push beyond the landmarks of the fathers.

Eliot was not happy about the democratic trend in American education:

> I trust that an habitual regard for masses and majorities is not going
> to render Americans less mindful of the value of noble family stocks,
> or of the immeasurable influence which individuals of extraordinary
> worth are capable of exerting. Republican institutions, with their
> great new merits, must not fail to secure also those proved advan-
> tage of aristocratic institutions, which are sure, because founded
> upon natural law.

Eliot was glad that Phillips Academy charged tuition fees and thought that
free tuition above the elementary grade was "of very doubtful advantage
to the morals of the community. Some people seem to think it more democratic to get a benefit without paying for it; but, if self-government means
self-respect and self-reliance, democratic practice should reject gratuities,
especially from government."

He supported the Academy's attempt to exert "a positive moral and religious influence" on its pupils and stated that he had no interest in separating adolescents from their families for a purely secular education. "Does
this mean denominational schools?," he asked, and then answered his own
question: "It does." He went on:

> I have no peculiar interest in the denomination to which the founders
> of this academy sought to attach it forever, except that, like all lovers
> of freedom, I am grateful to it for its strenuous maintenance of the
> right of private judgment, for its resistance to every form of eccle-
> siasticism and priestcraft, and for all the gallant service it has ren-
> dered to the cause of civil, as well as religious, liberty. Before this
> audience frankness requires me to say further, that there is probably
> not one of the distinctive tenets of orthodox Congregationalists, not
> one of the doctrines which characterize them as a sect, which I should
> personally accept. None the less I do rejoice that the hundreds of
> boys who gather here . . . come under the influence of a vigorous
> branch of the Christian church, and receive instruction in their duties
> and responsibilities which is given with all the weight of sincere
> conviction and consistent example.

And President Eliot closed by predicting a strong second century for Phillips Academy, as more and more people turned to educational institutions
of proved excellence and long-established traditions. Unlike most of the
speeches that afternoon, Eliot's was not one of fulsome praise for the
school or sentimental reminiscence about the past. It is extremely unlikely
that the faculty of the Theological Seminary could have liked what he said.
But he certainly gave his audience something to chew on.

If Eliot represented the new in American education, the next speaker, the venerable Professor Edwards A. Park, represented the old. He spoke for the Andover Theological Seminary and devoted himself to a long tribute to Eliphalet Pearson. Before launching on this main theme, however, he had some fun with the religious differences that existed at the time of the Seminary's founding:

> The first of these classes consisted of men who were Calvinists; the second, of men who were Calvinistic; the third, of men who were Calvinistical; and the fourth, of men who were Calvinisticalish. The second of these parties, *i.e.* the Calvinistic, was subdivided into two: the "Semi-Calvinists," whose heads were inclined toward Calvinism, and their hearts toward Arminianism; and the "Semi-Arminians", whose heads were turned toward Arminianism, and their feelings lingered around Calvinism.

And then Professor Park, like his son the evening before, embarked on a long, scholarly tribute to the great Eliphalet.[50]

On and on the speeches went. Josiah Quincy, Jr., told an amusing story of the time he had accompanied Lafayette on his visit to Andover. Before they arrived, Lafayette had pumped Quincy about the Theological Seminary, so that when the party arrived, the Frenchman could talk very knowledgeably about the institution. Later in the day Quincy returned to Andover to visit one of his old teachers. The master had been tremendously impressed with Lafayette:

> I was aware that our institution occupied a distinguished place in the religious world, but was unprepared to find that a man who had spent his life in courts and camps, and had gone through the horrors of the French Revolution, should have known so much about our school of the prophets.

Quincy concluded:

> I did not dare enlighten him on the subject, remembering that he always considered the tendency that boys had to prompt one another, as proof of total depravity. . . . and left him with a vague impression, which I doubt not he retained to his dying day, that in the *salons* of Paris, and among the officers in the French army, there was no subject more generally discussed than the orthodoxy of the institution at Andover.

There were still more speeches as the afternoon wore on,—President Noah Porter of Yale, Gustavus V. Fox of the Navy, a memorial poem for Andover men killed in the Civil War, composed for the occasion by Elizabeth Stuart Phelps, Professor A. C. Perkins, the Principal of Exeter, President S. C. Bartlett of Dartmouth, Horace Fairbanks, Governor of Vermont, and an assortment of clergymen. For some inexplicable reason the three main speakers of the Centennial—Annalist Park, Orator McKenzie, and Poet Holmes—were all called on *again*. Dr. Holmes announced that he would read the translation from Virgil that he had recited at his own graduation in 1825. At this Professor Churchill, who was always fast on his feet, "announced in a stentorian voice, after the manner of a pedagogue, '*Expectatur poema ab Olivero Wendell Holmes.*'" Way down on the list came Frederic W. Tilton, Dr. Bancroft's predecessor as Principal, and new Headmaster of the Rogers High School in Newport, Rhode Island. He was almost the only person during that long afternoon who mentioned actual teaching in a classroom. And he had a good story to tell to illustrate his point. He was, he said, trying to explain to a Phillips boy the axiom that two things equal to the same thing are equal to each other:

> I was anxious to present the matter clearly to him, and I said, 'Three and two are five; four and one are five; what then must be true of three and two, and four and one?' No response. I repeated. Still no response. I then tried a new experiment. I said, 'Here is a little boy of the same age as that little boy; and here is another little boy of the same age as that little boy; what must be true of these two little boys?' Still no response from the student. The large class of forty boys was becoming very attentive. I repeated the last question. All was still as death. After a moment, the face of the student lighted up, as he exclaimed, 'Oh! they must be *twins.*' All efforts to continue that recitation were useless.

Instead of dwelling on the past, Tilton then addressed himself to contemporary American problems. He pointed out that the public high schools were under attack, "not only by demagogues, but by men whose high position as teachers and scholars gives their opinion great weight." Under these circumstances the role of the privately endowed school might become even more important in the future, especially since private institutions were not prohibited from giving moral and religious training to their pupils, a training denied to the public schools under the Constitution. Tilton then touched on the problem of corruption in the country—the scandals of the Grant administration were still fresh in people's minds:

> On the one side, crime in high places; corruption of the most flagrant kind in comparatively intellectual circles. Our national name disgraced by men of liberal education; families worse than widowed and orphaned by the dishonesty of a husband and father, strong enough in intellect but only too weak, morally and religiously, to resist temptation. And then, on the other side, men doing all they can to eliminate from the training given to the great body of youth in our country all that tends to develop the spiritual side of their natures.

In such a situation Phillips Academy could play a vital role, perform a national service, and Tilton foresaw "a century of great usefulness and honor . . . dawning upon her." It was a thoughtful speech, with a fresh point of view, and it must have come as a welcome contrast to the rhetorical performances of most of the other speakers that day.

And that was about it. The exercises ended at seven o'clock with a vote proposed by the Reverend E. G. Porter thanking everyone involved in making the Centennial such a success—the Town of Andover, the citizens of Andover, all the speakers, the musical groups, the Associated Press, the Boston & Maine, and "every person . . . who has in any way contributed money, time, and labor of hand, tongue, or pen to the success of the Centennial Celebration of Phillips Academy." Presiding Officer Churchill spoke of cherishing the Centennial "as we cherish the blossoms of a century-plant" and finished with a prophecy:

> A century hence, when every eye that has beamed today is forever closed, and every tongue that has spoken here shall be hushed in eternal stillness, may the children's children feel the influence of this day's commemorations. *Esto perpetua.*

The assemblage then sang a Centennial ode to the tune of "Fair Harvard," went on to the Doxology, and concluded with a benediction. That evening the alumni gathered in the Academy Hall to reminisce.

It had been a demanding two days, particularly for Dr. Bancroft. Yet after the celebration was over, he and the Trustees still had enough energy left to meet in the Mansion House for an informal session. As they reviewed the events of the past two days, they might well take pride in what had been accomplished. Of the original aims for the Centennial, most had been achieved: documents pertaining to the Academy's past had been collected, mainly by the Reverend William Park; the portrait collection had been substantially expanded; though the $100,000 aimed for in the Fund Drive had not yet been raised in full, it soon would be;[51] a new Alumni Association had been organized; the Academy's statement of principles and history had been presented, not only to the Andover family, but to the general public; and a "large home gathering" of alumni had taken place. The general catalogue of graduates and teachers would never be published, nor is there evidence that significant additions to the library were made. But on balance, the Trustees must have been content with what had transpired. At a meeting later that month the Trustees sent a "thank-you" resolution to the Town of Andover,[52] and with that the formalities of the Centennial were over.

One cannot do better in concluding an account of the Centennial than to quote the passage that Dr. Bancroft wrote into the Trustee Records the evening after the celebration had been completed. By pure chance his statement rounded out the last page of the record book that had been begun one hundred years earlier with a copy of the Constitution of Phillips Academy. The good Doctor wrote:

> Mansion House, Andover, June 6, 1878. The Trustees of Phillips Academy, informally assembled in their ancient room in the Mansion House, on this the Centennial Anniversary of the founding of the Institution, place on record their profound sense of the eminent wisdom, the clear foresight, and the large Christian benevolence of its Founders. They remember gratefully the long line of wise and godly men who have presided over the Academy in the office of Principal; and the still larger number of scholars and faithful assistants who have labored in the various departments of instruction.
>
> They review with thankfulness and exultation the historical facts, that more than nine thousand students have enjoyed its advantages; that it is richly honored in its Alumni, among whom are many distinguished merchants, manufacturers, inventors, scientists, College Presidents and Professors, lawyers, doctors of medicine, statesmen, Missionaries and Ministers of the Gospel: that large numbers of its graduates have risen to high places of trust and honor; that not a few, for various eminent services, have been placed on the roll of the most distinguished men of our age; and that this Academy has been a fountain of measureless influences, which through many channels have flowed forth for the good of our Country and of the world.
>
> They desire likewise to acknowledge the great goodness of God in bestowing his favor so largely and continually upon the Institution, and in still raising up for it true friends and generous benefactors.
>
> And to Him, in whose name the Academy was founded, the Trustees desire to dedicate it anew for the promotion of good learning; for the instruction of youth respecting 'the true [*sic*] end and real business of living'; and for the upbuilding of his Kingdom throughout the world.
>
> Adjourned. Attest C. F. P. Bancroft, Clerk.[53]

A few weeks later the following item appeared in a local newspaper:

> Principal Bancroft, of Phillips Academy, has taken passage for Liverpool, in the *Batavia,* leaving Boston July 6th, expecting to spend a few weeks in England and Scotland, and returning before the commencement of the Fall term.[54]

Cecil Franklin Patch Bancroft had earned his vacation.

CHAPTER ELEVEN

THE BANCROFT YEARS:

ADMINISTRATION AND STUDENTS

T HE POSITION of Principal of Phillips Academy in the last third of the nineteenth century was a back-breaking one, particularly if, like Cecil Bancroft, one had set the highest of standards for the School. Dr. Bancroft became Principal of the Academy before the Trustees had realized that he would need help if he were to carry out effectively the manifold duties of the position. It was not until 1888 that George D. Pettee, Instructor in Mathematics, was appointed Secretary of the Faculty and began to assume some of the routine responsibilities that hitherto had devolved solely upon the Principal. Up until that time Cecil Bancroft carried on all the correspondence—with parents, with prospective parents, with alumni, and with a wide variety of people interested in the School—and did it in longhand.[1] This was in addition to the classes he taught, the discipline cases he and the Faculty had to deal with, the Faculty concerns that demanded attention, the problems of the boarding-house ladies, the complaints from Abbot Academy, and the myriad other demands that his position as Principal brought him. Friends worried about his health. One thought he was not getting enough rest and offered to nurse the children and look after Mrs. Bancroft if only he would go away for a few weeks of complete freedom before School started.[2] A colleague wrote, "I am afraid you will get sick. I hope you won't try to teach any next year. I don't believe in suicide."[3] Though he did take several leaves of absence during his twenty-eight years as Principal, his death at the age of sixty-one was undoubtedly hastened by the demands of office. Cecil Bancroft burned himself out in the service of Phillips Academy, but that was the way he wanted it.

Dr. Bancroft's task of running Phillips Academy was not made easier by his Board of Trustees, who provided little assistance. Ever since the founding of the Andover Theological Seminary, that institution had taken up a large part of the Trustees' time and energy. In the 1880's and 90's, as the difficulties of the Seminary multiplied, this situation became worse. The so-called heresy trials, the decline in enrollment, the problem of holding strong professors all combined to concentrate the attention of the Trustees on the Seminary, at the expense of Phillips Academy. The minutes of meeting after meeting read, "No Academy business transacted," and at times there was no quorum. The nadir was reached in 1893 when Clerk Bancroft's minutes read, "The Clerk only was present at the hour to which the Trustees adjourned."[4] What a blow to Dr. Bancroft's morale it must have been. On the other hand, the Trustees were most considerate of the Principal himself. In 1876 a dispute developed over Edward G. Coy, the Professor of Greek, presumably because of his refusal to teach more than eighteen hours a week. Apparently the Trustees split on this issue, and some hard words were said to Dr. Bancroft. Trustee E. K. Alden wrote Bancroft, "You ought to receive a most humble apology for what was said to wound your feelings; and yet I am afraid you will not. . . . For one, I engage to use appropriate instrumental agencies . . . to reach the source of your chief annoyance, and to make it sure that your official relation is treated with its due respect."[5] The Reverend Seth Sweetser, President of the Board, urged the Principal not to resign because of this flap and added, "You have, I may not doubt, sufficient confidence in your own integrity, not to be moved by groundless assertions."[6] The crisis passed, and there is no record of further difficulty between Cecil Bancroft and his Board. The Trustees were understandably concerned about the Principal's health and were generous in giving him leaves of absence. In 1881 they gave him a vacation with an extra two hundred dollars; in 1888 they granted him a year's sabbatical with an extra one thousand dollars. In 1895 they granted five hundred dollars for a vacation abroad.[7] But for the most part they concerned themselves with routine financial matters, accepting gifts to the School, voting salaries, and appropriating money for building repairs. Evidence that dissatisfaction with the Trustees was fairly widespread can be seen in the move on the part of some of the younger alumni—for the most part pupils of Dr. Bancroft—to get the Phillips Academy Charter amended so as to provide for alumni trustees. This group petitioned the Massachusetts legislature in 1893, citing among other things that the membership of the Board had been more than half clergymen, in violation of the Constitution, and hoped to get some younger men chosen. The legislature turned a deaf ear, however, and the matter died quietly.[8] During the days of Samuel Farrar the Treasurer was a powerful force in support of the administration, but during the Bancroft administration Edward Taylor and Alpheus H. Hardy, though dedicated and conscientious Treasurers, stuck closely to purely financial matters and contributed little to Dr. Bancroft's broad program. This is not to denigrate the Trustees but rather to demonstrate the extent to which Cecil Bancroft had to go it alone in achieving what he did for Phillips Academy.

A major problem throughout his entire administration was the proper housing and feeding of the undergraduate body. In these areas Phillips Academy lagged far behind other schools. Writing to the Trustees in 1875, the Principal said that there were six New England schools, including Exeter and Williston, that had equipment superior to Andover's. Four years later he reviewed the whole problem of student boarding and housing:

> Our commons and club arrangements are a serious drawback. As compared with Easthampton [Williston], Exeter, Quincy, St. Johnsbury, New London, Wilbraham, Dean, St. Paul's and several other academies our accommodations are mean, expensive, and very unattractive. The unsightliness of commons is of little account, but it is too true, that our supervision of them is insufficient, that the care of rooms is left to the boys entirely, even to the removal of wastewater and ashes, the sweeping, bed-making and cleaning. The boarding arrangements are capricious, the room often unduly crowded, the table manners boisterous, the expenses considering the quality of food and cooking too high. Nothing saves the system from breaking down utterly but the average high moral sense of the boys, their interest and determination to obtain an education, and their previous home training in self-help and self-reliance. I know how difficult it is to improve accommodations without increasing the general scale

36. *An undergraduate relaxing in his room in the Latin Commons in the mid–1880's.*

of expense, but if the Academy is to be a great educational establishment it must regard the physical, social, and esthetic requirements of its pupils, and it may be a serious question whether we are not sanctioning or tolerating conditions too perilous to the manners, the morals, and the health of our boys.[9]

In 1882 two members of the examining committee for the Seminary inspected the Phillips Academy plant while they were about it and steadfastly backed Dr. Bancroft. They urged the construction of a Commons Boarding House and suggested a program whereby cottages would be built to replace the old Commons barracks. "Both called my attention to our public privies as an outrage on health, comfort, and decency," wrote Dr. Bancroft, "and requested me to speak of them to the board."[10] As late as 1893 the Principal was worrying about the increasing cost of board at the boarding houses and the effect on the School that this might have:

> The tendency is to the community life of minimum expenditure, as at Moody's schools [Mt. Hermon and Northfield] and at Kimball Union Academy, or to the conventual life of aristocratic flavor at St. Paul's and Lawrenceville. Andover is very likely to be the chief representative of a school ministering to all social classes from the richest to the poorest, and providing a wide range of accommodations for the various pecuniary ability of its pupils. . . . The immediate danger is that the school will divide as some of the great English schools were once divided into a group of rich boys on the one hand, and a group of poor boys on the other. In the English schools the poor boys were gradually crowded out. It is our present obligation to make it possible for persons of moderate means to get good accommodations at Andover at a moderate price.[11]

A striking evidence of his genius was his ability to see the long-range implications of developments taking place around him and to move vigorously to deal with them.

When Dr. Bancroft reported to the Trustees on the problems of room and board, he knew whereof he spoke, for each year he was obliged to spend a vast amount of time dealing with unhappy landladies, obstreperous undergraduates, irate parents, and complaining townspeople, all of whom were dissatisfied with the workings of the Commons and the boarding house system. Major William Marland, who ran the so-called Commons boarding house in what is now Clement House, was a frequent object of attack. One mother described the Major as getting old and easily teased, his house so ancient that plaster fell down whenever the boys ran up stairs. She wanted a place for her son "where the boys do not feel as if in the hands of an enemy."[12] On another occasion, the Principal received an anonymous letter signed "One of the sufferers," complaining that the Major, in a fit of pique at some rough-housing in his dining room, had locked out all the boys in bitterly cold weather and made them wait outside a long time before being served.[13] Since all the Commons boys had to eat at the Major's, the situation was unhealthy, as Dr. Bancroft realized. Sarah Abbot wrote plaintively to the Principal, "What shall I do with my boys who break into my house by smashing glass, after eleven o'clock at night?"[14] A parent complained, "Miss Wiggins is so exceedingly particular in her description of the only kind of a boy that she will consent to take that I would not dare send a boy who fell very short of an angel."[15] Mrs. Davis complained that she could never tell where her boys were in the evening and that furthermore they had been abusing the boy who delivered papers.[16] Mrs. John Smith was worried for fear her boys would sneak off to a "colored" ball in Lawrence.[17] Mrs. R. A. Tilton wrote the Principal that she did not want any more Roman Catholics in her house and was trying hard to stop card-playing.[18] At the heart of the discipline problem was the fact that the landladies depended on the income from the boys for their livelihood and thus were unwilling to enforce the rules too strictly for fear of losing customers.

In the 1890's the Faculty moved to improve the difficult situation. They believed the board prices too high and suggested that contracts with the landladies be made a regular procedure. They also refused to grant licenses to three of the ladies.[19] Obviously there could be no adequate supervision of undergraduates under these circumstances; yet Dr. Bancroft was invariably kind to the ladies. Shortly after Alfred E. Stearns became Principal, he received a letter from a landlady asking if she could see him to discuss boarding house regulations. "I would like to tell you all about it as I used to tell Dr. Bancroft," she wrote.[20]

It was not merely the landladies whom Cecil Bancroft had to deal with. There was a hue and cry from parents, Abbot Academy, and townspeople as well. Mrs. Butterfield's boarding house on School Street was close to Abbot Academy, with unfortunate results for that institution. One of the Abbot teachers, Laura Watson, complained that Phillips Academy students climbed onto the roof of Butterfield's and shone a large mirror into her classroom, making it necessary to pull down all the shades. Miss Watson also complained of "insults" shouted from Butterfield's at Abbot teachers. "One ox-like creature," she reported, had called her "darling" and "birdie dear."[21] And Headmistress Philena McKeen wrote the Principal asking that Mrs. Mason not be allowed to rent a certain room to a boy because it looked out on the Abbot campus and the girls would be constantly watched.[22] But it was not just Abbot that was bothered by the boys in Butterfield's. John Phelps Taylor, a Professor at the Theological Seminary, lived nearby with his wife. In 1892 Mrs. Taylor delivered herself of the following jeremiad to Dr. Bancroft:

I should like to call your attention to the fact that we are no longer able to enjoy our grounds with any comfort, owing to the encampment of Phillipians who at *all* hours and every day are lying on the grass at Mr. Butterfield's *just over our borders*. . . . On Sunday I counted seventeen—yesterday there were ten—this morning I find on our *grounds* numberless stumps of cigarettes, paper wrappers of 'straight cut tobacco', and half eaten bananas, as well as their skins. I cannot work in my flower beds or take my little sick dog out for a quiet stroll without countless eyes upon me—my maid servants, both young women, are whistled to if they appear in the clothes yard.[23]

Mrs. Taylor wanted the practice "checked at once."

Parents tended to complain about the price and quality of the food. One irate father threatened to send his son elsewhere if the food prices were not lowered. He thought that Andover was the best School in the country, but he refused to put up with "extortion." "I can room and board at the Grand Pacific, Chicago, for less than you are paying Mrs. Butterfield," he concluded.[24] Another father was shocked that there was no "WC" in his son's house and only a very inferior one outside.[25] In addition, the cooking was poor, the food scanty, the rooms and bedding dirty. Another parent withdrew his son because "plain, nourishing food" could not be obtained at his boarding house.[26] The most aggressive father of the lot inspected the room in Commons where his son was to live, was dissatisfied with it, went down town and hired workmen to paint, paper, and repair it, then sent the bill to the Trustees. He did not think much of the plumbing facilities for the Commons either. "Worse water does not exist in a civilized community. I wonder you have not had typhoid fever, diphtheria, and other things from it. It certainly is in a dangerous proximity and relationship, and the pump ought to be taken out and the well filled up."[27] One of Cecil Bancroft's favorite stories was of a distinguished parent who was trying to decide between Andover and Exeter for his son. After he had been given a tour of the Commons buildings, he announced that Phillips Academy was the place for his boy. "Any institution which can keep the fine reputation which Andover has, and yet lodge its students in such disreputable barracks, must have about it some miraculous quality which I want my son to learn to know."[28]

Though the parents were probably more dissatisfied with the living arrangements at Phillips Academy than the boys themselves, the facilities were in many cases substandard, as the Principal would be the first to admit. In 1885 he reported to the Trustees:

The wants of the Academy are chiefly now in the way of buildings. Something has already been accomplished, but the main thing for many years was the perfection of our courses of study, the coordination of the Faculty, the winning of the confidence of the Colleges and the public, the raising of funds for the support of instruction, the payment of the debt, the improvement of the discipline of the academy.

He went on to list important needs—repairs to the Main Building, improvements for the Gymnasium, completion of the Science Building, better dormitories, and above all a new Dining Hall for the boys who lived in the Commons.[29] Dr. Bancroft was not able to accomplish all these projects during his administration, but he did at least make a start, and his program provided a blueprint that would be completed under his successor, Alfred E. Stearns. In 1881 a laboratory was constructed behind the Main Building, and ten years later a large addition was built, making the present Graves Hall. The new building not only provided excellent facilities for the study of science but relieved the pressure on recitation rooms in the Main Building. In 1883 the Trustees voted $10,000 for the construction of a small administration building with offices for the Principal and the Treasurer and a room for Trustee meetings. This building, later used as a Faculty Club, now houses the staff of the Office of the Physical Plant. Some new equipment was purchased for the Gymnasium and housed in the old Brick Academy, now Bulfinch Hall, but the facilities left much to be desired. For one thing there were no showers or baths in the building, a lack the *Phillipian* called attention to regularly. In 1896 after the Brick Academy was gutted by fire, the Trustees and Alumni had to build a new gymnasium, and the interior was eventually repaired to provide a school dining hall. But these two improvements were not accomplished until after Cecil Bancroft's death.

It was in the development of new dormitories that the Principal made his greatest contribution to the physical plant of the School. Ever since Phillips Academy had first opened, the undergraduates had been housed in private homes, with resulting disciplinary problems stemming from lack of supervision. Squire Farrar had made a stab at reforming this situation, particularly for the scholarship boys, by erecting the Latin and English Commons, where at the start rent was one dollar a term. But despite efforts on the part of the Faculty to police these buildings, inspection and supervision were never adequate, and the boys who lived there were pretty much on their own. The heating and plumbing facilities were antediluvian; the danger of fire constant. Cecil Bancroft dreamed of being able to house all the boys in modern buildings, with modern facilities and a resident Faculty member in charge. The first step in the implementation of the dormitory program came in 1891. At the New York Alumni Dinner of that year, Alpheus H. Hardy, Treasurer of the Board, announced to the assembled gathering that the Trustees would be happy to receive gifts for buildings and pay an annuity of five percent on the gift for the lifetime of the donor, the building becoming the property of the School at the donor's death. Melville C. Day, of the Class of 1858, who had lived in the Commons as an undergraduate and remembered them well, was greatly taken by this idea. He had made a fortune in the law, had no close relatives, and was about to retire from practice. He consulted with his old friend, John Phelps Taylor, Professor at the Theological Seminary, who urged him to support Dr. Bancroft's dormitory program. Accordingly he gave eight thousand dollars to construct a "cottage" to be named "The Taylor," after his friend.[30] At about the same time Professor Taylor was attempting to stir up interest in the Town of Andover in helping Phillips Academy meet its needs. In an article that appeared in the *Andover Townsman* he made a strong case. The Theological Seminary, he said, was relatively wealthy, but none of that money could be used for the Academy, even though the two institutions had the same Board of Trustees. He thought the School must have a new Science Building, a new Dining Hall, a new Gymnasium, "two blocks of modern Cottages," and endowments for teaching professorships. Following Professor Taylor's article was one by Warren F. Draper, an old friend of the Academy, showing that the Town received about $170,000 a year in the form of payments for food, rent, and labor. Shortly after these articles had appeared, a mass meeting of townspeople was held at which Miss Emily Carter announced that she had already collected over $1600, and before the meeting was over pledges brought the total close to $7,000. Thus a second cottage, "The Andover," was made possible.[31] The *Phillipian* suggested that Miss Carter's portrait should be painted and hung in the new building.[32] Inspired by all this, Warren F. Draper agreed to finance the construction of a third cottage if an annuity were paid to his wife. And finally, Melville Day was so pleased with his first cottage that he financed another the following year. To site the buildings properly, the Trustees engaged the firm of Frederick Law Olmstead, which placed three cottages in a group on the south side of Phillips Street and the fourth, "The Draper," near the English Commons. Thus by 1893 four cottages had been built as a start toward the realization of Dr. Bancroft's dormitory program.[33]

Those who live in these cottages today and compare them with the facilities of the new dormitories around Rabbit Pond may find it difficult to realize how proud the School was of these new buildings in the 1890's. Designed by the architect A. W. Longfellow of Boston, they were considered the last word in student comfort. An article in the *Masque*, the senior yearbook for 1893, said of the new buildings: "One of the features is . . . the most excellent view that can be seen from their windows. The rolling hills of the western landscape extend away towards the horizon, where the peaks of Wachusett and Monadnock may be seen faintly outlined against the sky."[34] The Taylor had large spacious study rooms, with two ample bedrooms connected, was heated by indirect radiation, and had hot and cold water baths in the cellar. The rent for Draper Cottage was

37. Andover Cottage, built in 1893.

less because it had no furnace at the start. The Andover was handsomest of all:

> The building is situated on an elevated knoll and presents a commanding appearance. Its architecture is more pleasing than that of the other cottages, and its rooms are considered the most attractive. The structure is built of brick having granite trimmings. An arched entrance opens into a spacious hall from which one ascends a broad staircase to the rooms above. The inside finish is in hard polished pine. Each room is provided with an open fire-place as in the other cottages. The building is heated by steam. The characteristics of the Andover cottage are its roominess and its light.[35]

The Trustees decided that the new buildings should be income-producing. A statement in the School catalogues for the late 1890's says that the income will be used first for maintenance of the buildings, secondly to help pay the annuities, and third to provide help for needy students. The prices were as follows:

For a double suite, each boy	$ 80.00
For a double suite in Draper	40.00
For a single suite	100.00
For a single room	35.00 to 45.00[36]

It is obvious that at these prices no scholarship boys would be living in the cottages, when the rent of a Commons room was $5.00 a term. One former Faculty member wrote Dr. Bancroft that the cottages would simply provide rooms for those who had previously been living in the boarding houses and would depress the Commons boys even further. He hoped that the time would come when the whole School could be in cottages.[37] This was certainly the wish of Dr. Bancroft and the Trustees; as the catalogue stated, the cottages were part of a plan "to replace, as fast as funds are provided for the purpose, the present Latin and English Commons with modern buildings, as favorable as possible to the best student life."[38] Yet there was still a long way to go. In 1895, for example, there were 524 students, but the cottages housed only 44 boys and four teachers.

Just at the close of the Bancroft administration, the Principal received additional support for his program. Indeed, as he sickened in 1901, his last days must have been made more bearable by the knowledge that more and more friends of the School were coming forward to help with his plan. In 1898 Melville C. Day, who, until Thomas Cochran, was the School's most generous benefactor, wrote Treasurer Hardy to ask if he would like another dormitory. His only stipulation was that any surplus income from his gift, after maintenance and annuity charges had been met, should be under his control. The Trustees were more than willing to agree to this mild restriction, and accordingly work was started on what was to be named Bancroft Hall. Bancroft Cottage's name was changed to Eaton Cottage, after

James S. Eaton, of the English Department in the 1850's and 1860's. Unlike the cottages, Bancroft Hall was to be a full-sized dormitory, combining, as it were, three cottages together in one building. Erected on Phillips Street, across from the Latin Commons, in what is now the Vista, it was finished in 1900 at a cost of about $42,000.[39] The new building provided eighteen double suites for the accommodation of another thirty-six boys, making it possible to have better than one fifth of the student body housed in modern facilities. Dr. Bancroft's project for a new gymnasium was close to realization before he died. After the burning of the Brick Academy, a drive was instituted to raise $50,000 toward a new building. Mainly because of the Principal's untiring efforts, the goal was reached and the new building, named Borden Gymnasium after the principal donor, Matthew C. D. Borden, was completed a year after Cecil Bancroft's death.[40] As part of the athletic program, a new playing field, given by George B. Knapp and called Brothers Field, was not completed until after the end of the Bancroft administration.[41] Finally, the Principal was still alive when Robert Singleton Peabody gave the School an extraordinarily generous grant to establish a department of archaeology at Phillips Academy. The gift was to be used to construct a museum to house a collection of some forty thousand American archaeological specimens, to provide for its maintenance, and to endow the salary of a curator.[42] In summary, Dr. Bancroft had, during his administration, made a strong start toward realizing the physical needs of the Academy; he had developed plans that would show the way for future expansion and development; and he had provided the momentum that would make it possible to achieve all his goals—far beyond his wildest dreams—in the next administration.

In 1877 there were 177 boys enrolled in the School, the smallest number of the Bancroft years; this was followed by a steady increase throughout the 1880's until a high of 524 was reached in 1895. Even though this number fell off to around 400 during the last three years of the Bancroft administration, physical growth was extraordinary. Though the English— and later the Scientific—Department was always smaller than the Classical, each department contributed about equally to the growth. Another characteristic of the students was their increasing geographical distribution. In 1884 a little over one half came from the New England states, while fewer than one third came from New Jersey, New York, Ohio, and Pennsylvania, and there was scattering representation from such faraway places as California, Iowa, Florida, Quebec, Chile, Turkey, and the Hawaiian Islands. By 1892 the New England states had dropped to 44 percent of the School, while New York, Pennsylvania, Ohio, Illinois, New Jersey, and Missouri accounted for 38 percent. In addition there were now 42 states and foreign countries represented, including many southern ones, Japan, and Ontario. In 1900 the figures were almost exactly the same as in 1892, except that places like Africa, England, Greece, Nova Scotia, and Prince Edward Island had been substituted for similar ones in the 1892 list. Certainly Andover's geographical distribution was infinitely wider than in the early days, and it looked as if it had become a permanent characteristic of the School.[43] Unfortunately there is nothing in the record to indicate whether this was a conscious policy on the part of Dr. Bancroft and Mr. Pettee, but the presumption is that it was. The *Phillipian* had no doubts about why these boys were coming to Phillips Academy from all over the country; it was because of the School's wide reputation,[44] and Dr. Bancroft echoed this explanation in a report to the Trustees. Though there had been two black students at Phillips Academy in the early 1850's, in 1870 the first post-war black student entered and for the rest of Dr. Bancroft's administration there were usually several in the undergraduate body.[45] Just at the end the number increased a little, with four in 1899 and 5 in 1901.[46] At least some of the blacks seem to have been protégés of Booker T. Washington at Tuskegee or of the Hampton Institute.[47] A black preacher spoke to the School in 1884, and in 1899 Washington visited the Hill in person. The following year the *Phillipian* was suggesting that the School found a scholarship at Hampton, and generally the presence of a few blacks on the campus was accepted with equanimity.[48] Not that complaints were nonexistent. In 1899 a Mississippi father who was considering sending his son to Andover wrote, "The only objection I have to your Institution is this, that you do not draw the color line, and that you have colored people in the Institution, but . . . there is no trouble arising from this irregularity, inasmuch as the white boys are kept away from them."[49] The following year Dr. Bancroft received a letter protesting because a black was captain of one of the School teams.[50] A second group to appear on Andover Hill during the Bancroft years were the Orientals. Joseph Hardy Neesima, later founder of Doshisha University in Japan, had attended Phillips Academy for two years in the 1860's as the protégé of Alpheus Hardy, a Trustee, and then had gone on to Amherst. The most famous Oriental of the Bancroft era was Pi Yuk, as he was known here, later Sir Chentung Liang Cheng, Chinese minister to the United States in the early 1900's. He had been sent to this country by the Chinese government, which later reversed its policy and recalled all the students in the United States, preventing Pi Yuk from finishing his study at Phillips Academy.[51] Just how many more Chinese came during this period is difficult to determine, but there are several letters in the Bancroft correspondence from former Chinese students, and there are five listed in the 1880 catalogue. When one student shirked his work and a report to that effect was sent to the Chinese government, the reply, according to tradition, was, "Send him home and we will behead him." This story got in the newspapers and poor Dr. Bancroft had to spend many hours assuring anxious correspondents that this dread event would not take place.[52] In the 1890's there was occasionally a Japanese student or two, but they had stopped coming by the end of the decade. Finally, in an attempt to add a further dash of spice to the undergraduate body, a gentleman wrote to sponsor two Sioux, George Frazier and Chauncy Yellow Robe. George wanted to go into the ministry, while Chauncy, aged twenty-six, wanted to improve his English. Unfortunately, they never made it.[53]

Though the religious affiliations of the families of Andover boys tended to follow the traditional Calvinist doctrines of earlier days, there were signs that this monopoly was weakening. Reporting to the Trustees in 1885, Dr. Bancroft said:

> As compared with the patronage at Exeter, it appears that we have a much larger proportion from Presbyterian and Congregationalist families than they, and our quota from Episcopal, Catholic, and other denominations is much less. We have almost no patronage from Methodist, Unitarian, and Universalist families. For the first time in twelve years we have had a Jew.

That there was a group of Catholic boys in 1898 is indicated by a letter from Father O'Mahony of St. Augustine's Catholic Church in the Town of Andover to George Pettee. He was concerned about a belief among the Catholic students that they did better at Phillips Academy, especially if they were on scholarship, if they attended the School's services rather than going to the Catholic Church in the town. Father O'Mahony hoped that Mr. Pettee would disabuse them of that notion.[54] The chances are that the image of the Theological Seminary in the public mind, particularly after the so-called heresy trials, was a strong influence against increasing religious diversification. It is easy to see why a Unitarian would not think of Phillips Academy as suitable for his son. It would not be until after the Seminary had moved to Cambridge that the School would become more diversified religiously. One of the School's basic policies at the time of its founding was to assist "indigent" young men in getting an education, and this policy was continued vigorously under Dr. Bancroft. In the 1874 catalogue, under the heading "Beneficiary Aid," it was stated that the income from two scholarship funds of about $20,000 would be used for aid, with an additional $80.00 from a special fund. The grants, it added, would range from $3.00 to $25.00, with pecuniary need, scholarship, and conduct all being taken into consideration. When it is considered that tuition alone was $60.00 that year, it can be seen that the beneficiary aid was hardly munificent. There is, unfortunately, no record of the number of boys aided, but if the grants were small, it could have been a substantial number. In 1900, at the end of the Bancroft regime, the scholarship aid program had grown considerably. There were now seventeen separate funds amounting in all to just under $52,000. For the first time there is a statement about the number of grants made—forty, each covering a year's tuition.[55] In addition, boys of modest means could earn money waiting on table and doing other useful jobs around the School. Just how much diversity the scholarship boys contributed is difficult to say with precision. Relatively, however, the Andover undergraduate body was much more diversified economically and socially than the other preparatory schools, with the exception of Exeter.

Starting in 1882, the senior classes of Phillips Academy began publishing little books of statistics that give additional dimensions of the undergraduate body during the Bancroft years. Data on the occupations of parents, the physical characteristics of the class, their interests and college choices, and their eventual career plans were included. In the class of 1883 there were 9 ministers' sons, 3 doctors', 6 lawyers', 2 teachers', 12 businessmen's, 3 farmers', 2 mechanics', and a scattering of others. Five were sons of Yale graduates, 2 of Amherst, 2 of Bowdoin, 2 of Union, and 5 scattering. The average age was just over 19, with the extremes being 27 and 15. Seventeen graduated at 18, 10 under 18, 16 over 18, and 9 over 21. The average height was 5 feet 8¼ inches, with extremes of 6 feet 1¾ inches and 5 feet 5 inches. The average weight was 143½ pounds, with extremes of 165 and 117. The average chest measurement was 36½ inches, with extremes of 40½ and 32 inches. The average hat size was 7⅛, the average shoe size 7. Thirty-three were Republicans, 8 Democrats, and 2 Independents. There were 16 Congregationalists, 9 Episcopalians, 5 Presbyterians, 3 Baptists, 1 Dutch Reformed, 1 Universalist, 1 Unitarian, and 7 with no religious views. The Class of 1883 disliked mathematics the most and thought that Greek was the best; 33 played cards, with whist the favorite game; 17 smoked; 24 swore "on more or less important occasions;" 10 drank; and 25 liked to dance. The class had spent an average of $624.56 a year at School; 16 had kept their expenses below $500, 9 below $350; while 8 spent between $1000 and $1200. One member managed to earn $800 during his whole course, the largest amount in a single year being $350. As far as college choices were concerned, 22 intended to go to Yale, 12 to Harvard, 4 to Amherst, 2 to Princeton, and 5 to other colleges. Nine planned on careers in the law, 5 in teaching, 12 in business, 1 in the ministry, 1 in music, and 1 as a rancher. These figures are for the 45 seniors in the Classical Department, but those for the 22 seniors of the English Department are very similar. In reporting on their habits, the English seniors said: "Our class is unanimous only in one habit—they are all lazy." Their average expenditure for the year was definitely higher than that of the Classical Department—$998 as compared with $624.56, presumably because there were fewer scholarship boys in the English Department.[56] Nor are the statistics for the Class of 1883 in any way abnormal. For the Class of 1890 41 parents were college graduates, with Yale leading the pack with 10. Forty-three parents were listed as businessmen of one kind or another—manufacturers, bankers, merchants, and the like. There were also 1 carpenter, 6 farmers, 11 ministers, 2 druggists, 12 lawyers, 8 doctors, 1 hotel keeper, and 1 pawnbroker. The college choices for the seniors of both departments were Yale (including Sheffield) 49, Harvard 18, Amherst 10, M.I.T. 7, Pennsylvania 4, Princeton 3, Williams 5, and 14 to other colleges. An unusually large number went to college in 1890 because 20 boys were admitted from their Middler or 11th grade year, a practice that was to become more and more common in the coming century.[57] A few generalizations can be drawn from these data. The Andover undergraduate in the Bancroft years was physically smaller than his counterpart today, a fact that has been determined for college students of the period as well. Generally he came from a conservative, Republican, middle-class background and looked forward to a career that would mirror that of his father. Although the largest number—in some cases, a majority —of the graduates chose Yale, there was an ever-increasing distribution among other colleges, and the statement that Andover was simply a Yale "feeder" was no longer valid. Yet there was heterogeneity in the Andover student body, particularly that provided by scholarship boys, and little evidence of social, as distinguished from economic, elitism. To a very real extent the aim of the founders to have the Academy open to "youth from every quarter" was being achieved.

A charming picture of undergraduate life at the end of the Bancroft years is given by Lee J. Perrin of the Class of 1902 in a little book he wrote entitled *My Three Years at Andover* under the pseudonym "Ewer Struly."[58] Perrin obviously had a very successful career at Phillips Academy and enjoyed himself tremendously during his stay on the Hill. He recounts how his father brought him to the School, admonished him to be a "Christian gentleman" and particularly to avoid indecent language and slandering other people, and then left him to his own devices. Perrin lived in one of cottages, and on his first night was treated to "prepping"—the hazing of new boys. He was invited to the room of one of the old boys, where he was suddenly seized and blindfolded. He was taken to the cellar and ordered to strip, then forced to jump into a tub of cold water, during which exercise he managed to splash most of his tormenters. To teach him a lesson he was required to run five miles in laps around the cellar, each lap being one two-thousandth of a mile. While he was running he was paddled by the old boys, who kept urging him to smile throughout the whole performance. Perrin felt humiliated by the treatment he had received, and he wept; but his spirits were greatly restored when an old boy took him aside and explained that he was "a bit too fresh" at present and that the hazing was for his own good. On reflection Perrin came to believe that the practice was a useful one and that he learned that night a lesson he remembered long after he had forgotten his Virgil and Homer.

Chapel the following morning was memorable. First Dr. Bancroft welcomed the School and told the students that while there might be distinctions between old and new boys among the undergraduates, there were none as far as the administration was concerned. The good Doctor's words were spoken from the heart, to the heart, Perrin thought. Once the formalities of Chapel were over, the football captain rose to give a fight talk about supporting the football team, which was followed by a long cheer for him. The Chapel was used frequently that fall for football rallies and the like. On the Friday before the Exeter game the entire School assembled there to cheer the team and various faculty speakers. The football manager urged that the meeting be such an uproarious affair that no one would be able to sleep until Exeter had been beaten again. Then Dr. Bancroft made some appropriate remarks, followed by more cheering, hat-tossing, and dancing on the benches. Matthew S. McCurdy of the Mathematics Department was next called on. He said he wished he could get his students as interested in mathematical problems as they were in the problem of beating Exeter. This produced a special cheer:

> Mac! Mac! Bully for Mac!
> Andover! Andover! Rah, rah, rah!

There followed remarks from Charlie Forbes of the Latin Department and several others, all of whom were cheered to a fare thee well. The next morning in Chapel there appeared a large dummy, dressed in a football suit, suspended from the rafters. Toward the end of the meeting an alarm clock in the dummy went off. Dr. Bancroft never turned a hair; "Gentlemen," he said, "the day is yours." And Perrin goes on to describe the special train to Exeter, the School marching through the town of Exeter singing a football song to the tune of "My Girl's a Corker", the great victory itself, and finally the victory celebration, with the team on a large barge, the undergraduates carrying red flares, and the town band leading the procession marching through town until every student was completely hoarse and exhausted.

Despite Dr. Bancroft's many attempts to get a proper dining hall, the aim was not realized until after his death, and as a result the boarding house continued as the standard institution where the boys got their meals. Perrin boarded all of his three years at Aunt Hattie Crocker's establishment, paying four dollars a week, which was about average. His descriptions of life at Aunt Hattie's, if nothing else, show that adolescent male table manners change very little over the years. In the first place, in order to realize the maximum income from her establishment, Aunt Hattie took more boys than her dining room could comfortably hold, with the result that the chairs at adjoining tables touched each other, making it almost impossible for the waiters to get through. Aunt Hattie followed the usual practice of serving excellent meals for the first week or so and then gradually reducing the quality as the term wore on. To meet this problem the boys began consuming vast quantities of shredded wheats—known as "bath mitts"—and on one occasion conducted a contest to see who could eat the most. When they told Aunt Hattie that raw eggs and breakfast foods were the best things she served, she simply cut off the shredded wheats except at breakfast. The consumption of pancakes—"pen-wipers"— was tremendous, even though they were described as having a tough and cold outer rim and a faintly warm heart somewhere inside. Furthermore, pancakes made excellent "scalers," and on special occasions like the morn- ing of the Exeter game, the room would be full of them. Aunt Hattie also produced a kind of muffin, the top part of which was edible, the bottom part not. The boys used to take the bottom parts, squeeze them into small balls, and then when Aunt Hattie was near, drop them on the floor with an accompanying stamp of the foot to indicate how heavy they were. And there were the usual butter throwers who managed to cover the ceiling with pats of butter, as successive generations of Andover boys have done in various dining halls since that time. The boys always wanted seconds of almost everything, but when Aunt Hattie produced a special dish like apple pie, seconds were out. Despite the confusion and plain fare, Perrin accepted her establishment with good grace, and since he remained there for three years, he could not have found the board too bad.

Perrin liked girls and took full advantage of the few opportunities that were presented to visit with those at Abbot Academy—the Fem Sem. He tells of how certain daring boys would occasionally visit Abbot at night, throw a pebble against a girl's window, and hope for a short visit. Abbot girls and Phillips boys used also to meet occasionally on the old railroad track going toward Ballardvale. When Abbot had a field day, the boys would climb trees and watch them engage in three-legged, wheelbarrow, and sack races. One occasion which the boys were allowed to attend was an annual softball game between two Abbot teams. Alfred Stearns was always umpire for this contest. Some said he was chosen for his baseball prowess but Perrin thought it was because he had a degree from the Theological Seminary. The playing left a good deal to be desired, but the pleasure of watching the girls was intense.

The normal procedure for visiting an Abbot girl was to call on her from nine to nine-thirty on Friday evening. After permissions and various other red tape had been taken care of, the boy would present himself at Abbot, where his name was checked off in a book called "Love's Ledger." There was an alcove in the visiting area that was much more secluded than the rest and was, therefore, in great demand. In order to get a seat in the al- cove one had to arrive about seven o'clock and stand in line. On one occa- sion Perrin obtained a seat in the alcove and then decided to go one better. He asked the girl to show him the library, which was off limits. The girl took him there and then abandoned him, with the result that he crashed around in the dark for some time before finding his way out. The next day he received a note from Abbot rescinding his permission to visit. Nor was his reputation with the Abbot authorities improved when he joined a group of Abbot girls on a bobsled and managed to steer them over an embankment into a snowdrift. Perrin's last escapade with Abbot reveals great ingenuity, if nothing else. He had purchased a second-hand Virgil in the flyleaf of which was inscribed "Minnie Burdett." As he leafed through the book, he found delightful witty comments. Assuming that Minnie was at Abbot, he wrote her a letter introducing himself and asking her to write. Since there had never been a Minnie Burdett at Abbot, the letter was referred to Dr Bancroft. Perrin was afraid he was in for real trouble, but he need not have worried. The Registrar told Perrin that Dr. Bancroft had laughed until he cried and said that the letter had prolonged his life by at least a year.

Since Perrin had no talent for athletics, he determined to try for a place on the board of the *Phillipian*. In the spring of his first year he heeled— tried out—for the board. He carried a notebook wherever he went and was forever interviewing people and ferreting out interesting bits of news. The success of the heeler was determined by the number of inches he got printed; by the end of the term Perrin had four hundred inches more than his nearest competitor and made the board easily. Given this drive, it is not surprising that he became editor-in-chief during his senior year. As is often the case, other members of the board left most of the work to Perrin so that he had a busy year of it. One of the main problems was obtaining enough copy to fill the paper, and he spent a lot of time urging on new heelers. On Wednesday and Saturdays, when the paper came out, he rose at six o'clock and went to the printing shop in the center of town, where he fed copy to "Mack," the genial Irish foreman. When material was short, he used to write communications to the paper signed "Freethinker" or "Fairplay," hoping that they would elicit a response that could be used in the next issue. On one occasion he dreamed up an obituary for a nonexistent Andover alumnus, Ebenezer Brockton Smith, P.A. Ex-'63. He was fearful lest he be found out by a member of the faculty who was reputed to know every Andover alumnus, living or dead, but apparently he never was. By ten o'clock in the morning he usually had the paper in shape, whereupon he would repair to "Chap's" grill, where Ovid Chapman, who often waited on table in his bare feet, would cook him some breakfast.

At the close of his little book Perrin makes a powerful statement on the quality of Phillips Academy under Dr. Bancroft and, incidentally, on one of the proudest hallmarks of the modern Andover:

> To Dr. Bancroft's administration is mainly due the sturdy spirit of democracy for which Andover is famous. Under his guidance the school assumed its present proportions as the most distinctly *American* institution of its kind; a school where wealth, antecedents, and locality count for nothing; where a boy is judged for what he is and

for what he does; where character and ability are the only passports to distinction. It is good to know that in this miniature republic the son of the eastern capitalist is, on the field and in recitation, shoulder to shoulder with the ranchman's son; that the petted bearer of a great name is on a footing of equality with the plucky orphan whose destiny is in his own hands; that distinctions of north and south, rich and poor, city and country, are here subordinate to the supreme test of intrinsic worth. In my senior classes I sat between a fellow whose income was practically unlimited and one who for more than five years had slaved in the city to lay by money for his education. And yet we three—two extremes and the mean—were the best of friends; that a disparity of purse was any barrier to our intercourse and sympathies as men, never entered our heads; and with any one of us the consciousness of that disparity made for nothing but admiration that the others could be such good fellows *in spite* of it. Altogether, I believe that in all the world there is no place where wealth and name count less, and personal worth more, than at Andover.[59]

Henry L. Stimson, who graduated from Phillips Academy in 1883, also remembered the democratic quality of the school.

But at thirteen there came a great change. My mental and physical horizons broadened before me. My father, dissatisfied with the conditions in New York, placed me in Phillips Academy at Andover, Massachusetts. I was much younger than any other boy in the school but the new surroundings were like heaven to a boy who craved escape from city life. I have heard the discipline of Phillips Academy of those old days described by an alumnus as "perfect freedom, tempered by expulsion." Of the outdoor life of the students that was a fair description. There was football, baseball, skating, bobsledding, and walking over the hills and woodlands of northern Massachusetts within generous limits, quite untrammeled by authority.

But once we entered the classroom it was quite a different matter. Andover fitted a boy for college and it fitted him well. The courses taught were fewer than they are today, but they were taught with extreme thoroughness. And the numbers of each class being large, the mere experience of standing up before a good-sized audience and answering tough problems before a rapid-firing instructor was in itself a stiff discipline to the average boy. To me it opened a new world of effort and competition. It also opened to me a new world of democracy and of companionship with boys from all portions of the United States. At that time Phillips Academy contained about two hundred fifty students, many coming from rural New England, but the remainder from nearly every other state in the Union. A large percentage of them were working their own way in whole or in part.

School life was extremely simple and inexpensive. The cost of tuition was sixty dollars a year. The school possessed no dormitories except the Latin and English Commons, in which nearly a third of the students lived. These consisted of two rows of very cheaply built three-story wooden houses, each house containing rooms for six students. The rental for each student was three dollars a term. There was no sanitation or water except from a single outdoor pump from which each student carried his own requirements, and no heat except that which came from each student's stove. And as the two rows of Commons stood on the northwestern slope of Andover Hill facing the distant New Hampshire hills on the horizon, winter life there was neither soft nor enervating. Some of the remaining students roomed in the houses of instructors but most of them were in boarding houses approved by the faculty in the town of Andover.

The result for me was association with a very different group of young men from those I had met in New York; they were representatives of homes of many varieties scattered all over the United States—most of them simple homes—but in general the boys were drawn to Andover by the desire to get the teaching given by a school which was known to have represented for over a hundred years the ideals of character and education believed in by the founders of our country.

I was too young to appreciate the full advantages of these new associations at first, but as the years of my course rolled by they were brought home to me, and I can never be sufficiently grateful to the school for the revolution it worked in my own character . . .[60]

Before Dr. Bancroft's time the undergraduates had shown little interest in what was going on in the world outside Andover Hill. There is, for example, no evidence that the students concerned themselves with national elections in the early years. Starting in the 1870's all this changed, and led by the *Phillipian*, the undergraduates began to show a lively interest in national affairs. In April 1880 a student poll was taken to determine preferences in the coming presidential election. It was clear that the boys were strongly Republican, for Blaine received 60 votes, Grant 59, and Edmunds 30, while Democrats like Tilden and Hancock got 5 and 1 respectively. The redoubtable Benjamin Franklin Butler managed to corral 2 votes.[61] That fall a school meeting was called for the purpose of organizing what was named "The Garfield and Arthur Battalion" with 150 members. This outfit even went so far as to produce uniforms consisting of red Turkish hats, white cutaway jackets trimmed in red, and white leggings. The members were to carry swinging torches while electioneering.[62] After Garfield's victory the *Phillipian* wrote an "I told you so" editorial, extending sympathy to the School's few Democrats.[63] Four years later, after Cleveland's victory, the *Phillipian* sourly suggested that at least the results of the election must have pleased the 30 to 40 Democrats in school.[64] There was interest as well in local politics. One of the hot issues was the liquor question. The towns had local option. In March 1885 the *Phillipian* reported that there was to be another year of prohibition in Andover, since the license men were beaten by fifteen votes.[65] In October 1888 the Democratic students perked up and put on a demonstration for Cleveland. They marched around the campus and the town, bearing a banner that read "Cleveland Cadets, No Free Whiskey"; but when the election itself came along, the *Phillipian* reported that there was very little excitement anywhere in town.[66] The faculty apparently wished to encourage interest in political affairs, for they voted a half holiday so that undergraduates could attend the town meeting of 1889. One of the things the students learned from attending the meeting was that all the faculty voted for prohibition.[67] in 1892 the students conducted a mock election, with the following results: Harrison 274; Cleveland 104; Bidwell, the prohibition candidate, 12. It was also reported that the football team was made up of 17 Republicans and 2 Democrats, while Abbot Academy had 110 Republicans and 33 Democrats.[68] As the Spanish American War approached, undergraduate interest was again intense. Forum, a society organized in 1892, debated the resolution that President McKinley should have demanded an indemnity from Spain for the *Maine;* and when war was declared, a mass meeting was held in the Academy Building to make preparations for raising a military company. "The whole front of the platform was draped with a large American flag, making an imposing spectacle," the *Phillipian* reported. Interestingly enough, at this meeting one undergraduate made a speech charging that the war was unjustifiable.[69] Finally, Forum passed a resolution in 1901 condemning Theodore Roosevelt's hunting activities in the West, on the ground that it was cruelty to animals and might poison the minds of school children who read it. Unfortunately, this bit of fun got in the Boston and New York newspapers and caused a contretemps.[70] Interest in political affairs is a clear indication that the School was becoming less parochial than it had been earlier in the century.

During the Bancroft years the undergraduates also began to question various aspects of the religious program. There had doubtless been earlier complaints, but they had tended to be muted; now they became more outspoken. One of the major undergraduate dissatisfactions was with the two long Sunday services conducted by professors from the Theological Seminary, and they were greatly heartened when a member of the Phillips Academy faculty said he thought the time would come when only one service would be required.[71] Though the boys did not know it, Principal Bancroft agreed with them, and hoped that the School could have its own pastor to work directly with the boys.[72] Shorter sermons helped. In 1881 the *Phillipian* reported that twenty-five-minute sermons were so popular "that many start for church at the first ringing of the bell."[73] Dr. Bancroft was continually distressed at the number of students who were lukewarm toward religion, but he was never able to modify the existing program enough to make it truly attractive to the students. One new student, "shocked at the depravity of the Academy boys," began circulating a temperence pledge. The success of this venture is unrecorded.[74] On the other hand, in morning chapel when Cecil Bancroft talked to the boys on the evils of tobacco, the *Phillipian* reported that he had been "interesting and convincing."[75] It all depended on the speaker, for at about the same time it was praising Dr. Bancroft, the *Phillipian* reported: "The sermons of Mr. Hincks seem to have a remarkably soporific effect upon his hearers, especially upon such are are fortunate enough to secure a corner seat." Mr. Hincks was a professor at the Theological Seminary.[76] Indeed some of the undergraduate resentment in the religious area was directed against the Seminary itself. In 1890 it was pointed out that the Seminary had 9 professors, 2 lecturers, and a librarian to deal with 48 students, while Phillips Academy had 12 teachers for 360 students. Three years later there were attacks on the *Phillipian* policy of printings news about the Seminary.[77] In 1894 Philo debated the topic: Resolved, that compulsory church attendance at Phillips Academy should be abolished.[78] Boys who were Congregationalists, Baptists, Episcopalians, or Roman Catholics were allowed by Dr. Bancroft to attend town churches for one of the Sunday services, and this doubtless ameliorated some of the opposition to the School program, but not until the twentieth century were any real changes made.

The latter part of the nineteenth century saw a proliferation of student extracurricular activities that ended by transforming undergraduate life markedly. At the start, at least, all of these activities were student initiated, since the administration offered no programs in this area; and for the most part the administration and faculty were content to allow the boys to run the enterprises with little official interference. The most notable developments were in the field of sports. In the period before the Civil War there was little athletic activity among the undergraduates. Swimming in the Shawsheen River or Pomp's Pond, sledding during the winter, and walking around the Andover countryside were the only opportunities for physical exercise open to Phillips boys. Occasionally there is mention of a game called "rounders" (a crude form of baseball) and a rudimentary form of football, but for the most part Uncle Sam Taylor believed that the boys should concentrate on their studies, their religious activities, and a little debating. There was no comprehension of the important part that a well developed program of physical education could play in the total development of the adolescent boy. After the Civil War, however, the undergraduates took over, and teams began to develop rapidly. In baseball both school and class teams were formed, and before long the pressure to play games with other institutions mounted. The teams played not only other schools but also Tufts and Harvard and later Yale, among the colleges. In 1878 came the first game with Exeter, which Andover lost 11 to 1, but the School redeemed itself in succeeding contests. The development of this program involved, as time went on, training tables, the purchase of athletic equipment, and the hiring of coaches. At this point the faculty assumed direction of the program, establishing rules for eligibility, financial responsibility, and the like. By the start of the twentieth century, with the construction of the new Borden Gymnasium, the School was in a position to develop a full-fledged athletic program of its own. What had been true of baseball was equally true of football. The same pattern was followed: undergraduate initiative, rapid development of the sport, scheduling of games with outside institutions, and eventually faculty control. The most remarkable aspect of the Andover athletic program was that the driving force behind it and its early administration were provided by the undergraduates themselves.[79]

The Bancroft period also witnessed the development of undergraduate musical activities. There had always been an interest in the Academy, from the days when Eliphalet Pearson sang bass and played the cello, and the early records of the Trustees contain frequent votes appropriating small sums for instruction in music. But there is no evidence that early musical activity extended beyond drill in hymn-singing in chapel and church. After the Civil War all this changed, once again the boys taking matters into their own hands. In the late 1870's a glee club was organized and gave its first public performance in early 1879.[80] Shortly afterward an orchestra was established, though the *Phillipian* was less than enthusiastic about it. " 'Music hath charms to sooth the savage beast' " [sic] the paper wrote, "but it is inclined occasionally to reverse the order and to make savage the tranquil mind of the average student when he hears a member of the Phillips orchestra practicing."[81] Nor was the paper more generous to a group of visiting musicians. "There was a very small audience at the concert given by the twelve beautiful (?) ladies of Warren's Military Band. . . . The concert began at 8 o'clock and dragged along for two hours, and then came to a close, to the delight of the audience."[82] There was also interest in finding a new school song, the *Phillipian* offering a prize of $15.00 for the best one.[83] Despite some shaky starts, by the 1890's several undergraduate musical organizations were going strong. In 1895, for example, there was a glee club of sixteen, looking resplendent in their white ties and tails in the yearbook. A banjo club of eleven—in tuxedoes—played "banjearines," guitars, and mandolins, as well as banjoes, while a mandolin club of twelve, also tuxedo-clad, included guitars, a flute, and a violin.[84] These clubs must have become proficient, for they gave concerts outside the School. The number of students who participated was not large, especially because some musicians were in more than one organization, but the clubs none the less provided a new dimension to undergraduate life. Also in the field of the arts there was in 1895 a thriving camera club of 73 and a small dramatic club of 11,[85] though there are no references to dramatic performances in the *Phillipian*.

A student organization that concerned itself with the religious life of the School was the Society of Inquiry, which had had a long history. It had been founded in 1833 as a Missionary Fraternity, by "a few pious members of Phillips Academy" "to enquire into the moral state of the world, and to effect a mission to the heathen in the persons of its members." The Society held monthly meetings focused on foreign missions, but in 1839 it was decided to broaden the scope of the organization and to change its name to the "Society of Inquiry at Phillips Academy." The emphasis now shifted to home missions, and the Society became active in the town of Andover. It undertook the distribution of tracts and missionary literature to all the families in the town, and in the 1850's volunteered to supply teachers for the Abbot Village Sunday School and the Scotland District Sunday School. The superintendents of these two schools were elected each year by the Society. It also decided to establish a library. Great care was taken to prevent unsuitable books from reaching the shelves. When someone presented it with a set of the Universalist Library, it was voted to burn it forthwith, and a committee was appointed to determine the propriety of books presented to the organization. In the 1850's the Society established a newspaper called the *Observer* and the character of the organization began to change. Instead of purely religious activities, emphasis was placed on literary productions, debates, and criticism. In 1882, for example, the preamble to the revised constitution read, "In order to gain for ourselves literary culture, and by appropriate exercises to prepare ourselves for life and its work." Aping the Philomathean Society, Inquiry began to stress debating and argued questions on divorce, the elective system, international coinage and woman's suffrage. In 1875 a delightful proposition was "Resolved, that intercollegiate boat racing is detrimental to good morals." The difficulty with the shift to debating and literary exercises was that it tended to make the Society of Inquiry indistinguishable from the Philomathean, and the School could not support two organizations so similar. In 1882, therefore, the Society reverted to its original purpose of being primarily religious. The debates ceased, literary exercises were abandoned, and prayer meetings were restored as the characteristic activity of the organization. One might think that in the more secular days of the late nineteenth century the popularity of Inquiry might have declined, but such was by no means the case. Membership went from 61 in 1883 to 123 in 1886, while in 1888 the average attendance at the Sunday evening meetings was 97. Visits were also exchanged with the Exeter Christian Fraternity. Principal Bancroft remarked on the success of the prayer meetings in the 1887 Report to the Trustees; he detected "a decided quickening of religious interest and many hopeful conversions." For the remainder of Dr. Bancroft's administration the Society of Inquiry, remaining true to its original purpose, provided for devout members of the undergraduate body an opportunity for religious activity beyond the regular church and chapel services.[86]

The Philomathean Society, oldest in the School, was the hardy perennial. Founded in 1825, it had had a long and distinguished career as a debating society, for much of which membership in the organization was a mark of distinction. During part of the Bancroft era Philo ceased to occupy a position of respect among the undergraduates, but it started off this period with éclat. In 1875, on the occasion of its fiftieth anniversary, for example, it managed a celebration that was a dress rehearsal for the Centennial three years later. The exercises opened in the hall of the Academy with a series of speeches interspersed with musical selections by Brown's Brigade Band. The Honorable Samuel B. Noyes read a long history of the organization, and Charles A. Dickinson recited a poem entitled "Philo." After members of the audience had sung an ode especially written for the occasion, they dispersed to form a procession and march around the campus, winding up at a large dinner tent on the site of the old Stone Academy. The menu for the Centennial dinner has been lost, but it must have been similar to Philo's, which consisted of turkey, chicken, mutton, lamb, beef, potted pigeons, lobster salad, apple, cranberry, and Washington pie, four kinds of ice cream, walnuts, raisins, oranges, apples and tea and coffee. As to be expected in the Phillips Academy of that day, no alcoholic beverages were served. After dinner came the usual number of toasts and speeches, and when it was all over, Philo must have been very proud of its accomplishment.[87]

In the 1880's the Society began its decline. Instead of serious debating, it turned to various kinds of horseplay, especially mock trials. The program for the mock trial of 1880 is complete with Judge, Sheriff, Counsel for both sides, and a list of witnesses. For the prosecution there are Hans Dott, an honest tradesman, Miss Fannie Flyrte, a fair but frivolous Fem Sem, and Allen Hinton, a dealer in ice cream. The defense countered with Melancthom Smirke, a worthy and gentle theologue, Miss Prudence Primmer, a Fem Sem of principle, and others. Although these mock trials were popular with the undergraduates, they lacked the seriousness of purpose that had characterized Philo in its earlier days, and they contributed to a falling off in membership as the 1880's wore on.[88] The Society was also under attack from the *Phillipian* during this period for poor attendance at meetings and what were termed "disgraceful scenes."[89] Early in 1892, as noted, Forum was organized. Far from signaling the end of Philo, it stimulated reform in the old organization, and by the end of the decade the two societies were holding regular joint debates. For many years Philo had published a school literary magazine called the *Mirror*, which in recent times had become a kind of yearbook. In 1892 it was decided that the Society should continue to publish a yearbook, which was soon to be called the *Pot Pourri*, while the *Mirror* became a strictly literary magazine. Although readers did not know it at the time, a very early poem of Robert Frost was published in the *Mirror* for June 1892. A friend of Frost's named Ernest Jewell was a senior at Andover and heeling for the *Mirror*. He needed all the contributions he could get and Frost obliged with a poem entitled *The Traitor*, which was submitted in Jewell's name.[90] The Philomathean Society, therefore, after going through bad times, was full of life by the end of Dr. Bancroft's administration and was to make many contributions to the School in the twentieth century.

The most important new institution established during the Bancroft period was the newspaper, the *Phillipian*, which first saw the light of day in the fall of 1878. There was a mock publication of the same name published in 1857, and from time to time various *Phillipian* boards have attempted to claim that date as the proper one for the paper's founding, but since no numbers were issued between 1857 and 1878, their claim has not been taken seriously. The paper that first appeared in 1878 was apparently published as a result of the tremendous activity that accompanied the Centennial and with the hope that the interest aroused in the School by that celebration might be maintained. As with the other student activities during this period, the *Phillipian* was composed and published by the undergraduates. There was no faculty censorship; the only control the Faculty exercised was to approve each incoming board. The paper soon proved itself a very lively publication. Though it can hardly be called crusading, it did not hesitate to criticize a variety of School policies, and the Faculty demonstrated toleration by allowing these criticisms to be made. The *Phillipian* came down hard on parts of the disciplinary system. It deplored the presence of student spies and complained that the Faculty kept classes late.[91] It thought there were too many rigid rules governing visits to the center of town and was outraged when a boy who broke a window was given eighty demerits and fined ten dollars.[92] It protested when the School refused to make Washington's Birthday a holiday, but agreed that the painting of mottoes on fences and walls had to stop.[93] It complained about the landladies and the high board and thought that School meetings were a farce.[94] Finally, it called attention to the absurdity of the new eligibility rule under which a boy, after declaiming in the Draper Prize Contest, had been declared ineligible.[95] The paper carried on a long-standing feud with the town of Andover on the subject of coasting. From time to time the town would ban all coasting; then the *Phillipian* would write steaming editorials; and usually the town would relent.[96] The paper was interested in girls in general and Abbot Academy in particular. It demanded more opportunity to see the Abbot girls and printed a mock diary supposedly written by Miss Flyrte, an Abbot student.[97] It complained that when an Abbot girl met a Phillips boy on the street, she would look at him "much as she would look upon some animal on exhibition at a circus."[98] The paper also extended its coverage to Bradford Academy: "Why are the Bradford Fem-Sems like the Apostle Paul?" "Because they write epistles to the Phillipians."[99] The publication was heartened when Principal Bancroft and his wife gave a party for both Phillips and Abbot seniors, but when it was announced one year that the Abbot Easter vacation would end the very day the Phillips vacation was to begin, the *Phillipian* charged conspiracy between the two administrations.[1] The paper took up other causes as well—for instance, it charged that a gift to the Theological Seminary had been meant for Phillips Academy, and it circulated a petition to help the Utah Indians.[2] Apart from the causes that it embraced, it did an admirable job of reporting School activities. Each spring it duly noted the first appearance of Allen Hinton, a black who lived on a farm off South Main Street and who sold delicious Harlequin ice cream. On one occasion he managed to sell 58 quarts to Andover boys.[3] It reported that the undergraduates had decided on a hat and had chosen a red fez. The question of the virtue of cane rushes was also debated.[4] The paper suggested that the cost of replacing the windows broken in the Commons was greater than the value of the buildings themselves. It commented on how much the undergradu-

38. The A.U.V. society coach in front of the Latin Commons at the Andover-Exeter baseball game in June 1898.

ates were enjoying their evening walks to Pomp's Pond in June.[5] Generally it presented the School as it really was. Getting out the paper was hard work, as Lee Perrin noted.[6] But it was rewarding work, and the freedom the board was given, coupled with the responsibility for what was printed, made the *Phillipian* experience one of the most valuable that an Andover undergraduate could have.

In 1874 there appeared the first of what were to become extremely significant and controversial student organizations—the secret society (below, pages 503–529). The Andover secret societies were part of a movement among college undergraduates two generations earlier, started as a protest against the monotony of student life. The college Greek-letter fraternities had spread rapidly throughout the East, Midwest, and South in the period before the Civil War, developing elaborate rituals and driving many of the college literary and religious societies out of existence. The appeals of these institutions was their privacy and the opportunity to form friendships undisturbed by the undergraduate body as a whole. In this sense they were frankly elitist.[7] At Yale, in addition to Greek-letter fraternities for the underclassmen, there were for the seniors, before 1883, two prestigious societies, Skull and Bones and Scroll and Key.[8] It is generally agreed that the Andover societies were modeled on the Yale senior organizations rather than on Greek-letter fraternities. In the 1870's the ties between the two institutions were close, and it is easy to conceive of a Yale alumnus returning to Andover to suggest the formation of secondary school societies modeled on Yale's. The first Andover society was K.O.A., founded in 1874. It met in the basement of what later became Chap's eating house, worked up a secret ritual and initiation ceremonies, and engaged in late-evening horseplay of various kinds. Shortly afterward came A.U.V., also established secretly. By the end of the Bancroft era two more, P.A.E. and P.B.X., had been organized, as well several others that did not survive for long.[9] At first the School's attitude toward these organizations was hostile; reporting to the Trustees in 1877, Principal Bancroft wrote: "Secret societies so-called have caused us some anxiety but the Faculty have taken a positive stand forbidding them and it is hoped to quite crush them out next year." This was easier said than done, and in a few years Dr. Bancroft came to the conclusion that it was wiser to regulate the societies than to try to eliminate them. When P.A.E. was founded, the experiment was tried of having a Faculty guardian for the new organization, and Professor Edward Coy was selected. In 1883 the Faculty voted to substitute stricter regulation for the policy of suppression. In the future all societies were required to have Faculty guardians, no member of the School could join one without Faculty approval, and no new society could be formed without a Faculty charter. Evening meetings, except on special circumstances, were limited to Saturday nights.[10] By the turn of the century there were four firmly established societies and several others destined to fail. After initially trying to suppress them, the School had adopted a set of regulations governing their conduct, and a measure of stability had been reached. The twentieth century would see the construction of handsome society houses, growth in power of the societies, and, eventually, a serious controversy over their role.

Cecil Bancroft, in his relations with the Andover undergraduate body during his term as Principal, displayed an extraordinary combination of tolerance, tact, and firmness. He understood that many of the student riots and roughhouses were the result of excess animal spirits rather than viciousness, and he had no feeling of *amour propre* about his position as chief disciplinarian for the School. "There are some things," he used to say, "which a teacher will do well never to see."[11] The difficulties in controlling the boys arose from the almost complete absence of Faculty supervision in the dormitories and the dependence upon landladies for disciplining of students who lived in boarding houses. The Faculty could pass rules about the boys being in at eight o'clock, but if there was no one to see that the rule was enforced, the rules were an empty gesture. The problem grew in difficulty as the School expanded in size. Whereas his predecessors, particularly Uncle Sam Taylor, had enforced discipline without reference to the record of the transgressor, Dr. Bancroft and his Faculty began to use a sliding scale in dealing with student misbehavior. A boy who had been thoughtless or stupid in the commission of some undergraduate crime might well be given a second chance, whereas another who had been malicious, vicious, or mean in the commission of the same crime might be expelled. Dr. Bancroft also meted out punishments quietly, with little or no publicity attending them; there was no more drumming culprits out of school before the whole student body, as was the case in the early days. Boys who had been expelled by Uncle Sam resented the cold and mechanical way in which the punishment had been meted out; a boy expelled by Cecil Bancroft wrote, "Banty fired me, but it woke me up, and was the best thing that ever happened to me."[12] Although it would be too much to say that Eliphalet Pearson's system of discipline based on fear had been abandoned, it was certainly modified; understanding, explanation of the reason for punishment, and more humane treatment came to be characteristic of the Phillips Academy disciplinary system.[13]

Principal Bancroft, more interested in developing the character of his boys than in adhering to a rigid system of rules, strove manfully to inculcate in his charges concepts of human decency and proper behavior. A clergyman himself, he was concerned with the spiritual welfare of the boys, and nothing gave him greater pleasure than to report to the Trustees that a substantial number of undergraduates had become converted. He was deathly against swearing and wrote a sermon entitled "The Guilt of Profanity." Insisting that the usages of good society forbade profanity, that it was the worst men who swear most, and that the worst places are the most filled with their blasphemy, he cited a number of Massachusetts statutes that forbade profanity, and reminded his readers that profane swearers were law-breakers. The excuses for swearing were pitiful—"I don't mean anything by it," "I don't swear much," "I can't help it," and "I didn't think." Finally, he quoted the Biblical injunction "The Lord will not hold him guiltless who taketh his name in vain."[14] What effect this sermon had on the Andover undergraduates is, of course, impossible to determine, but it is clear that the good Doctor wrote from the heart. Another *bête noire* of Principal Bancroft's was smoking, and he worked constantly to combat the habit among his students. Yet he was intelligent enough to realize that an outright ban on smoking would be unenforceable, and that education in the evils of the habit had more chance of success. In 1882 he reported to the Trustees:

> I have sent to the Trustees and every parent and guardian and to some forty distinguished physicians and school and college officers a circular letter and tract on the use of tobacco by boys. Two of the Trustees and 139 others have replied not only opposing the use of tobacco by boys, all but one who confess to using it regarding it as a damage to themselves, and the vast majority wishing us to forbid its use in school by a rule which they think would be both "reasonable and practicable," but the weighty letters from those best acquainted with the difficulties and the alternate evils are against the rule and in favor of constant argument and personal advice and persuasion.

When Dr. Bancroft cared about something, he really worked at it.

One gains insight into the way Cecil Bancroft handled disciplinary problems by examining a speech he made to the undergraduate body after

39. *The undergraduates have some fun at the expense of the Faculty. About 1894.* Left to right: *Allen Benner, George Pettee, William Graves* (behind bar), *George ("Pap") Eaton, Henry Boynton, Charles ("Frenchy") Stone, Cecil Bancroft, and William Terrill.*

the "stacking" of senior rooms. One of the traditional events of the Senior Year came in the winter, when the whole class went on a long evening sleigh ride. Since all the seniors were out of their rooms, it was an ideal time for the lowerclassmen to engage in a favorite trick: piling furniture in the middle of the room, dismantling beds, and the like. In 1890, however, the stacking operation went far beyond previous practice and resulted in the destruction of property. Alfred Stearns, a senior that year, describes what happened in a letter to his sister:

> We struck Andover at quarter before three o'clock, and I was soon in bed. Some of the other fellows were not so lucky however, for the middlers had been busy during our absence and every room in Commons was stacked to a certain extent. Some of them were all torn to pieces with pictures smashed, ink poured over books, and coal shoveled over the carpet, bed [clothes] scattered over the campus or hanging in trees, and in fact a general wreck. Stacking is an old institution in this school, but never before has it been carried to such an extent that property has been destroyed outright. The faculty are wild about it, and held two special meetings yesterday. . . . One fellow's room up in Latin Commons was so badly smashed up that he has given up all hope of trying to get it straightened up again and is going to room elsewhere. Among other things they tied a large Newfoundland dog saturated with some sort of horrible smelling acid to his bed post. When found the dog was nearly suffocated and the fellows had to hold their noses while they went in and untied him.[15]

Principal Bancroft reacted strongly to the outrage:

> I can appreciate the not very dignified but not very reprehensible satisfaction that one gets from stopping his neighbor's alarm clock, putting salt in his sugar, and tying up the sleeves of his dressing gown. But when fun goes over into open disorder, putting men to great inconvenience, exposing[?] in some cases their health, interfering with their school work, damaging their carpets, curtains, bedding, clothing, upsetting for a time the only Andover home they have and almost driving them out of it, when things get to such a pass, then every man arrived at years of discretion and actuated by a sense of honor, every man who values the good name of the body in which he is a part, stands off and denounces the rowdyism, and lifts up his protest against it.

The Principal then examined the various reasons people gave for engaging in vandalism of this kind. The commonest reason was that it was fun; Dr. Bancroft had no patience with this excuse; he and the Faculty were not trying to stop innocent fun, but when it became brutality, it was time to

call a halt. A second reason often given was that stacking was traditional—
it was always done at the time of the winter sleigh ride. The Principal dismissed this argument summarily; in the first place the tradition was only
two years old, but even if it were one hundred years old, it would not
make such behavior noble or venerable. A third reason was that the seniors
were off having a good time, so the underclassmen should be allowed to
enjoy themselves too. Dr. Bancroft insisted that in a School a boy receives
more privileges each year as he grows up and that special privileges for
seniors were a normal and healthy practice. A fourth reason was that the
seniors had stacked rooms the previous year and deserved to get the same
treatment this year. This, according to the Principal, would lead to a kind
of lynch law at Phillips Academy. A fifth reason sometimes given was that
it was a challenge to break into a senior room that had been locked and
barricaded. That kind of reasoning, thought Dr. Bancroft, was like saying
that a burglar's interest in opening a safe was to show that he was smarter
than the bank officer. Finally, the vicious behavior was justified by a mere
desire to settle old scores, to get revenge on another student; and it was
easier and safer to do this in the company of a mob than by oneself. Dr.
Bancroft thought this was like thinking of the shotgun and the dagger as
instruments of reform. Having disposed of every possible justification for
the recent malicious behavior, the Principal closed:

> But, gentlemen, this is not a question of *stacking*. It is a case of
> *rowdyism*, rampant and offensive. Under cover of *stacking* the worst
> exhibition of rowdyism we have had since 1873 has displayed itself.
> Boyishness and foolishness we have had, mischief we have had,
> occasional crimes we have had, sporadic cases of theft, and a murky
> stream of immorality all the time creeping its stealthy way under the
> proprieties and decencies of a school of good and pure-minded men
> and boys. The punishments we have in mind are not for *stacking*. . . .
> But rowdyism like that of last week is worthy of a worthy punish-
> ment. The good order and the good name of the school demand it.[16]

Unfortunately, there is no record of what punishments were meted out to
the guilty parties. One group of culprits met and collected $14.85 to pay
for at least some of the damage.[17] But since a large number of undergraduates were grilled by Dr. Bancroft and the Faculty, the presumption is strong
that a number who were found guilty were punished. What is impressive
is the Principal's concentration on the case. He and the Faculty spent a
week discussing all aspects of it before any action was taken; furthermore,
before any action he gave the undergraduates a thorough analysis of all
aspects of it, so that they would know just where the administration stood.
His procedure apparently worked. The *Phillipian* wrote an editorial against
stacking, and there is no evidence that the problem reappeared during the
rest of Cecil Bancroft's term.[18]

Like every other school principal, Cecil Bancroft had to deal not only with the undergraduates but also with their parents. To judge by the number of letters he wrote, he must have spent a prodigious amount of time on parental matters. And the requests, pleas, complaints, and attacks that he received were varied. A mother reported that her son had sat next to a boy who had died of scarlet fever and wanted him sent home if there was the slightest evidence of illness.[19] A father wrote that he was pleased with Andover, and all the more so because a son at Exeter was smoking and had developed "a terrible passion for Billiard playing."[20] An angry mother whose boy had been expelled accused the Principal of lacking "moral courage."[21] Another father complained that one of the Academy's teachers had been trying to catch his son in a lie.[22] A concerned parent wrote that the School was working his son so hard that he was developing nervous prostration and might well commit suicide (he solved the problem by withdrawing the boy).[23] Financial matters continually bothered parents; one asked Dr. Bancroft to talk to his son about his extravagant habits,[24] while another sent the Principal $150.00 and asked him to dole the money out to his son.[25] An unhappy father insisted that his son could not have been involved in an attempt to blow up the Lawrence depot.[26] A particularly difficult problem arose when there were complaints about the Faculty, sometimes justified; one father asked that his son be changed from a teacher who was teaching him nothing to another whose class was learning a great deal.[27] Some parents wanted the Principal's help in planning a boy's future career, like the one who wanted his son to become an electrician.[28] A grandmother wrote that she wanted her grandson to go to Andover, but only if the School refused to admit a vicious acquaintance of his.[29] An anti-athletic parent wanted his son to withdraw from all baseball and football games and leave them to the "sporting fraternity."[30] Hazing was always difficult to deal with; one parent wrote that what was being done to his son would be considered criminal conduct if done outside the School.[31] A bitter parent wrote Dr. Bancroft, "I expected that Christ ruled on Andover Hill. I am being convinced otherwise,"[32] and a less religious parent asked if his son could cut church on Sundays to study; the boy's weak eyes, he added, made evening study difficult.[33] Secret societies came under attack; "I would root out K.O.A. and A.U.V. if I didn't have any graduating class for two years," said one man.[34] A sardonic communication read, "I cannot help being amused when I think that last year I decided against Exeter because of the much drinking there and am wrecked upon this Charybdis of play [gambling for money] in Andover."[35] Unbelievably, a concerned mother asked Dr. Bancroft to see that her son was wakened in time for breakfast.[36] On and on.

One might think that Dr. Bancroft's exacting duties as Principal precluded his participation in activities outside the School, but such was not the case. First of all, he had a keen interest in the Town of Andover. John

N. Cole, one of the leading citizens, wrote at the time of his death that he was "the first citizen of the town" and knew almost everybody. Though his duties prevented him from holding regular offices in town government, he was Chairman of the Committee to celebrate the town's 250th anniversary in 1896. He was also a director of the Andover Bank and of the local insurance company. A fellow director of the Bank, impressed with his business sense, remarked, "Had Dr. Bancroft been a business man he would have become a millionaire." He also was asked by the State to assist in the administration of the Tewksbury almshouse.[37] Apart from his local interests, he was in great demand as a speaker. Mention has been made of the large number of addresses he delivered before various educational organizations on a wide variety of subjects. In June 1887 he journeyed to Yankton, Dakota—it was still a territory—to deliver the address at the first Commencement of Yankton College, of which an old friend was President.[38] He was constantly in demand to fill pulpits on Sundays. People were forever trying to enlist his help in worthy causes. Anti-tobacco groups found a champion in him and wanted copies of circulars that he had prepared.[39] Prohibitionists wanted him to help spread their gospel at the School.[40] An antivivisectionist lady sent him a batch of clippings, explained how she loved animals and hated those who abused them, and asked for his support in her crusade.[41] And the redoubtable Anthony Comstock, of the New York Society for the Suppression of Vice, wrote to warn of peddlers of dirty books who were infiltrating the schools.[42] When M.I.T., in financial difficulty, sought a grant from the Massachusetts legislature, Dr. Bancroft was asked to help.[43] I. K. Funk asked his advice on how to deal with unprincipled attacks made on his dictionary for including "indelicate" words.[44] The editor of *Child's World* asked him to write articles for that publication and also to submit a piece on Bible study at Andover.[45] And individuals continued to pester him with requests that had nothing to do with the School. One correspondent asked for a character reference for a man who wanted to rent a typewriter from him.[46] Another, who was responsible for selection of West Point students, asked Dr. Bancroft to be President of the Committee of Selection, set the exam, and make the final choice.[47] An anonymous group of local workers wrote protesting the hiring by Phillips Academy of immigrants from Lawrence when native-born workers were unemployed, and also the hiring of married women when single girls were unemployed; according to this communication, the Phillips Academy Superintendent said to applicants for work, "Get to Hell out of here and keep off this Hill."[48] Governor Dummer Academy wanted to enlist Dr. Bancroft's help in getting better boys; they had been accepting students expelled from other schools and the quality of the student body was deteriorating.[49] When the Presidency of Yale became vacant in the 1890's, an enthusiastic supporter of Cecil Bancroft for the position wrote, "I wonder if Banty keeps up his old time energy. He is a wonderful man.

If we could knock out the congregational Connecticut trustees and place a handful of live active men on the board under Dr. Bancroft what a rustler he would be and what strides Yale would make."[50] Finally, the Principal's help was enlisted to find a suitable military school for the adopted son of Jefferson Davis' widow.[51] When it is remembered that Bancroft took each one of these requests seriously, it is not surprising that, even with the help of George Pettee, he burned himself out in the performance of his duties.

In the late 1890's he began to fail. Part of the problem was a kidney complaint, but general exhaustion contributed a great deal. He received a crushing blow early in 1898 when his wife died. A quiet unassuming woman, she had nonetheless been a pillar of strength, and he never recovered from this loss. Later that year the Trustees sent him to Europe in hope that he would recover completely, but when he returned, he was still weak and listless. In 1901, as his condition deteriorated, the Trustees once again granted travel funds. At first he refused to accept, saying there was not enough money in the Treasury, but he was finally prevailed upon to go.[52] After his return to Andover in the late summer of 1901, it was clear that he could not last long, and on 4 October 1901 he died. His death caused widespread and genuine grief in all parts of the School community, and the town as well. At his funeral the entire undergraduate body assembled in a double line in front of the School buildings to pay their respects; he would have liked that. They then marched into the Chapel, where Dr. Bancroft's old friend President William J. Tucker of Dartmouth conducted the service. The brief committal service at the Seminary graveyard was conducted by another old friend, Professor John Phelps Taylor. Twelve Academy boys acted as bearers.[53] One of the bearers wrote, "Seldom have I seen grief so general and so sincere. For days not only the school, but the entire village was in mourning; tributes from friends and alumni poured in from all parts of the country in loving profusion." All wished to honor "the memory of a friend who had helped them by reproof and encouragement, and by example, to strive for manliness and nobility of character."[54] Dr. Bancroft had received his share of honors during his lifetime. He was President of the Dartmouth Alumni Association and later a Trustee of that Institution; he had been President of the Headmasters Association of the United States; and he had received an honorary Ph.D. from the University of the State of New York, an L.H.D. from Williams, and an L.L.D. from Yale.[55] He had transformed Phillips Academy from an eighteenth-century institution to a modern one and set a pattern that would be followed by his successors for many years. Impressive though his achievements were, it was the quality of the man that was his most enduring monument. A colleague spoke of his "power of sustained waiting."[56] This was not foot-dragging but a determination not to move until the time was ripe. Stories of his kindnesses to boys are legion, and when discipline had to be administered, infinite care was taken to explain the reasons for the punishment. In sum-

40. *Cecil Bancroft at work in his office near the end of his administration.*

ming up Cecil Franklin Patch Bancroft's career as Principal of Phillips Academy, one cannot do better than quote from the Resolution that the Trustees passed at the time of his death:

> After many years of distinguished service he rests from his labors. His administration of the interests of the Academy has been eminently successful. By large ability and discretion he so fulfilled the varied duties of his office that he readily commanded the confidence of those associated with him, and the respect and grateful affection of the thousands of boys who have been under his care. He has kept the school in its high place before the colleges and the world. He will always and everywhere be named with honor.
>
> Beyond all which was official, he has endeared himself to those who have stood with him by his fine qualities of heart, his unalterable courtesy, his constant courage and patience, his cheerfulness and hopefulness, and the full measure of his friendliness.
>
> Every thought of him is pleasant. His work will abide and his memory be an encouragement to fidelity. He has gained the blessing which belongs to him who has lived in the love of God and the service of men.[57]

CHAPTER TWELVE

ALFRED E. STEARNS: A STRONG START

BISHOP HENRY W. HOBSON once said that there was really only one important thing that the Board of Trustees of a School like Andover had to do and that was to choose the Principal or Headmaster. If the Board chose wisely, he added, they would have relatively few troubles; if, however, they made a poor choice, their troubles would be unending. The Phillips Academy Board, charged with finding a successor to Cecil Bancroft, understood the point. By proceeding slowly and cautiously, they succeeded in finding a man who was to become another of Andover's great Principals. After Dr. Bancroft's death, they had appointed Professor William Graves as Acting Principal, and appointed a committee to consider a permanent successor. The committee worked diligently, for at their next meeting, in February 1902, the Board considered the committee recommendations and voted unanimously to elect Professor James Hardy Ropes of the Harvard Divinity School the next Principal.[1] Since Professor Ropes had himself been a member of the Andover Board for some years, he was well known to the Trustees and a man whom they could choose with enthusiasm. Still in his thirties, Ropes had had a brilliant career ever since he had entered the Academy in 1881 as a student from the Town of Andover, where he had lived all his life. At the School he was class valedictorian, president of both Philo and the Society of Inquiry, editor of the *Phillipian*, and a prize-winning speaker. Of his oratorical ability one judge wrote, "A simple, manly, direct style."[2] He was also one of the founders of the P.A.E. Society. At Harvard he had an equally distinguished career, being a member of numerous student organizations as well as editor of the *Advocate*, and graduating *summa cum laude*. After graduation he spent a year doing geological work in the West and then returned to enter the Andover Theological Seminary, where he graduated in 1893. His work at the Seminary was so superior that he was awarded a fellowship to study in Germany and for the next two years he was enrolled at the Universities of Kiel, Halle, and Berlin. His European work completed, he returned to the Harvard Divinity School, where he became first Instructor and then Assistant Professor in New Testament Criticism. One admirer said of his election, "The athletic and popular sides of the school may well be trusted to care for themselves, if the scholarship is directed by such a scholar as Prof. Ropes."[3]

It was one thing to elect James Hardy Ropes; another for him to accept; and it soon became clear that he would take the position only if the Trustees met his demanding requirements. In a letter to the Board he spelled out these conditions. After paying tribute to the achievements of Dr. Bancroft and to the reputation of Phillips Academy generally, he hit hard at the housing and boarding conditions in the School, which he thought behind those of every other school in the country:

> Only 70 boys out of a total this year of about 340 boarding pupils have proper rooms provided by the Institution. The sanitary and other evils of the old Commons are well known to the Board, and are intolerable. The demoralizing arrangements of the Commons dining hall, the only provision for the boys' meals which the Academy can at present make, have lately been vividly set before the Board by the Treasurer. In consequence the daily life of the greater part of the boys is largely out of the control of the administration of the School, with the result of serious moral evils and constant danger of greater ones. I believe it is absolutely essential to any successful administration of the Academy and to the retaining of public confidence in the School that the boys' life should be brought again into the hands of the authorities of the School by the institution of sufficient dormitories and of a suitable dining hall, in which at any rate the larger part of the School, and not, as at present, only the poorest boys shall board, and where the influence shall be civilizing and not the reverse.[4]

Professor Ropes admitted that these changes would cost money, but said that he could not undertake to raise it. He concluded that if the Theological Seminary left Andover and the School acquired its property, he would accept the position if an additional $50,000 were raised. If the Seminary remained in Andover, a much larger sum would have to be raised before he could accept the position. The Ropes conditions were harsh but realistic; perhaps he wanted to see if the Board really meant business. In any event it was not long before he received word from the President of the Board that the Trustees could not accept his conditions; whereupon he declined election as Principal.[5] Professor Ropes would remain on the Board for another thirty years and perform many useful services for Phillips Academy, but he would never be its Principal.

Once again the Trustees began the search. Since Professor Graves was old and unwell, it was incumbent upon them to find an Acting Principal while they continued their search. A month after Professor Ropes turned them down, they selected a promising new teacher who had been Director of Athletics and Assistant to Dr. Bancroft—Alfred E. Stearns. There is reason to believe that some of the Trustees, particularly Treasurer James Sawyer, Stearns's dear friend, wanted Stearns elected then and there. Other members of the Board, however, wanted to wait a year and see how things went. When the year was up, their doubts were completely removed, and in March 1903 Alfred Stearns was unanimously elected the ninth Principal of Phillips Academy.[6]

Al Stearns was a natural in many ways to be Principal of the School. First of all, he had many forebears who had been associated with the Academy or with education. Two of his great-grandfathers—Josiah Stearns and Jonathan French—had been on the first Andover Board of Trustees. A great-great uncle, Jonathan French Stearns, had gone to Phillips and had been one of the founders of Philo. His grandfather, William A. Stearns, graduated from the Academy in 1823 and went on to become President of Amherst College. It was only Al's father who had no Andover connections. William French Stearns chose to go into business and became a merchant in India for fifteen years before Al was born. The family lived at Malabar Hill, just outside Bombay, and had a busy and interesting social life. Lord Napier was a frequent visitor, David Livingston stayed there before embarking on his expeditions to Africa—which Al's father helped finance— and Richard Henry Dana had spent a period of convalescence there following a serious illness. Although William French Stearns was very successful with his mercantile enterprises, the strain of living in India began to take its toll, and just before Al was born in 1871, they all returned to this country and settled in New Jersey, where they planned to live off the fortune that Al's father had made. Then came disaster. A Hindu employee of the father's firm was discovered to have embezzled almost all of the business's assets. This news broke Al's father, who never recovered from the shock and died shortly thereafter, leaving Mrs. Stearns and seven children almost penniless. She soon decided that the most sensible procedure was to go to Amherst, where her father-in-law was still President, and open a girls' school. This she did, and when President Stearns died in 1876, she was allowed to use the President's house for her school by Stearns's successor, Julius Seelye, who already had a handsome residence of his own. Thus it was that Al grew up in a girls' school, called "The Convent" by Amherst undergraduates.[7]

In a delightful book entitled *An Amherst Boyhood*, which he wrote after his retirement from Andover, Al Stearns recounted in a mellow mood his youthful experiences in that college town. The 1870's and 1880's were the heyday of fraternities, so Al and his friends formed one of their own, called Chi Delta, complete with ritual, grip, and regular meetings. While still very young, he began playing baseball on pick-up teams and thus started an interest that was to last his entire lifetime. Some of his closest friends were the sons of William B. Graves, who had left Andover in the early 1870's and was presently teaching at the Massachusetts Agricultural College at the other end of the town from Amherst College. Graves returned to Phillips Academy in 1881. Al had a scientific bent as well and established what he called the "Stearns Zoological Cabinet," which contained a miscellaneous collection of birds' nests and eggs, butterflies and beetles, shells and minerals. It received a tremendous boost as a result of a fire that had burned down the building where the College mineral collection was kept. Al sifted through the ashes, rescued many of the specimens, and was rewarded by being given a number of interesting rocks for his cabinet. One might think that living in the attic of a building that housed a girls' school would have cramped his style, but apparently it did no such thing. Sometimes, however, it could be embarrassing. On one occasion Al was asked to drive the girls to nearby Mt. Toby for a picnic. As he drove through the center of town, he saw a group of his cronies, who roared with laughter at the sight of Al with all those girls and yelled "Oh you Sissy" at him. Not infrequently he served as a go-between for girls at the Convent and Amherst undergraduates, his most famous courier service being performed for a beauty named Anna Barkley and Robert Lansing, later Secretary of State under Wilson. Long after, Al met some of Anna Barkley's relatives and found them still enraged because she had turned Lansing down. Al remembers the future playwright Clyde Fitch as a real fop—supercilious, always dressed to the nines, anything but masculine. Al and his friends used to waylay Fitch and roll huge snowballs down a deep slope at him.[8]

It is a sad commentary on the state of medical knowledge of the day that Al's mother, with her usual kindness, was allowed to take into her school a girl who was dying of TB, in hope of making her last days more pleasant. The result was tragedy. Four of Al's siblings died of the disease, and for a while it was thought that he had contracted the malady also. He was sent to Florida to recuperate and spent two winters there. When he returned to Amherst, he was at loose ends. At this point it was decided that he should go to Phillips Academy, where his uncle, Cecil Bancroft, was Principal. Since the Stearnses had no money for room and board, an arrangement was worked out whereby Al would live with the Bancrofts, while his cousin, Fanny Bancroft, would go to the Convent in Amherst. So it was that Al Stearns first came in contact with the School to which he was to devote most of his life.[9]

During his four years at Andover Al Stearns roomed at the home of his uncle the Principal, a good part of the time in company with James C. Sawyer, who became a dear friend and who later, as Treasurer of the Academy, became his strong right hand. Al had a distinguished record at Phillips Academy: he was captain of the baseball team, a good football player, the School tennis champion, editor of the newspaper, and president of Philo. Though he was a good scholar, his interests lay primarily in non-academic matters, particularly sports. Fortunately a series of letters written to his sister Mabel over the four-year period of his stay at Andover have been preserved, and they reveal a great deal about the schoolboy. He could enjoy a joke with the best. One of Al's teachers caught a boy chewing Black Jack tobacco and warned the rest about chewing. He then called on a boy in the back of the room who was also chewing tobacco but who managed to spit his quid out on the floor when the teacher was not looking. "I nearly rolled off my seat laughing," Al reported.[10] Undergraduate relations with the Faculty outside of class were pretty much a matter of cops and robbers. Al described a particularly telling encounter by the cops: "Last night the Profs. made a raid, that is they went around to all the different fellows' rooms to see how many were out of their rooms and they found about 150 out. A number of these will probably get bounced and all will probably get no small number of demerits."[11] He wrote that Edward Coy, under whom he had Greek, "looks as though he was going to bite your head off if you make a mistake," but that Algebra under Pap Eaton was a "regular gut." He wrote apprehensively of a coming Cane Rush, where his class was to take on the Middlers, who had three times as many members and were a lot heavier. He expected some broken bones, but apparently survived the ordeal successfully.[12] For all his uncle's lecturing on the evils of smoking, Al and Jimmy Sawyer occasionally smoked in their room in the Principal's house, but, perhaps as a compromise with his uncle, Al smoked mainly Cubebs. The two boys were amazed to discover later that Cecil Bancroft had known what they were up to all along.[13]

In his senior year Al Stearns had an experience that illustrated how divisive an influence the Societies could have on the School. He was a leading candidate for Class President, but the non-Society boys, most of whom roomed in the Commons, decided to unite and elect one of their number. At the election meeting one of the non-Society men got up and said he had nothing against Al Stearns but that he thought he had enough honors already. Al's friends were furious at this tactic, but when the vote was taken, Al lost 26 to 22. Al and his friends determined to retaliate by boycotting the Commencement festivities and refused to serve on any of the Committees. In the late spring Al wrote his sister, "I don't care about having you here for graduation for unless I am very mistaken, it will be pretty 'cheesey.' All the Society men in the class resigned from the Class Day Committee, so as to show them we didn't want to 'run the class' as they had the gall to say we did. I was appointed Chairman of Executive Committee which is next best to President, but I declined with thanks and told them that as long as I had been accused of being a hog, I wished to show them that such was not the case. They were all broken up over the whole business and tried to make us change our minds, but we pulled their legs badly." Eventually the Class of 1890 managed a respectable Commencement, but the struggle between the Society and non-Society men left scars none the less.[14]

In sports Al Stearns made his most important contribution as an Andover undergraduate. During his first year he was only a spectator, but he records cheering the football team despite a 26–0 loss to Exeter. "We yelled for about an hour steady for all we were worth and I was so hoarse when I got back that I could hardly speak," he wrote his sister.[15] In the spring of that year he was a member of a pick-up baseball team called the "Faculty Nine" and recorded with pride their defeat of Cheever House, 5–2. They were going to take on a team from the Theological Seminary the following week, Al wrote.[16] The following year he pitched for the varsity and beat Exeter 6–4, despite "the most continued yelling, hooting, rattle-shaking, and every conceivable annoyance" from the Exeters. Al wrote his sister a glowing account of the victory celebration afterward—the team on a barge escorted by a band and the whole School with horns, proceeding to the Fem Sem, then to the teachers' houses, for speeches, then to the campus for the bonfire. The team was carried on the shoulders of their supporters, then Professor Gile was carried around on student shoulders, and finally there were speeches from the team. "We broke up at midnight after a game of leap-frog and went to bed," he wrote. As for an Andover-Exeter game, "It is for blood and nothing else."[17] The following year—Al's third—came one of his most famous exploits. His pitching arm had been badly strained, and it was agony for him to throw, but since there was no one else on the Andover team who could pitch, he agreed to do his best against the Exeters. Jimmy Sawyer describes his arm hanging "limp as a dishrag" and how he had to lie down and rest the arm on his chest while Andover was at bat. Despite this handicap, Al kept the score down, and the game was finally called on account of rain with Exeter leading 3–2.[18] Following the game there was a riot at the Exeter railway station, which resulted in a suspension of Andover-Exeter contests for two years, so that Al never had another chance at the School's chief rival. But there were other teams to play. During his senior year he reported: "Last Friday we played the Yale Freshmen and beat them easily 13–7. We had a fine day for the game and had a tremendous crowd including the whole Fem. Sem. and a lot of Bradford girls. Then all the Societies had Tally-ho's trimmed with Andover colors and as there were lots of other teams besides, the ground presented quite an animated scene."[19] Though Al would never pitch at college, he was destined to become one of the great infielders of his generation.

Throughout his career at Andover Al Stearns developed a keen interest in girls and availed himself of every opportunity to be with them. In his first year he attended a meeting of the Sewing Society and played games with the girls until nearly nine o'clock.[20] That same year he went to a lecture at the Fem. Sem. He sat in the back near all the girls and came to the conclusion that they were not as good looking as those at his Mother's school in Amherst—"though of course there are some that are prettier," he added gallantly. A second visit changed his opinion somewhat: "There are some daisies down there and don't you forget it."[21] On another occasion the Fem. Sems. came to a boxing match at Phillips. Whenever a boy got hit, there would be a sympathetic "O-H" from all the girls that "sounded very funny and in some cases broke up the boxers for the time."[22] During his senior year Al complained, "The only trouble is that as I have to play ball every afternoon after school, I get almost no chance to see the dear Fem. Sems. This of course is terrible, but owing to the pressure of other duties I don't get much chance to lose flesh over it."[23] Just watching the girls was fun, too, as many an Andover student has discovered. "This afternoon a whole crowd of us went out in the orchard back of the K.O.A. house and watched the Fem. Sems. walking in their grove. . . . We lay around on the grass from the time that church let out until nearly supper time. It is great sport to watch the Fems. sporting around in their gay spring rigs."[24] All this was but prologue to Al's part in the Abbot Commencement festivities during his senior year. Headmistress McKean had asked him to be an usher—presumably because, as Cecil Bancroft's nephew, he would be considered safe. Al was delighted with his assignment; the girls looked "too smooth," he thought, and besides he got cuts from all his recitations. And were not his classmates jealous of him! On Monday evening he ushered for the Draper Prize Speaking and carried out flowers to the contestants. Some had so many that it took three ushers to carry them, he reported. The next morning he stayed in a room back of the stage during the Commencement exercises where there were a lot of girls and "raised cain." After serving as a waiter at the Commencement luncheon, he had the pleasure of sitting at the head of a table of girls. This ended at 2:15, at which time Al and a nameless young lady went out in the grove and stayed until 5:30. At 11:00 o'clock that night Al and a group of friends returned to the Fem. Sem. to serenade the girls, but since they had not rehearsed, they made "a pretty bad mess of it." Whatever Al might have to say about flappers and loose women later in his life, as a student at Andover he had a wholesome interest in the opposite sex.[25]

In the field of unorganized sports Al's passion was coasting. One hears almost nothing in the records of the day of skating, but coasting was a popular pastime. We have already noted the continuing wrangle between the School and the town about coasting on town streets and the amount of ink that the *Phillipian* spilled on the subject. Al Stearns's account of his coasting experiences do much to demonstrate why there was so much undergraduate enthusiasm for the activity. During his first year he writes, "We had some fine sliding yesterday and all the bobs in town were out." The next year he speaks of "one continual ding dong of gongs on different bobs" and how they could start at the corner of Phillips and Main Streets and go all the way to the railway station.[26] The winter of 1888 brought ideal conditions: "The road was all ice and we would start way up by the Graves's and go all the way to the depot. They shut down on our going to the depot, however, so we had to turn off into a side street by the Episcopal church. The whole slide was just a mile and I never went so fast on a rack before. In the evening nearly all racks had headlights so that when a rack was in front of our house, those way down by the church could see it coming."[27] Sometimes coasting was dangerous. "After we had been down several times the P.A.E. bob, which is the largest one, went down with about 20 fellows on it and just before they got to the Fem. Sem. a big dump cart drove out and they tried to turn to one side and just grazed it as it was. In trying to turn out, they got to slewing and just below the Fem. Sem. they struck a tree and went flying in all directions. We hastened to the spot and found one fellow senseless and several others badly bruised. We carried the fellow into the Morrill House close by and soon after he came to and is now all right. The accident put a damper on the rest of us and we decided to quit sliding."[28] But if one did not want to go coasting, there were always snowballs. "We have had some pretty good snowballing during the last 2 or 3 days and at the end of recitation hours the snowballs will be flying like hail out in front of the Academy."[29]

41. *A group of Phillips Academy students ready to go coasting.*

There were other lighter episodes during Al Stearns's stay at Andover. When his family was living in India, they had adopted the Indian custom of wearing pajamas to bed at night, and they continued to do so when they returned to this country. Al naturally brought pajamas with him to Phillips when he enrolled. When he put them on the first night, his roommate, Jimmy Sawyer, who wore the traditional nightshirt, said that it was one of the greatest shocks of his young life. He passed the word around among the other students and Al came in for a good deal of joshing. But when Sawyer hung the pajamas out the window for all the School to see, that was too much. Al had red hair and a temper, and this time he got so angry that he would not speak to Jimmy for three weeks. They finally made up, however, and Al got revenge by emptying a box full of June bugs into Sawyer's bedroom one warm spring night.[30] Al could usually control his temper, but there were occasional flashes. He was Chief of the Phillips Academy Fire Department and took his responsibilities seriously. On one occasion they had been called to help put out a fire in an ink factory nearby. When a group of townies began heckling the Academy firefighters, Al solved the problem by turning the hose on them.[31]

When the time came to make application to college, problems developed. Jimmy Sawyer and most of Al's other friends were all going to Yale, and he naturally wanted to go along with the gang. His Mother, however, would have no New Haven nonsense. The Stearnses were an Amherst family, and particularly in view of the College's generosity in letting Mrs. Stearns use the President's house for her school, Amherst was where Al must go.[32] Sick at heart, Al matriculated at Amherst in the fall of 1890. Fortunately, it was not long before he had no regrets about his choice.

Al's record at Amherst was as distinguished as the one he made at Andover. His Mother wisely insisted that he should room in the College, not at home, and thus avoid some of the disadvantages of being a day student. Though he used to eat meals occasionally at the Convent, he was for the most part a full-fledged boarding student. He was a good scholar, though he just missed making Phi Beta Kappa because he had cut some classes to go on an athletic trip and the professor, outraged at Al's sense of priorities, gave him a low mark. In order to make Phi Beta, *all* marks had to be above a certain level.[33] He joined the Psi Upsilon fraternity early in his career and made many close friends there. One of his happiest associations at Psi U. was with the black janitor, one George Davis, who used to lead the brethren in song on warm spring evenings.[34] Al did not get along with President Merrill Gates. When he was elected Chairman of the Junior Prom during his junior year, President Gates apparently considered this a sign of total depravity. He called Al into his office and told him he had been chosen to represent the College at a Y.M.C.A. conference in Princeton, to take place the same time as the Prom. Al was not a member of the Y.M.C.A. but could see no way of avoiding the assignment. His temper was not improved, however, when he arrived at Princeton to find that the conference had been the previous week. He also got into a bruhaha with the President over the powers of the student Senate, with the result that the Senate was finally abolished.[35] A good friend was Harlan F. Stone, who transferred to Amherst from the Agricultural College after having accidentally roughed up a professor there in a student free-for-all. This friendship was to continue throughout Al's entire career. Like many men of his day at Amherst he valued most highly the teaching of Charles Garman in philosophy. Garman was a chronic invalid who always kept the temperature in his room above eighty and wore a green eye shade. He used a kind of Socratic method to discuss with his students basic philosophical questions after they had studied pamphlets that he had composed and had printed. Garman's class was the last one in the morning, and often, according to Al's account, the students would stay an additional half hour or more to continue the discussion, even though it meant missing their dinners.[36] But again it was in athletics—particularly baseball—that he made his reputation. He got so good that he used to play semiprofessional ball in the summers; and when he graduated, he had many offers to join professional teams. Since he had permanently injured his pitching arm at Andover, he played second base and became one of the great infielders of his generation. One of his favorite baseball stories was of an episode that occurred during a Williams game. An Amherst batter hit a Texas Leaguer that the Williams outfielder dived for. The umpire ruled that the ball had touched the ground first. The outfielder, who knew the Amherst captain, Cornelius Sullivan, came rushing up and said, "Sully, honest to God I caught that ball." Sully looked at him and then to the umpire and asked him to reverse his decision. This was greeted with tremendous applause from the Williams stands. So Sully turned to the spectators and said, "You should all know that that outfielder is the one person in all of Williamstown whose word I would take."[37] Amherst was—and is—a singing college, and Al, who had a deep resonant voice, loved to sing. One friend remembers driving back with Al from a trip and singing continuously for two hundred and seventy-five miles.[38] Despite occasional disappointments, Al's Amherst years were full of rewards, and the relationship he established with the College was to remain strong for the rest of his life.

After graduation Al decided to go into teaching—among others Garman had urged him to do so—and got a job at the Hill School, where he taught history for three years. Mike Sweeney, the famous Director of Athletics at the Hill for many years, had this to say about him:

> He was very popular with the boys, who would go any distance with, or for, him, as he was the personification of tact, wholesome vigor, and good fellowship, an ideal man to lead and influence adolescent boys. He carried this personality to his class room, dormitory, dining room and chapel; a good scholar without the human weaknesses that

some scholars display during the early years; a quite remarkable all-round athlete; a born teacher; and a man who impressed one as having the ability to go a great distance, no matter what he undertook; as he proved subsequently as headmaster of Phillips-Andover Academy.[39]

The high point of his career at the Hill, according to Al, came when a huge rat attacked him in bed one night. In an effort to catch and strangle the animal Al upset his bed, and the noise was terrific. The entire dormitory was soon at hand to witness this titanic struggle and to see Al eventually subdue his attacker.[40] After three years at the Hill, Al's uncle, Cecil Bancroft, turned to him for help. He was beginning to weaken physically, and the chance to have a young assistant whom he knew and trusted must have been appealing. Al was hired to teach history, be Director of Athletics—the first in the School's history—and generally assist the Principal in whatever ways he could. An added inducement must have been the chance to study at the Andover Theological Seminary—Al had a strong rel:gious streak—and to get a degree there. He performed all these duties with distinction during the four years that his uncle was still alive, and when Dr. Bancroft died, his nephew was among the most promising men on the Phillips Academy faculty. As we have seen, after James Hardy Ropes turned down the Principalship, Al was chosen to that position in 1903.

The letters Al wrote to his Mother during that period provide an enlightening picture of his first two years as Principal. Al had always worshiped his Mother, and he was a faithful correspondent. Of his election to the Principalship he wrote: "And in many ways I am glad that it has come about in this gradual way. There is not the overwhelming sense of responsibility that would have come with a sudden and full appointment last year. . . . Last year some of the trustees were in doubt and had I been appointed then some people might have felt that Sawyer and perhaps one or two others had been over-zealous in my behalf. Now those who were formerly in doubt have expressed themselves as my warmest supporters. They have watched my work and have been satisfied with it and that fact alone gives me great confidence. The faculty and boys too seem to be wholly with me."[41] Discipline cases always bothered Al. While dealing with several, he wrote, "I feel like the weather (rainy and dark)."[42] And there were many problems with Abbot. He thought that his training at the Convent would serve him in good stead. In this case Abbot had expelled a girl who had gone off with a Phillips boy, and Al was afraid he would have to act too.[43] Sometimes he felt despair: "after reaching home after midnight, I began another similar session at 8:15 the next morning, a session which has lasted throughout the entire day and so it has gone on ever since. . . . parents, heartbreaking letters and the boys themselves. At times I have felt like taking to the woods and giving up the whole business. I don't wonder that Dr. Bancroft aged early. As for myself I feel 10 years older than I did a week ago."[44] A few days later he concluded, "I realize

42. *Alfred Ernest Stearns, Ninth Principal of Phillips Academy, at about the time he became Principal in 1903.*

. . . that Dr. Bancroft was right when he said that a school master lives on the edge of a volcano."[45] A Principal could never tell where his duties might take him: "Today I spent the whole day in Salem hanging around the County Court House waiting for the case to be tried against some of our boys for ringing false fire alarms."[46] Not long afterward he spent "two entire days. . . . thwarting the attempts of one of our boys to run away to Japan. I had explicit orders by telegraph from the boy's father to seize the boy's goods and to cut off all means of securing income. This I did, stopping payment on a loan he had just negotiated and appropriating about $500.00 worth of jewelry, watches, scarf pins, studs which the boy was endeavoring to sell. The youthful explorer accepted the situation gracefully."[47] At Commencement time there were additional burdens: "To add to my other duties I have been obliged to drill our Commencement speakers as we have no regular men in elocution this year."[48]

There were compensations as well. When the Head of Hampton Institute visited the School in 1904, he thought that there had never been a time when the atmosphere and general tone had been so good.[49] That summer another one of the Commons buildings burned down, despite all the fire department could do. The Reverend C. C. Carpenter "remarked that the Lord had done his best to help us out, but that the fire company had interfered."[50] When School started the following September, Al wrote his Mother of his concern that all the places be taken. They had admitted enough to fill the School, but there were anxious times until all the boys actually showed up. His burden that fall was made heavier by a history teacher who had left at the last minute to accept a better position. Al had to teach two classes and make trips to Cambridge to find a replacement.[51] Exeter that year had the largest school in its history. Al explained their success as a result of a scholarship program that was twice as large as Andover's, no entrance examinations, and a special lower school for younger boys, which provided special treatment for them.[52] Al was particularly pleased with the New Vesper Service that, at long last, he was allowed to introduce. No more would the Phillips boy have to sit through an hour-long sermon from a Seminary Professor on Sunday afternoon. The new service was one half hour in length, had plenty of music and a short talk, and began at 5:15, so that the boys could have almost all Sunday afternoon to themselves and go directly from Vespers to supper.[53] The landlady problem was still a time-consumer. Al called on one lady who was downcast because she had no boys at all. He suggested that if she put in a furnace and a bathroom, she would get some.[54] Along with his other concerns, he worked with the undergraduates to establish a student council.

At times his multifarious duties almost overwhelmed him:

If only I could work without interruption . . . but day and night I must break off again and again to interview a boy, listen to a land-lady's complaint or cheer a parent until any trend of definite thought that may once have existed in my brain is sadly broken . . . I don't wonder that Dr. Bancroft used to say often that when he accepted his position here, he gave up all idea of gratifying his longing to pursue a literary or scholarly life.[55]

So he went on, breaking up a Halloween march to Abbot by the Phillips boys, entertaining forty undergraduates and twelve Abbot girls on Thanksgiving evening, and journeying to Exeter to confer with Principal Amen about lowering faculty salaries.[56] His baptism was of fire.

If Al Stearns thought that his life as Principal would become easier with the passage of time, he was sadly mistaken. During his entire thirty years as Principal the demands on him were unending—indeed they could well have broken a weaker man—and if the problems he had to face changed but little, neither did he. When he retired in 1933, he was very much the same kind of man who assumed office in 1903. He had inherited from his uncle Cecil Bancroft a strong School and dynamic program for future development. He considered his major task the completion of the Bancroft program, rather than educational innovation, and he remained dedicated to the Bancroft principles throughout.

A difficult problem faced Al even before he had been formally elected Principal: the "Princeton Cribbing Case." In the days before the College Board Examinations each college gave its own, and if there were a large enough number of candidates, they held them at individual schools rather than a central place. In the late spring of 1902 plans were completed to administer Princeton examinations at Andover. The candidates had been notified, a Harvard professor engaged as proctor, and the papers received from Princeton and locked in the School safe. The night before the exam a group of Andover undergraduates, most of them not even seniors, waited on Al Stearns and said they wished to take the exams. Al explained that there were not enough papers, that they had not registered, and that they were therefore ineligible. Much to his dismay he received the following morning a telegram from Princeton that read: "Admit all candidates. Divide papers when necessary." The Harvard professor was outraged at this development but was finally prevailed upon to go ahead with the exam administration. After about an hour he was back in Al's office in a fury. "It's a damnable farce," he said. "Two to five boys huddled together working on the same paper. Not one of them could help cribbing if he tried." Again the professor was persuaded to return to his post, and eventually the examination was completed. When the papers were sent to Princeton, a strong letter of protest accompanied them—a letter to which the Princeton authorities never replied. To add insult to injury, shortly after this the New York *Daily Tribune* printed a story recounting how twenty-two out of thirty-one Andover boys had been rejected at Princeton for cribbing on their entrance examinations. At this point Al Stearns, who was never one to avoid a confrontation, hopped a train to Princeton, but the Registrar and the President were both out of town. He finally found a member of the Admissions Committee and presented his case to him. The only result of Al's trip was a short statement given to the press by the Princeton authorities that perhaps the Andover boys were not wholly at fault in the episode. But this retraction received little attention, and Al was snowed with protests from friends of Phillips Academy wondering what had happened. Finally a full statement of the Andover case was published, and things died down somewhat. The next year Phillips Academy refused to take any responsibility for the administration of the Princeton entrance exams, but they agreed to allow a Princeton professor to come to the school for that purpose. One might think that Princeton would have tried to reform the procedure, but nothing of the sort happened. The professor who arrived from Old Nassau was a cultured Southern gentleman whose solution to the proctoring problem was to put all the students on their honor, as was done at Princeton. He then settled down to read the newspaper. When Al Stearns's curiosity could restrain him no longer, he went over to the examination room to see how things were going. He found an unconcerned proctor, widespread use of trots, and generally a repetition of the previous year's experience—but with one big difference. This year no one at Princeton suggested that the Andover papers were not in perfectly good order. The whole episode illustrated the many difficulties that accompanied entrance examinations by individual colleges; once the College Board was established, most of the trouble faded away.[57]

Like his uncle before him, Al Stearns was constantly concerned with the problems of feeding and housing the boys properly. A great step forward in the boarding problem came in 1902 when Bulfinch Hall, the old gymnasium that had burned in 1896, was remodeled to serve as a Commons. Still, the new dining hall could not accommodate the whole school and a substantial number continued to board in private homes, some happily, some unhappily. At the start of Al's term, prices in these private boarding houses varied from $3.50 to $7.00 a week, and $4.00 a week in the dining hall. One of Al's first assignments when he returned to Andover was to board for a week at Major Marland's, in what is now Clement House. The Major had a $5.00 table and a $3.50 table. The latter complained that they were getting scraps from the higher-priced one. After a week's eating there, Al agreed, and the Major was prevailed upon to shape up. There were seldom any complaints about the highest-priced tables; thus Al was surprised one day to have a group of boys come to him with the accusation that the landlady was keeping all the white meat in the kitchen when goose was served, and giving the boys only the dark meat. Al never got tired of telling this story at alumni gatherings. Housing was another matter. While progress had been made toward having all the boys in school dormitories, with faculty supervision, there was still a long way to go. In 1900–01 out of 428 boys, 80 lived in the English and Latin Commons and 47 in the new cottages; 10 were day students; and 291 were scattered around in 48 private homes. The idea that the School could find 48 ladies who could ride herd on 291 undergraduates was obviously unrealistic, and because a landlady who was conscientious about the rules was liable to wind up without any tenants, the problem was that much more difficult. The location of the rooming houses was another important consideration; those near Abbot Academy were very popular, as were those on the outskirts of town, where expeditions to Lawrence could be undertaken with impunity. The boys were often heartless in teasing some of the older landladies. An aging spinster who was in charge of Pease House had an unreasoning fear of fire. When her boys learned this, they managed to produce several conflagrations in the house, on one occasion burning a vast amount of toilet paper up the chimney. In another house there was a removable register in the kitchen ceiling. The boys used to remove it and then send down a hook on a rope, catch the teakettle, pull it up and empty it, and then put it back on the stove, much to the mystification of the couple that ran the place. But it was the lack of adequate supervision that troubled Al the most. One house was reputed to have "the best stocked bar north of Boston." Others were convenient starting places for parties in Lawrence. With the coming of the street-car line, a new headache developed for Al—the "chippies." These ladies came over from Lawrence on the trolley and attempted to strike up conversations with Phillips boys. The chances are that in the great majority of cases nothing very serious was intended. One alumnus told Dr. Stearns some years after his graduation: "You know, Mr. Stearns, there were mighty few fellows in our time who really meant anything serious in fooling with those 'chippies.' They liked to chin with them, jolly them, and thought they were getting a thrill out of it. Once in a while if a more daring fellow slipped his arm around one of them, he thought he had got a big kick out of it. That's all there really was to it. But nowadays, when a fellow can squeeze and pet a Prof.'s daughter on the family sofa what's the use of looking for trash in the streets? The lure is gone." Al, however, was not content to accept this easy explanation of the problem. He and the Faculty set out to drive the chippies off the Hill. It was made clear to the boys that even talking to a chippie meant instant expulsion. Then Al began to chase them off in person on weekend evenings. On occasion he got help from the boys. One group lured a group of young ladies close to the Latin Commons and then poured the contents of ash cans and slop pails on them. Another group got whips and gave the girls a whipping. From then on, things improved, but like so many other problems, their solution had to wait the completion of the school dormitory program. Once all the boys were housed under Faculty supervision, problems of discipline were drastically reduced.[58]

A regular part of Al Stearns's duties as headmaster was breaking up undergraduate riots and fracases of various kinds. Al was a sensitive and wise disciplinarian in dealing with cases of individual boys, and he soon developed a reputation in handling problems that involved the undergraduates en masse. The first fall that he was at Andover, in 1897, he was not a full-fledged member of the Faculty. He lived with his old friend Jimmy Sawyer and his wife on Abbot Street and was not expected to enforce school discipline. Yet he wanted to help his Uncle Cecil Bancroft, and before long he was in the thick of the fray. Andover won the Exeter football game that year, and the usual celebration occurred after the contest. Much to Al's surprise, he found that most of the undergraduates vanished immediately after the celebration; they had not returned to their rooms, and he could not find out where they had gone. Dog-tired after a long day, Al repaired to the Sawyers and went to bed. His head had hardly touched the pillow, however, before the most horrid sounds of revelry were heard from the street outside as about two hundred Phillips Academy students danced and sang and stumbled their way back to their rooms on the Hill. Al decided that he was in no position to interfere with this saturnalia at the time, but later he used his position as coach to elicit from the boys just what had been going on. It turned out that several years earlier a group of adventurous souls had decided that the regular victory celebration after the Exeter game was not enough and had instituted the practice of repairing to Pomp's Pond, with a keg of beer, where they continued to celebrate. These festivities had proved such a success that as time went on, they were enlarged, with recruits from the town and other friends of merriment being included. The number of kegs of beer had increased in proportion. Al knew that if he turned this information over to the Faculty, the result would be a raid on one of the parties, the apprehension and expulsion of a lot of boys, and general bad publicity for the School. Fortunately for Al there was in the School at the time an extremely popular Texan who was a football player and a born leader. Al went to this boy with his problem, told him that Andover graduates were unwilling to send younger brothers to the School because of these orgies, explained the unhappy alternative of Faculty action, and asked him to clean the whole thing up. The boy demurred at first, explaining that he was one of the ringleaders in the Pomp's Pond parties, but he was finally won over. He asked Al if he could get a few of his "jock" friends to help him and also suggested that few school rules might be broken in the process. Al promised to give him full support, and for the rest of the year nothing was heard of these revels. Al did not know what his deputies were doing, nor did he try to find out. Late in spring he asked the Texan how things were going. "I guess we've finished the job," the boy replied. He said he and his friends had broken up party after party by pretending to be police, and that the participants were getting tired of the whole thing. The climax had occurred a short time before when six die-hards made a final try. The Texan and his henchmen had driven them away, and then to prove their point, had carried the beer keg all the way back to the Hill and placed it on Al Stearns's porch, much as a head might have been placed on a pike to dramatize an execution. And so the Pomp's Pond parties became a thing of the past—for the time being at least—and Al Stearns began the practice of enlisting undergraduate aid in the solution of school problems that he was to use many times again in the future.[59]

Hazing was something that Al refused to condone; on one occasion he used a novel way of breaking up a hazing party. One evening Jimmy Graham, the Chemistry teacher, called up Al and said a hazing party had just passed by his dormitory. Just why Jimmy could not do something about it himself is not clear; perhaps he had to stay in his dormitory. Al promptly high-tailed it over to the designated area and saw a procession of "preps," or new boys, led by several hazers. Rather than drive them all away, Al chose to join the procession as a "prep" and marched along with the rest. The "preps" were soon ordered to kneel down and "Pull up grass." When they obediently tugged at the grass, the order was stern: "With your teeth." At this point Al stood up suddenly and in that deep bass voice of his demanded of the hazers, "What are you doing here?" This move struck consternation into the hearts of the tormenters, who rushed away, tripping over rocks and logs, but not before Al had recognized one. The poor "preps" were completely at a loss, not knowing whether this was part of the hazing process. Al gently told them to go back to their rooms, and the exercises were closed. The hazer whom Al had recognized lived in fear and trembling for the next several weeks, but Al never turned him in; he thought he had probably suffered enough.[60]

In the 1890's the *Phillipian* had remarked that the annual cost of replacing broken window panes in the Commons was greater than the value of the buildings themselves. One of Al Stearns's early assignments was to do something about the problem. It had been exacerbated by the opening of Bancroft Hall right across the street, with its relatively luxurious accouterments. For one thing, Bancroft had toilets and showers, both unheard of in the Commons, and the Commons boys soon began to "borrow" them, all the while dubbing the Bancroft inhabitants "Gold Coasters." The latter retaliated by pulling up the Commons pump, and an unconscionable number of window panes were broken. Again Al decided to enlist undergraduate help. The football captain lived in the Commons, and it was to him that Al turned. It was finally decided to create a "Commons Glass Committee," with the football captain as chairman and two husky athletic types as aides. The committee was to have a free hand in dealing with the problem, and their existence and powers were duly announced to the student body in daily chapel. Returning from Boston late one night, Al was startled to find on his desk a note from the football captain asking him to come and see him at once. Late as it was, Al decided that he had better support his deputy. When he arrived at the boy's room, it was to be greeted with the news that the committee had had a very important meeting and had voted to expel one boy, put another on probation, and force a third to leave the Commons and room elsewhere. The chairman explained that the expelled boy was a "rotter" who had broken all kinds of rules; if the Faculty knew half of what he was doing, they would fire him. The boy on probation needed it to get straightened out, and the third simply did not belong in the Commons. As may be imagined, Al was horrified at the summary action, but after sleeping on it, he decided to back up his committee. It was not long before an irate father appeared on the scene, demanding to know what kind of School this was where the undergraduates rather than the Faculty expelled boys. Al handled him like a baby. He said he had not asked the boys for the reasons why they had expelled his son, but he was sure they would give them to him if he were to ask. As it stood, he told the father, there was nothing in the record against the son, and he could withdraw without prejudice. If he forced the issue, the chances were that damning evidence against the boy would come out and the Faculty would expel him. The father left in a huff, but a few days later he wrote that he would drop the matter. In the meantime the "Commons Glass Committee" kept at its work, and the number of broken windows decreased markedly. It would be only a short time before the problem was permanently solved by the removal of the Commons buildings lock, stock, and barrel.[61]

In the days before the development of an adequate system of athletics, and with the School divided into four clubs, class contests provided a means of letting off a lot of surplus energy. Shortly after he arrived on the campus, Al Stearns was asked by his Uncle Bancroft to inspect a class game. The Principal was well aware that these confrontations tended to get a bit rough, and he wished to be reassured that things were under control. When Al arrived on the field, he found the air blue from the smoke of exploding firecrackers hurled at the players by the respective oppositions. In addition, a small cannon was installed near first base. Loaded with grass and dirt, from time to time it added to the hazards of trying to play on the diamond itself. Any base runner had to bury his face in his arms to protect his eyes, if not his life. As Al watched, a boy was hit in the side of the head by a firecracker and collapsed in a heap, stunned. Fortunately, he soon recovered, but Al had seen enough. On his recommendation the Faculty voted to outlaw all explosives at class games. If the Faculty thought that was the end of the matter, however, they were sadly mistaken. At the next contest rotten eggs replaced firecrackers. It was not long before all the contestants were dripping with egg slime. This operation proved to be no laughing matter; one boy, hit squarely in the eye with an egg, lost his sight in that organ for life. Once again the Faculty moved, outlawing the use of eggs at class games; but the boys' resources were by no means exhausted. At the next contest the field was very wet, making possible the use of mud. As in past fracases, all the players were soon covered, and the spectators had as much fun as ever. Once compulsory athletics for all were introduced, much of the reason for class contests disappeared. A final practice associated with class games was the kidnapping of important players, in hopes of preventing them from playing. Al Stearns spent a great deal of time trying to prevent this from happening, and on one occasion drove out of one Commons building a large number of boys who were bent on kidnapping the class baseball captain, who lived on the top floor. Actually, however, he arrived too late to save the boy from his fate and later discovered that the captain had been locked in a barn on Salem Street. But his supporters managed to rescue him just in time for the game the next day. Shortly afterward, class games were banned.

Alfred Ernest Stearns not only developed techniques for dealing with the undergraduates *en masse*; he showed unusual sensitivity in handling individual cases. A good example of this talent was the way he dealt with the son of a prominent Washington politician. The first confrontation between Al and this boy occurred when Al surprised him leading a group of preps on a hazing party. Recognizing Al, the boy turned tail and ran, with the Principal, having shed his raincoat, in hot pursuit. The race proved to be a dead heat until suddenly the boy rose unexpectedly in the air and fell at Al's feet. Unable to stop, Al fell on top of him, at which point they both burst out laughing. It turned out that the boy had been done in by a tennis court net that he had not been able to see in the darkness. Al suggested that they return to the preps, and then proceeded to introduce each prep to the would-be tormentor. Everyone returned to bed. But that was just the beginning. At this time the School had been embarrassed by a large number of false fire alarms from boxes on Academy property; things had got so bad that the town fire department said they would answer no more alarms from the School area until a second alarm had been sounded. One night another false alarm was sounded from the box on the corner of Main and Morton Streets. Unfortunately for the alarm-sounder, as he was running away from the box, he lost his cap, and when Al was shown it by the police, he immediately recognized it as belonging to the prominent politician's son. Al decided on a novel procedure in dealing with the case. The next morning in Chapel he gave a talk on the evils of false alarms and then proceded to describe the kind of boy who would do such a thing. His description tallied precisely with that of the suspected culprit. After Chapel the boy came up to Al in a rage and demanded why he had been singled out for such treatment. All the undergraduates had known who was being described. When Al informed him that the police had his cap in their possession, he collapsed. By chance a trolley car was passing at just this time. The boy rushed out of Al's office, boarded it, and disappeared. The problem then entered a new phase; Al had to make special trips to Washington and New York to confer with the parents, and he was bombarded by various politicians, including Henry Cabot Lodge, pleading that he let the boy off and spare his parents the disgrace of arrest. The father in particular tried to impress on Al what a disaster it would be for his political career. Al held firm, pointing out, however, that the boy had committed a civil offense and had not broken a School rule, and promising that if the boy would clear himself with the local police, he could return to School. A few days later the boy appeared with a statement from the police that he had cleared himself and was duly reinstated. It would have been much easier to expel the boy in the first place, but Al's imaginative procedure managed to salvage him.[62]

Al showed a different kind of sensitivity in connection with the tragic case of a boy who was accidentally shot and killed. It seems hard to believe, but early in the century the undergraduates were allowed to take pistols to pre-Exeter game rallies and fire off blank cartridges to add to the general enthusiasm. The morning after such a rally, one boy dropped in to see a friend who had a pistol. How one chamber came to be loaded with a real bullet was never explained, but while the visitor was fooling with it, it went off and the bullet severed his jugular vein. Al Stearns and the school physician, Doc Page, were called to the scene immediately and were soon joined by a local physician, but all their efforts were in vain, and in a few minutes the boy died. Al soon realized that there was nothing to be done for the boy who had died and turned his attention to the owner of the pistol, who was wandering around in a state of shock. Al called on some of his dormitory friends to stay with him, and one of them gave up the Exeter game that afternoon to take him on a long walk. Soon the grieving parents of the dead boy arrived, and arrangements were made to have the body sent to the family's home. Before the parents returned, Al told the father that he wanted to ask a favor of him. The broken-hearted owner of the pistol had a new and terrible burden to carry for the rest of his life, and Al hoped that the father would be willing to talk to him. The father turned him down flat. His boy had been killed and he was not about to communicate with the person responsible for his son's death. Al continued to plead with him, pointing out how desperately the boy needed help—how he was, after all, the son's best friend. At last the father relented, and the boy was brought in, "limp and white-faced." When the father saw him, he burst into tears and took the boy in his arms, sobbing "My boy, my poor, poor boy." Later the dead boy's family invited the pistol owner to visit and help fill the gap caused by the death of their son. Though Al could be a stern disciplinarian, his action in this case indicates that he had many sides.[63]

Some of the more difficult and time-consuming disciplinary cases involved Andover undergraduates in trouble with the police. In the course of his career as Principal, Al Stearns spent many long hours trying to get his charges out of hock. During one of the class games, the usual amount of extracurricular activities had taken place, involving, among other things, the exploding of a large number of firecrackers.. One boy with a firecracker sputtering in hand looked hurriedly for a place to deposit it and spied a mailbox nearby. Without thinking, he opened the lid, deposited his firecracker, and ran off. In a few seconds an explosion occurred, and the top of the mailbox went flying off into space. On this occasion the police moved promptly, discovered the perpetrator, and arrested him. The case was all the more serious because it involved a federal offense, and the boy was summoned to appear before the Postal authorities in Boston. Al accompanied him, and when he and the boy entered the hearing room, Al's heart sank, for he saw before him a group of frowning officials headed by a big, burly Irishman who looked particularly foreboding. As the testimony of the Andover police was presented, the tribunal nodded with apparent approval of the case that was being presented. When the evidence had been completed, the Andover police and the boy were dismissed, but Al was asked to meet with the Chief Postal Inspector in his office. Al expected to be bawled out for not disciplining his boys properly, but much to his surprise, when he reached the Chief's office, the official burst out laughing. By way of explanation the Chief told Al that when he was first appointed, he had promised to be really tough and to bear down on anyone who violated any postal laws. One day he was called by the Cambridge police and told that three Harvard boys had blown up a mailbox. He ordered them brought before him immediately and prepared to throw the book at them. Much to his amazement, when the three were brought in, one of them turned out to be his own son. He immediately revised his tough speech and wound up putting the three on probation. The Chief said he was reminded of that incident in this case; he knew the boy meant no wrong, but he suggested that Al let him sweat for a few days before telling him that the charges would be dropped if he kept out of trouble from then on. Al followed his advice and kept the boy in suspense for some time. The boy was later to say that he had sweat more in those few days than he had in all the remaining days of his life.[64]

In dealing with disciplinary cases—as indeed in all he did—Alfred Ernest Stearns was primarily a moralist, for whom religious and moral training was at the heart of any successful education. He came from a long line of clergymen, and as a child had received a thorough grounding in Calvinist religion—family prayers, the saying of grace, regular church attendance, and all the rest. During his first years at Andover he attended the Theological Seminary and, as noted, earned a degree in Divinity. He did not think much of the course of study, but his Uncle Cecil Bancroft assured him that a graduate degree was worth getting.[65] Throughout the rest of his life he strove to transmit to his boys the moral precepts that he had learned and to give them the same exposure to religion that he had received. That he was strongly dedicated to these aims was clear to anyone who heard him conduct morning chapel at Andover. Generations of Andover graduates will never forget that tall, imposing figure praying. Eyes tight shut, that rich sonorous voice filling the building, he asked that undergraduates be kept from the things that were base and sordid in life and be led to the things that were pure and good and true. He reinforced his points by kicking the bottom of the pulpit. Al saw all of life as a struggle between the forces of good and evil, with temptation ever present. Duty and discipline were, he believed, the keys to the good life. In essence he was a. nineteenth century man, the last of the Calvinist Principals, whose outlook was essentially Victorian. Samuel Phillips would have approved of him, for he accepted most if not all of the religious tenets in the School's constitution. Given this background and these beliefs, it is hardly surprising that he thought moral education of prime importance.

"Education is commonly classified under three headings," he wrote, "primary, secondary and higher. . . . to these three add a fourth . . . the highest education is religion."[66] "The country's greatest menace is not the uneducated masses but clever, intellectual crooks who mold the masses to their will,"[67] and only too often the "intellectual crooks" had little interest in either religion or morality. One gathers a clear picture of Al Stearns's attitude toward religion from correspondence he had with President George Olds of Amherst about the question of compulsory chapel at that institution. The college paper had polled the undergraduates and found that 424 were against compulsory chapel, 16 were for, and 1 was indifferent.[68] As a member of the Alumni Religion Committee at Amherst, Al wrote President Olds:

> I have a strong conviction that the feeling against compulsory chapel is not nearly so deep as we are sometimes led to believe. The religion element has played a small part in [required weekday chapel services], as we all know. In many institutions the services have been nothing short of a travesty on religion, and the boys have naturally rebelled. Where the services have been kept on a truly spiritual level, I have never been able to find any vigorous opposition on the part of the student body as a whole.

He continued with bitterness:

> Not only would there be a loss on the religious side, but there would

be a distinct loss to the morale and spirit of the college. The thing that has troubled me most . . . is that the pronounced and pugnacious agitation against compulsory religious exercises has come almost wholly from a conviction [sic] of clever and noisy Hebrews, plus a group composed of the type . . . who have practically no religious background themselves and are like iconoclasts.

He concluded:

If we had to give up religion here, I should feel that we had knocked the bottom completely out of all that is of prime interest and concern to me in connection with the responsibilities and opportunities that I face in my job as Headmaster.[69]

On another occasion he asserted that if he could select only two courses for a school curriculum, they would be on bible and public speaking.[70]

One can get a clear understanding of Al Stearns's basic beliefs and attitudes from a little book that he wrote in 1923 entitled *The Challenge of Youth*. Youth, Al thought, had a dual nature—there was always a struggle going on in young people between temptation and vision, between shame and grandeur. Yet the potential for youth was unlimited if only the institutions of society could maintain the old virtues, the old discipline. The question was, Al believed, whether the "agencies which civilization has developed to aid in this eternal fight for virile and self-controlled manhood and womanhood" were still strong.[71] It was Al's considered opinion that the influence of the home was on the decline, that parents were failing to instill in their children the old discipline, the old respect for virtue. He was particularly distressed when parents attempted to prevent legitimate punishments from being meted out to their children. If parents were failing their children, the church and religion were not doing much better. Gone were family prayers, the saying of grace, the reading of the Bible. Indeed for most youth the Bible had become a closed book. What Al called "Modern Substitutes" for the home and church were positive forces for evil. He quoted with approval a statement by "Dr. Max G. Schlapp, Criminologist" that blamed the increase in inmates in insane asylums on "the motion picture and the motor car, almost exclusively" as well as "the general jazz environment which surrounds the race." The titles of currently popular movies simply reinforced the point: "Why Trust Your Husband? The Fruits of Desire. The Woman of Pleasure. His Temporary Wife. Playthings of Passion. His Bridal Night."[72] A new and alarming pattern of social behavior had developed among young people. "Joyrides," "petting parties," and all-night dances seemed to be the order of the day, and anyone who protested these activities was sure to be labeled a "Grundy" or a "Grouch." Though it seems unlikely that Al had ever read John Dewey, he does not hesitate to excoriate the new approach to education—"self-expression, self-realization, self-determination—what their advocates refuse to tell us is that in the last analysis these all spell Selfishness, and with a large 'S.' "[73] This new permissive attitude was not limited to education. "The classic expression of an old-time railroad magnate, 'The public be damned,' represents an all-too-common attitude of mind in these later days. Woman shouts for her 'rights'; labor joins the chorus . . . and the sterner sex [a favorite Stearns expression] screams for its 'personal liberties.' Seldom, in all this noisy turmoil, do we hear the inspiring words 'duty,' 'service,' 'sacrifice.' "[74] Finally, Al was dismayed at the change in the position of women in society. Today, instead of finding women serving as "an ideal, as an inspiration, as a challenge," one sees the "flapper"—hard-drinking, promiscuous, with painted face and rolled stockings. And he closed on a somber note:

> experience teaches us only too plainly that youth must have the help of its elders if it is to reach the high goal that these visions challenge us to seek. It is our duty and it is our privilege as well to face this task and accept this responsibility. We are not doing it today.[75]

Al Stearns's conservative view of society was reflected in his political beliefs as well. He was unreserved in his enthusiasm for General Leonard Wood, certainly a conservative figure in his day. His admiration for Calvin Coolidge was equally strong, partly because he and Coolidge had been at Amherst together and had worked together on various Amherst committees. In 1926 arrangements were made to have Sherwood Eddy, son of a popular visiting preacher, D. Brewer Eddy, come to the school to speak, presumably on some religious topic. Al was dismayed when he was offered a choice of three topics "What I Saw in Russia," "Russia—A Warning and a Challenge," and "Bolshevism and Fascism—The Danger Zones of Europe."[76] Al wrote to the father:

> I did not realize for a minute, when I accepted your suggestion that Sherwood should speak to the boys this fall, that he was going to talk on Russia and the Russian situation. Not that I object to knowing more about that big and complicated problem, but I do feel that the complications are so many and so far not fully disentangled that it is a risky topic to try to present to school boys. Were the audience made up of college students, even, I should feel very different about it. The boys are [so] apt to be interested and influenced by striking phases or phrases that I honestly question the wisdom of using this topic for the meeting suggested. If Sherwood is going to use it, I can only say that I feel justified in asking him to treat it with the utmost mildness, regardless of his own personal feelings.[77]

He went on to say that there was a member of the faculty who was apt to be "a bit hysterical" on the subject. It was finally decided that Sherwood should take on the Faculty after his talk to the boys. Despite Al's fears the whole evening was a great success. "Even our most rabid conservative pronounced Sherwood's philosophy sound," Al wrote after the talk.[78] Nor did he approve of people who tampered with national stereotypes. He was outraged at Rupert Hughes's life of George Washington and at Sinclair Lewis's *Elmer Gantry*. In a sermon delivered at Cornell in 1931, he referred to these authors as "buzzards hovering over some new-found piece of carrion." Lewis either ignored or was oblivious of Al's blast, which was reported in the New York *Times*, but Hughes hit back. After defending his treatment of Washington, he wrote, "Of course, it is to be expected that anyone who prates of Christ and of charity in judgment is using this as a preface to savage injustice and falsehood, and you have conformed to type. I have made few efforts to answer the many lying misrepresentations of my spoken and written references to Washington, but I have yielded to the impulse to inform you that your assault on my work and my character is viciously false both as to my motive and my publication."[79]

When it came to supporting his Faculty in the exercise of their Civil Rights, Al Stearns's record leaves a good deal to be desired. A striking

43. *Bernard M. Allen, Instructor in Latin at Phillips Academy from 1894 to 1919.*

example was the case of Bernard Allen, a Classics teacher at the Academy who became involved in a strike in neighboring Lawrence.[80] Allen was one of five brothers born to a prosperous contractor in Walpole, Massachusetts, all of them independent thinkers. The oldest brother took over his father's contracting business in Walpole; another, Philip, went to Andover and Yale, became President of the Bird Roofing Company in Walpole, and was eventually a member of the Board of the Federal Reserve Bank in Boston; a third devoted himself to the stock market, made a great deal of money, and finally came a cropper with Kreuger and Toll; a fourth was a distinguished engineer at Clark University. Bernard took a different course. He attended Phillips Academy, graduating in 1888, went on to Yale, where he graduated four years later, and after a year of teaching at a school in Newbury, New York, joined the Andover Faculty. From the start he proved himself an effective teacher and a dedicated scholar who demanded precision from his students. No one ever seems to have questioned his competence as an instructor. Yet his position as a teacher at Phillips Academy was always insecure because of the political beliefs that he held. Just how these beliefs developed is difficult to say; certainly he was a "sport" in the family, where the other members were conservatives. In 1912 he became an enthusiastic supporter of Theodore Roosevelt and the Bull Moose Party. When that movement failed, he moved forward to become a Socialist. It should be remembered that the Socialists polled over one million votes in the Election of 1912. At one point in his career, Bernard Allen had "I.R.R." put on his license plates, indicating his support for Initiative, Referendum, and Recall. Though it is difficult to prove the fact conclusively, the presumption is strong that Allen was the only Socialist in the Andover community. There seems to be no question that his unorthodox beliefs made the administration uncomfortable. After he had taught at Phillips Academy for twenty-five years, he still had no permanent appointment, and his salary remained well below that of his contemporaries. Between 1908 and 1918 his stipend went up only five hundred dollars, from fifteen hundred to two thousand. A characteristic salary letter was written to him by Dr. Stearns in 1911; it spoke of a possible "readjustment of our teaching force" in the near future and thus the impossibility of giving "definite assurance at this time of a permanent position for the future."[81]

Despite the fact that Allen was suffering financially for his beliefs, he continued to teach at Andover until an episode in 1919 that was to change his whole life. At the end of World War I working conditions in American factories were difficult at best. Inflation was cutting into real wages, soldiers were returning to the labor force, and foreign competition had revived. Lawrence, Massachusetts, was feeling the full effects of all these forces. The labor leaders in the city determined to push for a forty-eight hour week, instead of the old fifty-four hour one, but to demand the same pay they had received previously. The mill owners, during a slack period, were glad to cut the working week to forty-eight hours, but they balked at giving the same pay. The result was a strike that started in January and was to last well into the spring.[82] There could be no question where Bernard Allen's sympathies lay. He believed that William Wood, President of the American Woolen Company, "was one of the greatest menaces to New England Industrial life."[83] Intent upon seeing the strike at first hand, he went to Lawrence on Sunday, 16 February 1919. Here is his account of what hapepned:

> In Lawrence, four miles away, a strike of textile workers was going on, caused by the refusal to grant a demand for an increase in wages which would make up only in part a much larger increase in the cost of living. This demand, it was clearly shown, could easily have been granted without appreciable effect on profits, and in fact, was granted a few months later. It would be difficult to find a strike carried on with less violence on the part of the strikers than this, or one conducted with greater moderation. . . .
>
> In company with a small group from Boston, led by Mr. Rotzel, I visited Lawrence one Sunday morning. Our purpose was to show our sympathy for the strikers, and to learn as much as possible about the situation at first hand. I had also in mind the possibility of trying to remove some common misunderstandings by writing to the press. . . .
>
> Under conditions somewhat different, publicity might justifiably have been sought for the sake of calling attention to the fundamental principles of civil liberty involved. . . . At this time, however, I could see no advantage in publicity and did not seek it in any way. The wide publicity which followed came solely from the utterly unprovoked attack upon us by mounted police, who dispersed us with blows as we were quietly leaving the railroad station.[84]

The Lawrence *Eagle-Tribune*'s account, while generally substantiating that of Bernard Allen's, adds some interesting details:

> . . . the police made it very evident to the visitors that their presence here could be well dispensed with and that Lawrence could quite ably adjust her differences without their help. The crowds were kept moving by the police and there was considerable excitement. . . .
>
> Instructor Bernard M. Allen of Phillips Andover Academy had an exciting time when he was put to rout by the policemen who broke up crowds in the vicinity of the depot. Mr. Allen had a card inscribed "48–54" in his hat and when chased by the police ran up the Post Office steps and later toward the transfer station where he boarded a car for Andover.
>
> When interviewed last evening Mr. Allen said that he came to

Lawrence to investigate for himself the conditions here. He admitted having a card in his hat and said that he wore it because he was in sympathy with all who endeavor to secure better wages and better working conditions. "At no time did I hesitate at all to follow the directions of the police officer or attempt to answer him back. I simply waited and tried to find out what he wanted me to do," said Mr. Allen.[85]

The story in the *Eagle-Tribune* did Allen in. It was widely copied, and soon letters, mostly protesting Allen's behavior, began arriving on Al Stearns's desk. Later in the week the New York *Times* produced an editorial entitled "Bolshevism in the Schools." It read in part:

Are the preparatory seminaries of America to be nurseries of its overthrow?

A teacher of an old eighteenth century school, Phillips Andover Academy in Massachusetts, descends upon the industrial city of Lawrence, as a "Comrade of the World", crying for a strike, and imagining in his vealy way, that it is a clever and noble thing to associate himself with the forces of trouble.[86]

Occasionally Al received a letter sympathetic to Bernard Allen. One man wrote, "they [the police] made the Goddess of Liberty feel for an hour or so last Sunday that Lawrence officials were no friends of hers."[87] But for the most part the letters were highly critical of Allen's action. J. A. Macdonald of the Arlington Mills wrote, "As a Lawrence mill man and the father of a boy attending Phillips Academy it seems incumbent upon me to express to you the resentment which many here feel, that one of your faculty, B. M. Allen, should inject himself into a situation already discouraging and difficult enough." After explaining how the forty-eight hour week would handicap American mills in meeting foreign competition, he went on, "but not content with this a radical Socialist element joining with the worst element among the foreigners, has demanded 54 hours pay for 48 hours work. The real leader of the movement is a Russian Jew, who claimed exemption as an alien, and it seems too bad that just after this war, men of this type should be encouraged by educated men, under whom we place our boys for instruction in the formative period."[88] Al's reply to Macdonald made it clear that Bernard Allen could expect little sympathy from him:

I have your letter of February 17th. There is not a word or suggestion in it with which I do not sympathize to the fullest extent. . . . I venture to say that as a headmaster I have been more distressed and disgusted with what occurred in Lawrence last Sunday than have you as a father. That very Sunday afternoon . . . I had made as a basis of a talk to the boys in chapel the growing menace all over the world revealed in socialistic and anarchistic tendencies of various kinds. I had emphasized as strongly as I could the unstable character of the leaders and promoters of these movements. . . .

I prefer not to discuss at this moment the special problem that confronts us in view of the unfortunate activities of a member of our faculty at a time of real crisis. . . . The fact that he was present and evidently expressed his sympathy with the strikers in general furnishes fuel enough for my indignation; and the matter is not likely to rest where it is.[89]

The matter did not rest there. Key members of the Board of Trustees were convinced that the School's reputation had been severely damaged, and action had to be taken. Elias B. Bishop wrote the Headmaster asking if he would object if Bishop demanded Allen's resignation.[90] Alfred Ripley, President of the Board, expressed a similar point of view. Finally a decision was reached: Allen had to go.

A few days later Allen was asked to meet with a group of Trustees in Boston. Among those present were President Ripley, Headmaster Stearns, and Professor James Hardy Ropes of Harvard. What happened is best described by Allen himself:

At that meeting I began to give my reasons for thinking that this strike deserved the support of every believer in social justice, but was cut short by the President of the Board, who said, in substance, that they were not concerned with that question at this time, but with whether I had shown such a lack of judgment and loyalty to the school as to prove my unfitness to continue as a teacher. The failure of this statement to bring forth a protest from any other Trustee present made further defense seem useless.[91]

Trustees Ripley, Ropes, and Stearns flatly requested that Allen submit his resignation, and he agreed to do so. He stayed up all that night, in company with his brother Philip and two friends, writing his letter.[92] When completed, it was a moving document. After explaining how his presence in Lawrence was perfectly legitimate and the action of the police unjustified, he went on:

. . . after careful consideration I have decided that the only thing for me to do is to relieve the Trustees of all further embarrassment, so far as that is possible. I therefore tender my resignation as instructor in the Academy, to take effect as soon as you can conveniently arrange for my work.

It is not an easy thing thus to sever connection with the school to which I came as a boy, and where I have taught for nearly twenty-six years. But the interests of an institution like this must always be of more importance than those of any individual, and a deep feeling of loyalty to the Academy has been the controlling influence in this decision.[93]

The Trustees did not formally accept Bernard Allen's resignation until their meeting on 21 March 1919, and their action on that occasion indicates that there must have been some regret about the way the whole affair had been handled. To ease their consciences a bit, Al Stearns wrote Allen:

> As an appreciation of your constant loyalty to the school and your deep interest in all that pertains to its welfare the Trustees voted unanimously to pay you in full your salary for the current school year, even though your official connection with the institution has already terminated. It is a real pleasure to me to be able to advise you of this action.[94]

Bernard Allen went from Andover to teach in Cheshire, Connecticut, where he had a distinguished career. He published three Latin grammars and wrote numerous articles for Classical journals. A professor of linguistics at Yale wrote of him, "among American schoolmen he has not more than two or three rivals."[95]

In 1938, though sixty-nine years old, Bernard Allen decided to reopen the case. He wrote to the Trustees, suggesting that their action in accepting his resignation was in part due to the hysterical atmosphere of the times and wondering whether due weight had been given to ethical considerations. Appended to his letter were a number of character references from distinguished Classical scholars.[96] The Trustees, understandably, were unwilling to reopen the case. They pointed out that all the Board had done in 1919 was to accept a letter of resignation that had apparently been freely tendered and that the Board's action did not cast any reflection on Bernard Allen.[97] But this could not satisfy the old man, and he went to his grave still bitter at the treatment he had received from Phillips Academy. There is no question that the handling of the case was in part a result of the Red Scare that was sweeping the country in 1919. The Trustees, in taking the action they did, were behaving as did much of the rest of the country. Yet it should not be forgotten that some stood fast against the hysteria of the day. At the time of the Boston Police Strike, which also occurred in 1919, Harold Laski, then a young instructor at Harvard, raised alumni hackles by speaking out in favor of the police. A movement was started to demand Laski's resignation. President Abbott Lawrence Lowell of Harvard disagreed completely with Laski's position on the Strike, but he felt that freedom of expression was more important than a particular point of view. As he said to a friend, "If the Overseers ask for Laski's resignation they will get mine!" and the affair soon died down.[98] It is regrettable that no one at Phillips Academy in 1919 had enough conviction of the importance of civil liberties to take Lowell's position.

When it came to dealing with minority groups among the undergraduate body, Al Stearns followed no consistent policy. Generally speaking, he sought to have Andover students represent a broad cross-section of the American population, and he always had a soft spot in his heart for boys on scholarship. When it came to blacks, however, he was more ambivalent. Writing to Arthur Drinkwater of the Class of 1896, who wished to found a scholarship for black students in memory of a black classmate, Al said:

> In my earlier years as head of the school I fought vigorously for the colored boys in our midst and for those who sought to enter. As years passed I began to grow increasingly doubtful as to the wisdom of my position, for it seemed to me that these fellows were being harmed more than helped by the school. . . . As the doubts grew, I decided to discuss the matter frankly with the best informed man I could find. Dr. Frissell, then of Hampton Institute, had a boy in school at the time and was a graduate himself. I talked the situation over very carefully with him and was assured that my doubts were fully justified and that in his judgment we were harming more than helping the colored boys who were admitted to the school. Later I talked to Booker Washington and found that he felt, if anything, more strongly than did Dr. Frissell that it was unwise to take colored boys into the Academy. Both of these eminent authorities expressed the opinion that these fellows were pretty sure to have their heads turned and be cut off more or less from the natural work among their own people which was their lot and their privilege. . . . I decided that except in very rare instances colored boys ought not to be encouraged to come to the school. The last two who have been here have done exceptionally well, and one of these is now about to graduate from Harvard.[99]

On the other hand when a black alumnus, much more aggressive than Washington, charged that the American history course at Phillips Academy was presenting the viewpoint of white superiority, Al took pains to reassure him that this was by no means the case.[1]

Each class at Phillips Academy had a certain number of Jewish boys in it. Though there is no evidence that there was ever a formal quota for their admission, the Admissions Office appears to have acted informally to keep their numbers down. Few Jewish students were ever admitted to the school fraternities. When a lady in Cambridge wrote Al asking him to list the members of the Andover delegation going to Harvard who would make good ushers for her Brattle Hall Dances, he reported to her on the Wasp types and simply wrote "Hebrew" by the names of the Jewish boys.[2] Yet the discrimination that existed was almost entirely social. In the classroom and in extracurricular activities Jewish boys had as much opportunity as the other undergraduates.

One group of special students in whom Al took a particular interest was the Chinese. Phillips Academy had begun enrolling Oriental students as early as the 1860's, when Joseph Neesima attended. Throughout the rest of the nineteenth century there were a few present each year, but with the coming of the twentieth the number increased substantially, and Al himself played the leading role in dealing with them. After the Boxer Rebellion the powers involved in its suppression imposed on China an indemnity of about $335,000,000. The United States believed the sum too large for China to meet and, when protests were to no avail, decided to turn its share over to the Chinese Government to establish a fund for the education of Chinese students in the United States. The Chinese responded by establishing Tsing Hua College, an institution devoted to preparing Chinese students for matriculation at American colleges and universities. Since the standards of Tsing Hua College were extremely high, and since there was

44. Sir Chentung Liang Cheng in 1903. He studied at Phillips Academy from 1879 to 1881 and served as Chinese Minister to the United States from 1903 to 1907.

a growing desire on the part of progressive Chinese to emulate the United States as they modernized their empire, a growing number of Chinese students who were unable to get admitted to Tsing Hua sought other ways of preparing themselves for American higher education. The reason why Phillips Academy became particularly involved was that Sir Chentung Liang Cheng, Chinese Ambassador to the United States, who spoke at the commencement ceremonies in 1903, had studied at Andover in 1880–81 and distinguished himself in the Exeter baseball game of 1881 by knocking a three-bagger and a two-bagger. In his speech at the Commencement luncheon, the Ambassador, who had a deep affection for his old school, predicted that more and more Chinese would want to come to American schools, and he promised to send qualified youths to Phillips Academy. From that time on, the number of Chinese at Phillips Academy mounted steadily. Sir Chentung Liang Cheng personally recommended one of the first groups to come, and many others from the educational mission of Dr. Yung Wing in Tientsin followed. In 1920, for example, fifteen Chinese students came to the School, and during the period from 1903 to 1920 close to one hundred entered. The success of the program is indicated by the statement of a newly arrived Chinese boy who said, "Everyone in China knows about Andover. . . . it is about the only school we hear about over there." Al Stearns, very high on these students, thought they did much to modify the provincialism of the American boys, and he admired their high moral standards. But they needed to relax and play more, he thought. Though they were participating in tennis, track, swimming, and especially soccer, they were still an over-serious lot.[3]

Successful as this program may have been, it added a tremendous burden to Al's already busy life. Sir Liang Chentung Cheng's first group of boys were under the personal care of Al, and that established a pattern followed by most of their successors. In a sense the Chinese boys were sent not so much to Andover as to Al Stearns. In the files there are four fat boxes filled with correspondence between him and various Chinese parents, missionaries, educators, and the like. Among them are letters concerning the Sun children. In 1920 Al received word that seven Chinese students were on their way to Andover—five the children of Mr. C. Y. Sun and two friends. As one correspondent wrote, "He [Mr. Sun] sends them all to be in the care of Principal Stearns of the Academy as a sort of guardian."[4] The first contingent of four were to sail from Shanghai on the *Nanking Maru* and then proceed directly across the continent to Andover, arriving in time for the opening of school. In due course Arthur, Charles, Thomas, and Mary Sun arrived in Andover, and since only Arthur could go to Phillips Academy, the rest were taken into the Stearns household. The boys might have to eat at the school Commons, Al wrote, so as not to put too great a strain on his kitchen arrangements.[5] This would certainly satisfy the desire of the parents that the children be placed in a "Christian home" and that they be given "a training that would tend to strengthen their character, both morally and intellectually."[6] In due course reports on Arthur were received; they indicated a satisfactory record at Tsing Hua College and listed the English books that he had read, among which were *Ivanhoe*, *Sohrab and Rustum*, and *Quentin Durward*.[7] It was finally decided that Arthur should go to Phillips Academy and the other three to the Andover public schools, and by November, Al was able to write Mr. Sun that they had all settled in very well. The Stearns family were anxious to demonstrate to their visitors what an American Christmas was like, and plans were made for a big party, with a tree. All the Chinese students in Phillips Academy were invited—some twenty.[8] Lest Al fail to understand the kind of training a Chinese child should have, Mr. Sun spelled it out. The ideals were "Punctuality, Frugality, Discipline, Self-sacrifice for a good cause, Self-respect, self-denial, self-control, self-defence, Respect for righteousness, Exactness." It was a tall order.[9]

One has only to read the correspondence between Al and his Chinese friends to be appalled at the amount of work they involved him in. And his letters were no short notes; many of them were three or four pages of single-spaced typewritten communications. In February, 1921, for example, Al reported on the problem of room and board. He did not want to make any money on the students but he had to meet expenses at a time of rising food costs. In addition, "the advent of these young friends at my house brought me immediately face to face with a demand from the kitchen for an increase in wages."[10] On the other hand, there were compensations. In February Mr. Sun wrote that he was sending Al "a fur overcoat skin and a fur collar. . . Had I known your fit I would have had the overcoat made complete here."[11] When summer came, Al was faced with a difficult problem: what to do with the Chinese students during vacation. He finally solved it by sending them all to summer camps.[12] As if he did not have enough Chinese problems, Mr. Lin of Tientsin wrote, asking Al "to act as Guidance of my boy," who was also at Phillips Academy.[13] Later in the summer Mr. Sun reported, "Mary wrote to me about the ball game, Andover vs. Exeter. I am much astonished at her excitement she betrayed upon Andover's victory and how she went to ring the school bell."[14] The following year Arthur went to M.I.T.—without a Phillips Academy diploma—while Mary went to Northfield and the two younger boys entered the Academy. If Al thought that his guardianship would end when a boy went on to college, he was sadly mistaken. Two years later he was sending Arthur checks, and Mr. Sun urged Al to see that Arthur got a good Christian training while at M.I.T. Mary found Northfield too difficult, and returned to the Stearns household to go to Abbot as a day student.[15] For a while she appears to have caused trouble, becoming deceitful and disobedient, but later Al reported that she had shaped up pretty well.[16] Charlie developed an interest in music and began playing the banjo; this created the problem of music lessons.[17]

After Christmas 1923 Al wrote Mr. Sun begging him not to send such expensive Christmas presents to the members of the Stearns family: the duties on them were killing him. He was also disturbed by the statements of the Sun children that the value of the presents was far greater than that indicated in the inventory.[18] And so it went. It should be remembered that the four Sun children represented only a small percentage of all the Chinese students that Al was responsible for. Incredibly, Al survived the ordeal, and in the process broadened the make-up of the Phillips Academy student body and did much to build good relations between China and the United States.

The difficulties of Alfred Ernest Stearns's life as Principal of Phillips Academy were matched by those of his personal life. In 1900 he married Kate Deane of Springfield, Massachusetts, whom he had first met when she was a student at his mother's school. The couple had three children: Alfred, who died in infancy, Charles, and Marjorie. After a little over ten years of married life, it became clear that Kate Stearns was seriously ill emotionally, and Al was obliged to have her institutionalized for the remainder of her life. His mother-in-law extracted from him a pledge not only to continue to support her in the institution but also to agree not to remarry while she was alive. Since he could not very well raise two children and do the entertaining required of the Principal of Phillips Academy while carrying out the manifold duties of his position, he engaged Miss Grace Clemons, a native of Ballardvale, who had been teaching a small school in the home of Bartlett H. Hayes, to be his hostess and a governess for his children. She was to remain in this position until Al's retirement in 1933, and after the death of his wife that same year, to marry him. The two children presented problems also. Charlie was never successful either in school or later in making a living; he gradually drifted away from the family and finally lost all contact with them. Marjorie, though a charming and sensitive girl, was never strong physically and needed special care. As often as not when Al returned home after a hard day, it was not to the serenity of an easy-going establishment but rather to new problems and new challenges.[19]

Alfred Ernest Stearns was nevertheless a strong Principal in an era when schools were usually known by their Principals. Whenever he appeared at a Phillips Academy happening, his presence was immediately felt. He emanated a sense of integrity and morality. Yet his allegiance was to the past. The nineteenth-century moral code he had learned as a young man he carried with him to the grave. He was no innovator. With minor exceptions, for example, the curriculum that he inherited from his uncle Cecil Bancroft remained unchanged at the end of his term as Principal. He was uninfluenced by modern trends and usually deplored them. No intellectual, he preferred people who did things to people who thought about them. His capacity for concern for others was vast, and despite his stern exterior, he could be soft-hearted and generous. He often gave money to poor students and to faculty members out of his own pocket. He could take the trouble to call on a prep the night of his arrival in Andover and give him a warm welcome.[20] His students had differing opinions of him. One wrote, "Al Stearns towered above all of his contemporaries in the skill with which he developed character among his students."[21] Another said, "I was in awe of him; his moral perfectionism image was hard to break through, and I never had any warm relationship with him. He was so austere that the students often nick-named him 'base and sordid,' quoting a cliché he used too often in his chapel sermons."[22] There was no question about his being respected, however. Year after year in the poll in the school yearbook he won by a landslide the title "Most Respected."

CHAPTER THIRTEEN

GROWTH OF THE PLANT

T HERE IS a story—probably apocryphal—of an alumnus who returned to visit Andover in the early 1930's. He had not been back to his old school since his graduation in 1916, and as luck would have it, he arrived on the Hill after dark. Wishing, first of all, to pay his respects to his old Headmaster, Al Stearns, he went around to his house only to find himself confronted by a huge new Chapel. Still eager to see Al, he walked over to the Inn, where he thought he could get directions. But as he approached the Inn, he saw that the old stone building with the wooden annex was no longer there; in its place was an imposing new structure made of brick. Not sure that this new building was an Inn, he finally decided that the best thing to do was to call on his old English teacher, Jack Fuess, and see if he could straighten things out. Alas, when he arrived at the spot where Jack Fuess's house had stood, there was now simply open space, and as he looked up and down, he could see that a long vista extended from a large pillared building well down Phillips Street. According to the story, that did it; despairing of finding anything familiar in its accustomed place, he went back to the railroad station and took the next train back to Boston.

Apocryphal or not, the story illustrates the tremendous physical changes in the Phillips Academy plant that took place during the Stearns era. When Al Stearns took over as Principal in 1903, the physical facilities of the School were still woefully inadequate. Well over half the boys, for example, still lived in boarding houses. By the time Al left in 1933, every boarding student lived in a school dormitory and a host of new buildings had been constructed, with the result that the campus of Phillips Academy had acquired a breath-taking beauty. To be sure, important additions to the plant have been made since Al Stearns's time, but the basic plan of the school as it is today was determined during this period.

The head of an institution naturally receives credit for accomplishments achieved during his term of office, and Al Stearns deserves a full measure of applause for his part in developing the physical plant of Phillips Acade-

45. James Cowan Sawyer of the Class of 1890, Treasurer of Phillips Academy from 1901 to 1939.

my. Yet an equal share of the credit must go to the Treasurer, James Cowan Sawyer, who was Al's alter ego in this work.[1] Together they worked as an extraordinarily efficient team to build the beautiful Andover that we know today. James Sawyer was born on 30 March 1872 in Dover, New Hampshire, the son of a former governor of the state. In 1886 he entered Phillips Academy, where he roomed for four years with Al Stearns in Abbot House, now called the Double-Brick and then the home of Principal Cecil Bancroft. Unlike Al, Jimmy Sawyer was no athlete, but he was active in other areas: manager of the football team, a member of the *Phillipian* board, and a leader in the K.O.A. Society, perhaps the strongest of the fraternities. From Andover he went to Yale, where he was equally active, serving as manager of several undergraduate organizations and joining Psi Upsilon and Scroll and Key. At Yale he made many important friendships, which were to be important for Andover in the future—with such men as Thomas Cochran, Judge Elias B. Bishop, George B. Case, and Fred T. Murphy, all of whom later became Trustees of Phillips Academy. After graduation from Yale he married Mary Frost of Durham, New Hampshire, and decided to try his hand at running a travel business. Apparently this venture proved not to his liking, for he soon gave it up and moved to Andover. The presumption is strong that Cecil Bancroft and Al Stearns were important influences in his decision to move. In any event they had plans for him: early in 1901 he was elected a Trustee of Phillips Academy and a few months later was made Treasurer. By the time he retired in 1939, he had held the office longer than anyone in the Academy's history. The Trustees Records in the years immediately following Sawyer's assumption of the position as Treasurer show what a live wire he was. He announced that he was going to hire expert accountants to deal with the School's finances and to replace the rather slipshod procedures that had existed up to that time.[2] In June 1902 he presented a five-point program for Trustee consideration: rent Bartlet Hall from the Theological Seminary as a dormitory for Phillips boys; put steam heat in Phillips—now Foxcroft—Hall; construct a heating plant for the entire School; make Bulfinch Hall into a dining hall; and demolish the Latin Commons.[3] When it is remembered how little attention was paid the School by the Trustees in the previous decade, James Sawyer's incisiveness was like a breath of fresh air. From the very start he and Al Stearns worked closely together. They were often on the same Trustee Committees, they took a trip to Washington together on behalf of the Academy,[4] and they generally complemented each other in working for the School. It was not long before they could report real progress in the development of the Phillips Academy plant.

Before any new construction could be attempted, however, the existing buildings had to be put in good repair. For years there had been rumors that the Academy Building (the main classroom building) was unsafe. To investigate it, Guy Lowell, the School's architect, sent an engineer named

John Buttimer, later to be the Academy's Superintendent of Buildings and Grounds. What he discovered horrified everyone. He ripped up the flooring in the third floor, which served as an assembly hall, and found that the smaller beams running from the sides of the building to a huge beam in the center had all pulled loose. They were supposed to overlap the center beam by five inches, but were doing so by no more than one inch, and in some cases even less. Buttimer remarked on the good luck that only quiet religious services were held in the room; any jarring would have loosened the side beams and the whole building would have collapsed. Al Stearns, turning pale, explained to Buttimer that they had just had a rally with lots of shouting and stamping. "Good God," Buttimer replied, "you can only thank Divine Providence that you escaped a terrible tragedy." The building was immediately vacated, chapel was held in the Theological Seminary Chapel and classes in faculty homes, the whole third floor of the Academy Building was removed, and by the opening of School the following fall, the building was usable again. Al Stearns had nightmares about this episode for the rest of his life. "Suppose those displaced beams had given way when the entire student body and faculty were assembled in that big hall carrying them all to the basement with the roof on top of them?" he wrote. "Could the school ever have recovered from the blow?"[5]

When Al Stearns became Principal, he inherited a project that had been started under his predecessor, Dr. Bancroft—namely, the establishment of a Department of Archaeology. The donor, Robert Singleton Peabody, had, according to generally accepted reports, originally planned to give his money to the Peabody Museum at Harvard, named after his Uncle George Peabody, the noted philanthropist. Unfortunateely for Harvard, the Director of the Museum insulted Robert Peabody in some way, which led him to call in his lawyer and make Phillips Academy, of which he was a graduate, his beneficiary.[6] In a long letter addressed to the Trustees and dated 6 March 1901, Mr. Peabody spelled out the terms of his gift.[7] He had, he wrote, amassed over the years a collection of some 40,000 archaeological specimens and wished to establish a museum in which to house them. He also wished to establish a separate Department of Archaeology at Phillips Academy, with a curator for the museum and such other staff as might seem appropriate. He wanted the new department and the funds to support it, which he proposed to give, to be entirely separate from the rest of the Academy but to be under the control of the Trustees. If at some later time it seemed advisable, branches in Ethnology and Paleontology could be set up. Mr. Peabody hoped that the Phillips undergraduates might, as a result of his gift, come into contact with the science of Archaeology and be broadened thereby, but he had no desire to force a compulsory course in the science on the already heavily burdened boys. He hoped that the building to be erected could be particularly attractive, so that it might serve as a kind of social center for the undergraduates, thus filling a great need of the Academy. Finally, though he had no wish to dictate to the Trustees, he hoped that his friend Warren K. Moorehead might be named Curator. Professor Moorehead had helped to organize his large collection of specimens, was intimately familiar with it, and could display it effectively. He also hoped that his son, Charles Peabody of Cambridge, Massachusetts, could be given some part to play in the enterprise. Two days later Mr. Peabody wrote the Trustees that for a starter he would pay over to them the sum of one hundred and fifty thousand dollars, one hundred thousand for the foundation itself and fifty thousand for the building. It was no surprise when, at their meeting of 21 March 1901, the Trustees voted to accept the "municifent gift" of Mr. Peabody. They then proceeded to follow his suggestions as to personnel and named Warren K. Moorehead Curator and Charles Peabody as Honorary Director.[8]

Cecil Bancroft was ambivalent about the new acquisition. He was delighted, of course, at this handsome addition to the Academy plant; yet when he considered the other needs of the Academy—particularly new dormitories—he must have wished that the money could have been diverted to other purposes. He did convince Mr. Peabody, however, that the museum building should have facilities for a social center for the undergraduates, which he hoped, would broaden its appeal to the undergraduates and make possible a more enjoyable social life for them. In actual practice it was soon found that the space allotted in the museum for a social center was needed by the department, and as a result, a few years later, funds of the Peabody Foundation were used to construct a building named Peabody House, next door to the museum on Phillips Street. A grille was established in the basement of Peabody House and for many years served as an undergraduate hangout—the boys could smoke there—while the upper floors of the building provided rooms for meetings, debates, small lectures, and the like.

The Trustees decided that the proper site for the museum was the northern corner of Phillips and Main streets. This spot had had a long history. The first schoolhouse was located there when Phillips Academy had been established in 1778. In 1812 Squire Samuel Farrar had built a house there and taken care of Madame Phoebe Phillips in her last months. In 1881 the Farrar House was moved down Phillips Street to its present location, while a new edifice, Churchill House, was erected on the same site. Now it became necessary to move Churchill House to its present location opposite the juncture of Main and Salem streets. With the site clear, construction of the museum proceeded rapidly. Guy Lowell of Boston was chosen architect for the enterprise, and on 28 Mach 1903 the building was formally dedicated. Charles Peabody, the son of the donor, spoke at these exercises, as did Robert R. Bishop for the Trustees, Alfred E. Stearns for the Faculty, and Charles O. Day for the Theological Seminary. Professor Frederick

Ward Putnam of the Harvard Department of Ethnology and Archaeology gave the main address of the day.[9]

Despite attempts to make the Archaeology Department and its museum attractive to the undergraduates, the institution has always been something of an anomaly. From the first it was clear that Dr. Moorehead and his staff would devote most of their time to archaeological research, and this they did with distinction. The difficulty was that most of their sites were far from Andover. In the first twenty-five years of the Department's existence important archaeological finds were made in the Ozarks, in the Red Paint People country in Maine and other parts of New England, at the Etowah Mounds in Georgia, and finally, under the direction of Alfred V. Kidder, at the Pueblo of Pecos in New Mexico. In addition, Dr. Moorehead was frequently absent, working for the United States Board of Indian Commissioners and helping to recover for the Indians hundreds of thousands of acres of land and millions of dollars that had been wrongfully taken from them. As a result of this professional activity, there was little time left for the undergraduates of Phillips Academy. Elective courses in archaelogy were offered from the start till 1917, but the number of boys actively engaged in the subject remained small. Some four or five each year usually became vitally interested and often accompanied the staff on summer expeditions. To broaden the appeal, Dr. Moorehead tried to popularize archaeology with lectures on "The Story of Tecumseh," "Buffalo Days on the Plains," "The Custer Fight," "Exploring the Desert," "Prominent Indian Chiefs," and "The Lewis and Clark Expedition." Most of these lectures were historical rather than archaeological, of course, but they were usually well attended; Dr. Moorehead stated that attendance ranged from eight to one hundred and twenty. The problem of reconciling programs for the undergraduates and scholarly study on the part of the staff remains to this day. Probably in deference of Robert Singleton Peabody's original wishes, the Trustees have preferred to engage highly trained professionals and encourage them to proceed with their research rather than people whose main interest would have been in teaching archaeology.[10]

In the early years of the twentieth century occurred one of the most significant events in the history of Phillips Academy—the decision of the Andover Theological Seminary to move to Cambridge and the resultant acquisition of the Seminary property by the School. At one stroke the Academy was transformed from a second-class appendage of the Seminary into the dominant institution on Andover Hill. At the same time, the School acquired a Board of Trustees wholly devoted to its interests—something that had not obtained for one hundred years. In the 1890's and early 1900's the Seminary had begun to falter. Attendance had fallen off until by 1902 there were only three in the graduating class, and there were never more than four during the remainder of the Seminary's stay in Andover.[11]

Various reasons were given for the decline; certainly, the so-called "heresy trials" in the 1880's had given the Seminary a bad name. When relatively liberal theologians could be haled into court on some picayune matter of doctrine, prospective theological students could not help being put off. There was, in addition, a general falling off among candidates for the ministry, as many devout young men preferred social work of one kind or another. Andover's isolation, once considered an ideal setting for theological study, now seemed at variance with growing interest in the "social gospel," which involved work with the poor and unfortunate in the cities.[12] Whatever the main reason, it was becoming clear that if the Seminary did not correct the situation, it would die of inanition. What could one say of an institution where there were more professors than graduates? The Trustees of the Academy, who were also Trustees of the Seminary, realized that something drastic had to be done if the Seminary was to be saved. Early in 1902 they appointed a Committee to consider the removal of the Seminary to some other more appropriate place, and a month later the Committee recommended such removal. So far so good, but a few months later the Committee reported that it was unable to devise a way to remove the institution.[13] There the matter rested until 1906. In the meantime, the alumni of the Seminary made it clear that they wanted no part of a removal. They pledged to support the institution, raise money for it, and generally try to restore it to the position it had previously held.[14] Despite this opposition the Trustees kept at the problem, and by 1906 they were able to report progress.

The Gordian knot was finally cut by an agreement with President Eliot and various officers of the Harvard Divinity School that would provide for a merger of the two institutions.[15] The Divinity School, like Andover, had only a small number of students, and it was hoped that by joining forces, each institution might be strengthened. When the Trustees acceded to this arrangement, they undertook to provide positions for the Andover Theological Seminary faculty and to construct an Andover building in Cambridge near the Divinity School.[16] At the start, two plans were proposed— one that would effect a close union between the two institutions and another that would provide for a loose union. After proper deliberation the first plan was selected.[17] It should be pointed out that the Trustees were hampered in their decision to move; the original Constitution of Phillips Academy (which was to apply later to the Seminary) stated that the institution about to be founded should never be moved out of the South Parish of the Town of Andover "unless the good of mankind shall manifestly require it." Apparently the Trustees thought it did.[18]

Under the terms of the agreement with Harvard, Andover Theological Seminary was to have equal status with the Cambridge Divinity School. The curricula of the two schools were to be interchangeable, while the Andover professors, though bearing a slightly different title from their Harvard confrères, were to have fully equal status. In due course a handsome stone building called Andover Hall was constructed in Cambridge, and the physical translation of the Seminary was complete. The alumni of the Seminary were by no means happy. A majority voted to oppose the measure when it was still under consideration. One wrote, "An empty seminary is as well off at Andover as at Cambridge." But the Trustees pushed ahead with their plan, and eventually it was successfully achieved.[19]

It remained to work out the legal and financial aspects of the separation, both of which proved to be extremely complicated. It was clear that the Trustees of Phillips Academy could not, by their own act, divest themselves of the Theological Seminary. Both Harvard and Dartmouth had attempted similar moves in the past, and in both cases, after long lawsuits the courts had decided against them. The solution that was finally worked out was the work of a newly appointed Trustee, Henry L. Stimson, and Professor John Chipman Gray, of the Harvard Law School, who became counsel for the School in this matter. The plan that these two legal experts proposed involved petitioning the Massachusetts legislature to create a new and distinct Board of Trustees for the Andover Theological Seminary. At the start this Board and the Trustees of Phillips Academy would be identical and would wear two hats, so to speak. In one capacity they would meet as the Seminary Board, in another as the Academy Board. The Trustees of Phillips Academy were to make over to the Trustees of the Seminary all the property belonging to that institution as soon as possible.[20] The Massachusetts legislature dutifully passed an act to legalize the new arrangement and the separation of the two institutions was achieved.[21] Shortly afterward the Trustees began to choose which of the two boards they wished to serve on. Those with loyalties to the Seminary resigned from the Academy Board and served only on the other, while those whose primary interest was in Phillips Academy resigned from the Seminary Board to devote all their time and energy to the School. As Al Stearns put it:

> It would be difficult to overemphasize the benefits the school derived from this radical change in its governing body. For decades the Seminary had been the chief concern of the trustees, a goodly number of whom were retired ministers. During the hectic period of the heresy trials, involving seminary professors, from 1886 and for several years thereafter, academy affairs were given scant if any attention, and at many of the trustee meetings no academy business was included on their agenda. . . The creation of the new and separate board of trustees completely changed the picture and the Academy board set to work promptly to repair the damage. An Executive Committee which met monthly handled all the minor problems while the larger ones were settled at the quarterly meetings of the full board.[22]

Finally, there remained the difficult problem of determining what property on Andover Hill belonged to the Theological Seminary and what to Phillips. Some items were clear enough, but since others had been used jointly by both institutions, ownership could not be easily determined. To deal with this problem, the Massachusetts legislature, in the same act that established the two separate Boards of Trustees, authorized the appointment of three arbitrators, to be approved by both the Seminary Board and the Phillips Academy Board. After a certain amount of thrashing about, three gentlemen—Daniel Merriman, D.D., of Boston; Joseph A. Stuart of Andover; and Jeremiah Smith, Jr., of Boston—were selected.[23] The arbitrators went to work with a will and soon produced a report. The Trustees of Phillips Academy believed, however, that the report contained several important errors. They urged the arbitrators to review their work and also planned an appeal to the courts if the first report was insisted on. Fortunately, the arbitrators did some more homework and came up with a revised report that was completely satisfactory to the Trustees.[24] Since the Theological Seminary was moving to Cambridge, the purpose of this division of property was to determine exactly what Phillips Academy would have to purchase if it were to acquire the Seminary property on Andover Hill. It was clear from the start that the Trustees were determined to acquire that property. Even before the arbitrators were appointed, a draft of a purchase agreement was considered by the Board, and once the arbitrators' report had been filed and accepted, the Trustees moved rapidly. A special committee on the purchase was appointed to deal with the Seminary Board, which started out by offering $170,000 for all the Seminary's property in Andover. Apparently the Seminary people thought this offer too low; in any event, further negotiations followed and in May 1908 a final agreement was reached whereby Phillips Academy would purchase all the Seminary property on the Hill for $200,000—$50,000 to be paid when the agreement was formally signed, and the balance over a ten-year period. The long document spelled out the property to be acquired and dealt with such matters as interest on outstanding notes, mortgage arrangements, insurance, and the like. Once this agreement was formalized, Phillips Academy would become *the* educational institution on Andover Hill, with a plant that any college could be proud of.[25]

With the legal difficulties in connection with the Seminary's move to Cambridge successfully overcome, and with an agreement for the purchase of the Seminary property signed, sealed, and delivered, the last remaining problem was how to pay for it all. Since the Trustees had no money for this purpose, they obtained it by a fund drive, and in the fall of 1908 the "Seminary Purchase Fund" was established. In addition to the purchase price of $200,000, another $50,000 was added for the remodeling of Seminary buildings; Bartlett Chapel, now Pearson Hall, for example, needed to be converted into a recitation building.[26] In April 1909 it was reported that $96,000 had already been pledged; in addition Andrew Carnegie had promised to contribute the last $25,000 to the fund—after the Trustees had already raised $225,000.[27] The following September the figure of $125,000 had been reached,[28] but from then on, the campaign lagged. Despite heroic efforts on the part of Al Stearns and Jimmy Sawyer, who toured the country tirelessly visiting Andover alumni, it was not until 1916 that the goal was finally reached and Carnegie made the final contribution. Al Stearns told an amusing story of one attempt to raise money in this drive. He and Henry Stimson decided to take a shot at Michael Piel, the brewer who had made a fortune with Piel's beer and who had had two sons at Andover. They decided that evening dress would help create the proper impression and thus arrived at the Piel mansion in tuxedoes. Mrs. Piel, described as "an unpretentious but very motherly woman" met them in the reception room, listened to their story, and then said, "Mr. Piel must hear this; I'll call him." The two solicitors could hear sounds of revelry from the next room—clinking of glasses, bursts of laughter, the like—and they were apprehensive about disturbing Mr. Piel at this time. Finally Mrs. Piel appeared with a reluctant, if not surly, husband in tow. He plumped himself onto a spindle-legged chair that threatened to collapse under him and prepared to listen. It had been agreed that Henry Stimson would present the case; as federal District Attorney in New York City he would, it was thought, command respect. When he began talking about the need for endowment, Piel broke in, in his gutteral accent, "Vat is dis endowment? Is dat anudder dormitory?" Stimson went on to elaborate on the desperate need of the School for funds, but before he could finish, Piel burst out with, "Change de Management! Change de Management!" And that ended the interview.[29] Despite setbacks like this and many other discouragements, the Trustees and Administration of the School kept plugging at the fund drive until Phillips Academy owned the entire property of the Seminary free and clear.

And what a magnificent addition to the Academy plant this property was! In the first place, some of the Seminary buildings went far toward realizing Dr. Bancroft's dream of having all the boys housed in Academy houses. Bartlet and Phillips (now Foxcroft) halls were important additions in this respect, but the row of houses along Main Street that had been occupied by the Seminary professors were useful also. Many were remodeled so that eight or ten boys could be housed in each. Previously the School had taken over Farrar House on Phillips Street, the so-called "Brick House" (the relic of Warren Draper's printing establishment), Marland House, (now Clement House), and others in order to expand housing facilities. As the number of available housing units expanded, it finally became possible to get rid of the Latin and English Commons, so dear to the hearts of so many Andover alumni. Some of these structures were simply razed; two were moved downtown to an area behind Punchard High School, only to be razed shortly thereafter; and one exists to this day on Highland Road, though so completely remodeled as to bear little resemblance to its original form. As the last of the Commons houses were being moved, the undergraduates celebrated their departure by painting slogans on the sides and hanging placards from the windows. These were changed each night, so that each new day saw a fresh collection, much to the amusement of the townspeople.[30]

The Seminary property provided more than student housing. The stone Chapel not only served as a spacious church for the school's religious services but was used also for lectures, entertainments, and meetings, thus making it possible for the top story of the Academy Building, hitherto an assembly room, to be remodeled into additional recitation rooms. More recitation rooms resulted from the remodeling of what is now Pearson Hall. Brechin Hall, the Seminary library, located west of the present Oliver Wendell Holmes Library, was a welcome addition. After its ground floor had been remodeled to provide adequate space for the School's administration, Al Stearns and Jimmy Sawyer no longer had to fall over each other in the tiny administration building near Graves Hall. That building was for a time a center for the Music Department, later a faculty club, and currently is the Office of the Physical Plant. Brechin Hall also made possible, for the first time in Academy history, a well-equipped library under the direction of a professional librarian, and the old student subscription libraries became things of the past. Finally, the Stowe House, which, with an addition, could serve as an inn, came under Trustee control. In short, the acquisition of the Seminary property transformed the School almost overnight; that property and the departure of the Seminary were absolutely essential to the development of the modern Andover.

Magnificent though the Seminary purchase was, it by no means solved the problem of housing all the undergraduates in Phillips Academy dormitories. Until more buildings could be constructed, the unsatisfactory system of boarding houses would have to be continued for roughly one third of the students. No sooner had the Seminary negotiations been completed than the Trustees began plans for a new dormitory to the south of Bartlett Hall. They planned to finance the new building, the cost of which was estimated at $50,000, through notes bearing interest at $4\frac{1}{2}$ percent and sold to alumni and friends of the School. A good start had been made when Melville C. Day, one of the School's most generous benefactors, announced that he would foot the bill.[31] Mr. Day had already given what are now Draper, Eaton, and Pemberton cottages and Bancroft Hall; in the next few years his generosity was to be even greater. The new dormitory south of Bartlett was named Day Hall in his honor and was completed in 1911. Since the Trustees had already raised a large part of the money for a new dormitory through the sale of notes, they determined on a second one, which became the present Bishop Hall. Characteristically, Mr. Day made up the balance when the sale of notes did not quite reach $50,000.[32] Mr. Day must have developed a real passion for providing the Phillips Academy undergraduates with proper housing, for in 1912 he gave money for the construction of the present Adams Hall and the following year for Taylor Hall, named after his old friend John Phelps Taylor and not, as some think, for Uncle Sam.[33] Up until the construction of Adams Hall, all the dormitories had provided quarters for bachelor faculty members. The realization on the part of the Trustees that at least *some* of the faculty might get married prompted them to provide two suites for families in both Adams and Taylor halls. Finally, in 1910, the Trustees were able to acquire, at such a ridiculously low price that it amounted to a gift, property that became Williams Hall on Phillips Street. Professor Edward H. Williams, Jr., of the Class of 1868, made this acquisition possible, and it was decided to make it a dormitory for the youngest boys. A separate dining hall was soon established, and the master in charge was given a light teaching schedule so that he could devote most of his time to the needs of the juniors.[34] Though some of the alumni complained that the School was becoming a kindergarten,[35] many families who had hesitated to throw young boys into the rough and tumble of Andover life now felt reassured, and the junior class grew in size as a result. Furthermore, as the number of boys who attended Andover for four years increased, there was a corresponding improvement in the stability of the undergraduate body and in School spirit in general. In 1922 a wing was added to Williams Hall, providing room for eighteen more boys, and in 1936 what is today Junior House was remodeled to accommodate eleven additional students.[36] The Seminary acquisition, the four new Day dormitories, and Williams Hall came close to making it possible for all Phillips Academy students to be housed by the School, but since the Academy increased in size in the next twenty years, this goal could not be reached until the early 1930's.

Improvements in the athletic plant were also made during this period. Mention has already been made of the construction in 1902 of Borden Gymnasium, named after the principal donor, Matthew C. D. Borden. The drive for this building began after the present Bulfinch Hall, the old gymnasium, was gutted by fire in 1896. At about the same time George Brown Knapp provided funds for the purchase of land south of the Borden Gymnasium for additional playing fields. Though the School was eventually obliged to spend some $30,000 in addition to the original gift to drain and grade the land and to build grandstands, the resulting Brothers Field, dedicated in 1903, has been the focal point for Andover athletic contests ever since. During this same period the School adopted a policy of athletics for all, which created favorable comment all over the country. In the past School teams had been made up to a large extent of postgraduate students who stopped off at Andover on the way to college. The rest of the students either watched the games or involved themselves in other activities, not all of which were particularly savory. Al Stearns was sure that if all boys were involved in athletics, they could let off steam in wholesome contests. He remembered Dr. Bancroft's statement that a good gymnasium would cut discipline cases in half. The plan finally adopted was for the most part the brainchild of W. Huston Lillard, Instructor in English and later the first housemaster of Williams Hall. Lillard was a Dartmouth graduate, where he had been an All-American football player, and had spent the school year 1908–09 at Oxford, where he had become tremendously impressed with the system of intramural athletics. The original program envisaged a series of class teams that would compete with one another, but it soon became clear that the two lower classes were at such a disadvantage under this system that the contests would become noncompetitive. Accordingly, it was decided to divide the School arbitrarily into four "clubs"— Romans, Saxons, Greeks, and Gauls. Each student upon matriculation would be arbitrarily assigned to one of these four and would remain a member of that club during his entire career at Andover. First, second, and sometimes even third teams could therefore be organized in each sport from the membership of each club, and a large number of contests could be held. The great virtue of this system was that each team would be competing against another team roughly its equal in ability and strength. At the start it was thought that the varsity teams should be selected from among the best club players, but this proved impracticable, and the varsity teams continued to be recruited from among the whole student body. Though the club players were not as proficient as those of the varsity, many observers thought the club contests fully as hard fought as the ones at varsity level.[37]

The last change in the athletic program during this period came with the construction of a swimming pool, just before the war. The impetus was from the boys themselves, who set out to raise the necessary $25,000 through personal solicitation. Committees were formed that competed with one another for the largest amount raised, and Dr. Peirson Page, the Physical Director, lent a hand. It proved slow going. After almost a year only $3,300 had been raised, and it was clear that renewed efforts were necessary. A second drive added $8,200 and eventually about $15,000 was realized. At this point the Trustees agreed to loan the swimmers the remaining $10,000, to be repaid from fees charged for using the pool. As a result, on Memorial Day 1911, to the accompaniment of band music and speeches, ground was broken and about eighteen months later the first Andover undergraduates were able to dive in. The popularity of the pool is attested by the fact that it was open not only weekdays but Saturday evenings and Sunday afternoons as well.[38] Thus by the time that World War I broke out, Phillips Academy had a fine gym with a pool, handsome athletic fields, and a program of athletics for all—to the admiration of educators throughout the United States.

If one were to ask what the policy was for boys who got sick, the answer
—at least for the first century of the institution's existence—would have
been "None," or "Student, heal thyself." The remarkable thing is that the
School was able to survive for its first century without a serious epidemic
or even disasters to individuals. To be sure, boys living in Faculty houses
or in boarding houses run by solicitous landladies must have received some
nursing care on occasions. Though the Samaritan House was originally established to take care of sick theologues, it is possible that some Academy
boys were cared for there. But the standard procedure, particularly for students in the Latin and English Commons, was to have the sick boy remain
in his room until he got well; if he got sick enough, a physician from the
town would be called in.[39] Cecil Bancroft was disturbed at this state of
affairs and wished to improve the situation, but he was unable to accomplish anything during his term as Principal. It was not until Al Stearns
took over that progress in the area began to be made. The first step was to
find out who was sick and what was wrong with him. To accomplish this,
Al turned to Dr. Peirson S. Page, the Physical Director. Though Page had
an M.D. from the International Y.M.C.A. College, his main concern was
the program in physical education; he could usually diagnose an illness,
but he left the treatment to the physicians in town. Each morning Dr. Page
would ascertain what boys were absent from chapel; he would then go to
their rooms to find out what was wrong, and report to Al Stearns. Usually
his report was of colds and stomach aches, but on occasion it could be chilling. One morning he reported cases of scarlet fever. Nurses for the sick
boys had to be found. The Chandler sisters on Main Street were often willing to help out. If there were a large number of cases, the procedure was
to put them all in the same dorm and move out those still well. But that
was a makeshift policy at best. When a Boston physician, who had been
called in to advise on the scarlet fever cases, visited one of these quaran-
tined houses, he remarked that considering the outrageous condition of the
rooms in the house, it was a miracle that Phillips Academy had not been
visited by the Black Plague. In this particular scarlet fever epidemic it was
discovered that the children of the cook at the Commons all had the disease. Since the cook was a Christian Scientist, he had refused to have his
offspring examined by a doctor. When the cause, together with the cook
and his family, had been removed, the outbreak was brought under control; but the need for an adequate infirmary remained. In 1907 the Trustees voted that the old track house, located near what is now Adams Hall,
might be used for an infirmary. Though it was a flimsy wooden structure,
it at least had showers and toilets, and for three years it served to house
students with contagious diseases. In 1910, with the acquisition of the
Williams Hall property, it was found that the building where the coachman and his family had lived would make an adequate infirmary. Though
the facilities were excellent, the quarters were much too small to meet the

needs of the School. Thus in 1911 Al Stearns must have sighed with relief when he learned that Miss Flora Isham had decided to give the school $30,000 for a new infirmary in honor of her three nephews, all graduates of the School. Dr. William Graves of Boston, son of the old head of the Scientific Department, and Dr. Fred Murphy, later to become a Trustee, were called upon to draw up plans. Their original proposal would have cost $40,000, but Miss Isham said that $30,000 was her limit. There followed frantic pruning of the original plans to meet the financial requirement, and the new facility was opened in the fall of 1912. None too soon: a few years later the School had a polio epidemic, and seven boys were stricken. The new infirmary enabled the cases to be isolated, and with the help of the Harvard Paralysis Commission, all seven eventually came through unscathed. Perhaps more remarkable, as the result of a reassuring letter sent to all the parents by Al Stearns, only one boy was withdrawn because of the polio scare.[40] There was still plenty of room for improvement in Isham Infirmary, however; in 1935 a large wing was added, and today the institution has been designated a hospital, complete with all the latest medical equipment. The care that undergraduates get today in Isham Hospital is indeed a far cry from the "Student, Heal Thyself" program of the nineteenth century.

During the period of World War I almost nothing was done to improve the plant. Not that everything had been done. The old Academy Building was again considered unsafe and eventually would have to be torn down, and there was a continuing demand for more dormitories. The Peabody House, called at first the Phillips Union, was started in 1915; and Doc Page continued to raise money to pay off the debt on the swimming pool and construct a new track,[41] but for the most part it was not until 1919 that the pace quickened again. In the spring of that year the Trustees appointed a committee to make plans for the construction of a new main building. They were impelled to this action by the formation of an Alumni Fund Committee that promised to raise enough money to take care of the building and also substantially increase teachers' salaries, which were disastrously inadequate as a result of wartime and postwar inflation. Calling their venture the "Building Endowment Fund" drive, the alumni group, centered mainly in New York, planned a whirlwind campaign for the fall.[42] George B. Case was one of the most active workers, along with Thomas Cochran and Frederick C. Walcott. Claude M. Fuess of the Academy English Department was named Executive Secretary, and Al Stearns and Jimmy Sawyer were pressed into service to speak to alumni groups all over the country. The campaign got off to a flying start when gifts of $250,000 were announced at the first formal meeting of the Committee. After that it was a matter of sustained solicitation. Dr. Fuess tells the story of a luncheon given by Thomas Cochran for a wealthy alumnus. Fuess and

Al Stearns were the only two people there who were not millionaires. The guest of honor finally got the message and said to George Case, "How much is this going to cost me?" The reply was $20,000, which the guest pledged before the luncheon broke up.

The drive's biggest asset was Al Stearns, then at the height of his popularity and power. Jack Fuess was assigned to watch out for Al's welfare as the two of them traveled over the country visiting alumni groups. In his plea for improved teacher salaries, Al was, in a sense, speaking for all independent schools, and his message came through. The pair first took a trip to Buffalo, Cleveland, Detroit, Chicago, Minneapolis, Milwaukee, and then back to New York. Later they went all the way to the West Coast, visiting Denver, San Francisco, Portland, and Seattle. It was hoped that the entire sum to be raised—one and one half million—could be realized by late November, but it soon became clear that more time was needed. By early January over a million was in hand, and by the time of the victory dinner on January 28, 1920, the drive had gone over the top. The final success was made possible by some last-minute increases in pledges on the part of leading alumni. The magnitude of the venture and the organization that led to its success were unique in the history of independent schools up to this time, and in a very real sense Andover's success gave a tremendous boost to private schools everywhere.[43]

The purpose of the drive was to provide endowment for the improvement of teachers' salaries and to construct a new main building. The first of these aims was realized immediately—indeed before the drive had been completed. In January 1920 the Trustees voted an across-the-board increase of 10 percent in the salaries of teachers and other employees of the school, and they added a second 10 percent increase in April.[44] The question of where the new main building should be proved more controversial. Ever since the acquisition of the Seminary property, the location of the center of the school had been debated by the Trustees. Up until that time the only Academy buildings on the east side of the campus had been Bulfinch Hall and the Borden Gymnasium. The old Main Building and all the dormitories were on the west side, and it was naturally assumed that the School would grow around the already existing buildings to the west of Main Street. Indeed, in the April 1919 *Bulletin*, published just as the drive was getting started, there appeared an elaborate plan for the development of what is presently the West Quad, prepared by the school's architect, Guy Lowell of Boston. It provided for a Memorial Building located between the present Johnson and Rockwell dormitories but set back further west, as well as sites for new dormitories to be built sometime in the future. According to Al Stearns, the issue was far from decided, as the Trustees divided into East Siders and West Siders. The West Siders pointed out that the east side of Main Street was a poor place to expand because the Seminary buildings already dominated the area and because there was a large granite ledge behind them that precluded expansion further eastward. The issue was finally resolved by George B. Case, recently elected Trustee. He had been wandering around the campus early one morning and had conceived the idea of locating the new main building at the site of the ledge behind the Seminary buildings. The ledge could be removed, he insisted. Then to open up a vista from the new main building to Main Street, he proposed moving Pearson Hall from its position between Bartlet and Foxcroft halls and placing it at a right angle to those two buildings so as to provide another side of a large quadrangle. The School's new architect and landscape designer, Charles Platt, of New York, was enthusiastic about the scheme and insisted that it could be done easily. The West Siders were converted by Case's eloquent arguments, and his plan was followed. The first step was to move Pearson Hall to its present location and to remove the ugly clock tower that had been added long after the building was built. Then came the removal of the large ledge of solid rock located where the new main building was to be built. As bulldozers, giant cranes, and other modern machinery went about this task, the School community gathered to watch—perhaps to the detriment of School work but certainly to the enjoyment of all concerned.[45] Samuel Phillips Hall began to take shape. The plans were the work of Guy Lowell; the basic decisions had been made by the Trustees and the Alumni Building Committee; the inspiration for its location was the work of George Case. When completed, it was indeed a "main" building, consisting of twenty-six recitation rooms, two large examination rooms, a room for faculty meetings, and numerous small rooms for offices. It was certainly an imposing structure, with two long wings in brick and a central portico with pillars. For the first time it was possible for each instructor at Phillips Academy to have his own classroom—and a handsome one at that. Nor did the location of the new building on the east side of Main Street mean the abandonment of the west side. As the School grew during the 1920's it soon became clear that all available space would be needed, and while the central part of the School moved to the east side, the dormitories and other buildings on the west side continued to be used to the full. In effect Phillips Academy had developed two campuses —one on the west side of Main Street, one on the east.

When plans for a new main building were first discussed, the structure was thought of as a memorial to the Andover men who had died in the first World War. The reason this proposal was never carried out was that Samuel Lester Fuller, '94, had offered to give the School a bell tower in memory of the ninety Andover men who had been killed during the war.[46] "Something absolutely useless" was Fuller's characterization of his gift, but it proved far from that. Sited on high ground on what was known originally as the Training Field, across Main Street from Adams and Bishop Halls, this delicate brick "campanile" with a white cupola on top soon came to symbolize Phillips Academy for alumni and friends of the School. A

46. The Memorial Tower, given by Samuel Lester Fuller of the Class of 1894 in memory of the ninety Andover men who died in the First World War.

motorist driving to Andover from Boston along Route 28 sees the tower framed by elm trees long before he reaches the School. Ground was broken for this beautiful structure in 1922, and it was finished the following year. The indefatigable Jack Fuess, walking by the tower the day before it was to be dedicated, was horrified to discover that the word "descendant" in part of the inscription had been spelled "descendent." He immediately called the architect, who called the stone cutter, who worked all night so the error could be corrected by the time of the dedication the following day.[47] Mr. Fuller had been stationed in Fiesole outside Florence during the war and had been greatly impressed by the beauty of the bells of Florence as they sounded across the Arno valley. He wanted to install a set of bells in his tower to provide a similar beauty for the Academy. This proved to be easier said than done, for no sooner had the word spread that Phillips was in the market for bells than the School was deluged with promotional material from all over the world. Dr. Carl Friedrich Pfatteicher, head of the Music Department, was asked to investigate and spent a summer listening to bells in the United States and Canada. He was doubtless not impressed with one bidder who managed to spell his name wrong in every communication sent. One of Dr. Pfatteicher's responsibilities was to determine whether the Fuller tower should have a carillon, consisting of at least twenty-three bells, or a chime, consisting of a smaller number. The final choice was made easier by the fact that the Church of Our Lady of Good Voyage in Gloucester, Massachusetts, had recently purchased a complete carillon from the Taylor Company in Loughborough, England. Dr. Pfatteicher, Al Stearns, Jim Sawyer, Samuel Fuller, and other concerned Andover individuals went over to hear the Gloucester bells, and all returned convinced that this was what Phillips Academy should have. The Gloucester people had managed to work out a deal with the United States government whereby they were exempt from the 40 percent duty on imported bells, but Phillips Academy had no such luck. Apparently because of a new tariff law, there was no way to win exemption, and thus the cost of the carillon was substantially higher than planned. The Taylor Company moved so slowly on the Andover order that the carillon was not installed when the tower was dedicated. There were further complications when the bells did arrive, for the machinery to be used came into conflict with that of a clock with Westminster chimes already installed in the tower. Eventually all these obstacles were overcome, and the Phillips Academy community was treated to regular carillon concerts.[48] The Memorial Tower with its handsome set of bells was a welcome addition to the plant. As the *Bulletin* editorialized, Memorial Tower had become "the soul of the school."[49]

Other important additions to the plant were made during the early 1920's. At their meeting in January 1922 the Trustees voted to construct a new dormitory, similar to Adams and Taylor halls. This decision had

nothing to do with the Building Endowment Fund and was not designed
to provide for an expansion of the School. The Trustees had learned that
four boarding houses that had regularly served Phillips Academy undergraduates would be obliged to close, and some provision would have to be
made to house the students served by these houses. Since there were no
funds available for the construction of a new building, the Trustees
planned to amortize the cost over a period of twenty years from the room
rents that the dormitory would bring in. Like Adams and Taylor halls, the
new facility would provide quarters for two faculty families and forty boys.
The building was finally located on the West Quadrangle, at a right angle
to Taylor Hall, and was named for Osgood Johnson, Principal of the
School in the 1830's.[50]

Shortly after the Trustee decision to build Johnson Hall, Mr. and Mrs.
George B. Case announced their intention to give a baseball cage in
memory of their son, George B. Case, Jr., who had died the year before.
The location of this building presented a difficult problem. At first it was
thought that the cage should be attached to the Borden Gymnasium, but
the architects pointed out that such a solution would be unattractive from
an esthetic point of view and difficult because of grading problems. After
prolonged discussion it was determined to place the cage across Highland
Road from the Borden Gymnasium, even though this would mean en-
croaching on Brothers' Field and relocating the football field. The decision
proved to be a wise one, and the opportunities that the cage afforded for
athletic activities during the winter added a whole new dimension to the
school's sports program.[51] In part as a result of the construction of the
Case Memorial Building, the Trustees determined to improve the adjoining playing fields. The present football field, with stands capable of seating
about 10,000 spectators, was developed in 1924. Great care was taken with
grading and drainage so that the field could be used in any kind of weather.
An extra dividend was the 20,000 cubic yards of earth produced during
the excavation of the field and used as fill around the new main building
and Johnson Hall.[52] The School had recently purchased Pearson Farm, including extensive acreage to the south of the new football field. Here was
enough space for many new fields for club sports that could be developed
at a later date. The recent increased interest in tennis led to plans for
tennis courts to the north of the new football field, and some dreamers
even began talking of a covered hockey rink. Certainly the cage and the
accompanying development of new playing fields revolutionized the Andover athletic program.

At this point the physical expansion of Phillips Academy becomes the
work of one man—Thomas Cochran. To be sure there were others who
aided and abetted him in his many projects, but the dramatic transformation of the Academy that occurred during 1925–33 would have been impossible without his generosity and drive. He hoped that what he did for

47. *Thomas Cochran of the Class of 1890, Trustee of Phillips Academy from 1923 to 1936. Andover's most generous benefactor.*

Andover would serve as an example for other schools, and he would thereby help all independent secondary education. He was one of the great philanthropists of his generation. Although the precise amount of his total contributions to Phillips Academy varies slightly in different accounts, the figure was at least ten million dollars. When he was through, he had fashioned a plant that was breathtakingly beautiful, had established a number of foundations for the faculty, and had given many other useful things to the school he loved so much. Thomas Cochran was born in St. Paul, Minnesota, on 20 March 1871.[53] After attending public schools there, he came to Andover in 1888 as a member of the Class of 1890, which had among its members Al Stearns, Jim Sawyer, and George Case, all of whom would be working closely with Cochran on Phillips Academy projects in the years ahead. Cochran, Sawyer, and Case went down to New Haven together, with Cochran and Sawyer being college roommates, and graduated in 1894. Eighteen ninety-three was a year of panic, and Thomas Cochran's father apparently suffered severely from it. There was even some question whether the son could finish Yale. Tom was also concerned about whether his younger brother could come to Andover, as the family had planned, and wrote Dr. Bancroft to arrange for his admission.[54] The family managed to weather the financial troubles of the time, however, and after graduation from Yale and a year of teaching, Thomas Cochran entered business. He was successively a commission merchant, a railroad official, a corporation treasurer, and finally a banker. Until 1900 he worked in St. Paul; at that point he came to New York, where he was to be located for the rest of his life. In 1907 he became Vice President of the Astor Trust Company, which later merged with the Bankers Trust Company. In 1914 he became President of the Liberty National Bank. Finally, in 1917, he was invited to become a partner of J. P. Morgan and Company, a position he was to hold for the remainder of his life. As a Morgan partner his drive and his skill in financial matters enabled him to amass a large fortune. But like many business men of his day, he was interested not in money per se but in accomplishing good works with it.

Cochran's interest in the Academy was long standing. Indeed, it is doubtful if there was ever a time in his life when he was not concerned about Andover. In 1916 he wrote Al Stearns:

> I wish the time would come soon when I could do something more substantial for Phillips Academy. It is much in my heart and mind, and I dream about it. You and Jim are doing such fine work, that if some of us fellows could get rich, we ought to be able to give you a lift. You may rest assured that if I ever arrive, I will remember what I owe the old school.[55]

Again that same week Cochran wrote Al about organ repairs that the School needed:

when I do something for Phillips Academy I want to do more than
that, and I don't want to curtail the possibility of giving more by
giving a driblet. . . . I think of Andover a great deal, and I hope
the time will come when I can think of it substantially and not take
it out in hot air.[56]

Thomas Cochran had contributed one thousand dollars to the Seminary
Purchase Fund that year, and it would not be long before he would be giving a lot more than a driblet. When the Building and Endowment Fund
was launched in the fall of 1919, Cochran worked indefatigably for its
success. And he must have arrived financially, for he contributed $100,000
to the drive over a three-year period.[57] The real start of the Cochran philan-
thropies to Phillips Academy dates, however, from his election to the
Board of Trustees in April 1923. By that time his dreams for Andover had
begun to crystallize, his financial position was growing steadily stronger,
his wife had died in 1914, their one daughter had died, and the needs
of his old school could fill a void in his life.

Various influences worked on Thomas Cochran in the development of
a program to put his dreams into practice. First of all, he became excited
about the traditions of the School. As Claude Fuess tells the story:

During our Building and Endowment campaign of 1919–1920
[Cochran] one day picked up my book, *An Old New England School*
and seemed to be turning its pages rather lazily. A week later he
drew me aside and said in his forceful way, 'Jack, why haven't we
capitalized on our history? I never knew that George Washington
and those old fellows like Paul Revere and Oliver Wendell Holmes
had anything to do with this place. A school with a background like
ours should tell the world about it.' An idea had germinated which
was to fructify the remainder of his life. With the elation of an
explorer he discovered that Andover had unique traditions . . . and
he resolved that he would tell others what he had learned.[58]

This enthusiasm explains why so many of the Academy's buildings are
named for distinguished Americans connected with the School in its early
years.[59] The second all-important influence in shaping the Cochran program was that of the New York architect Charles Platt. He had been
recommended to Cochran by Miss Grace Clemons, Al Stearns's hostess, and
from the very beginning the two hit it off famously. Platt was not only an
architect but a landscape gardener, who approached his work from the
point of view of an artist, and his visions for Phillips Academy caught
Cochran's fancy. As Platt put it:

Why not surround the boys with the very best in architecture and
nature and the arts? Why not a bird sanctuary, a really fine library,
a topnotch art gallery, a good Colonial church with an organ? Why

not a few broad vistas, some lawns and terraces, even some notable lectures and concerts—all the instruments of culture? I'd just like to try my hand at it.[60]

Cochran decided to let Platt try his hand at it, and before they were through all the items that had been suggested had been realized. Fortunately for the success of the program, neither Platt nor Cochran cared what it cost.

In everything he did, Thomas Cochran was a man of mercurial temperament, impatient of delay, subject to fits of temper. His favorite verb when aroused was "bastardize." When he got in a rage at someone for a sin of omission or commission—which he did fairly often—he would burst out with "I'll bastardize the son of a bitch." Yet these fits of temper passed quickly, and he would move forward to meet the problem.[61] For all his enthusiasm for Platt, Cochran used to get enraged at him because of delays in the construction of buildings. Like many architects, Platt's main interest was in the creative work of drawing the plans, and he sometimes dragged his feet when it came to working drawings and the like. In 1927 one of the project engineers, Robert McCord, wrote to James Sawyer:

> Perfectly frankly we are having a hell of a time with Platt's office and if it were not for our relations with T.C. we would tell them to hire their own engineers and make their own design, which, of course, is their obligation. . . . The thing that hurts most and makes me so damn mad is fact that T.C. blames their delay on you and me and sets the real culprit up as a little tin god.[62]

When Sawyer relayed this to Cochran, together with a letter he had written to Platt, the latter exploded in a way that made it clear that he was not thinking of Platt as a little tin god:

> I think you should press Mr. Platt hard, hard, hard, hard! I don't like his dilatory method in handling Andover affairs, and if he should continue this way we will have to get another architect in his place. It is not efficient and it is not fair. . . . We might as well begin pounding him on the Oliver Wendell Holmes Library now, or plans won't be done until 1930.

And at the bottom of the letter in manuscript, Cochran added the succinct "Kill him."[63] Yet all these problems were eventually resolved, and one after another, handsome buildings arose to increase the beauty of Andover Hill. When Henry Hopper, the Academy Comptroller, wrote in 1930 that the Library and Paul Revere Hall would have a cost overrun of about $50,000, Cochran pretended to blow another gasket:

> I accept, without quibble, this new evidence of the gross incompetency with which these affairs have been handled at Andover. There is

nothing to do about it except to be a philosopher and I will prepare for this extra $50,000. . . . I would be insincere if I did not say to you that I think it is outrageous and you could not respect me if I thought otherwise. You fellows are gradually killing the goose that lays the golden egg and as soon as this party is over, I will be wise enough never to embark upon another of consequence.[64]

Yet Cochran and Hopper remained good friends, and later, Cochran invited the latter to take a trip to Europe with him.

The Cochran correspondence is full of sharp, salty passages. In 1929 he wrote his friend Jim Sawyer:

Just now I am on my way uptown to look at a new Winslow Homer that has come on the market, which they say is a pippin and costs $75,000. I am taking three or four extra pulls on my belt and am going to look for a drink of good Scotch whiskey, before I go into the art gallery, to see if I can get up my nerve to purchase it. . . .

I don't see how you are going to amount to much as the Treasurer of Phillips Academy any longer. You have got on your shoulders buildings, landscaping, pictures, books, ship models and silver, and God knows what else is coming. Why don't you commit suicide and end it all? I will go with you, hand in hand, and, perhaps, we can advertise Andover in a lasting and romantic way by both of us jump-off the Brooklyn Bridge together on the occasion of the 151st anniversary of the Academy.[65]

Cochran never wanted his generosity to Phillips Academy publicized. He tried to keep his gifts anonymous, and he refused to have any of the buildings he paid for named after him. His feelings on this general subject can be seen in his violent reaction when he learned that someone had sent the School a bust of him, done by Paul Manship. He wrote his friend Sawyer:

I am writing to tell you now that under no circumstances must this box be unpacked. If you can store it in your attic or in your cellar that is all right, but if that bust is unpacked and shown to anybody while I am alive it means that I will never set foot in Andover again. You yourself can determine which alternative is preferable to you, but it is final as far as I am concerned.[66]

This did not mean that Cochran was a modest man; he was not. It meant that he wanted to run the show his way, and he wanted to see his program for the School realized without reference to his part in it.

Thomas Cochran had very positive ideas about the financial policy of Phillips Academy. When he discovered that the school had paid for a special cab to take him from Andover to Groton and then to Boston, he wrote his friend Jim Sawyer, "Don't ever try to put anything like this on me, old fellow. As much as I love you and the Academy I can never allow my expenses to be paid by the Academy."[67] When the School ran a small deficit for the 1927–28 fiscal year, he threatened to cut off all connections with the Academy:

> I am so shocked that it is hard for me to say anything, but I have written a letter to Mr. Hopper . . . in which I tried to express my disappointment and at the same time present the problem that comes up with me as to what I can conscientiously do to maintain my connection with Academy under the circumstances. From my point of view it is very very serious.[68]

On the other hand, when Sawyer wrote to say that he thought some planting, originally budgeted for $21,000 could be done for $15,000, Cochran fired back, "I want the whole thing done, and I do not wish any curtailments."[69] Earlier he had said that he wanted Andover to have "the most lovely school buildings in America surrounded by the most lovely grounds."[70] At times his behavior could be quixotic, as when he charged the School brokerage fees and commissions for some stock turned over to him by Oliver G. Jennings, a generous benefactor of the School.[71] The presumption is that he did it out of pique; he did not wish to share with anyone the responsibility of providing for the School's financial needs. When he was starting to build the collection that would eventually be housed in the Addison Gallery of American Art, he wrote Henry Hopper: "I wish you to keep an account of all expenses involved with respect to these pictures, such as insurance, handling and any other items. . . . I desire to bear this expense."[72] In 1927 he wrote his friend Jim Sawyer:

> We have a big plan ahead of us and it is going to take five years to complete our ideal of Phillips Academy. You must do lots of it. As a matter of fact you are one of my great inspirations and I feel handicapped when I have a sub-conscious feeling that you are not always free on account of the petty duties of your office.[73]

Having got this off his chest, he wrote Sawyer four days later that he was taking a dose of his own medicine and resigning from "about 15 Boards of Directors. I can't advise you not to clutter yourself up and then not take the same advice and I have done so."[74] In addition to making many large gifts himself, Cochran prevailed on his friends to contribute also. In those days there was a tacit understanding among philanthropists that each would contribute to the projects of other members of the group. As a result, the Louis J. Horowitz Foundation, whose founder was a close friend of Cochran's, contributed $200,000; Dwight Morrow, another Morgan partner, contributed $15,000; Frank Stearns, the mentor of Calvin Coolidge, gave $50,000 for the Inn; and Alfred I. DuPont contributed $125,000 for Morse Hall.[75] The total was small when compared with what Cochran himself was doing, but they all helped. These vignettes reveal Cochran in action as a man often governed by his emotions and whims, but who never allowed fleeting fits of temper to deflect him from the great purpose he envisioned.

The first building to bear the Cochran hallmark was George Washington Hall, still in use as the main administration building. In 1925 Thomas Cochran announced that he would give $500,000 for this building, but before he was through it was over $600,000.[76] This was also the first building to be designed by Charles Platt. Cochran himself named the new structure in accordance with his deeply felt interest in the past history of the School. To give further emphasis to the name he purchased a Gilbert Stuart portrait of Washington, which hangs, with an appropriate inscription, in the main lobby. The building included a handsome auditorium, marred by the fact that the rows of seats are so close together that it is difficult to find leg room. Cochran also purchased the Martha Cochran Organ for the auditorium at a cost of $50,000.[77] The first two floors of the building housed various administrative offices, and the third floor contained at one end a gracious room for faculty meetings, and at the other, a magnificent trustee room. The completion of this last room was delayed, in part because Charles Platt was slow with the furniture, much to Cochran's rage;[78] but in the fall of 1927 the first trustee meeting was held in these beautiful new quarters.[79] A new science building, named, according to the Cochran formula, Samuel F. B. Morse Hall, was undertaken by the Trustees, who sought to raise $250,000 by themselves to pay for it.[80] Before it was completed, however, Cochran had contributed substantially and had purchased a chair belonging to Morse to ornament the new structure. Morse Hall was designed by Guy Lowell, who had until that time been the official School architect, but although Cochran had not liked some of his past work, he was reassured about this building when Charles Platt gave the plans his approval. The Trustees considered the original exterior of Morse Hall too ornate and asked Lowell to redraw them,[81] but aside from that all went smoothly. Taken together, George Washington Hall and Morse Hall fulfilled part of Cochran's dream, for they completed the so-called "Great Quadrangle," consisting also of Samuel Phillips Hall on the east, Bartlet and Foxcroft dormitories on the west, and Pearson Hall on the south. This cluster of buildings could serve as a focal point, to which structures yet to come could be related.[82]

Before he proceeded further, Thomas Cochran, wanting to plan his program as a whole, had a scale model of the School constructed, with every tree and building in place. With that as a guide, he felt more confident about proceeding.[83] In 1927 he took the next step when, in the names of his brothers, Williams Cochran and Moncrieff Cochran, and his sister, Louise Cochran Savage, he offered $500,000 for a new library. To be sure the School had a library in Brechin Hall, but the building was ancient and Gothic, and furthermore its location in the co-called "Great Lawn" would destroy the balance that Cochran was trying to establish with his new buildings. The library gift had a condition to it; the money would be turned over when ten teaching foundations of $160,000 each had been presented to the School. To start the ball rolling, Cochran himself gave the first foundation, which he named after the President of the Board of Trustees, Alfred Ripley. This condition of the library gift was never completely met. Cochran himself gave another foundation the following year, but the total never reached more than seven.[84] Nevertheless, construction of the library proceeded apace, and the building was opened in 1929 after the books and archival materials from Brechin Hall had been moved over to it.[85] The final step was the razing of Brechin Hall, part of which was accomplished by the undergraduates with block and tackle.[86] The new library was a handsome structure with a large reference room on the left, a reading and "browsing" room on the right, later named for Archibald Freeman, the distinguished instructor in American history. The stacks were open to the undergraduates, and soon a splendid collection of books (now over the hundred-thousand mark) was installed. If the library is the heart of an educational institution, Phillips Academy was well provided for.

One of Thomas Cochran's major aims was to create a "vista" that would go from Samuel Phillips Hall west to the distant hills. According to the story, he and Charles Platt were standing on the steps of Samuel Phillips one morning, looking westward. They were both distressed by the way Tucker House—described as "New Jersey Renaissance"—blocked the view.

48. Bancroft Hall in the process of being moved, as part of Thomas Cochran's plan to develop a "Vista" from Samuel Phillips Hall to the westward.

"That monstrosity is in the way," said Platt, whereupon Cochran said that he would move it, and in a few weeks it was put on rollers and moved to a site behind Taylor Hall.[87] The only problem now was that Bancroft Hall was blocking the view. It was one thing to move Tucker House, another to move a large dormitory and, furthermore, turn it around. Nonetheless this, too, was accomplished. People who remember this move tell of a large number of Italian workmen, each with a jack. When the foreman blew his whistle, each jack was given a quarter of a turn. Eventually Bancroft Hall was settled in its present site on the north side of the West Quadrangle. Yet that was not all. Pemberton Cottage was now in the way, so it, too, was picked up and deposited on its present site next to the infirmary. Lastly, some unsightly chicken coops were revealed, marring the view, and these were removed. When all of this had been completed, someone standing on the steps of Samuel Phillips Hall could enjoy a magnificent view across lowlands all the way to Mt. Wachusett and other hills. Once he had learned the effectiveness of moving buildings, Cochran did not stop there. The best location for the new chapel was at the site of the Principal's house, which would enable it to balance the Memorial Tower to the south. Over Al Stearns's strenuous objections, Samitaritan House was picked up and relocated on School Street. When it was decided to build a new inn on the location of Stowe House, it, too, was moved, to a new site on Bartlet Street. With all this relocation it was not surprising that older alumni, visiting the school, found it difficult to get their bearings.

When Charles Platt first talked with Thomas Cochran about making Andover a beautiful place, he had spoken of the need for "a top-notch art gallery" as an important item in his program. Apparently Cochran was greatly taken with this suggestion, and long before the construction of the gallery itself he appointed a committee to collect paintings and other works of art for the School. Early in 1930, with a major part of his program completed, he was in a position to house that collection, and on 10 January of that year he wrote a letter to the Trustees offering the sum of over $1,480,000 to build a gallery, endow it, and provide a fund for the purchase of works of art. His purpose was stated in the first paragraph of the letter:

> Bent on a desire to enrich permanently the lives of the students of
> Phillips Academy, by helping to cultivate and foster in them a love
> for the beautiful, I should be glad to establish at the Academy . . .
> an endowed Gallery of American Art.

That this project was especially dear to him is evidenced by the fact that, unlike many of his earlier projects, the gift was accompanied by many conditions. The building was to be called the Addison Gallery of American Art, in memory of Cochran's dear friend Keturah Addison Cobb; the location was to be east of the Elm Arch and south of Chapel Avenue so as to balance the new library. The main collection was to be limited to works of art by American artists, though temporary exhibits of the works of foreigners could be shown. No work of art could be added to the permanent collection of the gallery unless approved by an Addison Gallery Committee, to consist of Cochran himself, Charles Platt, Miss Lily Bliss, Mrs. Cornelius Bliss, and Mr. Robert McIntyre, all of New York. Cochran admitted that in certain areas the Trustees must have power, but he hoped that the Addison Gallery Committee could become a permanent part of the governance of the institution. Should the Trustees, at some later date, believe it necessary to modify any of the conditions stated in the letter of gift, they could do so by first passing such modification by a three-fourths vote and then getting the approval of the Chief Justice of the Massachusetts Supreme Judicial Court and of the presidents of Harvard and Yale. Finally, Cochran reserved the right, during his lifetime, to amend the terms of the letter of gift if experience should show that such changes were advisable. Four hundred thousand dollars of his gift was for the construction of the building itself, according to plans already drawn up by Charles Platt. Six hundred and fifty thousand was to be used for an Addison Gallery Endowment Fund to bear all the expenses of the Gallery in the future. Fifty thousand was to establish a Purchase Fund, the income from which could be used to add to the permanent collection. Finally, over $380,000 of the gift represented works of art that Cochran had already purchased to form the basis of the original collection. These items,—there are thirty-one listed in the letter of gift—included the works of such distinguished American artists as Gilbert Stuart, Rembrandt Peale, Winslow Homer, Abbott H. Thayer, Thomas Eakins, Paul Manship, Arthur B. Davies, and Mary Cassatt. It was a splendid start toward the establishment of a distinguished collection.[88]

Most of the Cochran buildings at Andover were planned and constructed with a minimum amount of difference of opinion among the Trustees. To be sure, there had been some arguments about the exterior of Morse Hall and disagreement about a proposal to build an el-shaped edifice. But these differences were resolved with relatively little difficulty. A sharper disagreement arose over the Addison Gallery. Platt and Cochran wanted it to be a "jewel of American art."[89] They realized the necessity of making provision for the teaching of art at the School, but they did not believe that such a program could be combined with the gallery. Trustee James Hardy Ropes thought differently. He believed that the teaching of art was a vital part of any overall program and was convinced that unless provision were made in the new building for studios where the boys could work at painting, drawing, sculpture, and the like, the usefulness of the building would be greatly reduced. For Ropes the art program should involve the boys in active participation as creators rather than as mere passive observers. To get support for his position, Ropes enlisted the advice of Professor Paul

Sachs of the Harvard Art Department. Sachs agreed with Ropes that studios should be provided in the new building.[90] All of this was frustrating to Cochran, who, characteristically, was in a tearing hurry to get the building started. He sent a memorandum to Jim Sawyer pointing out that if an addition to the proposed building were included, the site would have to be changed, the expense would be substantially increased, and the beauty of the Gallery would be fatally compromised. As far as studios were concerned, Cochran quoted Platt as saying than an artist needed a workroom where "he can sing and talk, throw his overalls around the floor, and so forth."[91] Such a work area was a far cry from the dignity and beauty of the Gallery. Eventually, as might have been expected, Cochran won. In part this may have been because of a hint he let drop that if the building were delayed, his promised contribution might not be realized. As a sop to Ropes, he promised to build a work area for artists at some later date.[92] As finally completed, the building was indeed what Cochran called "the real jewel of our crown." As one entered the foyer, it was to see Paul Manship's beautiful fountain entitled "Venus Anadyomene." In a room to the right were exhibited some handsome examples of early American silver. In a gallery at the back of the building was a striking exhibition of ship models, all built to the same scale. The advice of Professor Samuel Eliot Morison of Harvard had been obtained in selecting the models, and the collection was the particular concern of Treasurer Sawyer.[93] Upstairs was housed the permanent collection of paintings, and there was ample room in the building for the mounting of loan exhibitions. All in all it was a triumph—perhaps Cochran's greatest on Andover Hill.

When Thomas Cochran and Charles Platt were talking about their plans for Phillips Academy, the latter had also mentioned a bird sanctuary as one of his dreams. Other projects had priority, but by the end of the decade Cochran was ready to go ahead with the sanctuary. Originally it was to be limited to the Rabbit Pond area. According to the story, Cochran and a group of friends, including John Stewart, the witty manager of the Andover Inn, were sitting outside the Inn one evening when the subject of a bird sanctuary came up. Acting with his usual impetuosity, Cochran told Stewart to construct whatever was necessary to create a sanctuary at Rabbit Pond. Stewart got in touch with Dick Hoyer, a man of great ingenuity and a thorough knowledge of birds, and before long plans were ready for a duck house on the pond. Stewart then took off for Connecticut, where he purchased a large number of ducks and geese at Cochran's expense. The high point of this trip came when, on the way back, some of the cages broke and Stewart's car, by the time he arrived in Andover, was thoroughly covered with bird droppings. All those concerned with the project were delighted at this turn of events.[94] Dick Hoyer, who took over the management of the sanctuary, tells of building a fence all around Rabbit Pond and of constructing two islands in the middle, from rubble made available when Bancroft Hall was moved. These islands were put in so that the birds could nest. The original duck house was enlarged to take care of the birds in the winter, and steady additions were made to the supply of ducks, geese, and quail that were to inhabit the sanctuary.

One might think that this would have satisfied Cochran's interest in the subject, but that was by no means the case. He came to the conclusion that the Rabbit Pond sanctuary was too circumscribed for his purposes and determined to develop a much larger area that would provide space for the birds and also a wild woodland tract where the undergraduates could enjoy the beauties of natural surroundings. He proceeded, therefore, to purchase over one hundred and fifty acres of wild land to the east of Samuel Phillips Hall. When news got around that Cochran was buying, the prices of the various pieces of land went up sharply, but he went ahead and eventually acquired all that was needed. Running through the center of the tract was a brook that was dammed up to provide two artificial ponds where the birds from Rabbit Pond could be settled. In order to protect the birds from animal marauders a seven-foot-high fence was constructed around the whole property—over eleven thousand feet in all. To make the sanctuary doubly secure, the fence went into the ground for a foot and then horizontally underground for a foot, thus stymieing any animals that might try to dig under it. Finally, the lower part of the fence was sheathed in metal flashing. The fence cost $39,000 and accomplished its purpose so successfully that no animal has ever been able to circumvent it. The tract was well wooded from the start with oak, pine, larch, hemlock, birch, cedar, ash, and maple trees. To enhance the beauty of the natural surroundings, laurel, azalea, and blueberry shrubs were added, as well as large clumps of rhododendrons. Three miles of gravel road were constructed for walks in the sanctuary, but no automobiles were allowed.[95] To provide a center for the undergraduates, particularly on weekends, a log cabin was built on high ground in one part of the area, the rough-hewn logs being brought from Nashua, New Hampshire. This simple building consisted of one large room with a fireplace and facilities for serving simple meals. At the start a caterer was in attendance on weekends to serve the boys sandwiches, hamburgers, soft drinks, and the like. Outside the log cabin were two handsomely kept putting greens, where would-be golfers could practice. The development was of breath-taking beauty and added a new dimension to the School.

There was a problem at first as to what to call the property. One Trustee insisted that "preserve" was the proper term, but Cochran liked "sanctuary" and "sanctuary" it became, being named for his brother Moncrieff. As manager of the Sanctuary, Cochran chose his friend Augustus P. Thompson, a resident of Andover and a graduate of the Academy in the Class of 1892. Dick Hoyer became Superintendent. Hoyer remembers that for the first two years the main concern of the staff was stocking the Sanctuary with birds. Quail pens were built, a large number of beautiful pheasants were acquired, fifteen hundred duck eggs were purchased in the Midwest, and a lot of time was spent arranging for the breeding of the birds. In 1929 Edwin A. Potter, Jr., sent one hundred and two more pheasants,[96] and before long anyone strolling through the Sanctuary was sure to see one or more bright-plumed birds in the underbrush. Cochran's interest in this project remained strong. Hoyer remembers Tom paying early morning visits to talk with him while he smoked large numbers of Camel cigarettes. Cochran was a democratic man and insisted that Hoyer call him "Tom." Despite all the effort and money expended on the Sanctuary, it never completely fulfilled Cochran's dreams for it. As time went on, it was found that only a few boys came out to the Log Cabin, and it became necessary to discontinue serving food there. After that the Cabin was used on special occasions for Faculty parties, student meetings, and the like. After Cochran's death it was decided that the care of the birds was too expensive, and at the end of 1937 most of this part of the program was abandoned, some of the birds being turned loose, others sold.[97] The emphasis shifted to shrubs and trees, and the Sanctuary became an arboretum rather than a bird refuge. Later Wardens have concerned themselves with planting, pruning of trees, clearing out underbrush, and the like. The present Sanctuary is a joy to nature-lovers. Thanks to Cochran's vision, this beautiful addition to the Phillips Academy plant is unique among schools.

With the coming of the automobile and the truck, the Trustees of Phillips Academy were faced with an increasingly difficult problem of what to do about the traffic on Main Street. The problem was increased when the decision was made to locate a lot of important School buildings on the east side of the Campus while a substantial number of dormitories remained on the west side. This meant that a large number of undergraduates had to cross Main Street several times a day. Amazingly, there had been no serious accident, but the apprehension remained. In addition the automobile traffiic was noisy and dirty and destroyed the serenity of the Hill. As with everything else he did, Thomas Cochran believed in action, and he determined on a bold scheme to try to ameliorate this situation. Working with Comptroller Henry S. Hopper, he hired engineers to make a survey of a possible route that would by-pass the School to the east and join Route 114 east of the town. State approval would be necessary, and for this purpose the help of Trustee Philip L. Reed, a friend of Governor Frank G. Allen, was enlisted. On a cold January day in 1930 the Governor, the State Commissioner of Public Works, and various Phillips Academy representatives had lunch together in Boston and then drove out to Andover to inspect the proposed route. After extensive negotiations, it was finally agreed that the State would build the road if the Andover Trustees would purchase land and convey a hundred-foot right of way, approximately five miles in length, and pay the cost of construction of one mile of the road. The chances are that the State got the best of the bargain. Certainly, the project proved expensive. But Cochran never flinched. He ordered Henry Hopper to acquire the necessary land, which eventually meant fifty-six separate deeds and over four hundred acres, and the deal was on. But not without opposition. Farmers along the old route who had roadside stands protested vigorously that an important means of livelihood would be destroyed. Some merchants in the Town of Andover felt similarly. But the project went ahead nonetheless, and by the late fall of 1930 it was finished. Just how successful the "By-Pass" or "Cut-Off" has been is difficult to say. A study made shortly after the new road had been completed indicated that 45 percent of the traffic was being diverted to the new road. In recent times, with the tremendous increase in automotive traffic, Main Street is a busy highway. But one can take comfort from the fact that the existing situation would be infinitely worse had not Thomas Cochran built his By-Pass.[98]

All these projects were only a part of Thomas Cochran's program for Phillips Academy. In 1929 a handsome new dormitory, Paul Revere Hall, was completed, providing rooms for fifty-two boys and two bachelor masters. At the start Cochran conceived a novel plan for this building. He wished the income from the room rents to be used for another teaching foundation. Thus he could have both his building and his foundation from the same gift.[99] But various considerations convinced him later that the scheme was not feasible, and it was dropped. Paul Revere Hall was the final realization of Cecil Bancroft's dream of housing all the boys in School dormitories. Until its construction there had still been a few living in boarding houses. To complete what was at first called the "Little Quadrangle" and later Flagstaff Court, a splendid new dining hall was built on the south side and opened in 1930. Cochran estimated the cost of construction at $600,000 and offered to contribute $300,000 if the Trustees would raise another $300,000.[1] When completed, the building consisted of four large dining rooms, one for each class, handsomely paneled in wood, together with a faculty dining room and some smaller ones for group meals. At the time that the new dining hall, called The Commons, was opened, the School was still following the policy of having scholarship boys wait on table in return for their board, and the building was constructed with this procedure in mind. During World War II, when it was necessary to adopt a cafeteria program, lack of space in the serving areas presented problems, but recent remodeling has alleviated the difficulties to a large degree. The old Phillips Inn with its annex did not fit into the new scheme of things. Accordingly, it was moved to Bartlet Street and rechristened Stowe House, while the annex was torn down. In their place was constructed a gracious brick inn with a lovely garden behind it. To help pay for the Inn, Cochran induced some of his wealthy friends to contribute—a number of whom had no connection with Phillips Academy.

Like all small hotels, the Inn has had its financial problems, but it has survived to provide bed and board for Andover visitors and to serve as an additional ornament to the School.

Thomas Cochran's largesse to the Academy included other mundane things. When it became clear that the School needed a new heating plant, he provided the funds, using some of the income from the room rents in Paul Revere Hall that he had originally planned to devote to a teaching foundation. When Charles Platt told him that Bartlet and Foxcroft halls would fit better into the overall scheme of the Great Quadrangle if they were three stories rather than four, he again stepped forward and made possible the proposed change.[2] Having spent a sizable amount of money having the grounds landscaped and planted with shrubs and trees, he was concerned that their beauty be maintained; accordingly he gave one million dollars to establish the Emily Cochran Fund, the income from which had to be used on the care of the grounds.[3] Nor was his interest limited to building and grounds. Mention has already been made of his substantial contributions to the teaching foundations. He also contributed $10,000 to establish an annual concert named for his friend Jim Sawyer, in spite of the fact that Jim did not like music! When someone suggested that Al Stearns ought to have a similar honor, he gave another $10,000 to establish the Stearns Lecture—because, as he said, "Al doesn't like lectures."[4] Whimsical actions were characteristic of the man who at times had little patience with conventional modes of procedure. In 1928 he presented to the School an extraordinarily beautiful armillary sphere created by Paul Manship. Originally sited in front of Samuel Phillips Hall between Bartlet and Foxcroft Halls, it was later moved to a position in front of the Oliver Wendell Holmes Library.[5] Not everyone approved of the Armillary Sphere. One day a member of the Faculty noticed a workman polishing the Sphere, and asked him, "What are you doing? Taking some of the curse off the damn thing?" The workman, it turned out, was none other than Paul Manship himself.

His final gift—and a magnificent one—was the Cochran Chapel.[6] Given in the fall of 1930 and completed the following year, it was the only building in Andover to bear his name, and it completed his overall plan for the east campus. With its lofty spire it balanced the Memorial Tower to the south. Together with the Oliver Wendell Holmes Library and the Addison Gallery of American Art, the area west of the Great Quadrangle now presented a perfectly proportioned series of buildings. Al Stearns was not happy about the new chapel at first. Samaritan House, where he had lived for many years, had to be moved across the street, and to Al that was a kind of sacrilege. Furthermore, he had a sentimental fondness for the old stone chapel that dated from Seminary days. Yet he was finally won over. As he wrote Cochran:

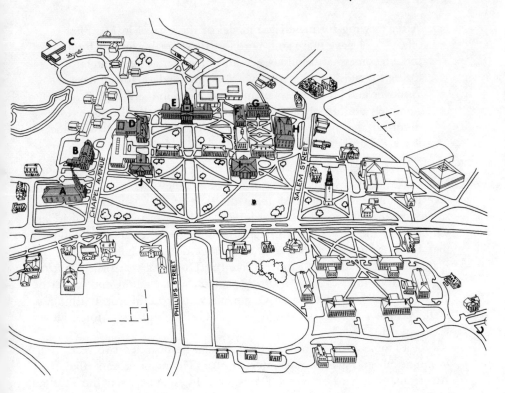

49. Projects on the campus of Phillips Academy constructed in whole
or in part from funds contributed by Thomas Cochran.
A The Cochran Chapel
B The Andover Inn
C The Moncrieff Cochran Bird Sanctuary
D George Washington Hall
E Samuel Phillips Hall
F Morse Hall
G Paul Revere Hall
H The Commons
I The Oliver Wendell Holmes Library
J The Addison Gallery of American Art

> After viewing for myself the model of the Chapel in Mr. Platt's
> office . . . I have more and more lost those qualms and natural,
> though somewhat nebulous, feelings of regret at the thought of
> losing the old building with which all my undergraduate days at
> Andover and all the years of my later work in the school have been
> so closely and deeply associated. The new Chapel will soon fill its
> dignified and influential place in our life and . . . I shall welcome
> it with real gratitude.[7]

When the Chapel was dedicated in the spring of 1932, Stearns, who had
been on leave of absence because of a serious illness, was able to return to
take part in the ceremony. At about the time of the dedication, someone
suggested that it would be appropriate to have memorial stained-glass
windows in the new edifice, to replace some of the clear glass windows
that Platt had installed. News of this suggestion sent both Cochran and
Platt into a rage, and the former wrote the Trustees a sharp letter, enclosing one from Platt as well, insisting that such desecration must never be
allowed.[8] The Martha Cochran Organ, previously in George Washington
Hall, was moved to the new building, and Cochran's program for Andover
was complete.

Not a moment too soon. Had the program been started two years later,
it might never have been completed, for Thomas Cochran, like most
Americans, was hard hit by the Depression. In 1932 he wrote the Trustees
requesting them to modify the terms of his gift of $650,000 to the Ad-
dison Gallery Endowment Fund. Were he obliged to raise the sum at that
time, he wrote, it would entail a very heavy sacrifice, and he asked that he
be allowed to spread the payments over a term of years. If the sum had
not been paid by the time of his death, he pledged one fifth of his estate
for that purpose. Naturally the Trustees were more than willing to grant
the request.[9] This was the last important piece of business that Cochran
did with the Trustees. After the dedication of the Cochran Chapel, he
never returned to Andover again. Throughout his life he had been subject
to fits of depression, and in 1932 he suffered a severe breakdown which
resulted in his becoming an invalid for the rest of his life, isolated from
all his former associates. It is sad to record that in 1936, just before he
died, he sent a check for five dollars to the Phillips Academy Alumni
Fund, explaining wistfully that it was all he could afford. His estate, however, proved to be over three million dollars, a substantial fraction of
which went, according to his promise, to the Addison Gallery Endowment
Fund.[10]

Expansion of the Phillips Academy plant under Al Stearns was an extraordinary achievement. A good start had been made before the Cochran
era, with the acquisition of the Seminary property and the construction of
the new dormitories and of Samuel Phillips Hall. Yet it was the vision of

Thomas Cochran and Charles Platt that transformed the Andover campus into one of the most beautiful educational areas in the United States. Cochran never stated his broad aims better than in a letter to Nathaniel Stevens, a generous benefactor of the School, written in December 1927:

> We are all trying to do a real job on Andover Hill and one that will affect the whole question of secondary education in America. It always has seemed a strange thing to me that the rich men of our country have lavished literally hundreds of millions of dollars upon the universities of the land and have almost entirely neglected the preparatory schools such as Phillips Academy. It has seemed particularly strange because every thoughtful man admits that character transcends intellect in importance, and between the ages of twelve and eighteen, when a boy is at preparatory school, his character is in a more formative state than when he takes up his university life later on. 'As the twig is bent so grows the tree,' and thus I believe that our rich men should pay more attention to the schools of the land than to the universities where the development of the intellect is the principal function. This is the great reason why I am interested in Phillips Academy. I believe if we can equip the Academy with adequate buildings and with a well paid contented inspiring faculty that we will place a beacon on Andover Hill, the gleams from which will spread to every state in the Union and will affect secondary education tremendously. At least this is our ambition and this is what we are working for.[11]

People may differ as to how much influence Thomas Cochran's beacon had on American secondary education generally, but there can be no question of that beacon's effect on Phillips Academy. As James Sawyer wrote him:

> I am sure that you are building much greater than you have any idea of. It is the result of a great vision and a generous heart, and it should be a great source of satisfaction and happiness to you as the years go on to feel that you have afforded so much inspiration and joy to these boys and their successors.[12]

CHAPTER FOURTEEN

THE GOLDEN TWENTIES

T HE PERIOD of the 1920's was indeed a golden time in the history of Phillips Academy. The program for the School which had been initiated by Cecil Bancroft was now completed under Al Stearns, and the result was an institution that bore little resemblance to that of Eliphalet Pearson and the early principals. Pearson's program emphasized academic excellence, concentration on the classics, discipline through fear, dictatorship of the Principal, dependence on town families for student housing, concern for the education of indigent young men, and an overriding interest in the moral and religious life of the student. By 1920 things were very different. There was the same insistence on academic excellence, but the classics, though still required, were in competition with a broad range of courses in other subjects. And it would not be long before even the classics requirement was dropped. The disciplinary system was still based to a large extent on fear, but it was administered primarily by the Faculty rather than by the Principal alone. The undergraduates, furthermore, considered disciplinary problems pretty much as a game of cops and robbers, particularly with respect to the younger members of the Faculty. The Principal was no longer dictator. Starting under Dr. Bancroft, the Faculty had come to assume a larger and larger role in the policy-making function for the school, and Al Stearns had not tampered with this system. With the construction of Paul Revere Hall in 1929, the last undergraduates who had previously been housed in private families could now move into School dormitories, and Dr. Bancroft's dream was realized. A second part of the Pearson program remained unchanged—the interest in scholarship boys, and the program in this area was as strong as ever in the 1920's and had become a hallmark of an Andover education. Throughout Al Stearns' tenure as Principal,[1] he remained deeply concerned about the moral and religious education of the students. There was a semi-religious chapel service every weekday and two religious services on Sundays. But the tone was relaxed when compared to the harsh Calvinism of an earlier day. There was a lot of music, and the favorite preacher was

William Lyon Phelps of Yale, who was not a clergyman and whose sermons would consist of three or four funny stories tied together with a moral. The morale of the School was high in the 1920's. There were certainly unhappy boys, those who resented not being chosen for membership in one of the School fraternities, for example, but School spirit, especially in support of athletic teams, was remarkably high. Some great teachers, many of whom had been hired by Dr. Bancroft, were in their prime and influenced boys in a way they would never forget. The excitement that accompanied the Cochran building program could not but foster pride in the School and convince the Andover community that the worth and prestige of the institution were increasing. Finally, in Al Stearns the undergraduates had a father figure who looked every inch the part and who seemed to personify what Andover was all about.

Phillips Academy entered the 1920's after a brief but exhilarating experience during World War I. As with earlier conflicts, World War I did not seriously disturb the life of the School, and the changes that did occur provided interesting varieties to the regimen of undergraduate existence. Late in 1914, after the struggle in Europe had beeen joined, Trustee Henry L. Stimson, fresh from his position as Secretary of War in President William Howard Taft's cabinet, suggested that training in rifle shooting be required of all Phillips Academy undergraduates.[2] Nothing as inclusive as that was ever introduced, but encouraged by a special visit of Stimson and General Leonard Wood, the Rifle Club was formed. At the start it was handicapped because it could not purchase rifles or find a suitable range, but eventually the Trustees built a range in the basement of Borden Gymnasium and some 140 boys took the training course.[3] In late 1914 the undergraduates, together with the Faculty and Trustees, contributed $750 toward the purchase of a Ford ambulance for use by the American Ambulance Hospital on the western front. In the early days of the war many Americans were raising money for this purpose. The following year the community was informed that the Andover ambulance was Number 127 and was operating in the area of St. Maurice. In 1916 the school received a long account of the activities of the driver of Number 127, and later that year a report that even though many ambulances had been destroyed, the Andover one was still going strong.[4] It is interesting to note that in the early years of the war both sides were represented in Andover news: early in 1915 it was reported that Herr Fritz Hellmuth, formerly a Prussian Exchange teacher at Phillips Academy, had returned to the front after having been severely wounded. For his exploits he had been awarded the Iron Cross.[5] For reasons that are not immediately apparent, the Academy undergraduates sent a large number of neckties to the wounded in English hospitals and received a warm letter of thanks from the physician in charge.[6] All these activities were extracurricular, however, and had little effect on basic routine.

All of this changed when the United States entered the war in April
1917. Some undergraduates who were old enough immediately volunteered
and left the Hill. Almost all of those who remained were soon enrolled
in an ROTC program, designed to prepare them for military service should
that become necessary. The program was compulsory for the two upper
classes and for everyone over sixteen in the two lower classes, and optional for any others who could get their parents' permission. Major Robert Davy of the Canadian Army was in charge. Drill started on 29 October 1917, with 510 out of 570 boys enrolled. It required three hours
a week, with the boys studying the School of the Soldier, the School of the
Squad, and the School of the Company. Monty Peck of the Physical Education Department was Battalion Adjutant. In addition there was a voluntary officers' school on Tuesday and Friday nights, though it was reported
that the "less proficient" had been dismissed from it. Wanting official
recognition as an ROTC unit, Al Stearns and Major Davy went to Washington and saw Secretary of War Newton D. Baker. Baker said that they
could not be official with a Canadian in charge, so a Major in Boston was
put in theoretical command while Davy continued to do the work. The
uniforms are described as barrack caps with the letters ROTC on them,
high-collared jackets, and "spiral puttees." Apparently many of the boys
wore these uniforms home at Christmas time. In addition there was a

50. *The Andover Battalion, 1918.*

Battalion band of twenty-two instruments. Target practice was conducted in the basement of Pearson Hall, where a new range had been constructed. An editorial in the *Phillips Bulletin* spoke of the change on Andover Hill: "The boys, erect and khaki-clad, the flags flung out from windows along the street, the flare of bugles and the roll of drums were, throughout the spring time, outward and obvious signs of change."[7] The *Bulletin's* description of the ROTC program ended on a self-satisfied note: Phillips Academy had solved the problem of military training without disrupting the School; the boys were willing to sacrifice their teams in order to perfect the ROTC; and it was predicted that by spring the unit would be indeed a crack one.[8]

This was all very well, but the *Bulletin* description hardly coincides with undergraduate opinion. One alumnus correspondent writes of the ROTC program:

> Those of us at Andover in '17 and '18 were victims of our pre-paredness rage. We were all put into olive drab, and drab and itchy it surely was. We were formed into companies and subjected to daily drilling. As if by magic, we found ourselves under the command of fellow students we had never heard of before who strutted around in Sam Brown belts and leather puttees while we wrestled with the infernal wrap around nonsense inherited from the British. A boy from Tennessee was head of the whole undergraduate business and as the companies were disbanded in '19 sank into oblivion where, so far as I know, he remains. The first year's training ended with a sham battle supervised by the school Medico Page who was known as "Paint it with Iodine" and who always wore bright yellow shoes and a blue suit which, with his short stature, dark black hair and black eyes, reminded one of a Mexican bandit. The battle was totally inconclusive and generally pronounced a crashing bore.[9]

Another alumnus correspondent agrees generally about the program but had a great time at another sham battle:

> During 1917 and 1918 most of the students were in uniform as members of the Andover regiment. As I recall, the majority of the boys resented the military program and especially having to wear those uncomfortable, high collared uniforms and the wrap around puttees. Many a boy was late for chapel or class due to putting on those 3 foot long puttees. In April a sham battle was to be staged at Pomp's Pond. The regiment was divided into two units—the blues and the whites. Much planning and study had gone into this exercise; it was to be a battle of strategy, one unit trying to outmaneuver the other and the one capturing the most prisoners declared the winner. Some groups disregarded orders and made a game of cops and

robbers of the military operation. They raced through the woods in all directions, out of touch with their command, and were soon in contact with the enemy. There was not supposed to be any physical contact; just the surrounding of a group meant surrender, but that was not the way some of the boys wanted to play. There was much rough and tumble hand to hand contact and the entire exercise developed into a gigantic wrestling match, fortunately without any serious casualty. One group had planned a surprise attack by using some six or seven canoes on the Shawsheen. When this unit rounded a bend in the river they were caught by a larger unit of the enemy which was supposed to mean surrender, but the boys weren't satisfied with that rule and proceeded to tip the canoes over with poles. In all, some twenty soldiers were dumped into the icy water, guns and all. Needless to say the staff officers were disgusted with the entire performance, but the rank and file of the regiment had one of their best fun days in uniform.

A secretary in the Alumni Office remembers a story from the military training days:

One amusing incident in connection with the Army Camp established on the Campus occurred when an employee of the engineering department, intent on pursuing the shortest path between the engineering office and an engineering problem in the general area of the Commons, was stopped at the entrance to the Campus by the guard on duty and asked for the password. Possibly a bit impatient with the whole idea of "playing soldier," no matter how commendable the purpose, the employee, who happened not to know the password of the day, kept on walking. At this effrontery, the guard, as he had been instructed, said, "Stop or I'll shoot." After a minute's consideration of the situation, the engineering employee remarked calmly, "Go ahead and shoot" and kept on walking. Obviously, military rules and regulations took a back seat to civilian expediency. No shots were fired.

An interesting sidelight in the history of Phillips Academy during the war years was Al Stearns's confrontation with Hearst newspapers. During the period before the entry of the United States into World War I, these newspapers had been printing articles and editorials which, if they were not pro-German, were certainly anti-British. Al was devoted to the cause of the Allies, and such writing he considered little short of treason. Accordingly, in chapel one morning he launched a scathing attack on the Hearst editorial policy and urged the undergraduates not to buy any more Hearst newspapers. Apparently his message came through loud and clear, for the sale of Hearst newspapers on the Hill dropped off to close to zero.

A few days later a representative of the circulation department of the Hearst newspapers in Boston called on Al. He explained that his job was to sell newspapers and suggested that Al's boycott was violating freedom of expression. Al insisted that he had not ordered any boy to stop buying the papers and that their decision to do so was their own. With the entry of the United States into the war, the Hearst policy shifted, and presumably the Andover boycott was relaxed.[10]

As 1918 wore on and it became clear that an Allied victory was only a matter of time, enthusiasm for the ROTC program dwindled, and at their meeting in December just after the Armistice, the Trustees voted that military training for Andover undergraduates should end.[11] It seems clear that such a program was not a wise one for secondary school students. Many undergraduates who were old enough volunteered for the armed services without any previous training. Furthermore, national leaders were urging secondary school students to remain in school and get a good academic training. When World War II came along, the School would develop a physical fitness program that was much better suited to the needs of the boys.

Whatever reservations one might have about military training, at least the end of the war was celebrated in style by the undergraduates. The first of the alumni correspondents cited above writes this description:

> The real Armistice Day was something never to be forgotten. The Inn was in the process of extensive alterations and there reposed on the ground a large pile of window blinds. They formed the base of a tremendous bonfire that consumed about every loose object available. The bell of the old chapel was rung by Al Stearns and his son until they broke the rope, I am told. All this was in the morning and was followed by a torch light parade around town that or the next night.

The war over, Phillips Academy reconverted to a peacetime basis almost immediately and embarked on what was to be a golden decade. Then as always responsibility for the School was in the hands of the Board of Trustees. The creation of separate boards for the Academy and the Seminary at the time of the latter's transfer to Cambridge paid off handsomely in the work of the reconstituted Board. In terms of service it was an old Board—only the New York financier and friend of Thomas Cochran, George B. Case, had been elected after 1913. At the head as President was Alfred Ripley, a very careful and conservative Boston banker. Harvard was represented by two professors: James Hardy Ropes, a *summa* at Harvard and now Hollis Professor of Divinity, a man with a keen but often inflexible mind; and Clifford H. Moore, Professor of the Classics at Harvard. Henry L. Stimson had already had a distinguished career as

United States Attorney for the Southern District of New York and as Secretary of War in Taft's cabinet. Before the decade was out he would be back in public service as Governor-General of the Philippines and then Hoover's Secretary of State. Elias B. Bishop was a Justice of the Superior Court of Massachusetts and the Board's authority on legal matters. All but Clifford Moore were Andover graduates, and Moore had taught at the School for a short time. In 1923 Thomas Cochran would be elected, and in 1926 Ernest Martin Hopkins, the President of Dartmouth and an old friend of Al Stearns. In 1929 Ripley resigned as President but not from the Board and was succeeded by James Hardy Ropes. In running the School the Board tended to follow the precedent of Uncle Sam Taylor's Board and let the Principal run the show. In an article on his relations with the Board, Al Stearns wrote:

> It was Dr. Bancroft's aim to guide and restrain when necessary but generally to carry out the expressed opinion of his faculty in all large matters of school administration. And this has been the aim of his successor. . . . In his relation to the trustees the principal of today then is largely the mouthpiece of the faculty. By his position as a member of both bodies he is given a unique opportunity to state the viewpoints of both and to harmonize conflicting opinions. With the internal administration of school affairs the trustees have little concern, preferring to leave all matters relating to discipline, curriculum etc. to the faculty for decision. But in the broader policies of school development . . . the trustees have wide authority and almost unlimited powers. . . . Some one man must be held responsible for carrying out the policies decided upon. . . . This responsibility is vested in the principal; and it is the function of the trustees to see that it is met, to supply needed backing if the occasion demands it, and to curb and restrain if the necessity for such action arises. . . . Having selected their helmsman, the trustees are not disposed to hamper him in the performance of his task. And they are free from serious anxiety as to the outcome, for if the course he steers is one of which they cannot approve, they have only to put another man in charge of the wheel.[12]

The Trustee Records of the 1920's do indeed indicate that they were willing to let Al Stearns run the School. A large part of the minutes of meetings deal with acknowledging gifts from Thomas Cochran and others, and most of the rest deal with routine matters. They voted $1000 to the Harvard Polio Commission for aid during a polio outbreak at Phillips Academy;[13] they passed a vote of thanks to the Cadillac Company of Lawrence for providing cars for the Sesquicentennial;[14] and they voted Al Stearns a year off to work with Henry L. Stimson in the Philippines, a sabbatical that never came to pass.[15] The only interesting thing they did in

51. Alfred Ernest Stearns in the 1920's.

the area of educational policy was to vote in favor of a five-year program, with a separate lower school that was not to be in Andover but nearby.[16] One criterion of a successful administration is its willingness to let competent people alone so that they can do their jobs; judged by this standard, the Andover Board in the 1920's gets high marks.

There is no question that Al Stearns ran the School in the 1920's. To be sure he had Lester Lynde to do a lot of the admissions work and Cecil (Pooby) Bancroft as registrar. To be sure there were regular Faculty meetings where important policy questions were often settled. But Al did not hesitate to step in and take over when occasion demanded. One of the attributes that humanized him for the boys in earlier years was his ability to coach and play baseball. He had to give this up in the 1920's and as a result he became a more austere, distant, and awe-inspiring figure for the undergraduates. He remained very conservative in his political and social outlook. He was outraged, for example, that anyone should suggest that Sacco and Vanzetti were innocent.[17] And when President Coolidge came to Andover at the end of the decade, Al accorded him something very close to adoration. But he was unquestionably respected by the entire School community. Year after year the seniors voted him "Most Respected" in their yearbook. Here are some impressions of Al written by various alumni correspondents:

> . . . to my mind, he was a terrifying creature and I think I would start shaking if he walked into my office right now. I do recall his praying morning after morning in Chapel for us to be forgiven for the base and sordid in our lives. [When I won a prize at commencement] 'eagle-beak Al' didn't know me although I had been on the hill for three years.

> About Alfred E. Stearns—it was him I saw in my mind's eye when I visited Geneva . . . and went to Calvin's church.

> Al Stearns towered above all of his contemporaries in the skill with which he developed character among his students. Al made perfectly clear the distinctions between black and white in such matters as honesty and integrity. . . . If ever a man taught and urged a boy to do the darndest he could with whatever talents he had available, it was Al Stearns. Moreover, if this boy did not dedicate his efforts to the best interest of everyone for whom he was responsible, he knew in advance that here or in some later world he would be called to account to Al Stearns for having failed to pay the price of the great privilege of having a superior education.

> Alfred Stearns, Headmaster, was not a lesser god, but the Jupiter of

this largely Latin pantheon. Tall and erect, he walked like a god
among us, head back with high beaked nose and eagle's eyes, and
full white hair with wind in its curl. I recognized his face at once,
years later, when I saw Michel-Angelo's Moses in San Pietro Vinculi.
. . . It was *his* school. He made all the decisions, hired and fired the
faculty, and handled all student discipline. . . . when two prominent
seniors had been fired for coming back from Boston to Sunday
vespers 'with liquor on their breath', we rushed through our work
[at the Commons] and ran all the way across campus to hear Stearns
thunder his angry indignation. We were rewarded. He was a magnificent speaker, and when he was angry made the rafters ring. We
trembled too, and resolved to sin no more.

I was scared stiff of all of them and particularly the Headmaster
from whom I got the impression, despite his cordial manner, that
he really had no understanding of boys like me. He seemed to be in
a world apart. . . . He always greeted us affably but not by name,
and I never thought he really knew one of us from Adam. Maybe
this standoffishness is what inspired our fear and led us to strictly
observe the rules and regulations.

Another virtue of Al Stearns: he emphasized the importance of the
faculty. Everything was done in the name of the faculty. I know that
he had almost dictatorial powers, but if he ever used them, he hid
the occasions from the students. All questions were subject to faculty
approval. The faculty, according to Al, ran the school.

Awed by the Dr. Arnold-ish Alfred E. Stearns—I don't suppose I
ever dared exchange a word with him. He was really God. Nor did
we ever question one of his rules or judgments. . . . One did not
love him or hate him, or perhaps even fear him. He was simply the
personification of cold authority. I can't remember enjoying one of
his sermons, and I certainly haven't retained any of his wisdom, or
to my knowledge, followed his moral or religious advice. I simply
knew that he made the rules, and it would never have occurred to
me to dispute them.

Stearns had one little weakness: he had a certain naivete about certain things that he should have understood. A story went around the
campus in my day (true or apocryphal) about the four boys who had
been caught gambling. Hauled before the Head, they were asked
what game they had been playing. 'Only bridge,' one replied. 'And
what were the stakes?' asked Stearns. 'Only half a cent' was the
reply. 'Oh,' said Stearns, 'that's not much, is it?'

I suppose I got to know Al Stearns as well as anybody—I served as a counsellor at his camp at First Connecticut Lake one summer. I was in awe of him; his moral perfectionism image was hard to break through, and I never had any warm relationship with him. . . . I was no doubt wary and defensive in relating to him, because my supposed religious 'kick' was fairly hypocritical.

But few of us had the privilege of experiencing the warm, affectionate nature which was his when engaged in relaxing conversation with friends and with the lucky students who visited him on informal occasions. These occasions were infrequent because Al, I am sure, felt that his job demanded of him the lonely eminence of a ship captain who must make decisions which are often unpleasant if not hurtful to his associates, his subordinates and those otherwise in his charge.

Principal Alfred E. Stearns, magnificent Christian athlete, made an indelibly favorable impression on me at my first assembly in the Chapel and it became apparent that he was universally admired by the students. He was approachable, not a bit awesome, a fair and genuinely concerned leader. He was also baseball coach, which meant a lot to me. As a senior I was a rookie pitching aspirant, with sand-lot experience in the outfield and none on the mound. Dr. Stearns indicated that he saw some potential in a strong arm and a good motion and though I did not earn a letter, I was indebted to him for the encouragement that led to a pitching role in college.

It was not until I was about to enter Yale that I had the good fortune to meet the real Al Stearns. I learned that I would be admitted to college on condition, so I returned to Andover for advice and Al Stearns happened to be the only one available at the time. To my surprise he greeted me warmly and took a personal interest in my problem. He said Amherst College would provide a worthwhile and happy experience for me. I unwittingly asked him where Amherst was. He then told me of his association with the college since boyhood. He even phoned Dean Esty to tell him I was on my way. . . . [In later years] I shall always remember how pleased and proud he made me feel when I would meet him on the street and he might be with some one, he would turn and say 'meet one of my old boys' and give my name.

The man's voice was his greatest asset. Deep and sonorous, he spoke from the pulpit or the assembly and at a rally with an air of conviction that was comforting at times and contagious at others.

I was attending a private, snobbish school south of Boston. It was the time of the financial crash, and the following fall I would have attended the local high school. Not for me. I wrote for information on the various prominent private prep schools. I decided that Andover was *the place for me*. This was a ridiculous decision, as it was pointed out by my family who were in no position to pay for tuition. Also my academic record was miserable and my athletic ability nil. There were no alumni to recommend me either.

So what to do? I wrote a five-page personal letter to Dr. Stearns. . . . Not once did I mention any attribute that might have qualified me as a student at Andover. I went on and on in an exaggerated, flowery language how I had flunked four out of five courses, how I was the most unpopular boy in school, and there was no money to pay for my support, that I had never participated in any of the school's extra curricular activities. I recall exactly the end of the letter, 'If there is any further information you may need, I will be glad to supply the same.' And I added a P.S.—'I'll be working at the Atlantic and Pacific store this summer and will have saved $250 toward the tuition.'

I was trusting that Al Stearns would be curious at the comical absurdity of my letter. And he was! I received a formal letter to meet him in his office the following week. I recall so vividly my first impression of the man. As I entered his office, naturally I was nervous, but that was soon dispelled. Dr. Stearns' solemn countenance broke into a large grin, and when he told me that he had never received such a letter as mine in all his years of academic life, we were both laughing. He went on to say there was a scholarship for a student who showed marked improvement his first year, and he roared with laughter when he said it wouldn't be difficult for me to show improvement over my past record! . . . As I left the office, I remember his exact words, 'Grow up!' and there was a warm smile upon his otherwise solemn face.

As can be seen by the above excerpts, Al Stearns was not an easy man to categorize. One's opinion of him would depend a great deal on chance and circumstance. Yet without doubt he was a dominant force in the school; Andover in the 1920's would not have been the same without him.

The Phillips Academy Faculty in the 1920's was a strong and colorful group of men. Some of the older ones who had been hired by Dr. Bancroft were then at the height of their powers, and there were able younger men to give balance to the whole. In 1926, for example, the Faculty consisted of forty-five instructors, which represented a ratio of one to fourteen boys. This ratio had not changed much over the past ten years, for as the

School grew in size, so did the Faculty. Like the undergraduate body, the Faculty came from a wide variety of geographical backgrounds. The forty-five had among themselves graduated from twenty-three different colleges. Only a few had more than two representatives: Yale, 8; Harvard, 5; Amherst, 4; Brown, 3; and Dartmouth, 3. The rest ranged as far afield as the University of Aberdeen. At the head of the Faculty roster was Charles Henry Forbes, who had attained his position by acting as Principal while Al Stearns was on sabbatical in 1913–14. Charlie Forbes sat on Al Stearns's right hand during chapel services. "Pooby," Cecil's son, sat on his left. The three of them made an impressive triumvirate. It was Pooby Bancroft's job to read the daily notices, and since he was so naive that he would read almost anything, the undergraduates soon developed a game of seeing what they could get Pooby to read. On one occasion Pooby read an announcement that a very effeminate boy was going to give flying lessons to anyone interested. On another, it was announced that a boy who had been remarked rubbing up against his girl at a recent tea dance would give boxing lessons. But the classic notice came on Good Friday, when Pooby read out in all seriousness that Father O'Leary of St. Augustine's parish wished to announce a steak dinner in the parish house, to be followed by Confession. It was clear that even Al Stearns thought this was great. But Charlie Forbes had nothing to do with this nonsense and maintained an imperturbable calm throughout.

Charlie Forbes was certainly one of the great teachers of his day, and his course in Virgil's *Aenead* was a must for most Andover seniors in the 1920's. Although he demanded a precise rendering of the text from his students, his classes included as well short homilies on a wide variety of other subjects—descriptions of Rome, the necessity of having regular bowel movements, political events at home and abroad, the virtue of mental discipline, and the like. His mind was facile, and perhaps superficial at times. He knew a great deal of Latin but he never produced any scholarly writing. Claude Fuess has written of him:

> Temperamentally he was a conservative, with a preference for traditions, established customs, and well-worn roads, yet occasionally he showed unaccountable flashes of liberalism. He disliked intensely all agitators, communists, "smart alecks," "flappers," and Democrats, as well as bad manners, flashiness, irreverence, and the *New Republic*.[18]

Charlie used to write some verse, which his friends thought consistently bad. He loved puns, which often made his students wince. On the other hand he wrote some beautiful prayers for use in the chapel services. Because he and/or his wife had substantial independent means, the Forbeses' life style was unlike any other on the Hill. He was driven to classes by a chauffeur in a large black limousine. His home was a striking example of

52. *Charles Henry Forbes, Professor of Latin, 1891–1932. Acting Headmaster, 1932–1933.*

careless opulence. Friends fortunate enough to be invited to dinner could count on a Lucullan repast. After dinner Charlie might entertain the guests with his gift of mimicry or take them to his wood-working shop and show them the admirable pieces of furniture that he had made. Their means enabled the Forbeses to play Santa Claus to all the children of the community at Christmas time, and they performed countless acts of generosity throughout the year. Charlie loved golf and played regularly until, in his later years, he was slowed down by the gout. Toward the end of his career he was delighted when Amherst College awarded him an honorary degree. Here, then, was a charming, Pickwickian man, a gifted teacher, beloved by students and Faculty alike.[19]

One alumnus remembers Charlie as follows:

> His full, florid face with bristling white eyebrows could be stamped on a Roman coin. While he wore well tailored English clothes, one remembers him in a flowing toga, like those on the statues pictured on his wall, for he inhabited Virgil's Rome as Zeus Benner did Pericles's Athens. All year we read the *Aenead*, nothing else. Written as a work of fiction, an epic poem to glorify the origins of what had become Imperial Rome, this had none of the ring of observed events we found in the *Iliad*. But it was a stirring tale, clothed in elegant language, and Forbes used it as a guide to Augustan Rome, bringing that world alive as no other Latin teacher had done. . . . Forbes was an urbane, witty man. His manner in the classroom was that of a gentleman entertaining us in his home. He was acting Headmaster that year . . . so when my parents came to visit we had dinner at his house, a beautiful Colonial one, elegantly furnished. He took us down to the basement to show us his woodworking shop, where he made fine furniture. Without Forbes, Rome and its great language would have remained dead for us. The others who taught Latin did it as a drill, with one goal in mind, high marks on the College Boards.

Another remembers a different aspect of Charlie Forbes:

> He was always driven to his class by a uniformed chauffeur in a large black car occupying the rear seat by himself. He usually allowed an insufficient margin of time and according to the traditions of the day, when the bell rang, students were permitted to leave without incurring a "cut." Several times as he came up the stairs about 30 seconds too late the entire class would hide in other empty classrooms and go down the other stairway.

Another former student remembers the charming way in which Charlie taught meter:

> He was a man of profound learning from the universities of Italy

53. Allen Rogers Benner of the Class of 1888, Professor of Greek, 1892–1938.

and Germany. . . . But his learning was never stuffy or pedantic.
I can see him at his desk, beaming at us from behind his round
spectacles and strumming out the rhythm of the dactylic hexameter
ending with phrases like:

> "Johnny, don't do that.
> Sister, be careful.
> Mama, come home now."

He would call out: "Think of a lovely girl's name; it had a dactylic
hexameter ending like this:

> Margaret Johnson."[20]

And a fourth:

> I did not find Latin an easy subject under Charlie Forbes as I tried
> to trot my way through his classes. I would like to have the money
> I spent on trots as each time Charlie caught me using one in class
> he took it away from me.

Another Titan among Andover teachers in the 1920's was Allen Rogers
("Zeus") Benner. He had graduated from Andover in 1888 and four
years later won his A.B. from Harvard *summa cum laude*. Cecil Bancroft
persuaded him to return to Phillips Academy after graduation, and he remained at the School until his retirement in 1938, first as Instructor in
Greek and later as Professor of Greek on one of Thomas Cochran's foundations. In 1928 he received an honorary Master of Arts from Amherst
College, and he authored several Greek texts as well as performing yeoman
service as Secretary of his Harvard class. Zeus was very conservative politically, and one of his pet aversions in his later years was Franklin Delano
Roosevelt. One day in class a boy asked what a "talent" was worth. Zeus
replied, "About $1000, that is before Mr. Roosevelt's administration.
Heaven knows what it is worth now." On another occasion Zeus tried to
mail a package on Washington's Birthday, a national holiday, found the
post office closed, and stomped down the steps, his arms stuck out like para-
vanes muttering "That man Roosevelt." Supposedly because of an unhappy
love affair, Zeus was very shy with women. On one occasion a mother was
visiting her son in Andover Cottage, Zeus's dormitory, when there came a
knock on the door. It proved to be Zeus, who asked the son, "Has Fred the
janitor made your bed?" The boy replied that he had. "Well he hasn't
made mine," said Zeus. The Mother, wishing to be helpful, said "Mr.
Benner, would you like me to make your bed for you?" Zeus's expression
was one of horror as he said, "Oooooh Nooo, Dear Lady, Oooooh Nooo."
But these are minor sides to him when compared to his power in the classroom and his lifelong devotion to his beloved Greek. It was his misfortune
to watch the number of students taking the subject gradually decline, first
when it was no longer required, and later when it got squeezed out of the
curriculum by other supposedly more modern courses. Throughout his ca-

reer, though the numbers in his classes might decline, the boys who had him would never forget the experience. For him teaching was his whole life, and his students were his friends, as his successor wrote of him:

> But his whole life was really the school. Not long after his retirement he told me that scarcely a night passed that he did not dream of Andover. He left behind him the only monument any teacher desires, an abiding memory in the hearts of his pupils of a great subject greatly taught, and of a friendship which outlasts time and death.[21]

A former student writes of Zeus:

> Zeus Benner was a joy in every respect. Handsome and dignified, possessed of profound learning, he loved his Greek and he was zealous to impart that love and that learning to his students. Zeus expected much of us and was concerned that every one of his boys should do well. Therefore we generally were happy to oblige him and do the best we could. But occasionally we "goofed off," and were unprepared for the day's assignment. We therefore devised a lightning rod that was guaranteed to divert the Olympian wrath. Shortly after the class convened—and before our deficiences could be revealed—one of us would guilelessly ask Zeus to tell us something about Paris. Paris to Zeus was the very lowest rung on the ladder leading down to Hell. The question, therefore, was sure to evoke a sermon on the iniquities of the City of Light, its denizens, its works. It was always good for the balance of the hour.

The following presents a different aspect of Zeus:

> One of my pleasantest recollections of Andover days is the close association that I had with "Zeus" Benner. I lived across the hall from him on the top floor of Andover Cottage. Early in the year I convinced him that he should have an automobile so he purchased a Studebaker coupe and I proceeded to teach him how to drive, which was really a terrifying experience. However "Zeus" had it set with Al Stearns that he could take me out of town any time he wanted to and the result was that we left Andover every Wednesday at twelve o'clock, went to Boston, where Zeus would purchase tickets for the third row center at the best musical comedy in town, and then after the show, Zeus would always take me to dinner in some very nice restaurant and then thank me most kindly when we got back to Andover for having gone with him.

Not all his students were enthusiastic about Zeus, however:

> Zeus Benner was, I thought, an eccentric but fascinating person. But he did me, and others studying Greek, a great disservice. When he

saw us wearying as we marched 16 parasangs a day to the next "beautiful city" in Xenophon's Chronicles, he would say that our struggles with grammar and endings would be over when we got to the *Iliad*. But alas, at the first lesson senior year he wanted to know the difference between the classical and ancient endings. This finished me. I quit and have regretted it ever since.

And this extraordinarily sensitive account of Zeus by Amory Bradford, '30:

At Andover Cottage I climbed to the third floor and knocked on the heavy oak door of Benner's room. A rich deep voice, appropriate to Zeus the Thunderer, boomed out: "Come in." I remember the room as filled with sunlight, but so are all my memories of him. Seated in his big Morris chair by the window, his powerful body and strong, lined face radiated a calmed energy.

After reading the note, he put it aside, and turned to me: "You're Bradford, aren't you?"

"Yes sir."

"I hear you are a very good student. Why aren't you taking Greek?"

Startled, I explained that I had added French this year as a fourth course and second language, thinking that a modern foreign language would be more useful to me, but that I was disappointed in the way Mr. Parmalee was teaching it.

"It's a complete waste of time for you," he said. "You should transfer to Greek right away."

"Can I do that?"

"Of course! Of course! I'll write a note which you can take back to the Office." He scratched one out. Taking it back, I felt a new excitement, full of expectation. This was soon fulfilled. Once the strange alphabet, with its sense of mystery, was learned, which took about two days, Greek proved to be an easy language, much easier than Latin. Its sentence structure, more like English, did not involve the gymnastics of rearranging subject and verb, and the vocabulary exercises seemed more direct and meaningful. Benner helped this by tracing many roots from Sanskrit through Greek, Latin, German, French, and English, giving us a sense of the evolution of this family of languages.

By the end of the first year we were marching across Asia Minor with Xenophon, parasang after parasang, and finally rejoicing in the cry "thalassa, O thalassa" when we reached the sea. It was a small class, of about a dozen, all eager students, since it was an elective course and Benner taught with infective enthusiasm. His stories of Fifth Century Athens, of Pericles, Alcibiades and Socrates, of the plays from Prometheus to the Frogs, of customs and manners, were told us as if he had been there—as indeed he had. In his visits to

Athens over thirty years his vivid imagination, fired by constant reading, had recreated there the people, the buildings, the very mood and spirit, of the Fifth Century B.C. In the classroom he was usually on his feet, striding up and down in front of the class as he talked, or leaning on a tall pointer he carried like a billiard cue to listen to someone recite.

Over half the desks were empty, and we were allowed to scatter among them, which gave an informal feeling. As I recall, though it seems unlikely, we remained seated to recite. At any rate, the feeling was that of taking part in an even conversational exchange on an interesting subject, in contrast with the master-pupil discipline encountered in most other classes. When a student came unprepared, Zeus was not angry, but seemed hurt, as if a friend had let him down. Seldom were any unprepared, since all preferred to risk anger elsewhere. . . .

His need for companionship was filled by friendships with some of his students. During the fall and winter, I frequently went on long walks with him over the surrounding hills, sometimes with others, sometimes just the two of us. As we talked, a strong friendship formed. In the spring, on Sundays and free afternoons, we drove in his blue Nash coupe to the nearby town of Ballardvale, on the Shawsheen River, to canoe and swim.

That summer he invited me to spend the month of August with him on his island near Waldeboro, Maine, where his family had been early settlers. I took the train to Rockland, where he met me. We spent the night in the house where he had grown up, one of the fine mansions built on Waldeboro's main street when it was a major port for sailing ships. . . . The next day, as we drove down to the shore of the tidal river, the name Benner appeared on many of the rural mail boxes. We parked the car near a dock which had a large lobster pound. He bought three wriggly lobsters out of the cold water, and rowed us in his dory a half mile to his island, one of a dozen scattered at the mouth of the river. His rough cabin consisted of a kitchen and two bedrooms. We bathed in the sun, on the smooth warm rocks outside, lunching on sandwiches of sardines and cheese. . . . Each day began with a swim off the pier in the icy water, which Benner, better insulated and more used to it, could take longer than I. Then we read in the sun, and canoed among the islands, and walked on them. All were wild and uninhabited. Terns and gulls followed us. Loons played and laughed off shore. A bald eagle, perched on a high dead tree, would soar out and dive on the hard-working ospreys, stealing fish they dropped before it hit the water.

Most of all we talked. Not constantly, since each of us enjoyed the outdoor silence, but a lot. I realize now that Benner guided much of this talk on the pattern of the Socratic dialogue, asking me a question, commenting on the answer, suggesting alternatives, and getting me to comment on them in turn. I felt free with him to open up inner thoughts, far more than I could with my contemporaries. . . . He revealed very little of his personal life. He did tell me that former students who had succeeded in business had given him tips on good investments, so that he had been able in the rising market—this was the 1920's—to run his meager savings up to over $100,000, and could afford to retire in about ten years, and live in Maine and travel, instead of teaching beyond the time when he could do it well, as he saw others doing. One of these businessmen came by one day in his big schooner. We sailed all day—my first time on the ocean—with him and his attractive family. I noticed that Benner, who with his students had the air of a rather eccentric scholar, when he talked with this man assumed the manner of a man of the world, knowledgeable about business and travel. For the first time I could imagine him moving at ease in a hotel in a big city, or on an ocean liner, enjoying himself in a way that my father, who was diffident about such things, never could.

He did tell me a lot about Andover over the years, drawing on his experience there to illustrate a point he was making, as he did also with stories from ancient Greece. . . . He had a poor opinion of most of the teachers, who made their subjects into a drill for high marks on the college boards. An exception was Charlie Forbes, who taught Latin as he did Greek, in the old classic tradition, as a study of a civilization for its own human values. He shared my growing distaste for the athletic, manly version of Christianity then in vogue at the school, which regarded all nonmarital forms of sex as sinful and ugly, to be put down by hard exercise and cold showers. It became apparent, though he did not proclaim it, that he had absorbed the pantheistic religion of ancient Greece, and at two levels: not just the sophisticated, more symbolic version of Fifth Century Athens, but the deeper Homeric one, when gods and goddesses did walk on earth, to make love and war with humans, and to enter other living things, animal, and plants. . . .

In 1932, when the Great Depression was getting deep, I visited Benner in Andover. The stock market crash had wiped out most of his savings, and he seemed broken in spirit. He believed that a revolution was coming, and kept his big blue Nash, full of gasoline, standing outside Andover Cottage ready to drive to Maine when it did.

Phillips Academy's great history teacher during the 1920's was Archibald Freeman, known to his students as "Bitch" Freeman. The origins of

54. *Archibald Freeman, Instructor in History, 1892–1937. From a portrait by E. Weber-Fülop in the possession of the Trustees of Phillips Academy.*

his nickname are obscure: one group claims that it represented his exacting demands in the classroom; another claims that it derives from the fact that he failed a boy with a 59 average. In any event he was a man who insisted on excellence with a vengeance; a boy who did well in his course not only knew a great deal of American history but could write it up effectively as well. For all his rigorousness as an instructor, he was voted Best Teacher eight years out of ten during the decade, while his American history course was voted the hardest for a similar eight years out of ten, dropping second to solid geometry on only two occasions.[22] There is something remarkable about the students' giving recognition to the difficulty of the course and the ability of the teacher at the same time. Freeman devised a system for the study of American history that involved the keeping of a notebook, wherein the student would take notes from a variety of different sources. The standard textbook, with its monotonous assignments of so many pages a day, day after day, was not for him. He was determined to train his students in making judgments on various kinds of historical materials and not simply in memorizing and regurgitating factual data learned by rote. For all his success, as measured by senior polls, few of his former students have written about him. One of the best descriptions is from a boy who never had his course but who heard about it from his friends:

> In the Upper Middle and Senior years, I had the privilege of living in Foxcroft Hall which was under the quiet but effective tutelage of Jimmy Graham and Archibald (Bitch) Freeman. It is one of the continuing regrets of my life that I had courses under neither one. I particularly regret my failure to sit under Bitch, for he enjoyed a reputation in the academic world of being one of the toughest but most stimulating teachers in the nation. He was called "Bitch" because he ran a taut ship in his American History classes; structured his course so that it would take brains and stamina to run; and he was less than lavish with "A's" and "B's". For example, the reading of an accepted text was not enough, should you be studying the Draft Riots in New York City in the early 1860's. No! No! You must read original sources A, B, C, and D, to the end that you might make an intelligent judgment regarding the actions of Ferdinando Wood, New York's Mayor. I knew Bitch only as a housemaster and he was the sort of man whose peace and quiet almost all of us thought it was sacrilegious to disturb.

But not all his pupils approved of his methods:

> Freeman's American history was taught in so disciplinary and rigid a fashion that he almost killed my love of the subject. No doubt I learned a lot, but the method was revolting, and I believe unnecessarily so. Fear is a poor teaching tool.

55. *Winfield Michael Sides, Instructor in Mathematics, 1919–1958.*

When it came to Mathematics, Winfield M. (Mike) Sides was in a class by himself. There were several competent mathematicians on the Faculty at this time, but Mike's dynamic personality made him unforgettable. Here is how three former pupils remember him:

> In recent years I have come to love the work of teaching, the meeting and clashing of minds in the classroom; and never far from my thoughts as I prepare for class or work in class is the lithe, crackling, passionate presence of Mike Sides. To be in class with Mike Sides was to sit tight, hold fast, and ride out a wild breathtaking storm of numbers that burst into the room with him and swirled to all corners as he moved quickly about, stabbing at the board, hurling questions, prodding for accuracy, pleading with us to stretch our minds. "Visualize! Visualize!" was the cry in this room. Never a slow moment was there, nor any let up in the electricity, but there was always kindness and patience, too, for the slow man earnestly struggling. And for all the hundreds he taught, for all the blinding storms of numbers, Mike Sides never lost track of an individual, and never once forgot an old boy—Mike Sides, surely one of the great teachers of all time.[23]

> To see Mike Sides after an Algebra class, hair all tousled, sweat dripping from his face after driving us through a hard session of logical reasoning and mental calculation was to recognize that he had in fact been working a lot harder than we had.

> Those who had the privilege of sitting at the feet of Mike Sides will never forget it. It is little to be wondered at that Mike's students had such extraordinary results on the College Boards. An average mark for all students over a 20 year span of 90 in Plane Geometry, 95 in Solid Geometry and Trig and 98 in Mechanical Drawing. He had a very lively mind and a very lively method of teaching. His favorite word was "visualize" and he drove students to see their mathematics problems and the steps of solution in the mind's eye. Of course the blackboard was necessary for the more complex problems, and it was one of his demonstrations on the blackboard that completely enchanted me and may very well have been the inspiration which sent some students on to the mastery of the deeper esoterica of mathematics. We had been working on "originals" in our Plane Geometry, and after sweating over a few thorny ones, we gave way to Mike, who posed us an original that was quite beyond the abilities of us pedestrian souls; so Mike began his analysis and demonstration. It was like a slow-motion picture of the flowering of a rose from the tight uncommunicative bud to its full blown glory. The problem

was solved, and we sat in silent awe at the beauty of the performance.

These four great teachers taught by pedagogical ability, without resort to fear. Bitch Freeman's stern insistance on excellence may have frightened some, but the respect in which he was held as the best teacher in the School means that only a few were put off. The success of these four in maintaining friendly relations with their students does not mean, however, that there were not other members of the Faculty who took a very different course. The leaders of those who believed in terrorizing their students were Horace Poynter and George Hinman, both Latin teachers. There appeared to be two Horace Poynters. On the one hand was a man who was an acknowledged leader of the Faculty, a dear friend and staunch supporter of Jack Fuess, a host whose hospitality was legendary in the Andover community. On the other hand was Horace Poynter the terror of the classroom who seemed to have divested himself of all the friendly, generous qualities that characterized the rest of his life. A former pupil writes, "I would warrant that not a single member of a Horace Poynter class remembers those long, terrifying recitations with anything but revulsion. . . . I don't remember ever going to his class without shaking. . . . I still shudder when I think of that man." John Monro, '30, has these recollections of Horace Poynter:

> I spent three years at Andover, and above all else I learned from Horace Poynter to be thorough, to get the lesson right and get it cold, and to take a daily drubbing in class as a matter of course. All primitive societies depend on a ceremony of ordeal as a way of shaping up the young bucks fast, and as preparation for the ruder parts of our own civilization for the past thirty years Horace Poynter's classroom had a certain merit. Twenty-five of us did Cicero with him daily at 8 o'clock. It was a rough way to start the day, but it had the immediate advantage of making the rest of every day seem easy. And it had the happily unforeseen long-run advantage of making a depression and war seem easy too. The subject matter was Latin but that was subordinate to the main thing, which was simply ordeal. The daily routine was uniform and merciless. Horace Poynter sat to one side, sharp pencil poised over his fine-squared grade book, and he called on us one after another in strict alphabetical order. When your name was sounded you stood up, struggled with your lot of translation, and braced yourself for iron questions. . . . If you missed something clean, the grade would be zero, as you could plainly see by watching the pencil top; and the question passed to the next man. If he missed, then the question started a murderous alphabetical round, giving all hands their fair chance at failure for the day. . . . How grateful we all were to the man who could stop Horace Poyn-

414 : THE MODERN ANDOVER

ter's steamrolling questions! There was no nonsense in this classroom about culture or the fun of learning; what mattered was getting the stuff right and getting it cold and standing up to take your dose when your name was called.[24]

Another story is of Horace Poynter the disciplinarian outside the classroom at a time much earlier in his career. A group of boys in his house had climbed out the second-floor window one evening and gone to Lawrence. On their return they managed to hoist one another back into the house—except for one boy, a track star. Just as he was being hauled up, Poynter appeared, at which point his two hoisters let go and dropped him into Poynter's arms. He managed to break loose and dashed off, with Poynter after him. They ran all over town before Poynter finally pooped out at the cemetery, and the boy was able to get back to his room. The next day he had Poynter in class and feared the worst, for he was unprepared. Strangely enough Poynter never called on him. After class Poynter asked to see the boy, who approached in fear and trembling. After letting him sweat for a few minutes, Poynter reached out his hand and said:

> Shake. I did not think you could do it, as I was a two-miler on the Yale track team and I did not think there was a boy in school who could beat me.
> Is that all, sir?
> I did not call on you today because I knew you did not do your homework, but be sure that you are prepared tomorrow.

And the writer sums up his impressions of the man:

> That was typical of Horace Poynter, who showed that in spite of being a strict disciplinarian, he was human and a good sport. I never heard anyone who studied Latin under him have anything but praise for him as a teacher and they said they learned more from him than from any other teacher.[25]

Another terror to many undergraduates was George Walker Hinman. He had graduated from Andover in 1894 and from Harvard in 1898, in both places making a name for himself as a scholar. He returned to Andover in 1907 and soon became a legend on campus. At some point in his career he had lost a leg, and wore a wooden one. Legend has it that one Christmas a group of his students sent him a present of a pair of garters, one of which had a thumbtack in it. Georgie was quite popular with the boys in his house during his early years. As time went on, however, his behavior became more and more eccentric. Here are some recollections of Georgie:

> Hinman was my housemaster for almost the whole of my four years because I stayed in Abbot House for all of that time except for the

first term of my Junior year when I roomed alone. The initial terror
of him as my first Latin teacher, who wrote across my first paper
"your father would be ashamed of this paper" eventually gave way
to warm friendship and great respect. Senior year I read Horace with
him. Indeed all of the boys in his house admired his gruff manner
because they knew he would be in their corner in any matter involving
them with the authorities. One incident proves it. On a very cold
winter night a car stalled in front of Abbott House and its occupants,
somewhat the worse for wear, got out and began shadow boxing and
making a tremendous racket. We were all watching them from our
windows when Georgie stomped down the walk and told them to be
quiet. They began to give him some lip, whereupon he turned around
and called, "All right, boys." Immediately a torrent of pajama clad
youths burst from the house and the occupants of the car beat a
hasty retreat.

In the course of a year I got to know Georgie well and liked him.
When he made his rounds at night for a bed check he would often
stop for a friendly word and always showed a willingness to help
any of us with our studies or school problems. He was very loyal to
the boys who lived in Abbot House, as he was to the members of
PBX fraternity, where he served as faculty advisor. His appearance
was deplorable, especially his dress. He went about the house in shirt
sleeves, an open vest, well spotted with gravy, and often his fly was
undone. Some years out of Andover I returned to the school with a
friend and as was our custom we dropped in for a visit with Georgie.
Going up the walk to Abbot House, my friend said, 'I'll bet you a
quarter Georgie's fly is open.' He was right and I paid the quarter.
   The incident that I want to describe occurred one night late in
the Winter Term. We were aroused from our studies by Georgie's
thundering voice coming up the stair wells, shouting "House! House!
all down to my office at once!" We all knew of his terrible temper
and this time he was boiling over. It seems that when he was making
the rounds he found one of the boys' room had been "stacked." The
unfortunate occupant of the room was a student who had lost both
his hands in an accident earlier in his life; furthermore, he had just
that evening returned from a few days' confinement in the infirmary.
Georgie demanded to know which one of us was responsible for this
trick. Finally a boy confessed. Georgie immediately phoned the Headmaster telling him he had a disciplinary problem and asked permission to handle it in his own way. With Al Stearns's OK, Georgie
announced that such a rotten trick called for physical punishment
and that the boy would be blindfolded and beaten with a paddle by

one of us—i.e. the boy who drew the slip of paper with the cross on it. Of course, I, being the smallest and youngest, drew the marked slip. However, with Georgie's assent, the slip was passed to the football captain, and the beating was severely administered in the presence of all. The guilty boy did not return to school for the Spring Term.

These first two passages describe Georgie fairly early in his career. As time wore on, he became more and more violent in class, and his temper became almost uncontrollable. Here is a description of him near the end of his career, by Amory Bradford, '30:

Georgie Hinman glowered at us over his desk, an ugly, disturbed face, with big, pock-marked nose, wide mouth with turned down corners and loose lower lip, dark-circled eyes with sadness in them, and high forehead. His ill fitting black suit was spotted with food, the vest, supporting a gold chain and Phi Beta Kappa key, often buttoned wrong, the shirt and tie crooked. His method was the deliberate use of terror. We were reading Caesar, and stood to recite. When a student made a mistake, Hinman would roar at him: "Sit down, you imbecile", or "Write it a hundred times on the blackboard", or "Go stand in the corner, you dunce." It was the tone, a mean one, in which these things were bellowed that hurt. Also the gestures that accompanied them. He would pound his fist on the desk, or slam open a drawer, take out a steel pen, and jab it into the desk top, leaving it quivering there as if it were in the body of his victim. We were seated alphabetically, which put me in the front row, but with three others ahead of me, who recited first, as we always went in alphabetical order. They often made mistakes, which gave me an advantage in taking the same line. With this, and hard work, I seldom made mistakes. When I did, he did not yell at me, but said wearily, "Sit down." . . . In spite of his ways, most students liked him, and enjoyed telling others about his latest antics. But a few were really upset. All worked hard, and our average on the College Boards was in the high eighties, one of the best in the school. I became friendly with Hinman, who could be agreeable out of class, and used to babysit with his children when he and his wife went out in the evening. But he treated his children the way he did his students, and it was not a happy family.

One of Georgie's favorite disciplinary measures was to throw students who had displeased him out of class, often adding one thousand demerits for good measure. One alumnus who did not have an eight o'clock class remembers clocking his roommate, who had Georgie at eight o'clock. The average time the roommate lasted with Georgie was twenty minutes, and the alumnus would see him walking back to the dormitory at 8:20. A few times he made it until 8:30. But never, the alumnus remembers, did he make it for a whole period. In the early 1930's various parents protested so vigorously about Georgie that he was removed as a classroom teacher and made a tutor, in the belief that a with a one-to-one relationship he might do better. Yet it must be admitted that, like most schoolboys who remember best the teachers who were holy terrors, the Andover graduates of this general era probably remember Georgie better than almost any other member of the Faculty.

Limitations of space preclude discussion of most of the other Faculty members, though a number will appear later in these pages. Generally speaking, the Faculty was conservative—educationally, politically, and socially. When it came to curriculum matters, there had been little change since the early 1900's. The so-called Classical course at the turn of the century put great emphasis on Latin, Greek, modern languages, English, and mathematics. There was one two-hour required course in natural sciences for the juniors—the equivalent of 9th graders—and it was possible to elect some history in the senior year; but the whole was language-oriented. The so-called Scientific Department required some work in history and the sciences, but it, too, insisted on a heavy dose of languages.[26] In the late 1920's little had changed. This was the heyday of John Dewey and progressive education, but there is no evidence that any of these educational reforms had any effect on Phillips Academy, aside from eliciting anguished cries of outrage from Al Stearns. Two changes had been introduced: Greek was no longer a required subject, much to Zeus Benner's dismay, and the distinction between the Classical and Scientific departments had been abolished, thus putting all the boys on an equal basis. The number of elective courses had been considerably broadened, but it was still possible to get an Andover diploma without having taken any course in either science or history. Yet the winds of change were beginning to reach even Andover Hill.

In 1929–30 a new course called "Science and Religion" and later "Religion and Modern Life" was introduced. It was to be offered for one hour a week for the last three years of a boy's course. The teacher was Alexander Buell Trowbridge, a former Rhodes scholar who had made a fine record with a course of this kind at the Hill School in Pennsylvania. Al Stearns was greatly taken with him and hoped he would enliven and modernize the religious program of the school. The only course offering in the field before then was in the Bible, taught by "Inchy" Spencer, a diminutive English teacher. Unfortunately, "Religion and Modern Life" never came off at Andover. For one thing, Buell Trowbridge expected all the upperclassmen to write theses, and this was rough for a one-hour course. He was also at times naive. He told his classes he was sure that many boys were having difficult sex problems and added that if they were shy about coming to see him, they should write him unsigned letters. This opportunity was too good to miss and writing letters about sex to Buell became a favorite indoor sport. On one occasion he announced that he simply must see the boy who had written him a letter signed "Desperate." The basic idea of the course—to bring religion up to date for the boys—was admirable, but unfortunately, it never realized its objective. In 1933 would come a major curricular revision—the first since the days of Cecil Bancroft.

Politically, the Faculty was apparently strongly Republican. The only straw poll conducted during this period was done by the *Phillipian* in 1924. According to that poll 19 Faculty members were for Coolidge, 15 for Davis, and 1 for LaFollette (who could he have been?)[27] At first glance this result might seem to belie the Republican strength of the Faculty, but it must be remembered that John W. Davis was a very conservative figure, a Republican in all but name, and although there is no record available, the chances are that in 1928 (when Al Smith, a real Democrat, ran), the Faculty closed ranks behind Hoover. Social life was very formal. When a new man and his wife came to Andover, older Faculty members would first call and leave cards. Then the new couple would return the call and leave cards. Then, after an appropriate interval, the new couple would receive an invitation to dinner. This was always a black-tie affair, with a maid waiting on table. When it came time for the new couple to return the dinner invitation, it usually knocked the family food budget galley west for a week or two.[28] But this formality, inherited from the Theological Seminary, did not last the decade, and the depression killed whatever was left of it. A central place for Faculty socializing was the Faculty Club, previously the office of the Administration before it moved to Brechin Hall. Apparently this small building was used a great deal by most of the teachers. There was a pool table, card tables, a coffee mess, and, above all, a chance to smoke. Because the Faculty were not supposed to smoke in public, the Club filled a definite need. Generally speaking, the Faculty was a congenial hard-working group. Al Stearns's often impulsive way of hiring Faculty resulted in wide diversity.[29] To be sure, there were occasional feuds. Archie Freeman and Charlie Forbes had not spoken to each other for twenty-five years, for example. But for the most part it was a strong and dedicated group of men.

The Phillips Academy undergraduate body in the 1920's had not changed markedly from the period before the war. During the decade the student body continued to grow, from 582 in 1921 to 667 in 1930, but not until 1937 did the total pass the 700 mark.[30] The distribution of the students among the four classes did not change much either. In 1921 there were 172 seniors, 163 uppers, 143 lowers, and 104 juniors. Ten years later there were 193 seniors, 185 uppers, 170 lowers and 111 juniors. The proportions remained almost exactly the same; the differences in the figures represent the increase in the size of the School. The geographical distribution of the undergraduates also remained fairly stable during this period. In 1921, 1925, and 1931 the top five states represented were Massachusetts, New York, New Jersey, Pennsylvania, and Connecticut, although there was a slight variation in rank according to numbers. Massachusetts dominated throughout the period from 173 in 1921, 196 in 1925, and 168 in 1931. The five top states accounted for more than half the School in each of these three years. After the top five, representation scattered broadly. In 1921 36 states and 16 foreign countries were represented, the foreign students coming mainly from the Orient and South America. In 1925 38 states and 14 foreign countries were represented, while in 1931 it was 40 states and 9 foreign countries. When it came to college choices, it was clear that the tradition of going to Yale, established under Uncle Sam Taylor, was still strong. 65 out of a senior class of 161 went to New Haven in 1921, 74 out of 168 in 1925, and 89 out of 201 in 1931, this last figure approaching half the class. Harvard was next with 38, 31, and 29 in the three years studied, while Princeton enrolled 29, 30, and 11, this last figure marking a sharp drop in interest in Old Nassau. M.I.T. was the only other college to have matriculants in two-digit figures, with Amherst, Williams, Dartmouth, and Brown having each a handful. Compared to college admission records later in the century, the number of colleges selected by Andover graduates—and nongraduates as well—was relatively small. The careers chosen by the Phillips Academy graduates were for the most part fairly conventional. The Class of 1927, for example, produced 28 businessmen, 28 lawyers, 15 managers, 11 insurance salesmen, 10 bankers, 10 teachers, and 8 doctors. On the other hand, there were 8 in Civil Service, 8 newspapermen, 5 writers, 4 in the Foreign Service, 3 farmers, 2 publishers, 2 ministers, 2 architects, and 1 librarian—and, of course, many others who were single representatives of a variety of other occupations. The prevailing impression to be gained from these limited statistics is of a student society characterized by stability in mores, with a consensus on what was proper procedure for undergraduates, for college choice, and for later careers.[31]

One alumnus who calls himself "Phillips" describes student life in this period. When he came to Andover in the fall of 1929, he found that he had been assigned to Andover Cottage—one of the school's most modern dormitories in 1895. Out of respect for the architectural integrity of this structure, the School authorities had done nothing to change it since it had been built, aside from slapping a heavy coat of varnish on floors, woodwork, desks, and chairs every summer. This had the effect of permanently sealing into the wood all the ink blots, scars, initials, and doodles, and by 1929 the collection was impressive. The overwhelmingly dominant color of the rooms in Andover Cottage was brown—good taste, he says, prevents him from being more specific as to the exact shade—which produced a sombre Victorian atmosphere. In an effort to save space above ground, the shower room and toilets had been installed in the basement, which also served as a kind of social and athletic club, since it was far from the eye and ear of Zeus Benner, the Housemaster. Phillips spent many a happy time that fall swinging from the basement water pipes and trying to do belly grinds. He heard that in Bancroft Hall, where the plumbing was also in the basement, there was a practice of urinating out of the third-floor windows to avoid the long descent into Avernus, and that the Housemaster used to sit up late at night with his window open, waiting for the pitter-patter outside in hopes of catching the culprits; but there is no record of such goings-on in Andover Cottage, presumably because Zeus Benner was installed on the third floor himself.

When Phillips' alarm went off at 6:45 in the morning, he often didn't have to shut the windows, for the simple reason that they weren't open. If there was a wind outside, plenty of air came in through the loose-fitting window frames, and in the winter, when gales blew straight across from Mount Wachusett, the bedroom was no place for brass monkeys. Phillips did not eat at the Beanery but at Berry House, because he had been signed up by a friend of his on scholarship to fill up a table. Berry House was then presided over by Rocky Dake, recently married and still more recently a father. Rocky ran Berry House in a firm but good-humored way. Every now and then, when food was being tossed around, he would come over and tell us that our table was worse than the pig-sty on his family farm in New York state. Ruth Dake believed in giving her young son plenty of sunshine, and on warm days used to put the baby in its pen with no clothes on. It was reported that Mrs. Arthur Leonard, stopping to see the baby on one of these days, had stared fixedly at the naked child for a minute or so and then remarked, "Wouldn't you just *know* he's a boy?"

After breakfast came chapel, in the old church that Andover had acquired from the Theological Seminary. It was a gloomy structure, and Phillips felt that the fall-out from Calvinistic sermons of the past had not been entirely dissipated. After singing scales and going through other vocal gymnastics for that fierce lover-of-Bach Carl Friedrich Pfatteicher, Phillips had made the Choir and Glee Club, and since at morning chapel the Choir sat in the stalls at the front of the church, he had a ringside seat for the daily performance. On the platform sat that great triumvirate Al Stearns, Charlie Forbes, and Pooby Bancroft. Phillips could not imagine Andover without Al Stearns—without question one of the most powerful personalities he had ever known before or since. He reminded Phillips of a battle-scarred eagle. His glance scanned the assembly each morning like a radar device, unbelievably sensitive to any "bogey" of student misbehavior that might appear on his screen. Phillips would never forget how he prayed—eyes tight shut, reinforcing each plea to the Almighty with a short forward movement of his foot. Charlie Forbes, by contrast, lent an aura of Pickwickian geniality to the proceedings, as he twinkled benignly on the undergraduate body. And then there was Pooby, stumbling through the daily notices.

By some strange quirk of Freddie Boyce's scheduling procedure, Phillips found that he had no classes before ten o'clock on any day. Thus each morning, after chapel, he would trudge back to an empty Andover Cottage. It didn't stay empty long, however. By 8:15 the first refugees from Georgie Hinman's Latin class would come straggling in. In addition to the fugitives from Georgie Hinman, a regular morning visitor at Andover Cottage was Freddie Grant, the janitor. Freddie was a sprightly little grey-haired man with an unlimited fund of stories, most of them dirty. He also had a distinguished collection of old magazines of the *Captain Billy's Whizbang* variety, which he used to dole out to undergraduates who he thought could profit from reading them. What with Al Stearns's prayers and Freddie Grant's stories, Phillips usually felt well fortified to meet his first class of the day with Liz Parmalee in French 3 at 10:00.

Charles ("Liz") Parmalee, as Phillips was to learn later, was a man of taste and sensitivity, but not much of this came through to his classes—at least in the fall of 1929. The first order of business was to send everyone to the board, where what passed for a French sentence was scrawled by each student. When this was finished, Liz would haul himself out of his chair, seize two or three pieces of new chalk, and advance on the undergraduate efforts spread out before him.

He usually started off making corrections in a weary, pained way, but before long, as he observed one grammatical horror after another, he would lose his temper and begin striking huge X marks on the sentences, scattering chalk in all directions, and uttering cries of "Piffle" "Pish" and the like. The class always enjoyed these performances immensely and Phillips had a suspicion that Liz did too. After the chalk dust had settled and Liz had lowered himself back into his chair with a sigh of relief, the class attacked *Lettres de Mon Moulin*, and soon succeeded in driving Liz to distraction again. The book was a delicate and whimsical one, and delicacy and whimsy were not favorite commodities to Andover students in 1929. Phillips remembered that the translations of a huge boy called Swede caused Liz particular anguish. Swede's approach to translation was simple and direct; he looked up all the words in the passage, wrote them in over the French text, and then, when asked to translate, bulldozed his way through the passage, giving the English in the order of the French, whether it made any sense or not. After one particularly gruesome performance, Liz said, "Swede, you have just finished murdering one of the most beautiful passages of French prose." Phillips was a conscientious student, and at the beginning of the course did his homework faithfully. But one day his morale received a shock. He had inadvertently left a book in Liz's classroom and had gone back to get it. As he entered the door, a few minutes after the class had ended, he saw Liz reach languidly over toward the pile of homework on the corner of the desk and gently push it off into the wastebasket.

After Liz came Cicero with Jackie Phillips. Phillips the student placed at the head of his list of blessings the fact that he had drawn Jackie for Latin and had escaped the Buchenwald of Poynter and the Dachau of Hinman. And it would be hard to find a greater contrast among teachers. Where Georgie Hinman would wrathfully eject a student and give him one thousand demerits, Jackie would say quietly—almost apologetically— "I'm afraid that's not quite right." Yet Phillips could not remember anyone taking advantage of Jackie, and the soft-spoken statement "The translation was an extremely good one" made the day for anyone lucky enough to receive it.

Afternoons Phillips spent on the old campus playing soccer under the watchful eye of Jim Ryley. During the two years that he spent with Jim, Phillips was never able to fathom the mystery of Jim's success as a coach— yet it was there for all to see. The team had no regular drills, no calisthenics, no secret weapons. Most of the time they scrimmaged, with Jim admonishing, cajoling, exhorting. Jim's most fearful weapon, however, was the silent treatment. If a player goofed in some way, Jim simply wouldn't speak to him for several days. Phillips remembered a South American student who considered himself a finished player. When varsity uniforms were handed out to a chosen few, the South American was not among them. "Where's my uniform, Jim?" he wanted to know. Jim turned purple. "I'll tell you where your uniform is," he said, "there's a beautiful one waiting for you on the Saxon club team." And with that the Latin was cut to the clubs, in a manner hardly in keeping with the spirit of the Alliance for Progress. Jim was full of other surprises, too. Phillips remembered well a scrimmage in front of the goal where he had been knocked flat. The ball was rolling along the goal line in a tantalizing and frustrating manner. Since he couldn't kick it in, Phillips hit it in with his hand and then turned, horrified, to receive a blast from Jim. But Jim was grinning from ear to ear. "I know how it is," he said "and you did just right. Besides," he added, "you never know. Maybe the referee wouldn't have been looking."

After athletics Phillips paid for his relaxed mornings by having both a four and a five o'clock class. The four o'clock was English with Frankie O'Brien, and it was a tough time of day. Most of the inmates had been exercising vigorously for the past two hours and entered the classroom exuding excess animal spirits. The room was warm and Frankie never raised his voice. Phillips' friend Swede was in this class also, and he used to go bye bye regularly about ten minutes after the period had begun. Frankie believed in putting first things first. If he couldn't read your handwriting, he argued, there was no point in going any further until that was corrected. Accordingly, a couple of weeks after the term had started, Phil-

lips was tapped by Frankie for a special group that had penmanship homework as well as English homework. "But Phillips," Frankie would say,
"you have written 'said' with the dot over the "a" not the "i". Of course
it's misspelled."

Frankie also believed that a book was not worth classroom study unless
it had been proven by time. Thus the class read *The Odyssey, Old Testament Narratives*, and a book of essays, the most modern author in which
was Charles Lamb. Phillips occasionally used to envy the Uppers in Al
Blackmer's sections, who, it was reported, were studying the unexpurgated
edition of *Lady Chatterly's Lover*. Still Phillips had to admit that life with
Frankie was probably good for his soul, and there were occasional satisfactions to boot. One day Phillips was the only one in class who knew
what Jephthah's curse was.

Phillips' last class of the day was in algebra with Guy H. Eaton, not to
be confused with the legendary Pap Eaton, also of the Mathematics Department. Guy Eaton was unlike the rest of Phillips' teachers in dress, if in
nothing else. Where the rest of the staff had the usual professional seedi-
ness about them, Guy was a dude. He had pince-nez on a long black ribbon,
and fancied ornate vests, loud tweeds, white sport shoes, and flamboyant
ties. The 1931 *Pot Pourri* printed a list of popular songs with supposedly
appropriate faculty names alongside. For example, beside the name of Miss
Alice Whitney, guardian of the "cut" list, was the title "Where Have You
Been?" For Guy Eaton it was "Tiptoe Through the Tulips." Guy Eaton
was not very strong on mathematics; it was rumored that when he got
stuck with a problem in class, as happened occasionally, he used to high-
tail it over to Ozzie Tower to find out the answer. But he was a kind man
and a good drill-master. His method was to rush through the book, finishing the course in March. Then every period in the spring term the class
would be given old college boards to take. By the time the real boards came
along, the Math exam was just another afternoon class with Guy.

Phillips' final appointment of the day came at eight o'clock sharp, when
Zeus Benner checked up on Andover Cottage. Zeus didn't do any housemastering in the modern sense of the term; he checked up on his charges
every night, bawled out various individuals for playing a phonograph in
study hours, and occasionally broke up riots. But Phillips never saw the
inside of Zeus's apartment during his whole year, and he missed the chance
of getting to know a man whom the boys taking Greek were never tired
of praising as one of the school's greatest teachers and personalities. Phillips used to hear stories of canoe trips on the Shawsheen, with Zeus, a sun-
worshipper from way back, stripped to the waist in the stern and his
favorite Greek student in the bow; of huge full-course dinners at neighboring inns; of invitations to spend summer weekends at the Benner farm in
Waldoborough, Maine. Although Phillips could not give Zeus very high
marks as a housemaster, he was always conscious of an aura of Olympian

grandeur in Andover Cottage. All in all, life at Andover in the late 1920's was a good one. There were frustrations, disappointments, successes, satisfactions. And always enough surprises to keep the School interesting.

Dormitory life in the 1920's varied a good deal according to the Housemaster. There was always more or less of an adversary relationship between boys and masters, but it seldom became rigid or bitter, and both sides tended to respect the position of the other. Liz Parmalee ruled the roost in Bartlett South. One alumnus has these memories of him:

> I never had him in French. I am told I didn't miss too much. But as resident master in Bartlet Hall he became my great friend. We thought he was so funny—as indeed he was. And he was certainly an old lady—fussy, peculiar. But he craved friendship—as who didn't—and it all worked with us. We all loved his Venetian palace of a sitting room—intricate gold mirrors, baroque furniture, agony paintings, rich objects everywhere, a crystal chandelier. There couldn't have been any place like it near Andover—it was the Paris flea market transported across the Atlantic. I can still hear his voice booming up to the third floor whenever there was too much loud talk or acrobatics. The racket would temporarily subside. Liz wasn't strict. . . . But he was a personality.

Another recalls Liz as follows:

> Parmalee taught the language, but he also introduced us to the history and customs of the French people. (For example, he told us about sending out his laundry in a paper bag and having the same bag go back and forth all summer long.) Parmalee was fun, too. One day . . . several of us tried to translate and display on the blackboard a then popular song: we wrote, "Oui, nous n'avons pas de bananes, nous n'avons pas de bananes aujourd'hui; nous avons haricots verts, etc." Well Liz thought this was great, congratulating us for our enterprise and correcting our mistakes.

Another amusing episode:

> Parmalee was the Proctor at Bartlett Hall and decided one spring that it would add a little color to the old building if each boy placed a pot of flowers on the window sill of his room. The boys got together and decided to buy every comode or champerpot in town and fill them with dandelions. The pots were placed on the sills before they retired and the next morning the ceremony was held of inspecting the decorations. Naturally Liz Parmalee was dumb-founded at what he saw but took the joke in his usual good-natured way and seemed to enjoy the prank as much as the boys.

Dormitory life was often hard for younger boys:

> I was small and timid and had never really been away from home
> before, so had little idea of how to mix with many of the boys in
> Taylor Hall. This held a broad cross section of new and old boys
> from all backgrounds including some who had just been discharged
> from the Service after World War I. They were grown men and I
> was a little boy. I was afraid of them and must have been obnoxious
> the way I shut myself in my room, which luckily was single. There
> were others like me, but we had a hard time getting together at first.
> Gradually, however, things changed—I'm not sure why. . . . A few
> were never able to adjust, however, and how well I remember one
> down the hall who became the butt of every joke or prank that took
> place. He was miserable and had no one to turn to, so finally left
> school. . . . He should probably never have entered Andover until
> he was older, much less assigned to Taylor Hall, where gory fist
> fights were not uncommon, particularly on Saturday night after the
> movies and after our housemaster Freddie Boyce had made his casual
> room check. Usually all Hell broke loose then.

The School was well aware of the problems that really young boys had at
Andover and in 1907 had moved to meet them with the acquisition of
Williams Hall. Here was a large, comfortable house that seemed more like
a home than a formal dormitory. A separate dining hall was installed, and
generally the boys were more restricted than the older ones on the main
campuses. For many years John L. ("Jackie") Phillips and his wife ran
this establishment with a friendly gentility that was just what a lonely little
boy needed. The difficulty was that there were not enough rooms to house
all the juniors who might profit from such an environment. In 1923 a
wing was added, increasing the spaces from 27 to 42, and in the 1930's,
Junior House was remodeled for another 9 students. In 1929 the supervision of Williams Hall was entrusted to Frederic and Ruth Stott, a perfect
pair for the job. Fred Stott was serious about this work and saw to it that
the rules were faithfully obeyed. Ruth Stott, with a heart as big as a whale,
was like a mother for countless boys over the years, as the many former
Williams Hall boys who came back to see her and her husband could have
testified. Still, the Williams Hall facilities would never be able to handle
more than about half the junior class, and it was not until the construction
of Rockwell House, in 1935, that the problem of dealing with little boys
was finally met.

The undergraduates in the 1920's were subjected to a large number of
rules and regulations covering a variety of matters. Yet compared to most
other schools the regimen was relatively free. The basic principle of the
Academy system was that a boy had certain appointments to keep and for

the rest of the time he was on his own. He was to attend chapel, classes, and athletics, and was expected to be in his room by eight o'clock at night. A premium was placed on a good scholastic record. A boy with two or more failures was placed on the "No-Excuse" list, which meant that he could not leave town or play on a varsity team. More serious academic problems could result in Probation; if a boy's record had not improved after a term of Probation, he was likely to be dismissed. One of the worst sins was skipping out at night, usually to visit the fleshpots of Lawrence. If caught on one of these escapades, dismissal was the invariable result. The Faculty viewed boy-girl relationships with a jaundiced eye. If a boy were to talk to a girl on the street, he risked a severe penalty. In addition to these regulations, the rule book has a charming section entitled "Customs and Points for New Men." Here are some samples:

Remember that you are an Andover man from now on.

Watch the old men and pattern your conduct after them . . . it is not yet time for you to start new modes and customs.

Always speak to an Andover man on the street, whether you know him or not. . . .

You are responsible for the reputation of Andover from now on wherever you may be. This is no light responsibility.

All cheering is under the direction of the cheer leaders. Individual cheering is not allowable.

New men are expected to have the songs and cheers perfectly learned by the end of the first two weeks.

In leaving chapel . . . students go out by pews, the foremost pew first and the next following in order till the end. This is very important.

In all Fall term elections only old men are privileged to vote. . . .

Do not read or study in chapel.

It is not good form to cut or mark school furniture.

Try to keep enlarging the number of your acquaintances, but be slow to make intimate friends.[32]

One of the most famous disciplinary cases of this period concerns Humphrey Bogart.[33] According to a widely accepted story, Bogart was fired from Andover for helping to throw the manager of the Phillips Inn into Rabbit Pond. A variation of this story is that it was a Faculty member who got thrown in. This legend has undoubtedly been strengthened by the fact that a group of undergraduates *did* throw the manager of the Inn into

Rabbit Pond. The only trouble is that the event occurred over ten years before Bogart arrived on the scene. Other variations of the legend are that Bogart got fired for being insolent to a Faculty member or that he was expelled for getting caught drinking Scotch from a teacup. The presumption is strong that in later life Bogart liked to boast about his Andover exploits and appropriated some that he knew about and applied them to his own case. The actual record is much less glamorous. In 1917 Dr. Belmont De-Forest Bogart, a prominent New York City physician and an Andover graduate, wrote Dr. Stearns that he would like to send his son Humphrey to Phillips Academy the following year.[34] The boy took six months to fill out the application that was sent him, indicating, perhaps, something less than perfervid enthusiasm to come to Andover. His application was not improved when he failed almost all his subjects at Trinity School, which he had been attending in New York. Nonetheless, the following September Bogart arrived on the Hill, only to find that because of his poor record he was classified as a Lower Middler rather than as a Senior, as he had expected. He was given a small single room in Taylor Hall, under Freddie Boyce, the physics teacher. As soon as classes started it became clear that Humphrey did not like school work in general or Andover work in particular. One teacher spoke of him as "entirely uninterested in his work"[35] and a fellow classmate remembers how sullen and spoiled he was. "When things didn't go his way he didn't like it a bit."[36] By Christmas time he had failed three out of five courses, and since his record did not improve, in February he was placed on Probation. The parents were furious with their son. "The harder the screws are put on the better it will for my son," wrote Dr. Bogart.[37] Though there was some slight improvement for a month or so, in May Dr. Stearns wrote the family that the boy had not met the terms of his Probation and would be required to withdraw. Humphrey Bogart left Andover not in the debonair way he later remembered but simply because he refused to work. Since World War I was still in progress when he left, he was able to enlist in Naval Aviation, a move that Al Stearns applauded. Yet despite his miserable record at Phillips Academy, he always remembered his school days pleasantly and helped to create the legend that has always been associated with him and Andover.

Though there were many martinets on the Faculty, some of the sternest had the milk of human kindness in their veins. Here is an episode involving Archibald ("Bitch") Freeman:

> Well into the spring term of his senior year one boy found himself
> on Probation because of poor mid-term grades, which, of course,
> meant no out-of-town excuses. His housemaster was Mr. Freeman,
> who well knew that this boy was grounded. The boy was desperately
> in love and just had to go to Boston to see his girl, so one fine beautiful Wednesday afternoon he took off. Who would ever know that

he was away for a few hours? Imagine his consternation when he
ran smack into Mr. Freeman on the return train trip. They greeted
each other and that was that, but the poor boy knew the recognized
penalty was expulsion, and he waited for a week for the axe to fall.
It never did and he never heard another word, so maybe Mr. Freeman
did not really deserve to be known as "Bitch."

And another example:

> Another bizarre experience I am reminded of was my first weekend
> away in my first term. I had lived for this 24-hour privilege—so
> much so that it became a total reality with all permissions granted
> weeks before I left. I just took off on the train to Boston. On my
> return I realized with horror that I had to report in and hadn't re-
> ported out. Somehow Al Healy sternly accepted my apology and ap-
> peared to believe my forgetfulness. My punishment was "No
> Comment" until the end of the term. I suffered agonies of fear as
> to what they would do. Nothing, of course, because I think Healy
> sensed my awe at what I had not done as punishment enough.

But the more normal procedure for handling cases of boys off bounds
without permission is to be seen in the following account of what happened to a descendant of one of the School's most illustrious graduates:

> As was his custom on Wednesday, a free afternoon without classes,
> he put on his bowler and Chesterfield and took the train to Boston,
> where he had a girl, or girls. This day he had the misfortune to be
> seen by a master boarding the train. When he got back to his room,
> there was a note summoning him to the Headmaster. We waited his
> return with interest, hoping he would be able to talk his way out of
> it. He returned, flung himself on the bed, and said: 'Nothing doing.
> He wouldn't listen. Just bawled me out and said he wanted me out
> of town by nine in the morning.'

Among the more exuberant customs on Andover Hill was the "All Out":

> Every year, in the spring, there was an 'all out' night. On a warm
> evening, after eight, when we were supposed to be in our own
> dormitories, some restless students would leave theirs and cry 'All
> Out' under the windows. When all were out there, they moved on
> to the next dorm, shouting 'All Out' again. Soon a yelling mob was
> formed, which snaked around the campus until all six hundred boys
> were out. Then, before it came to harm, the mob always gravitated,
> as if drawn by a magnet, toward the Headmaster's big yellow house
> on Main Street, blocking all traffic. On the high stoop, he would
> appear. His great voice would roll out, calming the crowd, telling us
> we had had our fun, and that it was time to go home. We went.

On 1 May 1930 some of the undergraduate body staged a splendid riot in the Town of Andover. The occasion was the annual May breakfast served in the Town Hall under the auspices of the General William F. Bartlett Woman's Relief Corps, 127, a branch of the Ladies' Auxiliary of the Grand Army of the Republic. For a modest sum anyone who so wished could purchase a breakfast of oranges, rolls, doughnuts, coffee, and other comestibles. The Phillips Academy contingent arrived about 6:30 and, having soon finished their breakfast, amused themselves by pelting other guests with half-oranges, rolls, and doughnuts. When the ladies running the breakfast remonstrated, the boys simply stuffed their pockets with more ammunition, went outside, and began pelting the guests as they came out. Tiring of this sport, they moved out to Main Street, where they found two new ways of amusing themselves. When the trolley came through town, they pulled the pole off the wire, causing it to stop. The motorman would then get out, replace the pole, and proceed a few feet until the pole was again disengaged. It was also found that if several boys jumped on the rubber pads that controlled the traffic lights, the light could be kept red for through traffic almost indefinitely. At this point the strong arm of the law appeared in the person of Officer Frank McBride, who ordered the students to cease and desist. Unfortunately for him, the students had discovered some sacks of potatoes in front of the A & P and they proceeded to bombard the luckless officer with spuds until he was driven from the field. That was the boys' last triumph. Soon a large black car bearing a very grim Alfred E. Stearns appeared on the scene, and the rioters scattered like chaff. Everyone expected that Al would blast the School at Chapel that morning, but he surprised them. He said he wanted apologies made to the town officials and the potatoes paid for, and that was all. Unfortunately for Al, the story got on the AP wire, and for the next few days he had plenty to do explaining the outrage to interested parties.[38]

An important feature of the 1920's at Phillips Academy was the presence and influence of the scholarship boys. There are no records of precisely how many students were getting financial assistance at any given time, partly because many boys earned money from jobs over which the school exercised no control. There were a relatively small number of cash scholarships to cover tuition. Winning and holding these were dependent on having a strong academic record. Most of the scholarship boys were able to get free board by waiting on table, either at the "Beanery" (the dining hall) or at one of several private boarding houses. Another way of earning money was to work for pay in one of the offices or at the library. The School determined the arrangements for these jobs, which usually averaged an hour a day. But some of the most lucrative positions were concessions for firms outside the School. One boy might have a cleaning and pressing concession for Burns or Langrock, the town's two leading clothing stores. Another might have a laundry concession for a town laundry. Still another might handle subscriptions for one of the Boston newspapers. And substantial sums could be made selling ice-cream at athletic contests. Some of the more enterprising undergraduates were able not only to cover their school expenses but to salt away savings as well. An outsider, unfamiliar with Andover, might think that the scholarship boys were second-class citizens, but nothing could be further from the truth. If anything, the boys formed an elite within the School; they held many positions of leadership and often were outstanding athletes. One former scholarship boy has this to say about his status:

> The most outstanding characteristic of the student body . . . was their genuinely democratic outlook. No one seemed to care where you came from or what kind of pedigree you had. As a scholarship boy working in the Commons or at Jim Ryley's Grill for my board, I never heard anyone, in the two years I spent at Andover, make mention of the fact as a reflection or as a means of harassment. Indeed, the opposite seemed to me to be the case; the surest way for a boy to be unpopular with his fellows was to flaunt his money.

During the decade of the 1920's extracurricular activities flourished. Many had had long histories in the life of the School, as we have seen, but nearly all became more active during this period. In the musical area the Glee Club was booming. In 1928 it counted eighty members. Dr. Carl Friedrich Pfatteicher directed this outfit and tried his utmost to make everyone a lover of Bach, but even he knew that he would have to compromise with his singers and throw in some sea chanties to lighten the fare. One reason for the Glee Club's popularity was that it had concerts with girls' schools, particularly Bradford Academy and Rogers Hall, and that these concerts were followed by dances. There was still a Mandolin Club of sixteen in existence, but it was not long for this world. In 1930 it disappeared, partly, perhaps, because of the organization of a School band. Phillips Academy also boasted a small orchestra during these years. The difficulty of recruiting orchestras in secondary schools is borne out by the fact that there were only three first violins; and the presence of three saxophones suggests that the repertoire was not strictly classical. Indeed, the Andover undergraduate of the 1920's had little interest in classical music, and a boy who played it on his phonograph was suspected of being a "fruit." The School had a Dramatic Club of sorts, with a checkered history. Various members of the Faculty had tried their hand at coaching the Club, only to abandon the project because of lack of interest. In 1928 it had revived under the direction of Allen Healy and was putting on such plays as A. A. Milne's "Mr. Pim Passes By" and Booth Tarkington's "Clarence." Since there were no girls available to play the feminine parts—Headmistress Bertha Bailey of Abbot would have turned purple at the idea of her girls participating—the boys played them, and there was much amusement in the audience when they forgot and sat with their legs wide apart. Though the Dramatic Club put on some entertaining performances, it was a far cry from the productions of Shakespeare that would start in the late 1940's. The Philomathean Society, which had been founded back in 1824, continued healthy. The Society was divided into two groups for purposes of competition, and in 1928 it debated such subjects as the Cancellation of War Debts, Coeducation, and Mussolini. Forty-six members participated in the debates. For boys interested in religious and moral questions there was still the Society of Inquiry, founded in 1833. The old emphasis on theological discussion had been abandoned, to be replaced by informal discussion groups on modern social and ethical problems. The Society also conducted a fund drive that, in 1928, realized over $1400.[39]

School publications met with mixed success during the 1920's. The *Phillipian* flourished, while the *Mirror*, the literary magazine, ceased publication in 1924 and was not revived until 1929. The *Phillipian* was a truly ambitious undertaking, coming out twice a week and conducted with generally high editorial standards. The proudest boast that the newspaper could make was that it was published without any prior faculty censorship whatsoever. This gave the editorial board a kind of responsibility that few other boys in School had. If the paper stepped out of line, the Faculty or Headmaster was sure to move in promptly *after* the sin had been committed, but for the most part there was little need of adult supervision. The *Phillipian* of this decade was heavily oriented toward athletics; many of the lead stories on the front page were concerned with athletic contests, and many of the editorials were pleas for support for one team or another. There were attempts occasionally to include some news of events outside the School—developments in Europe, for example—but there was little coverage of domestic political affairs except at election time. One reason why the Faculty could be content with their no-censorship policy was that the paper invariably supported praiseworthy causes—good attendance at concerts, no coughing in chapel, the Red Cross, not walking on the grass, and the like. The paper also put in a plug regularly for the support of its advertisers. Occasionally it would criticize in a gentle way some School policy that the board disagreed with. When Al Stearns put a ban on all dancing at Phillips Academy, which lasted two years, the *Phillipian* insisted that modern dancing was not nearly so bad as the older generation thought.[40] It complained about unsanitary conditions in the Beanery, where, it was reported, rats, roaches, and various kinds of bugs abounded in the food areas.[41] It thought that Al Stearns was on the road too much, making it impossible for the students to know him.[42] It complained that playing the chimes every quarter hour was "nerve-wracking."[43] When the new Dining Hall was opened, the *Phillipian* opposed the attempt to have it called the "Commons," preferring, apparently, to keep the old name, "Beanery."[44] Finally, the paper expressed pleasure that anti-prohibition forces were active on college campuses.[45] There were in School at the time a rather unsavory group of boys who spent most of their free time in the Grill smoking and playing cards. These "Grill Hounds" the *Phillipian* thought were a very bad lot indeed.[46] The paper tended to remark on the passing of important people. When Woodrow Wilson died, they spoke of the "loss of a friend,"[47] and, strangely enough, they reported the death of Joseph Conrad and Anatole France.[48] They also wrote a story on the trage- dy of Floyd Collins, trapped in a cave in Kentucky.[49] Occasionally they could have some fun, as when they reported that Al Stearns had forgotten his tuxedo on a trip to New York and had had it sent to him there by airmail.[50] Overall, when one considers the amount of writing and printing that got done over those ten years, the record in an impressive one.

In 1929, after a five-year hibernation, the *Mirror* began to appear again. With Alan R. Blackmer of the English Department as Faculty adviser, the publication soon achieved distinction by the high quality of its writing. Several of the contributors became prominent in various fields later on. In the first issue, for example, there were pieces by Ring W. Lardner, Jr., son of the famous author, who later was to make a name for himself as one of the Hollywood Ten; a piece modeled on John Galsworthy by Henry Ehrlich, later an editor of *Look*; entitled "Soames Buys a Picture"; and an article on disarmament by Max F. Millikan, son of the famous scientist and later a distinguished scholar in his own right at M.I.T. There were well-written poems by Edward M. Barnet, some striking graphics by Mar- tin H. Donahoe, and, for relief, humorous sketches on such subjects as how to fly an airplane. The high quality of the writing suggested that it was per- haps a good thing for a literary magazine to lie fallow for a number of years.[51]

The third major publication was the *Pot Pourri*, the yearbook. These volumes were handsomely bound in leather and contained detailed records of the school year. At the start came individual pictures of the entire Senior Class, complete with nicknames—"Tubby," "Spike," and the like—and with their intended colleges. Underneath the names were lists of activities that the individual had engaged in while at Andover, and it was easy to identify the Big Men on the Campus. Several students might have over two inches of double-column listings. There were always a few who re- fused to list anything, in protest against the ostentation connoted by "BMOC." Then followed the Senior polls of the class for the "Hand- somest," "Most Eccentric," "Laziest," "Windiest," and the like. This was followed by a similar poll for the Faculty—"Hardest Subject," "Best Teacher," and "Easiest to Bluff." There followed well illustrated sections on all the School's organizations and athletic teams, the closing section en- titled "Quips and Cranks," in which the editors could have fun with vari- ous aspects of school life. In one part quotations were applied to Andover institutions: the Dining Hall was "This muddy vesture of decay"; the orchestra was "All discord, harmony not understood"; while the Tower bells were "Like sweet bells jangled, out of tune and harsh." Then there was a take-off on Samuel Pepys' *Diary*, a list of members of a Fat Man's Club, and a list of "Fem-Sem (Abbot Academy) Chasers."[52] Taken as a whole the *Pot Pourri* volumes did an admirable job of reflecting the spirit of the School in the 1920's and provided an extremely useful permanent record of each class.

Phillips Academy undergraduates in the 1920's were offered an extraordinarily rich program of lectures and concerts, particularly after Thomas Cochran established the Stearns Lectureship and the Sawyer Concert with endowments of $10,000 each. In those days the income on $10,000 was sufficient to get the very best, and the School had other funds available for this purpose. For example, in a little over a month, in 1928, an Andover boy could have heard the Flonzaley Quartet, Sergei Rachmaninoff, and Pablo Casals. Nor was this an exception. In the next few years Fritz Kreisler, Jascha Heifitz, and Jose Iturbi all appeared in George Washington Hall. The programs were not always as long-haired: the Hampton Quartet was a perennial favorite, as were the English Singers. For lecturers the School was treated to Rear-Admiral Byrd; Count Felix von Luckner, commander of the German *Seeadler* in World War I; Roy Chapman Andrews speaking on "The Gobi Desert"; Robert Millikan lecturing on "Fire"; and Marie, Grand Duchess of Russia. To provide variety there were plays by the Ben Greet players, Tony Sarg's marionettes, and Bruce Bairnsfather, the World War I cartoonist who created "The Better 'Ole." The lectures tended to concentrate on exploration, nature, and outdoor activities. Two home-grown performers who appeared regularly were Lawrence V. Roth, who lectured on historical subjects, and Carl F. Pfatteicher, who, one year, did a series on almost all of Wagner's operas.[53] And of course there were movies on Saturday nights. In 1929 the School invested in a talkie machine and then very unwisely chose as the first talkie Eddie Cantor's "Whoopee." The high point of this movie came when a procession of long-stemmed chorus girls descended a staircase and threw back their arms revealing some very scantily clad female figures. Naturally, the School went wild, and the Faculty seriously considered junking the new talkie machine.

But the best story about Andover lectures is one told by Jack Fuess about the visit to Andover of a famous arctic explorer who shall be nameless. Jack, who was in charge of entertainments at the time, went down to the station to meet this gentleman. At first he thought he was not on the train, but then there was a kind of commotion at the end of one car, and soon he saw several trainmen and conductors carrying out a huge bear of a man who was clearly "bemused with drink." Jack got him into his car and drove to the Inn. After a shower and hot coffee, the lecturer seemed to be in good shape. The title of the lecture was "The Land of the Midnight Sun," and it was to be illustrated with slides. The explorer suggested that he omit his introductory remarks and start right off with the slides. Jack, thinking that a great idea, introduced the speaker, had the lights turned off, and supposed he had it made. The first slide showed an expanse of open ocean with a small bright ball over the horizon. The lecturer began as follows: "This is a talk on the Land of the Midnight Sun. You see that lil ball there. That's the Midnight Sun." There was a long pause, after which he added, "Or is it the god-damned moon?"

What chance did the Phillips Academy undergraduate of the 1920's have to meet with girls? The answer is, very little chance indeed. The most natural place for a boy to turn if he wanted to see a girl was Abbot Academy, where several hundred young ladies were living, a mere stone's throw from the School. But Abbot was ruled at this period by the iron hand of Headmistress Bertha Bailey, who was sure that no good at all could come from *any* contact between Phillips and Abbot.[54] In earlier years there *had* been some contact—Abbot used to come to the Phillips Vesper Service, for example—but gradually a high wall of exclusion was erected around Abbot. Miss Bailey was reported as censoring all letters to Abbot girls if they bore an Andover postmark, and she was determined that no uncouth masculine influence should threaten her charges. In this, for the most part, she was joined by Al Stearns, who thought of Phillips Academy as a solidly unisex school. He was so dismayed by the style of postwar dancing that he banned all school dances for two years. Despite these two redoubtable champions of the separation of the sexes, there were some occasions when Andover boys could see girls. Abbot allowed Phillips students to visit girls, under heavily chaperoned conditions, on Friday nights, as previously noted. But there had to be a lot of preliminary paper work—permission from the girl's parents, permission from Phillips Academy, and the like. Some of the seats in the visiting area were around the corner from where the chaperone sat, and boys used to go down very early and stand in line, so as to get one of these coveted positions. Toward the end of the decade Abbot girls were allowed to come to Phillips tea dances and proms, again under stringent chaperonage. Bradford Academy and Rogers Hall were generally more relaxed than Abbot, probably because they were farther away, and girls from those two institutions were frequent visitors at Andover dances.[55] The School had a lot more trouble controlling the relations of the boys with Faculty daughters and girls in the town, both of whom were more readily available. Despite all the puritanical restrictions, the chances are good that there were many unrecorded assignations between Phillips boys and girls. The Abbot girls, particularly in winter, took walks in pairs for their exercise, and though the routes were carefully drawn, it was quite possible to meet the young ladies. Several boys were expelled for taking Abbot girls into school fraternity houses (the Abbot girls were, too), and there were probably a large number who never got caught. When viewed in the light of today's coeducational school, the repressive policy in this area seems harder and harder to understand.

In one sense the climax of the Golden Twenties came with the celebration of the 150th Anniversary of the School on 18 and 19 May 1928. The undertaking was the most ambitious that any secondary school had ever attempted in the history of the country, and when it had been successfully completed, the name of the school had been spread far and wide and all the members of the Andover family had renewed pride in their institution. The main reason for the wide publicity given the event was the visit of President Calvin Coolidge to Andover and the speech he gave. This was the second time in the School's history that a President had visited the school while in office, the first being the visit of President George Washington in 1789.[56] In short the Sesquicentennial was a *succès fou* from start to finish.

Some of the Academy's Trustees as early as 1924 were considering what should be done to celebrate the Anniversary. At a meeting in January 1925 the Board accepted informal memoranda on the subject. Among other things, it was agreed that apart from the celebration itself, the School should use the occasion to conduct a drive to improve Faculty salaries, enlarge and improve the plant, revise the curriculum, and increase the financial strength of the institution.[57] At this time informal committees were appointed, and there was preliminary planning in the course of the next two years. It was not until April 1927, however, that more formal action was taken, when a committee was appointed consisting of Alfred Ripley, President of the Board, Headmaster Stearns, and Charles Forbes and Claude Fuess of the Faculty. At that same meeting Thomas Cochran announced that he had the acceptance of Calvin Coolidge to attend the celebration, thereby making good on a promise he had made to the Trustees to produce the President at the appointed time.[58] Coolidge announced that May 19 would be the best date for him, and thus the time of the celebration was determined. At the Trustees' meeting the following June, further steps were taken. The April Committee, now designated the Executive Committee, was authorized to make specific plans, calling for expenditures of not more than $25,000. The Trustees insisted that all athletic contests held during the celebration be with Exeter, and also authorized Claude Fuess to prepare a book of sketches of famous graduates, to be entitled *Men of Andover*.[59] From then on, the work of planning the celebration devolved upon the Executive Committee. Indeed, there is no further mention of the coming event in the minutes of the Trustees. An Honorary Committee of distinguished alumni, chaired by Henry L. Stimson, was formed, as well as a number of local committees made up for the most part of Faculty and townspeople, to deal with such specific problems as invitations, procession, alumni luncheon, decorations, publicity, housing, music, and finance.[60] It was now a matter of sheer hard work, and all the committees performed magnificently. There were invitations to be sent out after the invitees had been chosen. There were programs to be printed, housing forms to be prepared, tickets to the various events to be produced. It was estimated that nearly 100,000 different pieces of paper of one kind or another were mailed out during the winter and spring of 1928.[61]

The most important guest, of course, was President Coolidge, and he gave the Committee some bad times before he finally showed up. In October, apparently, the President thought that he might go to his son's graduation at Amherst and could not make two trips. Later that month Al Stearns wrote Ted Clark, Coolidge's Secretary, that he was surprised that there was any doubt about the President's coming; he thought it was all sewed up.[62] The Headmaster also took a special trip to New York to talk to Frank Stearns, Coolidge's confidant, on the matter.[63] Thomas Cochran protested strongly that the President should not be let off the hook because of his son's Commencement.[64] Apparently Coolidge's indecision about coming to Andover was overcome, and matters proceeded smoothly until the following April. At that point a new monkey wrench was thrown into the machinery when it was suggested by Ted Clark that Coolidge come on the 18th rather than the 19th. This obviously necessitated changing programs, plans for publicity, and the like.[65] Again Al Stearns took to the road, traveling to Washington to see what the problem was.[66] It soon became apparent that Congress might adjourn on the 19th, in which case the President could not leave Washington. Al learned shortly after that the President could not come on the 18th either, if Congress were about to adjourn. This news must have been met with dismay by the Andover Committee, but eventually it was decided to go ahead and plan for the 19th and hope for the best. Why not bribe some long-winded Senators to filibuster, Al Stearns suggested.[67]

From then on it was a matter of arranging the myriad details. The President wanted an amplifier, he wanted a desk, he wanted to speak first, he wanted to be sure that he and his wife would be in the same car and that they would not come in to the luncheon until all the other guests were seated.[68] All these requests Al Stearns agreed to honor, but he had some questions of his own. Could guests sit on the platform with the President, or did security reasons forbid that? How many extra police were needed? When would Colonel Starling, Head of the Secret Service, arrive to check things out?[69] These questions were eventually answered, and Colonel Starling appeared two days ahead of time to make the necessary arrangements for the President's security. At the same time, the Headmaster received a telegram from Ted Clark announcing that the President would be accompanied by three army officers, seven Secret Service men, seven newsmen, five photographers, and one messenger. He also approved the order of the march for the procession.[70] So it was right down to the wire before the

Sesquicentennial planners could breathe easily about the President's visit.

In the meantime there were a host of other details to attend to. Charles Evans Hughes was invited but declined. Caps and gowns for Faculty, Trustees, and guests had to be rented from the Harvard Cooperative.[71] W. K. Dugan wrote Thomas Cochran that Boston and Maine train 183 left Andover at 1:15 and thus the Coolidge Special would have to leave a few minutes earlier.[72] Thomas B. Rines and some friends wrote the Committee to get permission to fly over the parade on Saturday morning. Rines said he had a cabin monoplane and an army biplane available and would only be around for about ten minutes. On Rines's letter there is written the single word, "No."[73] Shortly before the event Al Stearns wrote an apologetic letter to all the Phillips Academy parents telling them how sorry he was that none of them could be invited. The Alumni had first crack, he said.[74] He also wrote Henry Ford asking for the loan of a stagecoach from the Wayside Inn, a request that Ford graciously granted.[75] An attempt had been made to get Sir Edward Grey, Chancellor of Oxford, to represent the British nation at the celebration, but Sir Edward was in poor health and could not accept.[76] Then it was suggested that Edward Lyttleton, former Headmaster of Eton, be invited, but he, too, was unavailable. Finally Frederick Malim, Master of Wellington College, accepted the invitation. The School wanted an historian for the occasion and after two false starts chose President Arthur Stanley Pease of Amherst College. When it came to choosing the poet, the Committee had more trouble. Walter Prichard Eaton, a graduate and a poet, was approached but tried to decline by suggesting James Gould Fletcher. Fletcher had been living in England for some time, and the Committee much preferred Eaton. Finally Eaton wrote, "You have closed the loop hole through which I hoped to escape, and I guess it's up to me to buy a rhyming dictionary. You have spoiled my winter."[77] There were many other distinguished guests—for example, the Presidents of Harvard, Yale, Princeton, Dartmouth, Amherst, and Cornell. Nicholas Murray Butler of Columbia could not come. A long roster of headmasters, not to mention hundreds of eminent alumni, attest to those who could. It was to be quite a show. Strangely—at least from the vantage point of the 1970's— no public school representatives were invited.

At long last the great days approached. A few nights beforehand the School was festooned with over four thousand colored lights, and powerful floodlights were turned on the main buildings. The result was a fairyland of light, and the spectacle attracted the attention of all who passed by. On Thursday night, alumni and visitors began arriving, each receiving a packet of directions, tickets, room assignments, and a map of the School. By Friday noon more than a thousand had come, in time for lunch in the Academy Cage. Promptly at two o'clock the first exercises began in the Great Quadrangle before Samuel Phillips Hall. A platform had been constructed jutting out from the portico of the building with an awning over it to protect the speakers. An amplifying system stood at the top of a tall tower erected for that purpose, and Radio Station WEEI of Boston had provided equipment to broadcast the proceedings to some unable to attend in person. Four bands were stationed at various parts of the campus to provide musical interludes. The only thing that was not admirably arranged for was the weather. A mist had begun to fall, and many in the audience had already put up umbrellas.[78] It was decided to go ahead as planned, however, and soon the assembly was being treated to a rather sentimental address of welcome from Headmaster Stearns. The first reply was given by President James R. Angell of Yale, who made use of material Al Stearns had dug up for him to show the close ties between the two institutions.[79] He closed by claiming that the independent secondary schools were much better fitted than the public schools to make the experiments that were necessary if secondary education generally were to do its job. The next speaker was President John G. Hibben of Princeton, who elaborated on the desire of youth to find the truth about the world they lived in. President Hibben was the last speaker to make it out of doors. As he finished, the Heavens opened and the rains came, and the exercises had to be moved into George Washington Hall. Because of the foresightedness of the Committee in providing the guests with rain checks, this maneuver was accomplished with much less confusion than might have been expected. President Ernest M. Hopkins of Dartmouth, a Trustee of the Academy and one of Al Stearns's dearest friends, spoke next. He amused the audience with a story of a tour bus in the north of England. The guide said at one point, "We are now passing the oldest tavern in England," which led a tourist in the back to ask, "Why?" Hopkins went on to stress the great debt that American colleges owed schools like Phillips Academy for preparing their students so effectively. Next came President Arthur Stanley Pease of Amherst, himself a graduate of the Academy, whose father had been a Professor at the Theological Seminary. President Pease was a scholar and had done his homework; the result was a lucid examination of the early history of the School.[80] Finally came the sesquicentennial poet, Walter Pritchard Eaton, who read a nostalgic poem in which he compared the past of the School to its present, more or less after the manner of Oliver Wendell Holmes at the Centennial. Eaton closed:

> Great is our school, and greater yet shall be
> When you and I will not be here to see . . .
>   No more
> The old boy need postpone his tears—
> He'll not see Phillips reach two hundred years.
> Nor will there be anyone to care!
> The old boy ceases—and resumes his chair.[81]

After the speeches came an organ recital by Dr. Carl F. Pfatteicher, for those who wished to stay, and later the School undertook the task of feeding the guests. Class reunions were held in the Cage and other places, while the ladies were dined in Borden Gymnasium. The rain that continued to fall did not seem to dampen the enthusiasm of anyone.

That night the undergraduates had their share in the celebration with a mammoth parade. The newspapermen present were enthusiastic about this operation, as was reflected in their writing. Here is one account:[82]

With a wild and wooly torchlight parade featured by colorful costumes and weird lighting effects, the Phillips Academy boys tonight put the crowning touch to the biggest day of celebration the school has ever seen.

The afternoon portion of this sesquicentennial observance was rather heavy, being freighted with endless speeches from great dignitaries in the world of education. The evening, however, gave to thousands of persons one of the most spectacular shows in the history of education.

A steady drizzle of rain failed to halt the proceedings. The heavy mist rather added to the effect of the dancing torches, the red lights and the white flares of the movie men. The costumes and the various antique conveyances in the line, too, were set off to perfect advantage by the glowing banks of pink mist.

There was noise galore. Half a dozen blaring bands, screeching motor horns, applause from the masses of spectators, shrill whistles from squads of State Troopers and whoops and cheers from the boys in line made a first-class good-natured pandemonium.

As a feature of a howling big celebration the parade was a wow. The paraders and the specators began to gather hours before 8:30, the scheduled time for starting. The boys, resplendent in costumes of red, blue, white and combinations, formed on the grass beside Main St. in front of Bishop Hall.

Each had a kerosene torch on the end of a stick except for some who had sticks of red fire. The boys cheered every car that passed, and their yelling sounded like that for four touchdowns.

As the time for the start drew near the traffic grew thicker and the crowd began to line the streets on both sides for hundreds of yards. The State Troopers handled them well, but they made a trying problem.

As 8:30 sounded from the carillon a handsome chestnut horse, high strung and skittish, stepped into the highway. Riding him was a boy in Colonial costume.[83]

At this point there was a great deal of confusion, caused by motor horns, lights, whistles and yells from the crowd. The horse, obviously frightened, began to prance dangerously close to the massed ranks of the spectators. Then, to add to the uproar, a motor ambulance roared past. But the rider succeeded in calming his mount.

A great feature of the parade was a lumbering old stagecoach loaned to the academy for the occasion by Earl J. Boyer, manager of Henry Ford's Wayside Inn. It was driven by a coachman, a footman and a trumpeter, all in Colonial costumes, and it was filled to the brim with juvenile academy students, also attired in silk breeches, silk stockings and brown wigs.[84]

One fellow who got a big laugh was pushing a high-wheeled bicycle as he trudged along in the costume of 1885. Close behind him was "The Baseball Team of 1860." These boys wore a rudimentary costume, featured in some cases by trousers which looked like, and in fact were, the legs of white flannel underwear.

Somewhere in the line was the old Phillips Academy handtub [fire engine]. It was drawn by big platoons of boys in black derbies, black raincoats and artificial black mustaches.

One big division of boys wore orange gowns and four-cornered orange hats, like flopping mortar boards. Another group wore blue and white pyjama suits, one leg white, one leg blue, half the coat blue and the other half white. Another outfit wore blue coats and white trousers. Here and there was a nifty white trench coat.

The parade lasted about an hour in and around the campus and the adjacent streets.[85]

Then at 9:30 followed another scene even more spectacular. On the steps of Samuel Phillips Hall, on the side of a huge, illuminated quadrangle, group singing had been scheduled. The boys marched there, and they were followed by a crowd which may have numbered 10,000.

From the crowded portico of the hall as far as one could see, for at least 100 yards into the murky distance, the campus was covered with faces. Here and there in the crowd was a kerosene torch. Strung in lines were endless rows of colored electric lights. A quarter mile away, on the highway, motor lights blinked intermittently.

This entire vast chorus seemed to be hiding. It was under the direction of Frank H. Simmons, Andover, '94. A brass band followed him, the boys followed the band and the crowd followed the boys. They sang old songs like "The Good Old Summer Time", "Two Little Girls in Blue", "My Old Kentucky Home" and others of the same vintage. Ordinary "group singing" is usually pretty pale fun, but this was spontaneous, and, like the parade, a wow.

According to residents, there never was a bigger crowd or more traffic in town at once in the history of Andover. All the surrounding cities poured out their inhabitants to see the show, and all who got within sight of the gorgeously-illuminated grounds got their trouble's worth. Great batteries of powerful searchlights played on the tall carillon tower and whitened the face of Phillips Hall. It was a marvelous show.

If the powers that be wanted to have a real celebration as part of the Sesquicentennial, it is clear that the boys stole the show.

The next day the rain, providentially, stopped. While there were still clouds in the sky, they did not appear threatening, and as it turned out, the day's proceedings, except at the very end, were uninterrupted by the weather. Right on schedule, the Presidential Special arrived in the Andover station at 9:00, to be met by Headmaster Stearns, President of the Board Ripley, Thomas Cochran, James Sawyer, and Judge Elias Bishop as representatives of the School. A troop of sixteen cavalry officers from the National Guard was also on hand to greet the President. In an effort to impress the Chief Magistrate they performed some kind of elaborate equestrian maneuver that caused two of them to fall off their horses. The President's comment on this mishap was characteristically laconic: "Not very good horsemanship here." But the troop recovered and, together with a band, conducted the President and his wife, the Reception Committee, and the President's staff to the Headmaster's house on Chapel Avenue, where another distinguished group of guests, headed by Alvin T. Fuller, Governor of the Commonwealth, was waiting to greet him. As the members of the Presidential party entered the house, they were cheered by the Phillips Academy undergraduate body. Coolidge's first utterance on Andover Hill, after meeting the guests, was a question to Jack Fuess: "Where's the toilet?"

While the President and Mrs. Coolidge were at the Headmaster's house, he took occasion to present them with two gold Sesquicentennial medals, which they both wore for the rest of the day. In a short time the assemblage moved over to the Headmaster's Office in George Washington Hall, which was closer to where the President would speak. While there, Coolidge smoked one of his little cigars, the kind that had a cigar holder of its own. When he had finished, the butt was seized upon and placed in an envelope, where it still reposes in the Phillips Academy Archives.[86]

At ten o'clock the academic procession started from the Memorial Tower, led by a color guard from the Andover Post of the American Legion and followed by Trustees, distinguished guests (mainly college presidents and headmasters), the Faculty of Phillips Academy, and a long line of alumni. As the procession marched up the vista, they were joined at the entrance to the Great Quadrangle by the President, accompanied by Al Stearns; Mrs. Coolidge, accompanied by Mr. Ripley; Secretary of Labor Davis, accompanied by Judge Bishop; Governor Fuller, accompanied by Thomas Cochran; Mrs. Fuller, accompanied by James Sawyer; and Frederic Malim, the English visitor, accompanied by President Hopkins of Dartmouth.[87] There

56. The President and Mrs. Coolidge arrive in Andover for the
Sesquicentennial in 1928. With them are Headmaster Stearns and
Thomas Cochran.

was a minor foul-up as the guests took their seats on the platform; Secretary of Labor Davis got in the front row, while Governor Fuller was further back. Coolidge motioned to Jack Fuess, who was in charge of all this, and said, "Governor should be in front row," and the exchange was quickly made.[88] It had been learned that Mrs. Coolidge was very fond of the "Mercersburg Hymn" and so the Glee Club and a band were asked to sing and play it, almost without rehearsal. To Al Stearns it looked as if the band were starting off on one foot and the singers on the other, and he tried to stop the performance and get them straightened out. But all went well, and Mrs. Coolidge joined in singing with the rest.

Some of those present who were familiar with President Coolidge's speeches in the past may have looked forward to his address with apprehension, but it soon became clear that they need have no fears, for the Chief Executive had done his homework. His friend Frank Stearns later wrote Al Stearns that the President had worked harder on this speech than on any other he could remember, spending about one hundred hours on it.[89] Coolidge first spoke of Samuel Phillips and particularly of his part in drawing up the Massachusetts Constitution, which the President thought a superlative document. He suggested that the principles of that Constitution were translated by Phillips to the educational sphere and had a profound influence on the Constitution of Phillips Academy. The President praised the democratic character of the School:

> Our country and its government belongs to all the people. It ought not to be under the domination of any one element or any one section. For it to fall under the entire control of the people of wealth or people of poverty, or people who are employers or people who are wage earners, would be contrary to our declared principles.

In speaking of the early days of Phillips Academy under Judge Phillips, he said:

> He knew that unless correct habits of thought are formed at the very outset of life they are not formed at all. Two great tests in mental discipline are accuracy and honesty. It is far better to master a few subjects thoroughly than to have a mass of generalizations about many subjects. The world will have little use for those who are right only part of the time. Whatever may be the standards of the classroom, practical life will require something more than 60% or 70% for a passing mark. The standards of the world are not like those set by the faculty, but more closely resemble those set by the student body themselves. They are not at all content with a member of the musical organization who can strike only 90% of the notes. They do not tolerate the man on the diamond who catches only 80% of the

balls. The standards which the student body set are high. They want accuracy that is well nigh complete.

After suggesting that not enough attention had been paid to secondary education over the years, the President finished with this peroration:

The general advance made by our country is commensurate with the advance which has been made by Phillips Academy. As we behold it, our doubts ought to be removed, our faith ought to be replenished. Our determination to make such sacrifices as are necessary for the common good ought to be strengthened. We may be certain that our country is altogether worthy of us. It will be necessary to demonstrate that we are worthy of our country.[90]

The Presidential address was well received by the crowd, estimated as high as 15,000, and it received broad coverage in the press. Chief Justice Arthur Rugg of the Massachusetts Supreme Judicial Court said to Frank Stearns that he thought it was the best speech that Coolidge had ever given.[91] It must be admitted that it is difficult to think of another Coolidge speech that might challenge that judgment. In the last analysis the President had certainly done what those in charge of the Sesquicentennial hoped he

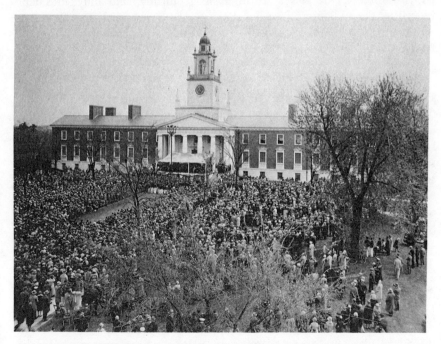

57. *The crowd that gathered to hear President Coolidge's address at the Sesquicentennial.*

would do—come to Andover, make himself visible, and then give an acceptable speech. They could not ask for more from him.

At the conclusion of the President's speech the invited guests moved promptly to the Cage for luncheon, except for an unlucky overflow of about three hundred that wound up in Borden Gymnasium. The ladies, in the meantime, were being served in the basement of George Washington Hall. H. J. Seiler Company of Boston did the catering and from all accounts did a more than satisfactory job. Shortly before one o'clock the Coolidges left for Washington amid the cheers of the crowd, and shortly thereafter the Senior Class arrived to sit on bleachers, from which they produced a lot of cheering. Once the ladies and those from Borden Gymnasium arrived, the program of speeches began, and before the afternoon was over the audience certainly had its fill.[92] In all there were nine speeches, and the whole program must have taken at least two hours. First came Governor Fuller of Massachusetts; then James J. Davis, Secretary of Labor; William Phillips, Minister to Canada and a direct descendant of the School's founder; Governor Spaulding of New Hampshire; President Lowell of Harvard; President Farrand of Cornell; Principal Lewis Perry of Exeter; Headmaster Malim of Wellington in England; and finally Al Stearns himself.[93] It was a distinguished company, and only President Lowell let the audience off with a short speech. Space precludes discussion of them; they were, for the most part, conventional statements of congratulation to Phillips Academy on her Anniversary. The two who stole the show were Lewis Perry and Frederic Malim. Perry, speaking from the point of view of Exeter, likened the celebration to the coming out party of the older sister, while Exeter remained a sub-debutante, and he proceeded to develop that theme in a witty and charming way. Malim spoke with deep feeling about education and closed his remarks with effective quotations from various psalms. Al Stearns had an unnerving time before his speech. Throughout the earlier addresses Thomas Cochran kept scribbling suggestions on small pieces of paper and passing them on to Al for use when his turn came. Al's speech had been written out and distributed to the press beforehand and it was obviously impossible to incorporate into it the last-minute suggestions of Cochran.[94] But the afternoon went off well, and certainly everyone got his money's worth. The guests were supposed to watch the Andover-Exeter track meet next, but had to abandon it when a heavy downpour intervened. The Andover boys beat their Exeter rivals decisively in what amounted to a millpond, but there was almost no one present to witness the victory.

That was about it. Some of the fraternities held reunions that night, and the boys had a very damp victory parade. By the next morning only wet remnants of decorations remained as testimony to the great things that had happened.

The Phillips Academy Sesquicentennial celebration had clearly been a great success. Largely because of the President's visit, the publicity the School received was both widespread and favorable. The affair put the School on the map as few other public relations campaigns might have done. It is impossible to say if this publicity was reflected in increased applications for admission, but that is possible. One of the Trustees' aims when the celebration was conceived was to improve teachers' salaries and thereby serve as an example for other independent schools. The teaching foundations that were established at the time of the Anniversary certainly went far to realize that aim, though it could be argued that Thomas Cochran would have established them with or without a Sesquicentennial. Another aim of the Trustees was the improvement of the Phillips Academy plant, and since the whole Cochran program was under way in 1928, that goal was well on the road to being realized. At a meeting of the Trustees the day before the celebration began, Cochran announced a gift of one million dollars for general endowment, in addition to grants for the Dining Hall, the Sanctuary, and other projects.[95] This in itself was enough to justify the Sesquicentennial. Another bit of fall-out from the drive was the collection of American art donated by Cochran for the yet-to-be-built Addison gallery. As is always the case with celebrations like this one, an important result was an increased interest in the School's past, with the result that additional archival material, art objects, and artifacts were acquired. Many of these accomplishments might well have been achieved without the Sesquicentennial, but it certainly added a new dimension to the School's energy, one that could last long after the event. Aside from these serious matters, there were a few loose ends to take care of after the show was over. Mrs. Frank Stearns had left her umbrella at Al Stearns's house but would drop by to pick it up sometime.[96] An alumnus wrote testily from New Haven that he had not been able to get in to the luncheon because the tickets had been taken out of his kit.[97] Secretary of Labor Davis was so impressed with the proceedings that he proposed to send 182 copies of his book *The Iron Puddler* for distribution to the Senior Class at graduation.[98] And Al Stearns was deluged with congratulatory letters and telegrams all praising the great show. Considering the work he had done to make the affair a success, these tributes were well deserved.

The Sesquicentennial was the high point of this era; the departure of Al Stearns from Andover marked its close. For almost thirty years he had served as Headmaster and in a very real sense had become the School. To have him no longer at Phillips Academy would leave a gaping void that anyone else would have difficulty in filling. Early in November 1931 Al was presiding over a Faculty meeting when suddenly he leaned forward and put his forehead on the table in front of him. For a few moments the Faculty thought he might simply be resting, but it soon became clear that he had fainted.[99] He was immediately taken to the School Infirmary and, when it became clear that specialists would be needed to diagnose his case, to a hospital in Boston. On 20 November he was operated on by Dr. Dellinger Barney for what proved to be a cyst of the kidney, the kidney itself being removed as well as the cyst.[1]

Al was miserable about the whole business. He wrote his friend Jim Sawyer: "I feel like a real quitter and don't know yet how to behave. I had thought that my innards would outwear my head. But it's my time, I guess, and so I have no kick coming. I do wish, though, that I had had a little advance warning and could therefore have kept my desk in better shape."[2] A month later he was able to return to "Archmeadow," the house in Danvers that he had purchased, even though his convalescence, according to his doctor, was "stormy and prolonged."[3] From then on, his recovery was steady, however, and by late January Jim Sawyer could write that he was on the "top of the wave."[4] Al was in a difficult situation financially as well, and his recovery may have been hastened when he learned that the Trustees had voted to assume all his medical and hospital expenses.[5] He was temperamentally anxious to get back in the saddle, and thus was of two minds about a Trustee vote that he take a leave of absence for the spring term. He did not want to dump the responsibilities of headmaster on Charlie Forbes, who had been acting in his place, he wrote Jim Sawyer; yet perhaps he should completely regain his strength. He was perfectly willing to have the School make use of his house in Andover, and if the Trustees wanted him to take the spring term off, he would agree, for "They are the 'boss'— and I won't fight them."[6] In the meantime, there was some talk of his being chosen the new President of Amherst, and some evidence that the Trustees of Phillips Academy might favor his accepting the position, should it be offered to him.[7] In May Al was able to participate in the ceremonies dedicating the Cochran Chapel and generally seemed to be regaining his strength. As James Hardy Ropes, President of the Trustees, wrote in June, "He fully expects to come back in full vigor in September, and his doctor, with whom I had a full talk, expected him to be able to do so."[8]

But it was not to be. Though there is nothing in the record, something happened at the Trustee Meeting of 16 June to change Al Stearns's future completely. In the light of what happened later, it is clear that a decision was reached to demand his resignation. In spite of disclaimers by the Trustees, it also seems clear than an important influence on the Trustee decision was Al's relationship with Miss Grace Clemons. It will be remembered that Al's wife had been in an institution for some twenty years and that he had engaged Miss Clemons to bring up his children. Miss Clemons proved to be a difficult person to deal with—emotional, opinionated, and hypersensitive. Many of the Faculty believed that one's success at Andover could be determined by her, such was her influence over Al Stearns.[9] She was at the same time a woman of great cultivation and taste. Al's mother-in-law had made him swear never to remarry as long as his wife still lived,[10] but it is clear that he felt a moral obligation, if not a genuine desire, to marry Miss Clemons once he was free. None of this can be documented, but the presumption is strong that this was the case. Professor Ropes wrote to the contrary:

> I told Stearns, I believe, that his household affairs had not been so much as mentioned in the Trustees' consultation about the matter, and I think it can be said with perfect truthfulness that they do not constitute an element in the present situation. Of course, they lie in the background of the thought of all of us, but are in no sense whatever an occasion of the present action of the Trustees or of myself. . . . Mrs. Stearns . . . is as well as she was a year ago, and for ought I can see she may live twenty years more in her present pitiable condition.[11]

In any event, Professor Ropes went in July to give Al the hard word:

> I first told him of the Trustees' plan to grant him $11,500 for his debts, and with some difficulty persuaded him to accept it. Then I gave him my advice to resign to take effect September 1, 1932, also telling him that his retiring allowance would in any case be $10,000 and that the Trustees earnestly desired it, if help from the alumni can be secured, to make it $15,000.
>
> He was naturally a good deal shaken up by the conversation, but had himself well in hand, and our talk was a very friendly one.[12]

After consultation with Acting Headmaster Charlie Forbes, Ropes modified his original proposal. It was now suggested that Al take a year's leave of absence for 1932–33 and then resign in 1933. There is no question that the Trustee decision hit Al Stearns hard. Nor was his life made any easier by Grace Clemons' charge that by that decision they were branding her a "scarlet woman" and attacking Al's character.[13] Throughout the remainder of the summer Charlie Forbes was a constant visitor at Archmeadow and did a great deal to reconcile Al to the leave of absence. But Charlie became more and more disturbed at Al's state of mind; he was not sleeping well, was "mulling over the whole business in his mind," and appeared "upset and muddled."[14] And well he might be. President Hopkins of Dartmouth, a Trustee, wrote sympathetically about the hard life Al had had:

> All in all, it seems to me difficult to imagine a worse fate than has been his. First of all, he was bred to such deference to his mother that he was compelled to marry one girl when all of his affection and desire were for another. Then he was obliged to live for years not only deprived of every solace and comfort of home life but in actual terror at times of the increasing mental unbalance of his wife lest it

result in personal tragedy to her or in violence to the children. Finally, he is bound by law to a being that is hardly a human being but simply an animate mass of matter while deprived of making any adjustment which would give him congenial companionship and offer him some of the peace and quiet of life which has never been his.[15]

On 27 July Al applied to Ropes for a year's leave of absence, but with no mention of his resignation a year later. Yet it was implied in a statement he made to the effect that the School could be administered successfully under Charlie Forbes and without him.[16] Shortly afterward the Trustee Committee on Exigencies met and granted Al's request for a sabbatical. They also voted to recommend to the full Board that Al be elected a Trustee to fill a then-existing vacancy. Ropes told Hopkins that he thought the idea basically bad, but he believed it would do much to heal any wounds that might be occasioned by Al's resignation, and he was sure that Al would not embarrass Charlie Forbes at meetings.[17] Hopkins wrote back that he hoped the matter could be deferred for the time being, and in fact Al's election as Trustee never did take place.[18] To make Al's life more difficult during this period a movement developed to get rid of his appointee Buell Trowbridge and his controversial course in Science and Modern Life. Part of the course was devoted to a study of Soviet Russia, in which Trowbridge had a keen interest, and the anti-Bolshevik forces in the Andover community wanted his scalp. But there was more to it than that; intelligent observers—particularly Charlie Forbes—did not have confidence in Trowbridge's ability as a teacher and scholar and believed he should go for these reasons; and he did go, the following year. This was a bitter blow for Al Stearns, who was sure that his protégé was performing a useful service for the boys, and he wrote Hopkins a long argumentative letter in his defense.[19]

Early in October James Ropes went to Archmeadow to visit Al. He was reassured to find him much like his old self, even though he was disturbed at reports from Charlie Forbes and Miss Clemons of Al's highly emotional state and his outbursts of temper.[20] Al was apparently able to get himself in hand, however, and on 14 October he, Miss Clemons, his daughter Marjorie, and a Mrs. Griffith sailed for Europe on the S.S. *Minnewaska*. He was never to hold an official position at Phillips Academy again.

The Stearns party traveled in Europe for the rest of the fall of 1932. New Year's 1933 found him in Nice, France, and it was from this beautiful resort that Al wrote his letter of resignation to the Trustees. After reviewing his thirty years as Headmaster, he said he had reached the conclusion that "the helm should be entrusted to younger hands." While he was feeling stronger, he was still "distrustful of the extent of my reserves" and thought that he should engage in less exacting work. Finally, he had great confidence in the men who were currently running the school and was sure that the future of the institution was in good hands.[21] Al's letter very nearly went astray; it was sent to Professor Ropes and apparently arrived just one day before Ropes's death. When Charlie Forbes went to Cambridge to look for Rope's notes for the coming Trustee Meeting, he found the letter and presented it to the Board. The Board accepted the resignation "with the deepest regret" and immediately and unanimously elected Al Headmaster Emeritus. They then passed a resolution expressing their affection for Al and their hopes for his increasing strength in the future. Finally, they voted that until further notice he was to receive the same salary that he had received as Headmaster. Thus the job was done.[22]

The rest of the Al Stearns story is soon told. In March 1933 he and Miss Clemons returned to Danvers, where they were to live for the next ten years. In June of that year his wife finally died, and in September he and Miss Clemons were finally married. He maintained distant relations with the School. In June 1933 he spoke at the Alumni Luncheon; each year in September he preached in the Academy Chapel; he made speeches and generally lent a hand with the fund drive of the late 1930's. Aside from his contacts with Phillips Academy, he was in great demand as a speaker and preacher, and the *Bulletin* used to print accounts of his engagements regularly. But his major interest came to be Amherst College. It was somehow fitting that he should return to his birthplace and his alma mater in his last years. He had always been active in Amherst affairs; he was a Trustee and in his later years became President of the Board. In 1943 Grace Clemons Stearns died, and he sold the Danvers house and returned to Andover with his daughter Marjorie, purchasing a house on Locke Street. When John Mason Kemper became Headmaster in 1948, he invited Al to address the undergraduate body in George Washington Hall. Al thought the boys would be interested in some of the early student riots that had taken place in his first years as Headmaster and recounted the story of them with great gusto. Later that afternoon John Kemper called him up and said that as a result of his talk the present undergraduates were staging a similar riot out on the football field. Al was chastened, but Kemper was highly amused. The following year Al suffered a heart attack and was confined to his bed. His last days were made immeasurably brighter by a new invention—television—on which he could watch baseball games. He died in November 1949.

Al Stearns was indubitably a great Headmaster, as the many tributes to him at the time of his retirement and of his death bear testimony. He had served Phillips Academy longer than any Headmaster except Uncle Sam Taylor, and when the increased size of the School is considered, more boys sat at his feet than at any other Headmaster's in the School's history. He was no educational innovator; the curriculum when he left Andover had changed but little from what it was in 1903. Many thought that his moral precepts were products of a forgotten world and had little relevance in contemporary society. But he had a tremendous concern for the boys in his charge, and few of them ever forgot that. His capacity for sheer hard work was almost unbelievable; indeed one wonders how he ever did as much as he did for the students, the Faculty, the alumni, the parents, and people in the town. He was fortunate in being Headmaster at a time when there was great loyalty to the School among the alumni and when the alumni had the means of translating that loyalty into tangible improvements for the School. The growth of the Phillips Academy plant during his administration was little short of breathtaking. But his life was a hard one. His family difficulties alone would have been enough to break another man. Despite blows and disappointments along the way, he finished strong—as dedicated to the principles he had lived by as he had ever been.

CHAPTER FIFTEEN

THE FUESS ADMINISTRATION

T
HE FIRST three months of 1933 were traumatic for Phillips Academy. In January Professor James Hardy Ropes, President of the Board of Trustees, died suddenly. At about the same time Al Stearns's letter of resignation was received, and though the Trustees had known that it was coming, it was a shock to the Andover community as a whole. On March 12 Charlie Forbes died of a heart attack. Thomas Cochran was in poor health, and although he had been able to attend the dedication of the Cochran Chapel in May of 1932, he never returned to Andover after that, and his driving force was missing from the Board. Finally, in the spring James Sawyer became ill and was unable to carry out the duties of his office for a year. It seemed as if some malign spirit were trying to destroy the Academy.[1]

At this critical juncture the Trustees turned to Claude M. Fuess, who had been teaching English at the School since 1908 and had performed many other services as well, such as editing the *Bulletin*, serving as Secretary to the Alumni Council, and arranging for the Sesquicentennial. Fuess had never considered the Headmastership; indeed he was at the time seriously considering accepting the post of Professor of Biography at Amherst College, where he would be free to write and conduct a few classes. When he explained this, Judge Bishop, who had just been elected to succeed James Ropes as President of the Board, replied, "Nonsense! You've just got to help us out here." "Do you mean to say," Fuess asked, "that I've got to be Headmaster whether I want to be or not?" "Not necessarily Headmaster," replied the judge. "This doesn't mean that you're not going to be Headmaster; on the other hand it doesn't mean you're going to be."[2] Fuess allowed himself to be persuaded, and the next morning took the Headmaster's position in Chapel, with, as he freely admits, his knees shaking. He had been elected Acting Headmaster, and the Trustees were now faced with the necessity of deciding who the new Headmaster should be —Fuess or some man from outside the School. Just how thoroughly the

Trustees canvassed the field outside the School is impossible to say. In mid-April a list of thirty possible candidates was circulated among them that was broad enough in scope. It included such people as Frank Boyden of Deerfield, President James Phinney Baxter of Williams, Henry Kittredge of St. Paul's, Professor Kenneth Murdock of Harvard, Louis Zahner of Groton, George Van Santvoord of Hotchkiss, and a number of other headmasters and college administrators.[3] It is hard to believe that the Trustee Committee entrusted with the task of recommending a Headmaster to the full Board could have interviewed all these distinguished people in the space of a little over a month. They doubtless decided early on that they should stick with someone whom they knew and respected, someone, furthermore, who knew Phillips Academy thoroughly and whose election would reassure the Andover community. In any event, at the Trustee Meeting of 28 May 1933 Claude M. Fuess was elected Headmaster. Writing to Judge Bishop about the choice, Jim Sawyer said, "Not for years have I been so contented as far as the school situation is concerned. With all my heart I believe we have a fine leader and under him the school will go forward to greater heights and prestige. The enthusiasm of every member of the Board over this appointment was certainly very gratifying . . ."[4]

The man who was to serve as the Tenth Headmaster of Phillips Academy had been born in Waterville, New York, on 12 January 1885, the son of Louis Philip and Helen Augusta Moore Fuess.[5] From the very beginning he had trouble with his name. No one seems to know why his parents picked "Claude," but it is certain that neither he nor his friends liked it. During his youth in Waterville, N.Y., he acquired the nickname "Dutch," and he was discouraged later to find that the tag had followed him to Amherst College. When he became engaged to Elizabeth Goodhue in 1910, she gave short shrift to "Claude," announcing firmly that she was going to call him "Jack"; and thereafter his friends knew him by that name. Students at Andover often referred to him as "Claudie," or, after he became Headmaster, "B.D." (Bald Doctor). Apparently Jack Fuess had no objection to his middle name of Moore, but he often bemoaned the wildly varied pronunciation of Fuess. As he put it, "I have become accustomed to Fuss, Few-ess, Fuse, Feis, and Foos," and finally someone wrote a bit of doggerel to illustrate the problem:

He'll exclaim, "Oh what's the use!"
When he hears you utter "Fuess."
And he'll like it even less
If you say it's Mr. Fuess.
If you want to hear him cuss
Just be sure to call him Fuess.
All his wonted calm he'll lose
If perchance you murmur "Fuess";

But he'll thank you on his knees
If you will but call him "Fuess."[6]

Despite these difficulties, he resisted steadfastly the suggestions of friends that he simplify the name; it was an honorable one in Germany as well as in the United States, and he was content to bear it in its original form.

Jack Fuess's grandfather, Jacob, was a native of Annweiler in the Bavarian Palatinate who had emigrated to the United States after the Revolution of 1848. He settled first in New York City and did well enough to send back to Germany for his sweetheart, Johanna Valeria Woerner. After the Civil War the couple bought a farm outside Waterville, and members of the family have lived there ever since. Jack remembers his grandfather as a dreamer with an Imperial beard who always spoke English with a pronounced foreign accent. His grandmother, with white lace collar and lace cap, reminded him of a Rembrandt portrait. He remembered particularly the Christmas celebrations, with a gorgeous tree, German cakes and cookies, and the singing of such songs as *O Tannenbaum*. But the German traditions vanished with the next generation. Jack's father Louis had a typically American education, going to Waterville High and then reading law in the office of a local lawyer and continuing his studies at a law school in New York City. He then hung out his shingle in Waterville, married Hannah Moore, who came from a long line of New England clergymen and magistrates, and began raising a family. Jack Fuess had an uneventful upbringing in Waterville. He enjoyed what he called "the democratic atmosphere of a New York country village" and followed his father's example by attending Waterville High, where he did well enough to win the chance of a college education. Friends of his father had gone to Amherst College, and one of his own best friends planned to go there. As a result, Jack applied for admission and was immediately accepted. It was a fortunate choice, and Amherst was to be one of his great enthusiasms for the rest of his life. He liked to tell the story of his saying good-bye to his Mother as he was leaving for college. According to his report, she said to him: "Claude, you certainly are homely, but you may do well."[7] Mrs. Fuess's prophecy was more than borne out by Jack's record at Amherst. As a member of the Class of 1905, he excelled in his studies, graduating Phi Beta Kappa. But he was no mere grind. He joined Alpha Delta Phi, one of the strongest social fraternities in the college, and soon became a leader in the organization. Nor did his interest in his fraternity end with graduation; he was a loyal supporter throughout his life and was at one time president of its national organization. But it was the friendships and student life that endeared Amherst to him and led him in later years to serve as President of the Alumni Association, to write a history of the college as well as countless articles for its alumni magazine, and to serve as one of the great presiding officers of all time for many college meetings. Jack's relationship to Amherst was clearly a love affair.

According to Jack, he first decided on a scholarly career when he heard the Amherst College professor George Bosworth Churchill read Wordsworth's "Tintern Abbey" to his class one gloomy November afternoon in 1904. In any event, after graduation from Amherst he proceeded to Columbia graduate school to pursue the study of English. He spent two years there, getting an M.A. along the way and passing the dreaded orals that were a requirement for the Ph.D. On the advice of Professor William P. Trent, his mentor, he decided to take a year off and try his hand at teaching, which he did at the George School, a Quaker institution outside Philadelphia. His experience there convinced him that he did indeed want to follow a teaching career, though he emerged with serious reservations about coeducation—the George School being a coeducational institution. After a summer of canoeing in the Canadian woods, he went back to Waterville, intent on returning to Columbia to finish his doctorate. Much to his surprise he received one day a telegram from Alfred E. Stearns asking him to come to Boston to discuss a position as instructor in English at Andover. He wired back that he was not interested. Another telegram came asking him to meet Stearns at Springfield. Again Jack said no. A third telegram suggested that a meeting be held at Albany. Jack's father suggested that this man Stearns must be pretty much in earnest about his offer and urged Jack to go to Albany. This he did and found that Al Stearns was offering him $1200 with room and board, which was pretty good for those days. But Al's trump card was a telegram he had from Professor George Carpenter at Columbia, one of Jack's teachers, urging Jack to accept the Andover position. As a result, thirty-six hours later he was ensconced in Draper Cottage to start an Andover career that was to last forty years.

In Jack's early years at the School he continued to work on his thesis, which finally was published as "Lord Byron as a Satirist in Verse" and which was accepted for his Ph.D. in 1912. In 1911 he had married Elizabeth Cushing Goodhue, a member of an old and distinguished New England family, and in 1912 their only child, John Cushing Fuess, was born. From the very beginning Jack did much more than carry a full teaching load. He was active in the alumni association and served for many years as the editor of the *Phillips Bulletin*, which became a distinguished publication under his leadership. In 1917 he published his first important book—a history of Phillips Academy entitled *An Old New England School*. That same year he was commissioned a major in the army quartermaster corps and spent an instructive time at a camp in Jacksonville, Florida. But it was not long before he was back in Andover to play a leading part in the fund drive of 1919–20. And when the Sesquicentennial celebration was being mounted, he had a responsible role to play. Considering the many ways in which he had served the school over the years, it is not surprising that the Trustees should turn to him when they needed someone to head Phillips Academy.

Jack's many peripheral activities should not be allowed to hide the fact that he was one of the great teachers of English in his generation. John U. Monro, '30, currently a Trustee of the Academy, said of his teaching:

> From Jack Fuess, in his big sunny classroom in Pearson Hall, I learned the joy and the basic skills of writing. Jack Fuess cared about writing, knew about it, and worked at it; and he liked students and wanted them to know, too, and he was crisp and good-humored and civilized about it all, and so he got through. I thought then, and I still think, that Jack Fuess was one of the two great school teachers of my time. His manner was to stand straight before us on the low platform, hands cocked on hips, heels together, a knee twitching, now and then the flat of a hand brushing back nervously over the bald head; his smile was broad and confident, his voice quick and firm; here was a friendly, lively, interested man, keen to have you share with him the fun, the work, and the importance of clear, expressive, disciplined writing. For most of college and all my working life I have thought of myself as dependent for survival mainly on writing, and the solid growing pleasure I take in the use of language I trace back easily to Jack Fuess.[8]

Another alumnus remembers his teaching:

> Among my own recollections of him as a teacher, one of the most vivid is of his reading poetry to us—Milton, Shakespeare, Keats, Swineburne, Frost, and many others. He had a voice that could thrill his listeners; and while the emotional message of the piece he was reading always came through loud and clear, he never slopped over into sentimentality. He had the somewhat old-fashioned notion that it was good pedagogy to make his students learn yards of poetry by heart, and I still think of him whenever I read "To hear the Lark begin his flight / And singing startle the dull night" or "Thou wast not born for Death, immortal Bird." As for prose, he was especially gifted at interpreting Boswell's Johnson to us, and seemed to enjoy immensely reading the great Doctor's replies to his Scotch friend's queries. " 'SIR,' said Johnson," Jack would boom, and we could all but see the Lexicographer standing before us. Hardly a class went by when we were not treated to an example of Jack's sense of humor, and he enjoyed nothing more—then as always during his lifetime—than turning a joke on himself. On one occasion we were all made to write some heroic couplets; much to Jack's delight one wag turned up with the following:
>
> > I see the bust of Plato on the shelf,
> > Methinks that Claudie should be there himself.

58. Claude Moore Fuess, Tenth Headmaster of Phillips Academy.

Another of his favorites was:

> Her lips were red, her neck was like the swan,
> And that's the neck I do my necking on.

Yet one should not get the idea that Jack's classes were mere vaudeville acts. He could be a brisk disciplinarian and on occasion would burst out with a long jeremiad on the stupidity of Andover seniors. And he could be savage with a sloppy theme. I well remember the bloody remains of a composition I wrote on Samuel Johnson in which I had spelled the name "Johnston" throughout. In short, Jack could combine a rigorous discipline in writing with a contagious enthusiasm for literature in the same English course, and make his students respect the one and respond to the other. It is small wonder that few of his boys ever forgot their work with him.[9]

This, then, was the man who took over as Acting Headmaster in March, 1933, and as Headmaster in his own right the following May. He was to continue in office for the next fifteen years—and they were difficult ones too. It was Jack Fuess's lot to preside over the School during the Great Depression and World War II, and this, almost by definition, meant that opportunities for innovation would be limited. One student of Jack's term of office after 1940 has characterized it as a "Holding Operation" and indeed this term could well be applied to all his years as Headmaster.[10] To be sure he was able to accomplish some useful things in the 1930's and generally to change the tone of the School in important ways, but there could be nothing like the excitement of the Cochran years. He succeeded in bringing about a major revision of the curriculum, but the change did not last much beyond his own Headmastership. He vastly improved the health services provided for the undergraduate body. In what was undoubtedly his most daring stroke, he attempted to abolish the School's secret societies, only to be stymied when alumni reaction proved too powerful. His major achievement was to modify the "sink-or-swim" policy that had been characteristic of the Academy for many years. He used to tell the story of a Faculty meeting that took place in the 1920's. As the meeting came to a close, one member of the Faculty remarked, in amazement, that not a single student had been fired. At this point a senior member roused himself, determined that the School's reputation for toughness should not be compromised, and announced, "Well, I have a candidate." He then proceeded with a short synopsis of the unfortunate boy's sins. Without further discussion—and apparently, according to Jack, with a good deal of relish—the Faculty then fired the boy and adjourned.[11] Under Jack such a cold-blooded procedure would have been impossible. From the start he insisted that each boy be treated as an individual, and that each boy's welfare be considered, as well as that of the School, when problem cases came up. Under Jack a much more detailed system of reporting on boys was instituted, so that a student would no longer be at the mercy of the whim of a single Faculty member.

For many years the person in charge of student records had been a sweet, birdlike woman named Alice T. Whitney. She kept account not only of the student's academic record, but of his cuts as well, and a large amount of her time was devoted to tracking down culprits who had failed to show up in class. And she performed this onerous task with a gentleness and understanding that made the whole School love her. When Dr. Willet L. Eccles became Registrar, after the death of Cecil Bancroft, he introduced a much more modern and scientific reporting procedure, so that a boy's entire record could be easily reviewed from a single small card. The result was that whenever the Headmaster or the Faculty wished to know about a boy, the record of his achievements and sins was easily available for all to use.

One of the most important achievements of the Fuess regime was accomplished before his election as Headmaster, while he was still only acting in that capacity. This was a major overhaul of the curriculum that was put through in the spring of 1933. For some time the Phillips Academy curriculum had been criticized by alumni and various college officials as not having kept pace with educational changes in the country. While adequate for college admission, it did not, it was charged, prepare the boys to meet the problems in the world around them—it was out of touch with life. The difficulty was that it lacked flexibility, variety, and proportion. Jack Fuess summed up its deficiencies for Judge Bishop, President of the Board of Trustees, as follows:

> It devotes relatively too much attention to foreign languages and to language study in general. It asks for too large an amount of mathematics, to the exclusion of other equally valuable subjects. It does not supply sufficient instruction in science, in history, and in the fine arts.[12]

Individual members of the Faculty had been concerned about these problems for some time, and the eight Class Officers appear to have been considering curricular reform as well. Jack Fuess himself was one of the leaders of this movement long before he became Acting Headmaster. But there were various roadblocks: the uncertainty following Al Stearns's illness and Charlie Forbe's position as Acting Headmaster militated against moving ahead in such an important area. And it may well have been that Forbes did not want to push a program that would seriously weaken his beloved Latin. One of the recommendations of the reformers was that American history should become compulsory for all Seniors. The then President of the Board, James Ropes, said that American history would become compulsory over his dead body. And that, as Jack Fuess was wont to point out, is exactly what happened.[13] With Ropes and Forbes both dead the way was at last open, and at the Faculty Meeting of 23 March 1933, Acting Headmaster Fuess appointed a curriculum committee consisting of Dean Lester Lynde as Chairman, Freddie Boyce of the Physics Department, Archie Freeman of History, Allan Heely of English, and Horace Poynter of Classics.[14] Curriculum revision usually involves long and acrimonious debate, with the gutters running with blood, before something is finally hammered out. This committee finished its job in about six weeks, and when its report was presented to the Faculty on 9 May, it was approved 46–0, with Allen Benner and Frank Benton, two Classicists, abstaining.[15] That such a fundamental change could be accomplished in such a short time and with such unanimity by the Faculty indicates that a great deal of discussion must have preceded the formal action.

Perhaps the most striking thing about the new curriculum was the introduction of a compulsory four-year History program.[16] In the past it had

59. Alice Thacher Whitney, Recorder, 1902–1950.

462 : THE MODERN ANDOVER

been possible to graduate from Andover without having taken any history at all, though there were elective courses in ancient, English, and American history. Now history was to be required each year, with the particular subjects to be studied following the recommendation made by the Secondary School committee of the American Historical Association back in the early years of the century. The Juniors (9th Grade) were to have a three-hour course in ancient history, presumably to complement their study of Latin or Greek, which most of them were beginning. In the Lower Middle year (10th Grade) there was a two-hour course in European history, focused on the Middle Ages, at a time when most of the class would be starting French. In the Upper Middle year (11th Grade) a three-hour course in English history was to be offered, again to complement the study of English literature begun in that year. And finally the Seniors (12th grade) would take a five-hour course in American history that would familiarize them with their country's past and its present problems. Before 1933 it was also possible to win an Andover diploma without having had any science at all. The new curriculum made the taking of one course in science a requirement for the diploma and provided for an introductory course in science for all Juniors. Finally, there was concern that the Phillips Academy students of the day would be illiterate in art and music. Accordingly, a course in these two subjects was to be required for most Upper Middlers. Obviously if these new courses were to be added to the curriculum, some of the older requirements would have to yield, and it was in the language area that the requirements were reduced. For the first time since the founding of Phillips Academy in 1778, Latin was no longer a required course. Now the student could choose from among Latin, Greek, French, and German and was required, in most cases, to take three years of one and two years of another. By the same token the old four-year requirement in mathematics was reduced to three. Yet these shifts were not sufficient to meet the demands of the new curriculum. As a result, the total number of hours a boy was to take was raised from eighteen to twenty or twenty-one. It was promised that the increase in hours would be accompanied by shorter homework assignments. The new curriculum provided for more variety and more choice on the part of the student; yet four of the required courses and a large number of electives were one- or two-hour courses in which it would be difficult to accomplish a great deal.

The new curriculum was a step in the right direction. The reduction in mathematics and language requirements and the inclusion of science and art and music as necessary for the diploma were all long overdue. The history program, however, failed to realize what had been hoped for it. Ancient history, taught in a fairly conventional fashion to the Juniors by Kenneth S. Minard, never meshed with the beginning classics courses as had been planned; indeed, the whole concept of the course bore testimony to the difficulty of establishing interdepartmental relationship between courses. The European history course, taught by the redoubtable Kilbrith J. ("Count") Barrows had similar troubles. In the first place, Barrows had six sections of two hours each, and after the first four or five sessions the bloom began to wear off. Nor did medieval France have much to do with starting the study of French. Barrows certainly did his best; he used to pep things up by calling the roll and conducting a brief conversation with each student; he introduced material on American railroads, a specialty of his; and he was regularly voted Favorite in the Classroom by many of the classes of this era. But the subject matter was wrong, the amount of time for the course was too short, and the students soon found themselves studying Barrows rather than Medieval France. The three-hour course in English history was something else again. The students in this course were more mature and thus more able to deal with historical material, and the techniques of the course were modeled on the Senior one in American history —taking notes in a notebook from assigned readings from books on reserve in the library. The course was designed to prepare for the Senior one and as a result emphasized British colonization, British constitutional history, and other subjects related to the United States. It was taught primarily by Leonard F. James, an Englishman by birth, who developed it into a truly meaningful learning experience. When the history sequence was abolished in the early 1950's, it was unfortunate that this course was not kept, for it served the dual purpose of acquainting the boys with the British past and of preparing them for the Senior courses in American history. This course, known for years as History 4, was the culmination of the history program and the most terrifying experience in the entire curriculum for most boys. The driving force behind History 4 was Dr. Arthur B. Darling, a former Professor at Yale who had come to Andover to succeed Archie Freeman, who was about to retire. When Darling took over the American history program, it was with a vengeance. He demanded extraordinarily high standards for all the students taking the course and soon became famous for the number who failed their diplomas in June as a result of failing American history. He was a brilliant teacher for able boys —challenging, incisive, exciting, and at the same time erratic, emotional, and at times confusing. He was the despair of slow students, who never understood what he was talking about a good part of the time. One year he had a so-called slow section of nine students whom he used to call the Nine Old Men and was forever bemoaning their stupidity. A graduate returned one year and asked where Darling was. "He was the greatest teacher I ever had," he said. When a member of the Faculty asked why this was so, he replied, "Because he was so god-damned unreasonable." And he went on to say that he had run into many unreasonable things in life, but none that could touch Darling. Another graduate remembers the time when Darling read aloud what he considered a good final exam. The class wanted to know what grade the exam had received. "80," said Dar-

60. *Arthur Burr Darling of the Class of 1912, Instructor in History, 1933–1956, and Head of the History Department, 1937–1956.*

ling, as the class moaned. But then he went on to say, "I'd have only got 85 myself." Darling's standards could be really rough; one June he failed 23 out of 70 boys, all of whom missed their diplomas thereby. Yet year after year he stood high in the Senior polls as "Best Teacher" and for those who could get his message, the experience was unforgettable. In addition to Darling, Bill Bender, later Dean of Harvard, and Miles Malone taught American history during these years, and although they were not as tough as the "Doctor," they, too, made the course sing for many students. This, then, was the new curriculum that, with minor adjustments, was to constitute the School's academic program until the early 1950's.

Jack Fuess became Headmaster in the depth of the Great Depression, shortly after Franklin D. Roosevelt assumed the Presidency. Despite the desperate condition of most of the country, the School managed to weather the hard times very well. Yet the Trustee Records indicate that there were problems. In 1932 Horace Poynter, for reasons of economy,[17] voluntarily gave up a sabbatical due him. In the same year, in an effort to help the town, the Trustees voted that all manual labor to be employed by the School be recruited in the town.[18] Tuition charges were a heavy burden on parents, and the Trustees recognized this by voting eight additional tuition remissions for "good" candidates.[19] Since, in the School's Constitution, Samuel Phillips had forbidden the reduction of teachers' salaries, the Trustees could not save money in this area, but they considered asking the Faculty to take voluntary reductions. Nothing was ever done about this, and actually the Faculty, most of whom were receiving salaries that had been set in the 1920's, lived very well during this period. It is interesting to note that when five new Faculty houses were built in 1938, each had a maid's room and bath, on the assumption that the teachers would continue to have maids, as they did in the 1930's.[20] As far as the financing of the School itself is concerned, the Trustees succeeded as well. Though there was a deficit of some $4,500 in 1934, the next three years showed surpluses of over $6,000. The years 1938 and 1939 were bad, however, with deficits of over $40,000 each year; but 1940 saw a return to a surplus. Considering the problems that other educational institutions were having, the record of the Trustees was praiseworthy.[21] Nor was there a falling off in the size of the student body. From 1931 to 1934 the number of students hovered around 650, but after that there was a fairly steady rise in numbers, the 700 mark being passed in the year 1936–37. By 1941 the number had reached 742, about one hundred more than ten years before.[22] What may have been a contributing factor in the School's growth was the introduction of a flat-rate, all-inclusive charge in 1934. Up until this time the charges for tuition, room, board, and other expenses had been computed separately, the dormitory rooms in particular varying a great deal in price according to their facilities and size. Now a rate of $1100 was established for all, regardless of where they roomed.[23] One effect of this decision was a program on the part of the School to improve some of the less desirable rooms so as to make them more nearly equal to the superior ones. The total of $1100 for room, board, and tuition was a bargain, even in the 1930's, and this flat-rate charge undoubtedly appealed to parents. All in all, the School weathered the Depression very well, and the institution was in general stronger at the end of the decade than at the beginning.

Perhaps the most important improvement accomplished during the Fuess years was in medical services. Before the twentieth century Phillips Academy had, in effect, no medical program. When boys got sick, they (as noted) stayed in their rooms until they got well, occasionally calling on physicians from the town if their condition became too desperate. Things changed for the better in 1902, when Peirson S. Page came to Andover as Director of Athletics and School doctor. From the beginning he devoted more of his time to the development of a strong program in physical education than to medical practice as such. He introduced compulsory physical examinations for each boy and a series of physical fitness tests that included such rigorous exercises as the rope climb, "belly grinds," and swimming and running events. Many an Andover undergraduate, attempting to do the arm-over-arm rope climb, will remember Doc Page saying, "Using your feet—F." Boys who were unable to meet these fitness tests were put in special classes for special training. This group was known variously as "P.I.'s" (physically inefficient) or, the favorite undergraduate designation, "P.W.'s" (physical wrecks). In 1912 a great step was taken in the area of student health when Miss Flora Isham gave the School a small infirmary. For the first time in its history boys who were sick had a place to go where they would receive adequate medical care. Dr. Page dealt with relatively simple ailments—sprained ankles, acne, colds, stomach upsets, and the like. When the complaint was more serious, he would turn to the town doctors or, in truly serious cases, to Boston specialists. Dr. Page's favorite remedy for any kind of abrasion was to "paint it with iodine" and this became one of his nicknames. He also was concerned about the prevention of a common athletic ailment called "jock itch" and used to lecture the whole School on the subject at the start of each year. The remedy, according to Doc Page, was to take "a clean pocket handerchief" and place it between the jock strap and the body. One alumnus remembers an epidemic of pink eye (conjunctivitis) that ran through the School in the winter of 1931. Even though it seemed to be having little effect on the infection, Dr. Page had everyone putting Argerol in his eyes, with the result that everyone looked like a raccoon and was unable to go to class. In short, as Director of Athletics, Peirson Page did a fine job; as a medical doctor he left a good deal to be desired.[24]

All of this changed in 1934 when J. Roswell Gallagher, the most distinguished physician in the history of the School, came to Andover. It is always difficult for an institution like Phillips Academy to attract a top-notch doctor. Most of the diseases of adolescence are hardly those to challenge a highly trained, aggressive physician. After a while athletic injuries begin to pall. Ros Gallagher came to Andover, in part at least, because he was interested in studying the adolescent boy and in establishing norms for the physical and psychological make-up of boys between the ages of thirteen and eighteen. Gallagher soon introduced the concept of the doctor-patient relationship, much to the rage of some of the Faculty. In the past a Housemaster had always been able to call the infirmary and find out what was wrong with one of his charges. Now he was met with a blank wall, for Gallagher believed that this was not the housemaster's business. He would talk with the parents if they wished to call up, but not to the School staff. In like manner he wanted the boys to feel free to talk with him about their problems, and thus it became understood that nothing would go outside his office, even if it involved the breaking of rules. Two examples of Ros Gallagher's *modus operandi* follow. He once wanted to talk to a boy who, he thought, was seriously disturbed emotionally, but he knew the boy would never come to see him if he called him in to his office. Accordingly, he called him up after chapel, together with a group of other ailing students. After asking how one boy's toe was, how another's cold was, he came to his boy and said, "What are you doing here?" The boy said he was told to report. The Doc looked in his book and then said, "Oh, your X-rays didn't come out. Come down sometime and we'll take some more." When the boy finally came down, Gallagher proceeded to take a lot of X-rays, without any plates in the machine, all the while talking to the boy and accomplishing his original purpose. The other example came as a result of a contagious disease that appeared in the School. Gallagher did not wish the boys to swim in the pool, but he did not want to alarm the school community. Accordingly, he went to the janitors in the gym and asked them what could go wrong with the swimming pool. They were puzzled at first but finally one said that the chlorinating system could break down." "It's just broken down," said Ros, and proceeded to put a notice to that effect in the School bulletin. All of this was a far cry from the health care that Phillips Academy students had had before the 1930's, and in 1935 the facilities for health care were further enhanced by the construction of a large wing on the rear of the old Isham Infirmary. Not only were additional beds made available but complete laboratory facilities as well. As a result, the Phillips Academy infirmary was recently classified as a hospital, and on the basis of its equipment it well deserves the designation.

Under Ros Gallagher the definition of health care was greatly expanded. No longer was it limited primarily to diseases and athletic injuries; every aspect of the adolescent was examined and tested in an effort to make his experience at Phillips Academy as rich and rewarding as possible. For example, Gallagher spent a lot of time testing boys for reading disabilities. He was convinced that in many cases—the national figure was 10 percent —failure in School was due to reading disability rather than to lack of academic ability, and he cited the case of a boy who had great difficulty with reading, writing, and spelling—for example, he always used very short words that he could spell—and yet scored 126 on the Wechsler-Bellevue test, one that puts little emphasis on reading and writing skills. This score indicated that he was in the top 3 percent of the country as far as basic intelligence went, even though he was having great difficulty with work that demanded verbal proficiency. If boys were tested early so as to discover language disability, remedial classes in language training could do much to correct the difficulty before the problem became acute.[25] Although Gallagher did a great deal of work trying to establish norms of various kinds for adolescents, he was under no illusion that there was such a thing as a "normal" or "average" boy. He was strongly opposed to attempts to establish rules for physical and mental development on the basis of age. For example, he cited the case of Sam, who was fourteen years old, weighed 150 pounds, was 5 feet 10 inches tall, was shaving regularly, but who seemed listless and was difficult for his parents to deal with. In contrast there was Billy, who had an upbringing almost identical with that of Sam, who at sixteen weighed 115 pounds, was 5 feet 4 inches tall, and had no reason at all to shave. He, too, was having trouble at School and was very hard to reach. Dr. Gallagher's point was that while neither of these boys was average, both were normal. The *average* weight of one group of schoolboys was 127 pounds, but the range was from 80 to 199 pounds. And his plea was that parents should stop worrying about averages; if they would only hide their anxiety, exhibit a great deal of patience, and above all give generously of their affection, the vast majority of the boys would sooner or later attain manhood.[26] Finally, during the war, under a grant from the Carnegie Foundation, Ros Gallagher studied the physical fitness of Andover boys and developed a program to promote it. He was convinced that too often the term was too narrowly defined. It included, he believed, *medical fitness*, which had to do with the condition of the eyes, heart, teeth, and so forth. It also included *dynamic fitness*, which had to do with the functional ability of one's heart, lungs, and circulatory system to respond to work. Finally, it included *motor skills fitness*, which had to do with the degree of skill, coordination, and strength with which one performs such acts as climbing, jumping, and swimming. Only if a boy were strong in all three of these areas could he be judged physically fit. In determining medical fitness Gallagher developed an elaborate set of physical examinations, conducted in large part by outside consultants at the Infirmary, that included dental X-rays, lung X-rays, blood and urine analyses, and many others. To determine their dynamic fitness, boys were required to take a step test, after which their heart rate was measured. And for motor skills testing, a pole climb, fence vault, jumping, and swimming were used. The whole program was an extraordinarily inclusive one and made a signal contribution to the health and welfare of the school.[27] Unfortunately, Ros Gallagher left Andover in 1950, first to go to Wesleyan and later to serve as Head of the adolescent unit at the Children's Hospital in Boston. But he left behind him a tradition of medical excellence that has been carried on by his successors down to the present day.

During the 1930's another interesting development on Andover Hill was the establishment of the Andover Evening Study Program.[28] Conceived by Alan R. Blackmer, who in the course of a long career was to make many important contributions to the school, with a strong assist from the Reverend A. Graham Baldwin, this program sought to provide the means for a continuing education for the inhabitants of the Merrimack Valley. The Directors insisted that their project must be completely distinct from Phillips Academy. To be sure they did use Phillips Academy buildings, but all other expenses—catalogues, advertising, janitorial services, and the like—were to be borne by the program itself. All of those teaching the courses—at the start they were almost all Phillips Academy Faculty—would contribute their services without charge, and the program generally was completely innocent of any commercial considerations. Particularly in its early years concerted attempts were made to attract factory workers from Lawrence and other industrial communities, and although this part of the program never achieved what had been hoped for it, the effort indicates clearly the highly idealistic aims of the founders. In its initial year, in 1935, 252 adults from the Greater Lawrence area took ten courses in such subjects as current events, modern art and literature, science, English, and German. The following year the program introduced what was to become a feature: a symposium entitled "Famous Men," with a series of lectures each given by a different instructor. Another very popular course was effective speaking, taught by Roger W. Higgins. Roger told the story of a young girl who was tongue-tied on her first essay at speaking and was unable to do more than give her name and address. In an effort to encourage her to continue, a male chauvinist in the back of the room cried, "What's your telephone number?" One of the decisions the directors of the program had to make was whether to insist on homework for the courses. A course in a modern language, for example, would be difficult to teach unless the class had done some preparation. Generally speaking, the courses that demanded preparation did not fare so well; it soon became apparent that most of the students preferred a passive role— to come to class and listen to someone talk. With the coming of the war, the curricular emphasis shifted to subjects that might be useful to the war effort—mathematics, science, first aid, and the like—but with the return to peace the program became once again strongly academic, with such subjects as "The Story of Russia," "State Government," "Seven Rebel Thinkers," and "Art and Mathematics." During this postwar period the number of students doubled, with 500 more or less enrolled each year. About 1952 the emphasis began to shift from purely academic courses to more practicall ones. During the next ten years, for example, such courses as "Coastal Piloting," "Spanish Conversation," "Blueprint Reading," "Laboratory Botany," "Chinese Cooking," and "Drownproofing" were offered. Though this shift represented a departure from the original goals of the founders, it may well have been what the community wanted. In any event, 753 people enrolled for the program in 1962. As the enrollment increased, the income from the program did likewise, providing the Directors with a surplus each year. They chose to distribute this money—over $11,000 in twenty-six years—to various worthy institutions—local libraries in the Greater Lawrence area; WGBH, the educational television station in Boston; and similar enterprises. In recent years the program has expanded its activities by joining forces with the Andover public school system and by including on its staff many teachers who are not members of the Phillips Academy Faculty. It is always difficult to measure the effect of a program of this kind—either on the individuals taking courses or on the community as a whole—but the chances are that Alan Blackmer was right when he spoke of "an enormous amount of good will" that had been gained, and added, "In short, it is our opinion that, in recent years, through no other single activity has Phillips Academy gained so much at so little cost."

The 1930's were certainly not a good time to raise money for plant expansion and new projects. Yet the School moved ahead during this period, though not, of course, with anything like the achievements of the Cochran era. By means of a bequest from the estate of Mrs. Fannie R. Dennis it was possible to build a large addition to the Infirmary, as has been mentioned; in addition, the bequest was large enough to make possible the construction of Rockwell House, a new dormitory for Juniors on the West Quadrangle. Williams Hall had never been large enough to hold the entire Junior Class, which had in recent years been increasing in size. Now it was possible to do so, with the older and more mature Juniors living in Rockwell, the younger ones in Williams Hall. In each case the purpose was to develop dormitory programs particularly designed for younger boys. In 1938, as a result of a gift from Edward Harkness, Bulfinch Hall, the former dining hall, was completely remodeled by Perry, Shaw, and Hepburn as a building for the English Department. The small classrooms, several with round tables rather than just classroom chairs, a handsome debating room, and individual studies for members of the English Department soon made this building a showplace on the Hill. Harkness also provided the money for the construction of five small Faculty houses beyond Hidden Field in what came to be known as "Little Siberia." These houses were constructed by Perry, Shaw, and Hepburn without the benefit of Faculty advice and as a result had very inadequate studies. Dudley Fitts, who lived in one, took over the master bedroom for his study and put a member of his family in the maid's room.

A matter that had been of concern to the Trustees for some time came to a head in the mid-1930's—namely, pensions or retirement allowances for the Faculty. When the Faculty was small, retirement did not present serious problems. There were seldom more than two or three Faculty members in that status, and in addition there was no compulsory retirement age, with the result that many teachers continued to teach after sixty-five, the present retirement age. George T. ("Pap") Eaton, for example, taught for fifty years at the Academy and retired in 1930 at the ripe old age of seventy-four. When there were only a few retired teachers to take care of, the Trustees simply dealt with each case on an individual basis and paid the pensions out of general funds. With the substantial increase in the size of the Faculty and in the number of teachers who were nearing retirement, a more comprehensive plan was required. Accordingly, the Trustees negotiated with the T.I.A.A. (Teachers Insurance and Annuity Association) a contract that would cover the Faculty as a whole. According to this arrangement both the individual teachers and the School would contribute regularly to funds that would provide teacher pensions. At the same time a compulsory age of sixty-five was established. Special arrangements had to be made for teachers who were close to retirement and who would not have time to build an adequate equity in a fund.

The compulsory retirement age angered some teachers. Allan R. Benner told Jack Fuess that he was as good as ever and that retirement would kill him, which it did. But the program was long overdue and was generally accepted with enthusiasm. In an effort to raise enough money to put the plan in practice—particularly for the older men—a fund drive was mounted under Lansing P. Reed of the Class of 1900. The goal was set at $750,000, and although this objective was never quite reached, a sufficient amount of money was contributed to enable the School to start the Retirement Program as of 1 July 1937.[29] The problem of pensions for the non-teaching staff remained, and the Trustees continued their old practice of handling these cases individually, providing pensions for retiring janitors, for example, of from $300 to $400 a year. It is interesting to note that while all this was going on, Headmaster Fuess, perhaps at the instigation of the Trustees, was working actively in opposition to the extension of the Social Security Act to private institutions.[30]

Phillips Academy survived the Depression with relatively little difficulty. There were, of course, special problems to be met, but no serious threat to the basic program of the School presented itself. Nor did World War II produce any basic change. Again, important modifications were made in certain areas of School life, but for the most part the Academy clung to the belief that the best preparation for a soldier was a solid secondary school training in the liberal arts. The School could feel close to the war

because of Henry L. Stimson, President of the Board of Trustees and Secretary of War during the conflict. Though Stimson had been a Trustee
since 1905, his public duties as Federal Attorney for the Southern District
of New York, as Secretary of War in the Taft cabinet, as Governor General of the Philippines in the 1920's, and as Secretary of State under
Hoover had prevented him from taking an active part in the life of the
School. With his retirement from public service in 1933, for the first time
in many years he had an opportunity to devote himself to Andover affairs,
and in December 1934 he spent four days at the School speaking and
talking to various groups. That same year Judge Elias Bishop, President
of the Board, died, and after talking with Alfred Ripley, Ernest M. Hopkins, and other members of the Board, Jack Fuess went to New York to
ask Mr. Stimson to become President. Stimson said that he was an old and
tired man but that since his public life was apparently over, he would
accept if he did not have to assume too much responsibility. At the next

*61. Henry Lewis Stimson of the Class of 1883, President of the Board
of Trustees, 1935–1946.*

meeting of the Board he was elected President unanimously and enthusiastically. Since he was without question the most distinguished living Andover alumnus, the Trustees might well have believed that they had made
a ten-strike. From that time on, Henry Stimson became a frequent visitor
at Andover. Unlike most of the Trustees, he enjoyed visiting classes, sometimes to the consternation of the instructor concerned. Miles S. Malone,
Instructor in American history, remembers one unnerving time as he was
discussing the Manchurian Crisis of 1931 when there was a knock at the
door, and, as Miles put it, "the Stimson Doctrine walked in in person."
But Miles was not to be fazed by this; he asked Mr. Stimson to take over
the class and for the rest of the period the boys got a first-hand account of
Far Eastern problems. Arthur Darling had a similar experience when lecturing on the Pullman Strike. He believed the Federal Government had
used the blocking of the mails as an excuse to intervene in the strike and
thus planned to discuss that topic at the end. But Mr. Stimson broke in in
the middle with "Don't forget the mails." Then as always throughout his
lifetime Stimson enjoyed walking, and often he and Jack Fuess would go
off for walks together around the School and in the Andover countryside.
It was clear to all who came in contact with him on these occasions that
Phillips Academy had a man of parts as President of its Board.[31]

With the outbreak of war in Europe in 1939, Mr. Stimson became more
and more concerned with the course events were taking. He was convinced
that if there had been strong action by the United States and other nations
at the time of the Japanese invasion of Manchuria in 1931, more recent
aggression by Mussolini and Hitler could also have been checked. Speaking at the Andover Commencement, on 13 June 1940, with the fall of
France imminent, Henry Stimson delivered the most important speech ever
given on Andover Hill. He said in part:

> Today our world is confronted by the clearest issue between right
> and wrong which has ever been presented to it on the scale in
> which we face it today. . . . The world today is divided into two
> necessarily opposed groups of governments. These governments are
> divided both by irreconcilable principles for international behavior
> without their borders as well as by irreconcilable principles of human
> rights and behavior within their borders. One group is striving for
> international justice and freedom, both without and within, while
> the other recognizes only the rule of force, both without and within.
> Over eighty years ago, Abraham Lincoln pointed out that a nation
> could not endure permanently half slave and half free. It would
> have to become all one thing or all the other. Today we are faced
> with that situation in the outside world, and the world has become so
> small that there can be no doubt of the truth of Lincoln's prophecy.
> The world today cannot endure permanently half slave and half

free. . . . In this great crisis, and in the decisions which you will
have to make, you will carry with you the confident hope and faith of
us who have the welfare of this academy at heart.[32]

Five days after this speech was delivered, Henry L. Stimson was appointed
Secretary of War in the Roosevelt cabinet. It should not be assumed that
the speech had any direct connection with the appointment, for Grenville
Clark, Felix Frankfurter, and others had been pushing for the Stimson appointment weeks before the speech was delivered.[33] But for the President
to appoint to a key cabinet post a man who had made such a strong policy
statement left no doubt as to where the administration stood, and in that
sense it became a kind of national policy statement. Another Andover
graduate, John D. M. Hamilton, called Stimson "a traitor to his party" for
accepting the post,[34] but most Andover men supported what the President
of the Board had done. The heavy new responsibilities that he had undertaken would mean that he would have little time for Andover for the
duration; it would be up to others to see that the School kept strong.

After the Stimson speech of June 1940 Phillips Academy became more
and more involved in the war, even though the formal entry of the United
States into the conflict was still over a year and a half away. In the fall of
1940 the School admitted a number of English boys who had been sent
overseas to continue their education in places that would be safer than England in the time of bombing raids. The tuition for these boys was raised
by alumni and friends of the School. At about the same time, the first
members of the Faculty began to leave for the armed forces. Some were
members of the reserves, others simply volunteered. Early in 1941 a comprehensive new work program was introduced for all boys. No longer
would janitors make the boys' beds; this was now the responsibility of each
student. No longer would waiting on table in the Commons be done only
by scholarship boys; now all would take their turn. It seems likely that the
administration used the war as an excuse to introduce reforms that had
been considered desirable for some years, for it is hard to see how making
beds and waiting on table had much to do directly with the war effort, but
regardless of motive the effect was salutary. As in World War I, the undergraduates contributed money to purchase a Phillips Academy ambulance, to be used in England to serve people who were victims of air
raids.[35] In the fall of 1941 the Trustees voted to allow boys who had their
parents' permission to take flying lessons. One adventurous student, mis-
taking the Shawsheen River for the Merrimack, ran out of gas, and wound
up landing on the lawn of the Tewksbury Asylum. Far from being reprimanded for the unexpected end to his flight, he was praised by his instructors for the intelligent way he had acted in time of crisis.[36] And thus the
School, like the country, drifted into war, almost without realizing it.
There is no evidence that the School community questioned the fact that

the cause of Britain was the cause of the United States. There was some criticism of Winfield Sides, who had a German wife, and of Walter Hasenclever, who was himself a German, but nothing much ever came of it, and early in 1942 Jack Fuess reported to the Trustees that the two were completely loyal.

All this was changed after 7 December 1941. It became imperative to put Phillips Academy in step with the rest of the country in an effort to win the war as quickly and efficiently as possible. And the plans for a wartime program that the administration developed were eminently sensible. Drawing on the experience of World War I, those in charge decided that any kind of military training per se would be a waste of time and that the most important thing the School could do was to turn out graduates who had been taught to think for themselves and who were in topnotch physical shape. Time enough to study the specifics of military science when they had actually joined the armed forces. As a result, the School's program remained much as it had been, with a few important modifications. Believing that mathematics was an important study for anyone about to enter the armed forces, the authorities stepped up programs in this area, putting fresh emphasis on basic mathematics and offering more advanced courses as well. Yet Mike Sides, Head of the Mathematics Department, insisted that the basic courses that had been given in the past were more than adequate for wartime preparation. There would be no need for "Victory Geometry" or "Defense Algebra," he said.[37] The same was true of the Sciences. Physics Instructor John S. Barss wrote, "In the selection of illustrative material [for Chemistry] preference is, of course, given to direct military applications: and the boys who are enrolled in the course this year will be somewhat better acquainted than usual, for example, with the manufacture and properties of the noxious gases, liquids, and smokes which some think the Axis may use before it is defeated. Where numerical problems [for physics] used to refer to baseballs and motor cars, they now sometimes talk of bombs and tanks."[38] The *Phillipian* reflected the change in curricular emphasis with the following comment:

> So help us we ran across a scared-looking fellow the other day who isn't taking Math, Physics, Chemistry, Communications, or Navigation. He figures that with so many guys concentrating on these courses, there will be a minimum of men who can really peel potatoes, so he spends his activity hour over in the Commons. He's getting so he can carve a mighty mean spud.[39]

In foreign languages there was a pronounced shift from the study of grammar and composition to learning how to speak the language. Under the leadership of Dr. James H. Grew a series of new courses were developed the aim of which was to make the student competent in speaking French so that if he should find himself in France, he would be able to communicate with the French. Since Dr. Grew had always thought that French should be taught this way, the war provided him with an opportunity to put his theories into practice. To complement the academic program, a large number of practical courses were offered on a voluntary basis. Over a hundred boys took a rigorous course in first aid; a larger group practiced every evening on the Rifle Range; others studied camouflage at the Addison Gallery; some took gasoline engines apart; still others learned to type. All concerned with the war program were agreed that Andover graduates should be physically fit at the time when they would be entering the service. Accordingly, a comprehensive program to develop physical fitness was introduced for all students. This involved a series of toughening exercises—walking up and down steps, climbing cargo nets, vaulting over high obstacles, running long distances. The effectiveness of programs like this is difficult to measure precisely, but the fact remains that the entire undergraduate body was put through its paces regularly throughout the year. In short, the specific modifications in the basic Phillips Academy program occasioned by the war were few and slight; the advice of all knowledgeable people was that the best thing the School could do was to graduate its students in the normal way and let them get their military training after they had entered the armed services.

Far and away the most important innovation of the war years was the establishment of the Andover Summer Session in 1942.[40] Although it was billed as a war measure, much of what happened there would have been valuable in peace as well, and the fact that the Session has been going strong ever since is proof that the program was not transitory. Its purposes as a wartime institution were very similar to those of the regular curriculum—emphasis on math, science, and foreign languages, a rugged physical educational program, and various activities that would be useful to prospective soldiers. Exeter and many other schools had had summer sessions for years, and in a sense the Andover move was simply catching up to the others. Many Phillips Academy people had long bemoaned the fact that the beautiful Andover plant should lie idle for a quarter of each year. The first session was placed in charge of Wilbur J. Bender, a popular American history teacher who had a rare gift of working with people. A staunch New Dealer, Bender had antagonized and alarmed some of the School community by his outspoken defense of the Roosevelt program, but with the coming of the war that was mainly forgotten. Bender insisted that the Summer Session should be democratically run. Accordingly, he held regular Faculty Meetings before the session started at which basic matters of policy were determined by majority vote. All the teaching staff, which was made up almost entirely of regular Phillips Academy teachers, would receive the same compensation and have the same amount of work to do. A man who happened to live in a dormitory would not, as in the regular session, have full responsibility for his charges; two other Faculty members, in each case, would be attached to his dorm so that each of the three would proctor two nights a week and every third weekend. This proved a great shot in the arm for Faculty morale. What was true of the Faculty was equally true of the students. Though a few monetary scholarships were offered, no distinction was made between scholarship boys and full-freight-paying customers. All were required to make their own beds, keep their rooms neat, and take their turn for a week of "KP" in the Commons. The only exception to this policy of equal treatment for all was in the case of boys who for minor disciplinary infractions were given an extra dose of "KP." Yet the disciplinary problem proved to be minor: of the 197 boys who enrolled only one had to be dismissed during the course of the summer.

The first Andover Summer Session proved to be larger than anticipated. The Director and his staff had expected somewhere between 125 and 150 but the School opened with 161 boarding students and 36 day students. Without adequate staff and no precedents to go by, the first days were chaotic; indeed it took two or three days to find out who were actually enrolled. But after that things shook down well, and the program proceeded smoothly for the remaining eight weeks of the session. The rules were few and simple; no "cuts" of any kind were allowed; all boys were to meet all their appointments, do their share of work in the Commons, and be in bed with lights out at ten thirty. As far as the curriculum was concerned, most boys took a major course, which met two hours a day, six days a week, and was roughly equivalent to a year's work in a particular subject. As previously noted, the emphasis was on the so-called war subjects. In addition, each boy took an "Activity" after lunch in a program that was, again, modeled on the voluntary courses of the regular session. Morse Code, coastal piloting, first aid, navigation, map interpretation, and practical electricity were some of those offered. After the Activity hour every boy reported to the field near the Cage for a half hour of body building. In the Summer Session this part of the program—partly because of the size of the student body—could be carried out more effectively than in the regular session, and bicycle and step tests, conducted by Dr. Gallagher at the end of the session, indicated that remarkable gains had been made by almost all the boys. The thin boys were fatter and the fat were thinner, for example, and the generally high degree of physical fitness of the undergraduates was borne out by Infirmary statistics that showed no contagious diseases, no injuries, and almost no patients during the entire session. At the start of the summer an obstacle run had been developed as part of the physical fitness program, but at the beginning it consisted of little more than a cross country run across the playing fields. By the end of the summer a boy would start by vaulting onto a platform, then drop off and turn three somersaults, repeat the process on another platform, "duck-walk" about one hundred feet, then climb a fifteen-foot rope hand over hand, then run backward for two hundred feet, crawl under four hurdles and jump over four more, climb to the top of the baseball grandstands, and finally climb two sets of steps and drop to the ground on the opposite side. And all this was done after twenty minutes of rigorous exercises. After body building there followed a conventional sports program, with volleyball achieving a surprising popularity, except for a few boys who made arrangements to work on neighboring farms, where labor was very scarce. All in all, the first Andover Summer Session was an outstanding success; apart from the war training given, the program put the Academy plant to good use at a time when it had previously been lying fallow; since many of the students came from schools other than Phillips Academy, it served to spread the School's reputation and led to many summer students applying for admission to the regular session; finally, it provided a means whereby prospective Andover students could test themselves for the coming regular session and acquire whatever additional training might be needed. And—though this was still in the future—the Summer Session could become a laboratory in which members of the Faculty might experiment with new programs they might be considering for use in the regular session.[41]

Increased emphasis on math, the sciences, and modern languages, the development of a more rigorous physical education program, and the establishment of the Summer Session—these were the major changes at Andover during the war years. For the rest, the wartime School was much like the Phillips Academy of the 1930's. The Summer Session made it possible for some boys to accelerate so that for the first time in its history a group of Seniors was graduated in February 1944 and for two Februarys after that. There was no sign that the excellence of an Andover education was being diluted by the war; in 1943, for example, 68 out of 69 Phillips Academy applicants qualified for the Navy's V-12 program.

A matter of continual concern to the Headmaster was the volunteering and drafting of members of the Faculty. It was not always possible to replace those who departed man for man, with the result that for many teachers more students, bigger sections, and additional responsibilities became the order of the day. Any teacher who entered the service was promised his position on his return, a policy that was to cause further difficulties after the war. The School played a leading part in the town of Andover's Civil Defense program. Leonard F. James of the History Department became Chief Air Raid Warden for the town and proceeded to organize a highly efficient organization. In addition he was active in many Civil Defense organizations and did a good deal of speaking and writing on the general subject. Many other members of the Faculty held subordinate posts in the Civil Defense organization of the town under Len James. As the war neared its close, the Office of Defense Transportation issued an appeal to cut all nonessential travel for the duration. In 1945, after checking with Colonel

Stimson, Jack Fuess proposed to the Faculty and students elimination of spring vacation and an early graduation. In that way some seven hundred boys would not be utilizing travel facilities in March. The plan was received with general enthusiasm. A member of the Student Council said, "Why do we go home at all? Can't we just stay here and attend classes as usual? Then we'll all get out that much earlier in the spring." Jack had more trouble with other Headmasters. When he called several of them to propose their joining Andover, the response was to question the real need of such a drastic step, and the final result was that Phillips Academy went it alone. Fortunately, the weather in March was dry and sunny and the whole plan went off smoothly.[42] It was only after the boys had left in May and the heating plant had been shut down that cold weather descended to make the lives of the Faculty uncomfortable.

The only new building project considered during the war years was a Student Union, plans for which were prepared in the last years of the war. As will be seen in the next chapter, this project became involved in the difficult question of Dr. Fuess's attempt to abolish the school's secret societies, and eventually nothing came of it.

The story of Andover graduates in World War II deserves a volume of its own and fortunately an admirable one was written by Leonard F. James and published in 1948.[43] The record is one in which all Andover graduates can take pride. One hundred and forty-two men died in the service of their country, while over three thousand were in the service in one capacity or another. And the number who were decorated for distinguished service, from the Medal of Honor on down, is impressive. If a main aim of the Academy is to develop leadership among its students, their record in World War II indicates that they were accomplishing this purpose.

So Phillips Academy came through the war years with flying colors. There were, to be sure, occasional alarming developments. In 1939 a communication from the State Department suggested in a veiled way that no more German exchange students be accepted. A more disturbing episode came in 1942 when an energetic Navy Lieutenant named Durgin threatened to close Andover and Exeter and use their facilities for the armed forces. Dr. Fuess wrote Secretaries Knox and Stimson and before long, apologies came in from every quarter, including Durgin's commanding officer.[44] But these were minor irritations; the main point was that the School had gone through the war years with relatively little change, and as a result reconversion would be easy. When the Academy opened in September 1945, all the special war courses were gone, and while the physical education program remained in an attenuated form, it no longer received the same emphasis. Of all the wartime programs, only the Summer School would remain as a permanent fixture in Phillips Academy.

An interesting aspect of reconversion was the appearance on campus of some twenty veterans, who enrolled at the School under the G.I. Bill of

Rights. They had entered the armed forces without finishing their secondary schooling and needed a year to win diplomas. Obviously, special arrangements had to be made for this group. Most were over twenty, had had two or three years of army life, and would not thrive under a regime that required them to be in their dormitory by eight o'clock and to refrain from drinking or smoking. So the veterans were all placed on the periphery of the campus, in Mike Sides's house on Bartlet Street, and promptly began to exercise an extremely beneficial influence on the rest of the School. As one Faculty member put it, "They knew why they wanted to be here and they worked like dogs."[45] If a twenty-year-old man took his work seriously, maybe there was something to it after all, the younger boys reasoned. A more difficult problem was dealing with the Faculty. When Andover teachers left for the service, they were promised, like other Americans, that they could have their jobs back when they returned. Jack Fuess added a gimmick in some cases by promising them that they could have the same houses as the ones they had left. Yet the School had to be staffed during the war years, and as a result many older men were hired to teach, many of them highly competent pedagogues. For several years this situation was extremely difficult particularly as regards housing. The Headmaster wrote one friend that all he could offer a returning veteran and family was the maid's quarters in one of the dormitories, and he wrote another Headmaster whose school was not fully staffed to see if he would not like some of Jack's cast-offs.[46] In the end the problem was eased when a large number of bachelors who had left in wartime either decided or were persuaded not to return. Generally speaking, however, reconversion problems were relatively minor, and were soon replaced by more immediate and pressing ones that the postwar period was to bring, not only to Andover but to the country as a whole.

During the last three years of his Headmastership—from 1945 to 1948 —Jack Fuess did little more than conduct a holding operation, as far as the School was concerned. He was still bruised from his ill-conceived attempt to abolish the societies; until he married Lulie Anderson Blackfan in 1947, he was a lonely widower; and finally his sense of hearing began to be seriously impaired. It is therefore not surprising that he rested on his oars. Yet a serious problem developed that had to be dealt with—namely, the increasing deficit under which the School was operating. For the first of the war years, as during the Depression, Phillips Academy managed its financial affairs quite effectively. There were deficits in those years, but they were all under $10,000. In 1943–44 the deficit jumped to $44,000 and continued in the same amount the following year. As postwar inflation developed, the situation grew worse. in 1945–46 the deficit was $89,000 and for the following three years it was $135,000, $184,000, and $98,000. In fact, during the years following the end of the war, Phillips Academy accumulated a deficit of some $500,000.[47] Fortunately, long before this figure had been reached, a group of Alumni and the Trustees moved to meet the problem. One of them describes what happened:

> On a pleasant spring afternoon in 1945 three class secretaries, William T. Kelly, Jr., '24, Joseph T. Hague, Jr., '25, and Carl Sandberg, '26, were sitting on the porch of the Andover Inn talking with Jim Gould, who was then Treasurer of Phillips Academy. . . . In the course of discussing the affairs of the school Jim Gould referred to the very serious financial problems the school faced which had now reached a point that he was finding it necessary to utilize principal from the endowment fund in order to meet the expenses of operating the school. This to us was shocking news and presented a problem that required prompt and positive action.[48]

The three secretaries proceeded to write the Headmaster and urge that the tuition be raised, that the size of the classes be increased, and that a new and more vital alumni organization be formed to enlist alumni support in meeting this problem. The most important thing to come out of this meeting was a thoroughly reorganized alumni organization—a new Alumni Council that was charged with interpreting the School to the alumni body and at the same time enlisting alumni aid for the institution.

The first step in building a more effective alumni organization was the appointment of an alumni secretary on a full-time basis. The School had never had such an officer before. Under Cecil Bancroft and at the start of Al Stearns's administration the Headmaster had the responsibility for whatever work with the alumni was done. After Jack Fuess joined the Faculty, he soon became interested in alumni matters and was able to relieve Al Stearns of much of his responsibility in this area. Jack edited the Alumni Bulletin, did a good deal of speaking before alumni groups, and finally was appointed Alumni Secretary as well. But it was still very definitely a part-time job. After Jack became Headmaster, much of this work was taken over by Scott H. Paradise, one of the School's most competent English teachers. Next to Jack Fuess, Scottie Paradise knew more about the history of the School than anyone else on Andover Hill, and he wrote extensively in the *Bulletin* on the School's past. His book *Men of the Old School* is a charming series of sketches of some Andover men of old. Yet Scottie never considered giving up his teaching, and for him, as with Jack Fuess, the job of Alumni Secretary was always a part-time affair. Now, with the war over and with the School in serious financial difficulties, the time had come to find a man whose primary responsibility would be to work with the alumni. The man the Trustees selected was M. Lawrence Shields, for some twenty years one of the most popular members of the Andover Faculty. A native of Westchester, Pennsylvania, he had attended Pennsylvania State College, only to have his studies interrupted by World War I, in which he served as a sergeant in the army. Completing his college course and doing graduate work in biology at the University of Wisconsin, he came to Andover in 1923, bringing with him a reputation as one of the great college milers of his generation. From the start Larry proved to be one of the liveliest personalities on Andover Hill. He had been hired to teach English, but he never enjoyed the work, mainly, he said, because he could not spell. According to his account, Al Stearns used to fire him regularly and then relent and take him back. He and Ray Shepard, the football coach, and Rocky Dake, then teaching math, enjoyed playing practical jokes on one another, with Shields always in the lead. He had an almost compulsive interest in fires, memorized the call numbers of all the fire alarm boxes in Andover, and, when the fire whistle blew, would take off. One of his proudest boasts was that he often arrived at the fire before the fire engines did. In 1926 someone woke up to the fact that Larry was no English teacher but an accomplished biologist, and he organized that department. Before long he put the biology course on a par with physics and chemistry and had developed a program that was really of college caliber. One day Larry arrived in class with a cage in which he said he had a rare Mexican lizard. He went on to say that the lizard would often sit motionless for hours on end, but if a student watched carefully and quietly, he might see it move. After several days of watching the class discovered that the lizard was a wax model.

There were some who thought that Larry's course depended too much on learning by rote and that the problems and theories of biology were slighted, but his students certainly learned a lot of biological material. In

62. *M. Lawrence Shields, Instructor in Biology, 1923–1945, Secretary of the Academy, 1945–1960.*

the meantime, he pursued research at the Woods Hole Marine Biological Laboratory, in the Sargasso Sea, and in northern Labrador. In May, 1942 he had been commissioned a Lieutenant Commander in the Navy and later that same year had married Ruth Noyes, a widow of some means. Now he was back from the wars with his wife, eager to assume the responsibilities of developing a more effective alumni organization.[49]

At about the same time as the Shields appointment an Alumni Steering Committee of eight was formed to draw up plans for a new alumni organization to be called the Alumni Council. By the fall of 1946 this group had presented a new constitution for the Andover Alumni Association and were gratified to have it approved.[50] "The purpose of the Association," said the constitution, "shall be to advance the interests of Phillips Academy and to increase its usefulness by promoting a closer relationship and better understanding between the Academy and the Alumni." Any one who had ever been a student at the School automatically became a member of the Association after his class had graduated. The management of the Association's affairs was given over to an Alumni Council of twenty-four members, six of whom were to be elected by the Association at large for three-year terms each year, and two of whom would be elected for similar terms by the Council itself. This was the first time in the history of the School that the Alumni had been given a share in the selection of their officers. In addition to the twenty-four elected members, the Council would include the School Treasurer, the President of the Class Agents' Association, the President of the Class Secretaries' Association, the Alumni Secretary, and three members of the Board of Trustees. There followed articles on officers, meetings, and amendments, and then a set of By-Laws, which listed the various committees. An Executive Committee of the Council was to consist of between seven and eleven members appointed by the President; its mission was to carry out whatever programs were entrusted to it by the Council as a whole. There was, of course, a Nominating Committee and various Standing Committees on such matters as scholarships, athletics, the library, and the Bulletin. The organization was logical, if conventional; what was new was the election of Council members by the Alumni at large. One of the major purposes in reorganizing the Alumni Association was to get it in shape for the fund drive, which was announced in the fall of 1946. As originally conceived, the drive for $3,500,000 was to include two million for general endowment, hopefully to check the deficits that had occurred with dreary regularity over the past years; one million for a new gymnasium; and half a million for a new dormitory. The dormitory project was later dropped, and the sum for endowment raised to two and one-half million. John P. Stevens, Jr., '15, was made chairman, and he moved purposefully to establish an effective organization. On 6 November 1947, in some thirty cities throughout the country, special dinners were held at which Bishop Hobson, Jack Fuess, Al Stearns, Jack Stevens, and others spoke to the guests by long distance telephone. The campaign got off to a fast start. At the time of the dinners $1,840,000 had already been contributed; three months later, on 11 February 1948, Chairman Stevens could announce a total of $2,365,000. Yet he was careful to point out that only 1100 of Andover's 11,000 Alumni had contributed, and he urged the rest to participate if the goal were to be reached. But the campaign languished. Over a year later, at the Alumni Luncheon in June 1949, Chairman Stevens said that there was still $750,000 to be raised and that he hoped it could be raised during the next year. The presumption is that this last amount did finally trickle in. The total that was contributed was immediately applied to endowment, with the result that the deficit for 1948–49 was cut to half of that of the preceding year. By mid-century, then, the Trustees, with Alumni support, had moved decisively to meet the financial problems of the School and had developed a new Alumni organization to tie the Alumni more closely to the School.[51]

In the mid-1940's Andover received country-wide publicity when two articles on the School appeared in national magazines. The first article appeared in *Fortune* in 1944; the second, written by the distinguished American historian Henry F. Pringle and his wife Katherine, appeared in 1947 in the *Saturday Evening Post*. Both articles were extremely favorable to the School, and it was clear that the writers were impressed with the institution and what it was trying to do. The *Fortune* writers entitled their piece "Andover: A Study in Independence" and added, "It is blessed with a freedom rare even among private schools." They thought the atmosphere of the School more like that of a small college than a secondary school and were particularly impressed with the School's scholarship program. In 1944 close to $100,000 was awarded to deserving boys in the form of cash grants and jobs, and 183 boys—about one fourth of the undergraduate body—were being aided. *Fortune* concluded: "Andover is not particularly a rich boy's school, but it is a rich school and has all the opportunities that institutional opulence has thrust upon it. If boys' boarding schools are really democratic internally, not only should more scholarships be given, but able boys from really poor families should be drawn in through substantial scholarships." The *Fortune* writers were impressed with the School's academic strength—100 percent success on one Navy examination, for example. They were impressed with the health program and the work of Dr. Gallagher, particularly the number of discipline cases that were referred to him. And they commented particularly on the work being done in art by Bartlett H. Hayes, Jr., and Patrick Morgan. The main criticism the *Fortune* writers levied against the school was its lack of pioneering work in curriculum and pedagogy: "Beyond the solid excellence of its instruction, is there not a place for educational research, frankly pioneering in aim, to exist side by side with the traditional system—much in the manner that pilot plants exist for technological research? . . . The result of such a pioneering program might well start a healthy ferment in secondary education that would have far-reaching effects on public as well as private school teaching." And they concluded: "The instructors who now want Andover to teach social responsibility, to serve the country even better than it has in the past, may be discouraged about the lack of visible effects on the students. The majority of Andover's students are still very conservative. But Andover is teaching the boys that the world moves and that they have a responsibility for the direction of things. It seems probable therefore that the boys will change too, even if only through a delayed reaction."

The Pringle article in the *Saturday Evening Post* was equally laudatory; like the *Fortune* writers, the Pringles were impressed by the scholarship program and the attempt on the part of the School to destroy the reputation for exclusiveness and snobbishness that plagued almost all private schools. They quoted Dr. Fuess's seven deadly sins of independent schools —snobbishness, bigotry, provincialism, "reactionarism," smugness, stupidity, and inertia and added, "During a fortnight's visit to the school . . . we saw few, if any, indications of the seven sins cited by Dr. Fuess." The Pringles could not agree with Dean G. G. Benedict's disgust at food throwing in the Commons and thought the boys were acting "like high-spirited youths everywhere." They listened to undergraduate complaints— American history was too tough, some Faculty members were rude, the marking system handicapped graduates in college admissions, and the like. They wondered if Phillips Academy had always been as tough in the past at its alumni claimed, and cited the case of a math teacher some years ago who changed a failure into a pass on condition that the boy would not take math in college. Unlike the *Fortune* writers, the Pringles took a position on the society issue. Commenting on the "unbelievable row" that was touched off in 1943 when the School attempted to close the societies, they went on to say that the Trustees had been right and that the Societies were a detriment. After a good deal of material on the history of the School, the Pringles concluded: "In these days of crowded public schools, nobody can deny that the best private schools supply superior secondary education. What Andover is seeking to accomplish is to provide that education to the boys of the United States who really want and deserve it, not to those who can merely afford it." The whole Andover community must have been heartened to have writers from such distinguished publications place an imprimatur of approval on what they were trying to do.[52]

A student's view of the School during the Fuess years is provided by the correspondence of Arleigh D. Richardson, III, of the Class of 1940 with his family. Dick Richardson was a one-year Senior who had the highly commendable habit of writing his family twice a week, and his letters are invaluable in revealing what the life of an undergraduate of this period was like. Indeed, had the School been able to acquire these letters at the time they were written, the Admissions Office could not have done better than use them for public relations purposes, for they show an undergraduate doing all the things it was hoped that Andover students would do while at the School. Dick arrived at Andover in September 1939 and was placed in Foxcroft Hall under the superintending care of Herbert Kinsolving of the Mathematics Department. He was prepped a bit, but generally enjoyed it; senior preps were treated pretty easily, he thought. He thought also that he was lucky in his Housemaster: "He is just swell. His rooms are very attractive. I know we are going to be good friends. . . . He goes to Fisher's Island and knows Bishop Hobson pretty well. We had a grand talk." A little later: "Mr. Kinsolving said I could use my electric shaver, in fact he is in favor of electric victrolas, and had a big argument with the powers that be over it this fall, but unfortunately he lost." Three weeks later: "The Yale Club tobacco is here too, and I am enjoying it. Mr. Kinsolving has us all in for a smoke almost every night, so that is when I use it the most. . . . Mr. Kinsolving plays the viola and Dick Richards, a fellow upstairs, plays the flute. Right now they are having a duet, and confidentially they steenk." In February: "Mr. Kinsolving had a waffle supper for us last night after the movies. It was really swell. We had waffles, bacon, coffee, milk, and potato chips. You know if you can I think it would be swell to send him a cheese. I know he would appreciate it." Clearly Dick was happy with his Housemaster, and the presumption is that the feeling was reciprocated. One of the most attractive things about Dick Richardson's letters is that they show him liking almost everything he experienced—"The fellows in our Hall are all pretty nice." "I like all of my teachers too." Fortunately, he was a conscientious and able student, receiving honors in everything but history.[53] The cost of books came as a shock. "I don't remember reading that we had to buy our own books, but we sure do. So far, however, I have had plenty of money so don't worry." A high point of the biology course he took with Bernie Boyle was a monkey named Jiggs. "He will untie your shoe and then take the laces out if you let him. They keep him very clean and wash him every day because monkeys do not know how to take baths and they get very dirty." The Andover countryside was beautiful: "The rolling countryside was so peaceful in the twilight. I'll never cease enjoying this country as long as I live. . . . Every day something happens to make things interesting." But not everything was perfect: "Bernie Boyle is getting under my skin. He's been nasty all term and today he gave me a demerit for throwing a snowball at a building when I didn't even do it in the first place. I will admit I was just going to, but hadn't." Yet it was not all that bad, for apparently Bernie never turned the demerit in. Things must have improved with Bernie for in June, Dick's mark on two comprehensive biology exams was the highest in New England.

Dick Richardson had many outside interests at Andover, but his first love was music, and his experiences in the field show how much was available to an interested undergraduate. In one of his first letters he wrote, "I am nuts about Dr. Pfatteicher. . . . He is a peach." Carl Friedrich Pfatteicher, in addition to being head of the Music Department, was an organist and musicologist of note, and the choirmaster. Dick made the choir and was enchanted with the robes: "You ought to see the classy robes that the choir wears in chapel on Sundays. They are all black with a square blue collar, a real rich blue and quite big with a small white stripe around it. They are really the stuff." And later: "The organ is wonderful, and it is a privilege to hear Doc. Pfatteicher play it. He is really supposed to be one of the best in the world, and so is the organ." Dick was in a very musical dorm, which prompted him to send on for "Pop's violin." Herbert Kinsolving had promised to give him lessons in the fundamentals. "Almost everyone here plays something. You never saw the like. There are two trumpets, a flute, a clarinet, a viola, and a trombone on our side of Foxcroft alone." By the middle of October he had signed up for symphony tickets in Boston. "We all sang and had a grand time in the bus both ways. . . . They played Debussy's 'La Mer', which was wonderful and they topped it off with Beethoven's Symphony No. 3 in C-Flat Major, the 'Eroica', which is one of my favorites. Koussevitsky is a marvelous conductor. I have never seen one so graceful. Boy! we got a real glimpse of Boston society. It was the first night of the season, and they were all there. I saw some of the most attractive girls I've seen this year there." Meanwhile, Pop's violin had arrived, and the redoubtable Dr. Pfatteicher had taken it to Boston to be fixed. In the meantime, Dick practiced on Mr. Kinsolving's viola. The more he saw of Dr. Pfatteicher, the better he liked him. He used to spend Sunday afternoons at his house listening to the Philharmonic. Late in February the Don Cossacks sang in George Washington Hall, and Dick was enthralled. "I never heard such low basses and high tenors. You'd swear it was a mixed choir, their falsettos are so good, and the volume is unbelievable. They just open their mouths and their beautiful church music rolls out and fills the room so that it goes right through you." Finally, early in April Dick went in to Boston to hear the Metropolitan Opera's performance of "Lohengrin," with Kirsten Flagstaad and Lauritz Melchior. Although he enjoyed the whole "immensely," parts were boring and over his head. "I never before saw two such hefties, however, and it was really funny when they were making love, and trying to be kittenish. It was just what might happen if the *Normandie* and the *Queen Mary* got together." All in all few students have taken fuller advantage of the musical opportunities available at the school than did Dick Richardson.

Not all his concerns were on such a lofty plane, however. Like many Andover undergraduates of that era he mailed his laundry home rather than entrust it to the mercies of local button-shuckers, and the problems that developed in this arrangement were never-ending. Early in October he reported: "My laundry came on Friday, and I guess you sent it on Wednesday, so that is not so bad. I am quite mad, however, because I got it all ready to send back Saturday morning, and Herbie (the janitor) told me that the Express man stops every day, and will take it if I leave it in the hall. He never got it Saturday, however, so I am waiting for him today." Apparently the Express man continued to prove unreliable, for later in the year Dick speaks of taking his laundry to the Post Office. One advantage of sending laundry home was that a boy's family could send back various goodies along with the clean clothes. Dick frequently mentions how much he has enjoyed cookies, nuts, cakes, and the like. A new crisis developed in February: "By the way, what on earth has happened to my underwear shorts? Six shirts came yesterday, and only two pairs of shorts. I really change shorts as often as shirts. Has Hanna swiped them for dust rags?" More trouble in April: "Did you send any laundry last week? I am very much afraid that if you did it is lost. I expected it Friday as usual, but it has not come yet. I waited until today to write you because often the old drunken express man brings it late, but when it didn't come yesterday I began to worry. . . . If it doesn't arrive, and you did send it, we'd better start sueing or something. I'm anxious to know." Similar problems were encountered in decorating his room at the start of the year. Dick's Mother had promised to make curtains for him, and there were the usual complications about measurements. When his Mother wanted to know the color of the rug in his room, furnished by the School, Dick wrote: "Our rug is many different colors. To be exact it is red, green, gray, blue, tan, and black, so you see that I can't exactly say." On the basis of this information Mrs. Richardson settled on green, and when the curtains arrived Dick was ecstatic. Other moves to improve his room included chipping in for a second-hand studio couch and purchasing a new set of andirons and fire tongs. Soon some pillows arrived from home for the couch, and by the middle of the fall term Dick and his roommate were very snug indeed.

In the meantime, Dick was becoming increasingly active in extracurricular activities and social affairs. He joined the Outing Club and reported a splendid trip to Kennebuck, Maine, where George Sanborn, the Faculty adviser of the Club, had a summer home. A Kenneth Roberts enthusiast, Dick was delighted to see the Arundel country at first hand. In October Cornelia Otis Skinner performed at Andover; "Everyone was in stiches," Dick reported. A little later he paid his first visit to Abbot: "I did not have a bad time, but I can't say that from what I saw, any of the girls are particularly attractive." Early in November came the first tea dance: "Dickie came over yesterday and brought with her a swell gal and we fixed her up with some of my friends. We all sat together at the football game in which we beat the Tufts Freshmen 19–6. The tea dance afterwards was swell and after the dance we had the girls stay for the Saturday night movies, and put them on the 10:33 train. Dickie invited me to a houseparty Thanksgiving weekend, but it is out of the question." One of the virtues of membership in the Glee Club was the chance to have concerts and dances with girls' schools. Early in December came the one with Rogers Hall: "they were a swell group of girls. We really had a marvelous time. After the concert they had a nice dinner for us, and a very enjoyable dance afterwards. Dates were hit or miss, but I was fortunate to get one whom I liked very much from Kentucky. She was grand." As vacation approached, Dick became concerned about the attire that he should bring with him for the Christmas parties at home in Columbus. Should he bring both his Tux and his tails, or only one, and in that case which one? The big social event of the Winter Term was the Prom, and Dick was determined to enjoy it to the full. Some of his friends had had trouble getting dates, so he ran a kind of dating service and lined up various Columbus girls who were at School in the East. The program promised to be lively. First came a tea at the Headmaster's, then a dinner at A.U.V., the Society that Dick had joined early in January; then the dance itself; then escorting the girls back to the dormitories where they were staying, with "breakfast in the beanery" the next morning. After breakfast Dick and his date would go to Boston together, where they would part.

Not all Dick's activities were social, however. One cold April morning a janitor picked up Dick and a friend and drove them to a pond in the Harold Parker forest to try their hand at fishing. Even though they left at five o'clock, by the time they arrived they found hundreds of other fishermen with every conceivable kind of pole and tackle engaged in the sport. One woman kept getting her fly caught in a tree overhead, others rushed to and fro looking for good positions, and pandemonium reigned generally. Apparently nobody caught any fish, but the experience was memorable.

Most Andover boys of that period paid little attention to what was going on in Europe, and Dick was no exception. There are only very occasional references to the world outside in his letters. In October he wrote one of his longer comments: "It seems to me that the foreign situation becomes more of a mess every day. Old Hitler was in too much of a hurry over the Polish Affair and his alliance with Russia. He scrambled onto the wrong horse and now it's running off with him. I have always thought of Russia as a place where nothing worked right and no one had any brains, but much to my consternation I find that I must change my opinion. . . . If only the two [Germany and Russia] could be played off against each other wouldn't it be swell? Oh well, this is probably boring so I'll stop." When the Headmaster spoke on the war, Dick was outraged: "Claudie gave a horribly sentimental and impassioned speech. . . . Everyone is very angry. He practically told us that it is our duty to go right over now. He said it is no longer a war of political philosophies, but a war between right and wrong. He continued in this vein for about five minutes, and then one of the students booed him." Finally, early in June, with the fall of France imminent, this comment: "The war is surely bewildering. I just can't understand how the Germans could be so much better than the allies. . . . The only thing for us to do is wait and take what comes. The world appears to be in a horrible state, but I still feel that things are no worse than they must have seemed many many times before in history. The Napoleonic years couldn't have been very comfortable ones for the people who didn't believe in aggression. All we can do is try to think sanely and if we get in, well, we just do that's all." And so Dick Richardson finished his year at Andover with much of the rest of the world crashing down around his ears. He had tried his hand at almost everything the School had to offer and had distinguished himself in many areas of activity. Above all, he had demonstrated that he was a boy of character and principle.[54]

Undergraduate life at Andover had its lighter moments during the Fuess years. One of the most famous episodes concerned a boy named Roger Kiley and "A. Montague Fitzpatrick," a fictitious student Kiley invented. Kiley had come to the School in 1935 and for his first year lay fallow. In 1936 he hit his stride, returning with a bicycle he used to ride furiously around the School while wearing a Napoleon hat. When told that he could not keep the bicycle in his room, he put it on the fire escape with a flashing red lantern attached. According to Kiley this was to ward off low-flying aircraft, in compliance with a state ordinance. But his main claim to fame was the creation of "Fitzpatrick." At first he proceeded slowly with his hoax. Fitzpatrick would sign in at the library, stay an hour, and then return to his dormitory and sign in there. Miss Alice Whitney, the sweet lady who had charge of cuts, had no reason to doubt Fitzpatrick's authenticity. The next day Fitzpatrick was excused from athletics to play in the School band, though suspicions might have been aroused when his name was greeted with much laughter by the students. Then Fitzpatrick really went wild. He signed out of Adams Hall, indicating his destination as the Sailor's Rest. He went back and forth among dormitories signing in at one before he had left the other. Meanwhile, he was handing in English themes and meeting various other appointments. Miss Whitney became greatly distressed by all this, all the more so as no one seemed to be able to find Fitzpatrick's class schedule. In desperation Miss Whitney turned to Dr. Fuess. The Headmaster said, "Fitzpatrick, Fitzpatrick. I seem to recall seeing him somewhere. Fine boy." Of course with the passage of time the hoax was revealed, and Miss Whitney's life became more placid again. But the tradition of A. Montague Fitzpatrick remained strong in the School for many years, and his story is revived from time to time right down to the present.[55] Though it happened long after the Fuess period, a similar spoof was worked in the Summer Session in 1967 when two Faculty sons who were working in the Summer Session office managed to get a fictitious character named Clinton LaGorce Mamorewski, III, actually

admitted to the Session. Mamorewski came from Moose Factory, Saskatch-
ewan, Canada, and was from all the evidence, which the boys forged, a
very promising candidate. Since the boys were working in the office, they
could intercept all the letters, and the rest was easy. One member of the
Admission Committee wrote, "Looks great" on his folder, and Clinton
was duly admitted. Not wishing to prevent some deserving boy from coming, the pranksters finally wrote that Mamorewski had changed his plans
and would not be able to attend.[56] Like Kiley, they had a great time blowing birds at the system.

Sometimes a spoof would involve the headmaster. A graduate writes: "I
can recall a student prank taunting Jack Fuess. He was known to have had
an aversion to a neighboring dog which belonged to Grenville Benedict. At
about 4 A.M. on the morning following a twelve-inch snowfall a group of
students living in Benedict's house filled a container with tea and poured
it carefully on the snow carpet in front of the headmaster's house—spelling the dog's name. Unfortunately, I cannot remember the dog's name."
Another time a boy dressed up as an East Indian potentate. He called himself Raja Ramchandrah and proceeded to take in the whole Andover community. First he went to the Art Gallery, where he was given a tour; he
thought the pictures "rather good for American art, but by no means extraordinary." He got a similar tour of the library and concluded, "Rather
handsome building, I guess, but the libraries in India are much better."
Finally he mounted the steps of Dr. Fuess's house and rang the bell. The
Headmaster greeted him warmly, insisted that he stay for tea, and wound
up spending most of the afternoon with him. It is generally believed that
Dr. Fuess never did find out that his leg had been pulled.[57]

One of the great Andover institutions during the Fuess years was the
hash house on Main Street run by Leon ("Doc") Davidson. Here is a fine
nostalgic piece, by Richard Woodbridge, '35, on going to Leon's on a
Sunday morning in winter:

> Imagine waking up on a frigid, winter morning and finding the first
> snow of the year. Through the narrow back window of Bishop
> Hall the whiteness goes on forever. One stares at it and notices how
> immense is the silence. It is Sunday morning! There is absolutely
> no sound.
>
> Sunday morning! There is a sudden feeling of release! A sensa-
> tion of confinement passes from one's shoulders. For a few hours
> there is freedom from academic apprehension and scholastic concern.
> And then dressing—and the warm overcoat and muffler and galoshes
> and the Andover Numeral Hat so proudly worn, dark-blue wool
> turn-down-all-the-way-around with '35 in small white letters (worn
> in the back). And then be-gloved out into the snow down the un-
> cleaned paths of whiteness where no one had trod—the fresh snow

going "qurinch, qurinch, qurinch" under heavy foot—out to Main Street—slowly down past the Headmaster's House—down to the warmth, tropical humidity and bright lights of Leon's with its Nickel-plated coffee urn and the smell of frying sausage—and Leon himself behind the counter. Leon was short, baldish and brown-of-eye. White-aproned Leon was well fed. His smile welcomed students, townspeople, faculty and all.

Honey (just crystallizing) on a hot waffle, with sausage on the side and a cup of the most delectable, aromatic coffee the Gods could brew—the thought will last forever. And then to pick up a copy of the Sunday New York *Tribune* to carry back to the room in Bishop Hall.

And on the cold way back (with icicles like illuminated drips of sun-filled glass from the tree twigs) to catch a smile from a feral Abbot girl all bundled up from her red wool pull-down cap to her plaid skirt with her red nose and pink chapped knees—well it made for a comfortable Sunday Chapel reverie much later in the morning.

Early in the Fuess years, in an effort to improve the generally barbaric conditions in the dining hall, the School hired a strong and very attractive woman to act as a kind of hostess there. An alumnus writes of this effort:

I can provide one incident which contained much of humanity and humor. The central figure had been engaged by the Academy to serve as a kind of hostess in the Beanery. The idea was to lend tone to the cheerful but noisy environment in which we bolted down our food, and her time of testing came on the very first evening of her new job. She was a tall woman with a posture that was almost regal, and she swept into the Commons that evening in an elegant dress to begin her work of uplift. The din was normal, the cynical greetings unpromising. Suddenly a bun was thrown from several tables away in her general direction.

But her three sons had trained her well in games played with balls of various sizes and shapes, so she knew what to do about the approaching bun. She caught it. An eerie silence fell in the crowded dining hall as she stood there, her dignified composure somehow not shaken, holding the bun in her hand. It seemed a very long silence, every young face turned to see what would happen next. Then she wound up and threw the bun back at the table whence it had come. Spontaneous applause greeted this athletic performance, and she was established as a good guy. From then on, when she walked into the Beanery, the noise level abated and boys would whisper of her exploit to guests and new arrivals.

Sex was naturally an area of great interest to the undergraduates of this period—as of all periods. One alumnus remembers a boy in his dormitory who had a book entitled *Flossie, a Venus at Fifteen,* which was one of the most sought-after volumes in the whole institution. Those who could get in to Boston often went to the Old Howard, then at the heighth of its popularity, with such strippers as Hinda Wassau leading the way. Individual exploits by more mature undergraduates were narrated by less sophisticated members of the student body when these lotharios returned from Boston and other spots. And there was, as always, an intense interest in Abbot girls.

It is usually assumed that undergraduate bull sessions take place at night. Here is a variation on that theme.

> Doc Chase's half of Bishop Hall was occupied by an essentially non-scholastic group. We had a number of athletes and we had people from the most diverse backgrounds, so that the conversations in that Hall, which went on for hour after hour at any time of day or night, while not always on an intellectual plane, were certainly racy, stimulating, and in their own way provocative.
>
> Our principal area of solving the problems of the nation, the world, and to a lesser extent Phillips Academy, were sessions at 10 o'clock in the morning, which lasted for an hour on the third floor. The fulcrum of these discussions centered around the use of one of the old, ugly, but reasonably comfortable, Morris chairs, with which the rooms were adorned and in which the back would be tilted. One of the school's leading athletes would sit back on that with a sheet around his chest and neck and one of his friends would lather him up and shave him with a straight razor. The athlete was old enough to need a shave every day, being then around twenty-one.
>
> There wasn't much we didn't discuss and there weren't many problems we didn't settle with finality. . . . No work was done, no studying accomplished, and I am sure the authorities would have frowned upon these sessions. Nevertheless, they are clear in my memory as part of the school.

The School had what were called "P.I." tests, designed to measure physical efficiency. A student had to make at least a minimum record in such things as high-jumping, running the half mile, and swimming one hundred yards. Some boys had a lot of trouble qualifying.

> There was a boy, a little on the plump side, physically extremely soft, and totally uncoordinated. He failed all his tests at first but finally got the minimum in all but high-jumping. His first efforts were totally unavailing, but a senior finally got him to the point where he believed that if the boy could move both legs together at the right time he could make it. The boy couldn't seem to solve this, and after an hour of trying, he was nearly in tears. The senior finally solved the problem by using a broom. As the boy approached the

bar and took off, the senior hit him in the backside with the broom. This caused the expected reaction; there was a slight lift in the rear end and the boy cleared the bar. By this time he was actively crying, but everybody was crowding around him, shaking his hands, patting him on the back and treating him like a fellow who had made the winning touchdown in the Exeter football game.

Undergraduate opinion of Headmaster Claude M. Fuess varied a great deal; on balance there were probably more who respected him than who did not. Some samplings:

> My memory of Claude Moore Fuess is of a remote, formal, aloof head whose professional life went well beyond the day-to-day opera- tion of Andover as a school. . . . I found it hard to think that at one time he had been a member of the teaching faculty. . . . He was rather the headmaster, appearing in the center chair at daily chapel, making well prepared and pompous comments on the state of the world and the state of the school, appearing rather incongruously to say things about an approaching athletic contest, but out of his element when that topic came before him. . . . In chapel, where my memory has him always appearing in a fashionably tailored suit, pre- cise and elegant, he spoke with left hand invariably in his pocket, his right hand used for a series of small gestures that emphasized this assertion or that.

And the writer went on to describe his resentment against Dr. Fuess for not allowing the Catholic students to attend a special service at the Catholic Church down town. Another writes:

> One thing is definite, however. He hadn't the slightest interest in boys. Out of roughly 700 boys at Andover, I would doubt that Mr. Fuess could name a hundred. Fifty had parents so rich that he could not ignore them in his money raising activities. Fifty were such hell raisers that he couldn't ignore them. I was in the latter category.

Another more favorable comment:

> I personally liked Jack Fuess. He was a tough disciplinarian and remained, by and large, aloof from the students, but he ran a good school. My classmates and I felt that more responsibility should be given to the student council but the good doctor never bought the idea.

From a student who saw quite a bit of him:

> I probably saw more of Dr. Fuess than most boys, since one of my scholarship jobs was to sit in the ante-room to his office and act as an office boy and messenger for 35¢ an hour. And yet I cannot re- member anything significant about him. He was always cordial and

pleasant with me, and wrote laudatory letters home to my parents
about me, so that I was well disposed toward him.

I don't remember that there was any serious faction among the
boys that disliked him. He was generally referred to as the "B.D."
(bald doctor) and his mannerism of taking off his glasses and blinking rapidly was widely imitated. However, he was an authoritarian
figure, difficult to draw close to.

From one who worked with Dr. Fuess on the Student Council:

> He was responsible for the school atmosphere and for the calibre of
> men that were on his Faculty. They could have taught elsewhere, at
> college level say, but they stayed at Andover. The administration
> must have been doing its job well. Perhaps a good administration is
> one you are never aware of—it does its job well, so well it is silently
> in the background.
>
> I recall my first meeting as a Junior on the Student Council at
> Dr. Fuess's house. He greeted me as "Jack," my brother's name, and
> for two years called me that. He made it clear that the Student Coun-
> cil was to take care of dances and such, was not to cause him trouble
> with wild ideas, was to set an example for the others and was to
> leave the running of the school to him. It was no nonsense and very
> direct and sobering. And I do believe correct.
>
> A classmate of mine was given a cut in Chapel for sleeping. He
> wore sun glasses the next Sunday and got hell again. His revenge
> was the alarm clock that went off Monday in Assembly when Dr.
> Baldwin was in the midst of a Bible reading. Dr. Fuess lifted not
> an eyelash, evinced no response whatsoever, but his eyes silently took
> in everyone with a single message: "Anyone who laughs will really
> get hell." It was a masterful demonstration of self control with
> enough left over to supply adequately 700 of us. Remarkable!

And another pro-Fuess statement:

> We thought Claudie was born to be a college president . . . and I
> think we admired him for putting up with the likes of us so patiently
> and so affably while he was waiting for the lightning to strike. I
> have no idea what his "policies" were. I just know he always per-
> formed as we thought he should. . . . I can see him now, dressed like
> a banker with pince nez in place, standing in the middle of a gym
> floor crowded with students, saying just the right thing. The charisma
> was several layers down, but it was there, and we knew it was there,
> and we loved him for it.

From an alumnus named Jack:

> I managed to do an incredibly good job keeping a comfortable
> distance between me and Dr. Fuess for four full years. . . . I remained

so remote that when I did graduate (by the skin of my teeth), Dr. Fuess looked me smack in the eye and said, "Congratulations, Bill." It could be that I did not impress him. My ego would prefer to believe that he was a touch vague.

Dr. Fuess and the *Phillipian*:

I suppose I was a fairly "cooperative" *Phillipian* editor. The paper did do things Fuess didn't like, however, and I must say that his expressions of displeasure were always gentle, never heavy-handed. And they always came *after* the fact. There was no effort to censor the *Phillipian* and for that I was (and remain) grateful. I think my sense of the meaning of a free press began to develop at Andover. . . . My deepest conviction today is that America can survive only as the First Amendment survives. Jack Fuess, Andover and the *Phillipian* played a part in developing my thinking on the subject.

Dr. Fuess and a bicycle accident:

One day I was riding down the path in front of the museum and I ran over Dr. Fuess with my bike. . . . when I ran over him, he immediately fell apart. . . . his pince-nez glasses fell off, his watch dropped on the ground, he dropped all sorts of things, and I had knocked the wind out of him. It was just a terrible disaster. You couldn't imagine anybody looking more discombobulated than poor Dr. Fuess at that time. Anyway, I got off my bike, picked him up and sat him on the bench in front of the museum and took all the various pieces that had landed on the ground and put them back where they belonged and had a nice chat with him. And he really didn't know who I was, which of course was his normal state, since he never seemed to know the names of anybody. What amounted to total terror in having flattened him faded quickly as soon as it was clear that even Dr. Fuess was human and breathed even though I had knocked the breath out of him, and that he was rather gentle behind his clipped and abrupt way of speaking. Moreover, he seemed quite interested in me.

Dr. Fuess and the war:

Back in World War II, there was a song that became popular entitled "There'll be Bluebirds over the White Cliffs of Dover." One morning in chapel, Fuess chose that song as the subject of his remarks and expounded at length and with some heat on what a terrible song it was. "There won't be bluebirds over the white cliffs of Dover," he said, "and there won't be love and laughter and peace ever after." Instead, he told us, after the war we should look forward to years of continued struggle, hardship and danger. Fuess's efforts did not have the desired effect. His audience was taken totally by surprise and sat there in amazement. As we left the building, I heard someone say, "Who ever heard of anyone getting so excited about a song?"

And on the other side:

> I can say very briefly that I am a tremendous admirer of Claude Fuess, whom I view as one of the truly great headmasters.

Jack Fuess's policy for dealing with his Faculty was unorthodox, to say the least. Once when Harold Gores, formerly Superintendent of Schools in Newton, Massachusetts, was asked how it was that the Newton High School produced so many National Merit Scholars, he replied wryly: "Well, we just kept out of their way." Jack must have had some such policy in mind for dealing with the Faculty: certainly it is hard to imagine a place with more academic freedom than Andover under his leadership. Emory Basford, for many years Head of the English Department, emphasizes this point in writing of his early days at Andover:

> My reception was casual; nobody took much notice of me. I was left to find my way around as best I could. There was little, if any, guidance or help from the administration. Fortunately, I had taught for six years before coming to Andover and had a fair command of my subject and some competence in schoolmastering. But I did not know how Andover wanted Paul Revere [a senior dormitory] administered and nobody told me. More surprisingly, nobody told me what texts to use in the classrooms. In my early years here there was never a department meeting, never any planning of work together. Everybody was friendly, to be sure, but everybody went his own way. There was a tacit assumption that men who came to Andover to teach knew what they were about and had best be left alone. Everybody had the maximum of freedom and independence and opportunity to experiment. I cannot recall that anyone ever asked me what or how I was doing or that anyone ever visited my classroom or criticized my work. Obviously so independent a way of life had grave weaknesses, but it had virtues too. The wonder is that it did not lead young teachers to extravagant and foolish experimentation. But there was always the sane influence of a group of great teachers. Without them the freedom of Andover might have been a heady tonic indeed. As it was the life was exhilarating. I liked it.[58]

By the end of Jack's term as Headmaster, some of this, at least, had changed: departments were more highly organized; younger teachers received more supervision; and there was a general tightening up. Yet Jack's basic conviction never changed—that his job was to find a promising teacher, lure him to Andover, and then let him teach what he liked in the way that he liked. The result was a Faculty community in an almost continual state of ferment. A scholar and a man of books himself, Jack never failed to encourage scholarly activities on the part of the Faculty, and he was genuinely proud of the intellectual achievements of his colleagues. His policy of hiring teachers was cut from the same bolt. He was much less impressed with a man's previous training than with his personality, his enthusiasm for teaching, his originality and élan. And he was always on the prowl for the kind of teacher he wanted. On one occasion a friend expressed surprise that he would travel a long distance for what appeared to be a minor ceremony at another school. "Oh, I'm not going down for the ceremony," he replied. "I'm hoping to steal the head of one of their departments." While Jack's unorthodox policy of recruiting teachers occasionally resulted in bizarre appointments, his batting average was very high, and he once said that his memorial would be the Faculty he had assembled at Andover. When it came to dealing with individual Faculty members on such practical matters as housing and salaries, the Fuess policy was well-nigh disastrous. There was no salary scale as such; there was wide variation in the amount paid members of the same general age group; and some older members of the Faculty had their salaries frozen for years. Harper Follansbee, recent Head of the Biology Department, remembers going in to see the Headmaster after the war and suggesting that his prewar salary was not impressive. "Well, Harper, we'll just double that," Dr. Fuess replied, and it was done. And the same doubling process occurred when Harper got married.[59] Generally speaking, those who demanded higher salaries got them, while the more timid teachers advanced slowly, if at all. The assignment of Faculty housing was equally without system; on one occasion the Headmaster apparently promised the same house to three different people, with results that were fatal for Faculty confidence in his word. The effect was low Faculty morale. Many teachers could never be sure where they stood. Suspicions were aroused that the Headmaster played favorites, as indeed he did. Dr. Fuess was not always able to command a united Faculty. It was strange that a man generally sensitive to other people could administer his office so insensitively. Jack Fuess must be given top marks on academic freedom, imaginative recruiting, and encouragement of academic excellence; but his disorganized administrative procedures did much to counterbalance his virtues.

Claude Fuess was never completely happy as Headmaster. He used to tell his friends how he would sit in his office before Assembly and read Macaulay's essay on courage before going out to face the troops. "I often wonder," he once told a visiting speaker, "what I would do if they all started swarming over the footlights and onto the stage right in the middle of Assembly." While he could be delightful in conversation with individual students, boys in the mass often alarmed him and made him appear stiff and stuffy. Alan Blackmer, who knew him very well, said about him:

"He was a paradox; he did more than any of his predecessors toward adapting education to the individual, intellectually and emotionally, but he did not know the kids any better than they did before him."[60] And he was very poor at names. There is a story told of his attending a dinner for Andover graduates at one of the leading colleges. The toastmaster was a distinguished member of the previous senior class who had worked very closely with Jack on student government. His name happened to be George, but during the evening Jack insisted on calling him Bill. But George took the last trick. At the end of the dinner he said, "Thank you very much, Dr. Perry, for coming down. And be sure to remember us to all our friends at Exeter." A more serious weakness than his inability to remember names was Jack's unwillingness to say no. Members of the Student Council during the early years of his Headmastering remember how he used to pretend to approve some of their suggestions for the School but would then go to a Faculty meeting and urge the Faculty to turn them down. He apparently hoped, rather wistfully, that he could keep everyone happy all the time, and often made promises to both students and Faculty that he was later unable to keep. This sometimes led to the very bitterness and misunderstanding he was trying to avoid. His instincts were of the best, but at times he simply was not tough enough or honest enough.[61]

Claude Fuess's effectiveness as Headmaster may well have been limited also by his determination to continue his career as a writer in the midst of the cares and burdens of office. By the time he became head of the school in 1933, he had an impressive number of books to his credit. In addition to *An Old New England School*, a history of Phillips Academy published in 1917, he had produced a large number of English texts, some in collaboration with Arthur W. Leonard, Head of the English Department. These volumes included selections of English letters, of essays, and of short stories, not to mention a spelling book, a rhetoric, and a manual on précis writing. In his spare time he wrote three books for boys—*All for Andover, The Andover Way*, and *Peter Had Courage*. Though these volumes may seem unsophisticated to today's youth, they are still read with pleasure by younger boys. It was as a biographer, however, that Jack Fuess made his reputation in the literary world. Before 1933 he had written four—the lives of Caleb Cushing, Rufus Choate, Daniel Webster, and Carl Schurz. Though some professional historians attacked some of these books, particularly the Webster, as not being scholarly enough, the general public received them well and Jack became one of the best biographers in the country. In addition there were countless articles, book reviews, pieces for the *Phillips Bulletin*, and papers read before historical societies. When he became Headmaster, he had already agreed to write a history of Amherst College and was negotiating to write a biography of Calvin Coolidge. Rather than drop these projects and devote all his time to the Headmastership, he chose to finish both of them, a task that was completed by 1940.

One marvels that he was able to do so. Throughout his life, he was able to accomplish a prodigious amount of work, mainly because he was highly organized and methodical. A book would progress from individual research cards, to clusters of cards arranged topically, to a first draft, to a finished product. More important, he got an early start on his work each day, usually being at his typewriter by five or six o'clock in the morning. Before he became Headmaster, he arranged to have no classes before eleven and was thus able to put in five or six hours before most people got started. He told his friends that he used to start writing immediately, even though he might have to discard some of the first material. As he warmed to the task, words would begin to flow and the book would begin to write itself. Yet Jack had no magic formula for composition; the true secret of his extraordinary output as a writer was his tremendous capacity for sheer hard work. He was only half joking when he once remarked that his epitaph should read: "He worked like Hell."[62] Still and all, though his writings undoubtedly brought renown to Phillips Academy, he might have been more successful as a Headmaster had he devoted all his time to the School. In short, any assessment of Claude Fuess's Headmastership is bound to be a mixed bag. There were some things that he did extraordinarily well; there were others that he did very badly. On balance he piloted the School through the difficult times of Depression and War and at the end of his term was able to turn over to his successor an institution that was stronger than the one he inherited in 1933.

In 1947 Dr. Fuess determined to retire the following year. He would have completed fifteen years as Headmaster, with another twenty-five as a member of the Faculty—in all forty years of service to Phillips Academy. The ostensible reason for his decision to retire was his increasing deafness. After a 1947 Trustee Meeting he told the new President of the Board, Henry W. Hobson, that he had not been able to hear much of what went on at the meeting and that he thought he should leave. The Bishop persuaded him to stay on for a year, which he did with the help of a hearing aid. Yet deafness was not the only reason for the decision. The Headmaster was still bruised from the controversy over the School Societies (the subject of the next chapter), and there is reason to believe as well that the New York research organization that the Trustees had hired to make a survey of Andover alumni for the coming Fund Drive had turned up a substantial amount of opposition to Fuess as Headmaster. Finally, Jack Fuess had been very happily remarried in 1945 and may well have wanted to be relieved of the burdens of office so as to be free to spend more time with his wife. In any event he finished his last year with the help of his hearing aid, retired in June to the plaudits of his friends, and was given a handsomely appointed testimonial dinner at which the Faculty presented him with the fanciest typewriter on the market as an aid to future literary production.

On his retirement his old friend Colonel Poynter wrote a letter to him that reviewed his accomplishments.[63] Horace Poynter thought first of all that Jack's insistence on full freedom of discussion at Faculty meetings was a signal achievement. No teacher had ever suffered for anything he said at Andover, even though on many occasions Faculty sentiments were most distasteful to the Headmaster. And the Colonel added wryly that it must have been a great comfort—as Jack became deaf and got a hearing aid— to be able to turn it off during Faculty meeting discussions. The second achievement that Colonel Poynter stressed was what Jack had done for the health program at the School. With a new and modern hospital and an outstanding School doctor and staff, a revolution had been accomplished in this important area. Third, the curricular change of 1933 was significant. The Colonel regretted the passing of the Latin requirement and thought too much history had been introduced, but he recognized the inevitability of change and congratulated Jack on engineering it. Finally, Poynter was high in his praise for Jack's insistence on treating boys as individuals, in abandoning the "Sink or Swim" policy of an earlier generation, in op- posing an arid rigidity in the enforcement of rules, and in discipline gen- erally. Pieces like the one Poynter was writing approach their subject with a kind of *de mortuis nihil nisi bonum* attitude; it was not to be expected that the author would deal with the less successful aspects of Jack Fuess's Headmastership. Yet the four achievements the Colonel stressed were real; no one could take them away from the retiring Headmaster.

The period after Jack Fuess's retirement was probably the happiest of his life. His first wife, Bess, had represented for him all the best of New England virtues. His second, Lulie Anderson Blackfan, brought all the warmth and charm of her native Kentucky, and the years that she and Jack spent together were an idyll. During the last fifteen years of his life the stiffness and seriousness that had hitherto characterized his speaking mel- lowed and his sense of humor took over, until he became one of the most sought-after speakers in the East and certainly one of the great toastmasters of all time. As always throughout his life, Jack enjoyed making jokes at his own expense. No better example can be given of his gifts as a speaker than the remarks he made at the dedication of the Claude M. Fuess dor- mitory, a year before his death. He started off by assuring his audience that the rumor that he had given the money for the dormitory on condition that it be named for him was without foundation. He then went on: "I may as well confess with undisguised humility that I never expected to have anything named after me in my lifetime—no cigar, like Henry Clay, no highway, like Daniel Webster, no rose, like Dwight D. Eisenhower. As for a dormitory, and a dormitory like this, that was beyond my most ex- travagant dreams." Then followed a moving account of the growth of Phillips Academy and of his own affection for the institution. His conclu- sion was: "Today this school is more respected and admired than ever before in its history. And both the respect and admiration are well-deserved. Let us, as loyal Andoverians, admit all this, meanwhile offering up our fervent prayer, 'Lord, have mercy upon us and justify the high esteem in which we hold ourselves!' " As usual, Jack had a perfect story for the occasion:

> After Melville W. Fuller, in 1888, had been appointed Chief Justice of the Supreme Court of the United States, he made a sentimental journey to his native city of Augusta, Maine. Getting off at what was always called the Dee-Po, he hired a decrepit cab to drive to the hotel. Thinking that he recognized the ancient driver, he asked, "Do you know who I am?" "Yep, you're Mel Fuller." was the reply. "Do the people here know that I've been made Chief Justice?" "Yep". "Well, what did they say?" "Oh, they laughed!"
>
> If any of my schoolmates at the Waterville High School or at Amherst College were here this morning, they would certainly laugh. And if any of my former pupils wants to laugh, now is the accepted time. If I myself laugh, it is "with a tear in the middle," as James M. Barrie once wrote, grateful for what Phillips Academy has done and is doing for me.

The dedication was a completely appropriate climax to Jack's long association with Phillips Academy. And how fortunate that he could be there to enjoy the honour! Less than a year later he was dead. Thus closed a long career of service with distinction. The epitaph on his gravestone in the old Phillips Academy cemetery reads: "Wit graced his learning and generous warmth his friendship."

CHAPTER SIXTEEN

THE SECRET SOCIETIES

OCCASIONAL MENTION has been made earlier of the Secret Societies that existed at Phillips Academy. In the 1940's the question of whether these organizations were desirable came to a head and produced bitter controversy between the Administration and various groups of alumni. The first attempt to abolish the Societies occurred in 1943 and resulted in failure. Under John Mason Kemper, in 1949, elimination of these institutions was finally achieved, and with much less bitterness than had accompanied the first attempt.

The Andover Secret Societies were unique among American secondary schools. To be sure there were various kinds of fraternities at high schools, and some private schools also had exclusive clubs. At Exeter, for example, Societies existed until World War II, but they were a pale copy of the Andover institutions. For one thing, the Exeter Societies rented their quarters, while at Andover there were eight Society houses owned independently of the School by separate corporations. For seven of these organizations handsome new houses had been constructed for the express purpose of providing quarters for them. After a short period of trying to suppress them, the School, under Cecil Bancroft, had decided to allow them to exist and to supervise and regulate them. The School cooperated further by selling land to the various Society corporations when they wished to build their houses. Al Stearns continued the Bancroft policy; indeed, he often turned to the Societies for leadership in undergraduate affairs.

In the 1930's the attitude toward them began to change. In part this may have been the result of the change in attitude toward American society generally that accompanied the New Deal. In part it came about because more and more of the Faculty were becoming disenchanted with the institutions. Though Claude Fuess took a leading part in the first attempt to abolish the Societies, he was in large measure reflecting the attitudes of the country and the Andover community. The issue was difficult and highly emotional; in no sense did it have a purely right or wrong side. Even today, twenty-five years after the abolition of the Societies, it is difficult to be objective about the problem.

There were eventually eight Secret Societies at Phillips Academy, although several were more fugitive and lasted for only a few years. The three oldest, and by far the most prestigious, were K.O.A., A.U.V., and P.A.E. These three, together with P.B.X. and F.L.D., were founded in the late nineteenth century; P.L.S., A.G.C., and E.D.P. were founded in the twentieth, the last in 1915.[1] When these organizations first appeared in the 1870's, the Faculty voted to forbid them, and for a few years entering Andover students were forced to sign a pledge that they would not join any Secret Society.[2] As a result, the early meetings had to be *sub rosa*, usually around midnight or in the early morning hours.

Yet the Societies were filling a definite undergraduate need. The School provided a solid academic program and was starting to develop an athletic one. Philo, the Society of Inquiry, and the musical clubs offered activities that might appeal to some boys but had no attraction for many. The Andover students of the 1870's were reacting much the same as college boys did a generation earlier when they established Greek letter fraternities. If colleges and schools were not going to provide institutions for the social life of their students, the students would have to develop them themselves.

In the 1880's the Faculty apparently had second thoughts about Societies; if they could not lick them, they had better join them. Accordingly, in 1883 the practice was instituted of each Society's having a Faculty

63. The old P.A.E. House at the turn of the century.

guardian. Professor Graves was chosen guardian for K.O.A. Once this had been accomplished, the School had given formal recognition to the Societies, and from then on, each organization, in order to be in good standing, had to have a guardian, chosen by the members and approved by the Faculty. Once a Society had come out in the open, it was decided that new members had to be approved by the Faculty, with the names presented by the guardian and resting on the table for a week before being voted upon. Apparently in the early days there was no restriction by classes as to which boys could belong, as there was to be later, nor was the number of late meetings that a Society could have determined by the group's scholastic average. Faculty policy toward the Societies can be seen from the charter of the S.A.O. organization, passed in October 1896. First of all, the life of the Society was limited until June 1897, presumably so that the Faculty could check on its progress. The membership was limited to sixteen. The group was to have a suitable house or rooms near the Academy which could be used during regular recreation hours and on alternate Saturday nights until 9:50 P.M. S.A.O. was to have a guardian, and was to initiate no new members without prior Faculty approval.[3] This policy of Faculty supervision was to continue with relatively little change down to the 1930's.

A charming account of the early days of K.O.A., the oldest of the Societies, was prepared by Jack Fuess, a member of the organization, on the occasion of their Fiftieth Anniversary.[4] The Society was founded in September 1874, with five members present at its first meeting. The treasury contained five dollars, gained from the dollar initiation fee that the original five had paid in. Monthly dues were twenty-five cents. A fat source of revenue was fines—absence from meeting, twenty cents, disorderly conduct, fifty cents, and the like. Each member had a special societal name— Don Santo, Thersites, Fra Diavolo. The group made a brave attempt to introduce literary exercises at their meetings, but after one session the members voted to abolish them. The Society first held its meetings in a room in the Latin Commons and later in a dilapidated structure below the Academy on the way downtown. Beer was drunk, and some of the meetings were boisterous. In order to get food for these gatherings a "Committee of Plunder" was appointed, and occasionally, when the treasury was flush, a society supper was held, fried oysters being served in one instance. To avoid Faculty detection, the day and time of meetings had to be changed frequently, and in 1881 the annual reunion was held in New Haven lest the Faculty find out about it. In school elections the Society was well organized, had its own tickets, and did surprisingly well. After a Philo election in 1878 the Scribe wrote in the minutes: "A glorious victory for K.O.A. and the gentlemanly element of Phillips Academy." The members also bought a bob-sled for seventeen dollars, painted it with a skull and crossbones, and made a great hit with spectators on School Street. The Society was apparently effective at disciplining its own members. In the mid 1870's, one student was "dishonorarbly expelled" for some unspecified crime. Interestingly enough the Andover K.O.A. attempted to establish a chapter at Exeter, a task made easier by the presence at Exeter of a boy who had recently been expelled from Andover. The chapter was indeed started, but faded soon after.

As was true with most secret societies in those early days, a major concern of the membership was the initiation ceremony. In K.O.A. the ceremony involved visiting one of the local cemeteries at midnight, various kinds of tortures, running the gauntlet—though the novice was apparently punched rather than paddled, being baptized in a water tank, being hoisted in the air by a pulley, and finally being placed in a coffin, where he was cross-examined by the members. It is interesting to note that in 1882 a black who was serving the Society as janitor was also initiated. Much of what went on may seem childish and unimportant today, but the fact remains that K.O.A. was able to hold the loyalty of its members over the years to become a powerful institution at Phillips Academy and to erect a handsome pillared Society house on School Street.

The second Society of the seven that would survive until 1950 was A.U.V. The letters stood for *Auctoritas, Unitas, Veritas*.[5] This organization resulted from a merger of two slightly earlier Societies, O.D.A. and Delta Tau Delta. O.D.A. had been born in the Brick House, formerly a printing shop, located in front of what is now Adams and Bishop Halls. The Brick House was isolated from the rest of the campus, as it then existed, and it was natural that the boys who lived there would develop close friendships. But O.D.A. did not prosper and in 1876 had only four members. Since Delta Tau Delta was not that strong either, and since the two groups had been engaging in a friendly rivalry for some time, they determined to merge, which they did in 1877. A new constitution was drawn up outlining the rules for the governance of the Society and providing for four chief officers—Imperator, Vice Imperator, Scriptor, and Quaestor—with a number of lesser ones as well. Like K.O.A. the Society depended on an elaborate system of fines for some of its income. Unlike some of the other Societies, which tended to become cliques, A.U.V. made a conscious effort to have variety in its membership, and apparently at times pleas would be made to the brethren not to blackball candidates that might provide such variety. Like K.O.A., A.U.V. had an elaborate initiation ceremony. Once a pledge had been approved by the Faculty, he was given a letter with a list of rules he was to follow. He was to be in the cemetery every night from 12:30 to 5:00, deliver a morning paper to each member of the Society each morning, must not comb or brush his hair nor wash his face or hands, smoke nothing but a clay pipe with Lucky Strike tobacco, and not speak to any student except members of A.U.V.

After the pledge had memorized these rules, his letter of instruction was burned. The pledge now became a "scut" and was compelled to learn many mottoes and incantations. On Friday night of initiation week the scut was taken to Hartigan's drugstore downtown and given a "scut sundae," which consisted of pepper, ice cream, oysters, and raw liver. Later that night he reported to the South Church cemetery, where he had to wait for two hours for the members to arrive. There followed the usual horseplay—the scut was used as a tackling dummy, threats were made to lock him in a tomb, and various other ceremonies observed. On Saturday afternoon the scut was taken on a long walk around town, being forced to stop at some houses and ask for food, to urinate on a few porches, and generally to make a fool of himself. On Saturday night came the initiation proper. The scut was prepared by reporting to the cellar in his underwear and having dirt and flour smeared all over his body. He was finally cleaned up and brought to the initiation room, where a solemn ceremony followed, ending with the longed-for words "Let him have light," at which point his blindfold was removed, some oaths were administered, and the boy was finally a member.

A.U.V. had better housing than the other Societies in the early days, for a new lodge was constructed in 1894. In 1902 alumni members of the Society incorporated it, and in 1909 purchased a lot on Wheeler Street from Phillips Academy. Shortly after 1915 the present house was constructed. From then until the Society crisis of the 1940's, A.U.V. continued strong and successful. There were, to be sure, some problems. In the mid-1920's, the scholarship average of the Society dropped abysmally. The members had also been pledging students illegally—without the approval of the Faculty guardian. In one initiation a boy had been so battered that he was unable to run in the Andover-Exeter track meet. The janitor forgot to turn off the water one winter vacation, with the result that the pipes froze solid. Yet the Society managed to overcome these problems and well deserved its position as one of the big three among the school's Societies.

A.G.C. was different in some ways from the other Societies.[6] Its founders—and many of its later members—believed that the true function of a Society should be "real interest in working for the school and scholarship." A.G.C. was also different in that its Faculty guardian—for most of its existence Allan Rogers ("Zeus") Benner—played a much more active role than did the other Faculty guardians. Perhaps this was because Zeus was the only Faculty member of the Society, while most of the others had several, but in any event his influence was profound. A.G.C. was founded in 1904 by ten students, nine of whom were members of the Society of Inquiry, an organization whose purpose was "to make Christianity not merely a pious creed, but the very core of daily living." This seriousness of purpose is reflected in the epithet that other members of the school applied to the members—"Christers." Bishop Henry W. Hobson, until

recently President of the Academy's Board of Trustees, remembers the
early meetings of the Society:

> We'd bring up subjects about the school which we would discuss,
> and discuss seriously. I mean some of the really important school
> problems and questions that students had in mind. We had some
> discussion of the things of the world. There was an occasional pre-
> pared paper read by one of the members. While we had a lot of
> good times together, there was always the underlying idea.that we
> were there for the purpose of trying to be of some use to the school.[7]

An important reason for the relative seriousness of the membership was
the interest that Zeus Benner took in the selection of students as prospective members. A scholar himself, he prized scholarship among the students
and often suggested one of his able Greek pupils for pledging. Partly as a
result, the scholastic average of the Society was nearly always higher than
that of the others. Yet it must not be supposed that the brethren of A.G.C.
were dour, joyless young men, forever concerned with life's most serious
questions. There is ample evidence that the members had a lot of fun.
The Society's first house, called "Bill's" was off Bartlet Street and was the
scene of "a lot of good times"—"feeds," "Hydrox cookies, ice cream, and
soft drinks." As one member remembers it, "How moving it was to march
up the hill on the clear, crisp nights singing our songs of brotherhood,
hearing our rivals singing theirs across campus, and reaching home as the
clock struck the hour. There was exaltation in it." The A.G.C. initiation
had much in common with those of the other Societies, with a few special
twists of its own. The pledge, called the "bird," might be asked to push
over a large stone wall—and be paddled when he did not succeed. Or he
might be taken on a long walk, asked to flag down the streetcar and then
wave it on, ask permission of a farmer to kiss his horse, and finally yell
"Cuckoo" three times through a window at a lady playing a piano.[8] The
ritual that followed the horseplay bore the imprint of Zeus Benner's
composition:

> The beautiful badge of Alpha Gamma Chi boasts few symbols, but
> these are very significant. . . . Its composition is gold and diamond.
> The former is symbolic of our high ideals; the latter, hardest of
> stones, suggests to us the difficulties involved in its achievement, as
> well as the value and worth of our goal, character and highest man-
> hood. The letters knit close in the monogram are indicative of the
> close bond of friendship and affection that knits our brothers together.
> The shield of Alpha Gamma Chi is the facade of a castle, the
> symbol of strength without and secrecy within. The sum of the num-
> bers on the seal and the number of panels around the door is ten, a
> number which we emphasize as a tribute to our ten charter members.
> The Eagle Knocker stands on a cord of many strands, each represent-

ing a brother. In its mouth this strongest of birds holds and protects a Key—our Key.[9]

When the ceremony was over, the new brother, according to one initiate, experienced "the warm sense of belonging to a gallant company."

In 1915 the corporation of the Society acquired what was described as a "cottage" on Salem Street so that the Society could be nearer to the School. Apparently it was no real estate bargain. When Mrs. Henry Hobson saw it, she remarked, "If the parents of the boys ever saw it, they'd demand that their sons resign, and if the building inspector or board of health ever came near this corner, they'd close the place up!"[10] A particularly unattractive feature of the building was "the dreadful condition of the porch." Yet the Society thrived in its new dwelling until 1927, when a group of alumni under the leadership of Henry Hobson determined to build a new house for the Society. Money and pledges were obtained, a plot of land was purchased from the School, a brochure entitled "Old Bill's is Crumbling" was distributed as part of the fund-raising effort, and the handsome structure known today as Benner House was built. The backers of the project had unwittingly picked a poor time to build; hardly had the new house been constructed than the Depression hit and for the rest of its existence A.G.C. was never free from financial troubles. Yet at least until Zeus Benner retired in 1938, its morale remained high.

One final example—E.D.P., the last of the Societies to be founded.[11] As the youngest of the eight Societies, E.D.P. suffered in competition with the others, particularly at first; yet like the others it managed to survive until 1950. When it was first founded in 1915, it was completely secret; it was not recognized by the School and had no Faculty guardian. During these first years it was handicapped because its members were often pledged to other societies as well, which produced divided loyalties to say the least. After four years, however, it was strong enough to apply to the School for recognition, and once that was received, E.D.P. became the eighth Society at Phillips Academy. It determined to be an "open" Society—that is, undergraduates who were not members could visit it, as they could P.A.E., F.L.D., P.B.X., and P.L.S. Three of the Societies—K.O.A., A.U.V., and A.G.C.—were closed, meaning that only members were ever allowed inside. E.D.P. acquired a modest shingled cottage on Highland Road, which remained its house until the abolition of the Societies in 1950. As the newest of the Societies, E.D.P. had trouble attracting campus leaders—particularly the captains of major sports. As one Faculty member put it: "All the fraternities wanted to pledge the same boys but only the name fraternities were able to acquire them. E.D.P. was more fortunate in pledging boys with latent qualities that the prominent fraternities might have overlooked."[12] The three qualities most sought after were athletic ability, personality, and scholarship, though not necessarily in that order. One way in which E.D.P. sought to strengthen its position was by pledging promising lowerclassmen before the other Societies had become aware of them, but the Seniors disliked the idea of having a lot of young kids around, and the idea never got very far.

Since there was a certain amount of confusion in Society affairs, especially regarding pledging, an Inter-Society Council was set up to try to bring some kind of order to the situation, and after its establishment in the 1920's, things did improve, but the members of E.D.P. showed little concern for it. On various occasions proposals for the construction of a new house for the Society were brought forward, but these never materialized, and E.D.P. remained throughout its entire existence the one Society that never had a new house of its own. One description of Society life at E.D.P. reads as follows:

> On a Saturday night the only place a Phillips Academy student could sign out for after the movie was his fraternity, where he could sip a soda, light up a cigarette, play cards, pool, ping-pong, or throw the "bull" with a student or faculty member. The atmosphere was congenial and the people friendly. Softball games, picnics, and special outings added to the social life of the members. The Society provided an oasis for students who were trapped in an age of strict discipline; it was a place where one could escape from the pressures of school, be with people of the same mentality, and have a feeling of belonging. The close proximity among fraternity members did indeed foster a special "intercourse" which was occasionally so powerful that a member would feel more loyalty to the Society than to the school.[13]

In short, though E.D.P. was never as strong as some of the other Societies, it did equally well in providing a place where its members could relax together in good fellowship.

For the first third of the twentieth century, therefore, the Societies prospered and provided a rich experience for many of their members. There can be no question that the friendships formed in these organizations were lasting. Furthermore, the loyalty of the alumni members of the Societies— for example, their return to Andover for reunion dinners each spring—is additional evidence that the Society experience had been meaningful. In most of the groups the alumni members were more than willing to open their purses when things got rough financially, and it is a truism to state the Societies would never have survived without alumni support. Under Al Stearns, undergraduate Society leaders were often asked to help with school problems. John Kemper reported on the following conversation with Al: "He explained to me the way in which they [the Societies] were particularly useful in his day. Whenever he had a problem that he felt the boys could solve better than the faculty—and there are always many such problems—he worked through the Societies."[14] Strong and generally well behaved as they were, they were by no means spotless. A certain amount of drinking went on fairly regularly, all the more so because it was difficult to apprehend the transgressor. Safe within the confines of his house, he was vulnerable only to incursions by the Faculty guardian, and these occurred rarely. In one Society, for example, bridge was played for one twentieth of a cent a point.[15] Occassionally a crap game developed. But most of the boys did not have enough money to engage in any large-scale gambling, and the problem was never serious.

Finally, there was the question of girls—particularly Abbot girls, who regularly took walks in pairs past some of the Society houses. In the "open" houses girls could visit if properly chaperoned, usually by the Faculty guardian. In the "closed" houses none was ever to enter. This did not prevent certain enterprising undergraduates from inviting girls in for a visit in both "open" and "closed" houses without benefit of chaperone. If they got caught, the penalty was often to close the entire house for a lengthy

64. The modern K.O.A. House, now Alumni House.

period. In the winter of 1931, for example, an amorous brother of AGC took a young lady into his house. Unfortunately for him, he was observed by the wife of the Head of the Math Department, and the house was closed for the rest of the year. On another occasion, when a P.B.X. brother took a girl into his house and was caught, Arthur B. Darling, Faculty guardian, was bemoaning to an alumnus brother how the boys had let him down. The alumnus listened for a bit and then said, "Well, Art, your parents didn't find you under any mulberry bush."[16] There is no evidence that anything very ambitious was attempted during these clandestine visits, but given the attitude of the School and, more important, of Bertha Bailey, Headmistress of Abbot Academy, the mere fact of an unchaperoned meeting between a boy and girl was shocking and intolerable.

During the 1930's some of the Societies ran into financial problems. P.L.S., for example, found itself unable to meet its obligations in the late 1930's, appeals for alumni support went largely in vain, and the organization was finally forced in 1939 to turn over its new house to the School, which held the mortgage. Hence as the 1940's opened, there were seven rather than eight Societies.

Despite various sins of omission and commission, there was no reason in the 1930's to believe that the Societies were not permanent institutions at Phillips Academy. In 1943 Headmaster Claude Fuess made a sudden attempt to abolish all of them outright. At the start he received the almost unanimous support of both the Trustees and the Faculty; yet it is difficult to determine precisely where the movement to get rid of the Societies came from. To be sure, there were straws in the wind. In 1934 one undergraduate had been killed during the course of a Society initiation. A group of alumni had joined the undergraduates for part of the ceremonies that were held in a barn on the outskirts of Andover. On the way back the initiate rode on the running board of a car driven by one of the alumni. The roads were slippery, and the car skidded and crashed into a telegraph pole, crushing the boy, who died in Dr. Fuess's presence in the hospital a few hours later. According to his own testimony, this tragic eposide had a profound impression on Dr. Fuess:

> I had known this kind of thing was going on, but up to that time the accidents had been relatively trivial; boys who had been beaten up considerably had emerged with bruises and sometimes with dislocations. But this was the first time anybody had been killed. . . . I made up my mind that [the Societies] would just have to go. . . . It was perhaps the most important factor in forcing me to reach a decision.[17]

One might argue that the accident was not directly connected with the Societies as such—a non-Society boy might have ridden on the running board of a friend's auto, for example. Unquestionably Jack Fuess never forgot the experience, and it contributed to his eventual decision to move for abolition. Other forces were also at work: a subtle change in attitude that may have been a result of the New Deal programs, the attacks on special privilege, the egalitarian character of the New Deal philosophy, the concern for the disadvantaged—all put the Societies on the defensive. A natural result of this change in national thinking was an increasing concern for the boys who were *not* in Societies. Though from the start many students were disappointed or bitter or insecure as a result of not having been chosen for a Society, no one seems to have worried much about it. It was the way of the world, and the unwashed could take their knocks like anyone else. Now there began to develop an interest in this group and also in their parents. Furthermore, the increasing influence that mothers began to have in their sons' secondary education played a part. A father might accept the fact that his son did not make a Society; for a mother such a state of affairs was unbearable.[18] The Faculty, which had accepted Societies without much question up to this time, also began to alter its position. Another straw in the wind came when Alan R. Blackmer, the distinguished English teacher, resigned from K.O.A. because he could not subscribe to what the Societies stood for. An attempt by the Faculty to ameliorate the whole situation came in 1935, when membership was limited to Upper Middlers and Seniors. Yet that exacerbated the situation: 40 percent of those two classes were Society members and 60 percent were not. When all four classes had been eligible, the percentages were not that close. Commenting on this, Dr. Fuess stated that he would be happier when 10 percent were in and 90 percent out, or when 90 percent were in and 10 percent out. Splitting the two upper classes down the middle was, he thought, the worst possible division.[19] Aside from limiting Society membership to the two upper classes, no action was taken on the question in the 1930's, but there were tides running that would have a deep influence on the attitude of people toward exclusive institutions both within and without the School.

As the decade of the 1940's opened, the position of the Societies at Andover seemed secure. Rumors that the School was considering some kind of drastic action toward them proved unfounded. When Charles L. Stillman, Class of 1922 and an alumnus member of P.A.E., wrote Dr. Fuess on the subject, he received the following reply:

> I can say briefly that my object for the past two or three years has been to improve the societies, and I am confident that when you understand what has been done, you will agree with the program which we have undertaken.

A few months after this, Stillman met with Dr. Fuess and others to discuss, among other things, the Society question. Stillman's report of this meeting included the following statement made by Dr. Fuess:

> Fuess said that the society situation was much better than it has been.

There is vast improvement at K.O.A. and signs of more life at
P.A.E. If all societies were more like A.U.V., in Jack's opinion,
there would be no society problem.[20]

These statements could not but reassure the Society alumni that at least the
situation was no worse that it had been; if the School were trying to improve them, the presumption was that they were to remain as permanent
parts of Phillips Academy. As we shall see, however, these statements were
to return to haunt Jack Fuess when the Society crisis broke three years later.

Then came the war, and most people had more important things to do
than to worry about Andover, let alone Andover Societies. In 1942 Dr.
Fuess decided to move for the elimination of Societies. According to his
recollection he had been discussing the problem with many people, he
would have behind him the almost unanimous support of the Faculty, and
he was confident of Trustee approval. He therefore met with the undergraduate heads of the seven Societies, told them of his plans, and won their
agreement to support the measure. Since Jack's recollections were dictated
twenty years after the event, the chances are good that he mixed up his
dates. It is hard to believe that an announcement of this kind would not
have leaked out long before the explosion in the spring of 1943.[21] Be that
as it may, the next step was to get the approval of the Trustees, which was
accomplished at their meeting of 10 April 1943, at which the following
Resolutions were passed:

> VOTED, that it is the sense of the Trustees that the existence of secret
> societies at Andover is not to the best interests of the school.
> VOTED, that after the close of the present school year on June 11,
> 1943, no boys be permitted to belong to or join any social organiza-
> tion not authorized by the faculty.[22]

On 30 April 1943 the Faculty passed the following Resolution at a special
meeting, with two dissenting votes:

> VOTED, that it is the sense of the Faculty that the existence of social
> societies, with restricted membership, is not in the best interests of
> Phillips Academy.[23]

Both the Trustee vote and the Faculty vote were to be kept in confidence
until adequate preparations had been made for presenting these decisions
to the Andover community at large. Yet the Societies were apparently
wiped out, summarily. There had been no adequate preparation for the
step, no opportunity for discussion with interested alumni, no openness.
Jack Fuess was later accused of trying to ram the measure through while
everyone was busy fighting the Nazis and the Japanese. Although no evidence in support of that charge exists, it is difficult to understand how he
thought he could accomplish his purpose of closing down in two months
seven institutions, several of which were over fifty years old and all of

which represented a substantial financial investment on the part of Andover graduates.

He soon learned that he could not. Although Trustees, Faculty, and the undergraduate Inter-Society Council had all been sworn to secrecy, leaks soon developed, and as the actions became more widely known, the undergraduates of K.O.A. believed that they were released from their pledge of secrecy and sent out an appeal to their alumni to come to their rescue.[24] Then the fat was in the fire, and Jack Fuess was deluged with letters from alumni, most of them protesting not only the action itself but the surreptitious way in which it had been carried out. Two of the more savage attacks follow. In the first a distinguished Andover alumnus telegraphed the Headmaster:

> I was called on the long distance telephone by a member of my old society P.A.E. who stated that the Andover Trustees planned to abolish the societies without giving them any hearing. I told him that this sounded so Fascist that I would not believe it. Certainly no such step should be taken without a full hearing at which the proper representatives of the alumni graduates of the societies could be present.

When Dr. Fuess asked him to wait the results of a coming meeting in New York, the alumnus let go another salvo:

> I am not interested in post mortems but only in fair play. That the societies have not received. Star chamber proceedings have been out of date since 1688. This telegram closes our communications on this subject.[25]

Another wrote:

> I have been compelled, after long thought and with regret for a pleasant past, to write . . . that I have lost my faith and friendship in you; and that I think your usefulness to Andover has ended.
>
> You yourself have destroyed my friendship and faith. . . . I have thought long and reluctantly before admitting it. Because I have liked you and backed you where I could for many years gone by.
>
> But I cannot approve the long, obvious, undercover course you have pursued with regard to the abolition of the societies; in our constant meetings you never once spoke of your plan. And secondly I am stricken with amazement at the complete obliviousness of wrong that you show in your letters to me.
>
> . . . in the army they sometimes decide that an officer is no longer fit to command brave troops. I feel that you have shown yourself no longer fit to lead straight-forward young Americans.[26]

He went on to comment on the bitterness toward the Headmaster—"which, to me is amazing in its depth"—and the resentment felt by Andover men in the armed forces "who feel that you have used their absence as a further aid to your secret effort." A hornet's nest had been stirred up.

Dr. Fuess did not take these attacks lying down. He prepared a memorandum on the Societies in which he stated his views clearly and strongly. First of all, he thought, the tremendous changes that had taken place on Andover Hill since World War I made many of the arguments that might have been relevant at an earlier period no longer valid. The improvements in School plant and equipment, the increase in the size of the Academy, the lowering of the average age of students—all had made Phillips Academy a very different place from what it had been a generation or two ago. When the Societies were founded, the School made little provision for undergraduate recreational facilities, and they served a definite need. At the time he was writing, with a broad program of recreational facilities, that need no longer existed. If there were no Societies, no one could ever think of establishing them. The Societies had contributed little to the School over the years. Their members' grades tended to decline after initiation, and there had been no Society programs designed to improve School life. Many members cared more for their Society than for the School. Furthermore, the system was promoting exclusiveness and gave official recognition to that exclusiveness. It tended to give members an unjustified sense of superiority—all the more so when the criteria for election were often capricious and sometimes discriminatory. Indeed, the Faculty had no trouble in recognizing the "society type" of student. The system also encouraged School politics and the manipulation of other students. The expense of membership was unjustifiably large. Even more important was the effect that the Society system was having on those who were not members. During the first two years of a boy's career at Andover, he would make friends with a variety of other boys. Then in Upper Middle year came the Society "rushing," and suddenly the class was divided into two groups, often for the most arbitrary of reasons. "The consequences are disappointment, concealed envy, and a sense of injustice, all the more devastating because so seldom revealed." Visitors to Andover were often amazed to learn that the School had Societies—Phillips Academy was the only strong private School in the country still to have them. When the Trustees, Headmaster, and Faculty were all but unanimous in their belief that the Societies should go, it should give proponents of the system pause. The possibility of attacks on private schools by those who wanted the state to control everything was a constant danger. How much more vulnerable would Phillips Academy be if it had to defend these special interest institutions from attack! The Trustees had no intention of eliminating the Societies without replacing them with new recreational facilities. Just what form these new facilities would take would have to await further study, but the time had clearly come to abolish an anachronism and replace it with something more in keeping with the Phillips Academy of that day.[27]

Others rallied to the Headmaster's support. Robert A. Gardner, a Trustee and a member of P.A.E., spoke for the Trustees on the matter. He pointed out that all the Trustees but two were members of Societies and that they had reached their conclusion only after a lot of hard thinking, fully cognizant of the storm that would break about their heads once their decision became known. He said that the claim that Society alumni were stronger supporters of the School than non-Society ones simply was not true. As far as financial support for the School was concerned, the support of the Society alumni was slightly less than that of the others. He then took up the problem of boys who were not in Societies and the often made statement that if boys were disappointed, it was good for their character and would prepare them to meet trials later in life. On this point he said that he was willing to take the judgment of the Faculty, who were all but unanimous in favor of abolition, even though most of the Faculty were not Andover graduates and even fewer were Society members. Gardner insisted that the Faculty were in closer touch with what was going on than any other group, including the Trustees, and he did not see how the School could be run successfully if their opinions were ignored. To make this point more emphatic, he used a business analogy: "If anyone were running a business and the department managers were unanimous as to a policy, it would be very poor judgment not to give weight to their advice."[28] There was no question that a strong case had been made for the abolition of the Societies. Unfortunately for the Administration, however, no case at all could be made for the manner in which the votes had been rushed through without any prior discussion or preparation. As a result, the Administration's case was fatally weakened before the issue was fairly joined.

It was the original intention of the Trustees to pass their vote, get Faculty approval of it, notify the Inter-Society Council, and then swear everybody to secrecy until a meeting could be held in New York, at which the decision could be explained to a representative group of Society alumni. Because of the leaks, Dr. Fuess and the Trustees who attended the meeting were forced to adopt an essentially defensive attitude from the beginning, with the storm of protest already raging. On 14 May 1943 the dinner was held, with Jack Fuess, Dr. Fred Murphy, representing the Trustees (President Henry L. Stimson was unable to attend), several other Trustees, and a group of Society alumni. Jack Fuess remembered the dinner as one of the most lavish he had ever attended; before dinner and during the meal everything was very pleasant; then after dinner the Society alumni opened up on the Headmaster. At this time they were not so much concerned with the merits and demerits of the Society system; they rather insisted that they deserved a day in court before such drastic action as that proposed by the Trustees were taken. Dr. Murphy, who, as Vice-President of the Board, was presiding, was ineffectual in support of the Administrative position;

when he was asked questions, he often replied that he did not know. The only support that Jack Fuess got that evening came from Allan Heely, a former Andover Faculty member, a member of P.A.E., and Headmaster of Lawrenceville. He rose and made a powerful statement in defense of the Administration position.[29] At the end of the evening the Trustees who were present retired, and when they returned, they announced that while their first vote that Societies were not in the best interest of Phillips Academy would stand, they would recommend to the full Board, at their meeting in June, that their second vote closing the Societies in June, 1943, be rescinded and that the actual abolition of the Societies be postponed.[30] Although those present at the dinner may not have realized it at the time, this meant that the movement to eliminate the Societies was dead. There were still many committee meetings to be held and a great deal of ink to be spilled, but no one in power ever again seriously considered abolition at this time.

A major reason why the drive for the abolition of the Societies stalled was the position taken by Henry L. Stimson. Stimson, as Secretary of War, more than had his hands full in Washington and was understandably unable to attend any of the meetings on the Society question. But he had been sent copies of the many letters of protest that had come to the Headmaster and somehow found time to read them all. On 31 May he wrote Jack Fuess a letter in which he said, "The reading of the letters . . . has given me the impression that we have made a mistake in bringing such a matter up at this time when all men were under nervous pressure and when harmonious unity in support of the war effort rather than discord on such a minor matter as this should have been aimed at. Furthermore I think we made a mistake in taking action in a way which has given the opponents of the step ground for accusing us of acting without any discussion and an opportunity to them for being heard on the other side." To soften these statements, Stimson wrote the words "may" and "may have" in the margin, so that the statements would read "may have made a mistake." But it was clear that the original phrasing represented his true position. Secretary Stimson went on to say that he thought some more modern reform of the Society system was contemplated rather than "complete annihilation of the societies," and added that he felt sympathetic with some of the Society alumni who had written moderately on the subject. He was impressed, too, by the importance and intelligence of the men who had written in. Stimson concluded:

> In short, I am inclined to feel that if it is possible we should not press this thing at present to a ruthless immediate decision. It seems to me the wrong time and the wrong method. . . . But I am very much impressed with the importance of keeping the unity of the body of the alumni preserved, and frankly I don't think this Society issue is one on which we should break it. I know enough of the men

whose names appeared as signers of these matters to feel that they represented an opposition which the Trustees should not brush aside as an unimportant minority. . . . it is needless to say that I shall loyally accept any decision the Trustees make.[31]

The Stimson letter was gentle but firm. A Headmaster who would have proceeded with abolition of the Societies without the support of the President of his Board would have been very rash indeed.

On 10 June the Trustees met. They accepted the advice of their members who had attended the New York meeting and rescinded their April vote, which would have closed down all Societies on 11 June of that year. At the same meeting a delegation of Society alumni requested permission to attend for a while, a request that was granted. They were bitterly hostile to the Headmaster, and their aim was to force his resignation. According to Jack Fuess's account, they realized that they could not accomplish this on the Society issue—for one thing the coverage in the national press had been universally favorable to the Administration position.[32] They believed that the new policy of treating each discipline case on its individual merits was a pernicious one that confused the present undergraduates and demanded a return to the old system where punishment was automatic for a particular crime. They charged Dr. Fuess with being "soft" and generally incompetent in the field of discipline and grilled him on the handling of recent cases. He explained that all disciplinary matters were now handled by a Faculty Discipline Committee, a competent group with whom he had no intention of interfering. After the Society group left, the Trustees gave the Headmaster a full vote of confidence, and he learned shortly thereafter that the Faculty had met on their own and passed a similar vote.[33] All this was encouraging and reassuring, but a personal tragedy was to cause Jack Fuess to give up the battle. His wife, Elizabeth Goodhue Fuess, had not been well for some time; in the spring of 1943 she became so desperately ill that it became more and more difficult for her husband to meet his appointments. On 26 July 1943 she died. Of the effect of her death on him he wrote:

> The situation was such, however, that with my wife as ill as she was, and with the necessity of my being with her virtually all the time, that I finally made up my mind that I would just let the thing lapse. And in a period of great emotional strain, during the summer, I simply dropped whatever steps I had made up my mind to take with regard to the societies. I think for a short period I was almost incapable of action, not because I was seriously ill but because I was emotionally disturbed.[34]

Secretary Stimson invited Jack Fuess to spend August with him and Mrs. Stimson at the Ausable Club in the Adirondacks, and there he recovered his composure. If he needed further encouragement to drop the Society question, Stimson provided it. He had, he said, received many letters from Andover alumni on all sides of the Society question, but one thing most of them agreed on—that it was unwise to try to settle the matter in the middle of a war. It was clear that Henry Stimson agreed with them.[35]

In the meantime, at the suggestion of the Trustees, a committee of Society alumni was formed to consider what improvements might be made in the existing Society system, since it soon became clear that the Trustee vote to rescind the closing of the Societies was to be more or less permanent. This Committee met with a Faculty committee twice in the summer of 1943 in long sessions and worked diligently to come up with something constructive.[36] Yet it soon became clear that there could be no real meeting of minds, for the two groups—the Faculty and the Society alumni—had basically different concepts of American society. The Faculty were generally egalitarian in outlook; they were primarily concerned with the boys who were not chosen for Societies, they disliked anything that smacked of special privilege, they believed that the influence of the Societies on their members was at best neutral, at worse negative, and they resented the air of superiority that Society students often bore. The Society alumni had what might be called for want of a better word an "individualistic" outlook on society. They believed, first of all, that it was absurd to claim that all men were equal, when they obviously were not. They insisted that disappointments like not making a Society were normal experiences in life and that Andover undergraduates would profit from learning how to accept such disappointments. They were convinced that the Societies had for years provided the School with an elite leadership that had done much for the institution. And they believed strongly that if there were things wrong with the present system, it should be reformed rather than abolished. Given these two diametrically opposed set of values, it is easy to see why agreement between the two committees was difficult to obtain.

Since Societies were to remain in existence, the Society committee set itself to devising programs for their improvement. Attempts were made to devise a system of Clubs for the non-Society boys, but this program was abandoned as unworkable. When the report finally came out in October— it was written by the Alumni Committee—it recommended essentially that the existing rules governing the Societies be kept, with the exception of a change in pledging procedure. Since 1936, all Upper Middlers had been pledged at one time, focusing too much attention, it was believed, on Society membership. The report proposed a return to the old system when boys were pledged individually throughout the year.[37] The report also reviewed the various reasons why the Societies were in trouble, as well as the changes that had taken place at Phillips Academy since 1930. The report put particular emphasis on the growing paternalism at the School, with the boys being subject to Faculty supervision in almost everything they did. In short, the report was unhappy about developments at Andover since 1930 and wanted the School to return to the good old days before 1930 when, it was believed, Phillips Academy was a stronger institution.[38] With the submission of this report, there ended what might be called Round 1 in the Society battle. As might have been expected, the undergraduate members of the Societies, realizing what a close call they had had, behaved in the most exemplary fashion for the next few years. Indeed a Faculty Committee appointed to supervise the Societies published a highly complimentary report for the School year 1943-44, in which they gave the boys top marks in almost every category. Especially noteworthy were instances of the Societies contributing to the School—establishing prizes, entertaining visiting teams, purchasing history books for the Library, and the like.[39] For the time being, at least, the Societies seemed to be safe.

Round 2 occurred in 1947, when Frederick S. Allis, Jr., Faculty Guardian of A.G.C., sent out a letter to the alumni of that Society expressing his concern over the condition of the Society. The undergraduates were having financial problems, the morale of the organization seemed to the Guardian to be far from high, and the Society's future seemed problematical. Allis added that he was becoming more and more uncomfortable as Guardian of an institution that he really did not approve of and was continuing more out of respect to "Cap" Benner than anything else. He added that he could find no qualified members of the Faculty who were interested in taking over the Guardianship. Shortly after this the undergraduates sent out a letter to the alumni insisting that they were a viable organization and asking for alumni support. On 6 June 1947 the annual meeting of the A.G.C. corporation was held in its house at Andover. After routine business had been disposed of, Brother Henry W. Hobson, newly elected President of the Board of Trustees, took the chair, and the meeting proceeded to a discussion of the future of the Society. First the undergraduates presented their case. They insisted that the Society was in good shape, that the financial difficulties had been straightened out, that the members were taking an active part in the life of the School and making important contributions to its welfare. Next the Faculty guardian stated his position and was politely mauled by the undergraduates for his pains. Bishop Hobson reported on the letters that had been written by alumni members unable to attend—some fifty in all. Of this number roughly one third unequivocally favored continuation of the Society, one third unequivocally favored dissolution, and one third qualified their position so much that it was impossible to categorize them. The meeting was then thrown open for general discussion, from which the following points emerged: It was agreed that the financial condition of the Society should not be a determining factor in any decision made about its future. A majority believed that the Society deserved to be continued. A minority believed that the Society was not in the best interests of the School. A majority wanted to know what the position of the Trustees was on Societies in general, quite apart from any particular problems of A.G.C. Finally, late in the evening, Bishop Hobson agreed to state that position. He reminded the brothers of his many years of loyalty to A.G.C. and of the leadership he had provided in the construction of the present Society house. He added that he had been strongly opposed to the action taken toward the Societies in 1943; he had been unable to attend the meeting in April 1943, when abolition had been voted, but he was confident that had he been there, he could have prevented that vote. Ever since his first arrival in Andover in 1909, he had been a loyal Society man.

But things had changed. Now the present Board of Trustees—all but one of whom was a Society man—had all but unanimously reached the conclusion that the Societies were a detriment to the School and that sooner or later they would have to go. He said that the Trustees planned no immediate action but he was not sure how long they would wait if the Societies did not dissolve themselves voluntarily. Bishop Hobson then presented six points on which the Trustee position was based. First, *the opinion of the Faculty*. With well over 90 percent of the Faculty in favor of abolition of the Societies, he found it difficult to believe that such a large majority could go wrong. He added that he had talked to many Faculty members and was convinced that they were not, as some had charged, simply echoing the Administration position. Second, *the loss of promising prospective students*. Bishop Hobson had had an opportunity to examine Exeter's admission correspondence and had found a disturbing number of letters that specifically stated that a family's choice of Exeter over Andover was the absence of Societies in the one, the presence in the other. Third, *the increasing protests of parents and alumni*. Bishop Hobson said he had been receiving a large number of letters on the Society question from parents and alumni. On the basis of these letters he would estimate that a large majority of parents and non-Society alumni and about half of the Society alumni favored dissolution. The School simply could not afford to have the Andover "family" split in this way. Fourth, *the testimony of a New York fund-raising organization*. The Trustees had engaged this firm to make a survey of the greater Andover community to determine strengths and weaknesses for the coming fund drive. The report of this firm stressed the Society problem as a serious handicap both for a successful fund drive and the selection of the best possible new Headmaster. Fifth, *the testimony of educators throughout the country*. Bishop Hobson said he had talked to many educators, both school and college men, and could not find one who thought that Societies were desirable in a secondary school. Sixth, *the problem of choosing a new Headmaster*. Bishop Hobson had heard from a number of quarters the statement that no really good man would consider the Headmastership of Andover as long as the Society question remained unsolved. He added that the choice would be the most important decision that the present Board would make.[40] The Bishop's speech was extra-

65. The Right Reverend Henry Wise Hobson of the Class of 1910, Bishop of Southern Ohio and President of the Board of Trustees of Phillips Academy, 1947–1966.

ordinarily effective, as evidenced by the fact that no one rose to challenge him when he had finished. After the speech some of those present wanted to move immediately toward dissolution of the Society, but instead a resolution was passed expressing the Society's willingness to cooperate with the Trustees in whatever proved to be for the best interests of the School and suggested the formation of a committee of Society alumni to work on the problem. The A.G.C. meeting accomplished little of a positive nature. What it did do, however, was to provide a platform from which Henry Hobson could explain the Trustee position. What he said that night went far beyond the confines of the A.G.C. house and did much to prepare the way for the final dissolution of the Societies in 1949.

John Mason Kemper became Headmaster of Phillips Academy in the summer of 1948 and realized from the start that one of the major problems facing him was to resolve the Society question. He started by doing an extremely thorough job of research on all aspects of the question, determined to approach the issue with an open mind. He talked and corresponded with many representatives of the Andover community—Faculty, undergraduates, Society alumni, non-Society alumni, parents, and educators.

In the meantime, the Inter-Society Alumni Committee, aware that a basic change was bound to come, had been meeting regularly in an effort to devise some plan short of complete dissolution. Much of the bitterness that had arisen from the ill-advised attempt to eliminate the Societies at one fell swoop in 1943 had disappeared; and there was a widespread desire to support the new Headmaster as he took over the reins. Yet some still refused to compromise on the issue. For example, an alumnus sent the following communication to the Inter-Society Alumni Committee:

> I feel that the action to abolish Societies was a distinct move to the
> Left, in the first instance, and that the present set-up is the beginning
> of the end of Andover as it has been known in the past. . . . Their
> term "un-democratic" or "democratic" as applied to Societies is a
> Leftist term, applied whenever Leftists subtly plan to undermine the
> foundations of an institution. . . . Is Andover going to join the
> parade of traitorous educators by glorifying socialism and atheistic
> internationalism? . . . I hope Bishop Hobson is there [at the meet-
> ing]. I have documentary evidence of his being associated with or
> sponsoring several Communist Front organizations or groups.[41]

John Kemper was not only studying the past history of the Societies but also seeing at first hand the effect they had on the School. He found that the Society boys were having a good time and were behaving in an irreproachable way, but also had to deal with a boy who tried to run away because he was unhappy over not being in a Society. He also became aware of four outstanding boys who were not considering Andover for their schooling because their parents disapproved of the Societies, and he began to wonder if Andover could have both Societies and full enrollment. He came to the wise conclusion that the arguments for and against Societies in the abstract tended to cancel each other out, and that no one who felt strongly on the matter could be induced to change his position by prolonged debate. But the unhappiness of non-Society boys at Andover and the unwillingness of many parents to send their sons to a School with Societies were disturbing facts that could have a profound influence on the future of the School. The conclusion was unavoidable that some kind of change must be made. Yet John Kemper kept an open mind on what that change should be and refused to close out any suggestion for reform.[42]

In his recollections, Jack Fuess describes his first talk with John Kemper on the Society problem and speaks of their being in "complete agreement."[43] This may well have been so, but any similarities in their approach to the difficult problem stopped there. Where Jack tried to ram through his program with no previous preparation among the interested parties, John Kemper took infinite pains to give everyone his day in court. While Jack tried to justify the abolition of Societies on ideological grounds, the Kemper approach was to avoid such emotion-packed areas and focus on the practical problems. While the Fuess plan plumped for complete, immediate abolition, John was willing to consider any alternative solutions that might be presented.

By the spring of 1949 the Headmaster had come to the definite conclusion that some kind of change was imperative. Once he had made up his mind—and he had canvassed the situation thoroughly—he determined to act. He believed that further postponement of the issue would be cowardly on his part; once his determination had been made, he believed he owed it to the whole Andover community to proceed. In addition, as a purely.tactical matter, he believed the alumni would be much more likely to support him during his first year on the job than if he were to wait. Accordingly, the Headmaster arranged with the Inter-Society Alumni Committee to have a meeting in New York on 13 May 1949, at which he told the group that he believed some definite change in the present Society system should be made. The Committee then presented what came to be known as the K.O.A. plan, whereby all Seniors would be taken into the Societies and, to provide continuity, ten Uppers would be elected by each Society in the spring. The Headmaster was asked to present this plan to the Faculty and the undergraduate Inter-Society Council as soon as convenient. It was characteristic of John Kemper that he agreed to do this. On his return to Andover, he called a Faculty meeting on the question. The Faculty reaffirmed (with one dissent) their vote of 1943 that Societies were not in the best interest of the School, thus demonstrating that there had been no change of opinion over the past five years. They then took up Plan A, as the K.O.A. plan was now called. They believed first of all that the boys would not like it, and they objected to the selective feature in the election of the Upper Middlers. As a result they voted Plan A an unsatisfactory solution (no dissenting vote). Shortly thereafter the Headmaster met with the undergraduate "Kings" of the various Societies. They were generally cooperative and understanding, though naturally apprehensive about what was in store for the Societies. Like the Faculty they could not accept Plan A and preferred complete abolition to it. The Headmaster believed their opposition to Plan A stemmed from the fact that they could not accept sharing their secrets and ritual with boys whom they had not elected. The next day the Headmaster took on all the undergraduate members of the Societies for a two-hour session. Many of the boys could see nothing wrong with the present system and presented eloquent statements in its defense. The Headmaster stressed a point he was to make again later—that the School must answer not the objections to the present system but the objectors, and that he doubted if they would be convinced by these arguments. Thus the Headmaster had presented his views and engaged in discussion with the Society alumni, the Faculty, the undergraduate "Kings," and the whole undergraduate Society group. Everyone directly connected with Andover had had his day in court.[44]

The climax came during the Commencement weekend of 1949, in a series of meetings. At a gathering on Friday afternoon the undergraduate members of the Inter-Society Council made a last-ditch effort to defend the existing system. The case against it was by no means conclusive, they said, but added that they would prefer complete dissolution to some compromise position like Plan A. Headmaster Kemper reiterated his position that the School had to answer the objectors, not objections in the abstract, and based his own case on two points: the harm done to non-members and the adverse effect the existence of Societies had on enrollment. Several alumni present thought that to take action at this time would be too precipitate and asked that discussion be continued for another year. Headmaster Kemper and others insisted that discussion had gone on since 1943 and that no useful purpose would be served by prolonging it. Dean Oswald Tower suggested that the best service the Societies could perform would be to abolish themselves voluntarily. At this point the meeting reached dead center. It was clear that if John Kemper were to ask the Societies to dissolve, they would do so to support him; this he was unwilling to do. At the same time, it was clear that the Headmaster hoped the Societies would move on their own initiative; this *they* were unwilling to do. To break the impasse Bishop Hobson, who had been sitting quietly in the back of the room signing diplomas, was asked to give his views. As he had done at the A.G.C. meeting two years before, the Bishop gave a masterful presentation. He reviewed his own dedication to Societies over a thirty-year period and refused to attack the institutions as bad in themselves. Most of the material in his statement was familiar to his audience; it was the tone—gentle and conciliatory—that gave it fresh vitality and power. When he was through, no one present could have resented anything he had said. If the proponents of the Societies were unable to agree with the Bishop's conclusions, they were at least able to accept them with no loss of self-respect.[45]

That same evening each of the seven Societies held a meeting to discuss the whole question and to take whatever action seemed appropriate. On Saturday afternoon the interested parties convened again to learn of the action taken by the individual Societies at their meetings and to see what further steps might be taken. As the individual Societies reported, it became clear that a widely varied series of actions had been taken. Two— P.A.E. and A.G.C.—had voted to dissolve their organizations and to take steps to arrange for the transfer of their property to the school. Two others —A.U.V. and K.O.A.—needed a two-thirds vote for action. The other three promised cooperation with a program of dissolution but had taken no formal vote. In the discussion that followed it was made clear that if the Societies were to be dissolved, next year's Seniors would be allowed to continue as members; they would simply not be allowed to elect any Upper Middlers. A final attempt was made to resurrect Plan A, but it soon became clear that support for it was minimal.

Toward the end of the meeting Bishop Hobson was asked if the Trustees were requesting dissolution, which indicated that there were still some who would find it easier to accept the decision if they were asked to do so by either the Trustees or the Headmaster. Bishop Hobson said the Trustees did not want to act for the Societies and much preferred that the Societies act together as a group in this matter, rather than for some to delay and thereby appear reluctant to support the decision. Thus ended Round 3 in the Society fight.[46] There were, to be sure, many loose ends to be tied up, but never again would an organized group of alumni attempt to preserve the Society system at Phillips Academy.

In the course of the next year the remaining Societies tooks the necessary steps to disband and to turn their property over to the School. Some financially strong ones established scholarship funds bearing the Society's name. In contrast to the bitterness that had characterized the earlier struggle, these final steps were accomplished in an atmosphere of good will that augured well for the future of the School. The Administration had no trouble finding uses for the Society houses, despite the fact that they had not been constructed for educational purposes. F.L.D., P.B.X., and E.D.P. became Faculty houses, which were much needed in a period when the Faculty was expanding. P.A.E., renamed Cooley House, became an extraordinarily useful social center for teas after athletic contests, alumni meetings, informal discussion groups, undergraduate and Faculty dinners, and the like. A.U.V., located as it was behind the chapel, became a center for the Religion Department and more recently for the School's counseling service. K.O.A. has been used for many purposes—as an alumni center, for Faculty housing, and for informal meetings. Finally, A.G.C., renamed

Benner House after Zeus Benner, was remodeled to become a grill for the undergraduates, where refugees from the Commons could buy hamburgers, cokes, and so forth. It is difficult to estimate the value of the real estate and invested funds turned over to the School, but the total must have been in the hundreds of thousands of dollars.[47] Whatever the precise value, the donations represented an extraordinary act of generosity on the part of the Societies and gave the lie to those who said that Society members were more loyal to their institutions than to the School. Phillips Academy owes a debt to these people that it can never repay.

So the Societies disappeared from Andover Hill. In bringing this about, John Mason Kemper deserves high marks for his eminent fairness, his insistence that everyone have his day in court, and his willingness to keep an open mind regarding alternative solutions. Yet it is doubtful if this difficult problem could have been resolved without Bishop Henry W. Hobson, the President of the Board of Trustees. His eloquence and perceptiveness convinced many of the proper decision to take and made it easier for all to swallow the bitter pill. It has now been over twenty-five years since the Societies were abolished. Few undergraduates today know anything about them, except as one may ask how a particular house came to be built in its present form. And the School has accomplished its two major purposes with the dissolution. The problem of unhappiness among boys who are not Society members has obviously gone. No longer can alumni write as did one who was at School in the 1920's:

> The only unhappy hours were Saturday nights in the Winter Term when the men with whom I had spent the whole day at classes, meals, sports and games would leave to go to their houses for the evening. The great event was when the fraternities were abolished.[48]

Nor could the Societies affect admissions. Generally speaking, the number of applicants has grown steadily each year, but whether the absence of Societies was responsible for this growth would be hard to prove. With the disappearance of the Societies, the School worked hard to provide alternative recreational facilities. The new dormitories constructed around Rabbit Pond all have common rooms, television, pool, and ping-pong tables. In an effort to bring the West Quadrangle dormitories up to date, a series of appendages was constructed to give them similar common room facilities. The undergraduates take these improvements pretty much for granted. Some had hoped that loyalty to dormitory—or more recently to cluster— might replace loyalty to Society, but for the most part this has not happened. In short, the School has never been able to find a replacement for the loyalty a Society man had for his Society. This is not surprising. The Societies became obsolete because they no longer represented the kind of social system that most Americans approved of. In the 1930's and the years following World War II there developed in the country an egalitarian outlook that was death on special privileges. In this atmosphere maintaining the Societies would inevitably have hurt the School. Those who said that Andover would never be the same without them were correct. Those now working at Phillips Academy hope that it is better. Certainly it is different.

CHAPTER SEVENTEEN

THE KEMPER ADMINISTRATION

WHEN THE Trustees learned of Jack Fuess's intention to resign in 1948, they immediately set to work to find a successor for him, a task that Bishop Henry W. Hobson, President of the Board, described as the only really important thing that Trustees have to do. The search was very open. Alumni, Faculty, students, and friends of the School were all invited to send in suggestions, either specific or general. Out of the large body of material that the Trustees received, a substantial number of correspondents suggested that what Phillips Academy needed was a man with a completely fresh approach—not necessarily a graduate of the School, not necessarily a graduate of an Ivy League college, but one who could look at the School without any preconceptions and judge its procedures and practices without being the prisoner of tradition. Although it is hard to say how much the Trustees were influenced by these opinions, the choice they made fitted their criteria almost precisely. The man who was solely responsible for bringing the name of the new Headmaster before the Trustees was James Phinney Baxter, President of Williams. During the war Baxter had been asked by the United States Army to join a group of professional historians in writing a history of the role of the Army in the conflict, and before long he was in Washington at work on the project. He and his fellow historians found themselves under the direction of a regular Army light-colonel named John Mason Kemper, who was then only thirty years old.[1] At the start many of the professional historians, most of whom were older than Kemper, viewed working under him with various degrees of apprehension; they simply could not believe that he had enough maturity and experience to ride herd on such a group of prima donnas. With the passage of time, however, the young colonel proved that he was more than up to his responsibilities. He arranged interviews between his historians and high-ranking Army officers; he got his people clearance to talk to soldiers on the field of battle; and he proved extraordinarily skillful at anticipating problems and dealing with them before they became serious. By the end of the war John Kemper had no more enthusiastic group of admirers than the professional historians who had worked with him on the Army history, and his chief, a Major-General, "treasured John Kemper as one would a jewel." Among his supporters, Phinney Baxter was one of the strongest, and when the Andover Headmastership became vacant, he pushed hard to get him the position. Baxter thought that if Kemper could manage him, he certainly could manage Andover. At first Kemper was amused at the suggestion. He knew nothing about private schools for boys and he was committed to an Army career, as so many of his ancestors had been. But Baxter continued to work on him and gradually effected a change in opinion. The period following World War II, as after most wars, was not easy for the Army, and career prospects were not particularly favorable. Temporary wartime promotions were rescinded and officers had to start again where they were before the war. John Kemper also remembered that the happiest time in his Army career was when he was a Company Commander, having full charge of a group of men; perhaps running a School would be something like that. He said later that if he had known the Korean War was coming, he would never have left the Army; fortunately for Andover, that conflict was still two years away. Finally, John Kemper agreed to meet with the Trustees and present himself as a candidate for the headmastership. At his first meeting with the Trustee Committee, Bishop Henry Hobson asked him: "What do you think you could do for Andover if you were Headmaster, Mr. Kemper?" To which he replied, "Isn't the question, Bishop, what I could get others to do with me to help the school?" A variation on this story has Kemper replying, "I don't consider myself a great man, but I have been able to do one thing. I can build a team. You have over eighty men on your faculty, and I think I could get them to work together as a team with a common purpose, and Andover would be great— not because of me, but as a result of the efforts of all those on the team."[2] This answer and the modest integrity of the man impressed the Trustees tremendously. Baxter's own testimony and that of several other historians who had worked with Colonel Kemper in Washington strengthened his case, and in a short time he was offered the position. The Trustees knew that they would be criticized for putting a regular Army officer in charge of the School, and when the choice was announced, there was a substantial amount of wailing and gnashing of teeth. But it took John Kemper only a few years to prove to everyone that they had nothing to fear.

Anyone who knew anything about Colonel Kemper's background should not have been surprised that he had chosen a career as an officer in the Regular Army, for his family tree bristled with military men.[3] Indeed, aside from a doctor or two, they all seem to have been army men, and the number was increased even further because almost all his female ancestors married army men as well. The earliest figure was Captain John Mason, who fought in the Pequot War in Connecticut in the seventeenth century.

For some reason the family seems to have skipped the Revolution, but an ancestor who was a naval officer fought in the War of 1812, and when the Civil War came along, many members of the family distinguished themselves. Two of his great grandfathers were general officers in the Union Army, both of them West Point graduates—Major General Edward Otho Cresap Ord and Brigadier General John Sanford Mason—while his Kemper grandfather served on General Halleck's staff. There were also Kempers in the Confederate army, though of a branch of the family only distantly related to John. One of them commanded a brigade in Pickett's division in the charge at Gettysburg and later became Governor of Virginia. John Kemper's paternal grandfather, Andrew Kemper, who was a doctor all his life, married a girl from Louisville, and his grandmother Mason was a dyed-in-the-wool Yankee. His own mother used to say that she could never have the two grandmothers in the house at the same time for they had not got the word that the Civil War was over. His grandmother Mason was perhaps the most colorful person in the whole family. As John remembers her early days out West:

> Whenever the infantry were ordered out on any kind of expedition, the column was always followed by a horse-drawn ambulance, and my grandmother, whenever she could work it, refused to be left behind, so that she accompanied her husband on a good many of these long hikes. . . . There were Indian scouts attached and after the troops were putting out the breakfast fire, she noted that the Indians were taking leftover flapjacks and sticking them in their breech clouts, and this would be their lunch. She always told the story of speaking to one and saying, "Well, aren't they kind of cold and soggy at lunchtime?" and the Indian's reply was, "Well, we'll get them down, fill up, it's all the same."
>
> The first baby, the one that died, was actually born in a tent, when they were out on campaign. And neither my grandmother nor my grandfather—it's amazing how little they knew about things—understood even how babies were born, and it was then that my grandmother made up her mind, having lost the first one because she really didn't know what was happening, to get busy and find out more about it. So she badgered doctors from that point on, and as a matter of fact was substantially a midwife for almost all of us who were her grandchildren. I think she presided over the birth of everyone of us.
>
> I guess it's fair to say that with a grandmother who lived that kind of life and with my mother and two aunts who kicked around all over in the Army that the women in the family were probably every bit as good soldiers as the men were.[4]

John Kemper's father, James Brown Kemper, was born and brought up in Cincinnati, where his father was a practicing physician. He went to Walnut Hills High School and to the University of Cincinnati, and hoped to win a Congressional appointment to West Point, but was beaten out by two other candidates who had higher high school records. Undaunted by this disappointment, he managed to obtain a direct commission in the Army and thus outranked the two who had beaten him for the Congressional appointments. Then began a lifetime Army career that included service in the Philippines in the early 1900's, in the Cuban pacification campaign in 1905, and in a number of posts in the United States, another tour of duty in the Philippines in the 1920's, and finally a position as recruiting officer in Manchester, New Hampshire, where he and his family remained until his retirement. John Kemper remembers his father as a man with a mechanical turn of mind. During his youth he had been a plumber's apprentice one summer, a carpenter's apprentice another, and an electrician's apprentice a third. In addition, he had learned a good deal of physiology from his doctor father and could, for example, name all the bones in the body. In the Army he was at one time post exchange officer and learned a good deal about wholesale and retail selling and buying. As a result, he was always getting good bargains. One Christmas he went from hardware store to hardware store buying broken or damaged electric train equipment for his son at next to nothing. Then he repaired it all so that John Kemper had the most elaborate electric train system in the area. As his son grew up, James Kemper saw to it that he learned many skills, took many trips, engaged actively in scouting, and generally was exposed to a wide variety of experiences. He could be stern with his son; when he gave him an order, he expected it to be obeyed. Above all, he wanted his boy to learn the code of the officer and gentleman. When he came back from the Phillipines in the early 1900's, he married Mercer Mason, who had just graduated from Abbot Academy, and the couple had two daughters as well as John. The marriage was extremely happy, and John Kemper grew up in a home where the qualities that were to distinguish him later were highly valued.

John Mason Kemper was born on 1 September 1912 at Fort D. A. Russell, Wyoming, where his father was stationed at the time.[5] The place of his birth was to cause him some embarrassment later when he wanted to get a passport and could not find his birth certificate. When he wrote to the Fort to get another copy, he was told that they had no record of his birth, nor was there any at the Army base in Cheyenne. Finally, availing himself of a special State Department dispensation, he got his sister to testify to the fact that he had been born, and the difficulty was overcome. The Kemper family were stationed at various posts in this country until after World War I—his father, incidentally, was bitterly disappointed that he was never assigned overseas—and then the family settled in Manchester, New Hampshire, which was to be more or less their home until James Kemper retired in 1935. We first hear of John Kemper's distinguishing exploits when he graduated as eighth grade valedictorian from Miss Alta Willard's Straw School in Manchester in 1926. For the next few years the family was on the move, as James Kemper was stationed first in the Philippines and then in Washington. As a result the son attended four high schools in the course of obtaining a secondary education. The two most important were the Central High School in Manila, and the Western High School in Washington, where he graduated in 1930. Early in his life John Kemper had set his heart on going to West Point, and once he finished high school, he set out to win an appointment. The strength of this resolve was tested when a cousin offered to send him to Princeton and then to the Harvard Business School, with all expenses paid, but the boy never hesitated; he thanked his cousin for the offer but turned it down. Obtaining an appointment for an Army brat was difficult because few officers were stationed long enough in any one state or in any Congressional district to be eligible for Senatorial or Congressional appointments, which almost always went to the sons of permanent residents. There were, however, a small number of competitive places reserved for the sons of Army officers; in John Kemper's year there were seventeen. Determining to compete for one of these places, he enrolled at the Columbian Preparatory School in Washington, a cram school for aspiring candidates for the Point. The schedule was rigorous; John Kemper would get up at five and study till breakfast, have classes all morning and for two hours after lunch, take an hour's break for exercise, then study two hours before supper, and finally work until ten o'clock. The plan was to take the students through the whole syllabus—mostly English, history, and mathematics—by Christmas and then go over it all again after Christmas. In addition the boys took practice exams each week. Finally, in March, came the real exams. The boys were kept on tenterhooks until May, but when John Kemper finally got the word, he found he had placed sixth out of about one hundred and was assured of a Presidential appointment. Ironically, after all that work, he soon learned that he had been named second alternate for a Congressional appointment from Vermont—his father knew one of the Congressmen there. When both the principal and first alternate failed their exams, John Kemper received the Vermont appointment, relinquishing his Presidential appointment to another boy further down the list. As the new appointee remembers it, he had never been in the state of Vermont in his life.[6]

John Kemper's years at the Point were in many ways golden.[7] Though he was no student, he had great capacity for leadership, and he graduated as one of the most outstanding members of his class. When he first arrived as a plebe in the summer of 1931, he was assigned, like the rest of his class, to the "beast barracks," where he was subjected to a certain amount of horseplay, though he always insisted that it was not hazing because there was nothing cruel about it. Plebes had to go everywhere at double time, and that, together with plebe maneuvers in the country around West Point, kept him in top-notch physical shape. He learned about the Honor Code and how, if a sentry called out "all right?" and a cadet answered, "all right," it meant that he was stating on his honor that he was bound for a legitimate place on a legitimate mission. The cadet companies were organized according to height, with the "flankers" being the tallest, the "runts" the shortest. John Kemper was about in the middle. During most of his career at the Point he had two roommates—in cadet jargon he had "a house with two wives." During his first year he aspired to become an athlete and went out for soccer, swimming, and track. Though he never achieved varsity standing in any of these sports, he did make the JV, which had a great advantage for him as a plebe. Members of the JV teams were not "braced"—that is, made to sit at rigid attention—during meals. Again as a plebe he used to take long Sunday afternoon hikes in the surrounding country, partly because he liked them and partly to avoid the horseplay he might encounter if he stayed around the barracks. The plebes had no Christmas vacation, but he was cheered when his sister and other members of the family came to visit him during the holiday season. He also had some histrionic talent and did tap-dancing in the cadet Hundredth Night Show. When his sister entered Vassar, he had a better chance of seeing girls than did most of his classmates. She used to bring a group of girls over regularly, and they all would engage in informal "hops." Though the cadets were paid modest salaries, they never had much spending money. Thus if a cadet wished to take a girl to the hotel that was located within West Point limits, it was wise to invite one who could pick up the tab. Otherwise, they would have to go to a rather sleazy restaurant called "Boodler's," where the cadets could use chits. It was during his plebe year that John Kemper first started teaching Sunday School at the Point. He admitted that he had little interest in religious training, but Sunday School teachers were given a weekend pass a term, which was something else again. His first year he taught a class of six small boys. He said he controlled them by seating them in two rows of three and then sitting himself in the middle and keeping poised above their heads a hymn book, so that he could play on their heads as on a xylophone. The next year he was promoted to teach thirteen-year-old girls, who thought all cadets were heroes, and he had no further trouble. His teaching must have been a success, none the less, for he was made Sunday School Superintendent during his last year. One of his weekend leaves he spent in New York with a very attractive Bostonian named Sylvia Pratt, a St. Catherine's graduate and the daughter of a distinguished Boston doctor, whom he had met on summer vacations. They danced to Guy Lombardo, lunched atop the Empire State Building, and generally had what John Kemper considered "a field day." It was his first heavy date, he thought. He complained about a very pedestrian course in European history that he had to take, but he worked at it and did well enough to have his name put in a file as a possible future history teacher at the Point. During his last year, as a firstclassman, important honors came his way. He was appointed Regimental Adjutant, the officer in charge of parades and drills and also the one responsible for reading orders during meals. Since the mess hall was anything but peaceful at mealtime, the Regimental Adjutant needed a stentorian voice and cast-iron lungs to make himself heard. He was at the same time elected Class President, perhaps an even more coveted honor, since he was elected to this position by his classmates. When he graduated on 12 June 1935 with a Bachelor of Science degree and a commission as a Second Lieutenant of Infantry, he was clearly one of the most distinguished members of his class.

If John Kemper had dreamed of leading troops into battle in the course of his up-coming Army career, that dream was to be shattered, for a good part of his time with the military was spent on the teaching, studying, and writing of history. He was first assigned to the Eleventh Infantry at Fort Benjamin Harrison, Indiana, and two years later attended the Infantry School at Fort Benning, Georgia. A year after graduation, after a courtship that was punctuated by a few squalls, he married Sylvia Pratt, and in due course the couple had three little girls. In 1939 he was brought back to the Military Academy to teach history; to improve his knowledge of his subject, he studied Far Eastern History at the Harvard Summer School and earned an M.A. in History from Columbia in 1942. That same year he was assigned to Military Intelligence in Washington and the following year was asked to develop and supervise a combat history of the United States Army in World War II. It was in this position, as we have seen, that he caught the attention of President Baxter of Williams, with such momentous results for Phillips Academy. John Kemper did not wish to follow in his father's footsteps and spend the entire war stateside, so in 1945 he was assigned to the Mediterranean Theater of Operations to survey the use of manpower in that area. In 1943 he was awarded the Legion of Merit and in 1945 the Oak Leaf Cluster in lieu of a second Legion of Merit for his wartime services. After the war he returned to Washington, where he was assigned to the Army Historical Division, where he was serving when the Trustees of Phillips Academy made their offer.[8] His career to date had been extraordinarily free of mistakes. The only one he remembered came when he talked back to an upperclassman at West Point; later he apologized. But above all he had a great gift for getting people to work with him in cooperative endeavor; he had proved that at West Point, he proved it again in dealing with the civilian historians during the war, and he was soon to prove it even more dramatically at Andover.

The entire Andover community eagerly awaited the arrival of John

Kemper, his wife Sylvia, and their three daughters in the summer of 1948. There may have been a modicum of apprehension as well, for unlike previous headmasters, John Kemper was an unknown quantity. When Jack Fuess assumed office, he had been a member of the Andover community for twenty-five years and was widely known among the alumni. He had merely to move from Tucker House to Phelps House and he was in office. When the Kempers finally arrived, it soon became clear that the new Headmaster would be very different from his predecessor. The Trustees had provided Jack Fuess with a large black limousine as the school car, and Jack had hired a chauffeur to drive him about. The Faculty wondered what kind of school car the Kempers would have. One morning there appeared in the Kemper driveway a new two-door Ford. This decision proved a ten-strike for the new Headmaster. It announced much more clearly than words that he had no intention of trying to achieve status through his automobile. There had been no children in Phelps House for many years; now the sight of girls' bicycles leaning against the front steps bespoke a family in residence. Once installed, John Kemper initiated a policy that was to continue throughout his entire administration of inviting any member of the Faculty or staff who had something on his mind to come in and talk it over. And he made it clear that this offer was open to *anyone*—not just department heads and administrative officers. The new Headmaster was an extraordinarily good listener, and many a Faculty member found comfort and understanding from a talk with the new Headmaster. In all he did during these early months he sought to establish the fact that he would play no favorites. Jack Fuess's record in this area was by no means free from blemish, with serious effects on Faculty morale, and John Kemper was determined to give everyone equal treatment.

Another point that he wished to have recognized early was that he was his own man and beholden to no one. Again his predecessor had often depended heavily on the advice and counsel of a few members of the Faculty and administration; John Kemper wanted to give everyone his day in court, but the final decision had to be his. And this applied to the Trustees as well as to the staff. He once said that if he had canvassed a question thoroughly, thought long and hard about it, and finally reached a decision, that decision was irrevocable and if the Trustees did not support him, he would resign and "pump gas." At an early Trustee meeting, for example, the question of wages for the nonacademic members of the staff came up. The new Headmaster believed them to be shockingly low and recommended raises. Some of the Trustees demurred, pointing to the sizable deficit the School had already incurred. John Kemper said that he simply could not head an institution where many of the employees were so badly underpaid, and he got his raise. James Gould, the Treasurer and an old hand in Andover matters, expected to take the new Headmaster under

66. *Lieutenant-Colonel John Mason Kemper at about the time he was elected the Eleventh Headmaster of Phillips Academy.*

his wing and advise him on many matters. The new man embarked on a policy of ostentatiously ignoring Gould's advice until it became clear to all that the Treasurer held no privileged position within the administration. Kemper also inherited an unsavory mess in the Music Department, occasioned by the fact that Jack Fuess had led two men to believe that they would be the next head. The new Headmaster worked out a compromise arrangement for one year, to give him time to study the problem, but one of the contenders refused to accept the arrangement and resigned. Some of his friends brought pressure to bear on the Headmaster to find some way of keeping the man at Andover. Kemper refused to budge; but he bore the man no ill will, as evidenced by the fact that he succeeded in bringing him back to Andover some years later. Finally, he went to the mat with J. Roswell Gallagher, the distinguished school physician, over a basic matter of administrative policy. Under the Fuess regime Gallagher had had a completely free hand when it came to student health. Jack Fuess never interfered, and if Dr. Gallagher wanted something, he got it. John Kemper had no pretensions of understanding student health problems, but he still insisted that final decisions in this area had to be his. To this Dr. Gallagher could not agree, and so they parted company. If the new Headmaster could best someone of Gallagher's stature—for the Trustees supported the Kemper position—it was clear that he was not a man to be trifled with. Thus after three years in office the new Headmaster had demonstrated that he could not be pushed around, that he was indeed his own man, and for the rest of his term no one challenged a decision of his, once he had made it clear that it was a matter of confidence.

None of this was easy, particularly when his policy of no favorites among the Faculty precluded his turning to them for reassurance. He found that there was a new employee in the Heating Plant and turned to him as someone he could talk to without jeopardizing his position. He used to wander around the campus at night, looking up at the lighted dormitories and wondering if the School were really functioning properly. Eventually he would wind up at the Heating Plant for a talk with his new friend, who was uncontaminated by Phillips Academy politics.

There were other new problems to meet. As part of a program to acquaint the undergraduates with the issues of the Presidential Election of 1948, the School invited representatives of the various candidates to speak in Assembly from time to time. To present the position of Henry Wallace and the Progressive Party, the Reverend Amos Murphy, pastor of the Unitarian Church in Lawrence, was invited to speak. Murphy was a private school and college graduate who never allowed the fact that his congregation was minuscule to deter him from dealing with issues head-on. He had recently campaigned for the Lawrence School Committee, riding his bicycle through the streets of Lawrence and haranguing the populace, only to be badly beaten at the polls. Murphy's appearance on the stage of George Washington Hall was electric; a huge bear of a man, with charisma to spare, he took a frankly pro-Russian position on the affairs of the day, echoing that of his leader, Henry Wallace. John Kemper was obviously upset by this, and underestimating the basic horse sense of the average undergraduate, he attempted a rebuttal of Murphy a few days later. Not only was his speech not very effective; he found that at least some of the undergraduates resented the fact that he thought he had to reply. He clearly learned his lesson from it, for when, two years later, in the midst of the Korean War, the Secretary-General of the Communist Party of Massachusetts, Daniel Boone Schirmer, was invited to speak, he took it in his stride. Schirmer accused the United States of starting the Korean War and made other far-fetched charges. The effect on the undergraduates, however, was anything but what the speaker had desired. Their reaction was rage, and, as someone said, had there been a recruiting sergeant outside George Washington Hall at the end of the program, he could have signed up most of the School. John Kemper's behavior during this episode was exemplary; he supported the invitation to Schirmer, he let nature take its course as far as dealing with what he said was concerned, and he defended the School's position to the few parents—he hated to admit that they were army officers—who protested the fact that a Communist had been invited to speak. Never again would he try to interfere with the free flow of ideas, as he did in the Murphy case.

In October of 1948 came the Inauguration of the new Headmaster. A ceremony such as this had not been considered necessary for earlier headmasters, but since John Kemper was not widely known in the academic world, over two thousand headmasters, college presidents, and the like were invited to install the new man properly. The auspices were favorable: the fall weather was gorgeous, the academic costumes, colorful, the mood, sanguine. The main address was given by President James R. Angell of Yale University, who had done yeoman's service at past Andover ceremonies as well; the new Headmaster, addressing himself primarily to the undergraduates, delivered a simple, sincere address; and Robert Q. Anderson, President of the Student Body, spoke for the undergraduates. When the festivities were over, it was clear that John Mason Kemper had been properly established as Andover's Eleventh Headmaster.[9]

John Kemper came to Andover convinced that his primary task was to build a strong and effective Faculty. In a report to the Trustees written after he had been at the School for five years, he spelled out a policy toward the Faculty that would result in his greatest achievement during his term as Headmaster. "A school can be only as good as its teachers," he wrote. "Andover's greatest asset is its tradition of great teaching. The tradition will survive and grow stronger as the spirit of the faculty is high, as living and working conditions are good, as an atmosphere of mutual respect and unity of purpose prevail."[10] On another occasion, speaking of Andover's policy of developing a strong Faculty, he wrote:

> It is remarkable also in that it so clearly accepts the premise that a teacher is not a hired hand, but a highly trained professional whose experience and judgment are vital assets to society, and for whom an adequate salary and satisfactory working conditions must be provided. It places the teacher in his school on a par with the lawyer in his firm or the doctor in his hospital. It is a way of persuading the teacher that others respect him and his calling.[11]

To achieve these lofty aims, he devised a series of programs to build Faculty morale and thereby effectiveness. For his own dealing with the Faculty he had four basic rules: One, play no favorites; two, consult the man concerned before making a decision affecting him or his work; three, recognize merit and a good job any and all ways you can; and four, build up the dignity of the profession of teaching.[12] These four rules indicate an extraordinary sensitivity to teachers and their needs; it is small wonder that as he began to put them into practice, Faculty morale soared. He was fully aware of the difficulties in the life of an average Faculty member, working as he did as teacher, housemaster, coach, and activity director, and spoke of "the special stresses and strains" that such a position entailed. Fairness was the number one virtue in dealing with teachers. Thus it was vital that in such matters as housing, committee work, classroom load, and the like, every effort be made to ensure equitable treatment. A school like Andover could not prosper, the Headmaster insisted, unless the Faculty had a large share in its government, and he cited such areas as admissions, scholarships, discipline, the awarding of prizes, and the determination of curriculum as legitimate areas for Faculty action. In some cases Faculty decisions might technically be in the form of recommendations to the Headmaster and Trustees, yet these were rarely, if ever, reversed. Another important ingredient in good Faculty morale was keeping them informed of what was going on in the school. Nothing was more destructive of good morale among the Faculty than to have things sprung on them without adequate warning. In the past the Trustees had usually been distant figures, whom most of the Faculty did not know. John Kemper was convinced that if the two groups were to work together in harmony, they must become better acquainted, and to achieve that end he arranged a series of Trustee-Faculty dinners. In similar fashion he believed that schoolmasters had a lot to learn from other professionals, and arranged meetings between the Faculty and leading psychologists and psychiatrists from Boston. Although the gatherings never accomplished as much as he had hoped, they were often thought-provoking. One Boston doctor, for example, rocked the Faculty by suggesting that Phillips Academy did its best job educating the sons of relatively wealthy people and that programs for poor boys, whom the Academy did not know how to handle, should be junked. But all these exchanges had a common theme—trying to keep the Faculty informed about the School itself and about the world of adolescent education generally.

These general programs might give the Faculty a sense of running the School and being fully informed about its problems, but it was in the disposition of material benefits that the greatest boost to morale could be achieved—all the more so because in the previous administration the disposition of such benefits had been done in an unsystematic and at times bizarre way. For the first time in the history of the School a firm salary scale was established, with fixed starting salaries for both bachelors and married men and minimum increments for future years. Provision was also made for merit increases above and beyond the minimum. In his first five years John Kemper succeeded in raising both the average and the median salary by one thousand dollars, had narrowed the gap between the salaries of bachelors and married men, and brought the foundation salaries more in line with the rest of the scale. Another problem concerned tenure. In the past the length of time of appointments had often been undefined and quixotic. Now a system was adopted whereby a young teacher would start with three one-year appointments, then three-year appointments until he was forty, and then five-year appointments until retirement. This procedure made it possible for the Headmaster to let someone go but with plenty of warning. For example, a man might be told at the end of his second year that he must go but would then be given the third year to find another job and appear to be leaving Phillips Academy through his own choice. This was true of the sixteen men who left during John Kemper's first five years; their departure was without loss of face or self-respect. Realizing how difficult it was for the average teacher to provide a college education for his children, the Trustees, at the Headmaster's urging, started a program of college grants of six hundred dollars a year for Faculty children. Finally, although the program was by no means fully implemented, the new Headmaster had started on a program of sabbatical leaves for the Faculty, in the belief that extended absence from the School once every seven or ten years would provide an opportunity for travel, study, research, or new and different experience that must inevitably refresh the Andover teacher and sharpen his teaching.

It was relatively easy to be fair with salaries and perquisites that could be measured in dollars, but quite another to achieve equity in the assignment of Faculty houses. The previous administration's housing policy had been practically nonexistent; there was, as noted above, the occasion on which Jack Fuess had led three Faculty members to believe that each would have a certain house. John Kemper was practically starting from scratch. The first decision was to award houses on the basis of seniority and to establish a Faculty committee to determine such seniority. This was more difficult than might appear, particularly for members of the Faculty who had joined the staff at a relatively advanced age. What to do, for example, with a fifty-year-old teacher who had been on the Academy Faculty for ten years and had taught in a day school previous to that? How should those with long terms of dormitory service be related to those who had served the School just as faithfully but had lived in houses with no boys? The committee, struggling manfully, devised a procedure that was a tremendous improvement over the old hit-or-miss system. There were clashes, nevertheless. Early on, a family with one child and a family with four children and one year less of seniority both wanted the same roomy house. The committee stuck to its seniority rule and assigned the house to the one-child family, but a serious flap was created. Indeed, John Kemper soon became convinced that this was an area in which he could not win, and he dreaded housing spats more than anything else he had to deal with. For one thing, most Faculty problems involved the husband alone; with housing, the Faculty ladies entered the arena, and the new Headmaster hated to disappoint them. He finally embarked on a scheme that he hoped would tend to equalize housing. Obviously, there was wide variation in the houses themselves, but at least they could all have equal kitchens. And so he proceeded to modernize the kitchens in all the Faculty quarters. Another housing problem developed from the School's practice of many years to depend largely on bachelors for the manning of dormitories. When John Kemper took over as Headmaster, there were sixteen Faculty quarters that were suitable for bachelors only. This often meant that the Headmaster would be unable to hire a married man, because the housing was inadequate, even though he might be much more desirable than the best available bachelor. To meet this problem the Headmaster started a program of remodeling bachelor quarters to make them available for married members of the Faculty. For example, Paul Revere Hall, Bishop Hall, and the three cottages, all originally bachelor quarters, were converted. As the Headmaster put it, most of the men he wanted to hire had already been latched onto by some girl, and this would help him meet this problem. John Kemper soon discovered that "hot-topping" was a real status symbol among the Faculty. To have one's driveway and front walk paved with asphalt was a sign that one had arrived. He also discovered that there was a great deal of bitterness over who got hot-topped. Accordingly, he took control of hot-topping himself, to make sure that it was done with an even hand. The result of all these programs for the Faculty, administered with extraordinary fairness, was higher Faculty morale, and this paid off in superior work with the students. As the Headmaster summed it up:

> My own faith is in the individual. A gifted youngster under the influence of a good man will develop into a good man, more likely than he will under an elaborate system of rules and regulations. A

system is both impersonal and inflexible, whereas a man is not. . . .
My colleagues are experienced enough, wise enough, and numerous
enough (one teacher to ten boys) to handle the number of boys we
have. Moreover, they are and have been doing a remarkable job
with energy and patience and spirit.[13]

When John Kemper became Headmaster, the Dean of the Faculty was
Oswald Tower, an elder statesman who had for many years been a brilliant teacher of mathematics at the School. He was also one of the country's
leading authorities on basketball and often served on committees to revise
various aspects of the game. Ozzie reached retirement age after the new
Headmaster's first year, and the question of who would be his successor
was a lively topic of discussion on the Hill. Characteristically, John Kemper
decided to appoint no successor immediately, to give him more time to
canvass the situation. And it was not until 1953 that he announced the
appointment of Alan R. Blackmer as Dean of the Faculty. This appointment recognized the academic and educational leadership that Al Blackmer
had already won for himself on the Phillips Academy Faculty and was to
provide him with a base from which he could make further important
contributions in the future. A graduate of Williams, where he had a distinguished academic record and had been, as well, one of the outstanding
collegiate basketball players of his generation, Al Blackmer had done
graduate work at the University of Chicago and came to Andover as an
English teacher in 1925. After spending a year in France at no pay, he
returned to Andover, where he would serve for the next forty-two years.
During his early years on the Hill he proved to be an extraordinarily gifted
English teacher with a contagious enthusiasm for his work that was immediately transmitted to his students. One alumnus writes:

> I am sure that no history of Andover over the last generation can
> fail to give an absolutely major place to the impact of Al Blackmer
> on the school. . . . he was by all odds (and by at least one order of
> magnitude) the best teacher I have ever known and one of the people
> who I can genuinely feel impacted in a major way on my intellectual
> development and on my life. . . . his upper middle special English
> course was by all odds the most stimulating, exciting and mind-
> developing course I ever took in school or college. . . . If I had to
> give up my entire college education, I am not sure that I would have
> sacrificed as much intellectual development as if I had failed to have
> that course experience. When we had finished dissecting *Othello*,
> reading *War and Peace*, and sharing (the only appropriate word)
> the *Ordeal of Richard Feverel*, we had a feel for literature even if
> we never read another serious book. . . . But it was much more than
> an English course. . . . he forced us into propaganda analysis. . . . as

a way of approaching learning with a healthy skepticism for what one reads and is told. . . . he gave us all, I think, a profound respect for intellectualism in the best sense of the word. . . . derived mainly from the exciting and valuable experience of associating with him as a man.

Henry Ehrlich, '30, writes:

First Alan Blackmer, who could be just as caustic and tough as Horace Poynter—but who cared, and genuinely wanted you to learn. His class was my first brush with Shakespeare—the beginning of my happiest literary association. Who but Blackmer would have chosen Richard II as an introduction to the world's greatest writer? The result was electrifying—I still never miss a performance if it is within 100 miles, and I can quote great gobs of the play. It was he who interested me in O'Neill—I read all that O'Neill had published to date during my last two years of Andover. And it was he who spurred—maybe dreamed up would be a better phrase—the revival of *The Mirror*. . . . Blackmer insisted on quality in *The Mirror* and while he may not have achieved as much as he might have liked in a literary sense, he certainly inspired a handsome publication. . . . In my senior year Mr. Blackmer contracted TB, and the treatment seems to have been bedrest. . . . Sick as he was, he always made us feel welcome at his house. . . . There was cider and cookies, a warm, always friendly Mrs. B. We used to stretch out on the rug in his living room and play the Tchaikowsky 4th, 5th and 6th over and over and over, on his new victrola, as we called a record player in those days, with its deep floor-shaking resonance. Those could have been my happiest hours at Andover.

Another evidence of Al's ability to appeal to undergraduates—at least the abler ones—was his Saturday night discussion group. Each year he would invite a dozen or so of his students to meet regularly at his house to settle the affairs of the universe. This, of course, meant giving up Saturday night movies for the year. Yet Al's boys remained faithful to this commitment while it was being conducted in the 1930's, and many of them remember with pleasure and excitement the lively give and take that went on in the Blackmer living room. As Al got more and more involved in administration, he was obliged to give up some of his teaching, and like many administrator-teachers he found it difficult to maintain the excitement of the earlier years. He was always, of course, a highly skilled practitioner of his craft, but his courses did not sing the way the early ones did. In his prime he was *sans pareil* on the Andover Faculty.

When Claude M. Fuess became Headmaster, he turned to Al Blackmer for help with a variety of projects. The Headmaster could no longer con-

546 : THE MODERN ANDOVER

tinue to edit the *Phillips Bulletin*, as he had done for many years, and he asked Al to be his successor. For the rest of the decade Al edited the magazine with flair and care and more than maintained the standard of editorial excellence that his predecessor had established. In 1935 he and some other friends on the Faculty founded the Andover Evening Study Program for Adults, as has been mentioned in an earlier chapter. Wilbur J. Bender, the first Director of the Andover Summer Session, enlisted in the Navy shortly after the close of the first session, and Al was drafted to serve as head of the Summer School for the next two years. During this same period he was acting as Head of the English Department, a position he held until succeeded by Emory Basford right after the war. In short, he was being bounced from one position to another without ever having time to get thoroughly established in any of them. By 1950 he was tired of the peripatic existence that had characterized his career in the 1940's.

Thus when John Kemper asked him to accept the permanent position of Dean of the Faculty in 1953, he agreed at once. He had had a variety of experiences to prepare him for the position. He was a brilliant teacher, a proven administrator, and a man capable of such imaginative projects as the Evening Study Program. Generally speaking John Kemper and Alan Blackmer worked effectively together as a complementary pair. The Headmaster had always insisted that he had no intention of trying to dominate academic matters, preferring to leave those to the Faculty and the Faculty's Dean. On the other hand, academic matters were Al Blackmer's specialty, and he was able to provide leadership in the very area where the Headmaster felt unsure of himself. Yet there was one area that caused friction between the two men. As Dean of the Faculty, Al Blackmer understandably thought that he should deal with the Faculty. John Kemper approved of this as long as it was limited to discussion of the curriculum and other School programs, but he insisted on reserving to himself all dealings with the Faculty that involved salary, tenure, personal problems, and the like. This was something very close to him that he refused to delegate. As a result, Al Blackmer found it difficult to deal with individual Faculty members when they knew that he had no power to affect their lives in any substantial way. One can argue forever as to which man was right in this difference of opinion. Yet the arrangement did not prevent either man from performing effectively in his sphere.[14]

Every new headmaster wants to examine his school's curriculum, with the possibility of devising a new one that will have his brand on it, and John Kemper was no exception. In 1950, therefore, he appointed a Curriculum Committee consisting of the heads of all the major departments, under the chairmanship of Alan Blackmer, to consider the problem. It will be remembered that the last important curricular revision had been in 1933, when the Latin requirement was dropped and a four-year History

67. *Alan Rogers Blackmer, Instructor in English, 1925–1953, Dean of the Faculty, 1953–1968.*

sequence introduced. After almost twenty years of operation under this curriculum, there had developed an increasing groundswell of opposition among the Faculty. The major objection was to the curriculum's inflexibility. There were so many required courses that the individual student had little chance to pursue in depth a subject that interested him. The curriculum also contained an excessive number of courses, particularly minor courses, that tended to force a student to scatter his shots over so broad an area that it was difficult to get a truly solid exposure in any. Finally, there was concern that the curriculum was too demanding for some boys—particularly Upper Middlers—with the result that there were too many failures and disappointments among the undergraduates.[15] The 1933 curricular revision had been adopted with the almost unanimous support of the Faculty. No such luck this time. The Committee could agree that each boy at Andover should have four years of English, three of mathematics, and three of a foreign language, but from there on, there was strife. As is always the case in discussions of this kind, each department was anxious to protect its own turf, and the Committee split into factions, no one of which could command a majority. Some wanted to have four five-hour courses each year and do away with minors; others wanted all courses beyond the basic core to be electives; and so it went. Dr. Arthur B. Darling of the History Department was also a strong supporter of requiring two languages and thus often found himself lining up with the language people. As the year wore on, the Committee meetings often became acrimonious, as it became clearer and clearer that there could be no common ground on which a majority of the Committee could agree. Finally, instead of reporting to the Faculty a single recommendation, the Committee presented four plans and in effect told the Faculty to choose the one they liked best.[16] Plans I and II were similar. They each envisaged the basic core of four years of English, three of mathematics, and three of a foreign language, to which was added a year of science and a year of American history. Minors in Bible and in art and music would account for a thirteenth unit. The diploma requirement would be sixteen units, thus allowing for three electives. Plan II in effect simply increased the diploma requirement to eighteen units and made provision for more major courses being taken. Plan III, conceived by Dr. Darling, pretty much kept the existing curriculum intact but provided for a committee of class officers to ensure flexibility in a boy's program. The implication of this plan was that some diploma requirements might be waived in particular cases. Finally, Plan IV was the existing curriculum, with suggestions as to how to lighten the burden of assignments in existing courses. The four plans were to be presented in order to the Faculty at a meeting in the fall of 1950. After Plan II had been presented, however, the Headmaster, whether inadvertently or not, indicated obliquely that he favored that plan. This so enraged Dr. Darling that he refused to present his plan, claiming that the Headmaster had already decided the outcome. The Faculty, many of whom were looking for leadership in this jungle, then proceeded to vote in Plan II, and the curriculum had presumably been revised. It is quite possible that John Kemper, hoping to avoid a curricular donnybrook at the meeting, decided to make his own view known; in any event his position on the matter was decisive. Like most curricular revisions, this one was hardly earth-shaking. Only one year of history was required instead of four; only one foreign language was required; there was some reshuffling of minor courses. But for the most part the courses that had characterized an Andover education in the past remained intact. Ray Wyman Wilbur once said that it was harder to change a curriculum than to move a graveyard;[17] his observation was borne out to a large extent by the Andover experience of 1950–51.

Even though the Phillips Academy curricular revision may not have been breath-taking, a development of great importance to American education grew out of it. In 1950 the Headmaster asked a group of alumni to make up an Alumni Educational Policy Committee whose charge was to work with the Faculty Committee and other interested persons in developing a new curriculum. While this Committee addressed itself to their basic charge, their discussions ranged over a wide variety of educational matters much broader in scope than the specifics of the School's problems. Members of the Alumni Committee from the colleges, particularly Wilbur J. Bender, then Dean of Harvard, and Thomas C. Mendenhall, Professor of History at Yale, enlarged the discussions to include the whole relationship between school and college and the problems arising from that relationship. In the spring of 1951 a much larger group of Deans and headmasters met to consider what might be done about some of these larger problems, and out of this discussion came the proposal that three schools—Andover, Exeter, and Lawrenceville—and three colleges—Harvard, Princeton, and Yale—should sponsor a study of the relationship between the last two years of school and the first two of college. The Fund for the Advancement of Education, an adjunct of the Ford Foundation, made a generous grant to support the study, and a six-man committee, one faculty member from each of the institutions involved, was formed to carry out the work. The Chairman was Alan R. Blackmer of Andover. Writing to Dr. Clarence Faust of the Fund for the Advancement of Education, John Kemper presented the problem:

> Perhaps because too little research and thought have been given to the matter in the past, it appears obvious that school and college programs, especially during the important years from the 11th through the 14th grade, have not been planned as coherent wholes. Boys from the best independent schools often report that their early courses in college are repetitious and dull. We are much concerned that some of our best boys seem to lose interest in their work during

their first and second years in college. It looks as though the country might no longer be able to afford the waste involved in the transition from school to college, especially for gifted and well-trained boys.[18]

The Committee went to work with a will, though only the Chairman was relieved of other duties so as to devote full time to the project. They first conducted a study of the 341 boys who were graduates of one of the three schools and currently enrolled at one of the three colleges as members of the Class of 1951. This served to point up duplication of courses taken, frequency of advanced standing, and the like. For example, the survey revealed that of 209 graduates of the the three schools who took physics, chemistry, or biology in college, almost half were taking the same course they had taken in School. Even worse, most engineering students spent four years—two in School and two in college—getting credit for elementary physics and elementary chemistry. In short, they repeated *both* subjects, yet their grades in the repeated courses were not noticeably higher.[19]

Next the Committee engaged a group of experienced teachers, most of them at the secondary school level, to make surveys of exactly what was taught in a particular subject in both secondary school and college. Sample examinations were studied, reading lists examined, and correlation between school and college courses checked out. These surveys tended to indicate an almost complete lack of contact between school and college teachers of the same subject. The third method of getting information was to send a detailed questionnaire to fifty-eight graduates of Andover, Exeter, and Lawrenceville who were in the Class of 1952 at the Big Three. Since the students were asked to comment on their education, the results, of necessity, would have to be judged subjectively, but the questionnaires yielded a rich mine of material nonetheless. Here is what one of the questioned had to say:

> My greatest dissatisfaction is that I wasted two years before getting to the business of getting a college education. My last year in school, though I did less work than before, was not a time in which I loafed. The same cannot be said of my first two years of college. I am to blame mainly for this, but the college bears some responsibility for letting itself be an anticlimax intellectually.[20]

Finally, the Committee held a series of panel discussions to which distinguished scholars in various fields were invited. The topics discussed were, among others, "Motivation," "Values," "Emotional and Social Development," and "Testing and Measurement," as well as the basic academic disciplines. From these various sources a substantial amount of relevant material was collected and digested, so that the Committee's final report was based on solid evidence.

The final report of this Committee was an impressive document that immediately had a wide influence on American schools and colleges. It began by stating certain convictions on which the report as a whole was based. First, the Committee believed in individual excellence and wished to foster programs that would lead to such excellence. They admitted frankly that in this report they were primarily concerned with the superior student. Programs and facilities for mass education in the United States had made rapid strides since World War II. It was now time to concentrate more on quality rather than quantity in educational matters. Providing imaginative programs for the superior student would affect all students, however; it was the Committee's belief "that standards can be pulled up from the top more easily than they can be pushed up from the bottom." And they cited the statement of one headmaster that the chief danger to American education was "contentment with mediocrity."[21] The Committee took a conservative position when they insisted that content was fully as important as method in present-day education. This point was to prove very important later in winning the support of conservative institutions for what became the Advanced Placement program. Finally, the Committee admitted that both mind and emotions were vital considerations in developing a successful educational system. This report would concern itself almost exclusively with matters of the mind, but the members were quick to admit that the physical, social, and emotional development of the student was equally important.

Space does not permit discussion of sections of the report dealing with the concept of a liberal education in general or with philosophical terms. Building on these general concepts, the Committee proposed several curricular programs covering the 11th grade through the 14th grade that were conceived as logical progressions over those four years and would avoid the sharp and often irrational break that was occurring between school and college. One of the major purposes of the program was to enable the student to progress steadily within a given field and not be obliged to submit to sterile repetition of material previously studied. With a series of basic programs established for these four years, the report proceeded to take up ten subject fields, examine the present correlation or lack of it between school and college courses, and make specific recommendations for improvement. For example, the report suggested that one of the worst areas of duplication was in introductory courses in American history, a subject taught in many schools at college level. The Committee believed strongly that colleges must give students from schools with strong American history courses advanced placement in college. One college man suggested that if this were done, the student would "wallow in difficulty," to which the Committee replied, "It is better for these students, we believe, to wallow in a few difficulties than to slumber in indifference."[22] And similar analyses were made for the other nine fields selected for study. At the close of the report the Committee proposed an experimental seven-year program whereby a student would enter college either from the eleventh grade of school or as a college sophomore from the twelfth grade. They were not interested in acceleration for acceleration's sake, but they were convinced that for some students eight years was a wastefully long time. Finally, the report closed on a specific note with a recommendation that the College Board make studies to see if valid tests for advanced placement could be devised for college freshman courses and to see if enough students and college people were interested to make a pilot program worth while. A lot of hard work and hard thinking had gone into the report, and the result showed it.

It would be nice to be able to say that *General Education in School and College* led directly to the establishment of the Advanced Placement Program and that thus Phillips Academy, which had done so much to initiate this study, could be credited with being the most important influence in getting the Advanced Program established. Such, however, is not the case. At almost exactly the same time that the Andover study was started, what came to be called the Kenyon Plan was initiated by President Gordon Chalmers of that institution.[23] Early in 1951 a group of eleven, later twelve, colleges met to consider the same problems that were the concern of the Andover group. With the exception of M.I.T. they were all small liberal arts colleges. At an early meeting Dean Frank Kille of Carlton presented a paper, later published in the *College Board Review*, that bore many striking resemblances to the Andover report. The Kenyon group, like the Andover group, were concerned with the superior students—the "able and ambitious student" they called him. They too emphasized course content and control of that content by the student. Both study groups believed that formal credit should be granted by the colleges for freshman courses passed on the basis of an examination, such examinations to be prepared by committees of school and college teachers. However one might try to divide the credit for the establishment of the Advanced Placement Program, there is no question that the effect of two distinguished and independent study groups arriving at almost identical conclusions speeded the process. In 1952–53 seven pilot schools began to develop Advanced Placement courses under the supervision of the College Board. By September 1953 twenty-seven schools were offering AP courses in one or more of the following subjects—American history, biology, chemistry, English, European history, French, German, Latin, mathematics, physics, and Spanish. At the same time, the program was given a boost when the twelve Kenyon Plan colleges voted to give credit for examinations taken as a result of these courses. In the spring of 1954 the first AP exams were administered, having been drawn up by committees of school and college teachers. To establish a point of reference, a group of college freshmen were paid to take the same exams, and it was soon found that the secondary school students did substantially better than the freshmen, possibly because the latter did not care so much about the exercise. From then on, the College Board took over, directing the Educational Testing Service to administer the program, and the Advanced Placement Program as it exists today was fully operative. There is no question that the program had led many schools to develop advanced courses for able students—courses that probably would not have been developed without the stimulus of the program.

Those who feared that AP courses would put the secondary school teacher in a straightjacket, no longer free to teach as he would, have generally been confounded. Although requirements in some subject fields are more rigid than others, in most cases the AP syllabi allow a large measure of flexibility. There were also those who thought that once the new courses had been drawn up, interest in the program would wane, but this, too, seems not to have been the case. Enrollment figures have varied from year to year, but the program is still going strong. Figures on specific advanced placement in colleges are difficult to obtain. There appear to have been relatively few students who achieved full sophomore standing through AP, but many able students have been able to avoid the drudgery of repeated courses.[24] Phillips Academy can be proud of her part in the establishment of the Advanced Placement Program. It represented the first time in the history of the school when something initiated at Andover contributed to the establishment of an educational program of national importance.

The effect of the Advanced Placement Program on Phillips Academy and its curriculum varied a good deal according to the department concerned. The School had provided students for the first pilot programs of the AP, and once the College Board had taken over, a large number of Andover undergraduates took the tests each year, with generally superior results. In the case of history, English, and the classics, the students took the examination without special training. Dr. Arthur B. Darling, Head of the History Department, announced that he had been giving a college-level course right along and saw no need to change it to meet the requirements of the AP. His position was borne out by the superior records that his students and those of the other teachers of History 4 made on the American history AP. Since the AP requirements in English were fairly flexible, Andover students were able to take the AP exam in English without special training, and the same was true of the classics. When it came to French, the AP requirements presented problems. Since most college freshman courses in French were devoted to the study of French literature, the examining committee naturally emphasized literature in the French AP exam. Dr. James H. Grew, Head of the Andover French Department, believed that the study of a language at the secondary school level should concentrate on getting command of the language itself and not on the literature of that language. Also, as the man responsible for introducing French courses taught entirely in French at Andover, he was disturbed by the use of English on the French AP exams. Eventually it was decided to offer a fifth year in French that would be devoted to literature, but to concentrate on the language itself for the first four years. In this case the AP requirements did, in effect, dictate part of the Andover curriculum, against the wishes of many of the department. The effect of the AP program on the sciences was to encourage science teachers to develop new and advanced courses to meet the AP requirements. Up until this time the various offerings in the sciences had been one-year elementary courses and minor courses for Seniors who wanted to keep in touch with the subject. Now in both chemistry and physics new advanced courses were offered to meet the AP requirements. Encouragement was also given to students taking the physics AP exam to take calculus at the same time. A variation on this was the science honors course, open to only a small number of very able students, which, in the course of two years, prepared the student for both the chemistry and the physics AP. It was assumed that these students would take calculus at the same time. Generally the AP program provided a strong stimulus to the teaching of advanced courses at Phillips Academy. Finally, the effect of the AP program on the Department of Mathematics was to make calculus the standard senior course, a full year beyond what had previously been fourth-year mathematics. This meant that some mathematical subjects like statistics and probability, solid geometry, and trigonometry had to be sacrificed to a certain extent, but most of the Department believe that the whole subject of mathematics is better integrated under the new course arrangement.

The Advanced Placement Program has not been an unmixed blessing. Although it has provided challenge for exceptional students, it has also led average students to attempt programs for which they were not qualified, often with disastrous results. Although the program has encouraged the development of advanced courses, it has also, in certain areas at least, tended to dictate what should be taught. On balance, however, the advantages for American secondary school students definitely outweigh the disadvantages.[25]

The revision of the Phillips Academy curriculum and the study that helped establish the Advanced Placement Program were both activities in the academic area. With the successful completion of these two projects, John Kemper was content to leave academic matters to the Faculty, at least for the time being. He became, however, more and more concerned with the development of adolescent boys, particularly how to make them what he called "decent" people. Mention has been made of his interest in bringing the Faculty and the medical profession together to exchange experiences on dealing with adolescents. He was always on the lookout for new programs in the nonacademic area that could improve the influence Phillips Academy had on its undergraduates. Thus he immediately became interested in the program known as Outward Bound. The development of that program in the United States was to a large extent an Andover affair. It started in 1950, when Trustee John P. Stevens, Jr., first heard of a German educator named Kurt Hahn, who had been working in England and on the Continent and who had developed innovative techniques for dealing with adolescents. Stevens asked his son-in-law, Joshua Miner, if he would like to spend a year or so at Gordonstoun, one of Hahn's schools in Northern Scotland, and Miner jumped at the chance. In the course of what came to be two years at Gordonstoun, Miner came to know an extraordinarily gifted educator.[26] At one track meet, for example, Miner noticed that the opposition was competing barefoot, and partly as a result of this his team was winning. Hahn appeared on the scene, discovered that the opposition could not afford track shoes, and immediately ordered the meet to be run over again with the Gordonstoun group barefoot as well as the opposition. Though Kurt Hahn did not slight the academic side of the program, his major interest was in producing good people. When the high jumpers on the track team became so proficient that they were swamping all opposition, Hahn told them they could not compete anymore. When the coach protested, Hahn said, "We want to develop people through jumping, not making jumpers out of people." Kurt Hahn had had an interesting background. Born and brought up in the Germany of the pre-World War I period, he had studied at Oxford, and after the war had worked in Germany to found Salem, the prototype of his later schools. But he could not accept the Nazis, and when Hitler came to power, he wrote the School's alumni saying that they must choose between Hitler and Salem. As might have been expected, he was jailed for this act of defiance, and it was only after various British friends put pressure on the German Foreign Office that he was allowed to emigrate to England. Again with the support of friends, he was able to found Gordonstoun, where one of his first pupils was Philip, later the Duke of Edinborough. One of the things Hahn stressed most at his school was service to the community, a group of programs he called "Samaritan services." A school Fire Service fought fires in the surrounding countryside as well as at the school itself; a Mountain Rescue Service was trained in rock climbing and evacuation techniques so as to save those caught in the mountains; and finally a Coast Weather Service maintained a twenty-four-hour watch over the coast and developed breeches buoys and other forms of rescue techniques for shipwrecked vessels. Hahn called these activities "experience therapy" and was convinced that they could make his charges emotionally healthy. With the coming of the war and the Battle of the Atlantic, British authorities were dismayed at the loss of seamen from torpedoed merchant vessels. Hahn and a Gordonstoun father named Lawrence Holt worked together to found what became the first Outward Bound School at Aberdovey, Wales, in 1941. Designed to train young Englishmen for survival at sea, the school became an instant success and before the war was over had provided many young men with techniques enabling them to stay alive. But the basic Hahnian concept remained: as Holt said, "The training at Aberdovey must be less a training *for* the sea than *through* the sea, and so benefit all walks of life." After the war Hahn returned to Gordonstoun, where he demonstrated that he meant it when he said that he was "an old man in a hurry." He often had three breakfast meetings simultaneously, he was forever wandering around the school to see what was going on, and at the end of the day he would take drives in his car, an authentic London taxi-cab, which he liked because it had more room than other cars. His attitude toward discipline was unorthodox; when a boy got into trouble, the whole adult community in the school were placed on trial rather than the boy; Hahn was always convinced that someone should have seen the trouble coming and acted to prevent it. Once when he visited Andover, he told John Kemper that a committee should never dismiss a student; "A committee has no conscience. Use it to investigate and advise, but you must make the decision. . . . Some one must carry the decision on his conscience." Perhaps the most interesting part of the Gordonstoun programs was "The Break"—a fifty-minute period in the morning devoted to athletics. The unique thing about this program was that each boy competed only against himself. Each day he tried to better his own record in one of five or six track events. The results were extraordinary. Many boys who started as physical misfits wound up making splendid records and at the same time banishing for themselves what Hahn called "the misery of unimportance." Hahn thought that team sports were good when they taught a lesson of "the good ally," teamwork, modesty in winning, and resolution in defeat. They harmed when they glorified individual performance or brute power. Before he died, Hahn embarked on some new ventures, particularly establishing four United World Colleges, which would enroll students from many lands in hope of breaking down national differences. It is easy to see that Hahn was a true educational innovator, and why John Stevens, John Kemper, and Joshua Miner should want to try to transplant at Andover some of the good things of the Hahn system.

John Kemper believed that some, at least, of the Hahn program might be introduced into Andover and serve to complement the strong academic program that was already established. Accordingly, in the summer of 1952, he invited Joshua Miner to introduce at Phillips Academy those parts of the Hahn program that seemed feasible. But he warned Miner that there could be no basic structural change in the Andover way of life to accommodate Hahn's theories. Miner accepted this difficult assignment and discovered, upon his arrival in Andover, something less than enthusiasm for the proposed changes. The School had a long tradition of doing things the way it was used to, and most of the Faculty were more than satisfied with things as they were. Few had ever heard of Hahn anyway. A vigorous athletic program was going well, and the Department of Physical Education believed that change was unnecessary. In addition, the leadership in the Department was undergoing change, and no one was willing to take the strong stand necessary if Miner's innovations were to be given a chance.

Faced with this roadblock, Miner decided to nibble away at the edges. He prevailed upon the Department of Physical Education to let him work with twenty of the most physically inefficient boys in school. Since it was difficult to fit this group into the regular athletic program, the Department was glad to get rid of them. Though it is difficult to measure achievement, there is no question that Miner's physical misfits prospered under his tutelage; they developed physically and, more important, they gained self-confidence. The following year it was arranged to have all the Williams Hall Juniors take the program, while the Rockwell House Juniors did not. At the end of the year a comparison was made between the two groups, with the Williams Hall boys coming out far ahead, not only in physical proficiency but in academic records as well. Other factors may have influenced the result, of course, but the comparison was too striking to be ignored. From then on, all the Juniors and later new Lower Middlers as well took the Hahn-inspired course. Those in charge of the program introduced the Hahnian concept of competing against oneself in track events, and a program called "drown-proofing" was introduced, in the course of which the student learned to stay afloat with both his arms and legs tied. A later development was Search and Rescue, in the course of which boys were trained in rock climbing and rescuing people in the mountains. This program involved taking overnight trips to the White Mountains and other appropriate places. As part of their training, boys learned to rappel—to let themselves down a sheer cliff on a rope. Since there were no cliffs near Andover, the Bell Tower was commandeered, and it soon became a familiar sight to see Andover students descending from the top of that tower. A much more recent program based on Hahn's principles was developed as part of the orientation program for new students at the beginning of the School year. Many of these new students testified that they made friends more easily working together in this program than in any other activity they had previously engaged in. So the Outward Bound principles were engrafted on part of the Andover program. These programs did not revolutionize the School, but unquestionably many boys profited enormously, both physically and emotionally.

Josh Miner, John Kemper, and Jack Stevens played a leading part in the development of Outward Bound schools in the United States as well. The first was established in Colorado in 1962 and five others followed in such places as Minnesota and on the coast of Maine. At this time of writing, about seven thousand students take month-long courses at these schools each year, and four hundred Search and Rescue type programs have been

68. *A student rappelling down Memorial Tower as part of the Outward Bound program introduced at Phillips Academy.*

established. Five thousand high school teachers have gone through one or another of the programs to enable them to work more effectively with their pupils. In short, Outward Bound has been an exciting innovation in American education, and the chances are that it might never have been established—at least as it is now—without the work of Phillips Academy people.[27]

Another innovative program introduced during the Kemper years was Schoolboys Abroad, known after girls were admitted as School Year Abroad. The idea had originated with Clark Vaughan, Head of the Language Department at Wilbraham Academy. Vaughan believed that the eleventh grade was an ideal time for a student to spend a year in some foreign country, becoming thoroughly familiar with its language and culture. An eleventh-grader was mature enough to take advantage of the opportunities the year could provide, yet young enough to be kept under a fairly tight regimen and not waste a lot of time horsing around, the way people in the college programs did. Since Vaughan's field was Spanish, he made preliminary investigations in Spain and came to the conclusion that the best location for such a program would be Barcelona. Catalan rather than Castillian Spanish was spoken there, but other considerations, he thought, more than outweighed that disadvantage. Vaughan presented his plan to the Trustees of Wilbraham, who, primarily for financial reasons, believed that they could not undertake to support it. Accordingly, Vaughan decided to try out his proposal on John Kemper. A program of this kind that could provide special enriched advantages for language students appealed greatly to the Andover Headmaster, and he determined to give it a try.

In a memorandum to the Trustees presented in the fall of 1963, Kemper stressed the advantages that might be gained from such a program; in addition to language proficiency and cultural studies, it would undoubtedly fit its students for the Advanced Placement exam and thereby increase their chances of college admission. Vaughan had already made arrangements with the Instituto de Estudios Norteamericanos in Barcelona for classroom space and had enlisted the help of Daniel Olivier, another member of the Wilbraham Faculty, as his second in command. One of the big stumbling blocks in a program of this kind was how to conduct it so that the students would not lose a year of secondary school in the process. To meet that problem it was agreed that Mr. Olivier would teach a regular eleventh-grade English course, while Edmond E. Hammond, Jr., one of the ablest members of the Phillips Academy Mathematics Department, would give a regular course in eleventh-grade mathematics. History courses would be taught in Spanish by teachers hired in Barcelona, as would be true of the language courses themselves. After an initial stay in a pension, the students would spend most of the year living with Spanish families,

thereby intensifying their experience in a foreign land. With tuition at
$3200 it was believed that the program could be financially self-supporting.
The Headmaster closed his recommendation to the Trustees by suggesting
that if the program in Spain worked well, Phillips Academy might well
want to consider establishing similar programs in other foreign countries.
Impressed with the possibilities of the program, the Trustees voted to support it for one year.[28]

Implementing the program proved to be far more difficult than planning it. The original proposal called for thirty students who had done
honor work in Spanish. Since it was clear that not all of them would come
from Andover, the program was opened to students of any reputable
school who could get the recommendation of their headmasters. Clark
Vaughan, a perennial optimist by nature, was sure there would be a waiting
list of students who wanted to go but could not get in. In the event, although there was a great deal of interest—requests for information and
the like—it was difficult to find candidates whose parents were willing to
make hard and fast financial commitments. As a result, when the first
group left for Spain in the summer of 1964, it contained eleven rather
than thirty. Despite the small number and some administrative foul-ups
that were unavoidable the first time around, the initial program successfully immersed the students in the Spanish language and culture. Here are
a few vignettes from the *Barcelona Bulletin*, a mimeographed paper published by the group:

> Barcelona traffic—Not only are there no speed laws or code of ethics,
> but the inability of the Barcelonans to park without running up on
> the sidewalk menaces the pedestrian even there.

> Spanish transportation—The language problem and the typical
> Spanish disregard for fixed time schedules caused much confusion.
> On our first trip to a beach forty-five minutes away, five of us took
> three hours to get there, and the rest never arrived at all. . . . The
> autobuses and streetcars are effective as long as they are not hit by a
> slow-down strike, which is the only resort of Spanish labor since
> regular strikes are forbidden by law.

> Bullfights—We were startled by the smallness of the arena, not
> bigger than an infield. Each movement, each stream of blood could
> be seen clearly. All six kills were done clumsily, and our reaction
> was one of disgust. Even experienced bullfight patrons called that
> day's *corrida* more butchery than art. . . .

> Athletics—The center of our athletic activities thus far has been a
> semi-public sports club. . . . At first swimming was most popular,
> but since it has become too cold, a new sport has been devised—
> roller skate hockey. . . . Starting the first of December we will have

membership in the *Club de Natacion*, oldest sports club in Spain, where we will take part in swimming, sailing, water polo, track, and gymnastics.

Dances—In the part of the program aimed at getting us to socialize with Spanish teenagers, we have attended several dances at the Instituto. The dances are strange—the Spanish are just now doing the twist and rock and roll, and the dances are always over before supper at 9:00—but they have been for many of us the best devisable Spanish classes. We make practical application of the language, talking with *chicos* and *chicas* with names like Margarita, Bella, Carlos, Jaime, and Josefina.[29]

The academic side of the program ran smoothly, and by late in the fall all the students had left the pensions, where they had lived at first, and were lodged with Spanish families. Some of these families were very lax in dealing with the American boys, and a general tightening up of discipline proved necessary in some cases, but aside from the inevitable student who drank too much Spanish wine, there were no serious disciplinary problems. During vacations the group went on trips: the first a tour of Spain itself in a bus; the second, visits to cities in other countries, with the group going by train.[30] When the potential difficulties inherent in trying to ride herd on a dispersed group of teenagers in a foreign country are considered, the first year of Schoolboys Abroad went off very well indeed.

In the years that followed, the sailing was not all smooth. At the end of the first year Harris Thomas of the Exeter Language Department visited Barcelona with Colonel Edward Harris, Executive Officer for the program in Andover. Thomas went on the trip because Exeter had agreed to join Andover in sponsoring the program, and a few years later St. Paul's joined also, making a troika. The visitors were generally delighted with what they saw. They did, however, make various recommendations for improvement. The administrative structure of the program was loose and needed tightening, particularly in connection with regular reports from the Director. They also had suggestions for the improvement of various classes. They warned strongly against having the boys engage in any kind of political activity in Spain, lest the program be irreparably damaged. And finally, they urged that preliminary steps be taken to establish another Schoolboys Abroad program somewhere in France.[31]

At the same time, the Barcelona Faculty produced an evaluation with suggestions for improvement. They thought the word "Honors" should be eliminated from the program literature, since it tended to frighten away prospective candidates and since all agreed that middle-of-the-road boys could profit greatly from a year in Spain. They questioned the value of the vacation trips to other countries, particularly since they were very expensive, and believed that the students should spend all their time in Spain.

Finally, they were unhappy about the absence of any organized athletic program. While they agreed that roller skate hockey, basketball, and touch football had gone well on an informal, pick-up basis, they still favored a more structured program.[32] Most of these recommendations were put into effect in the years that followed. In 1967, after long discussions over the most suitable site, a Schoolboys Abroad program was opened in Rennes, France, where it has been operating ever since. As with the Spanish experiment, American teachers from one of the three schools involved teach English and mathematics, while native teachers conduct classes in the language and literature of the country. An attempt was made to establish a program in Germany, but so many difficulties were encountered that it had to be abandoned. The most serious problem faced by the French and Spanish programs was financial. Despite heroic efforts on the part of the administration in the United States to recruit pupils, the optimum number was often not realized. Since administrative costs were high and fixed, this put a squeeze on the budget. And expenses in the foreign country were often more than had been expected. Ted Hammond, the first mathematics teacher to participate, wrote: "There is apparently no awareness on the part of the administration of the magnitude of expenses over here [Barcelona]. I am badly out of pocket for housing already, in what may become an involuntary personal subsidy of this program."[33] The programs ran deficits a number years, which the Trustees of the various schools picked up. Those in charge faced a dilemma. There was no question that a year in a foreign country was a tremendously valuable and enriching experience for the students involved. At the same time there was serious question as to how long such programs could be subsidized when they failed to be self-supporting. Happily, School Year Abroad has recently become financially independent, and its future seems assured.

Phillips Academy joined another off-campus program in 1969; the Washington Intern Program, which had been set up by Exeter four years earlier. Andover joined it in much the same way that Exeter had agreed to become part of Schoolboys Abroad. It differed, however, in that it required the student to be absent from campus only part of the year. The basic idea was to have a small group of undergraduates live in Washington for the spring term of the Upper Middler year and work full time in the office of a Senator or Representative. The belief was—and it was strongly supported by actual practice—that this would give the student an unusual insight into the workings of the Federal Government. Collaborating with Exeter on the program took some doing, for they were on a semester system and believed that the most eligible group to go to Washington would be Seniors who had fulfilled their diploma requirements in February, while Andover, on a trimester system, chose Upper Middlers who would return to school for their Senior year and, it was hoped, would share their experiences with other members of their class. In practice this meant that the Exeter boys would start their internships in the middle of February, while the Andover group would not begin until late March. None of the students was allowed to pick his Congressman; on the contrary, the various Congressional offices selected from detailed application forms the interns they wanted.

School Year Abroad had financial difficulties, and the Washington interns were plagued with the finding of adequate housing. At various times during the history of the program the students have lived in dormitories of the National Cathedral School for Girls, Mt. Vernon College, and various hotels. The difficulty can be understood by reviewing the facilities in Hearst Hall, where the first group of Andover Interns lived. An abandoned dormitory of the National Cathedral School for Girls, the building that spring housed on the second floor a Ballet School for girls; on the top floor, the Andover-Exeter contingent; scattered throughout the rest of the building, various old ladies who were former employees of the National Cathedral Scheool and were now on pension; and an assortment of theological students. Despite these handicaps in physical equipment, the program has been extremely popular, and each year since it was started in 1969 there have been many more applicants than could be chosen. Since it was the first program, aside from School Year Abroad, to involve absence from campus for a substantial part of the school year, the Faculty was understandably conservative on the matter of credits. At the beginning the student was to do his English while in Washington, reading and writing themes; then he would come to Summer School—first at Exeter and later at Andover—to make up the other work he had missed in the spring term. As time went on, these requirements—particularly attendance at Summer School—became more and more onerous both to the students and to those in charge of them. At last the Faculty relented, and today a Washington Intern gets credit for the courses he would have taken during the spring term had he remained in School.

A final problem involves staffing. Andover and Exeter have agreed that the program must be supervised by one of their own Faculty members, but hauling a teacher out of School half way through the year to oversee the program is difficult at best. Perhaps even more than Schoolboys Abroad, the program illustrates the complications involved in special opportunities of this kind—in this case to make it possible for fifteen students to spend one term in Washington. The reaction to the program ranges from enthusiastic to rhapsodic, but the number of man hours involved in making it possible is awesome.

A sensitive and incisive picture of the Washington Intern Program in action can be gained from the diary of James Stover, P.A. '70, a member of the first Andover contingent to go to Washington. He writes:

First Day—Today, of course, was the big day. . . . I arrived in the office before most of the other staff members. All were very friendly, everything on a first name basis. . . . . Mr. Watkins [a Congressional Aide] was on the run all day, talking on the phone and to visitors the whole time. The pace is very, very fast. At lunch he told me he'd try to talk with me in the afternoon. As I was leaving about 5:45 he said that he was sorry but that the afternoon had been busier than the morning. It was a good introduction. I realize now how nearly frantic the work can be. . . .

Typing—Actually, I've been typing most of the day. The Office is short a secretary and Larry and Bill discovered that I can type quite well. . . . I typed a letter to a churchman which states Denney's [Congressman Robert Denney of Nebraska, his Congressman] views on such things as the draft, the ABM system and the welfare programs. . . . I also typed up a reply to a letter from a man in Atlanta, Georgia that asked that Denney support the direct election of the President. The reply was a page and a half long. . . . It's amazing how much noise there is in the office. Several times I couldn't even hear the typewriter bell. . . .

Bill gave me a pamphlet from the Legislative Reference Service on "Preparation of Committee Legislative Calendars by Computer" (the Administrative Terminal System) and told me to read it over and write up a summary including my opinion of the system. . . . Certainly Washington is a very beautiful city, at least from Capitol Hill to the Lincoln Memorial. And probably no place is more gorgeous than the Botanic Gardens. Right now the Easter show is on and never in my life have I seen and smelled so many absolutely stunning flowers massed together. I was so carried away I used every flash bulb I was carrying. . . . At lunch today Bill told me that probably an average of 250 pieces of mail come into the office each day, five days a week. About 100 require replies. He figures that 25% of staff time is spent in handling correspondence. . . .

The polls started coming in today. I am the lucky fellow who gets to open all the envelopes, pick out any cards that are bent, spindled, or mutilated; if people have indicated that they want to get the Progress Reports, make sure that the addresses are legible; and stack the cards. Actually, there are cards of interest: bent ones, ones in which the choices have been indicated by checking instead of punching out the box, and ones that have mistakenly punched-out squares glued or taped back on. Many have comments scrawled on them. . . .

I am sick of being bored out of my mind by poll after poll, of coming back here to study history. . . . of having to shut the door so Michael can work and not be disturbed by having some one come in and talk. This isn't exactly my idea of great fun. But it's "good" for me, I suppose, I'm glad I'm here. . . .

As I strolled along the Basin, the sidewalk overhung by branches heavy with the white and pink flowers, a wonderful sense of peace took hold of me. This calmness was enhanced when I reached the Jefferson Memorial. This building, for my mind the most beautiful in Washington, is certainly worthy of the great man it honors, of the words inscribed on its inner walls: "We hold these truths to be self-evident. . . ." Seeing it framed by the blossoms is a truly unforgettable experience. . . .

Things began to look up today when an electric letter opener arrived at the office. Within an hour and a half, I had opened all the remaining letters, probably ten times faster than I could have done by hand. . . .

These last few days have been hectic, but I will never forget them. Wednesday I started a new job: calling up various agencies to try to drag information out of them. This sounds fairly easy, but in fact is incredibly difficult. It often takes four or five calls to get through to the right person, and then that person is on the phone or busy or doesn't have the information right on hand and so will call back. An example: trying to find out the status of pay TV from the Federal Communications Commission. Most of the information is needed to answer constitutent inquiries or complaints. . . .

One of the highlights of this whole experience was the seminar with Mr. Thomas Corcoran. . . . It was hard to comprehend that the man sitting right next to us was a man who had sat next to FDR so many times. Yet there he was, describing Franklin as a saint, a phenomenal political artist, a man with a great humanitarian heart who never took his eye off the ball, who was pragmatic enough to know that the world wasn't full of saints. . . .

Today I tried to rework Mr. Denney's Memorial Day oration of last year. I was really discouraged about the speech, even after managing to organize it a little. I was using the same words as last year, the same tired cliches. . . . I had to leave most of it alone. . . . but I did manage to slip Abe Lincoln and the Gettysburg Address in, which can never hurt. . . .

Tuesday I worked most of the day on a couple of articles the Congressman gave me to memo. . . . The second concerned President Nixon's proposed budget for FY 1970. I had real problems understanding why there are different totals for appropriations and expenditures, and even more, how it can be planned to spend more than is to be appropriated, but I struggled through. One other cheerful note: Larry ordered a brand new cabinet for all the address stencils, which means that I'll have to rearrange all 23,000 or so. Can't wait.

About 3:00 Mr. Denney came storming into the back office where

I work and started to give me hell about the memo I wrote on the Russian ABM system. He was upset about my last sentence which stated. . . . that there was no proof that the system worked. The Congressman. . . . said that someone in the office must be against President Nixon's safeguard system. I finally convinced him, I think, that I was justified in putting in the last sentence. . . . Later Bill said I handled the logical part of the discussion pretty well, but seemed a bit flustered. I was. He also said that the Congressman gave him a big wink as he left the office.

And a final entry a short time before the program ended:

I don't think I've ever been this happy for this long in my life. Love. Peace. A little sadness that it can't last. That's what I feel right now. Everything, everybody seems good today. . . . I've never been so conscious of other people. I've never really relaxed and enjoyed being alive as I am right now. That's not to say there isn't a hell of a lot of work, but its work that means something. It has a purpose, a purpose which is often lost amid the books at Andover.

There are few students who have the intelligence, imagination, and sensitivity to get as much out of the Washington Intern Program as Jim Stover did, but the batting average has been consistently high. What is frustrating to those in charge is that there seems to be no way of expanding it so that more students can have this unusual experience.

While these opportunities for off-campus educational opportunities were doing much to enrich the Phillips Academy curriculum, the main academic strength of the School remained in the resident Faculty. In the Kemper years a new group of outstanding teachers came to replace the Titans of the Stearns era. The leading Classicist was Alston Chase, who had one of the finest intellects of anyone who has ever taught on Andover Hill. Fully qualified to teach in college—he had been on the Harvard Faculty before coming to Andover—he preferred to work with younger boys, believing that the secondary school age group was most receptive to what he had to offer. A conservative in both political and educational matters, he insisted on the same precision in the study of Latin and Greek that his predecessors Horace Poynter and Georgie Hinman had, but he achieved his purpose without the use of fear. One can get a clear idea of his educational philosophy from "What is Andover?"—a paper he wrote the fall after John Kemper arrived. "Andover's primary duty," he said, "its only excuse for existence, is the education of an elite body of men whose intelligence and character shall provide the leadership so badly needed in a democracy." He hoped that the student body would be varied in character—some from the families of professional men, some from wealthy families, and some from the underprivileged—though he warned against romantic notions concerning the third group. Once at Andover, the boys should have fairly

69. Alston Hurd Chase, Instructor in Classics, 1934–1971, and Head of the Classics Department, 1954–1971.

rigid requirements. "My own conviction is that boys are happier when they are given a few rules with stated penalties for their violation and are then subjected to unvarying application of those rules." And in the last analysis it was the men who taught rather than what they taught that was important. "We teach not only in the classroom. Every hour that we dwell among those boys we are reaching them by our examples, with devastating effectiveness in some instances. They are shrewd and rather merciless judges, with all the perceptiveness of youth and none of the tolerance of age. If we teach one thing with our lips and quite another with our lives, they value each form of teaching at its proper worth. I fear that our particular generation has suffered from a peculiar shyness in testifying to moral truths." He closed by defining Andover as "a school made beautiful by nature and the living hands of many generations, where a group of men of the most varied gifts and interests and beliefs are united in dedication to the pleasant work of teaching boys to love the truth, to cherish honor, and to serve their fellows with wisdom and integrity and grace."[34] No one ever forgot Alston's classes. He was a redoubtable housemaster as well. Here was a perfect milieu where he could apply his doctrine of a few rules strictly enforced. One might think that undergraduates would prefer the more permissive housemasters, but this was not the case. Each year there was a race to see who could get into his dormitory. Interestingly enough, it was usually the school athletes who flocked to him. Though he was anything but a "jock" type in physical stature, the athletes believed that somehow he could get them through, whip them into line, and produce diplomas in June. And he was not always as strict as his stated policy would imply. One alumnus writes:

> Dr. Chase, the Cherubic Classics scholar who was my housemaster during the third year, caught me gambling at cards and informed me this was not permitted. I had studied the rule-book very carefully and told him I could find nothing about gambling. He said it fell into the "conduct-unbecoming-a-gentleman" rule. I reminded him of my readings at the time in 19th century literature, which was full of gentlemen who frequently gambled. He thought this was funny, and I became more careful about my gambling operations.

Another episode indicates more rigidity:

> In the springtime Dr. Chase found two boys sitting in an area marked "Keep Off the Grass." In a red-faced (more so than usual) fury, he called, "I'll give you as many demerits as you take steps to get off the grass." (fitting the punishment to the crime). Suffering under the pronouncement of this Rector of Justin did not snuff out the boys' cleverness; they *rolled* off the lawn. To this point the story is wonderful; the poor-sport ending is that the boys were given demerits anyway.

Alston Chase was a powerful intellectual force in the Andover community, and though many disagreed with him on basic matters of policy, he had the respect of boys and Faculty alike.

Another outstanding teacher during the Kemper years was Emory Basford, Head of the English Department for most of the period. He had been hired by Al Stearns and had taught at Andover during the Fuess period, but he reached his full height in the 1950's and 1960's. He was a craftsman who knew how to teach boys how to write, and his literature classes, particularly in American literature, were famous throughout the School. Like Alston Chase he was a bachelor, and like Alston Chase he took his housemastering very seriously. He was concerned that boys become *gentlemen* as well as pass their courses, and he labored long and hard to achieve this aim. One alumnus remembers the teas he used to give for his students:

> I always regarded Emory Basford as one of the finest teachers I knew in that school. From my own standpoint I found his teaching inspirational and I found his friendship, then and now, one of the warm aspects of the school.
>
> Nonetheless, Emory was himself cut of the mold that was somewhat different from most of us boys. He was almost studiously quiet, although a conversationalist in the classic mold. I never knew him to raise his voice. . . . But one of the things which he always did and for which happily I was often made a part, was his Sunday afternoon tea.
>
> In those days it wasn't terribly popular to be intellectual and certainly I was not tainted with that label in any form. Nevertheless, at those teas I think I was exposed to a little bit of this and made to think of some of the more intellectual and nicer aspects of living and particularly of writing and art, for these were the subjects that were discussed under Emory's sympathetic and gentle guidance. I might also say that I developed a taste for good tea, for Emory always had the very best and there were always some edibles that went with it. I must say that I also enjoyed those edibles because they were a marked contrast to the lousy food in the Commons. I have many happy memories of those afternoon teas during my senior year.

Another alumnus writes in a similar vein:

> The singular influence on my life was Emory Basford's. I impressed him once by knowing Max Beerbohm's *Zuleika Dobson*; from that moment he believed that beneath my playboy facade lay a seed of intelligence, and that belief may well have changed my life. Emory's belief in me was soon pitted against Bitch Freeman's conviction I was a worthless student and Andover would be a better place with-

70. *Emory Shelby Basford, Instructor in English, 1929–1964, and Head of the English Department, 1945–1964.*

out me. Emory prevailed and it made for a turnaround in my academic career.

The same alumnus concludes about Andover in general:

> I had a wildly good time at Andover, thanks to a sort of Foreign
> Legion, misfits from all over the eastern school system who arrived
> when I did in 1936, having proved too much for Groton and St.
> Paul's. We went into PAE and we tried and failed as athletes and
> scholars, but I have never laughed so often, nor so joyfully as I did
> in that first Andover year.

Finally, during these years Emory Basford served as a kind of conscience
of the Faculty. Time and time again in Faculty meeting he would call attention to the fact that the School was abandoning its principles. The
seriousness with which his statements were listened to, from the Headmaster on down, was a measure of the respect all had for the man.

Another unforgettable teacher during the Kemper years was Leonard F.
James, who succeeded Arthur B. Darling as Head of the History Department in the 1960's. As has been noted, the course in American history—
History 4—had been under attack for the excessive number of failures that
resulted each year. One of the difficulties had been that the students—and
particularly the slow students—did not understand the examination questions. Len determined to correct this fault and insisted that all questions be
crystal clear. As a result the failure rate dropped markedly in the 1960's
and much of the neurotic apprehension about the course disappeared. In
the classroom, however, Len really shone. A peppery man with a short
fuse, he used to stimulate his students to discussion through sarcasm, insult, gentle encouragement—in short every trick in the book. At times he
would take an outlandish position on a controversial subject and then defend it against student attack. The result was a constant ferment as boys
learned to think about the implications of what they were studying. He
was a hard taskmaster who had no use for shoddy work, and the record of
his students on the AP exam bore this out. In 1969 a group of his students
published a little pamphlet entitled "Quotations from Chairman Leonard,"
which reflects his classroom procedure.[35]

> On History 4— Preparation for this course should take you no more
>   than an hour a day.
> On Hitler— Hitler was a first class thug.
> To a Student— I defended you today. Somebody said you were a
>   very able person and I said you weren't.
> On Neckties— Did your dog buy it? You don't have to show it to
>   me, I heard it coming up the stairs.
> On Water— A glass of water is not a glass of water without the
>   glass.

71. *Leonard Frank James, Instructor in History, 1932–1970, and Head of the History Department, 1956–1970.*

On John Brown— John Brown was a first class thug.

On Idealism— Being an idealist is a lot of baloney.

On Punctuality— You know you're going to be late for your own damn funeral. People will be crying for you and you won't even be there.

On Monthly Tests— This exam is straight-forward.

On Coming to Class Late— Coming back from the dead?

On Submarine Warfare— The *Lusitania* got what it deserved.

On a Debate— Get off your duff and get down to brass tacks. Oh, come on, let's not talk puppy love. If you look at it from a non-SDS point of view . . .

On World War I— Germany was a thug surrounded by thugs.

On Disagreement— Well it is, you damn fool.

On China— It's about time Chiang Kai-Shek dropped dead.

On Arabs— Let's discuss the flea-bitten Arabs.

In addition to being a top-notch classroom teacher, Len James was also a housemaster of parts. One alumnus writes:

> he was my housemaster in Adams, where the atmosphere was soft-ened by his Scandinavian wife. . . . He was thought of as somewhat strict, and, as a result, the boys on the top floor devised an experi-ment: one would crouch on the mantlepiece and jump while his roommate hid behind the door with a stopwatch to time Mr. James's arrival on the threshold. As I recall, his record time was 10 seconds.

Although Len James wrote several textbooks and was active in the Advanced Placement Program, he will always be best remembered at Andover as one of the most stimulating and challenging classroom teachers of his generation.

Dudley Fitts of the English Department was *sui generis*. There had never been anyone like him at Andover in the past, and it is highly unlikely that there will ever be anyone like him in the future. A distinguished poet and translator, an accomplished musician, a man who seemed to have read everything ever printed, he held memorable classes in the basement of Bulfinch Hall, where his barbed wit constantly provoked sparks in classroom discussion. Just before he came to Andover in the 1940's from Choate, he came to the Hill for a visit and because of his musical talent was asked to conduct a Faculty madrigal group in the singing of "Happy, Oh Happy He." The group produced what they thought was a respectable rendition, only to have Fitts say at the end, with a baleful expression, "That was obscene." No one participating in that exercise has ever forgotten the experience—or Fitt's comment—and his students must have been treated to the same fare on many occasions. One alumnus writes:

> Fitts's ringing challenges were another matter—his is the last mind

72. *Dudley Fitts, Instructor in English, 1941–1968.*

by whom I have felt completely overawed—and his cultivation (whether by challenge or encouragement) of one's sense of personal strength gave me an intellectual character that has not changed, really, at all since I left PA. He gave my already synthetic mind a strong push towards questioning the nature of things. I remember walking into Fitts's class on the first day and being told to take a piece of paper and write for fifty minutes on the subject "Toasted Suzie is My Ice Cream" (a line from Gertrude Stein).

David Slavitt, the poet and novelist, P.A. 1952, knew Fitts intimately both at Andover and in later life and has written an admirable study of the man and his poetry.[36] A few excerpts:

Fitts missed more classes than any other Andover master. Sometimes he would show up, find that he could not face an hour's performance, and instead, scrawl something on the blackboard and say, "Write for an hour, gentlemen," and then leave. It was exhilarating that anyone could get away with such behavior, and because he was able to do so . . . his authority was enormously increased. That authority, however, was based on other, more general considerations. . . . And his manner was not only authoritative but authoritarian. He was famous for his wit and his sarcasm of which we, as an honors group, were prime beneficiaries and victims. It was a matter of pride to be insulted by Mr. Fitts.

. . . Fitts's high, rather nasal voice, to which from sickness or perhaps affectation there was an occasional quaver, was a perfect instrument for the delivery of quite withering but very elegant insults. . . . I remember, for instance, his scribbled notations in the margin of a paper I had written in which I had misused "should" and "would." The letters "I.E." and "E.I." appeared wherever I had erred. After class I went up to ask him what these letters meant, " 'I.E.' stands for immigrant English, and 'E.I.' means Ellis Island, and don't ever make that mistake again," he said, looking quite pleased with himself, for I had taken the bait perfectly and had been fairly gaffed.

. . . I looked up the usage of "should" and "would", learned it, and have not made that mistake since. I owe the man thanks, then, for doing his job, teaching me English. But what overkill! . . . we were right for each other. He could vent his anger with insults, the barbs of which were tricked out in the bright feathers of wit, and I could turn insults into solicitousness and friendship . . . At any rate I was not put off. Instead, I sought him out, brought poems I had written for him to read, and met with him in his study in his house in Hidden Field, once every week or so for most of the year. . . .

Once that initial salvo had served its purpose by demonstrating his authority and my respect for it, he could afford to relax a little, and at each visit he would go through the poems I had brought him, and, with much wit and energy, explain what was bad, why this didn't work, and that, and how I might have improved here, and where I was being imitative there. Line by line, and sometimes word by word, he would go over these hastily written attempts of mine, and, every now and then, discover a line, two, or even four that were interesting, promising, or even good. At the end of the session, he would give me tea and then dismiss me, usually with some joke or clever line, frequently one that was over my head and that sent me to the dictionary or the library where I would try to figure out what he had meant, sometimes succeeding, sometimes not.

Fitts's fame as an English teacher spread well beyond Andover. David Slavitt tells of his experiences at Yale, where, as a Fitts-trained student, he was encouraged to take advanced and graduate courses in English almost immediately. Jacques Barzun, in *Teacher in America*, remarked on the number of students trained by Dudley Fitts who knew how to write literate, if not polished, English.[37] For a good part of his last days at Andover, Dudley Fitts suffered from a crippling illness; yet his wit and his brilliant incisiveness never faltered, and he finished his career, as he had begun it, an inspiration to most of the students who sat at his feet.

Here is an unusually perceptive and thoughtful general account of the School in the early 1960's, written by James S. Kunen, '66.

In many ways P.A. from 1962–1966 was more similar to the P.A. of 1910 than to the P.A. of 1970. I was proud of the fact that Andover had a broad spectrum of students—that one third were on scholarship—that P.A. was not an elitist school. It did not strike me as strange that there were only three or four Blacks at P.A. It did not even strike me as strange that scholarship boys were set apart from the rest of us by having to do work around school—extended Commons duty and so forth. I had a white, middle-class background and that rather narrow world-view remained intact during four years at P.A. The seeds of rebellion had not yet poked above the soil during my P.A. years.

The great Northwest Power Blackout was metaphorically significant. A third of the nation was plunged into darkness, but P.A., with its own power plant, shone on. I noticed that the town street lights and traffic signals were out. Otherwise I wouldn't have known anything had happened. P.A. was quite insulated. We didn't have much time for newspapers, either. Wasn't there an enormous Civil Rights Movement at the time? We were not terribly aware of it.

Inside we lived in a male adolescent world exclusively. There was little evidence of adults around once classes and sports were over for the day. It was almost like *Lord of the Flies*. . . . Naturally, physical ability and cultural conformity were at a premium and pressures were extreme. . . . I know that some boys who were dubbed "Fliers" were terribly unhappy at Andover. Of course some people are going to feel rejected anywhere, but the problem was extreme at Andover because there were few sources of support other than peer group support—no parents, no family. There were few supportive relationships between faculty and students. For one thing a plethora of petty regulations which the faculty had to support created an adversary relationship. . . . The most vivid example of the gulf of distrust between students and faculty that I experienced occurred one night during upper year when a boy in my dormitory stayed up all night cutting himself with a razor blade, and we, his dorm mates, stayed up all night trying to stop him, and no one went to the housemaster for fear the boy would get *kicked out*.

In fact, some of the most creative kids in our class got kicked out. To this day that is the sore point in my relationship with Andover. . . . I will always resent the way P.A. dealt with boys who had difficult problems—get rid of them. Out of sight, out of mind. . . . It seems to me Andover was just typically American in its approach to people who cause problems—get rid of them, hide them.

The most valuable things I got out of Andover were the friendships I made there. I've been out ten years and my closest friends are still my friends from Andover. It may be that there is an extra dimension to friendships made in an all-male situation. What was especially valuable was that you had to come to terms with everybody. . . . There was no escape for the harpsichordist from the football player, or vice versa. . . . Though there was not as much socioeconomic diversity as I naively thought there to be at the time, there certainly was a wide range of characters there and we all got to know each other well. P.A. was our "army", P.A. friends our "army buddies."

We didn't think very much about P.A. while we were there—not critically, I mean. . . . Anyone who believes that sexual energy can be sublimated into creative activity could find great support for the theory in our P.A. years. . . . We were dynamos. Some of us have been resting up ever since. I have never taken a course of study as rigorous at college or law school. And at law school a physical education instructor doesn't tie you up and throw you into a twelve-foot pool for fifteen minutes. He made it very clear that there was something lacking in your masculinity if you didn't meet and beat such physical challenges. His "drown-proofing" exemplified the 19th century Capitalist values which were still going strong at Andover in 1962–1966. . . . We had to meet other people's expectations. We had to live by other people's values. We had to do things which seemed pointless and maybe were pointless. In short, *we were made to do things we did not want to do.* I don't know anyone who regrets that.

Andover was an institution which believed in itself. Mr. Kemper said that Chapel was optional because if you didn't like it you could go to school some place else. We called that "chapel reasoning", mocked the argument, and bridled at the school's intransigence, but at least we had something to rebel against which did not collapse before us. There was order in our universe. I think we felt secure.

As this passage suggests Phillips Academy changed very little in the 1950's and early 1960's. To be sure, the Societies were gone, but in almost all other areas of school life conditions were similar to those of the 1930's and 1940's. In part, at least, this static state of affairs was a reflection of the relaxed condition of the country during the Eisenhower years. For the most part, the undergraduates accepted the regimen that the Faculty and Administration had laid out for them. They were serious in purpose, aimed at admission to a top Ivy League college, and planned on graduate school after that. There were, of course, the usual student highjinks, but compared with what was to happen in the late 1960's, Andover Hill was a very peaceful place. The one thing that was new was the Headmaster and his relationship to the undergraduates. In dealing with the various constitutencies that go to make up the greater Andover community, John Kemper batted close to a thousand in dealing with Trustees, Faculty, parents, alumni, and general public. It was only in dealing with the undergraduates that he had any trouble. And this is hard to understand, for he was certainly the fairest and kindest of men. Those who worried about his military background and feared the establishment of a military system of discipline were soon reassured. John Kemper was more liberal in this area than his predecessors and believed in giving a boy a second, if not a third, chance wherever possible. Yet he was uncomfortable when addressing the whole School and some of his statements rubbed the boys the wrong way. Early in his term he returned from a long alumni trip and found that in his absence the students had engaged in some kind of reprehensible ructions. He then gave his famous "I'm tired" speech that antagonized many students. He said that not only was he tired, but he was "tired of being tired," seeming to imply that it was the undergraduates' fault. They felt the charge was unfair and reacted accordingly. On the other hand, a boy who was present for the speech came to believe that John Kemper moved Andover from strength to strength and became "a wonderful model of saintly mellowness of character" toward the end. Another alumnus who roomed in the Headmaster's house describes a very revealing episode:

The Headmaster used to have us in for milk shakes and snacks with his family on selected Saturday nights. One Saturday night a student was making a milk shake with great gusto when the top slipped and sprayed the shake across the kitchen. Kemper, in an attempt to make light of the matter, said, "I guess there are soda jerks and just plain jerks", but he didn't quite pull off the joke, and it took us some time later that night to convince the boy that no criticism was intended. It was particularly sad, though, because some successes along those lines would have made a big difference to the students.

When the students challenged him on legitimate grounds, however, he could act magnificently:

That year, John Kemper received as a gift a great black behemoth of a car, a classic in mint condition.[38] . . . Our consuming goal was to get a ride in that magnificent auto. Through one of our fathers we obtained a proper black chauffeur's hat with "Mason" emblazoned on its metal insignia. Summoning up our honours English, we composed a Victorian epistle, requesting that the recipient, one JMK, please be present to motor us to Commons the following day at 7:30 a.m. With some trepidation, we signed the note and mailed it to the Headmaster's house. To our awestruck delight, at the appointed hour, John Kemper showed up, wearing the hat, and duly ferried us to the Commons. Many may have thought him slightly aloof, but we knew better.

John Kemper believed that if a boy had to be dismissed, the School had somehow failed, and he did everything in his power to find new ways of dealing with undergraduate problems. When he found no mitigating circumstances, however, he could be as stern as Uncle Sam Taylor, as the following episode illustrates:

My last memory of Mr. Kemper is when he was presiding over the Discipline Committee that was to decide my fate after being caught selling phony I.D. cards to my colleagues, for use in buying liquor, the drinking age being 21. The cards were replicas of some White Citizens Committee organization in Atlanta, Georgia, with the forged signature of the Chief of Police of Atlanta. A picture of the card holder glued onto it made it complete and surprisingly effective. I got a dollar apiece and had been making beer and pool money for two years before being caught, one month before graduation, after four years of attendance. The main point Mr. Kemper made was that I had violated the law of the land and didn't I feel I deserved the worst? I asked him if he had ever had the occasion to drink alcoholic beverages during prohibition. He declined to answer and informed me of the Committee's decision to expel me.

Another anecdote:

> In the spring of my Lower year we arrived for morning chapel to
> find the ceiling of the Cochran Chapel covered with helium-filled
> balloons. . . . Shortly John Kemper arrived and walked into the chapel
> through the front doors. He halted, stunned, plainly angry. Then he
> moved determinedly through to the robing area. When he and the
> chaplains emerged, we were anticipating a serious tongue-lashing.
> Instead, Mr. Baldwin, the head chaplain, read e.e.cummings' "Chan-
> son Innocent."[39] By the end of the poem, John Kemper, too, was
> smiling.

Early in his Andover career John Kemper decided that he should do some
teaching so as to get the feel of the place and selected a class in Algebra I
for his experiment. A former pupil remembers the class with pleasure:

> I regard it as most fortunate that I was in the next to last Algebra
> class Johnny Kemper taught. . . . He often said that he "Kept his
> finger on the school pulse" thru the 15 or so Juniors to whom he
> taught Algebra I. Unlike many of my classmates, I and my Algebra
> students felt that we "knew" Johnny, and Andover was unquestion-
> ably a warmer and friendlier place for us from the experience. It was
> fun to be called by your first name by the Headmaster as I piled
> into the football stands as a French Horn player in the band. This
> was the 1950's version of an ego trip!
> What student doesn't like to get his teachers off the subject and
> our class with Johnny was no exception; it was even more exciting
> with the headmaster. We learned a lot of history of the Academy
> and Johnny got into the habit of using figures about the school's
> endowment, investments, and holdings to get us interested in the
> problems of Algebra I. We, of course, went off to our dorms with
> "inside information and deep dark secrets about PA's finances."

Another admirer writes:

> John Kemper carried himself like one of his ancestors who led at
> Gettysburg and in no little way did this impression lead me to favor
> the lost cause of the South. . . . Kemper was a gentleman from the
> way he observed our games to the way he addressed a chapel service.
> To grow up to be like John Kemper was an ideal at the time: he
> radiated dignity.

In the 1950's without question the great majority of Andover undergraduates respected John Kemper, even if they did not feel close to him. In the
1960's this relationship began to deteriorate, even before the crises evolving
out of student protest late in the decade. For one thing, the Andover Program drive forced him to be away a lot, and he lost his close touch with

the School. He had developed a nervous habit of clearing his throat frequently during his speeches, and the undergraduates, annoyed by this habit, used to clear theirs at the same time. When, after the Surgeon General's report, the School banned smoking completely, he continued to smoke, which angered some students. Most important, he was by training and principle completely opposed to the student life style of the 1960's— the drugs, the long hair, the general sloppiness, the mocking of old institutions and practices. Had John Kemper been asked about his relations with the undergraduates, he would undoubtedly have said that he was not running a popularity contest. It was his job to see that the School was running well, and it *was* running well. Yet it is sad to think that only a handful of undergraduates ever got to know him well enough to understand his extraordinary qualities of character and humanity.

In many ways the climax of the Kemper administration came with the Andover Program, initiated in 1959 and completed in the early 1960's. Up to this point in the history of the School, there had never been a program so carefully researched, so efficiently organized, and so successfully realized. Yet it was only the climax to a building program that had begun in the early 1950's. When John Kemper took office, it was clear that the School needed a new gymnasium. The Borden Gym, considered the most modern of athletic facilities when it was built in 1902, could no longer meet the School's needs. It was too small, its equipment was antiquated, and it could not provide adequate facilities for boys interested in particular sports, especially in the winter. For years student polls in the yearbook had placed a new gymnasium in first place as Andover's greatest need, and shortly after John Kemper became Headmaster, the students attempted to show that they meant business in this matter by raising about five thousand dollars toward a new gym. This was impressive evidence that the need was real, and in 1951 the Trustees took over and before long the building became a reality. There was no attempt to launch a special drive to raise the sum needed—more than one million dollars. A substantial number of gifts came in voluntarily, and the Trustees voted to borrow from the endowment for any additional funds needed.

Antiquated as it was, the Borden Gymnasium was still a useful building; to tear it down would be a real waste of facilities. As a result it was decided to tie the new facility into the old building. This presented some architectural problems, for Borden was Victorian while the new building was to be modern; but after a certain amount of flak the problem was happily resolved. In similar fashion it was decided not to build a completely new swimming pool but to enlarge and remodel the old one. When the building was completed, it more than met the hopes of those who had worked so long and hard to get it erected. The most striking feature of what was christened the Memorial Gymnasium, in memory of Andover graduates killed in World War II, was the main floor, large enough to contain three basketball courts. Previously, the single court in Borden had severely limited the number of boys who could engage in this sport. Movable partitions made it possible to divide the main floor into play areas of different size and gave flexibility to the physical education program. Another striking feature of the new building was the movable stands for spectators. Facing one way, they would command the basketball courts; turned around and facing the other way they would command the swimming pool. Over one thousand spectators could be accommodated—again a vast improvement over Borden, where only a few hundred could be crowded in. The swimming pool itself was enlarged from four to six lanes, and a special diving pool was added at one end, with a high board as well as a low board. In addition there were squash courts, wrestling rooms, and, perhaps most important, locker space adequate for the whole School. The building was dedicated in February 1953, with Admiral William Halsey giving the address.

With the completion of the Memorial Gymnasium the whole program of athletics and physical education at Phillips Academy took a great leap forward.[40] Hockey had been having a hard time of it for many years. Hockey players usually spent a good part of the winter running cross country because there was no ice on the outdoor rinks. If there was ice, there was the problem of shoveling off the snow. One Andover hockey team had not played a single game before it met Exeter in the Boston Garden. Again the undergraduates applied pressure to the Trustees and Administration, and in the late 1950's Sumner Smith, P.A. 1908, agreed to provide the funds to construct an artificial rink. This did wonders for the Andover hockey program, but it soon became clear that the uncovered rink could not function at maximum efficiency without a roof, and that objective was included as part of the Andover Program. Thus well before the program was launched, Headmaster Kemper could boast of two splendid new additions to the School plant.[41]

Any institution that embarks on a fund drive of the magnitude of the Andover Program must depend heavily—if not exclusively—on its alumni. Fortunately for Phillips Academy, the Andover Alumni Association had been thoroughly reorganized in 1956 and was in vigorous condition. It will be remembered that what was to all intents and purposes a brand new organization had been established in 1946. The experience of ten years had indicated the need for certain changes, and as a result a Committee was appointed under the chairmanship of Edward Robie, '37, to revise the Alumni Constitution. Alumni Council President David A. Dudley, '28, also provided strong leadership. The new constitution enlarged the Council to sixty-five members, reduced the previous number of committees, many of which had been moribund anyway, integrated the Class Secretaries Association and the Class Agents Association into the Council—they had previously been operating independently—and increased representation from the Trustees, the School Administration, and the Faculty. Without question the most important change was in the provision for Alumni Trustees. Hitherto the Board of Trustees had consisted of charter members and no one else. Now alumni representatives would sit with the Board and take part in their deliberations, though because of the School's Constitution, they could not vote. The President of the Alumni Council was automatically an Alumnus Trustee, and each year another alumnus would be elected by the alumni body for a three-year term. There is no question that Alumni Trustees quickened interest in the School on the part of the alumni body as a whole. In addition, they provided valuable counsel to the Board on many occasions. In several instances Alumni Trustees proved so useful that they were elected Charter Trustees after their term had expired. As a result of these changes, the Andover alumni body was a well organized group with a high morale. When the School turned to them for help with the Andover Program, they would not be found wanting.[42]

Speaking at the launching of the Andover Program early in 1959, Headmaster Kemper said:

> Education must meet our era of unparalled rapidity of change with new ideas, new attitudes, and new techniques and tools, while holding fast to the enduring values of the past. . . . By reason of its history, traditions, and present strength, including pre-eminently, the loyalty of its alumni body, Andover has an inescapable obligation for example and leadership.
>
> A deep, underlying cause for action now is clear evidence of the dangers facing the nation. To every thinking person it is obvious that our schools must be immeasurably strengthened—and rapidly—if the country is to survive what will undoubtedly be a long period of severe testing of its intellectual and moral resources.[43]

John Kemper was to play a leading role in this program. Donald H. McLean, Jr., '28, General Chairman of the Andover Program campaign, had this to say of the Kemper contribution:

> Throughout the campaign the Headmaster's leadership was vital in two areas—on the one hand as master planner, on the other as leading spokesman. . . . His determination was a continuing source of inspiration. And I suspect strongly that when future historians evaluate this period of Andover's history they will refer to it as the Kemper Program. In my opinion such a judgment will be entirely fitting.[44]

When the Headmaster announced the opening of the Andover Program campaign, a great deal of preliminary planning had already taken place. A Faculty Committee and a Trustee Committee had both worked on the needs of the School and had come to general agreement. Their recommendations were then turned over to the Alumni Council's Committee on Educational Policy and Administration, under the chairmanship of John U. Monro, P.A. '30. This group went over the recommendations with a fine-tooth comb, challenged the Faculty and Trustees on various matters, and were finally responsible for inclusion of a wing for the library in the program, in the belief that the program needed additional intellectual facilities to give it balance. With the goals agreed upon, Dean Alan Blackmer prepared a comprehensive workbook that would lay out the specific reasoning behind the various proposals.[45] As finally codified, the program included the following proposals:

> For Teachers and Students
> Phillips Academy's aim is to have a Faculty salary scale second to none, with a range of from $4,000 to $12,000 and with perquisites of from $1,000 to $3,000.
> The Andover Teaching Fellowship Program, initiated a few years earlier, whereby college graduates could serve as apprentice teachers at the school, must be continued and supported.
> Scholarship funds must be maintained at a high level so that the school could say that there was not a boy in America who could not afford Andover.[46]

In committing themselves to these objectives, the Trustees made a vital decision. They voted to depend on tuition, endowment income, and annual giving for the funds necessary to implement them. Thus none of the funds raised in the Andover Program campaign would go for these purposes. All the energies of the campaign could, therefore, be devoted to raising money for capital improvements, totaling a little over six million dollars. Specifically the program entailed the following projects:

> The Sciences A new Science building to meet the needs of the school. School enrollment had gone up 25 percent in the past twenty-five years, science course enrollment, 60 percent. The old building, Morse Hall, was clearly inadequate.
>
> A remodeling of Morse Hall to provide additional classroom space. Only 32 percent of Andover teachers had classrooms of their own.
>
> The Library The construction of an additional wing at the rear of the Oliver Wendell Holmes Library. Such a wing would relieve crowded reference rooms and provide a reading room for American history students and a place where they could write research papers.

The Arts	The enlarging and modernizing of the George Washington Hall stage; the construction of a workshop area for painting, sculpture, woodworking, metal working, and the like; the building of an Audio-Visual Center for producing films and slide-tapes; and the inclusion of a lecture hall with a small stage. The aim in all this was to have as many boys as possible engage in creative work of their own.
Housing	The construction of five new dormitories, the remodeling of old dormitories so as to provide commons rooms, and the elimination of old substandard housing.
Religion	The construction of a small chapel in the basement of the Cochran Chapel to provide for special services for boys of different faiths.
Athletics	The construction of a roof for the hockey rink, a crew boathouse, additional playing fields, and an extension to the Cage.[47]

It was an ambitious, exciting program. If realized, it would transform the School almost as much as the Cochran program of the 1920's. It now remained to raise the six million dollars.

That job was entrusted to Donald H. McLean, Jr., P.A. '28, and it is hard to see how the School could have picked a better man. He may have said that he thought the program should be called the Kemper Program, but it could equally well have been called the Kemper-McLean Program. A lawyer on the staff of John D. Rockefeller, 3rd, McLean had had wide experience in dealing with people in a variety of different situations, and this experience was to prove more and more valuable as the campaign developed. The prospect was an awesome one. Never before in the history of the country had a private secondary school attempted a campaign of this magnitude. When it became clear that all systems were "go," McLean began to build up his organization. For professional advice on money-raising he turned to the firm of Kersting, Brown and Company, and particularly to Robert F. Duncan, who conducted a survey among influential Andover alumni and parents to get a feel for the climate of opinion about a drive. Next McLean needed a right-hand man, whom he found in Frederic A. Stott '36. Stott had served as Alumni Secretary for several years previously and was an ideal man for Executive Secretary of the Campaign. A Steering Committee of Trustees, Alumni, and Parents would serve as the spearhead of the campaign for the next two years. Meeting in Andover in the fall of 1958, this Committee decided, first, that solicitation would be on a person-to-person basis. They drew up a table indicating the size and number of gifts that would be needed in different categories—one gift of over a million dollars, two gifts between half a million and a million, eight gifts between $100,000 and half a million, and so on. A campaign headquarters was established in New York City. Not only would that make life infinitely easier for Chairman McLean himself; most of the members of the Steering Committee and a substantial number of potentially large donors also lived in that area. The next step was to set up Special Gift Committees to deal with potentially large donors in areas where they were concentrated. Eventually, twelve such committees were established. For the general campaign, committees were organized in every city in the country where there were twenty-five or more alumni. Appalling though the magnitude of this task may seem, in a surprisingly short time volunteer committee organizations had been established in over two hundred and fifty different communities. McLean received staunch support from R. L. (Tim) Ireland, III, P.A. '38, who performed heroically as National Alumni Chairman, and from Thomas M. Evans, who agreed to serve as Parent Chairman. Mr. Evans' contribution may be seen in Stimson House, which was given by the Parents of Andover boys, and in his own generous contribution to the new Science Building that bears his name. The campaign got off to a fast start. When the Headmaster announced it in March 1959, the Trustees by themselves had already pledged over one million dollars. By that June, two and one half million dollars had been pledged by 187 donors. The fall of 1959 saw numerous trips by Headmaster Kemper and his Assistant, James R. Adriance, P.A. '28, to the increasing number of communities where Tim Ireland's volunteer committees were operating. The Headmaster, incidentally, was very diffident about fund raising; he knew he must do it, but he always felt uncomfortable asking people for money. The trouble was that because he was very good at it, the leaders of the campaign worked him hard. By the end of 1959 over four million dollars had been raised, including a gift for the new library wing from James S. Copley, P.A. '35. Those in charge of the drive did not limit themselves to the United States. There was a Canadian Committee and dinners for Andover alumni in both Paris and London. Early in 1960 the campaign seemed to drag, but all concerned with it received a shot in the arm when R. Crosby Kemper, Jr., P.A. '45, announced his intention of giving the auditorium for the Arts and Communications Center. When at Commencement 1960, a little over a year after the formal campaign had been announced, it was reported that the School had received over five and one half million dollars from 4,413 donors, there was clearly light at the end of the tunnel. By the fall of 1960 there was only $200,000 to go and by the end of the year the drive was over the top with a preliminary total of $6,235,000.

This was certainly a magnificent achievement, as to both the amount raised and the speed with which it had been raised. Characteristically, Chairman McLean had some thoughtful comments to make about the whole operation once it had been completed. He attributed some of the success to the generally favorable economic climate that had prevailed in the country during the campaign. Andover also benefited because Yale, where so many Andover graduates had gone, was not campaigning at the same time, even though Harvard and Princeton were. The success of the Harvard drive was probably a help, for many people believed that Andover was doing at the secondary school level what Harvard was doing at the collegiate level. The Chairman was convinced that the person-to-person approach had paid off also; although a large amount of attractively printed material had been prepared for distribution to those who could not be reached directly, it was the personal touch that counted. The costs of the campaign were modest: 5.6 percent of the total amount raised went for operating expense, a percentage generally considered low by professionals. And Chairman McLean went on to spell out the guiding principles that had governed the campaign:

1. Before contributions are sought a well-documented case must be prepared—one which can withstand cross-examination by reasonable men.
2. Those closest to the institution are those from whom major support should be expected.
3. People respond to other people, not to the mail of other people.
4. A number of substantial gifts must be secured as well as a large number of gifts.
5. The more people active in the campaign organization, the larger the number of givers.
6. People contribute when they are asked by others to contribute—and seldom until they are asked. Moreover, people are more effective in asking others to give when they have made their own commitment first.[48]

These principles provide food for thought for any would-be fund-raiser. In summing up the gifts, the Chairman reported that over 5,000 Alumni had contributed over five million dollars, over eight hundred parents had contributed over one million dollars, and something over $200,000 had come from Foundations, Corporations, and friends, for a final total of $6,763,971.[49]

Finally, in considering the implications of a campaign such as the Andover Program the Chairman wondered whether it was necessary every generation for private institutions to engage in ventures of this kind. He came to the conclusion that it was because there was no effective alternative. To try to raise capital funds from tuition would price a School out of the market. And he thought it a useful exercise for an institution to go through a process of self-analysis, as it must do if it is to present a case to the public. For him one of the greatest things about the Andover Program was the evidence it presented of the loyalty and generosity of countless friends of the school—evidence that made the institution's future look bright indeed.

The Andover Program buildings more than realized the hopes of their planners. As one after another of the new structures was completed, the face of the Hill was altered and excitement mounted. Benjamin Thompson, the member of Architects Collaborative of Cambridge who was in charge of the Andover Program buildings, came up with some brilliant solutions to the problem of fitting new structures with modern construction into the already existing older plant. Particularly successful was his design for the Copley Wing on the library, where the wing was to be virtually surrounded by older buildings. Without being imitative, he designed the wing so that it would be modern in concept and at the same time blend in easily with the older buildings. The Copley Wing immediately took much of the pressure off the older reference rooms in the Library and for a few years served as a study hall for American history students as well. When the American history course started using paperbacks instead of having the students read from texts on reserve in the Copley Wing, this function of the wing came to an end. Thompson was equally successful in his design for the new dormitories in the Rabbit Pond area, using glass and modern construction but retaining brick so as to make the new buildings fit the rest of the campus. Headmaster John Kemper had some new plans for the housemasters of these dormitories. He had come to the conclusion that there were not enough good housemasters to go around and so he proposed a scheme whereby a forty-boy dormitory, with two entries of twenty boys each, would have a senior housemaster and a junior housemaster responsible to the former. He hoped that the influence and expertise of an older, experienced housemaster could thereby be extended to the whole dorm. But he reckoned without the desire for autonomy on the part of the junior housemasters, who chafed under the control of their seniors and wanted to run their own show. As a result, after a few years' trial, the scheme was abandoned.

At the start the new dormitories in the Rabbit Pond area housed only Seniors, which led to the area acquiring the unfortunate name of "Senior City." Later, when vertical housing was introduced, this was changed. No matter what boys were living in them, however, they provided extremely comfortable living quarters, with spacious commons rooms to foster social exchanges among the students and Faculty. The new athletic facilities were equally successful. A handsome wooden roof on the Sumner Smith hockey rink made it possible to use that facility eighteen hours a day—for part of which time it was rented out to other institutions—and aroused so much interest in hockey and skating as to suggest the need for another rink. New tennis courts, new playing fields, an extension to the cage to make it possible to run a fifty-yard dash in winter track, a new boathouse—all these enriched the lives of Andover students. The new Science building was magnificent. Constructed with three wings—one for physics, one for chemistry, and one for biology—it was so flexible that the space for each of these three sciences could be adjusted to fit enrollment. A certain amount of flak developed over a Japanese cherry tree, located directly in front of the main entrance. Science building supporters wanted to chop it down so as to display the main entrance; environmentalists were outraged at the thought. Eventually the latter won, and the cherry tree stayed. The most interesting of all the buildings was the Art and Communication Center; its purpose was not only to house existing facilities in the arts, but to encourage the development of new activities that, it was hoped, would come into being once adequate facilities were provided. The remodeling of the stage of George Washington Hall made possible the production of much more sophisticated dramatic works, but it was the small, experimental theater below the main stage that attracted the most student interest. A generation before, the School might mount two or three dramatic productions a year; now there seemed to be nearly one a week. The provision for a well equipped photography workshop resulted in a burgeoning of interest in photography; and the Audio-Visual Center, under the brilliant direction of Gordon Bensley, was soon making it possible for all manner of classes to see movies and slide tapes that enriched their understanding of the subject under study.

The Kemper Auditorium, about a quarter the size of George Washington Hall, has been used on countless occasions for relatively small gatherings, and the Underwood Room has become a community center where, for example, Seniors come for coffee and cookies in midmorning. The remodeling of Morse Hall for the Mathematics Department, the remodeling of West Quadrangle dorms so as to provide them with Commons Rooms, the construction of two new Faculty houses, and, finally, the construction of what was named the Sylvia Kemper Chapel, after the wife of the Headmaster, who had died, all served useful purposes and stimulated undergraduate activities previously handicapped by lack of adequate facilities.[50] As always, there were some problems with the new construction, but in a few years these difficulties were surmounted, and the School was free to enjoy its new riches. The Andover Program was so well conceived and so well planned that the need for new buildings has been virtually nonexistent until recently. The merger with Abbot Academy, increasing the size of the School and introducing girls into the undergraduate body, has led to the demand for a new—or at least a remodeled—Commons and the construction of athletics facilities for girls, but given the undergraduate body they were building for, those in charge of the Andover Program did their job with rare vision.

A capstone was placed on the Andover Program and the achievements

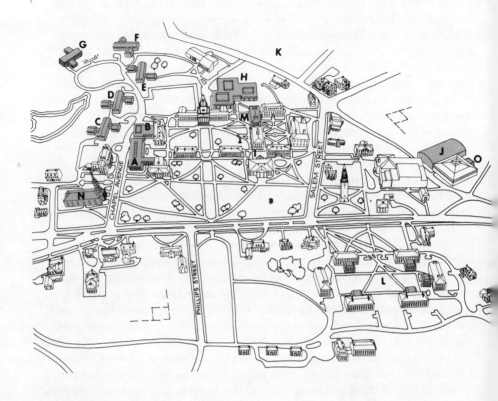

73. *Buildings on the Phillips Academy campus constructed under the Andover Program.*

A *Audio-Visual Center*
B *New Stages in George Washington Hall*
  Five new Dormitories in the Rabbit Pond Area
C *Stearns House*
D *Stevens House*
E *Stimson House*
F *Fuess House*
G *Nathan Hale House*
H *Evans Hall, the new Science Building*
I *The Copley Wing on the Oliver Wendell Holmes Library*
J *Roof for the Hockey Rink*
K *Rafferty Playing Fields*
L *Common Rooms for the West Quadrangle Dormitories*
M *Remodeling of Morse Hall*
N *Sylvia Kemper Chapel in the Basement of the Cochran Chapel*
O *Extension of Cage*

of the Kemper Administration when *Time Magazine*, in its 26 October 1962 issue, put John Kemper on its cover and devoted its cover story to Andover in particular and eastern preparatory schools in general. The theme of the article, as announced on the cover, was "Excellence and Intensity in U.S. Prep Schools," with the caption "Andover's John Kemper" beneath his picture. The picture itself made the Headmaster look pretty grim, with an almost sharklike mouth that many found uncharacteristic. According to the story circulated on the Hill, the artist's first rendition of the Headmaster made him look benign and benevolent, as indeed he was. But this did not fit the "intensity" theme, and the artist was ordered to make him look more intense. The result was a slitlike mouth that made him indeed look intense. He passed it off lightly, telling people that *Time* wanted the public to know that he could bite. Aside from the severe portrait, the article gave Phillips Academy very high marks indeed. It opened by citing the belief of Andover supporters that it was "the nation's best prep school." The authors were impressed by the dramatic changes that had taken place in private schools since the war: "By snubbing *Social Register* dullards and by combing the country for bright recruits of all races, religions, and incomes, they are fast becoming more democratic than homogeneous suburban public schools." And both Andover and Exeter were becoming "national public schools," with representatives from almost every state in the Union. As for the Headmaster, *Time* said, "Kemper's gifts for hard analysis and easy leadership galvanized Andover. Today, Harvard College's Dean John Monro calls Kemper 'one of the really great headmasters.' " Yet the Headmaster has plenty of problems: "He worries about the lucky-me attitude that affects many Andover boys. He wonders how to teach them a sense of humanity and public service. He wants the school to serve. 'We should be identified with public school,' he says. 'Our job is to be available to anyone who wants to use us. We must be of service." There was no question about the "excellence" part of an Andover education: "The average Andover graduate, says College Board President Frank H. Broyles, 'could enter junior year in a great many colleges without risk of failure.' " In speaking of his own upbringing, John Kemper said, "Father expected all of us to be officers and gentlemen, which was hard for my sisters but not for me." *Time* was impressed with the Andover Teaching Fellowship program, whereby a college graduate could spend a year at Andover practice teaching, to be followed by a year of graduate school paid for by the School. *Time* was also impressed with the foreign language programs: "Foreign languages begin without books, and English is banned from the classrooms. For nine hours a week, 14-year-olds answer one question after another in high-speed French and Spanish." Yet not everything was rosy. Some teachers were disturbed at the emphasis placed on grades, looking toward entry into prestige colleges. " 'The spirit of man is neglected in this school' fumes Emory Basford, veteran chair-

74. *John Mason Kemper with his second wife, the former Abby Castle.*
Mrs. Kemper graduated from Abbot Academy in the Class of 1931 and in
1964 was elected a Trustee of the Academy.

man of the English department. . . . 'This has become a strange, bewildering, killing place.' "

John Kemper agreed that the School might be trying to get the wrong kind of best out of its students, but suggested that parents should bear some of the blame for not placing enough emphasis on the old dream of being a good father and a good man. Despite these criticisms, however, it was the boys who made the School. As one teacher said, "And those great kids—where can a man find students who are so electrifying? There lies the dream of the good teacher. There is the significance and challenge here." As in all articles of this kind, the praise of Andover was qualified; without qualification the account would have been fatuous. Yet taken as a whole, the *Time* piece was a powerful endorsement of both the School and its Headmaster, John M. Kemper.[51]

CHAPTER EIGHTEEN

MID-CENTURY DEVELOPMENTS

DURING THE Fuess and Kemper administrations a number of developments occurred on Andover Hill that would alter the face of the School. Some involved changes in the curriculum. Toward the end of the period the English Department developed a new course entitled "Competence," designed, through a new approach, to teach students to write more effectively. The course was an instant success, as was attested by articles about it in national news magazines, and has had substantial influence on the curricula of other schools. The Mathematics Department, in addition to adding new courses in advanced mathematics, acquired a computer, which gave a new dimension to the teaching of mathematics and has been extensively used by the administration as well. The number of history courses increased from five to over twenty and offered students for the first time instruction in such subjects as the history of education, of the family, and of women, as well as more conventional fields like Russia. The Science Department, in addition to adding advanced courses in physics and chemistry, expanded their offerings in the life sciences with subjects like ecology. The Language Department developed new courses in Russian, Italian, and, for a time, Chinese, in addition to enriching already existing courses in French, Spanish, and German. The so-called direct method, whereby only the foreign language to be studied is spoken in the classroom, which had been pioneered by Dr. James H. Grew, was used not only with French, where it had first been tried, but with all languages. Dr. Grew also tried the interesting experiment of having qualified Seniors teach first-year courses in French. A fully equipped language laboratory was set up which enabled students to listen to tapes of the language being studied and also to test their own pronunciation. A brand new department came into existence with the establishment of courses in psychology, while the number of offerings in the field of Religion increased markedly. The Oliver Wendell Holmes Library steadily enlarged its collections, until today they consist of well over one hundred thousand books. A new Teaching Fellowship program was set up under which each year ten or so college graduates would come to the School as apprentice teachers who, it was hoped, would choose the teaching profession as their life work. Among other things, this program proved to be an extremely useful recruiting device in hiring new teachers. Meanwhile undergraduate extracurricular activities proliferated, particularly after the abolition of the Societies. The School publications like the *Phillipian* continued to flourish, and new clubs were formed. One year an energetic group of undergraduates set up a mock Senate, where they tried a President on impeachment, debated various pieces of legislation in the news at the time, and engaged in intricate parliamentary maneuvers. All of these changes were important and interesting, and all could well be discussed at length. They took place within the existing framework of the School and were, therefore, primarily evolutionary. This chapter, however, will be devoted to a discussion of five changes that broke sharply with the past— the explosion in the Arts, the transformation of Andover Summer Session, the reformation of the Department of Archaeology, the development of new policies and procedures in Admission, Scholarships, and College Admissions, and the development of cooperation between Andover and Exeter.

THE VISUAL ARTS

In 1955 Oliver Jensen, '32, was asked by the School to poll Andover alumni from representative classes to find out what they thought about the School. From among many interesting findings, the following was particularly striking:

> The most remarkable development, from the standpoint of the older classes at any rate, is the rise of art—which in my day was something we heard they kept in that new gallery, and which we left there, undisturbed. Obviously something constructive has been done to change the atmosphere. Whatever it was that once wrapped so fundamental an aspect of culture in an aura of sissification . . . seems to have disappeared. The art-loving class of 1951, in fact, still doesn't think the subject is getting enough attention.[1]

Though Jensen is talking about the visual arts, similar developments have taken place in drama, music, and, more recently, the dance. Many factors have contributed to this important change at Phillips Academy: in the first place the number of teachers in all phases of the arts has grown from four in the early 1930's to some fifteen in the early 1970's, not counting members of other departments who work in the field of drama; secondly, the various departments of the arts have not simply grown in size; a group of extraordinarily imaginative and forward-looking men and, more recently, women have developed programs in the arts with great appeal for the undergraduates; thirdly, the construction of the Arts and Communication Center in 1963 provided, for the first time in the School's history, adequate facilities for the study and practice of the arts; and, finally in the 1960's courses in the arts provided a welcome relief to an alienated generation from the rigidly structured cognitive courses that characterized most of the Andover curriculum.[2]

The first major breakthrough for the arts in the history of Phillips Academy, as noted earlier, was the construction of the Addison Gallery of American Art in 1931 and the acquisition of a distinguished collection of paintings and sculpture by native artists to go with it.[3] It was the hope of Thomas Cochran, who was responsible for the building and a good part of the collection, that if Andover boys could be surrounded by beautiful things, their lives could be immeasurably enriched. Cochran suggested that the first Director of the Gallery be Charles Sawyer, son of his dear friend James Sawyer, the School Treasurer. When Thomas Cochran suggested something, it was usually done, and Charlie Sawyer soon took over. Because he had some background in the law, in addition to his interest in the arts, he proved an ideal museum administrator. He soon had the permanent collection hung, and he worked hard at finding and purchasing new acquisitions. In this work he was assisted by the Addison Gallery Committee, which Cochran had established to oversee the purchase of new works of art. Charlie Sawyer also arranged a number of loan exhibits designed to attract the interest of the community. Among the more important were "The International Exhibition of Theater Arts," "Water Colors by Contemporary Americans," "The Works of John Sloan," "Works of Maurice and Charles Prendergast," a show of the drawings of Walt Disney, and "Water Colors, Drawings and Prints by Winslow Homer."[4] It was Charlie Sawyer's ambition to have the Gallery serve the community in general and the Phillips Academy students in as many ways as possible. He was particularly anxious to have the boys receive instruction in drawing, painting, and modeling. "But," he wrote, "The aim will not be to produce artists at Phillips Academy. It should rather be the purpose to show that an ability to draw represents neither eccentricity nor talent but may be as much a part of a complete cultural equipment as the ability to write."[5] At the time he took over, there was an informal Sketch Club that reached a few boys, but it was not until the appointment of Bartlett H. Hayes, Jr., in 1933 that regular instruction in painting and drawing was made possible. When the Gallery was built, no real provision had been made for studios, and so the painting classes had to be conducted in a spare room in the basement that was far from satisfactory. Though a start had been made, it would take a long time for the new Art Department to convince the undergraduates that art was something they should concern themselves with, and during the 1930's progress toward achieving this end was slow.

In 1940 Charles Sawyer left the Addison Gallery to become Director of the prestigious Worcester Art Museum, where he was to work until, later, he went to Yale. He had laid a firm foundation for the work of the Addison Gallery; it remained for his followers to carry through what he had begun.

Sawyer's successor was Bartlett H. Hayes, Jr., who would hold the position for twenty-nine years, from 1940 to 1969. During that period he made the Gallery—and himself—nationally, even internationally, known. Though Bart Hayes's interests were catholic, his greatest achievements were in the shows he mounted. Some of the most interesting were based upon pictures from the permanent collection, rather than imported works. For example, "Architecture of a Painting" was built around Edward Hopper's "Manhattan Bridge Loop," an item in the permanent collection. The purpose of the show was to teach viewers by a close examination of this one work of art. Limitations of space prevent mention of more than a few of Bart's exhibitions, but some of the more significant showed works by Mahonri Young, Hans Hoffman, and a group of European Artists Teaching in America. Each year there were striking exhibitions of the work of the students themselves. Accompanying all the important shows were handsomely printed brochures, reproducing important pictures in the exhibition and including perceptive texts. Bart the gallery director and Bart the teacher were never far apart, and several of his exhibitions were didactic. "The American Line: One Hundred Years of Drawing" traced the development of American drawing over the past century and illustrated how the changes that had taken place reflected changes in American society generally. "The Naked Truth and Personal Vision" instructed the viewer how to look at a work of art and how to distinguish between the raw material the artist had started with and what he had done with it. Finally, "A Layman's Guide to Modern Art" proved to be an immensely popular explication of this difficult subject, and the resulting book was widely sold throughout the country.

Bart was also interested in helping Andover alumni who were artists. For example, one exhibition presented paintings and mobiles by Donald G. Outerbridge, '42. Nor were the exhibitions limited to the Andover community; several traveled widely to other galleries and museums and brought the names of the Addison Gallery and Phillips Academy to many people throughout the country. It is probable that more people know about Phillips Academy through the Addison Gallery than through any other single agency of the School.[6]

The work of the Gallery since 1969 has been ably carried on by Chris-

75. *Bartlett Harding Hayes, Jr., of the Class of 1922, Director of the
Addison Gallery of American Art, 1940–1969.*

topher Cook, Bart's successor. He has focused particularly on artists who live in the area around Andover, with painters from Lawrence and Boston, for example, represented in exhibitions. Other programs illustrative of Chris Cook's determination to involve the Gallery with the surrounding communities have included the public schools of the area. The most innovative of his programs is one devoted to work with patients at the Danvers State Mental Hospital. Believing that the study and practice of art can help emotionally disturbed people deal with reality and not escape into fantasy, Chris organized classes in painting and drawing for the patients. One man who had not spoken for years started to talk again after working in this art program. Chris also had the patients make videotapes of themselves so that they could see themselves in action. Arrangements were made for the patients to visit the Addison Gallery on a monthly basis. The result of all this was a show that was astonishingly competent; it went on tour throughout the country. Chris Cook annoyed some people by moving the ship-model collection to the basement, but justified the move on the ground that no room in the Gallery should ever be permanently static.[7] The Addison Gallery has been fortunate in its three directors—Sawyer, Hayes, and Cook. They are all very different, but each has contributed innovative programs for the institution, and together they have made it nationally known.

At the same time that the Gallery was developing into a national institution, important changes were being made in teaching art to Andover undergraduates. The first breakthrough came in 1933, when the Faculty voted to establish a two-hour minor course for Upper Middlers as an introduction to art and music. Originally this course spent two terms on art and one on music, but later it was half and half. As first conceived, the art course was essentially a history of art, depending heavily on slides of famous masterpieces. It was not generally successful, the main reason being that it was another cognitive course, similar to those the boys were already taking; no chance was given students to learn about art by practicing it themselves. In an attempt to improve this situation in the late 1930's a course entitled "Studio Art" was offered; it would serve as an alternative to the introductory course. At about the same time "Advanced Art" was established for Seniors who had taken studio art the year before. Bart Hayes taught the studio course at the start, but he soon became Director of the Gallery and a new man was needed. The person selected was Patrick Morgan, an extraordinarily gifted art teacher. Not only did he make things sing in his studio; he and his wife Maud, a distinguished painter in her own right, became father and mother confessors for countless numbers of boys. At a time when many of the faculty still conceived their relationship to the boys as one of cops to robbers, Pat and Maud Morgan treated them as equals, and their house was continually thronged with undergraduates. Much of this general popularity was transferred to the art program and helped to make it acceptable to the undergraduates. Pat Morgan's job was not an easy one. In 1948 he wrote a perceptive article suggesting that there were two major hindrances to the success of an art program in a secondary school: lack of facilities and the curriculum. Though lack of facilities was bad enough—Pat was still teaching in the Gallery basement—the real problem was the curriculum. Not so far back, he suggested, it was assumed that a man would marry whatever culture he was to possess and thus there was no point in art programs. Some schools had used art as therapy for maladjusted students, with the result that art classes became a kind of asylum. But the real problem was the colleges, which looked with suspicion on art courses offered for admission. Until the colleges changed their tune, it would be difficult for secondary schools to develop adequate programs. And this was all the sadder because elementary school children loved art and wanted to continue with it. If only the curricular hurdle could be jumped, Pat predicted a flowering of art programs that could provide excitement and insight for many boys.[8] Pat, unfortunately, left Andover in 1957 and thus never saw the flowering he was talking about. But while he was here, he was a rare spirit.

Some minor changes were made in the art courses in the late 1950's and early 1960's. The studio course was modified and an art major was offered. But this was nothing compared with what happened with the completion and dedication of the Arts and Communications Center in 1963. This handsome complex consisted of a small auditorium, a lounge, rooms for painting and drawing, sculpture, photography, and manual arts, an experimental theater, and an audiovisual center. This latter included four small rooms, where three or four people could see a movie or a slide tape; a larger room, where a whole class could be handled; and facilities for movies to be shown in the Kemper Auditorium. John Kemper used to worry about this new building. Would it be used enough to warrant the large sum of money that had been expended on it, he wondered. He did not need to fear: the building was a catalyst, stimulating all kinds of creative endeavor on the Hill. In charge of the Audio-Visual Department was Gordon G. (Diz) Bensley, '42, who had joined the Faculty as a young art instructor in 1948. It was not long before he decided to develop an audiovisual department to serve the entire School, and despite handicaps of space and lack of equipment he made progress during the 1950's. In this venture he was ably assisted by technician Aloysius (Lolo) Hobausz and his wife Lillian. Midway in the decade Diz was given the old Faculty room in Samuel Phillips Hall, which could seat some seventy students, and began selling his services to his colleagues. The most obvious type of audiovisual presentation was, of course, the movie. If a French class could see a movie on Paris or an English class a movie like *Man for All Seasons*, it could greatly enrich their classroom experience. Yet movies had problems. They were prohibitively expensive to buy, which necessitated renting them; in addition, in many cases, the movie did not provide what the teacher wanted. Diz Bensley, therefore, became a great shouter for the slide tape. This involves making a number of slides of the teacher's choice and then recording a commentary on tape. In its most sophisticated form, the slides are put in a projector and synchronized with the tape through magnetic markings on the latter so that the whole show is automatic. Slide tapes take a long time to make, but they can easily be revised by introducing new slides and need never become frozen, like a movie. Under Diz's prodding more and more Faculty members began to make use of his services, and with the opening of the Arts and Communications Center the whole program was stepped up tremendously. Theoretically, five different showings could occur at the same time, and the small showing rooms made it possible for students who had missed an earlier showing to catch up. Partly as a result of the new facilities and the excitement of the new building, members of the Faculty began to make slide tapes. Wayne Frederick of the History Department, for example, produced a splendid one on the American cowboy. At the same time, the number of rented films increased. This is not to say that more use might not have been made of the facilities; many Faculty members have not found a way of adapting their class programs to them. But on balance the Audio-Visual Center has been a striking success, and Bart Hayes and Diz Bensley, who were responsible for the concept, deserve accolades.[9]

The Audio-Visual Center was only one part of the effect of the Arts and Communications Center on the art program in particular and the School in general. For the first time in the history of the School, adequate facilities for a wide variety of art courses were made available, and the Department was quick to take advantage of them. More important, it changed the whole concept of art teaching at Phillips Academy. The aim of the Department now was to give each undergraduate an experience in creative work in the arts. The old Introduction to Art, where the students were passive spectators and the material cognitive, was done away with the year after the Center opened. The following year there were new offerings in painting, architecture, furniture design, sculpture and photography, and in the next few years the list lengthened to include graphics, filmmaking, animation, ceramics, kinetic art, and a course called contemporary communications, given in conjunction with the English Department.[10] In making it possible for each student to have the experience of creating something in the art field, the Department found that photography was the most useful vehicle. A student with an inexpensive box camera could be turned loose anywhere on the campus to learn by experience the relationship between his picture and the object he photographed. Though some believe that too great an emphasis has been placed on photography, it is hard to fault the Art Department when the number of students that must be dealt with is considered. And the other art courses are flourishing as well. If anything else were needed to demonstrate the increased interest in art, course enrollments would furnish it. In 1976–77 Andover enrollment for term-contained courses in the field was 1041. To be sure, some students took more than one course, but at a conservative estimate over six hundred individual students took one or more art courses that year. Courses in the history of art have been transferred to the History Department, where they probably belong, and the present offerings of the Department are strictly non-cognitive. Though it is true that the most important parts of a school are the faculty and the students, a new building can sometimes bring about revolutionary change. That has certainly been the result of the Arts and Communications Center, as the flowering of art programs bears witness.

DRAMA

In large measure because of the Puritan antipathy to the stage and all its works, drama did not become a significant activity at Phillips Academy until well into the twentieth century. In the 1850's, for example, rumors that Harriet Beecher Stowe went to the theater in Boston did much to make her suspect in the Andover community. At the turn of the century a Dramatic Club was formed which presented, among other works, *She Stoops to Conquer*, with boys taking the girls' parts, but this organization appears to have died out in a few years. In the 1920's interest in the drama revived, and a newly organized Dramatic Club put on at least one production a year, again with the boys playing the female parts. In 1931, for example, the club presented *The Queen's Husband*, with the late Max F. Milliken, '31, in the leading part.[11] Drama at Phillips Academy continued pretty much in this same state until after the war. An exception occurred in 1937 when the Faculty presented Prissy Hallowell's *Many Happy Returns*. She not only wrote it but played the leading role of Mrs. Hogstrap. The production was directed by Allan T. Cook of the English Department. The play, a hilarious farce, included the delivery of a coffin to the wrong address, with Mrs. Hogstrap hiding in the coffin; the arrival on the scene of Dark Stable, a famous movie star; and various cloak-and-dagger complications that all eventually got sorted out.[12] The undergraduates were highly appreciative of this effort, which went far to convince them that the Faculty were human beings after all, not just policemen. (The production was repeated in 1955, with John M. Kemper playing the role of Wretch, the butler.)

A breakthrough in the direction of more professional productions came in 1948, when some students asked Pen Hallowell to put on *Othello*. No one had attempted Shakespeare before, though the Ben Greet players had occasionally performed plays like *As You Like It* before the School in the 1930's. Pen Hallowell decided to take the students up on their request, and thus began a series of distinguished productions of Shakespeare plays that would continue into the 1960's. Hallowell was interested in Shakespeare for two reasons: the challenge of producing him and the conviction that acting in a Shakespearean play would be a unique learning experience, far more valuable than anything to be learned in class. Once the Shakepeare tradition had become established, the Andover community was treated to *Macbeth, Hamlet, Antony and Cleopatra, The Merchant of Venice, King Lear*, and others. The beauty of these productions was greatly enhanced by the striking sets built by the stage crew under the direction of Hart D. Leavitt, with assistance from members of the Art Department. Instead of having boys play the female roles, Pen turned to the Faculty wives and discovered talented ladies able and willing to play the female parts. Particularly outstanding were Audrey Bensley as Cleopatra and Ethel Whitney as Desdemona. Director Hallowell describes his procedures as follows:

> The casts for our plays have usually been built up around one or two actors who seemed to be "naturals" for the major parts. . . . For them and their supporting casts, Shakespeare has become a part of their life. It means work, time and patience on their parts. On the average, each play is given 70 hours of rehearsal time on the stage. In addition, special drill in articulation, inflection, blank verse, posture, walking, gestures, even sitting, is necessary for individuals who, without the drill, might suffer by comparison with the better actors in the cast. In the interest of consistency, regional accents are levelled off as much as possible. Self reliance is encouraged by making it clear at the first rehearsal that no prompting is allowed, once the lines have been learned. The usual reason an actor forgets a line is that he has not learned to concentrate on the stage action. He allows himself to be distracted from this world of make believe. . . . If overall improvement is slow, scenes are recorded on a tape and played back to the cast. And so ad infinitum—work to eradicate any clumsiness which might tend to destroy the audience's illusion. Perfection can't be reached, of course, but we won't admit it until the play is over.
>
> There is just one question that I have been asked many times. I should like to answer before closing: "Must you spend so much time on the plays?" The answer is emphatically, "Yes!" To learn the lines is one thing. To declaim the lines with actions is another. To feel the lines is still something else. That takes time.[13]

It might be added that Pen Hallowell carried out his promise of no prompting by coming out and sitting in the audience on performance nights. Nor did the actors' academic records suffer, despite Faculty fears. For some time Faculty members had noticed that members of the football team did better in class during the season than afterward, when they had more time to study. The experience of the actors was another example of the same phenomenon. Taken as a whole, the Shakespeare productions were a smashing success, and the boys who participated in them never forgot the experience.

In 1955 a group of students organized the Drama Workshop, designed to give undergraduates more opportunity to engage in all phases of the drama. It was described as "an organization to teach boys, through experience, the mechanics and techniques of acting, directing, staging, designing, and producing dramatic productions."[14] The group believed that the Shakespearean plays, though admirably presented, did not give students a large enough share in the manifold activities that go to make up a dramatic production. They hoped to offer several one-act plays in the fall and a full-length play in the spring, leaving the winter for Shakespeare. The fall one-act plays or fragments of longer plays would be presented primarily to the members of the Drama Workshop, rather than to general public. Despite these praiseworthy aims, the Workshop never really got off the ground. In the first place, it had no permanent home and wandered about from White Auditorium to Peabody House to the Addison Gallery to George Washington Hall. Play production was obviously difficult under these circumstances. Nor was student support encouraging. The *Phillipian* panned many of their productions, and eventually the leaders came to the conclusion that they must present popular pieces like *Arsenic and Old Lace* and *The Ten Little Indians* if they were going to capture and hold an audience. The original aim of experimenting with different kinds of drama had to go by the board.[15] All of this changed when the Arts and Communications Center was completed in 1963. Part of that project included the construction of an experimental theater under the main stage of George Washington Hall. The main stage itself had been reequipped and modernized as part of the program. The Drama Lab, as the experimental theater soon came to be called, was another instance of how adequate facilities can stimulate activity in a given field. Once the Lab group had a place to roost, their activity increased tremendously. Partly because it was the 1960's and partly because of the facilities of the new building, students in the Drama Lab began to branch out into all kinds of experimental theater. They started slowly; in their first year they produced Saroyan's *Hello Out There*, O'Neill's *In the Zone*, and Beckett's *Waiting for Godot*, among other works. The next year saw the introduction of plays written by the students; after all, all activities were carried on by undergraduates. Some of the success of this venture was due to an arrangement with the Athletic Department whereby boys could be excused from a term of athletics to engage in various types of dramatic activity. The next year the Drama Lab group established a workshop in which Seniors instructed interested Lowers and Juniors through various kinds of dramatic exercises. From the late 1960's on, the Drama Lab has become more and more avant-garde. Works of Beckett, Ionesco,

LeRoi Jones, Pintner, and Brecht dominated, indicating the desire of members to look into every phase of the modern drama.[16] All of this led to a rivalry of sorts with the main-stage productions in George Washington Hall, the Drama Lab group insisting that Faculty direction was not necessary for the successful production of a theatrical work. Yet the two different dramatic activities have each continued without serious opposition from the other. Dramatic activity reached such a peak that in 1973 Headmaster Theodore Sizer appointed Harold Owen, '42, a member of the English Department, as Chairman of the Committee on the Performing Arts. As such he also has supervision of Dance, which Phillips Academy acquired as a result of the merger with Abbot and which has grown in popularity among both boys and girls ever since. Like the visual arts, drama provides the undergraduates with the opportunity for a noncognitive personal experience in art. This was a major purpose of the Arts and Communications Center, and in the field of theater the hopes of its builders have been richly fulfilled.

MUSIC

Unlike the visual arts, music has had a long history at Phillips Academy. While at Governor Dummer, Samuel Phillips told his family of the "superior singing" that the undergraduates were producing. Eliphalet Pearson was a musician of note: he played the cello, trained the school choir, and was a musicologist of sorts. In the early days of Phillips Academy the Trustees voted to provide a music master, though none seems to have been found. At the early Exhibitions, musical selections appear on the program, often with imported groups like the Germania Band or the Boston Cadet Band. After the 1870's the students took an active interest in music. As noted previously, there were a School choir and glee club, various quartets, a banjo club, and a mandolin club. Like athletics during this period, these organizations appear to have been primarily student inspired; certainly the Faculty provided no rigorous musical training.

The modern period of music at Andover started with the appointment in 1912 of Carl Friedrich Pfatteicher as Director of Music, a post he was to hold until 1947. In many ways Pfatteicher was not suited to teach music in a boys' school. He was first and foremost a scholar, his specialty being the work of Johann Sebastian Bach. He edited a learned edition of Bach's works that is still highly respected among musicologists. Though he would never have admitted it quite that bluntly, he really thought that no music worth the name had been written since 1900, and except for Wagner, he had doubts about nineteenth-century works as well. He waged a continual war against modern jazz, barbershop songs of the nineties, and sentimental Victorian music generally, and he complained vigorously when he was criticized by musical illiterates. For him there was no substitute for the best, and that meant, for the most part, German music of the seventeenth and eighteenth centuries.

Over the years "Pfatty" Pfatteicher was able to develop an excellent choir and glee club, a small orchestra, and a number of students who excelled as soloists. To encourage boys to join the choir, three bribes were offered: a free cut from chapel each week, or credit for a minor course on their schedule, or a small weekly stipend. Partly as a result of this system there were always more applicants for the choir than could be accepted. Applicants may also have been influenced by the fact that for concerts with girls' schools, the choir became the glee club and could enjoy the dance that followed the concert. It was always a hard fight to field an orchestra. Because there were not enough instrumentalists among the students, the orchestra had to be strengethened with various ringers from time to time. Dr. Pfatteicher's instrument was the organ, and he was never tired of bragging about the magnificent Martha Cochran Organ in the Cochran Chapel. In large part because of his enthusiasm for the instrument, a number of boys each year took organ lessons from him. Mention has been made in an earlier Chapter of the distinguished concerts held at Andover in the 1930's and 1940's. These were, for the most part, a result of Dr. Pfatteicher's taste and drive. Yet despite his accomplishments, he always bemoaned the fact that so few boys at Andover were musically literate. He liked to tell the story of a boy who came to him and said, "I play cello, but my mother wants me to play football." And then the good doctor would go on to say that until music had the same respect among the undergraduates that football did, the situation would be unsatisfactory. To buttress his case he used to remind boys that Bach sired twenty children— certainly no sissy could have done that. Next to his complaint about undergraduate lack of interest in music was his dissatisfaction with existing facilities for music. To be sure, with the construction of the Cochran Chapel an excellent choir practice room had been provided, but there were still not enough practice rooms for individual students and not enough instruments for those who could not afford to buy them. What was needed was a new building, designed for musical activities, that would both meet the present demand and encourage others to elect music as a field.

A student who knew Carl Pfatteicher remembers him as follows:

> As I saw it then and now, Dr. Carl Pfatteicher of Park House remains a kindred soul. *Gemütlichkeit* flowed from him, from his wife Lillian, and even from the overstuffed Dalmatian, Specky. Many a Sunday afternoon was spent, alone, in that Bavarian study overlooking the soccer fields, listening to the New York Philharmonic and occasionally looking greenwards through the leaded windows. The whole Park House group were congenial; the leader most of all.

Dr. Pfatteicher conducted the glee club and choir, played the organ in post-chapel Sunday recitals, dispatched brass quartets to the top of the Bell Tower; and otherwise sustained the musical life of Andover. Philosopher, theologian, and musician all in one, he was (except for the medical degree) our *alter*-Albert Schweitzer. Andover was his Lambarene. He was not really happy there. He escaped briefly on Saturday nights, going to Symphony with his students. . . . When once, ill-advisedly, he returned to see the changes which Art Instructor Pat Morgan had made in Park House—conservative pictures having given way to Avant Garde Modern Art—his wisdom seemed corroborated.

Yet for a long time Andover was his locus. Who of us in the glee club can forget the admonition: "Remember, lads, this is a concert followed by a dance—not a dance preceded by a concert!" He was hurt when some in the community objected to the choice of "The Mikado" as a Phillips-Abbot enterprise in 1943, while the war was going on. Individuals like my roommate took it amiss that Pfatteicher stressed performance on the trombone rather than motivation. Many did not share his enthusiasm for J. S. Bach, or his high-decibel interpretations of the master. Freddy Boyce, the Physics master, publicly disparaged the notion that sympathetic vibrations could shatter glass, on the grounds that (were the theory valid) the chapel windows would have been long since gone.

One Saturday afternoon my roommate and I went up in the chapel organ loft on a surreptitious inspection. Unbeknownst to us, the good doctor was about to practice. Suddenly, the "St. Anne's Fugue" broke forth, shaking all the pipes in the forest. As the poet says: "Such violence. And such repose." The doctor, in his wisdom, would surely have understood. It was he who allowed a student into the Bell tower, ostensibly to play "Ein' Feste Burg" for the general edification. When, instead, "Little Brown Jug" emerged, the master's chagrin knew no bounds.[17]

Toward the end of his career Dr. Pfatteicher finally agreed to put on a Gilbert and Sullivan opera with Abbot Academy as the spring musical. He was dubious about the project from the start, but at least it was not jazz. Much to his surprise he found himself enjoying the production thoroughly, and when the actual performance was received with acclaim by the undergraduates, he was as pleased as punch. For that rest of his career a Gilbert and Sullivan was mounted each year. How sad that he waited so long to compromise a bit with the Phillistines. He was a man who set high standards for himself and the School and who could be easily wounded by some imagined slight. He once wrote Al Stearns a letter accusing Al of cutting him dead after a Vesper Service. Al replied that he had not remembered seeing him on that occasion. Yet for many boys his contagious enthusiasm for great works of music rubbed off on them and stayed for the rest of their lives.

With the retirement of Carl Pfatteicher in 1947, the driving force went out of the Music Department for some time. The essentials of the Pfatteicher program were maintained, with choir, glee club, and orchestra continuing to function. Some distinguished spring musicals were given jointly with Bradford Junior College and with Abbot Academy—*Carousel* and *Brigadoon*, for instance. During this same period a School marching band was organized; its productions between the halves at football games were stirring.[18] But when plans for the Andover Program were drawn up, Music found itself the stepchild of the arts. The Department was then housed in Graves Hall, a building that had gone through various reincarnations since its life as the Science Building. For a while the School Laundry was there; junior members of the Faculty had taught there; after the war it had been used as a Civil Defense Headquarters. The building was old, the walls were thin, the acoustics disastrous, and it could not provide adequate quarters for the Music Department. Yet the Andover Program made no provision for correcting this state of affairs, and partly as a result, music did not share in the explosion of the arts that followed the construction of the Arts and Communications Center. Inadequate facilities can adversely affect student interest in a field, and this was undoubtedly true to some extent with music. Interest was rekindled after the merger with Abbot, and in the last few years William Thomas and a group of able assistants have bucked up the program. If, at long last, it can get adequate facilities, Music should once again take its rightful place among the arts at Andover.

THE SUMMER SESSION

During its thirty-five years of existence, the Andover Summer Session has gone through several metamorphoses until today it bears little resemblance to the institution established in 1942. Originally designed as a war measure to help Academy students accelerate their secondary education, build them up physically, and teach them skills useful in the armed forces, the session became, after the war, basically a testing ground for prospective students and gave the School's Admission Office a chance to select the most promising performers for admission in the fall. This role was continued throughout the 1950's until, in 1960, it was decided to make the Summer Session almost completely independent of the Winter Session, to eliminate make-up courses, and to recruit public school students vigorously. In 1964, for the first time in the history of Phillips Academy, girls were enrolled, and since that time a number of experimental courses and programs have been instituted. More recently, attempts have been made to recruit minority students, a program that, on balance, has probably been more successful than the similar one in the regular session. What those in charge of the Summer Session have been aiming at is a "national public summer school."

Mention has already been made of the first Summer Session in 1942 with its aims of enabling Andover boys to accelerate in order to graduate before the age of eighteen, to develop physically through a demanding body-building program, to give them experience in various kinds of manual labor, and to offer repair programs for those who had failed courses.[19] Later wartime sessions followed much the same course as the first one, though the curriculum was broadened to include more liberal arts courses in the belief that these would be useful to future officers.[20]

A high point of the 1945 session was the announcement by President Truman of the surrender of Japan. All the school bells were rung, and the students assembled in George Washington Hall to sing the Star Spangled Banner and listen to a short address from the director.[21] After the war the Summer Session adopted a conservative stance, its major purpose being to help Phillips Academy students who needed extra study, or prospective students who needed a preliminary experience with Andover standards. For a while the Admissions Office sent to the Summer School a substantial number of applicants to the regular session, after which they would compete for ten or fifteen places that might still be open in September. This exercise was brutal, as numbers of small boys tried frantically to beat one another in the competition; often at the end of the Session there were more eligible candidates than there were places. Fortunately, the practice was dropped after a few years. From the beginning, the Summer Session was conceived as an institution where experiments of various kinds were made in order to see if particular policies or courses should be adopted in the regular session, but in the years after the war the Summer Session was essentially conservative. Writing in 1949 Floyd T. Humphries, the Director, spelled out some of his suggestions for the future.[22] He hoped to see the introduction of courses in Greek and Latin; more emphasis on music, the visual arts, and reading; and departmental experimental courses. He thought a major effort should be made to help boys with language disabilities and blind spots in mathematics and suggested the establishment of clinics for each group. Interestingly enough, he thought the Session should have a stand-by program ready for use in time of war and recommended getting advice from the military for such a program. He pointed out that most of the Andover Faculty who taught in the Summer Session did so from economic necessity and expressed the fear that they would go stale if they continued to teach summer after summer. He hoped that every third year a member of the Summer School Faculty might receive a summer sabbatical with pay. Finally, he hoped that the Session might develop policies to attract more public school students, and hoped that a more generous scholarship program might be established to that end. But the Session was still to be tied closely to the regular session as the remedial programs and the testing of candidates for entrance into the Academy in the fall indicated.

As time went on, the Summer Session became more and more divorced from the regular session, until today it is for all intents and purposes a completely independent institution. In 1960 the first big changes were made, under the Directorship of Robert Hulburd. After that year, no Summer Session course carried Phillips Academy credit; the Session was reduced from eight to six weeks; a mandatory six-hour course in English composition for all students was introduced; review and make-up courses were dropped; and the screening of prospective candidates for the regular session was eliminated. Coupled with these changes came the gradual elimination of grades. From the start no grades were given in the English composition courses, and bit by bit the other courses fell into line. The result was that teacher and student alike could concentrate on achievement rather than worry about marks. There was also a proliferation of new courses, such as The Art of Communication, Probability with Application to Elementary Statistics, Research in Biology, Contemporary Drama Workshop, and Atomic Physics. Those in charge of the Session were apprehensive that these changes might result in a falling off of applications, but the reverse proved to be true, the student body increasing by over 50 percent between 1960 and 1964. In 1964 came a truly momentous change when, for the first time in the history of the Academy, girls were admitted. Despite dire predictions of sexual orgies among the students, the transformation to coeducation was accomplished smoothly and, as we shall see, played an important part in preparing the way for coeducation in the winter session. The Faculty became coeducational as well. Another innovation was the engaging of ten Teaching Assistants—able college students who assisted in many aspects of the Summer Session program and worked closely with an experienced teacher.[23] Now, with increased scholarship funds available, the Summer Session has been able to diversify the student body far beyond what was true in its earlier years and has been particularly successful in enrolling representatives of minority groups. In this respect it has been able to go further than the regular session. Since the mid-1960's, therefore, the Summer Session has continued to grow toward its aim of becoming a national public summer school. It has served as a laboratory for experimental courses, many of which have later been adopted in the regular session, and for other experiments, like coeducation and elimination of grades. Finally, it has meant that instead of lying fallow all summer, as was true in the pre-War period, the Phillips Academy plant is being used constructively during almost the whole year.

ARCHAEOLOGY

You know, I don't think many alumni know anything about the Peabody Foundation, and I'm sure that very few undergraduates do," remarked a recent alumnus who was always one for perceptive remarks.

His words, classic in their understatement, report all too truthfully the fact that the Andover family goes happily on its way in complete ignorance of a side of the Academy that is known to scientists concerned with man and complexities of his life, throughout North America, Great Britain, and Europe, and even behind the Iron Curtain.[24]

This statement by Douglas S. Byers, Director of the Robert S. Peabody Foundation for Archaeology from 1939 to 1968, points up a dilemma that the Foundation has had to face almost since its inception. It will be remembered that Robert Peabody, in his letter of gift to the Trustees, said that he hoped that the building to be constructed would be pleasant and attractive, that the Curator would be "of such a character and manner as would invite the approach and inquiries of students who might feel an interest in any point and desire to obtain explanation regarding it; to make it a pleasant place where students might find an agreeable relaxation during the broken moments which occur in the lives even of those most closely pressed."[25] This desire of Mr. Peabody's has, over the years, proved impossible of fulfillment, and for good and understandable reasons. In the early years of the Foundation lectures on archaeological subjects were given frequently and were well attended. In addition, a few boys studied under Dr. Warren K. Moorehead, the Director, and sometimes accompanied the staff on summer expeditions. As time went on and the space in the museum became more and more in demand for collections and exhibits, it became clear that Mr. Peabody's hope that the Museum might become a social center for the students was not going to be realized. Accordingly, in 1911 Dr. Moorehead suggested to Dr. Charles Peabody, son of the founder and a top-flight archaeologist in his own right, that a kind of annex be constructed near the Museum to provide such a social center, the money for construction to be taken from the Peabody funds. With the approval of the Trustees what became known as Peabody House was built and dedicated in 1915. But this did not solve the problem either. Although some undergraduate activities took place in the house, they usually consisted of special meetings, and the building never became a center to which students would repair. In the basement, as previously noted, there was a grill, run by the redoubtable Jim Riley and his wife, where undergraduates could buy sandwiches and where they were allowed to smoke. Populated by what were called "grill-hounds," this establishment eventually became so unsavory that it was discontinued. Finally, nothing that went on in Peabody House had anything to do with archaeology. In the 1930's some of the staff of the foundation, resentful that Peabody Foundation money had been used for the construction of the building, investigated the original letter of gift and with the aid of counsel came to the conclusion that the money spent on Peabody House had been in effect a breach of trust. But the Trustees insisted that they were trying to carry out Robert Peabody's desire for a social center for students and refused to budge. Since the staff were not about to go to court, the dispute finally died, and the various attempts to tie the School into the Department of Archaeology failed. One of the major reasons was the steadily increasing professional work of the staff—work that forced them in 1917 to abandon lectures and classes for the undergraduates. It was clear that if the staff had to choose between professional work and popularizing archaeology for the students, they would opt for the former.

But if Mr. Peabody's dream of undergraduates swarming around the museum, being introduced to archaeology, never came to pass, his basic aim of establishing a scholarly Foundation that would contribute to the knowledge of ancient man was realized many times over. Under Warren K. Moorehead, Douglas S. Byers, Frederick Johnson, and Richard Mac-Neish, the Foundation has engaged in a wide variety of archaeological digging and has published a distinguished set of scholarly bulletins. Dr. Moorehead—later known as "Wigwam Willie" because of his work with Indians[26]—had, as first Director, to get the Museum's collections in shape, especially the one donated by Robert Peabody. Additional gifts swelled the collection, until by 1905 it numbered over 60,000 artifacts. That same year Moorehead wrote to Charles Peabody, "the cases are not only full inside but underneath every case is packed solid with thousands and thousands of implements. . . . all the closets in the building are filled to over-flowing."[27] With the Museum itself under control, Dr. Moorehead turned to other matters. In 1909, at the request of the United States Commission on Indian Affairs he investigated the claims of the Chippewa Indians that their land and timber were being stolen from them. He was able to prove that many of these claims were true, and the grateful Chippewas presented him with a ceremonial war flag. Starting in 1912 the Foundation began a series of expeditions to the Penobscot River in Maine to study the past history of the "Red Paint People." Not only did they find a large number of artifacts, but they also discovered the source of the Indians' paint, thereby disproving the claims of another group of archaeologists who believed that European explorers had furnished the paint. While this was going on, the Foundation embarked on what was to be a long study of the Pueblo Indians in the Pecos Valley in New Mexico. This enterprise was under the direction of Dr. Alfred Kidder of the Peabody Museum in Cambridge, who was, in effect, loaned to the Andover Foundation for this purpose.

Before he was through—in 1958—Dr. Kidder was able to reconstruct a Pueblo town and acquire a large number of artifacts.

His major contribution, however, involved stratigraphy in American archaeology. According to the law of stratigraphy, in a series of strata the lowest is always the oldest, the uppermost the youngest. Many American archaeologists had been convinced that while stratigraphy might apply in the Old World, the record of man in the New World was too short for its application. Dr. Kidder refused to accept this. At the Pecos site he found nine layers, indicating nine different periods of habitation. As Douglas Byers has put it, "All modern archaeological research is based on the foundation which Kidder cemented into place."[28] In addition, foreign artifacts at the Pecos site indicated the existence of trade with other tribes, while European china and iron dated the arrival of the Spanish.

Space does not permit a detailed account of all the other projects undertaken during the period when Warren Moorehead was Director. He investigated the Cahokia mounds near St. Louis and was instrumental in preventing their destruction as a result of the city's expansion; at the request of the Department of the Interior he visited an Iroquois tribe in Northern New York and recommended that the government should leave them alone; as a member of the Board of Indian Commissioners, a position without power and without pay, he fought hard to get politics out of Indian affairs and to get better people into positions of responsibility. He was active in so many things that he may have spread himself too thin. In his later years he had little time for the Museum or the Foundation collection, and both suffered as a result. Yet a start had been made: the Museum had been built; a large collection had been acquired; and a number of expeditions had been mounted.

The Peabody Foundation entered a new era in the 1930's when Douglas S. Byers and Frederick Johnson were appointed to the staff. Byers was Harvard-trained and had been a "baby dean" at Harvard. Johnson, from the age of thirteen, had spent summers in company with an older friend in the wilds of Northern Quebec and had then studied at Tufts and the University of Pennsylvania. Each had acquired a high degree of professional competence. For all his enthusiasm, Wigwam Willie Moorehead had never been fully accepted among professional archaeologists, and one of the aims of the two newcomers was to establish the reputation of the Foundation among scholars throughout the country and convince them that Phillips Academy was no longer supporting a moribund institution. One of their first tasks was to renovate the Museum itself and to refurbish its collections. This involved the remodeling of three exhibit rooms so that items from the Foundation's collections could be properly shown, and washing, sorting, and in some cases cataloguing the thousands of items in the collections so that they could be properly stored. Doug Byers also reintroduced a course in archaeology for undergraduates that has been taught, in one form or another, to a small number of students ever since. At about the same time Stuart Travis painted one of his striking picture maps on the west wall of the museum, a work that combined cartological and archaeological information in a most effective way. With the museum in better order, Byers and Fred Johnson were able to begin studies on the archaeology of New England, particularly to try to establish stratigraphic sequences in the area. In order to determine the difference, if any, between remains in various parts of New England, they worked one summer on Martha's Vineyard and published an article on their findings. They later moved to Maine, where they discovered a sequence, but one very difficult to interpret. This led to consultation with scientists in other fields—botanists, geologists foresters, zoologists—and helped pave the way for the interdisciplinary, cooperative ventures that have become a characteristic feature of modern archaeology. It should be added that much of the manpower for these excavations was furnished by Phillips Academy undergraduates, who worked for $1.00 a week but ate high on the hog. One of the most interesting opportunities for research came in connection with the so-called Boylston Street Fishweir, parts of which were uncovered when foundations were being sunk for three new edifices in Boston's Back Bay —the New England Mutual Life Insurance building, The John Hancock Life Insurance building, and the International Business Machines building. The foundation for each was sunk through a structure of poles and brush. thought to be an Indian fishweir, giving archaeologists a rare opportunity to study what was surely a very old structure. Commenting on the work done at this site, the present Director of the Foundation, Richard Mac-Neish says: "the Boylston Street dig saw a real use of interdisciplinary techniques with studies of pollen, sedimentation, botany, chemistry, mollusks, oysters, foraminifera and so on."[29] Stakes from the IBM site yielded a radiocarbon date of approximately 2500 B.C. Frederick Johnson was the member of the Foundation staff most actively engaged in this study. Finally, a group of studies in Maine and other parts of New England enabled the Foundation staff to push back the date of the earliest human societies in the area to 8000 B.C.

Both Doug Byers and Fred Johnson retired in the late 1960's, to be succeeded by Richard MacNeish, an archaeologist of wide experience and a prolific scholar as well, with more than one hundred titles in his bibliography. One of his major concerns was the origin of corn, the resulting development of agriculture, and its effect on the rise of civilization. Much of his recent work has been centered on the so-called Tehuacan Project in Mexico. Several volumes on this project have already been published, with more to come. When completed, these studies promise to be an outstanding contribution to archeological literature.

The staff of the Peabody Foundation has done much more than dig.

They have enhanced the reputation of the Foundation by participating actively in professional organizations and in the editing of scholary articles. Doug Byers, for example, became editor of *American Antiquity*, the journal of the Society for American Archaeology, just before the war and managed to publish a distinguished journal despite such handicaps as wartime shortages and authors who vanished into the service. He is also editing Scotty MacNeish's studies on the Tehuacan Valley, a monumental job in itself. Different members of the staff also held leading offices in various learned societies. Alfred Kidder held many positions in the American Anthropological Association, including its Presidency, and Fred Johnson also served as Treasurer and President. Fred received an honorary degree from his alma mater Tufts, in 1966 and in 1977 was cited by the Department of the Interior for his contributions to archaeology. Scotty MacNeish was recently elected to the American Academy of Sciences, one of the highest honors an American scientist can receive. These offices and honors are a clear indication of the respect that professionals have for the staff of the Peabody Foundation. In addition, the Foundation mounted a number of conferences, the first held by Alfred Kidder at Pecos in 1927 and later ones at Andover. These conferences were true pioneering efforts and did much to advance the concept of cooperative effort among archaeologists.

The position of the Foundation in Phillips Academy is unique. Though based in Andover, all its archaeological work is done elsewhere—sometimes at very considerable distances from the School. This also means that it is difficult for the staff to integrate closely with the School community. As a result (noted above), most of the community is unaware of what the Foundation is doing. Yet if the success of the institution is to be measured by its reputation in the outside world, there are few departments of the School that can equal Archaeology. If Robert Peabody could have seen all this, he would have believed his gift to Phillips Academy to have been worthwhile.

ADMISSIONS, SCHOLARSHIPS, AND COLLEGE ADMISSIONS

During the mid-century period Phillips Academy policies on admissions, scholarships, and college admission all changed from operations that were played pretty much by ear to highly organized, scientific procedures that made all three areas big business at the School, far beyond anything dreamed of in the earlier years. At the turn of the century most of the admissions work was done by the Headmaster, with assists from other members of the Faculty and Administration. From the very start, a good character was a prime requisite for admission, but there was no elaborate system of entrance examinations. When boys who had been admitted found that they could not do the work, they were simply transferred to a lower class.

As a result, boys of eighteen or nineteen were regularly classified as Juniors or Lower Middlers.

After World War I admissions procedures became better organized when Lester Lynde, Dean of the Academy, was put in charge and a system of entrance examinations was instituted. The examination system had its difficulties, however; examinations were given in Andover and New York in the spring for boys who could get to those places, but the rest had to take their examinations locally under conditions that the School had no way of checking. The tests helped to determine which boys should be admitted and in what class.

In these days of Fair Educational Practices Acts, it is hard to remember how easy it was to discriminate against minority groups before World War II. Phillips Academy was no exception to a practice that was followed by most American colleges and private schools and was probably neither worse nor better than any of the others. It used a quota system, as did most of the rest. Writing to another school in 1935, Dr. Fuess said, "It is just too bad about the little Jewish boy, but I can't very well blame Dean Lynde for trying to keep our school as predominantly Aryan as possible. If we once start to open our doors freely to members of that race, we shall be overwhelmed by applications. As a matter of fact we have hundreds each year as it is."[30] On another occasion, writing to the Headmaster of a British School, Fuess reported that at Phillips Academy there were thirty to thirty-five Jewish students out of a school of 690. "We shall never," he said, "have a larger percentage, and I am trying to reduce it just a little. On the other hand some of them make first class students and real leaders, although very few of them are permitted to hold important social positions."[31] In another letter to the same man, he added, "The pressure to get Jews into Andover is tremendously strong, especially from bankers among our alumni body, but so far we have been able tactfully to resist it."[32] Occasionally, Jewish students who had managed to jump the admissions barrier met with anti-Semitism within the School. An alumnus writes of his first years at Williams Hall, where there were a few Jewish students enrolled. It was decided to give them the so-called "silent treatment," and as a result none of the other students in the dormitory would speak to them. The alumnus went along with this vicious performance, at the same time hating himself for doing so, but he did not feel strong enough to defy the herd. Generally speaking, however, most of the Jewish students were well accepted, and some of them made distinguished records during this period. Jack Fuess's attitude toward black students was of a piece with his attitude toward Jewish students. Replying in 1944 to a request from an alumnus for more blacks at Andover, he reported that there were two in school at the time, one of them a member of a Society. But he felt that more might make trouble.[33] In short, Andover had a few token blacks, but no concerted effort was made to recruit any.

The admission picture changed with the arrival on the Hill in 1934 of James Ruthven ("Spike") Adriance. A graduate of Phillips Academy in the Class of 1928, where he had been Class President and a school leader par excellence, he had gone on to Yale, where, among other things, he had been a member of the Whiffenpoofs. After a short tour of duty at the Hill School, he returned to his alma mater, first as Assistant Dean and then, in 1942, as Director of Admissions. It would be hard to find a man better fitted for his post. Wherever he went, he exuded a geniality and affability that soon put people at their ease. His concern for all kinds of people was genuine and contagious. As Director of Admissions he spent countless hours trying to help parents whose sons had been rejected at Andover find other schools for the boys. Spike and his talented wife, Nancy, did a lot of traveling for the School, not only on admissions business but for Alumni dinners as well. They soon became great favorites, and before Spike retired from Phillips Academy he was widely known as "Mr. Andover."

After he had been Director of Admissions for six years, Spike wrote an article summarizing admissions procedures that can serve very well as a statement of the School's policy in 1948.[34] At the head of the organization was the Admissions Committee, made up of the Headmaster (when he was available), the Director of Admissions and his Assistant, the Deans of Faculty and Students, the Director of the Summer Session, and four members of the Faculty. This group would meet regularly after the May entrance exams and also at the end of the Summer Session and at the opening of school in September. In most cases Spike's recommendations were simply approved, but with difficult ones long wrangles often took place. In the main the Committee was looking for boys of good character, with satisfactory school records, who had also distinguished themselves in some kind of extracurricular activity. In reaching their decisions the Committee depended on the form filled out by the boy's previous school; it would include his academic record and any comments the school might make. For example, under the topic "Principal Weaknesses" one school wrote, "He has a math blind spot, and a mother who is just short of being batty." Boys who were able to do so were urged to come to Andover for an interview; in other cases the interview was conducted by an alumnus nearby. Each applicant was asked to produce three letters of recommendation, two from teachers and one from an outsider. The School also gave entrance exams (this was before the SSAT tests) that included a spelling and an aptitude test, as well as subject exams. The spelling test often revealed reading disabilities that would make the applicant's chances at Andover very poor indeed. When a boy wrote "annusement" for "announcement" and "touploup" for "tulip," the danger flag went up.

The Committee's task was complicated by the wide variations in the quality of education at the applicants' previous schools. A boy in the top 10 percent of his class in a big city high school wrote a paper that the

Phillips Academy English Department pronounced completely illiterate. A school mathematics teacher obtained a copy of the Andover entrance exam in algebra and gave it to his class. Much to his dismay only two out of sixty passed. Yet Spike refused to yield on this point. Phillips Academy was a school with high standards, and he insisted on keeping them so. Generally speaking, the character of the undergraduate body changed very little during Spike's term as Director of Admissions. For a good part of that time applicants were not numerous, and the School would not have been able to engage in social engineering to change the make-up of its student body even if it had wanted to. During a ten-year period after the war, every year the five states from which most of the Andover undergraduates came were Massachusetts, New York, Connecticut, New Jersey, and Pennsylvania, and the representation from these five accounted for well over half of the undergraduate body. To be sure, there were about forty states and a number of foreign countries also represented, but in a large number of these cases it was only by one or two boys. Having the son of an Andover alumnus from Idaho may look good in the catalogue, but it contributed very little to the diversification of the student body. The fact of the matter was that in the postwar years Phillips Academy was happy to fill the School with able boys and did not concern itself about what social class they came from. It was not until the 1960's that the School would make a conscious attempt to control the make-up of its student body through the recruiting of different kinds of students.

In 1955 Spike Adriance left his position as Director of Admissions to become Assistant to the Headmaster, a post from which he could continue to exercise his considerable gifts with the Alumni and the general public. As his successor the Headmaster appointed Robert W. Sides, who had been Assistant Director of Admissions up to this time. Bob Sides was different from Spike; though warm and friendly with people, he did not have Spike's effervescence. His approach to admissions problems was more scientific, less intuitive. Perhaps it reflected the fact that in addition to being Director of Admissions he taught Mathematics and Navigation. Bob's sensitivivity to boys and his ability to go beyond superficial impressions are illustrated by the following episode. A boy arrived with two very high-powered parents who spoke glowingly of their son's abilities and his keen desire to go to Andover. The boy himself said very little. After some conversations, Bob told the parents he would like to interview the boy alone. When they were together Bob said, "Nothing that is said in this room will ever be told your parents. Now tell me honestly, do you really want to come to Andover?" "Hell, no," the boy replied. "Don't worry," Bob said, "you won't have to." And in due course the application was rejected.

One of Bob's first innovations was to involve the Faculty more with admissions decisions. Though the old Committee had had four members of the Faculty, it was dominated by representatives of the Administration.

The admissions people were regularly attacked by members of the Faculty who wondered how so-and-so could possibly have been admitted. To give the Faculty a greater share in selecting boys for admission and at the same time to silence the Faculty complainers, Bob Sides instituted a new procedure. The folder of each applicant would be read by three Faculty members of the Admissions Committee and by one of the Admission Officers. Each reader would vote on a scale of five—one being a shoo-in and five being hopeless. Then the total would determine whether the boy would be admitted, rejected, or put on a waiting list for further study. A score from four (the lowest possible) to eight was a sure admit, from sixteen to twenty a sure reject. That left a large pool of boys with scores from nine to fifteen for the Admissions Office to agonize over. Alumni sons were recognized by having three points subtracted from their total, while applicants with other alumni relatives received lesser bonuses. One disadvantage of this procedure was that it took a tremendous number of man hours to implement, and this necessitated increasing the number of Faculty members on the Admissions Committee markedly. But as more and more of the Faculty came to understand the difficulties in the admissions process, complaints about decisions almost disappeared. In addition, it seemed logical to have those who were going to teach the students have a say about whom they were going to teach. Finally, instead of admissions being handled by an elite group dominated by administrators, the new procedure was broadly democratic. Aside from the work involved—the number of applicants was often over one thousand—the new system brought nothing but plusses to Andover admissions.

Bob Sides was also one of the leaders among a group of schoolmen who established the Secondary School Admission Test, administered by the Educational Testing Service. Known to thousands of boys and girls as the SSAT, these tests replaced the individual school entrance exams and did for secondary education what the College Board had done for the colleges. Though charges have been made that too great an emphasis is placed on these aptitude tests, the scores provide one item in an applicant's total record that has proved very useful in predicting his future success in school.[35] During Bob's term as Director of Admissions the Commonwealth of Massachusetts proposed, and eventually enacted into law, a Fair Educational Practices Act that would make any kind of discrimination in admissions procedures on the basis of race, creed, color, or national origins illegal. Phillips Academy supported that Act in general but was unhappy with some of the proposals for implementing it. For example, the Act banned the use of pictures of applicants in the admissions process. Bob Sides and other members of the School went to Boston to protest some of these features. Bob pointed out that since practically every Andover applicant was interviewed, if the School was going to discriminate, it would do so on the basis of the interview, and he insisted that he used pictures to remind him of a previously held interview. But it was politically difficult to oppose any part of the Act; anyone doing so immediately became suspect. The great many schools and colleges that had reservations about certain parts of the Act eventually had to accept it pretty much as originally drawn.

After the passage of the Act in 1956, any quota systems that educational institutions in Massachusetts may have used in the past became dead letters. This was accomplished without any school or college ever being haled into court. Perhaps the provision that in case a school discriminated, the Headmaster and the Director of Admissions could be put in jail had something to do with it. Phillips Academy's acceptance of the Act was made even clearer when, under Bob Sides, the first concerted efforts were made to recruit minority students to make the Andover student body more diversified. Since these programs were intimately connected with the School's Scholarship Program, they will be discussed below.

In 1972 Robert Sides resigned as Director of Admissions, his place being taken by Joshua Miner. In general Josh Miner has continued Bob's basic policies, though he has stepped up the recruiting programs significantly. In recent years the number of applicants has steadily mounted, and although a variety of factors are responsible, especially the advent of coeducation, one of the major reasons is the skill and sensitivity in dealing with people that Josh and his staff have demonstrated.

If procedures for admissions became more scientific during the Mid-century period, those for awarding scholarships became equally so. The tradition of helping poor boys get an education is as old as the School itself. In the Academy's Constitution, provision is made for aiding what were then called "indigent" students, and early in the school's history special funds were set aside for that purpose. This tradition continued without much change well into the twentieth century. Some deserving students were given cash grants, others were given jobs in the School—waiting on table being one of the most popular. A scholarship student was expected to maintain a respectable academic average and could well have his scholarship revoked if he failed to do so. This all seemed to work pretty well; yet there was no rhyme or reason in making awards. The parents submitted no financial statement to determine if they were eligible for a grant, nor was there any scientific method for determining the size of the grant. Scholarships were usually awarded after conversation with the parents, and the School official involved had to play it pretty much by ear. At times mistakes were made, and members of the Faculty would become enraged when the parents of a boy on scholarship would come to pick him up in an expensive new car.

Andover was no different from all the other schools and colleges in this respect, and the wonder is that it took so long for somebody to do something about it. That somebody was John Monro, '30, at this writing an Academy Trustee and at that time in charge of financial aid at Harvard. He was the moving spirit in the establishment of the College Scholarship Service, which at long last put the awarding of financial aid on a scientific basis. It also encouraged foundations and corporations to make grants for scholarships because they could have confidence that the money would be awarded fairly. The procedure that CSS developed involved the submission by parents of a detailed financial statement not unlike an Income Tax form that listed all income, assets, expenses, other children, and the like and then asked the parents to indicate how much they could pay toward the student's tuition. Computation developed what the parents *should* pay on the basis of the statement submitted. The balance, if any, could be made up by the college in the form of grants, loans, or jobs, or a combination. One of the major aims of the Service was to eliminate the size of grant as a factor in the student's choice of college. If all colleges followed the same procedures, that should automatically be the case, and to ensure it, all colleges had to report all the offers they had made to applicants, so that comparisons could be made. Frederick S. Allis, Jr., of the Andover Faculty was a member of the first College Scholarship Service Committee, representing the schools, and he also served as Chairman of the CSS Subcommittee on Computation. As a result he became familiar with the new procedures and determined to introduce them at Phillips Academy. The School's Scholarship Committee under Dean of Students G. Grenville Benedict had already moved in the direction of the CSS program by working out a rough table of grants that related the size of the grant to net income, but the procedure was not nearly so sophisticated as that of CSS.[36]

In the course of the next few years Fritz Allis, who had been appointed Director of Financial Aid, was able to implement the CSS policy at Andover. Permission was obtained to copy the CSS financial statement, and at first the computation was done at Andover by some very sharp Faculty wives. If this was good for Andover, it should be good for other schools as well, and before long the School Scholarship Service was organized, closely modeled on the College organization. Eventually the schools stopped doing their own computations and turned the job over to the Educational Testing Service at Princeton, as the colleges had done from the beginning. The new procedures in the awarding of financial aid enabled the Director to act with infinitely more confidence than was the case in the old hit-or-miss days. The job was difficult, for it involved making decisions about a family's life blood. What were legitimate expenses, for example? Should the family of an applicant for a scholarship own an expensive boat? One angry mother wrote the Director that he was so stingy that he probably cut his own hair. Another parent insisted that he was a tither and therefore could not afford to send his boy to Andover on the grant offered. The Director suggested that in effect he was asking that Andover scholarship

76. *The author deciding a difficult scholarship case in the early 1960's.*

money be given to his church, but the boy never came to the Academy. A distressed mother arrived with her family budget and asked the Director to go over it with her. She did not see how she could possibly pay what the School expected her to. The Director, who usually did not get into family budgets, discovered an item of fifty dollars a week for the husband's "beer and bowling" and suggested that that was where the tuition money could come from. In this case the boy came and the father presumably found some less expensive form of recreation. With the passage of time the whole business of financial statements and computation became routine both for parents and for the Scholarship Office. Some modifications were made, like the introduction of a loan program for families on the borderline; but generally speaking what had been a jungle of confusion and uncertainty became a policy of clarity and equity.

A second major alteration in the Scholarship Program during the mid-century period involved a change in the status of the scholarship students in the School. Before World War II no one had considered whether it is a good idea to have the scholarship boys labeled as such. They were a clearly identified group, recognized primarily by the fact that they had jobs to do around the School. In addition, those in the know realized that scholarship boys had to maintain good academic records, or they would lose their scholarships. It must not be supposed that this necessarily was a hardship to those on scholarship. Each year many of the School leaders and outstanding athletes were on scholarship. Indeed, one reason why Al Stearns had insisted on spreading the scholarship boys throughout all the school dormitories, after the disappearance of the Latin and English Commons, was to prevent a special clique of mature, tough boys from dominating the School. In the period between the two wars the boys on scholarship considered themselves an elite group in the school. Ted Harrison, '38, later Director of Athletics, can speak eloquently about this. He was a headwaiter in the Commons and always thought that he and his friends had the best deal of anyone at Andover. In the first place they had a shot at the best food, and in addition they had positions of authority that brought respect. After World War II, however, there was growing concern among the Faculty over what was called the double standard. If a full-freight-paying customer committed some crime, he would be put on probation. If a scholarship boy committed the same crime, he would likewise be put on probation and also might have his scholarship revoked. He was thus in a double jeopardy that to many seemed unfair. And the same situation obtained with regard to academic performance: a full-tuition boy might fail two courses and be put on No-Excuse; a scholarship boy might get No-Excuse and lose his scholarship as well. During the 1950's the Scholarship Committee had great difficulty with this double jeopardy policy, particularly because, in many cases, taking a boy's scholarship away was the equivalent of expulsion. As the decade wore on, the Committee gradually moved further and further away from the double jeopardy policy. The first step was to eliminate taking away a boy's scholarship during the school year; only at the final Faculty meeting in June could this be done. A second step was to remove scholarships only by a vote of the Faculty as a whole in June. After a year or so, the double-standard policy was dropped entirely, simply because the Faculty refused to vote any more removals. From then on, if a scholarship boy got into trouble, he was not punished more than anyone else.

A second area in which potential scholarship boys were discriminated against was in the matter of admissions. In the period immediately following World War II there were, in effect, two Admissions Commitees—one for full-freight-paying customers and one for scholarship boys. The two worked closely together and had the same general standards for admission. The major difference was that when the scholarship funds ran out, the Scholarship Committee came to a halt, even though they might still have some very promising candidates. As time went on, it became more and more frustrating for all concerned to have good scholarship applicants turned down for lack of funds while mediocre boys whose parents could pay full tuition were accepted. When the problem was presented to John Kemper, he characteristically met it head on. First, he found ways of supplementing the scholarship budget so as to enable the Scholarship Committee to accept more good boys. Then, with the strong support of Trustee Jack Stevens, he revolutionized the whole procedure. Jack Stevens had often said that there were only two really important items in the Academy's budget—teachers' salaries and scholarships—and it was up to the Trustees to find whatever money was necessary for both. In the late 1950's the Trustees, egged on by Jack Stevens and John Kemper, voted to wipe out the distinction in admissions between scholarship and nonscholarship boys. The Admissions Committee and the Scholarship Committee were to be merged and instructed to get the best boys they could find, regardless of whether they needed financial aid. The Trustees would foot the bill that resulted. This courageous act on the part of the Trustees meant that a promising boy would no longer be penalized because of his father's financial status and would improve the quality of the student body. A most important contribution to the success of the new policy was the grant by the Independence Foundation of Philadelphia, under the leadership of Robert A. Maes, '27. The Foundation granted the School $50,000 a year for Scholarships for a twenty-year period, 1952–72.

The term "Most Qualified" or MQ has been applied to this policy, and though the Admissions Office has had to fudge a bit occasionally, generally speaking it is still in effect today. Those who feared that the policy would mean a majority of the School on scholarship, with astronomical scholarship budgets, have been proved wrong. The fraction getting financial aid has never gone much over one third. The financial aid budget has certainly grown tremendously over the years—it is now pushing one million dollars a year—but this has been due more to inflation than to an increased percentage of scholarship students. In a very real sense the MQ policy is a logical culmination of Samuel Phillips' original desire to help indigent boys of good character.

The final step in changing the status of Scholarship boys at Phillips Academy came in the late 1960's when the Faculty voted to have all students do work around the School. From the very beginning, boys receiving financial aid from the School had been expected to do some kind of useful work in partial repayment for their grant. Some boys were given a chance to earn part of their tuition money through concessions. The difficulty with this arrangement was that no one could predict how much money a boy could make from his concession. A high-powered leader with an effective sales pitch might sell contracts with the laundry he represented to a large part of the School, while a timid boy from a rival laundry would wind up with almost no sales at all. An even more callous part of the system made the youngest boys on scholarship deliver newspapers before breakfast. The sight of a small Junior making his rounds in a blizzard to deliver his papers was reminiscent of something out of Dickens. Gradually the use of concessions as a means of helping boys on scholarship pay part of the tuition expenses was abandoned. In part this resulted from a decline in sales—today, for example, most students do their own laundry in washing machines in dormitory basements—and in part because there was too much variation in the amount of money that different boys made. Newspaper deliveries have been stopped, in part because the School decided that the labor of boys on scholarship should not be used to subsidize Boston papers. But the other jobs—working in the Commons and in school offices—remained. As the 1960's wore on, more and more of the Faculty became uncomfortable with a system whereby the scholarship boys did useful work while the rest of the students watched. Furthermore, there was pressure from other quarters. One mother wrote to see if there was not some way that her son could be on scholarship. She knew she was not eligible on the basis of need, but she said that the boys on scholarship were getting the best education at Andover and she wanted her son to gain the experience that working for the School could provide. This feeling grew steadily until in the late 1960's the Faculty finally voted to have *all* students share in the work to be done around the School. Thus the last vestige of a policy that had distinguished boys on scholarship from other students disappeared. Scholarship students were no longer identified as such, the amounts of their awards no longer appeared on their record cards, and generally every attempt was made to give them a status of complete equality in the School. Some of the Faculty believed that this was going too far, that it was bad education to encourage students in the belief that the financial condition of their families made no difference in life. These

Faculty members also feared that the scholarship students would be in for a rude awakening in college, where such an egalitarian policy did not prevail. For example, colleges sometimes admit an Andover scholarship student even though at the time they have no scholarship funds to award him. But the great majority of the Andover community believe that the present system, despite some drawbacks, is preferable to the old one, in which scholarship students were a group apart in the School.[37]

When, in 1954, the Supreme Court of the United States handed down their now famous decision in *Brown vs. Topeka*, in which the Justices ruled that separate educational facilities were inherently unequal and mandated a policy of school desegregation, their ruling had no direct effect on Phillips Academy. Aside from relatively small grants from the Federal Government under the hot lunch program, the School received no money from either the federal or state governments, and the Trustees had made it clear that they did not want any. At the same time there were many in the Andover community who did not wish to hide behind legal technicalities. They believed that integration was the law of the land and that Phillips Academy should do its share in helping to implement this vital national policy. Certainly up to this time the School had done little if anything for blacks. For the previous century there had been one or two in School about half of the time, but there were long periods when there was none. From 1911 to 1934, for example, only four had enrolled. Both Al Stearns and Jack Fuess were dubious about the value of an Andover education for blacks and had discouraged their admission. Now, in the mid 1950's, the School's policy toward the admission of blacks was to change dramatically. Partially, one supposes, as a result of the Supreme Court decision, the numbers began to increase; in 1956 there were twelve, with the numbers for the next three years, 11, 10, and 10. The black students were still, for the most part, children of black professional people— those who had already made it. Not until the 1960's did the School embark on a concerted program to recruit black students—not just sons of professional people but disadvantaged ones as well. At the heart of this drive was an organization formed by a group of independent schools called ABC—A Better Chance.[38] Before the formation of this program, the School had worked with the National Scholarship Fund for Negro Students—known familiarly as Nessfeness—which had developed a recruiting program for blacks; but their main focus was on collegiate education and it was believed that a separate organization for schools was in order. Those behind ABC were all the more determined to develop school programs because of the testimony of sociologists to the effect that if one waited to help a black student until he was old enough for college, it was often too late. In the fall of 1963 Dr. Howard Jones of Northfield-Mt. Hermon and President John Dickey of Dartmouth began planning for a program the following summer designed to prepare black students for entrance into independent schools. As the program developed, schools were found willing to accept black students and provide them with scholarships. Dartmouth was able to get the Rockefellers to subsidize the summer program, and the college itself agreed to pay for the overhead. At the same time, plans were made for an Independent School Talent Search Program designed to identify black secondary school students of promise. The first summer program was held at Dartmouth in 1964 under the direction of Charles Dey, now head of Choate-Rosemary Hall, and a high proportion of the black students who attended went on to independent schools in the fall. Headmaster John M. Kemper had been enthusiastic about ABC from the very beginning—indeed he helped to set it up and he made the substantial resources of Phillips Academy available for the program, for it was going in precisely the direction that the School had been heading since the mid 1950's. One year, for example, when two promising ABC students could not find places in independent schools, he accepted them at Phillips Academy, even though the School already had its quota. Once the ABC program had been established, it expanded rapidly. Additional summer programs were set up at other colleges besides Dartmouth, and eventually Phillips Academy decided to start one of its own as part of the Andover Summer Session. The general aim of the Andover authorities was to have about 10 percent of the undergraduate body black, roughly the same percentage as in the nation as a whole, but this goal was never achieved. In the School year 1969–70 the high point was reached, with fifty-four black students or 6.2 percent of the student body and with a record number of fifteen blacks in the Class of 1971. After this peak year the number dropped to an average in the mid 30's.[39] But it was not simply a matter of identifying promising black students and getting them placed in independent schools. The culture shock of entering a white environment on a twenty-four-hour-a-day basis was acute. As one of the first students to enroll at Andover under the program put it:

> I knew it would be hard work, but it was more than that. There's a dislocation. When someone is transplanted from one environment to another, he can't grow without some very abrupt adjustments. When I was here . . . there was no social scene at all for Blacks. . . . On the other hand, you were forced into new social situations—getting to know new people—opportunities to have new experiences. But it wasn't easy at first.
>
> But you never gave up. No matter what. When you were down in the depths about your situation, you still felt that commitment, that charge you had to keep. And you kept it.[40]

Some of those in charge of the ABC program at Phillips Academy hoped that the black students would become integrated into the School community but, for the most part, this did not happen. Blacks and whites might work together in class, might compete together in sports, might live together in dormitories, but in other areas the blacks tended to constitute a distinct group. For example, they all sat together in the Commons at meal time. As time went on, it became clear that the black students were not going to integrate socially with the whites and that they needed a social center of their own. Though John Kemper had reservations about such an institution, he finally agreed to the establishment of the Afro-American Society, later called the Afro-Latino-American Society, and turned over to the new organization the upper floor of Peabody House. Here the black students could put up posters reflecting black accomplishments, have their own music, and serve their own food. Even though such an institution ran counter to the goal of integration, it filled a crying need of the black students to have a place of their own. At times there was racial friction. When a black student with an unusually fine voice was refused the chance to try out for the leading role in the spring musical, *The Boyfriend*, because, according to the Director, the part called for a white, undergraduate resentment was so strong that the entire production had to be abandoned.[41] A program like ABC was full of risks. Despite summer preparation for the independent school experience, some of the students found the adjustment too difficult and had to be sent home. But the majority came through with flying colors and went on to college. They provided a new meaning to the phrase "Youth from Every Quarter." Douglas Suisman, '72, who made an admirable study of the Andover undergraduate body over a fifty-year period, concluded in 1972 that *"socially* Andover now has reached the fullest integration into, and the greatest compatibility with American society" of any time in its history.[42]

COLLEGE ADMISSION

As was true of both the admissions and the scholarship areas, Phillips Academy's policy on counseling boys on their choice of college was a relaxed business before the 1930's. Much of the work was done by teachers and housemasters, and no single person was in charge. To a large extent this situation was due to the fact that Andover boys had little trouble getting into the colleges of their choice, whether they graduated or not. Each year, for example, there were a certain number of "Non-Returning Upper Middlers" who were not returning because they had already received admission to college without diplomas. On one occasion Al Stearns got into a fight with the Director of Admissions at Amherst because of the college's rule that a boy must take mathematics the year before entering college, but for the most part it was a matter of letting nature take her course. When Willet Eccles became Registrar in the early 1930's, he introduced more system into college counseling, as he did with so many other aspects of his office, and when he left to become Headmaster of St. George's in 1943, he was succeeded by G. Grenville Benedict, who took college counseling very seriously and developed a highly sophisticated system for helping boys gain admission to the college of their choice. "Geegee" or "G squared," as he was known to the boys, each year became father confessor to the whole Senior class—and many of their parents to boot—and achieved a high degree of success in this work. As Dean of Students he had many other responsibilities as well. He was Chairman of the Faculty Discipline Committee and fought many a fight with the more conservative members of his committee trying to save some unfortunate youth who had committed some heinous sin. In both his disciplinary work and his counseling, the undergraduates came to understand that he really did have their best interests at heart, and until he retired in the 1960's he was one of the most popular and respected members of the School community.

In the 1930's college admissions won by Andover undergraduates followed a very consistent pattern. The most striking thing about this pattern was the large number who went to Yale, as noted frequently above. The tradition went back to the days of Uncle Sam Taylor. A high point was reached in 1936, when 90 boys went to New Haven, which meant that about one freshman in ten on the Yale campus was an Andover man. This was also about three times as many as went to Harvard that year. Harvard usually ran second during this period, with Princeton third, but only once during the 1930's did more than twenty boys go to Princeton. Then followed Dartmouth, M.I.T., Brown, and Amherst, the order of these last four varying from year to year. Wartime figures are unreliable because of the number of accelerations and entries into the armed services, though a new high of 95 going to Yale was registered by the Class of 1942.[43] Once the war was over, the whole college admission picture changed drastically. Returning veterans, supported by the GI Bill, swelled the number of applicants for college places. In addition, the rise in national income made it possible for more families to send their children to college than had been the case in the 1930's. Just as after World War I a high school diploma became for the first time the expected goal of most adolescents, so after World War II that goal became a college degree. The effect of all this on Phillips Academy was to make it more and more difficult for Andover graduates to get accepted at their first-choice colleges and thus to make effective college counseling essential. In the early 1950's, for example, Harvard had 3500 applicants for 1100 places, Yale 4000 for 1000, Princeton 3000 for 750, and Amherst 1200 for 250. It was clear that what Gren Benedict called the "Edwardian Era" in college admissions was gone.[44] All of this came as a shock to Andover graduates and particularly their parents. As one disgruntled student put it, "If I can't get into my first-choice college, why bother to come to Andover at all? I could have done just as well from high school." When a mother was told that her son could not get

77. *George Grenville Benedict, Dean of Students, 1944–1967.*

into Yale, she replied, "What do you mean he's not going to Yale? I've told everyone in Darien that he was going there." And the situation was not helped by colleges like Amherst, the Faculty of which believed that the college had too high a proportion of private school graduates and wanted to increase public school representation. In the 1940's Amherst had been very generous about admitting fourth-quarter Andover boys, but no longer. The effect of this squeeze for college admission on Phillips Academy graduates soon became clear; a much smaller percentage of the graduating class was admitted to the Big Three—in 1937 74 percent of the class went to Yale, Harvard, and Princeton; in 1957 the digits were reversed: 47 percent went to those institutions.[45] A second result was the increase in the number of colleges that Andover boys attended. Before the War the number of institutions attended was seldom more than twenty. By 1959 the number had increased to 40, and by 1965 Andover seniors applied to 96 colleges and wound up attending 66. It was Gren Benedict's job to get Andover seniors and their parents to accept the facts of life in current college admissions, and though there was plenty of parental outrage when a boy had to enroll in a non-Ivy League college, other families discovered that there were many relatively unknown institutions where a student could get a fine education. One Yale graduate who had set his heart on having his son go to Yale was told by the New Haven admissions people that he would not be admitted. The boy wound up in a small Midwestern college. After several visits to this college, the family became so enthusiastic about it that they in effect transferred their allegiance to it and kissed Yale goodbye. The percentage of boys admitted to their first-choice colleges also declined steadily in the 1950's and 1960's. In 1951 91 percent were admitted to the college of their first choice; by 1959 the figure had dropped to 73 percent; and by 1965 to 56 percent.[46] Part of the reason for this decline was the growth of multiple applications; a boy might apply to as many as eight or ten colleges. In many of these cases the indicated first choice was unrealistic, and the boy settled down in a less prestigious institution. In addition to these changes the pattern of admission to prestige colleges changed also. The number attending Harvard increased markedly during this period until it approached that of Yale; in 1950, for example, there were actually more admitted to Harvard than to Yale—64 to 46. With the increase of Californians in the Andover student body, Stanford became a strong contender, often ranking fourth in number of Andover boys admitted. Finally, the University of North Carolina —in part because of an outstanding Freshman Honors Program and in part because of the highly publicized Moorehead Scholarship Program— became a popular choice. In the midst of all these pressures and confusions Gren Benedict each year managed to get all but a very few Seniors settled in respectable colleges. And the wonder is that he could do such a job when all his other responsibilities as Dean of Students are taken into consideration. Occasionally he would get an encouraging note from a former Senior. One boy wrote, "Blank University is not the best, but it's good enough for me. A year ago I didn't think so." In 1965 Gren Benedict turned college counseling over to Robert P. Hulburd, a graduate of Exeter and Princeton, who was particularly successful at making friends with college admissions officers, so that they could all work together in the best interests of Andover boys. Today it is big business, with the counselor devoting virtually full time to the job. And there is no reason to believe that things will change in the future.

ANDOVER AND EXETER

Finally, an important mid-century development was the increased cooperation between Andover and Exeter. For nearly two hundred years these two great schools had existed side by side, and many people never thought of one without the other. Yet during a good part of their history, relations between the two institutions were characterized first by apathy and later by hostility. At the time of the founding of the two academies there was, of course, close cooperation because of the interest that members of the Phillips family took in both institutions. Uncle John Phillips, one of the founders of Phillips Academy, a Trustee for the rest of his life and President of the Board from 1790 to 1795, never let his interest in Exeter crowd out his concern for Andover. As we have seen, he made a generous contribution for scholarships in 1789, and when he died, he left one third of his estate to Andover.[47] Samuel Phillips, Jr., reciprocated by serving on the Exeter Board of Trustees from the founding of the Academy until his death in 1802, and while there is no record of his making any donations to Exeter, his presence on the Board must have provided strong support for Uncle John and the new institution. As noted above, the two Boards cooperated in arranging a settlement with Uncle John's widow, with the Andover group generously suggesting "one other cow" for the lady.[48] The Andover Trustees attended Uncle John's funeral, and the Exeter Board were present at Samuel Phillips, Jr.'s last rites.[49] Finally, the Exeter Board asked the Andover Trustees to make suggestions as to a suitable tombstone for Uncle John.[50] In short, as long as these two Phillipses were alive, cooperation between the two institutions was close.

With the passing of the Phillipses, relations between Andover and Exeter all but ceased. There was really no reason for their working together. Uncle Sam Taylor, for example, admitted that he had met the Principal of Exeter only once during his term of thirty-four years.[51] One of the reasons for this lack of contact was that the two institutions were pursuing different courses. Andover sent a large number of its graduates to Yale, for example, while Exeter favored Harvard. With the founding of the Andover Theological Seminary, Phillips Academy became more committed than ever to a very conservative position on religious matters, while Exeter became more liberal in this area. Until after the Civil War, there is no record of significant contact between the two schools.

Things began to change when Cecil Bancroft became Principal of Phillips Academy. The Exeter Trustees and Faculty were invited to the Andover Centennial in 1878, at which Principal Albert C. Perkins of Exeter spoke, while the New Hampshire institution made similar overtures to Andover at the time of its Centennial in 1883, at which Cecil Bancroft spoke. But it had taken Centennial celebrations to get the two groups together. In the 1880's there were a few exchanges between the Society of Inquiry at Andover and the Christian Fraternity at Exeter, with members from each organization meeting together, but nothing much came of this either.[52] As has been noted, Bancroft, unlike his predecessors, sought advice about his School from a variety of sources, including Principal Perkins. The two administrators corresponded fairly regularly during the late 1870's and early 1880's about such matters as the two Centennials, school catalogues, record-keeping, financial and boarding arrangements, the problem of smoking, and Faculty salaries. Incidentally, Perkins thought that Bancroft was underpaid.[53] Bancroft does not seem to have been as close with Perkins's successors—Walter Scott, Charles Fish, and Harlan Amen, but at least he was on speaking terms with the last.[54] It should be stressed, however, that this cooperation between the principals of the two schools was essentially a personal one. Of institutional cooperation, with one notable exception, there was almost none. But that the principals could discuss things together, and that their successors would continue to do so, with varying degrees of intimacy right up to the present, was an important step forward.

The one notable exception to the absence of close relations between the two schools was varsity athletics, which brought the institutions into intimate contact. In 1878 the first Andover-Exeter baseball game was played, which Exeter won handily, 11–1. From then on, the rivalry between the schools in sports became bitter, with charges by each school that the other was hiring ringers, and with a bad riot at Exeter in the early 1890's leading to suspension of competition for two years.[55] Indeed, much of Cecil Bancroft's correspondence with Exeter principals concerned the problems of athletic contests. Nor did the rivalry on the playing field become any less bitter with the passage of time. I can well remember the outrage of the whole Exeter community, from the Principal on down, when, in 1937, a football official ruled that an Andover man had caught a pass when the Exeters thought it had touched the ground first. A similar rivalry developed in debating, which became, in effect, a contest between the two English departments. Each department used to meet to think up arguments for its team. In the areas in which the two schools came into closest contact, their relations were characterized by suspicion, if not outright hostility, until very recent years.

Alfred E. Stearns of Andover and Lewis Perry of Exeter strengthened the tradition of cooperation between the heads of the schools which had been initiated by Bancroft and Perkins. The two men had a lot in common. Though he tried to play it down while he was at Exeter, Lewis Perry had gone to Andover for one term, only to be withdrawn when his father became enraged at a comment about his son made by Professor David Comstock. Al had had Comstock in class also, and thus they had had a common experience at the secondary school level. Though Lewis Perry went to Williams while Al went to Amherst, their college experiences were certainly similar. Perry was one of the great college tennis players of his generation, and though Al's athletic interest was primarily baseball, he was no slouch on the tennis court, and the two men enjoyed matches together over a number of years. Again, however, their relationship was essentially personal; the same kind of intimacy did not exist between the faculties of the two schools. Al and Lewis corresponded—or telephoned each other—about a wide variety of school matters. In many cases their exchanges concerned the problems of individual boys. They were both active in the Headmasters' Association and usually worked together in dealing with various problems presented to that organization. As has been noted, Lewis Perry, one of the wittiest and most urbane speakers of his era, almost stole the show at the Andover Sesquicentennial celebration. Perhaps the most important aspect of friendship was the support that Lewis gave to Al during the difficult times at the close of his career at Andover.[56]

It was not until after World War II that true institutional cooperation began. Coupled with that development came the gradual dissipation of the suspicion and distrust that had characterized the relations between the Faculties of the two Schools up to that time. The change in attitude was accelerated by a slackening of the athletic rivalry. In the 1930's for example, any student who did not attend an important Andover-Exeter contest was liable to be ostracized by the undergraduate body. In the 1960's this attitude changed markedly. Only a handful of undergraduates attended regular football games, and nothing like 100 percent went to the Andover-Exeter contests. There were even complaints that the Andover-Exeter weekends were "closed"—that is, students could not leave the campus for a visit away from school. This change in the climate of opinion made possible a new order of cooperation between the two institutions. Only a few instances need be mentioned to make the point. In the early 1960's Exeter established the Washington Intern Program. A few years later Andover asked if it might join, and since that time it has been jointly administered by both schools.[57] At about the same time Andover set up School Year Abroad, designed to give students a year in either France or

Spain. Shortly thereafter Exeter, and later St. Paul's, agreed to help sponsor this project, and the enterprise has been a cooperative one ever since.[58] Most of the academic departments of the two schools now meet informally every year or so to have a good dinner together and discuss common problems. Such behavior would have been branded treasonable consorting with the enemy a generation ago. Another activity that tended to bring the faculties together was the reading of Advanced Placement Exams. Each June representatives from schools and colleges gather at Rider College in New Jersey to read the essay questions on these exams. Apart from the professional job to be done, these gatherings made possible long, usually alcoholic evenings of discussion during which the Andover and Exeter representatives often found themselves side by side on a disputed point (they fought a lot, too). But the end result of these meetings could not help bettering understanding. Incidentally, the Advanced Placement reading sessions provided an extraordinarily valuable recruiting opportunity for both schools. Their representatives had a chance to meet able teachers whom they could never have located otherwise. For example, Wayne Frederick, one of Andover's most distinguished history teachers, was a member of the faculty of the Isadore Newman School in New Orleans before coming to Andover. Had he not been an AP reader, it is inconceivable that the Andover department would ever have found him.

Yet none of this explains the importance of Exeter to Andover, which feels that if Exeter had not existed, it would have been necessary to invent it. The chances are that this feeling is reciprocated in New Hampshire. Exeter is important because it is a school of comparable endowment, comparable faculty, and comparable leadership which will always serve as an institution for Andover to emulate. When Andover received a vast amount of money from Thomas Cochran to build a number of new buildings, a member of the Exeter faculty was reported to have said, "We're beaten. Exeter can never catch up."[59] Yet in a few years the Harkness grants to Exeter enabled them to equal, if not surpass, the Andover program. This competition, friendly as it now is, has been the hallmark of Andover-Exeter relations in modern times.

CHAPTER NINETEEN

REVOLUTION

IN THE early 1960's the average Andover student was reasonably content with his lot. If asked what was wrong with the School, he was apt to reply, "the food." He attended daily chapel, and church on Sunday (attendance being taken in both instances), with resignation if not enthusiasm. He had an allowance of cuts that enabled him to miss a few of these exercises, and if he was careful, he might be able to take a nap during church. When he got up in the morning, he put on a coat and tie without thinking about it very much. The only hassle over student dress was the question whether blue jeans could be worn as trousers. It was pointed out that scholarship boys would profit greatly from the legalizing of jeans, which were much less expensive than woollen trousers, but the Faculty refused to yield on the point. Sam the barber in the basement of the Andover Inn was doing a thriving business and turning out neatly coiffured students, some of whom had crew cuts. All the courses were year-long, at which attendance was taken each day, and an elaborate system of recording absence from class had been developed, presumably to ensure regular attendance. In the evenings, except on Saturdays, he was expected to be in his dormitory, the library, or some other authorized place after eight o'clock.

An undergraduate Student Council met regularly with the Headmaster, but although students could make suggestions and assist at various School functions, they had no real power. Occasionally someone would complain about this in the *Phillipian,* but for the most part the undergraduates were content with the system. If membership on the Student Council meant little more than recognition of positions of leadership, maybe that was the way it should be.

Outside the School there was little to disturb this relatively peaceful scene. The country was prosperous, and overseas there was little cause of alarm. To be sure, everyone was galvanized by the Bay of Pigs episode and the

Cuban missile crisis. The latter was made all the more meaningful by the presence on the campus at that time of a group of visiting Russians, who, during the crisis, held meetings in the middle of the vista so as to avoid possible wire taps. But these crises passed; Viet Nam, except for the insiders, was still a cloud no bigger than a man's head. Blessed with the new buildings that the Andover Program had provided, the students could, presumably, look forward to a peaceful and productive time during their stay on Andover Hill.

Ten years later a great deal had changed. Perhaps "revolution" is too strong a word, but Phillips Academy neverthlees underwent more basic changes during this decade than in all its previous history. Daily chapel had been abolished, and attendance at church on Sunday was on a voluntary basis; as a result, only a handful of undergraduates showed up. The requirements for coats and ties was gone, and many student costumes were bizarre, to say the least. The hair style of the undergraduates had changed markedly also, with various types of long hair-do's predominating. There were pigtails, braids, Afros, and some that resembled bird nests. Many wore long sideburns, full beards, and moustaches as well. Instead of taking only year-long courses, the student now had available a smorgasbord of term-contained courses so that he might, during his Senior year, take as many as fifteen different courses. The cut system had been abolished, and attendance was no longer taken in class. Each student was simply expected to attend all his classes. The hour at which he must be in his dormitory had been extended to ten o'clock and on some occasions to eleven; up until that time he was free to go where he wanted on campus. A so-called "cluster" system had been developed in an attempt to decentralize the nonacademic life of the School, with each cluster having autonomy in the administration of discipline. Students sat on all important Faculty committees and often attended Faculty meetings as well. Events in the world outside were of urgent concern to many of the undergraduate body, particularly the war in Vietnam and the draft. The problem of the blacks in America was brought home to the students by the presence on the campus of a much larger number of blacks than ever before in the history of the School. The environment, the plight of the cities, and many other contemporary concerns were now discussed seriously. The most important change of all, of course, was the fact that the School had gone coeducational. For the first time in its history, girls were actively participating in all phases of school life. It is hard to believe that this Phillips Academy bore any relationship to that of ten years before.

Any attempt to explain these momentous changes must focus on two important forces: first, the work of the Steering Committee, established by Headmaster John Kemper in 1965; and second, the influence of student protest movements, with their demands for change that would make their education more "relevant." These two forces were by no means independent of each other; some of the recommendations of the Steering Committee met demands that the students were making, while student pressure on occasion helped to achieve programs that the Steering Committee were advocating. Despite this interrelationship, it will be convenient to treat the two forces separately.

The Steering Committee was appointed by the Headmaster in June 1965 "to consider the current effectiveness of the policies and practices of the Academy and to make recommentations for its development in the future." The eight-man committee, under the chairmanship of Simeon Hyde, Jr., of the English Department, believed that "its function was to be the stimulation and coordination of a wide range of planning activities rather than the formulation of detailed plans in every area where a need for change or development was seen. It was left to the Committee to determine the areas in which it wished to make specific recommendations and the areas which appeared to require investigation by additional, properly representative committees."[1] Behind all the Committee's work was the belief, as stated by Chairman Hyde, that "American culture was changing rapidly."[2] If American culture was changing rapidly, it behooved Phillips Academy to adapt itself to that change if it wished to maintain its position of leadership among American secondary school institutions. The Committee believed that in the past, Phillips Academy had approached change in too deliberate and conservative a manner. The aim usually was to get a majority, if not a consensus, of the Faculty to subscribe to a new program that would replace an old one. The Committee was convinced that there must be a spirit of "optimistic venture"[3] in approaching new conditions, that frankly experimental programs should be undertaken alongside older, more traditional ones. Or, as the Committee put it, an established institution's "opportunity to poise experiment against experience is the basis of its peculiar strength."[4]

With this by way of general background, the Committee stated that Phillips Academy's basic aim should be to provide "a broadly human education" for boys of high intelligence who planned to go on to college and a career. The word "human" should be stressed here, for the Committee believed strongly that in the past the Academy had placed too much emphasis on purely academic areas and that there was great need to fashion programs that would develop the emotional, social, and spiritual side of the adolescent. To use the jargon of the time, they wanted less emphasis on "cognitive" courses and more on "affective" courses. If the student were to learn values while at School, the Committee believed that he must be offered three things: an active religious program that would present values; a Faculty that would, in their lives, represent these values; and, the creation of situations that would require the students to make value judg-

78. Simeon Hyde, Jr., of the Class of 1937, Instructor in English, 1950–1968; Dean of the Faculty, 1969–1972; Associate Headmaster, 1972–1973.

ments for themselves.[5] When it came to Instruction, the Committee limited itself to a few broad statements. It believed that in the past, Phillips Academy had placed too much emphasis on rote learning, and hoped that in the future principles and concepts could be stressed more than mere facts. But they realized that no single innovation could change this situation and hoped rather for a series of experimental programs that might blaze trails for others to follow. Nor did they believe that Andover should conduct the experiments in a vacuum; they hoped that the School would pioneer programs in cooperation with other schools, both public and private.[6] At the close of their first summer of deliberation, the Committee, it was realized, would need help with specific aspects of School life, and as a result four subcommittees were formed: one on the Composition of the Student Body, under Frank M. Eccles; one on the Demands made upon the Student, under John B. Hawes; one on the Counseling of Students, under Dean G. G. Benedict; and one on New Media and Methods of Education, under Dean Alan R. Blackmer and, later, Edmond E. Hammond, Jr. Thus the Committee completed its first summer of work with its general goals determined, four working subcommittees ready to go into action, and a vast amount of educational material gained from reading and from specially invited leaders in the field of education.

The Steering Committee spent the next summer in further discussion of subcommittee reports and other material and the following year began to issue its findings in a series of separate reports. One of the first was a statement on the Composition of the student body. The Committee believed that the Academy's Admissions Office was placing too much emphasis on test scores in determining who could come to the School. There were many promising students with considerable talents in a variety of areas who did not test well, and as a result, in many cases, the School was failing to admit some potentially admirable citizens. As the report stated it:

> Phillips Academy should value positive moral qualities as much as intellect. It should value social competence—that is, an interest in others and the ability to work with them—as much as creative imagination and originality of mind. It should recognize that academic brilliance and common sense, or good judgment, do not necessarily coincide. It should value generosity of spirit and social concern and should seek boys who seem to have the capacity for constructive influence and leadership. It should also value physical hardiness, skill, stamina, and courage.[7]

In addition to encouraging the admission to Phillips Academy of low-testers who had promise in other fields, the Committee urged that the School step up its program, already begun, of bringing to Andover boys of varying backgrounds. The report spoke of drawing students "from diverse social, economic, cultural, racial and ethnic backgrounds in order to

draw upon the diverse strengths of the nation's population and to maintain a school community which represents and contributes to the openness
of our democratic society."[8] In this recommendation the Committee was
trying to broaden and make more effective a basic princple of Phillips
Academy that had existed since the School's founding. At the time the
Committee met, various proposals had been made to convert Andover into
a junior college, teaching from the tenth through the fourteenth grade.
There had also been talk of abolishing the Junior or ninth grade, so that
more boys could have an Andover experience. The Committee refused to
buy any of these suggestions. The members believed that it was better to
strengthen the Junior program than to abolish it, and they recommended
establishment of a Junior complex, centered on Williams Hall, with its
own dining facilities and enough dormitories and houses to accommodate
the whole Junior Class. If this were done, it would be possible to develop
programs especially designed for younger boys and to make the transition
from home to a big impersonal school more gradual and thus less traumatic. In like manner, the Committee recommended that a Senior complex
be established in the new dormitories around Rabbit Pond, again with
special rules and regulations appropriate to Seniors. In both the Junior and
the Senior complexes it was hoped that the housemasters in charge would
be able to assume a large part of the administrative work and handle all
but the most serious disciplinary cases. The Committee hoped that similar
complexes might be developed for the two middle classes, though this
presented more difficulties because there was no natural grouping of dormitories to give such complexes physical unity.[9]

Finally, the Committee wanted Andover students to have more contact
with girls. They applauded the steps that had been taken to have more
social events, more extracurricular activities, and a few classes where girls
participated with Academy students. But the School had not gone far
enough. "The heart of our recommendation is that Phillips Academy encourage creative cooperation with one or more of our neighboring girls'
schools to develop various kinds of co-educational enterprises ranging
from social activities to joint instruction." This was coordinate education
rather than coeducation proper, but it was moving purposefully in the direction of the latter.[10] Were all these recommendations on the composition
of student body to be carried out, Phillips Academy would become a very
different place from what it had been.

Mention has been made of the Committee's proposals for the housing
of students—a Junior Complex with separate dining facilities, a Senior
complex of the new dormitories around Rabbit Pond, and one or more
Middler complexes. Such arrangements implied substantial decentralization of administrative responsibility for the students in their nonacademic
activities and would relieve the present pressure on the Dean of Students,
the Discipline Committee, and other central offices. The Committee also

made new recommendations for the school work program. Until this time, work around the School—in offices, in the Commons, and on the grounds —had been done only by scholarship boys. The Committee believed that since the previous double standard for these boys had been abolished, as far as admission to the School was concerned, it was only logical to erase the distinction in this area as well. They therefore recommended that the work program be distributed among all members of the School. The Committee was disturbed as well by eating conditions in the Commons, where noise and confusion reigned and very little gracious living was possible. They realized that the only effective solution to the problem would involve substantial remodeling of the building, and they realized that such remodeling might not be possible in the immediate future. But they did suggest that the serving and disposal areas could be vastly improved without great cost.

Improved living arrangements could contribute greatly to student welfare, but there would always be boys who needed special help. The Committee recommended that the system of counseling boys be overhauled and made more effective. The key figure in such a system would be the housemaster, but his effectiveness was often limited by the number of other responsibilities he had and by his ignorance of modern counseling methods. The Committee recommended that housemasters with large counseling responsibilities be relieved of some of their other work and be encouraged to attend summer conferences on counseling so as to improve their expertise. In addition, the Committee believed that a strong professional counseling service should be established to backstop the housemasters.

The Committee took a conservative position on the School's religious program, recommending that the existing provision for Wednesday and Sunday chapel be maintained. They believed that the students were still too young to make wise decisions in this area and if exposed to religious services might well profit from the experience. That section of the report, which is unlike most of the rest in that it does not propose innovative changes, may well have been included out of deference to Headmaster John Kemper, who had made it clear that he believed the religious program to be of vital importance to the welfare of the School.

As for discipline, the Committee sought to change the system of automatic penalties that had prevailed in the past. Such a system made no allowance for individual situations and often acted unfairly on individual boys. What the Committee wanted was a flexible system, whereby the housemaster, who knew the boy best, could deal with disciplinary cases on an individual basis. As an example of this change in procedure, it was recommended that Demerits be abolished, because they were too rigid and impersonal, and "Comments" be substituted for them. According to this procedure a member of the Faculty who believed a boy should be reported for some infraction of a rule would write a comment on the case, which would be referred to the boy's housemaster. In like manner they proposed that the old "Posting," whereby a boy was denied all outside activities for a period of two weeks, should be replaced by "Restriction," which could be tailored to meet the individual case. And finally, they suggested that a new publication on rules and regulations be prepared that would stress general principles of behavior and the reasons behind them, rather than merely publishing a long list of offenses, all of which were negative. If all these recommendations for student life at Andover were to be adopted, it was believed that the School could do a much better job in dealing with the individual boy and his problems.[11]

Just as the Committee sought more flexibility and variety in dealing with students outside of class, so they believed that there must be similar flexibility and variety in the academic program. Unless the student were exposed to new courses and new methods of instruction, he was liable to go stale and believe that his education had no "relevance." In order to accomplish these aims, the Committee recommended that off-campus programs like Schoolboys Abroad be encouraged and independent study projects, whereby the student could work on his own in consultation with a Faculty member, be made more easily available for Upper Middlers and Seniors. They also recommended that there be an "Activities Week" at the end of the winter term, which would allow a student to pursue an activity of his choice—not necessarily an academic one—in a non-classroom situation. The Committee also recommended, as a kind of off-campus project in reverse, that professionals from various walks of life be invited to the campus to spend time with the students, giving lectures, conducting discussion groups, and meeting with individuals. Such a program could help provide the curricular variety that the Committee was searching for.

The Committee was disturbed at the amount of "grade-grubbing" that went on, a good part of it prompted by a desire to get into a good college. They admitted that the School would always be competitive, but, seeking ways of reducing at least the outward and visible signs of this competition, they recommended abolition of class ranking, which often worked unfairly, unless it was absolutely essential for a college recommendation. And they proposed the institution of a new marking system in which grades would run from a bottom grade of zero to a high of six. By dividing the marking scale into seven segments, it was hoped that there would be less emphasis on grades than in the 1–100 marking scale of old. They recommended that the old rigid effort-marking system be abolished and that written teacher comments be substituted.

The Committee made few specific recommendations about the curriculum itself. One of the most interesting was its proposal for a four-year sequence built around the question "What is Man?" According to this plan, a Junior course would concentrate on how man perceives things and how he expresses himself. It was believed that this focus would involve the student in English courses, supplemented by work in the visual arts, music, and drama. Thus this course would be interdisciplinary. The course for Lower Middlers would deal with man and his environment and would focus on the physical world. The Upper Middler course would concentrate on man as a social animal and utilize various courses in the Social Sciences to illustrate human social activity. Off-campus programs might well play an important part in this course, enabling the student to see how other people lived. Finally, a Senior course, drawing heavily on the humanities, would examine the inner man and explore "some of the ways in which man has conceived of himself and his place in the order of things." Such a four-year sequence, by cutting across departmental lines, could contribute greatly to the flexibility and variety that the Committee sought. Almost every course at Phillips Academy consisted of a certain number of fifty-minute periods. Day in and day out these never changed. The Committee believed that the lengths of classroom periods should be adapted to the type of course taught. Some courses would profit from as many as ten short periods a week, others might benefit from two two-hour periods. To achieve this purpose the Committee recommended the establishment of a system of twenty-minute modules that would enable a scheduling officer to set up classes of varying lengths. Those who thought that the system was extremely complicated were assured that it all could be worked out by the computer. In similar fashion the Committee proposed a revision of the calendar that would provide for three terms of equal length rather than the current system in which the fall term was much longer than the other two. Though it was not stressed in the report, a system of equal terms would encourage the establishment of term-contained courses. Finally, the Committee had some recommendations about the Faculty. They could take as their point of departure a statement of Headmaster John Kemper:

> At the heart of secondary education is the relationship of man and boy. Therefore, as we plot the future of the school, my chief concern is the quality of Andover's teachers. In his every contact with a boy a great teacher communicates what he is and stands for as a person; his love for things of the mind, his integrity, his moral values. From the example and encouragement of such a man, a boy sets his sights high and grows in self-reliance, self-control, and confidence. In the last analysis he will probably not learn in any other way.[12]

To find such a Faculty and to hold it at Andover, the Committee had several suggestions. They wanted more active recruiting of new members rather than appointment from among candidates who had already made applications. They wanted the Faculty to have more free time, in order to attend, for example, meetings of professional societies that might give them perspective on what they were doing. They wanted to equalize the Faculty workload at Andover, so that an undue burden would not fall on those who were teaching and housemastering and coaching. On the other side of the coin, they wanted an increased workload for those who were only teaching. In short, they were convinced that if Faculty morale was to be maintained, they must all be treated fairly. The concluding section of the report recommended establishment of an Office of Research and Evaluation, whose purpose would be to "plan and carry out studies of the educational functioning of the school, using appropriate sociological, psychological, and statistical techniques." To emphasize how important they believed this institution to be, they recommended that one percent of the School's income each year be devoted to the project. Then, having covered almost every phase of life at Phillips Academy, the Committee rested its case.[13] It remained to be seen what the Faculty would do with their reports.

As is almost invariably true of programs as broad and inclusive as that of the Steering Committee, its record in getting its recommendations implemented was win a few, lose a few. Phillips Academy was changing rapidly during the years after the reports were issued, and in some cases other solutions to the problems the Committee had dealt with replaced the Committee's recommendations. As far as the make-up of the student body was concerned, the Admissions Office continued to pursue a policy that followed the Committee line. The A.B.C. program, as previously indicated,[14] brought a much larger number of disadvantaged students, mainly black, to the Academy, and the diversity of the student body was increased. Low-testers, as distinct from the disadvantaged group, did not receive the same amount of attention, however, and experimentation with that group remains to be tried at the Academy. The Committee's recommendations for Junior and Senior complexes were never realized, mainly because an alternative system of housing developed in their stead. The Senior housing unit around Rabbit Pond was in effect for several years, and a start was made toward developing the Junior complex. Then a basic change was made with the introduction of the Cluster system. First developed on an experimental basis by K. Kelly Wise of the English Department, this system envisaged the grouping of dormitories so that there would be clusters of roughly two hundred students housed in them. A major aim of the Steering Committee was incorporated into this arrangement when administrative and disciplinary responsibilities were decentralized. Another feature of the cluster system that negated the plans for Senior and Junior complexes was the practice of vertical housing—each dormitory was to have representatives of three, if not four, of the school classes. Eventually there were six clusters, and the system became standard for the School. The Committee's recommendation that the Academy should have closer relations with girls' schools was, of course, more than realized when full coeducation by means of a merger with Abbot Academy was effected in 1973. A more detailed account of this development will follow. As for the School work program, the Faculty, as previously noted, voted to accept the Committee's recommendation, and ever since that time all members of the undergraduate body have shared in work to be done around the School. What the Committee had to say about the Commons remains true—the eating facilities leave much to be desired. The lobby of the building was redecorated and changes were made in the decor of the dining halls themselves, presumably to please the undergraduates, but the basic problem of the building remains unsolved to this day. The Committee's concern about counseling was generally implemented. A professional staff under the leadership of Dr. Karl Roehrig was created, and a substantial number of Faculty members attended special conferences on counseling methods. The Committee's concern about compulsory religious services was knocked out by the undergraduates in the early 1970's, with the acquiescence of the Religion Department, and to all intents and purposes the great majority of undergraduates today have little if any contact with formalized religion. The Committee's recommendations on discipline were appropriated and modified by those in charge of the various clusters. The cluster discipline committees included undergraduate representatives, gave the accused a much better day in court than had been the case under the old centralized Discipline Committee, and generally developed a more flexible disciplinary system. In this respect the recommendations of the Steering Committee were definitely carried out, for the old rigidity became a thing of the past. The Committee's recommendation for increased off-campus programs was generally accepted at first, and for a few years there was a great deal of interest in such alternatives to regular classroom work. More recently, interest in these programs has declined, some have been abandoned, and the future of all is problematical. Independent study projects have been thriving, however, and each year a substantial number of students pursue work of their own under the general supervision of a member of the Faculty. The Committee recommendation for an Activities Week was implemented by vote of the Faculty in a program called "February Week" and lasted for several years. It was found that the program proved valuable for about 80 percent of the undergraduate body, who engaged in a wide variety of projects, both off campus and on. About 20 percent were not interested, and it proved extremely difficult to decide what to do with them. In addition, dealing with the entire student body, each of whom had to have a project approved, made the administration of the program extremely difficult. After a few years the program was quietly dropped, having been a valuable one for many students, something less than that for others.

The Committee's hope that rank in class could be de-emphasized has not been completely achieved. Although attempts have been made to play down this statistic, the insistence of colleges on the School's providing this information has made it a matter of common knowledge. Yet the competition that accompanied such ratings in the past has undoubtedly diminished.

The Committee recommendation that a grading system from zero to six be adopted has been accepted by the Faculty and is now in effect. It has probably helped to lessen the emphasis on grades per se. These seven numbers cover a fairly broad band of achievements and do not correspond to other marking systems, like, for example, the letter method. Just what a "4" means in relation to other marking systems varies a good deal according to the individual member of the Faculty concerned; as a result, invidious comparisons of grades becomes more difficult. The ambitious proposal for a sequence of courses to be entitled "What is Man?" has never been fully implemented. A course for a selected group of Juniors entitled "Perception and Expression" and taught by Harold Owen of the English Department and Gordon Bensley of the Art Department has successfully combined the two disciplines so as to achieve much of what the Committee intended. Concentrating on how humans perceive things and how they express themselves, this course is still being offered today. The Lower Middler course on Man and his Environment has never been developed, presumably because those on the Faculty competent to offer such a course were too busy with other things. For the Upper Middler course on Man and his Social Relationships, two very interesting courses were developed, taught by Thomas Lyons and Wayne Frederick. As originally conceived, the course would undertake a study of American urban society and Mexican agrarian society, with a view to comparing the two. The class would study both societies in the fall term, then one group would spend the winter term in Boston's South End studying conditions there at first hand, while the rest of the class would spend the winter term in a Mexican agrarian village. The two groups would return to Andover in the spring to compare notes. It was soon found that the program was too ambitious; as a result, two distinct courses were offered, one dealing entirely with Mexican agrarian society and one with American urban society.

At the beginning there was great interest in these courses, a substantial number of applicants, and a rich learning experience for those enrolled. As time went on, interest in off-campus programs declined and the administrative problems connected with offering the courses increased. Today they have been abandoned, at least temporarily. But the basic concept was challenging, and it may well be that others will attempt to revive them in the years to come. Finally, the Senior course, like the Lower Middle one, has never been developed. The idea of the sequence was highly imaginative; it is unfortunate that staffing and other practical problems prevented it from becoming a reality.

When it came to scheduling recommendations, only part of what the Committee proposed has become actuality. The plan for modular scheduling during the school day was never seriously considered by the Faculty, despite assurances that a computer could make it work. The proposal for three equal terms was also turned down by the Faculty when it was first presented. Many believed that a long fall term was important in getting students off to a good start. A later reconsideration was approved, however, with extremely important results for the School. Three terms of equal length made it much easier to offer term-contained courses. Furthermore, such courses could be offered in the first, second, or third terms, since all were of equal length. The proliferation of term-contained courses, an outstanding characteristic of Andover's recent curriculum, would not have been possible without this change. As far as the Faculty is concerned, few of the Committee's recommendations have been fully implemented. The recruiting of teachers has become something of an academic question, for the merger with Abbot Academy caused temporary overstaffing. In addition, budgetary considerations in recent years have dictated against many new appointments. Attempts have been made to develop elaborate point systems to measure Faculty loads, but again it has proved difficult to apply precise measurements to many of the things that a teacher does. Finally, the School accepted the Committee's recommendation for an Office of Research and Evaluation. Under Frederick Peterson this office conducted studies on such subjects as blacks at Andover, undergraduate use of drugs, and undergraduate attitudes toward various aspects of School life. Valuable though these investigations were, the Office has recently been abandoned, for budgetary reasons. (The subject of coordinate education and coeducation will be discussed later in this chapter.) Thus the Committee had some of its recommendations accepted—although some were accepted only to be discontinued a few years later—and some turned down. Yet the influence of the Committee's work on the School cannot be measured by a box score. Its main contribution was to open a lot of windows and let fresh air into the Andover community, to challenge old practices, to encourage experiment in all phases of School life.

> Something has gone sour in teaching and learning. It's almost as though there were a widespread feeling that education had become irrelevant. . . . I think I know what is bothering the students. I think what we are up against is a generation that is by no means sure that it has a future.[15]

This statement by Professor George Wald of Harvard, though referring to college-age students, can apply equally to the *malaise* that affected secondary school students in the 1960's. As a leading headmaster put it, "Every schoolmaster knows that the patterns set by college students, whether in dress, behavior, or thought, tend to repeat themselves in due course, at the secondary level."[16] Except for use of physical violence, the college protest movements of the period were reflected in secondary schools in general and at Phillips Academy in particular. When the smoke had cleared and stability had been restored, many things had changed. The undergraduate protest movements of the 1960's were therefore the second important force to produce profound changes at Andover, to make the School of the 1970's a very different place from what it had been in the early 1960's.

Anyone who attempts to explain the unrest among independent school students in the late 1960's is fortunate in having at his disposal an admirable study of the subject, prepared for the National Association of Independent Schools by Alan R. Blackmer, who produced the work just after he had retired as Dean of the Faculty at Andover. In examining this subject, Dean Blackmer first reviewed the explanations that various writers had given for the unrest of college students during the period. After acknowledging that "the idealogy of rebellion is a confused one, a crazy-quilt of many strands," he goes on to define the student activist as one unlikely to come from a small town or rural area, a member of the upper class, enrolled in a large university or college rather than a small one, in an institution with high academic standards rather than mediocre ones, where freedom of expression had always been encouraged.[17] This by no means suggests that all the students in the group were activists. Lewis Feuer believed that the protesting students were acting out hostility toward their parents, that student uprisings were "symbolic parricides" designed to attack the authority of their fathers and to overthrow their institutions. Jacques Barzun believed that the straight-jacket pressures of the modern, competitive educational system were to blame: "in order to achieve any goal, however modest, one must qualify. Qualifying means having been trained, passed a course, obtained a certificate. . . . The young in college were born into this system, which in this country is not much older than they, and they feel, quite rightly, intense claustrophobia. They have been in this groove since sandbox." Another explanation for student unrest is resentment of the Establishment and its emphasis on material success in the world. "The generation gap is now a moral chasm," says one writer, "across which the young stare at their elders with distrust, convinced that the values which make for success are fake." Or, as a Harvard undergraduate put it, "We live with the horrible feeling of being a pawn caught in some one else's chess game." Archibald MacLeish suggested that the source of the contemporary feeling of frustration was that "we, as Americans . . . have somehow lost control of the management of our affairs, of the direction of our lives, of what our ancestors would have called our destiny." For all its faults, he added, the young generation does possess one virtue "to a degree not equaled by any generation in this century. It believes in man. Its resentment is on behalf of human life." And Barzun again: "What, then, is being fought against on our campuses? The answer, apart from the explicit opposition to the war in Vietnam, is: The whole of modern life."[18]

Blackmer tended to play down the Vietnam War as a cause of unrest.

650 : THE MODERN ANDOVER

His report appeared early in 1970, before the Vietnam issue had attained the white heat that it would later. He wrote, "To many, there seems little ground for the belief that student unrest would end with the termination of the Vietnam war. Vastly deeper than protest against the war and the draft, the revolt of disenchanted youth appears to be directed against the quality of contemporary life."[19] Time was to prove him wrong, but when he wrote, there is no question that the student protest movement covered a broad spectrum of dissatisfactions and, as the various viewpoints above indicate, was a highly complex phenomenon.

When it came to independent secondary schools, a survey conducted by Dean Blackmer revealed the following student grievances, listed in the order of what the students conceived as important:

1. Lack of student influence in shaping school rules and policy.
2. Poor communication between students and faculty and administration—students not "listened to."
3. School life too tightly scheduled and regimented; too little time for oneself.
4. Overly strict regulations of dress codes and hair styles.
5. Too much pressure for grades.
6. Boredom.
7. Lack of relevance of education to the "real world."
8. Too much emphasis by the school on getting into college rather than on what is learned.
9. Compulsory attendance at religious services.

Dean Blackmer points out that the relative importance of some of these grievances needs to be qualified. About a fifth of the responding schools, for example, had no compulsory religious services, and in these schools that could not be a grievance. Likewise, some of the respondents were not taking college preparatory programs and could not resent too great an emphasis on getting into college. Even so, there is no question that the listed grievances reflect widespread dissatisfaction among many independent schools. But it was not merely the listing of grievances that was significant—many of them had been voiced in more peaceful times—the novelty lay in the intensity with which reform was urged. As Blackmer put it, "In the opinion of experienced schoolmasters, the new tensions between students and faculty are a far cry from the old, relaxed, good-humored cops and robbers relationship, when the cops did not try too hard to find the robbers at their nefarious activities and the robbers accepted 'capture' without bitterness or loss of confidence in authority or in the system." As one housemaster put it:

> This has been a year of really serious questioning of the school's authority, of its standards, rules, and traditions; students are demanding justification in all areas of school life, and resisting the old

take-it-for-granted, if-you-say-so-it-must-be-true-Sir line of non-reasoning. For the first time they are aware of their own power; for the first time, it occurs to them simply to say "No."

Central to all the student grievances was the problem of communication. It was not, for example, the decisions the Faculty made for the School that were necessarily resented; it was that the students had had no share in making these decisions, particularly the ones that would have a profound effect on the students' lives. A basic cause of poor communication was a difference in attitudes toward the institution; a student who was to be a member of the School community for only a few years was obviously less interested in the long-range effect of a decision than on its immediate effect on his life; a Faculty member, often with a lifetime's emotional commitment to the institution, was likely to be deeply concerned with the future. As if this were not enough, the increased use of drugs in independent schools made communication even more difficult. One student-faculty committee wrote: "Drugs splinter the school, separating students from faculty and students from one another. The drug problem's strongest dimension may be its divisiveness."

Still another problem plaguing those charged with dealing with student protest was the cleavage among the larger School community regarding how best to proceed. To the statement "The best way to cope with the growing trend of student militancy is to apply firm discipline," sent out to headmasters, faculty, parents, and trustees, three fourths of the parents and trustees expressed themselves as in agreement, while in almost every case well under half of the headmasters and faculty expressed similar agreement. Such a difference of opinion could not help weakening the hands of those in charge. Many of the schools had had traditions of developing *human* excellence; it was now felt by many of the students that *academic* excellence had been given such an important place in the life of the institution that it had crowded out all the other values. Some student comments bear this out:

> The school quite simply fails to develop a boy emotionally so that he can handle situations outside the realm of academics in a responsible and mature way. . . . The emphasis on intellectual achievement and the encouragement of a spirit of intense competition are grossly exaggerated, and are in many ways detrimental.

> The schools are threatened by a failure of purpose, a failure to relate academic learning to a full and useful life. . . . They are threatened by the apparent inability of so many students and faculty members to laugh or to love—and hence to know each other as human beings.

> The school has become so involved in maintaining academic success that it is not meeting the most important needs of its students—per-

sonal and social experiences which alone can give substance and life to the intellectual and other activities of the school.

And finally a member of a girls' school quotes from the children's book *Madelaine* to make her point:

> In an old house in Paris all covered with vines
> Lived twelve little girls in two straight lines
> In two straight lines they broke their bread
> They brushed their teeth and went to bed.

The student desire for more warm, human relationships was particularly strong in the independent boarding schools. No matter how unsatisfactory his environment might be, a day school student was assured of going home in the late afternoon. But the totality of the boarding school environment made alternative methods of finding human relationships more difficult and thus tended to increase the pressure for reform exponentially.

In this discussion of student unrest among independent schools, the scope of the movement should not, however, be exaggerated, for in some schools students accepted the old ways without protest. In schools where unrest was substantial and many students refused to go along, even some of the most critical leaders of the movement agreed that there was much good about the schools they were attacking. Alan Blackmer draws a nice balance:

> A few students suspect that the education to which they are subjected is outmoded to the point of loss of validity and authenticity. Most disagree with a rejection so total. But many of the ablest, there can be no question, urgently seek a vastly expanded educational environment and one which is not only larger, freer, and less sheltered but more varied, warm, and human than the one they now know.[20]

Almost all the grievances and discomforts that were found in independent schools as a group were reflected in Phillips Academy as well. And the size of the School tended to make student protest activity more powerful. In a small school the chances of finding enough dynamic leaders to galvanize the whole institution into action were greatly reduced; at Phillips Academy throughout the 1960's and early 1970's there always seemed to be plenty of leaders ready to carry one or another banner.

In discussing student actions of this period it is difficult to distinguish between sincere protest and traditional horseplay. Undoubtedly many students were acting on principle when they demanded a greater share in running the School, when they fought against dress codes and compulsory chapel, when they protested such outside developments as the war in Vietnam and the violence at Kent State. On the other hand, some of the most malicious activity of the period seemed to be mindless attempts to destroy School property. And some actions were participated in by both groups. For example, some of those who demanded the abolition of classes after Cambodia cared little for the issue involved but thought a free day would be great. And when free days were granted, it was noticed that many students utilized them to stay in bed all morning. It is nevertheless true that a substantial number of Andover undergraduates were deeply concerned with the issues of the day and sincerely wanted to take a position on them. Although student protest activities at Phillips Academy were chronologically intertwined, a clear presentation can best be achieved if they are treated topically.

As noted, one of the major grievances of students was their lack of participation in the decision-making process. This was certainly true at the Academy as the 1960's developed. At the start of the decade, however, there was little interest in the problem. A 1960 *Phillipian* poll for example, found a majority of the students opposed to undergraduate representation on the Discipline Committee.[21] Although there was some opposition to the cut system and compulsory chapel during these early years, nobody appears to have done much about the issues. After 1965 the pace was increased. A dramatic confrontation took place on 3 May 1967, when some two hundred and fifty students staged a sit-in—on the steps of Samuel Phillips Hall after supper to protest the action of the Discipline Committee in dismissing a student. Dean G. G. Benedict agreed to talk to the student body at the following Saturday morning assembly and explain the reasons for the Committee's actions.[22] During the next twelve months undergraduate dissatisfaction with the existing student government and its failure to accomplish anything steadily mounted. The Student Council, the main agency for student opinion since the advent of the Kemper administration, was a generally conservative group made up of Big Men on Campus of the old mold. The Council met regularly with the Headmaster and served as a sounding board of student opinion; they also could make recommendations to the Faculty on matters they believed to be in the best interest of the School. By 1968 the Council no longer represented the views of an increasing number of students who wanted a larger share in decision-making at Phillips Academy. To be sure, students had made a number of recommendations to the Faculty, but the latter had turned them all down. Particularly galling to the undergraduates was the Faculty rejection of a petition to allow three student representatives to attend Faculty meetings on a nonvoting basis.[23]

By June of 1968 undergraduate frustration and dissatisfaction had reached a point where some change in the existing system was essential if the morale of the School was to be maintained. The Administration, sensitive to undergraduate feelings, took steps during the summer to establish a new form of student government to replace the old Council. In the two days before School opened in September 1968, a conference was held to which all the Faculty and all the returning old boys were invited. About half the Faculty and about one quarter of the old boys attended. The first aim was to establish better communications between the two groups, and therefore a series of seminars made up of both students and Faculty were held, to give everyone his day in court. The conference was under the direction of William Torbert, P.A. 1961, then a graduate student in psychology at Yale. Torbert's approach was relaxed and low key, and he was successful in defusing both student hostility and Faculty skepticism. The result was a frank and open discussion in which both students and Faculty expressed themselves freely, and when the conference ended with a picnic at the home of Dean of Students John Richards, there was general agreement that communication between students and faculty had been tremendously improved. Torbert reported on the student enjoyment of the conference and "their interest in *influencing* the faculty rather than *sharing decision-making power* with them."[24]

The purpose of the conference had not been to do anything substantive about student government itself, but out of later meetings what was called the Student-Faculty Cooperative (the Coop) came into being. This organization, open to all students and Faculty, was governed by an Executive Committee consisting of three students who had been elected by the undergraduates and three Faculty members who had been elected by their colleagues. The three student members also served as the officers of the Coop, while the role of the Faculty members was purely advisory. Subcommittees were appointed to deal with specific issues, and an attempt was made to involve in one way or another all the students who showed deep interest in school problems. As far as decision-making was concerned, the students failed to get what they were after, for the Faculty reserved to itself the final decision on issues that came before the Coop; but the three Faculty members of the Executive Board tried hard to represent the student point of view to the Faculty, and soon the practice developed of inviting student members of the Coop to attend selected Faculty meetings. During the first year of its existence the Coop focused on two issues—required chapel and coordinate education with Abbot Academy. From the student point of view, some progress was made in both areas. Wednesday morning chapel was made voluntary, and a special "Coeducation Week" was held with Abbot, during which the students of each institution were free to attend classes at the other. The following year the Coop took up many new issues, such as vertical housing, student membership on the Discipline Committee, and the Intensive Studies Program, but in most cases the Faculty ruled on these issues before the Coop had had a chance to discuss them. The following year, interest sagged to such an extent that a "Save the Coop" Committee was appointed. Two of the officers wrote, "Because of a lack of proper leadership, the Coop has run into great difficulty within the past year. This has created and compounded a great many of its problems, among them: poorly run meetings, apathetic committees, and a lack of compliance with its constitution on the part of the Coop Executive Board."[25] The fact of the matter is that the Coop could not be effective unless a strong group of students was willing to put a lot of work into it, and although this was true at the start, it proved very difficult to maintain. The Coop got a temporary respite in the spring of 1971 when David Lipsey, a student activist leader, became President, but the recovery was short-lived. It is hard to predict what the future would have been had the cluster system not been established and student government not decentralized. Under the cluster system students play major roles in governing the cluster, serving on cluster discipline committees, managing cluster social events, and generally participating actively in cluster affairs. Thus, even though the Coop died, the major aims of the movement—improved communication between students and Faculty and a larger role for students in the running of the School—were achieved in another form.

Another highly emotional issue that exercised the School community in the late 1960's was student appearance—particularly length of hair and coats and ties. Whoever started the craze for long hair among college and school students in the 1960's could not have picked a more frustrating practice for administrations to deal with. How a student wore his hair was considered a matter of personal choice, a basic individual right. And from an administrator's point of view it was difficult to deal with the problem. No one wanted to hold the students down and shave their heads, nor in cases of defiance of School rulings in this area did they want to dismiss students. The issue polarized the Phillips Academy Faculty. To some the long, messy, unkempt hair of many students was an insult to decency; others thought that long hair did not seriously interfere with school life and were willing to let students do as they wished. The football coaches made their players who had long hair cut it, but the reason given was that otherwise their helmets would not fit. Finally, after a heated Faculty discussion on the subject, Headmaster John Kemper announced that he was going to become a "czar" of hair at Andover. The duty was unpleasant. It would have been hard to find a practice that ran more counter to his army training. Yet, as usual, he was determined to be fair to all sides. Under the czar plan, members of the Faculty who thought a boy's hair was completely beyond the pale could send him to the Headmaster, who would then decide whether to force him to cut it. This was done in a few cases and may have mollified some of the anti-hair Faculty, but it could work both ways. One boy had a beautiful page-boy haircut, with his hair coming down to the nape of his neck. He must have spent a long time grooming it, for aside from the length, his appearance was impeccable. After he was ordered to get it cut to earlobe length, he emerged looking much worse than before. As time went on, the czar program was in abeyance, and the community came to accept weird hair-dos, some albeit grudgingly.

In the great hair battle the boys therefore won hands down. They won on the issue of coats and ties as well. From time immemorial, Phillips Academy students had been required to wear coats and ties to class. In the 1960's this, too, became an emotional issue. As with hair, the student claim was that an individual's attire was a personal matter and he should be allowed to wear what he wanted. Abortive attempts were made to get the whole student body to agree to go to class without coats and ties in order to force the issue, but only a few of the most dedicated ever actually did this. One teacher remembers three or four boys coming to class one morning without coats and ties. He told them they would have to leave. When one asked what a coat and tie had to do with his education, the teacher replied, "Nothing. But it has a lot to do with my contract with Phillips Academy." This apparently presented the problem to the boys in a different light. At any rate, they left the classroom and returned later

79. *A student comment on the hair problem. Cartoon by Andrew Rutherford of the Class of 1971, reproduced with his permission.*

more or less clad in coats and ties. And the teacher did not mark them late. As time went on, more and more of the Faculty became convinced that coats and ties were not all that important, and eventually the matter came up for a vote in Faculty meeting. There was some concern lest the Teaching Fellows, who were unanimously opposed to the requirement, might cast the deciding votes and then the following year not be around to face the results of their decision. Indeed it was suggested, that the Teaching Fellow vote should not be counted, so that the decision could be made by the regular Faculty. But no one need have worried. When the vote was taken, a substantial majority favored elimination of the coat-and-tie requirement, and that was that. The change was put into effect gradually; for the first year informal attire was allowed after May first. The following year, the requirement was done away with altogether. Those who feared that sloppiness in dress would be reflected in sloppiness of academic performance were generally proved wrong. Some of the finest work was done by the most disreputable-looking students in the School.

A long-standing grievance of the undergraduates was compulsory chapel, and in this area the students of the late 1960's succeeded in revolutionizing the whole religious program of the School. As long as the Andover Theological Seminary stayed in Andover, it dominated the religious life of the School; students were required to attend daily chapel and two long church services on Sundays. With the departure of the Seminary for Cambridge, Al Stearns took over and for a while was School Minister as well as Headmaster. Midway in his term the Reverend Markham W. Stackpole was appointed School Minister, but though he contributed a great deal to the Andover community, he did not remain on the Hill long enough to establish any new programs. First he entered the army during World War I as a chaplain, and soon after the war was over, he resigned to join the Faculty of Milton Academy. It was not until the very end of Al Stearns's career that A. Graham Baldwin was appointed to the Department of Religion and, when Jack Fuess became Headmaster, was made School Minister. Gray Baldwin proved to be an admirable choice for a very difficult job. He was an outspoken liberal; one of his proudest boasts was that he had been listed in an anti-communist publication called *The Red Network*. He believed in the gospel of service and was not troubled by theological niceties. Since Jack Fuess before becoming Headmaster had usually played golf on Sundays, he needed a lot of help in this area, and Gray became his strong arm. As Jack wrote about him,

> I asked my younger friend, the Reverend A. Graham Baldwin . . .
> to fill the position of school minister. His acceptance was a guarantee
> that I need have no more worries about a field in which I was cer-
> tainly without experience. I believed then—and still believe—that
> the school physician and the school minister occupy unique positions

80. *Alfred Graham Baldwin, Instructor in Religion and School Minister, 1930–1968.*

and must be selected with the greatest care. No man could have been more cooperative than Gray Baldwin—or better suited to his job.[26]

One great difficulty in establishing religious services for a nonsectarian School was the necessity for compromising on the form of service. The strength of an established and traditional ritual in church schools could make their services much more meaningful to the students. Gray Baldwin dealt with this problem very effectively. He started with the framework of the Congregational service but included material from other denominations as well—from the Book of Common Prayer, for example. And he tried very hard to get speakers who would interest the boys—men who would often speak on important social issues of the day. There were complaints, of course: Unitarians complained about the presence of the cross in the Cochran Chapel; a student from the back country of North Carolina said wistfully that nobody did any "preaching" at Andover. Certainly a sizable number of students were apathetic about the whole program, but until the 1960's that was as far as it went.

The religious program of the School received strong support from Bishop Henry W. Hobson, President of the Board of Trustees, and from Headmaster John Kemper, both of whom believed strongly that it was an integral part of a boy's education. In 1966 Gray Baldwin retired and was succeeded by James Rae Whyte, who had been school minister at Northfield and Mount Herman and who had had a church in Pittsfield, Massachusetts. Jim Whyte was a man of rare sensitivity and open-mindedness. He was determined to make the School's religious program meaningful to the students and willing to go a long way to accomplish this purpose. He believed strongly that religion need not be lugubrious and delighted in introducing humor into all he did. He began publishing a witty pastoral letter called *The Epistle* that was enjoyed by the whole community.

All this was done with such gentleness that no one could take offense. The idea of forcing religion on boys was abhorrent to him, and thus he was vulnerable to student demands for change. With the construction of the Sylvia Kemper Memorial Chapel in the basement of Cochran, it became possible to hold special services for Catholic and Jewish students as alternatives to School chapel. As the 1960's wore on, the question of compulsory attendance at chapel became more hotly debated. Here was another issue that involved the right of the individual to run his own life in an area that the students considered very personal. They refused to accept the Steering Committee's dictum that students were not yet old enough to decide for themselves such an important matter as religious training. They started a campaign of trying to make life miserable for those who conducted the chapel services. By refusing to participate in singing and responsive readings and by openly displaying contempt for the very fact of chapel, they gradually demoralized the Department of Religion and made its appointed task almost unbearable. In 1969 the Faculty tried to meet this difficult situation with a compromise. Daily chapel had earlier been limited to Wednesday mornings; now this one service was eliminated and replaced by School "gatherings" on topics of concern. At the same time, more options were offered for religious attendance on Sundays. As always, students could attend town churches instead of the School service. There were in addition special services for Catholic and Jewish students. A new alternative was provided—a meditation service, after the manner of a Quaker Meeting, where students were to sit quietly in a special room instead of going to chapel. These stop-gap measures proved insufficient for the undergraduates. The pressure to make *all* religious services voluntary continued, and finally Jim Whyte came to the conclusion that compulsory attendance at religious services was a lost battle at Andover. John Kemper had always insisted that compulsory chapel would never be abolished while he was Headmaster, but he could not very well carry on the program if his Department of Religion believed that the task was impossible to perform effectively. Jim Whyte makes his position clear in the following statements:

> I know the arguments for compulsory chapel and have used them in a defensive holding action against adult and youthful opponents. As a minister I have always felt somewhat guilty about my own position because I defended compulsory worship on practical and educational grounds while my antagonists spoke from a devotional, idealistic and spiritual position. I envied them their stand because where worship is concerned they were right. . . . perhaps the most sacred area of worship in the Christian tradition is the Service of Holy Communion. The service in the Protestant tradition could never be a compulsory service. The question? If one cannot justify compulsion at the most sacred level, then how can one with a clear conscience justify compulsion at any level of worship?[27]

> From the liturgical point of view, from a worship perspective, required chapel is an insult to the participant and to Him whom one is to celebrate. It is the kind of praise I don't think God needs.[28]

The Faculty accepted the Reverend Whyte's arguments, and an old, old tradition was no more. The results were what most people had expected. Attendance at the Sunday services in the Cochran Chapel dropped off to twenty-five or thirty Protestants, while attendance at the Catholic and Jewish services ran about seventy-five each. These last two groups became the leading religious forces in the life of the School. Recently, an experiment with a plural ministry has been tried: A Catholic priest, a Jewish rabbi, and a Protestant clergyman have all been made members of the Faculty with part-time teaching assignments. This works well for the Catholic and Jewish students, but the problem of dealing with the hundreds of Protestants remains. Religious enthusiasm and dissatisfaction come in waves, and it could well be that in the years to come, most of the undergraduates will return to the kind of religious devotion in which Samuel Phillips, Jr., put great store.

Student protest activity in the late 1960's was devoted in part to effecting changes at Phillips Academy, but it also concerned itself with leading national problems as well. As was true of many other schools and colleges, Phillips Academy students engaged in protest marches, demanded moratoria on classes, struck occasionally to obtain their ends, and generally behaved much the same as college students, with one difference: there was no physical violence. No offices were occupied. Despite that, the students on many occasions managed to make the lives of those in charge miserable. No attempt will be made here to cover all aspects of student opposition to such things as the Viet Nam War; rather a few examples may indicate the quality of the disturbances. One of the early episodes occurred on Memorial Day, 1969. An alumnus participant remembers:

> Traditionally, the town of Andover had joined with Phillips Academy to celebrate through speeches and parades in honor of those who lost their lives in service to their country. However, during the spring of 1969 the opposition to the war in Viet Nam had reached the most vocal point to date; many of the students also felt committed to somehow sharing our concerns about what we perceived to be a costly and immoral war.
>
> As an expression of our opposition to the War, we decided to wear white armbands engraved with the insignia of the peace symbol. As we viewed our actions, we stood as active participants in a national rite to honor America's war dead, yet unlike the American Legion and other patriotic organizations involved in the parade, we wished to register our opposition to the present war in which American lives were being lost.
>
> Prior to the ceremonies a few faculty members attempted to dissuade us from wearing the armbands. Somehow, the image of an Andover boy registering an independent and potentially unpopular political viewpoint was not one easily embraced by those who experienced the burning of a neck-tie in front of the Commons as a radical, extremist act.
>
> During the parade we silently watched the passing entourage of veterans dressed in army uniforms, of high school bands and of local politicians. Some people noted our white armbands, whispered to their husbands or made disparaging remarks about the political leanings of American youth. Yet the parade passed without any notable incidents. After the ceremonies were over, a few of us wandered to the local coffee shop on Main Street. When we entered, we sat down at the counter and ordered some ice cream and doughnuts. The waitress looked at us, noticed our armbands and quickly

81. *An early example of protest by Phillips Academy students. Andover boys march in Boston to protest the city's segregated school system, 1965.*

rushed behind the grill, where she exchanged some hurried words with the manager. We waited for about ten minutes for our food, but instead of doughnuts, we were greeted by the manager. "Do you kids come from the Academy?" he queried. When we replied affirmatively, he said, "You'd better leave, we don't serve Communists in here." Immediately our youthful moral feelings were aroused by such a demand. Armed with visions of Selma and Birmingham, we stated the principles of the Bill of Rights, as enunciated in our American History class. It was illegal, we argued, to be denied service in a public place because we were wearing armbands. . . . The manager called the police. They arrived and ordered us to leave. As intelligent Andover men, we knew better than to confront the uniformed authorities; yet our sense of justice had been wounded in the most direct way most of us had ever experienced.

The protestors decided on two courses of action to support their position; one was to organize a boycott of the Coffee Mill, the other was to get publicity for their cause. They made contact with both the Boston *Globe* and the Boston *Herald*, and the next morning full articles appeared in both papers. The story was taken up by other media and soon obtained widespread coverage indeed. The *Herald* editorialized:

It appears that peace has become a fighting word in Andover. . . . On second thought, perhaps Mr. Nixon should visit Andover. He not only wants peace in the world. He also wants domestic tranquility. Andover might offer him a challenge.

No formal disciplinary action was taken by the School in this matter. The students had broken no school rules, and besides, if there was one thing that Headmaster John Kemper believed in, it was the right of the individual to voice his own opinions. But it was clear that the Faculty strongly disapproved of the whole business. "Many prominent members of the Andover faculty were not pleased. . . . We were told not to talk to reporters any more, as we had brought the Academy into disrepute. Not one faculty member ever voiced a word of praise or support for our actions." And the Director of College Placement informed the leader of the protest that he had been obliged to report the matter to the college to which the boy had already been admitted and that his admission might be revoked. As it turned out, it was not. A year or so later, student protests of this kind would receive some Faculty support, but in 1969 such action was considered unacceptable.

A much more traumatic experience for the Andover community came at the time of the Cambodian crisis. Student and Faculty outrage at this governmental policy was supplemented by similar outrage at the Kent State killings a few days later and to a lesser extent by the treatment of the Black Panthers in New Haven. The morning after the announcement of the invasion of Cambodia, many of the students wore black arm-bands and prevailed upon some members of the Faculty to do so.[29] Tension mounted over the weekend, and on the morning of Tuesday, 5 May, at about 7:30 A.M. a group of students gathered outside the library and began discussing Cambodia and Kent State. One observer said it was as though individual members of the group were reaching out toward one another in search of a hand to grasp for comfort. In the middle of that afternoon a group of students from Merrimack College, who had struck their classes, arrived on campus, only to find most Phillips Academy under-graduates engaged in sports. They returned later, their forces augmented by some Andover alumni from Harvard, and circulated through the dining halls drumming up support.

The next day, Wednesday, was a half holiday. In the afternoon a group of Phillips students marched to Merrimack College, where they were joined by students from Abbot and the Andover High School. There they conducted a rally. Headmaster John Kemper drove over and watched the proceedings for about an hour. That evening representatives from the administrations of Exeter, Groton, and St. Paul's came to Andover to discuss the situation and the policies that should be developed to deal with it. Headmaster Richard Day of Exeter had already sent a strong letter of protest to President Nixon. Thursday saw some two or three hundred Andover students on the steps of Samuel Phillips Hall with placards labeled "strike." The Headmaster and Dean of Students John Richards talked with them and urged discretion; somewhere between fifty and one hundred cut the rest of their classes that morning. At mid-morning assembly the Headmaster announced that there would be a twenty-four-hour moratorium on all School appointments. Since the long spring weekend followed immediately after the end of this period, the undergraduates would have four days to cool down. But the School had no intention of making the moratorium simply a free day. At very short notice a long list of faculty-sponsored discussion groups and seminars was prepared, while other members of the Faculty simply listed themselves as available for consultation in their classrooms or their homes.[30] Headmaster John Kemper canceled an engagement that he had in Washington that evening so that he could be in his office from seven to ten to talk to students. A special Communications Center was established in the Underwood Room to provide students with information on what was going on at Phillips Academy and in the world outside. During this period 92 percent of the students answered a poll of student and Faculty opinion; 27 percent of the Faculty responded. Solid majorities in both groups expressed themselves as wishing to protest the American involvement in Indo-China and the Kent State killings; 56 percent of the students and 46 percent of the Faculty felt similarly about the Black Panthers. A strong majority of each group favored petitioning local, state, and federal officials to correct these abuses, and a somewhat smaller majority supported meetings, demonstrations, and the distribution of pertinent information. Forty-six percent and—interestingly enough—20 percent of the Faculty favored strikes of required appointments as a form of protest.[31] It soon became clear that although many students might have cooled off over the long weekend, a substantial number were as hot as ever.

On the following Monday the Faculty approved a two-point program to deal with the latter group—and a wise and understanding program it was. Students were permitted to withdraw from campus for an indeterminate period if they had their parents' permission, if they wrote for Dean Richards an explanation of why they wished to withdraw, and if they agreed not to return to campus until they were ready to rejoin the School. If a student returned before the end of the academic year, he could take the final exams in his courses and thereby receive credit for them. Otherwise, he could take a make-up in September. A second option allowed students to remain on campus and, with special permission from an ad hoc committee, to be absent in order to participate in protest activities. A handful of students opted for the first plan, and a few more for the second. Most of the first group were away for a week or ten days, many having gone to Washington, and generally the response to these two proposals indicated that the long weekend had defused more students than the administration had at first thought.[32] The Cambodian crisis showed that a large number of the Faculty agreed with the students' opinion of the war. A Faculty petition, signed by almost the entire membership, was sent to President Nixon urging him to confer with the Congress on the proper policy for the Viet Nam War. It was a difficult period for John Kemper, many of whose West Point classmates were in leadership positions during the war. He could not bring himself to sign the Faculty petition, but he encouraged its circulation, and his understanding of the feelings of the boys marked him as a rare leader of youth. And so Phillips Academy weathered another storm. Unfortunately, there was worse to come.

The period of 1971 and early 1972 was the most difficult in the history of the Academy. An alumnus who was a student during that period speaks of this time as the nadir of the School. Students were frustrated, the morale of the community was low, and the undergraduates engaged in a number of "pranks" that were really not pranks at all but rather conscious attempts to disrupt the workings of the School. Another alumnus who was present during this period writes:

> The first thing that could be said about the Class of 1972 is that we were alienated. Nobody seemed to like the administration, the rules, the faculty, each other, or the school itself. . . . In general, my class was rebellious and distrustful of authority, and were mad—mad at the school, mad at our parents, mad at Nixon, mad at the country.

Perhaps the tone of the period was set in February 1971, when a bomb was discovered near the Bell Tower. That the bomb was not properly armed and that there was no evidence that a Phillips Academy student was involved did little to dispel the chilling effect of the episode. Participation in protest movements continued. In April a group of Andover and Abbot students traveled by bus to Washington to take part in an antiwar march, a trip that had the blessings of both faculties. When, however, in May seven students took illegal day excuses to attend an antiwar demonstration in Boston, they were put on probation, much to the anger of the undergraduate body. The *Phillipian* wrote a scathing editorial attacking both the decision and the School's announced reason for it. According to the School, if these boys were to go to Boston, Phillips Academy would lose its position of neutrality in these difficult times. Quite apart from the fact that many other groups had been allowed to attend such demonstrations, the *Phillipian* believed the policy to be unneutral in itself:

> The school, in punishing students for speaking out against the war, suppressed the expression of anti-war sentiments and thus acted in defense of present U.S. policy in Indo-China. . . . The decision is the result of faculty priorities. In order to follow written rules, the school denied students the right of free speech. Sometimes people at PA seem to care more for legality than they do for morality.
> The students . . . were punished for following morals instead of rules.

The paper went on, after the example of many college papers, to list school investments in various war-making industries, and suggested that these holdings of themselves put the Academy in an unneutral position.[33] That same spring life at Andover was further disrupted by the election of David Lipsey of the Senior Class as President of the Coop. Lipsey had many gifts of leadership. He was highly intelligent, extremely articulate, and capable of exerting a profound influence on those who listened to him. His tactics were often those of a demagogue, but this disturbed the students not a whit. During this whole period at Andover, Lipsey was the only student who approached the kind of radical leadership that was making the lives of college administrators miserable. He believed that the School's progress toward coeducation, the abolition of the cut system, and the abolition of compulsory chapel had been inexcusably slow, and he sought to light a fire under Administration and Faculty to speed things up. Lipsey and the Coop won on the chapel issue in May of that year, but there seemed to be a lot of foot-dragging on the other two. As a fitting climax to the spring of 1971, about 160 members of the Senior Class, just before graduation, signed a statement that was interpreted to mean a lack of confidence in the Faculty and Administration. The *Phillipian* wrote as follows:

> Members of Phillips Academy's senior class signed a petition last

week to express their "lack of confidence in the administration and faculty of Phillips Academy." Almost two-thirds of the class, 160 out of 246 members, supported the statement.

Senior David Lipsey, one of the originators of the petition, stated that people entering PA have a lot of expectations which they never realized. Lipsey added that he wanted to give seniors an opportunity to express their disappointment. He stated, "I feel the response is a reflection of the unrest in the school."[34]

The best statement during this whole unhappy period was made at the Senior Dinner by Dr. Alston Chase, who was retiring that year. He pointed out that the true revolutionaries of modern history—Darwin, Mendel, Marx, Freud, and Einstein—were mild-mannered men who worked quietly by themselves; yet each had had a more revolutionary influence on the world than the would-be revolutionaries who took to the streets and engaged in acts of violence. For all their disaffection most of the seniors were impressed with Dr. Chase's profound observations, but when the class rose to applaud him at the end, there were some who remained seated. No wonder that at the end of the year John Kemper wrote in the *Pot Pourri*:

Tension between faculty and students reached an unfortunate peak toward the end of the year.

As individuals, teachers sought to be sympathetic and understanding, but as a body, the faculty was painfully slow to institute vital change. Conflicting values and growing frustration needlessly hindered communication. Amidst all the tension faculty and students alike often failed to come to terms with human nature and human needs.

Too many of us isolated ourselves from each other, losing the rapport between teacher and student which should have been the most valuable part of our Andover education.[35]

Hardly had School started in the fall of 1971 when the basic stabilizing force in the Andover community was removed by the resignation of Headmaster Kemper. He had had an operation for lung cancer the previous spring and it was hoped that a complete cure had been effected. In the fall there was a recurrence of the disease of such virulence as to make it impossible for him to continue. An alumnus who was in School at that time writes the following account of the Headmaster's resignation:

Headmaster Kemper personified the traditional force of Andover. He presented something of an enigma to the students. Dressed in white shirt and Andover tie, with a short haircut, he seemed out of place in the jeaned, long-haired world of the 70's. Students did not understand Mr. Kemper and they were certain that he did not under-

668 : THE MODERN ANDOVER

stand them. But for some strange reason this distance also created respect as having been a great headmaster at one time and symbolizing a once-great Andover.

At an assembly in October Mr. Kemper resigned because of poor health. The entire student body was stunned, and rose, spontaneously and unanimously, in ovation. Why students, often puzzled and frustrated by the Headmaster, should have risen together in such a tribute and afterwards gathered together in sadness and shock I am not certain, but we knew that Andover and the traditions embodied by this one man would not be the same. Perhaps, having faced for so long the prospect of an unchanging Andover, the students experienced the sudden uneasiness that change was going to occur.

Granting that John Kemper may have been out of touch with the rebel undergraduates of the previous few years, he still led the School—indeed the whole Andover community—through those difficult years with extraordinary patience and fairness. And this was all the more difficult for him because the life-styles of the period must have been extremely offensive to him. His loyalty to the Army precluded his joining in any protests against the war in Viet Nam. He must, during this time, have been a lonely man. Yet there is in his record no attempt at the suppression of student or Faculty opinion. To be sure he sought to channel these opinions and make them constructive. But he had too much respect for the individual personality to try to impose any of his views on others. It was unfair that after more than twenty years of extraordinarily distinguished service to the School, he should, during his last years, have been plagued by the disintegration of old values and by disease. Despite the unhappy end of his administration, when his Andover career is viewed as a whole, he clearly deserves to be considered one of the School's great Headmasters.

John Kemper died about two months after his resignation, and there followed a frightening period. Dean of the Faculty Simeon Hyde, who had been appointed Acting Headmaster when John Kemper resigned, struggled manfully to deal with the manifold problems that developed. But it was understood by all that he would not be made Headmaster in his own right—indeed a Trustee Committee was at work searching for a new headmaster. Dean Hyde was prevented from making basic decisions because he did not wish to tie the hands of his successor. Early in 1972 a wave of vandalism swept the School. Most alarming was that much of it seemed to be mindless, unconnected with any student demands. Early in the winter of 1971 the School's cut records had been stolen from George Washington Hall. If no record of class and athletic absences existed, students could not be disciplined for overcutting. In the next issue of the *Phillipian* appeared an anonymous letter from the thieves stating that "cuts are a false impetus to attend classes" and closing "In any event change must, and will, occur. We will not wait much longer."[36] Early in

1972 the crime was repeated, though without any newspaper communication. Dean Hyde could not find any connection between this second offense and the student activists; it was apparently an unprincipled act.[37] The community was shocked again when undergraduates stole all the Commons silver and put it on the roof of the building. The School had to eat with its hands until the lost cutlery was finally found. A much more serious act of vandalism was the emptying of card catalog drawers in the library and scattering the cards all over the place. The School might get along without cut records and silverware, but this struck at the very heart of the institution. A student of the time writes: "These acts, almost of terrorism, caused the community to despair, waiting during agonized weeks for the next inevitable 'prank.' Without a Headmaster, in the midst of a struggle between tradition and dissent, Andover was repeatedly shaken by paralyzing acts." The climax came in late winter when three students attempted to steal the cut records for the third time. Entering George Washington Hall, they were met by an off-duty policeman whom the School had hired to protect the building. The students immediately separated and ran, with the policeman in hot pursuit of one of them, yelling at him to stop. When they reached the vista, the officer drew his gun and threatened to shoot if the boy did not stop, and when he continued to run, the policeman fired a warning shot in the air and the student then stopped. The same alumnus correspondent comments:

> As the student froze, so did the whole community. A single shot of a pistol awakened everyone from their fatalistic lethargy of the past weeks. . . . Nearly everyone was horrified that events had deteriorated to a point where a gunshot had been fired.

Fortunately, the end was in sight. In March the Trustees announced the appointment of Theodore R. Sizer, formerly Dean of the Harvard School of Education, as the new Headmaster, and after a period of drifting, the School once again had direction. Ted Sizer visited Phillips Academy often in the spring of 1972, met many members of the School community, and made it clear to all that he had a positive program and that he intended to move decisively when he took over in the summer. The students took him at his word, determined to wait and see what the new administration would bring, and abandoned their acts of destruction. But for many in the Andover community the vandalism of the winter of 1972 left scars that would take some time to heal.

It remains to speak of what was far and away the most important change in the nearly two hundred years of Phillips Academy history—the coming of coeducation. New dress codes, new chapel attendance requirements, new forms of student government all fade into insignificance when compared with this momentous change. The decision to go coeducational was very difficult to reach. At the start, the Andover community was sharply divided on the issue. The Faculty was split, the Headmaster had serious reservations, the Trustees were determined to move very slowly. Most of the undergraduates favored coeducation and became more and more impatient, as time went on, with what they considered the snail-like pace of the School. The issue was also complicated by the relationship between Phillips Academy and Abbot Academy. The two institutions had enjoyed more or less amicable relations over the years, and Phillips felt an obligation toward the sister school. If Andover were to start admitting girls on its own, as Exeter had done, the impact on Abbot was sure to be disastrous, especially since Abbot was having financial difficulties. Yet there was a substantial group among the Faculty who favored doing just that. On the other side it could be argued that if the School were to go coeducational, here was a way of accomplishing its purpose immediately, with some three hundred girls, an experienced Faculty, and a useful plant all ready to enter into a relationship with Phillips Academy if some kind of agreement could be reached. Another possibility was coordination—a system whereby the two institutions would remain distinct and under separate administrations but there would be cross-enrollment in courses at the two schools and most extracurricular activities would be open to students of both sexes.

A question of this magnitude naturally fell in the province of the Trustees, and from 1967 to 1972 they moved slowly through a mass of claims, counterclaims, suggestions, and demands on the subject. Though the ultimate responsibility lay with them, all the elements in the School community had a keen interest in the problem. The Faculty, split though they were, provided many committees to study various aspects of the problem. The Headmaster tried to give the discussions focus and to prevent the school from moving too fast. The undergraduates, who were convinced that coeducation would solve most of the School's problems, worked through the Coop and the *Phillipian* to keep the pressure on. In a very real sense the solution to the coeducation problem was the result of hard work on the part of the whole Andover community.

It has been claimed that early in the nineteenth century two girls attended Phillips Academy for a short period. The documentation for this claim is dubious; in any event, it did not lead anywhere.[38] Had relations between Phillips and Abbot been closer and the rules and regulations governing the mixing of the two sexes been more relaxed, it is conceivable that some kind of shared educational experience might have evolved, but the ferociousness with which Abbot headmistresses like Bertha Bailey guarded her charges precluded any such development. Some relaxation of the restrictions on the mixing of Phillips boys and Abbot girls occurred in the early 1960's, but it was not until later in that decade that the pace quickened. Meanwhile, Phillips Academy had taken its first step toward coeducation when the Summer Session of 1964 admitted some girls as an experiment. This decision, incidentally, was striking evidence of how useful the Session could be as a laboratory for the winter School. If coeducation did not work, it could be dropped; if it did work, it could provide a testing ground for possible action later on by the winter school. In actual fact, it worked very well, and ever since, the Summer Session has been coeducational. Director Frederick A. Peterson agonized over a rule to govern the conduct of boys and girls when they were together and finally came up with a real gem. It read: "Couples must take care not to find themselves in circumstances suggesting that they sought deliberately to avoid observation."[39] The first move in the long series of steps that was to lead eventually to coeducation was the part of the Steering Committee's report which read: "The heart of our recommendation is that Phillips Academy encourage creative cooperation with one or more of our neighboring girls' schools to develop various kinds of co-educational enterprises ranging from social activities to joint instruction."[40] This recommendation was approved by the Faculty in the spring of 1967, and during the fall exploratory meetings were held between the administrations of Abbot and Phillips academies with a view of implementing the plan.[41] Since Donald Gordon, '52, the Principal-elect of Abbot Academy, would not take office until the fall of 1968, it was decided to wait until then before proceeding further on major questions; it was possible, however, to develop a program of increased joint social activities early in 1968. Yet things moved slowly, and it was not until over a year later—in the spring of 1969—that further progress was made. At that time an experimental "coordinate education" week was scheduled, during which Abbot and Phillips students might visit each other's classes. A real breakthrough came about a month later when the two schools agreed to a limited number of coeducational courses for the School year 1969–70. The Phillips courses open to Abbot students would be advanced art, religion major, Italian, Asian history and some minor science courses. In addition, the two schools agreed to merge their fourth-year Spanish courses, while a few German students from Abbot could enroll in Phillips courses. It will be seen that no provision for cross-enrollment in any of the basic sequences like mathematics and English was made.

This modest proposal did not accomplish much during its first year, mainly because the two schools had different class schedules. As a result, only about fifty enrollments in the available courses resulted, mostly Abbot girls in Phillips classes. In November further progress was made toward coordination when a group of administrators from the two schools recommended that the various departments at Phillips and Abbot meet to discuss the possibilities of cross-enrollment in major sequential courses as well as those already available, and that the two schools agree on a common calendar for the year and compatible daily schedules. In the meantime, the

Faculty-Student Coop recommended the enrollment of girls at Phillips Academy while continuing the coordination program with Abbot. At this point Headmaster John Kemper urged students and Faculty to go slow. He reminded them that decisions in the area of coordination or coeducation were the responsibility of the Trustees and that he was sure they would move slowly and not reach a decision before at least two years. He presented a series of questions on coeducation that would have to be answered before further steps could be taken.

When the Trustees met in April, they charged their Educational Policy Committee to make an in-depth study of the whole question, while the Alumni Council, meeting at the same time, supported some kind of co-ordination or coeducation. After further studies by members of the ad-ministration of the two schools in the summer of 1970, the Faculty, in September, finally approved meetings between the various departments to try to enlarge the number of courses that could be coeducational and also to develop a common calendar and daily schedule. None of this, however, could apply for the School year 1970–71; thus the relatively small number of cross-enrollments that had obtained the previous year continued. That same fall Dean Simeon Hyde, Jr., prepared a powerful statement in sup-port of coeducation. Space prevents mention of more than a few of his points; but he believed that from both the sociological and educational point of view coeducation was a must. "As the roles of men and women become less differentiated," he wrote, "differentiated education loses its validity. . . . The separation of the sexes in secondary boarding schools is a kind of hiatus in the normal process of growth, a period of artificial separation, discontinuous and out of harmony with the stages immediately preceding and following it. It is also at odds with the experience of all but a tiny minority of the American population, a status no longer supported by the concept of a special mode of education for a special class."[42] Having made a strong case for coeducation in general terms, Dean Hyde turned to Phillips Academy in particular and came out strongly for a merger with Abbot. His conclusion:

> A merger with Abbot, though full of difficulties, seems practical, ethical, and educationally sound. A true merger would bring to either partner the insight, experience, and resources of the other; and with no alteration of numbers the combined school would have a better start toward an acceptable ratio of boys and girls and of men and women than would be possible at the beginning of any one school's solitary effort. . . . If Abbot and Phillips could together commit them-selves to the development of a school in which boys and girls and men and women shared equally, they would be far ahead of other institutions striving to escape from the limitations of sexually segre-gated education.[43]

Later that fall the Trustees gave Dean Hyde's position a measure of support when they resolved that "Phillips Academy should be involved in the education of women" and that it should pursue that goal not "independently but in close association with Abbot Academy."

But by no means all the community agreed with Dean Hyde. The leading spokesman for an all-boy School was Richard Pieters, Head of the Mathematics Department and one of Andover's leading teachers, who was asked by the Trustees to present the opposing position. He viewed the coming of coeducation with alarm. A colleague describes his position:

> One of my strongest memories about Dick Pieters goes back to the days when the great debate was on about Andover's going coed. Dick was a dedicated and articulate spokesman for the opposition, and at one point, in the face of strong evidence of inevitable change, he prepared a formal statement for those who wanted the school to remain as it was. Although I felt otherwise, I recognized the intensity of their emotions, and I know that when the vote went against them, it was a difficult defeat.
>
> If my memory is accurate, it was only a short time later when Dick stood up at Faculty meeting and said, "As you all know, I opposed this action; but the vote has been taken, and now let's make this the best damned coed school in the country."[44]

There were further complications. Many of the strongest supporters of coeducation on the Andover Faculty did not wish to join with Abbot but wanted Andover to select its own girls for admission. They believed that the Abbot girls were inferior students, and they were anxious to maintain Phillips' high standards. Just why this caused so much concern is not clear. In the case of a merger there would be no old Abbot girls in School after three years, and the new merged Academy would be selecting all its own pupils, both boys and girls, the selecting being done, presumably, from a common admissions office.

Some idea of the splintering of opinion among the Faculty can be obtained from the results of a Faculty poll taken in March, 1971. At that time it was found that 15 percent of the 96 voting wanted an all-male School, 41 percent wanted coordination of some course offerings, 5 percent wanted complete academic coordination, and 39 percent wanted a coeducational School. When the Faculty were asked to choose between the second and fourth options, 56 percent wanted coordination of some courses, and 44 percent a coeducational school. Finally, when asked to vote on how to achieve a coeducational school, 63 percent wanted Phillips to take its own girls, while 37 percent wanted to merge with Abbot.[45] A similar poll sent out to the alumni showed the same scattering of opinion, though, since only about 3 percent responded, the figures are not firm. Generally, those before the Class of 1940 opposed coeducation by a two to one margin while those after that class supported it by a four to one margin.[46] The School also conducted a series of ten Alumni Forums without getting a clear message on the subject of coeducation, though there was general agreement that the question should be raised and discussed. That same spring the Trustees made the problem more difficult by resolving that "financial considerations make a merger with Abbot impractical at this time" and suggesting further study of coordination.

The school year 1971–72 was the first when fairly extensive cross-enrollment between the two schools became possible. There had been departmental meetings the previous year, and a common daily schedule had been drawn up. As a result, during that year 193 girls took 302 courses at Phillips, while 327 boys took 376 courses at Abbot. Yet Dean Hyde reported that the program had its difficulties. The lack of a unified administration made it hard to settle issues; differences in pedagogical approach and standards caused trouble, leading to withdrawal of girls from Phillips classes; some feared that Abbot classes were not up to Phillips standards; and the establishment of a fifteen-minute interval to allow time to get to and from Abbot meant the loss of a class period in the morning, with concomitant scheduling difficulties. An example of the kind of difficulty that developed is the case of a very attractive young lady who taught American history at Abbot. Since the two departments had agreed to cross-enrollment in American history, it was possible for Andover boys to take her course. It was soon discovered that this lady's procedures and standards were very different from those of the Andover course. One by one, boys began to transfer to her course, until the Acting Head of the History Department had to forbid further transfers. The problems of coordination strengthened the position of those who wanted Phillips Academy to go it alone. In the fall of 1971 Richard Pieters moved in Faculty meeting that the School should admit its own girls and hire its own women teachers. Since this motion was liable to pass, it put the administration on the spot, for it was equally probable that the Trustees would refuse to accept it and an impasse would result. In the last Faculty meeting John Kemper would attend, shortly after he had announced his resignation, he made a powerful statement against the Pieters motion. He said that a merger with Abbot Academy was the logical solution to the problem of coeducation and reminded the Faculty of the contributions that Abbot could make, particularly in plant, endowment, and expertise in handling girls. He spoke of the long relationship between the two schools and of the damage in public relations that would result if Phillips abandoned Abbot. Finally, he said he thought that the new Headmaster should be given a chance to deal with the problem, since he would have to live with the results. As a result of this appeal, the Faculty voted to table the Pieters motion. By this time things were in a mess. The Faculty were frustrated by indecision and not sure whether there was an option to have Andover go it alone. The students were puzzled over why Andover could not make up its mind, as other schools had done. The Admissions Office reported parental uneasiness at their inability to find out what the School intended to do. Alumni Class Agents were impatient over the delay in reaching a decision and thought it might harm the fund-raising effort. In short, all members of the Andover constituency wanted decisive action and wanted it right away.

Phillips Academy and Abbot Academy remained on dead center as far as coeducation was concerned until the announcement, early in March 1972, of the appointment of Theodore Ryland Sizer as Andover's twelfth Headmaster.[47] Dr. Sizer moved aggressively to deal with this thorny problem, and within six months he, Headmaster Gordon of Abbot, and the two Boards of Trustees had been able to resolve it. The new Headmaster had had a distinguished career in education. A graduate of Pomfret and of Yale, he had served two years in the Army before turning to his chosen career. He taught for a year at the Roxbury Latin School and then earned a Master of Arts in Teaching degree at the Harvard School of Education. There followed a year in Australia, where he taught at a grammar school in Melbourne and studied the educational system of the country. On his return to this country he resumed study at Harvard and earned a Doctorate in History and Education under the colonial historian Bernard Bailyn. With the completion of his graduate work he accepted the position of Director of the Master of Arts in Teaching program at the Harvard School of Education. An extremely effective part of this program was the Harvard-Newton summer project that Dr. Sizer ran, whereby apprentice teachers could gain experience in the classroom under the watchful eyes of master teachers. When Francis Keppel, Dean of the Harvard Graduate School of Education, resigned to go to Washington in 1964, Ted Sizer was named to succeed him at the tender age of thirty-one, and for the next eight years he held that post with distinction. He played an active role in dealing with the student troubles that beset Harvard in the late 1960's and generally opposed the use of force as a solution to the problem of student unrest. In the meantime, he had published several books and a large number of articles, the best known books being *The Age of the Academies* and *Secondary Schools at the Turn of the Century*, both highly relevant to a school like Andover.[48] The former of these works contained many documents on the history of the early academies, including, interestingly enough, the Constitution of Phillips Academy. In addition he and his wife, the former Nancy Faust, a scholar in her own right, had published five lectures on *Moral Education*. With the coming of the Bok administration, Ted Sizer decided that he had been at Harvard long enough and resigned his position as Dean of the Graduate School of Education. Shortly before he left, he and his family spent some months in England, where he studied British education at secondary school and graduate levels. He had proved

82. *Theodore Ryland Sizer, Twelfth Headmaster of Phillips Academy, shortly after he took office.*

his ability as administrator, as head of one of the great graduate schools of education in the country; he was a scholar and author of parts; and his experiences in both Australia and England ensured that he would not have a parochial outlook. In view of all this, it is hardly surprising that the Trustee Search Committee asked him to serve as Andover's Headmaster. Since he had spent most of his career working with prospective teachers, it was appropriate that he work directly with secondary school students themselves, and when the Trustees offered him the position of Headmaster, he accepted with enthusiasm. It is interesting to note, however, that he told the Trustees that he had no interest in heading a single-sex school. Since the Trustees had already determined to address the question of women's education, this was no obstacle. Although his term of office did not begin until 1 July 1972, he spent at least a day a week in Andover during the spring, getting to know the place and lending his support to the establishment of the Cluster System, which was to go into full effect that fall.

Once Ted Sizer had officially taken over the reins of the School, he moved rapidly to deal with the coeducation issue. At his first meeting with the Board of Trustees on 14 July 1972, he presented a paper entitled "Speculations on Andover—I," in which he outlined his thoughts on what a School like Andover should be. Though many interesting points were made, the one that dealt with coeducation is especially pertinent. Proposition I read: "Andover should vigorously recruit an international student body, boys and girls, of social, racial, national, and religious diversity."[49] The Trustees accepted this proposition and instructed the Headmaster to explore with the appropriate officials of Abbot Academy how best to proceed. Less than a week later Ted Sizer and Donald Gordon, Abbot's Headmaster, drew up a paper entitled "Specifications for a Possible Andover–Abbot Agreement." The two must have had many talks together before the Trustees gave the green light; in any event, this document was extremely sensible and sensitive. That Donald Gordon subscribed to these specifications is remarkable because in so subscribing, he was doing himself out of a job. The Headmasters confronted the problem that had bedeviled the two schools ever since talk of coeducation had first begun— namely, what their relationship would be. The first specification read: "P.A. would absorb Abbot, i.e., Abbot as a corporate entity would cease to exist and its assets would be transferred to P.A."[50] The name of the new coeducational school would be Phillips Academy, but an attempt would be made perpetuate the name of Abbot in some fashion. Starting in September 1973, Phillips would absorb all Abbot students, except that those enrolled at Abbot before the merger would have the option of getting an Abbot or an Andover diploma. Abbot would be incorporated into the Andover cluster system, necessitating the formation of at least two new clusters. It was hoped that each cluster could have a girls' dormitory. Phillips would attempt to absorb as many Abbot personnel as possible into

678 : THE MODERN ANDOVER

its operations. The Dean of the new Academy would be a woman. A single Admissions Office would be established by November 1972. In addition, plans to consolidate various services in the two schools would be made to determine what should be kept and what disposed of. Since the combined schools would number well over twelve hundred students, a study of the ideal size of the community would be undertaken, and the result of the study would govern admissions policy in the next few years. Finally, it was agreed that the Trustees of Phillips Academy would be the governing body of the new School, but efforts would be made to add women and/or former Abbot Trustees to the Board as soon as possible. In retrospect these agreements spell out the only possible solution to a very difficult problem, and it is greatly to the credit of Headmasters Sizer and Gordon that the final settlement followed them closely.[51]

The climax came in September. Shortly before the Trustee Meeting on the 16th, Headmaster Sizer distributed a powerful paper in support of co-education in general and, in particular, the plan to incorporate Abbot into Phillips. He pointed out that although the Trustees, Alumni Council, Faculty, and undergraduates had all indicated strong support for coeducation of some kind, the specifics for the accomplishments of that goal remained elusive. He suggested that there were four possible approaches: coordination, Phillips Academy to admit its own girls, merger through the creation of a new school and a new corporation, and incorporation of one of the schools into the other. The Headmaster came out strongly for the fourth choice, pointing out that coordination had not worked well and quoting John Kemper to the effect that coordination only leads to some kind of merger. Although he admitted that Phillips could admit its own girls, he said that the effect on Abbot Academy could well be disastrous and that he did not think the Andover community would want that responsibility. There were many legal and financial difficulties in setting up a new corporation that would combine the two schools in one. Thus the incorporation of Abbot into Phillips was the only workable solution. He was fully aware of the traumatic experience that this might be for Abbot, but he was confident that, particularly with the passage of time, this could be overcome. To soften the blow to Abbot, the Headmaster made three proposals: one, the naming of Carolyn Goodwin, Director of Studies at Abbot, as Dean of Phillips Academy; two, the construction of a new dining hall and student center to be named Abbot Hall; and three, an invitation to three Abbot Trustees, at least two of them women, to sit with the Phillips Academy Board with the same authority as Alumni Trustees, it being understood that the Phillips Board would elect women as Charter Trustees as soon as possible. And he went on to spell out ways of dealing with legal, financial, and social problems that the joining of the two schools would bring. The twenty-two-page document was inclusive, and the case it presented was extremely persuasive.[52]

With the terms of the marriage contract more or less drawn up, it remained to get the bride and groom to agree to them, then to solemnize the pact, and finally to get the bride and groom to the marriage bed. Agreement by the two took some doing. It was obviously difficult for the Abbot Trustees to vote elimination of their school as a separate legal entity, while it was equally difficult for some of the Andover Trustees to accept the idea of having women in their midst. From time immemorial the Andover Board had considered itself an exclusive men's club, and new Trustees were chosen fully as much for their ability to fit in with the already existing Board as for any other qualifications. Ladies in the club were like ladies invading barber shops and pool parlors. Yet these obstacles were eventually overcome. The man who probably did more than anyone else to bring it about was Philip K. Allen, who had the unique distinction of being both Charter Trustee of Phillips Academy and at the same time Chairman of the Board of Abbot Academy. He was convinced that the incorporation of Abbot into Phillips was the only workable solution, and he bent every effort to bring it about. His task was the more difficult because his membership on both boards made him suspect by each. As Donald H. McLean, Jr., President of the Andover Board, pointed out, "There were those on the Andover side who regarded him as a Trojan Horse and . . . there were those on the Abbot side who regarded him as somewhat of a Trojan Horse."[53] In any event, when the Andover Trustees met on 16 September, Phil Allen started the proceedings with a proposal from the bride. This proposal authorized him as President of the Abbot Board, together with Headmaster Donald Gordon, to negotiate with the Trustees of Phillips Academy an agreement based on the Sizer-Gordon Memorandum of the previous July. The Abbot proposal contained four supplementary suggestions: one, that there be drawn up a memorandum of future educational policy for the combined schools; two, that there be a firm commitment to add Abbot representatives to the Andover Board; three, that all members of the Abbot staff be considered on the basis of merit only if cuts in staff had to be made; and, four, that the name of Abbot be perpetuated in the new institution. Having presented Abbot's offer, Mr. Allen left the meeting. After due deliberation the Andover Board passed resolutions introduced by Headmaster Sizer, designed to reassure Abbot of Phillips' good intentions. Miss Carolyn Goodwin was to be appointed Dean of Phillips Academy, starting 1 September 1973; three members of the Abbot Board —at least two of whom were to be women— were invited to sit with the Andover Board with the same rights and responsibilities as Alumni Trustees; and it was the intention of the Andover Board to elect women Charter Trustees at an early date. The Board then adjourned without really biting the bullet; their resolutions were clearly based on the assumption that the two schools would merge, but it was not until a meeting a week later that the terms were agreed to.[54] At that meeting Philip Allen presented a firm commitment from the Abbot Trustees to incorporate Abbot Academy into Phillips Academy. The groom finally accepted the offer on 23 September 1972, when the Trustees passed the following resolution:

> Voted, that this Board welcomes and accepts the proposal of the Board of Trustees of Abbot Academy . . . to transfer to Phillips Academy the educational undertakings and assets of Abbot, and instructs the President and Headmaster to accomplish this incorporation effective 1 September, 1973.[55]

It remained to legalize the union, a process that was achieved in two parts. On 24 February 1973 the two Presidents of the boards, Donald H. McLean, Jr., for Andover and Philip K. Allen for Abbot, together with the two headmasters, Theodore Sizer for Andover and Donald Gordon for Abbot, signed the documents necessary to legalize the incorporation.[56] Later that spring the last step in the laborious legal process of incorporating the two schools was accomplished at a so-called wedding when

83. Signing the Merger Papers, 24 February 1973. Left to right: *Headmaster Sizer; Donald Gordon, Headmaster of Abbot; Philip K. Allen, President of the Board of Trustees of Abbot Academy; and Donald H. McLean, Jr., President of the Board of Trustees of Phillips Academy.*

84. Coeducation comes to Andover

Melville Chapin, acting for the Abbot Trustees, turned over his School's property to Donald H. McLean, Jr., acting for Phillips Academy. On that occasion Mr. Chapin said, "In consideration of the payment of one dollar, all assets of Abbot now become the property of Phillips—entrusting to them our greatest asset, young ladies of inestimable value."[57]

One might wonder how the Trustees of Phillips Academy could vote against merger in November 1971 because of financial considerations, and then support such a move eight months later. The answer lay in the agreement to reduce the size of the combined schools over a three- or four-year period. The first year of merger would produce a school of over twelve hundred, but the Admissions Office was instructed to reduce the size to something under one thousand in the coming years. Since a school of this size would be more manageable financially, the Andover Trustees agreed to accept the plan, and after a great deal of agonizing, the greatest change in the history of Phillips Academy was brought about. Despite the fears of the timid and the conservative, the new School has been a smashing success from the very beginning. Those who took this revolutionary step should derive satisfaction from their share in strengthening the principle that only institutions which adapt to changing circumstances can remain strong.

With the introduction of coeducation into Phillips Academy, this history comes to an end. One is too close to the dynamic and innovative programs of Ted Sizer for anything like objective analysis. Yet wherever one looks on Andover Hill today, he sees activity, experimentation, creativity, and élan. As Phillips Academy enters its third century, who can doubt that it will continue to teach its students—in twentieth century terms, to be sure—"the great end and real business of living."

APPENDIX

THE CONSTITUTION OF

PHILLIPS ACADEMY

A SHORT reflection upon the grand design of the great PARENT OF THE UNIVERSE in the creation of mankind, and the improvements, of which the mind is capable, both in knowledge and virtue as well, as upon the prevalence of ignorance and vice, disorder and wickedness, and upon the direct tendency and certain issue of such a course of things, must occasion, in a thoughtful mind, an earnest solicitude to find the source of these evils and their remedy; and a small acquaintance with the qualities of younger minds,—how susceptible and tenacious they are of impressions, evidences that YOUTH is the important period, on the improvement or neglect of which depend the most important consequences to individuals themselves and the community.

A serious consideration of the premises, and an observation of the growing neglect of YOUTH, have excited in us a painful anxiety for the event, and determined us to make, in the following Conveyance, a humble dedication to our HEAVENLY BENEFACTOR of the ability, wherewith he hath blessed us, to lay the foundation of a public free SCHOOL or ACADEMY for the purpose of instructing Youth, not only in English and Latin Grammar, Writing, Arithmetic, and those Sciences, wherein they are commonly taught; but more especially to learn them the GREAT END AND REAL BUSINESS OF LIVING.

Earnestly wishing that this Institution may grow and flourish; that the advantages of it may be extensive and lasting; that its usefulness may be so manifest, as to lead the way to other establishments on the same principles; and that it may finally prove an eminent means of advancing the Interest of the Great REDEEMER, to His patronage and blessing we humbly commit it.

Know all men by these presents that we, SAMUEL PHILLIPS of Andover in the County of Essex and State of Massachusetts Bay, Esquire, and JOHN PHILLIPS of Exeter in the County of Rockingham and State of New Hampshire, Esquire, for the causes and considerations, and for the uses and purposes, herein after expressed, have granted, and do by these presents grant unto the Hon. William Phillips, Esq. Oliver Wendell and John Lowell Esquires of Boston in the County of Suffolk and State of Massachusetts Bay, the Rev. Josiah Stearns of Epping in the County of Rockingham aforesaid, Elias Smith of Middleton, William Symmes and Jonathan French, Clerks, Messrs. Samuel Phillips, jun. and Eliphalet Pearson, Gentlemen, and Mr. Nehemiah Abbot, Yeoman, all of Andover, aforesaid, and to their heirs, all the Right, Title, and Interest, either of us have in certain parcels of land, hereinafter mentioned, viz.

In three several pieces of land, situate in Andover aforesaid; the first of which contains about twelve acres, the second piece contains about twenty eight acres, the third piece contains about thirty acres, being lately part of the Estate of George Abbot Esq. deceased, and conveyed by Capt. Joshua Holt, Administrator on said Estate, to SAMUEL PHILLIPS Esq. aforesaid, March first one thousand seven hundred and seventy seven;—likewise two other parcels of land in said Andover, situate near the two first mentioned pieces, containing about thirty nine acres, conveyed by Solomon Wardwell to said PHILLIPS January twenty fourth one thousand seven hundred and seventy seven, together with all the buildings on said lands; —likewise two other pieces of wood land, situate in said Andover, containing about thirty two acres, conveyed by Nehemiah Abbot to said PHILLIPS January twelfth one thousand seven hundred and seventy eight; —likewise about two hundred acres of land in the town of Jaffrey in the County of Cheshire and State of New Hampshire, conveyed by John Little to said PHILLIPS September fourth one thousand seven hundred and seventy seven.

And the said SAMUEL PHILLIPS and JOHN PHILLIPS do also farther give, assign, and set over unto the said William Phillips, Oliver Wendell, John Lowell, Josiah Stearns, William Symmes, Elias Smith, Jonathan French, Samuel Phillips jun. Eliphalet Pearson, and Nehemiah Abbot, and to their heirs, the sum of one thousand six hundred and fourteen pounds, to have and to hold the same land and the same sum of money to them and to their heirs, to the USE and upon the TRUST, hereafter mentioned.

The lands shall be let out on proper terms, and the said sum of money put to interest on good security, or both improved in such way, as shall be found to the whole most beneficial; and the whole of the Rents, Profits, Issues, and Interest of said land, and of said sum of money, shall be forever appropriated, laid out, and expended, for the support of a public FREE SCHOOL or ACADEMY in the south parish in the town of Andover aforesaid in manner and form following.

The said SAMUEL PHILLIPS and JOHN PHILLIPS shall, together with the beforenamed William Phillips, Oliver Wendell, John Lowell, Josiah Stearns, William Symmes, Elias Smith, Jonathan French, Samuel Phillips jun. Eliphalet Pearson, and Nehemiah Abbot, be TRUSTEES of said School; and hereafter the Master for the time being shall ever be one of the TRUSTEES;—a major part shall be laymen and respectable freeholders;— also a major part shall not consist of the inhabitants of the town, where the Seminary is situate.

The TRUSTEES shall meet on the last Tuesday of April instant; and ever after, once in every year, on such day, as they shall appoint; also upon emergencies, when called thereto, as hereafter directed; and a major part of the TRUSTEES shall, when regularly convened, be a QUORUM; of which QUORUM a major part shall have power to transact the business of their TRUST, except in cases, hereafter excepted; and their final meeting shall be at the dwelling house on the lands, purchased of Capt. Joshua Holt, where Samuel Phillips jun. now resides, at which shall be chosen the Officers of the TRUST; a name shall be given to this Seminary and its principal Instructor; and such other business, relating to this Institution, transacted, as the TRUSTEES shall think proper.

There shall be chosen annually a President, Clerk, and Treasurer, as Officers of the TRUST, out of their own number, who shall continue in their respective offices, till their places are supplied by a new election; and, upon the decease of either of them, another shall be chosen in his room at the next meeting. The Master shall not be chosen President, and no member shall sustain the office of Clerk and Treasurer at the same time.

The President shall, in all cases, give his voice and vote in common with any other member; and, whenever there shall be an equal division of the members on any question, it shall determine on that side, whereupon the President shall have given his vote; and in his absence, at any meeting of the TRUSTEES, another shall be appointed, who shall be vested with the same power, during such absence;—he shall call special meetings upon the application of any three of the TRUSTEES, or upon the concurrence of any two of the TRUSTEES in sentiment with him on the occasion of such meeting. And upon the decease of the President, a special meeting may be called by any three of the TRUSTEES. All notifications for special meetings shall express the business, to be transacted, if convenient; and be given at least one month previous to such meeting, if not incompatible with the welfare of the Seminary; and, when a special meeting shall be called for the appointment of an Instructor, or to transact other business of material consequence, information shall be given by leaving a written Notification at the house of each TRUSTEE, or in such other way, as that the President, or members notifying, shall have good reason to believe that each member has received the notice.

The Clerk shall record all votes of the TRUSTEES, inserting the names of those present at every meeting. He shall keep a fair record of every

Donation, with the name of each Benefactor; the purpose, to which it is appropriated, if expressed; and of all Expenditures; and a true copy of the whole shall be taken, and kept in the Seminary, to be open for the perusal of all men; and, if he shall be absent at any meeting of the TRUSTEES, another shall be appointed, to serve in his room, during such absence.

The Treasurer shall, previous to his receiving the Interest of the Seminary into his hands, give Bond for the faithful discharge of his office, in such sum, as the TRUSTEES shall direct, with sufficient Sureties, to the TRUSTEES of the Seminary for the time being by name; said Bond to express the USE both in the obligatory part and in the condition. He shall give duplicate Receipts for all monies received, countersigned by one of the TRUSTEES; one to the Donor, the other to be lodged with such member, as the TRUSTEES shall from time to time direct; and the TRUSTEES shall take such other measures, as they shall judge requisite, to make the Treasurer accountable, and effectually to secure the Interest of the Seminary.

The TRUSTEES shall let or rent out the lands in such a manner, as they shall find on the whole most profitable. They may make sale of any kind of Estate, make purchases, or improve the property of the Seminary in any way, which they judge will best serve its Interest.

Upon the death, resignation, or removal of the Master, appointed by the said SAMUEL PHILLIPS and JOHN PHILLIPS, the TRUSTEES shall appoint another in his stead; and ever after from time to time, as there shall happen any vacancy in this office, they shall supply it.

Whereas the success of this Institution much depends, under Providence, on a discreet appointment of the principal Instructor, and the human mind is liable to imperceptible bias; it is therefore required, that, when any candidate for election, as a principal Instructor, is so near a kin to any member of the TRUST, as a nephew or cousin, in determining that election, any member, to whom the candidate is so related, shall not sit.

The TRUSTEES are empowered to appoint such Assistant or Assistants in and for the service of the Seminary, as they shall judge will best promote its usefulness, and as may be duly encouraged.

No person shall be chosen, as a principal Instructor, unless a professor of the CHRISTIAN RELIGION, of exemplary manners, of good natural abilities and literary acquirements, of a good acquaintance with human nature, of a natural aptitude for instruction and government; and, in the appointment of any Instructor, regard shall be had to qualifications only, without preference of kindred or friend, place of birth, education, or residence.

The TRUSTEES shall make a contract with each Master and Assistant, before their entrance upon office, as to Salary; of which there shall be no alteration, but in their favour; which the said TRUSTEES are empowered to make, as to them shall appear reasonable, and as the income of the Seminary will admit.

It shall be their duty, to inquire into the conduct of the Master and Assistant, or Assistants; and, if they or either of them be found justly chargeable with such misconduct, neglect of duty, or incapacity, as the said TRUSTEES shall judge renders them, or either of them unfit to continue in office they shall remove the Master or any Assistant, so chargeable.

The TRUSTEES shall determine the qualifications, requisite to entitle Youth to an admission into this Seminary.

As the welfare of the Seminary will be greatly promoted by its members being conversant with persons of good character only; no Scholar may enjoy the privileges of this Institution, who shall board in any family, which is not licensed by the TRUSTEES

And, in order to preserve this Seminary from the baneful influences of the incorrigibly vicious, the TRUSTEES shall determine, for what reasons a Scholar shall be expelled, and the manner, in which the sentence shall be administered.

The TRUSTEES at their annual meeting shall visit the Seminary, and examine into the proficiency of the Scholars; examine and adjust all accounts, relative to the Seminary; and make any farther Rules and Orders, which they find necessary, and not inconsistent with any Rule, that is or may be established by the FOUNDERS.

They shall, as the Funds will permit, without affecting the support of the Master or any Assistant, have power to erect such buildings, as they may think necessary; and at a convenient season, when of sufficient ability, shall erect a large, decent building, sufficient to accommodate at least fifty Scholars with boarding, beside the Master and his family; unless it shall be the determination of a major part of the TRUSTEES, that the true design of this Institution may be better promoted by the Scholars boarding in private families, and by some other improvement of the Interest of the Seminary. They shall from time to time order such repairs, as they shall judge necessary.

Upon the death, resignation, or incapacity for the service, by reason of age or otherwise, of any of the TRUSTEES, the remaining TRUSTEES shall supply the vacancy by a new election.

In settling the Salary and Perquisites of the Master, and in the consideration of every other question, in which the Master is particularly interested, he shall not sit. And, if any question shall come before the TRUSTEES, where the Town or Parish, where the Seminary is situate, may be a party or particularly interested, and any Minister, belonging to such Town is a TRUSTEE; in the consideration of such question he shall not sit.

At the meetings of the TRUSTEES there shall be made decent, not extravagant entertainment. Economy is to be ever viewed by the TRUSTEES and Instructors, in their respective capacities, as an object, worthy their particular recommendation.

The Master, when appointed, shall receive applications for the admission of Scholars, and determine them agreeably to the Rules, respecting the same.

He shall conform himself to the Regulations, established by the FOUNDERS and TRUSTEES, and have power from time to time to make such other consistent Rules and Orders, as he shall find necessary for the internal management and regulation of the Seminary; which Rules and Orders shall be subject to the examination, amendment, or discontinuance of the TRUSTEES, at their discretion.

It shall be ever considered, as the first and principal duty of the Master, to regulate the tempers, to enlarge the minds, and form the Morals of the Youth, committed to his care.

There shall be taught in this Seminary, the English, Latin, and Greek Languages, Writing, Arithmetic, Music, and the Art of Speaking; also practical Geometry, Logic, and any other of the liberal Arts and Sciences, or Languages, as opportunity and ability may hereafter admit, and as the TRUSTEES shall direct.

The Master is to give special attention to the health of the Scholars, and ever to urge the importance of a habit of Industry. For these purposes it is to be a part of his duty, to encourage the Scholars to perform some manual labor, such as gardening, or the like; so far as it is consistent with cleanliness and the inclination of their parents; and the fruit of their labor shall be applied, at the discretion of the TRUSTEES, for procuring a Library, or in some other way increasing the usefulness of this Seminary.

But, above all, it is expected, that the Master's attention to the disposition of the *Minds* and *Morals* of the Youth, under his charge, will exceed every other care; well considering that, though goodness without knowledge (as it respects others) is weak and feeble; yet knowledge without goodness is dangerous; and that both united form the noblest character, and lay the surest foundation of usefulness to mankind.

It is therefore required, that he most attentively and vigorously guard against the earliest irregularities; that he frequently delineate, in their natural colours, the deformity and odiousness of vice, and the beauty and amiableness of virtue; that he spare no pains, to convince them of their numberless and indispensable obligations to abhor and avoid the former, and to love and practise the latter; of the several great duties, they owe to GOD, their country, their parents, their neighbour, and themselves; that he critically and constantly observe the variety of their natural tempers, and solicitously endeavour to bring them under such discipline, as may tend most effectually to promote their own satisfaction and the happiness of others; that he early inure them to contemplate the several connexions and various scenes, incident to human life; furnishing such general maxims of conduct, as may best enable them to pass through all with ease, reputation, and comfort.

And whereas many of the Students in this Seminary may be devoted to the sacred work of the gospel ministry; that the true and fundamental principles of the Christian Religion may be cultivated, established, and perpetuated in the Christian Church, so far, as this Institution may have influence; it shall be the duty of the Master, as the age and capacities of the Scholars will admit, not only to instruct and establish them in the truth of Christianity; but also early and diligently to inculcate upon them the great and important scripture doctrines of the existence of One true GOD, the FATHER, SON, and HOLY GHOST; of the fall of man, the depravity of human nature; the necessity of an atonement, and of our being renewed in the spirit of our minds; the doctrines of repentance toward God and of faith toward our Lord Jesus Christ; of sanctification by the Holy Spirit, and of justification by the free grace of God, through the redemption, that is in Jesus Christ, (in opposition to the erroneous and dangerous doctrines of justification by our own merit, or a dependence on self righteousness), together with the other important doctrines and duties of our HOLY CHRISTIAN RELIGION.

And, whereas the most wholesome precepts, without frequent repetition, may prove ineffectual; it is farther required of the Master, that he not only urge and reurge; but continue from day to day, to impress these instructions.

And let him ever remember that the design of this Institution can never be answered, without his persevering, incessant attention to this duty.

Protestants only shall ever be concerned in the TRUST or Instruction of this Seminary.

The election of all Officers shall be by *ballot* only.

This Seminary shall be ever equally open to Youth, of requisite qualifications, from every quarter; provided, that none be admitted, till in common parlence they can read English well, excepting such particular numbers, as the TRUSTEES may hereafter license.

And, in order to prevent the smallest perversion of the true intent of this Foundation, it is again declared, that the *first* and *principal* object of this Institution is the promotion of true PIETY and VIRTUE; the *second*, instruction in the English, Latin, and Greek Languages, together with Writing, Arithmetic, Music, and the Art of Speaking; the *third*, practical Geometry, Logic, and Geography; and the *fourth*, such other of the liberal Arts and Sciences or Languages, as opportunity and ability may hereafter admit, and as the TRUSTEES shall direct. And these Regulations shall be read by the President, at the annual meetings of the TRUSTEES.

Whereas, in the course of human events, the period may arrive, when the prosperity of this Institution may be promoted by removing it from the place, where it is founded; if it shall hereafter be judged, upon mature and impartial consideration of all circumstances, by two thirds of the TRUSTEES, that for good and substantial reasons, which at this time do not exist, the true design, herein expressed, will be better served, by removing the Seminary to some other place; it shall be in their power, to remove it accordingly; provided that, if this event shall ever take place, there shall be fairly and truly entered on the Clerk's records all the reasons, whereon the determination was grounded; and the same shall be subscribed by the members, who effected the determination; but unless the good of mankind shall manifestly require it, this Seminary shall never be removed from the South Parish in the town of Andover.

And we hereby reserve to ourselves, during any part of our natural lives, the full right, jointly to make any special Rules for the perpetual Government of this Institution; which shall be equally binding on those, whom they may concern, with any clause in these Regulations; provided, no such Rule shall be subversive of the TRUE DESIGN, herein expressed. We also reserve to ourselves a right, jointly to appoint one person, to succeed in the TRUST after our decease or resignation; to whom shall be transferred the same right of appointment, and to his Successors in the said TRUST forever.

In witness whereof we, the Subscribers, have hereunto set our hands and seals this twenty first day of April in the year of our LORD, one thousand seven hundred and seventy eight.

Signed, sealed, and delivered	SAMUEL PHILLIPS (S.)
in presence of	
JOHN ABBOT,	
HANNAH HOLT.	JOHN PHILLIPS (S.)

Essex ss.

The foregoing Deed of Samuel Phillips Esq., and John Phillips Esq., founding and instituting the Academy at Andover and this Deed of release of Samuel Phillips Esq., son of Samuel first named, were received in the Registry of Deeds July 13, 1793, and are recorded Book 156, leaves 192, 193, 194, and 195 and examined by

JOHN PICKERING, *Registrar*

BIBLIOGRAPHICAL NOTE

THE basic sources for this book are materials in the Phillips Academy Archives and in the Andover Collection at the Oliver Wendell Holmes Library at Phillips Academy. In the early days of the School, records were kept in the offices of the Principal and Treasurer, but no attempt was made to organize them. Early in the twentieth century Sarah Frost, the Academy Librarian and a sister-in-law of Treasurer James Sawyer, began to develop a collection of printed materials on the School's past which came to be called the Andover Collection. It contained copies of the School's publications: *The Phillipian*, the newspaper; *The Pot Pourri*, the yearbook; *The Phillips Bulletin*, later *The Andover Bulletin*, the alumni magazine; catalogues; rule books; and other academy publications. In addition a sizable number of alumni memorabilia were added to the collection—scrapbooks, diaries, and the like. Finally, an attempt was made to collect books that had relevance to the past of the School and of the Andover Theological Seminary, as well as copies of books by writers who were Andover graduates. Though the Andover Collection is for the most part limited to printed material, some manuscripts were obtained. The collection has been completely catalogued, and cards are included in the Library's main card catalogue file. After the retirement of Miss Frost, Ruth Brown continued to work on the collection, with the result that today it contains about four thousand items. In addition, there is the so-called "Andover Vertical File," with some 360 folders of clippings on the history of the School, some, but not all, of which have been catalogued.

In 1955 Headmaster John M. Kemper asked the writer to set up an archive to preserve the manuscript records. We were fortunate in obtaining the advice of Clifford K. Shipton, Harvard Archivist for many years, who explained the cataloguing system for archival material and made many other useful suggestions. Juliet R. Kellogg, who had had wide experience in this field, was named Associate Archivist and has since done 99 percent of the work in the Archives. When it was established, School records were scattered all over the Academy. The first task was to assemble them, organize them logically in boxes, and shelve them in the stacks on the fourth floor of the Library. Once this was done, arrangements were made for the orderly transfer each year of the manuscript productions of the various departments of the School. Today the archival collection is substantial, filling almost one floor in the Library stacks.

Basic to any study of Phillips Academy are the Trustee Records, fortunately complete from the first meeting in 1778 to the present. The records for the last thirty years are kept in the Headmaster's Office and are not open to the public. The Trustee Records are particularly important for the first hundred years of the School history, when few other records were kept and when the Trustees concerned themselves with many more details in the running of the School than is the case today. Until Cecil Bancroft became Principal in 1873, there are, unfortunately, no files of the Principals' correspondence, though there is a file of Samuel H. Taylor's reports to the Trustees. Starting with Dr. Bancroft, the Principals' and later the Headmasters' correspondence is very rich. There are 15 boxes of Bancroft correspondence; 47 boxes or file drawers of Alfred Stearns's correspondence, and an additional 12 letterbooks; 22 boxes of Claude Fuess's official correspondence, with an additional 47 boxes of his private papers; 116 boxes of Headmaster John Kemper's official correspondence; and 30 boxes, so far, of the correspondence of the present Headmaster, Theodore R. Sizer. In addition to this basic material there are 372 boxes of records of the Alumni Fund and Alumni activities; 161 boxes of records from the Dean of Students' office; 127 boxes of records of the Admissions and Scholarship office; 82 boxes of correspondence from the Treasurer's office, and 126 boxes of receipted bills, as well as 59 old leather account books covering the period 1795–1929; 16 boxes on student activities; 32 on the Faculty; 79 on the various academic departments; 34 on School Year Abroad; 26 from the office of the Dean of the Faculty; 22 from the office of James R. Adriance, Director of Admissions and later Assistant to the Headmaster; and a host of smaller collections. Far and away the most valuable sources for an understanding of the School are the Trustee Records and the correspondence of the various Headmasters; these are the materials used most extensively in the writing of this book. The Minutes of Faculty Meetings from the 1880's on are kept in the office of the Dean of the Academy (formerly the Dean of Students) and are generally disappointing. Until very recently they record little more than the bare bones of Faculty decisions, seldom including reasons for Faculty action or any accounts of Faculty debates. Taken as a whole, the material in the Phillips Academy Archives represents an invaluable asset for anyone wishing to learn about the past of the School.

Though the Archives and the Andover Collection are technically distinct and under different oversight, I have not attempted to distinguish between them in footnotes. As a general rule, as noted above, the reader can expect a printed document to be in the Andover Collection, a manuscript document to be in the Archives.

Two books, each covering a substantial part of the School's two hundred years, are extremely useful: Claude M. Fuess, *An Old New England School: A History of Phillips Academy, Andover* (Boston, 1917), covers the story from the School's founding until 1917; and *Terms of Trusts and Other Records* (Andover, 1932) contains the record of all major gifts to the School from its founding through 1932. One serious drawback in Dr. Fuess's book is the complete absence of any kind of bibliographical information.

Part I. The Early Years

The definitive study of George Phillips is Henry Wilder Foote, "George Phillips, First Minister of Watertown," *Proceedings of the Massachusetts Historical Society*, 63 (1930), 193–227. For the first Samuel Phillips see John Langdon Sibley, *Biographical Sketches of Graduates of Harvard University* (Cambridge, 1873) I, 221–228. For the third and fourth Samuels see Clifford K. Shipton, *Sibley's Harvard Graduates*, V, 432–440 and IX, 431–436. For John Phillips of Exeter, see Shipton, IX, 560–570.

The fullest work on Samuel Phillips, Jr., is John L. Taylor, *A Memoir of His Honor Samuel Phillips, LL.D.* (Boston, 1856). This work is uncritical but contains a substantial number of Phillips family letters. For changes in the town of Andover during Samuel Phillips, Jr.'s youth, see Philip J. Greven, Jr., *Four Generations: Population, Land, and Family in Colonial Andover, Massachusetts* (Ithaca, 1970). For Harvard College when Sam went there, see Samuel Eliot Morison, *Three Centuries of Harvard, 1636–1936* (Cambridge, 1936), 76–163, and Sheldon S. Cohen, "Harvard College on the Eve of the American Revolution," a paper soon to be published by the Colonial Society of Massachusetts. See also the same author's "The Turkish Tyranny," *New England Quarterly*, 47 (1974), 564–583, for an account of the disorders of 1768. There are a few letters between Sam and his family while he was at Dummer Academy and a manuscript diary and additional family letters while he was at Harvard in the Phillips Academy Archives. There is also a fairly substantial correspondence between Sam and Phoebe Foxcroft, later to become his wife, in the School Archives. There are some materials on Sam's gunpowder making in the Pearson Papers in the same Archives. See also Charles H. Lyon, "Eliphalet Pearson: Puritan Educator," an unpublished Senior Honors Thesis written in 1963 and now in the Harvard University Archives.

For secondary education in colonial Massachusetts I have dependend primarily on Robert Middlekauff, *Ancients and Axioms: Secondary Education in Eighteenth-Century New England* (New Haven, 1963); the appropriate chapters in Lawrence A. Cremin, *American Education: The Colonial Ex-*

perience, 1607–1783 (New York, 1970); the appropriate chapters in Samuel Eliot Morison's *The Puritan Pronaos: Studies in the Intellectual Life of New England in the Seventeenth Century* (New York, 1936); and James Axtell, *The School upon a Hill: Education and Society in Colonial New England* (New Haven, 1974).

Samuel Phillips, Jr's earliest thoughts on founding a school are contained in two undated documents addressed simply "Dear Friend" and "Hon'd Sir" in the Phillips Academy Archives. There are also several early drafts of the School's Constitution. That document, in addition to being printed as an Appendix to this volume, has been reprinted in Theodore R. Sizer, *The Age of the Academies* (New York, 1964), 77–89. There is a scholarly account of the founding of the School in William E. Park, "The Earlier Annals of Phillips Academy," a speech delivered on the occasion of the School's Centennial in 1878. It is printed in a volume on the Centennial (pp. 62–72) in the School's Archives. There is also some interesting correspondence between Sam and his Uncle John on the founding of the School.

Two boxes of Pearson Papers in the Archives contain among other items a manuscript diary for 1777 and a biographical sketch of Pearson by his son Henry. There is also some pertinent Pearson material in the Park Family Papers and the Edwards A. Park Papers at the Yale University Library. The best recollections of Pearson's school, though written many years later, are those of Josiah Quincy in Edmund Quincy, *Life of Josiah Quincy* (Boston, 1868), 24–28. The Trustee Records for this period, when the Trustees were interesting themselves in almost all aspects of the School, are also valuable.

There is almost no material on either Ebenezer Pemberton or Mark Newman in the Archives. For Pemberton, see C. K. Shipton, *Sibley's Harvard Graduates*, XVI, 197–200; for Newman see Charles Mooar, *Memorial of Deacon Mark Newman* (Andover, 1859). A very useful work on the first 52 years of the School is C. C. Carpenter, *Biographical Catalogue of the Trustees, Teachers, and Students of Phillips Academy, 1778–1830* (Andover, Andover Press, 1903). There is also useful material in Harriet W. Marr, *The Old New England Academies* (New York, Comet Press, 1959). The records of the Select Committee appointed to ride herd on Mark Newman are important for the early 1800's, while a run of letters from Henry Pearson to his father Eliphalet gives a good picture of undergraduate life during that same period.

Part II. Interlude

For the story of the Andover Theological Seminary I have depended primarily on the following works: Leonard Woods, *History of the Andover Theological Seminary* (Boston, 1885); Henry K. Rowe, *History of the Andover Theological Seminary* (Newton, 1933); three articles by J.

Earl Thompson, Jr., Professor of Church History at the Andover Newton Theological Seminary (see the notes for specific citations); Sidney E. Ahlstrom, *A Religious History of the American People* (New Haven, Yale University Press, 1972); Sarah Stuart Robbins, *Old Andover Days*, (Boston, The Pilgrim Press, 1908); and Daniel D. Williams, *The Andover Liberals* (New York, King's Crown Press, 1941).

Almost all the material for the Farrar and Taylor chapters is based on documents in the Phillips Academy Archives, with the Trustee Records and Principal Taylor's Reports to the Trustees being particularly useful. In 1814 the School started printing annual catalogues, and these, too, have been valuable. A collection of letters from James A. Burrill to his father gives a good picture of the School during 1819–20. For undergraduate life in the 1850's, see Henry M. Saville, *A Schoolboy's Letters of Seventy-Seven Years Ago* (Boston, R. G. Badger, 1930). The only significant printed work on this period is M. E. and H. G. Brown, *The Story of John Adams, a New England Schoolmaster* (New York, Scribner's, 1900). For an interesting account of some of the experiments in secondary education during this period, especially Round Hill outside Northampton, Massachusetts, see James McLachlan, *American Boarding Schools: A Historical Study* (New York, Scribner's, 1970). As usual, Fuess's *An Old New England School* is valuable. A folder of student reminiscences from the Taylor period that he solicited for his book is in the Phillips Academy Archives. There are also a number of articles and documents printed in the *Phillips Bulletin* that deal with this period.

Part III. The Modern Andover

The most important single source for the three Bancroft chapters is his correspondence (15 boxes). Also important are his annual reports to the Trustees, some of which are very moving documents. Of lesser importance are William B. Graves's reports to the Trustees on the English Department. The establishment of *The Phillipian* in 1878 adds a whole new dimension to the material on the history of the School and continues to be invaluable down to the present. The Minutes of Faculty Meetings in the 1880's and 1890's are often enlightening. The basic source for the School's Centennial in 1878 is a single volume that I have entitled *Centennial History*. The School planned to publish this work but got only as far as page proof. To my knowledge only the single copy in the Phillips Academy Archives is in existence. There is also a useful box of material on the Centennial in the Archives containing many newspaper accounts of the celebration, among other things. For a delightful account of undergraduate life during Bancroft's last years as Principal, see Lee J. Perrin, *My Three Years at Andover* (Boston, Mayhew Publishing Co., 1908).

Again, the basic sources for the three Stearns chapters are the papers of Alfred E. Stearns himself. These include not only his official correspondence but a series of letters to his sister Mabel while he was an Andover undergraduate, a similar series to his mother Mary after he first became Principal, and some twenty-odd short chapters recounting some of his experiences as Principal, which were apparently intended for eventual publication but never got that far. These last three collections were graciously turned over to the School by his daughter Marjorie. For his earliest years, see *An Amherst Boyhood* (Amherst, Amherst College, 1946). A statement of Al Stearns's basic beliefs about American adolescents is in his *Challenge of Youth* (Boston, W. A. Wilde, 1923). Just as *The Phillipian*, starting from the Bancroft period, added a new dimension to the history of the School, so the *Phillips Bulletin*, founded in 1907 and edited for the Stearns period by Claude M. Fuess, provides not only a compact record of events at the School but also a number of articles and documents on the School's past. Dr. Fuess's autobiography, *Independent Schoolmaster* (Boston,1952), picks up at about the time his *An Old New England School* leaves off and is a highly readable account of his years at Andover, especially from 1920 to 1948. In 1962 Dr. Fuess was interviewed by Frank W. Rounds, Jr., '34, in connection with a Columbia University Oral History Research Project. The tapes from this interview have been transcribed and the result is an unusually frank account of, primarily, the Fuess administration. Yet there is some material on the Stearns period as well. This interview was conducted just before Dr. Fuess died, when he was an old man, and his recollections of events that happened twenty or thirty years earlier are not, I believe, always trustworthy. As noted in the Preface, an important source on the Stearns, Fuess, and Kemper administrations is the series of letters written to me by some one hundred alumni, giving their reminiscences of their Andover experiences. Covering the same three administrations is *In My Time*, edited by Claude M. Fuess (Andover, 1959), a delightful collection of reminiscences by Andover graduates. Since it was already in print and thus available to the public, I have used these reminiscences sparingly, favoring instead hitherto unpublished material.

With the decentralization of administrative authority, starting under Claude Fuess and continuing under John Kemper, the files of Headmaster's correspondence become less important for the major theme of this volume. Much of what had been in the province of the Headmaster in earlier years was now transferred to the Office of the Dean of Students, the Admissions Office, or the Alumni Office. Thus the Headmaster's correspondence during roughly the last forty years covered by this history is concerned primarily with such matters as Faculty salaries and problems, financial matters, some alumni affairs, and relations with other schools and colleges. Much more important for the story of the Fuess administration is his own autobiography, *Independent Schoolmaster*, and the Oral History he dictated for the Columbia project. For a short sketch of his career, see my own memoir of him in the *Proceedings of the Massachusetts Historical*

Society, 76 (1964), 137–153. Two interesting evaluations of Andover during the Fuess regime are "Andover: A Study in Independence," *Fortune* (May 1944), 167–168, 226–236, and Henry F. and Katherine Pringle, "America's Oldest Private School," *Saturday Evening Post* (27 September 1947), 32, 100–107. The relevant alumni letters for the Fuess administration are, again, important sources. The writer joined the Phillips Academy Faculty in the fall of 1936, early in the Fuess administration. From then to the end of the story, except for three years in the Navy and two sabbatical leaves, he was always an observer of, and sometimes a participant in, what was happening at Andover. For the last five chapters of this book his personal recollections have been used extensively.

For the chapter on the Secret Societies the major sources have been the records of each organization in the Archives and research papers on individual Societies written, for the most part, by students in my seminar in the History of Phillips Academy. Outstanding among these studies is the one on A.G.C. written by my colleague H. Schuyler Royce. Most of the reports, statements, letters, and other documents produced during the various attempts to abolish the Societies are available in a single box of records in the Archives.

I found it difficult to deal with the very recent material covered in the last three chapters, primarily on the Kemper administration and particularly the period 1963–1973. Because of this, reliance was placed for the most part on published articles in the *Phillips Bulletin*, later the *Andover Bulletin*, the *Phillipian*, and the *Pot Pourri*. For John Kemper's early life the transcript of his interview with Frank W. Rounds, Jr., '34, as part of the Columbia Oral History Project, was invaluable. Almost all of John Kemper's correspondence deals with specific, practical, administrative problems; when he wanted to say something important about the School, he almost invariably put it in the form of a report or an article. These reports have therefore been particularly useful. On the subject of coeducation Dean Simeon Hyde, Jr.'s admirable summary of all the various steps taken in the direction of coeducation, entitled "The Case for Coeducation," has been almost the only solid source for the period before the arrival of Dr. Sizer. Dr. Sizer's files on the final resolution of the coeducation problem contain many important documents that illuminate that momentous decision. As with previous administrations, alumni letters, selections from *In My Time*, and recollections of the author have helped to flesh out the story.

NOTES

Introduction

1. For descriptions of Andover Hill in 1778, see John L. Taylor, *A Memoir of His Honor Samuel Phillips, LL.D.* (Boston, Congregation Board of Publication, 1856), 213, 230; Claude M. Fuess, *An Old New England School* (Boston, Houghton Mifflin, 1917), 62; and Sarah Nelson Carter, "The Old Mansion House," in *The Andover Magazine* (n.p.,n.d.), 4.
2. The original Constitution of Phillips Academy is in the Academy Archives. The School has published several editions in pamphlet form; the most convenient is Theodore R. Sizer, *The Age of the Academies* (New York, Teachers College, Columbia University, 1964), 77–89. The full text of the Constitution is printed in the Appendix, above, 683–690.
3. John C. Fitzpatrick, ed., *The Writings of George Washington* (Washington, D.C., Government Printing Office, 1934), XI, 284–293.
4. Pittsfield Memorial, quoted in Oscar and Mary F. Handlin, *Commonwealth: Massachusetts, 1774–1861* (New York, New York University Press, 1947), 2.
5. For a convenient collection of the important documents on Bay State constitution-making, see Robert J. Taylor, *Massachusetts, Colony to Commonwealth* (Chapel Hill, University of North Carolina Press, 1961).
6. The standard histories of Andover are Abiel Abbot, *History of Andover from Its Settlement until 1829* (Andover, Flagg and Gould, 1829); Sarah L. Bailey, *Historical Sketches of Andover* (Boston, Houghton Mifflin, 1880); and Claude M. Fuess, *Andover: Symbol of New England* (Andover, Andover and North Andover Historical Societies, 1959). Miss Bailey's work has recently been reprinted by the Andover and North Andover Historical Societies.
7. This letter is in the Park Family Papers, Sterling Memorial Library, Yale University.
8. The most complete account of Andover in the Revolution is in Bailey, *Historical Sketches,* 286–409.
9. For a more extended account of Samuel Phillips' powder-making, see 31–34.
10. Quoted in Abbot, *History of Andover,* 61.

1. The Phillips Family

1. Horace E. Scudder, "A Group of Classical Schools," *Harper's New Monthly Magazine,* 55 (September, 1877), 563.

2. In a manuscript account of his forebears, Samuel Phillips, Jr., had this to say about some of them: "But alas! Their 2 eldest Sons did not conduct with that Care & Caution which their Father had done, & it proved accordingly. We hope better things concerning the youngest Son William, whom we pray God to direct and bless."

3. The definitive study of George Phillips is Henry Wilder Foote, "George Phillips, First Minister of Watertown," *Proceedings of the Massachusetts Historical Society*, 63 (1930), 193–227. Unless otherwise noted, all the material on George Phillips has been taken from this work.

4. Quoted in Taylor, *Memoir*, 334.

5. The material on the first Samuel is taken from John Langdon Sibley, *Biographical Sketches of Graduates of Harvard University* (Cambridge, 1873), I, 221–228.

6. At Samuel's death his son-in-law, Edward Payson, wrote a long elegiac poem that is printed in Thomas Gage, *The History of Rowley . . .* (Boston, 1840), 79–84.

7. For the goldsmith, see Albert M. Phillips, *Phillips Genealogies* (Auburn, Mass., 1885), 13–14, and the manuscript account of his forebears by Samuel Phillips, Jr. Among the Phillips Papers is the following statement, written in a notebook: "Samuel Phillips Senior do freely for Ever give to my son Samuel Phillips junior a Seal ring; 3 pair (or 1 sett) of shirt buttons and a shirt buckel, all of Gold and weighing 11 penny weight. Witness my Hand Sam: Phillips. This 23d of Sept: 1709."

8. Unless otherwise noted, the material on Parson Phillips has been taken from Clifford K. Shipton, *Sibley's Harvard Graduates, V*, 432–440.

9. There are several documents among the Phillips Papers that deal with the Parson's salary problems. These include tabulations of arrears of salary, parish committee reports on the subject, and a letter from the Parson to his congregation dated 8 June 1762, beginning: "Beloved Brethren, With respect to the Business which, I perceive, you are now met together upon, I shall say, The Parish can witness for me, that in years past, I sent in one Memorial after another, frequently entreating that Justice might be done me with regard to my Salary." This letter and some of the other documents in the Phillips Papers on the subject of the Parson's salary have been printed in *Historical Manual of the South Church in Andover, Mass.* (Andover, 1859), 41–45.

10. This quotation is from a long letter among the Phillips Papers, dated 27 September 1738, written by the Parson to his son Samuel and daughter-in-law Elizabeth. In it the Parson also urges the newlyweds to be thankful for their blessings, to examine themselves regularly, to make family prayers a part of their daily life, to behave properly toward their fellow men, to contemplate mortality, and to use their time well and practice thrift. The passage quoted in the text has been printed in Bailey, *Historical Sketches*, 154.

11. For this story see Fuess, *Old New England School*, 10.

12. *Historical Manual of the South Church*, 68.

13. Bailey, *Historical Sketches*, 446.

14. Ibid., 444–445.

15. In a manuscript book entitled *Genealogy of the Phillips Family*, prepared in 1856 by William Gray Brooks, there can be found (139–142) annotations that the Parson wrote in his almanacs for the years 1739–46 recording family and parish matters, natural phenomena like earthquakes, and political events like the siege of Louisburg. The original is in the possession of C. Lloyd Thomas, present owner of the old Phillips mansion in North Andover, who

has generously allowed me to make a copy for the Phillips Academy Archives.

16. Unless otherwise noted, the material on Squire Phillips has been taken from *Sibley's Harvard Graduates*, IX, 431–436.

17. William E. Park, "The Earlier Annals of Phillips Academy," an address delivered at the Centennial of the School in 1878. Apparently the School planned to print the record of the Centennial: it reached page proof only. There exists a single copy of the proof in the Phillips Academy Archives. This statement is on page 57.

18. Park, "Earlier Annals," 56.

19. The complaint, with notations on further court proceedings, dated May–June 1758, is in the Phillips Papers.

20. For an account of this episode see William G. Brooks, *Proceedings of the Massachusetts Historical Society*, 9 (1866–1867), 252–254. The original of the letter from which Brooks quotes, dated 29 August 1769, is in the Phillips Papers.

21. Squire Phillips to Sam Phillips, Andover, 7 July 1768, Phillips Papers.

22. Ibid., 5 November 1769.

23. Ibid., 20 November 1769.

24. This letter in the Phillips Papers is addressed to "Mr. Samuel Phillips in Cambridge" and is signed by the Squire.

25. Squire Phillips to Sam Phillips, Andover, 20 November 1769.

26. Unless otherwise noted, the material on John Phillips is taken from *Sibley's Harvard Graduates*, IX, 560–570.

27. Myron R. Williams, *The Story of Phillips Exeter* (Exeter, N.H., Phillips Exeter Academy, 1957), 9.

2. Samuel Phillips, Jr.

1. Bernard Bailyn, *Education in the Forming of American Society* (Chapel Hill, University of North Carolina Press, 1960), 14. Bailyn believes that educational historians in the early years of this century sought to find in the colonial period the roots of nineteenth-century educational institutions and thus concentrated too much on colonial formal education, failing to grasp the significance of agencies like the family and the church, which probably played a far more important part in the education of children than did schools and colleges themselves. For these writers, as Bailyn put it, "the past was simply the present writ small" (Ibid., 9).

2. For a penetrating study of these changes, see Philip J. Greven, Jr., *Four Generations: Population, Land, and Family in Colonial Andover, Massachusetts* (Ithaca, Cornell University Press, 1970).

3. For the other children see Albert M. Phillips, *Phillips Genealogies*, 18. Sam's sister Hannah lived until he was twelve years old, but she was ten years older than he.

4. For the early town schools in Andover, see Bailey, *Historical Sketches*, 517–522. Edward Wigglesworth, who taught in Andover in the early 1760's, had this to say about his position: "I am staffed way up here among a Parcel of stupid Monsters (except a few) that are as ignorant as the Caffaries of Madagascar. But then I have a plenty of harmless Country Lasses, fat as Butter and make a body sweat all Night as tho they were hard at work." See *Sibley's Harvard Graduates*, XII, 509.

5. Taylor, *Memoir*, 14–15.
6. For the Barnards, see Bailey, *Historical Sketches*, 426–439.
7. Taylor, *Memoir*, 16.
8. Elizabeth Phillips to Sam Phillips, Andover, 4 May 1766, Phillips Papers.
9. Ibid., 13 June and 29 July (no year given).
10. Ibid., undated but addressed to Sam at Cambridge.
11. Ibid., Andover, 4 May 1766.
12. Ibid., 25 March 1765 (copy).
13. For an admirable discussion of catechizing colonial children, see James Axtell, *The School upon a Hill: Education and Society in Colonial New England* (New Haven, Yale University Press, 1974), 5–50.
14. On Moody see *Sibley's Harvard Graduates*, XII, 48–54, and John W. Ragle, *Governor Dummer Academy History* (South Byfield, Massachusetts, Governor Dummer Academy, 1963), 13–27.
15. One of Master Moody's favorite injunctions to his boys was "Credo quod Possis, et potes." (Sibley, 51).
16. Lawrence A. Cremin, *American Education: The Colonial Experience, 1607–1783* (New York, Harper and Row, 1970), 509, says of Moody: "No provincial schoolmaster was more respected during the eighteenth century, and none made a greater impact on the later life of the Republic."
17. Undated fragment of a letter from Sam Phillips to his father, Phillips Papers.
18. Squire Phillips to Sam Phillips, Andover, 5 December 1767, Phillips Papers.
19. Sam Phillips to Elizabeth Phillips, Newbury Falls, 21 March 1765, and Byfield, 5 April 1765, Phillips Papers.
20. Ibid., Byfield, 5 April 1765.
21. Ibid., 29 June 1765.
22. Quoted in Taylor, *Memoir*, 18. The original is no longer in the Phillips Papers.
23. Sam Phillips to "Honoured Parents," Newbury, 15 June 1767, Phillips Papers.
24. The material in the last two paragraphs has been taken from Samuel E. Morison, *Three Centuries of Harvard, 1636–1936* (Cambridge, Harvard University Press, 1936), 76–163, and Sheldon S. Cohen, "Harvard College on the Eve of the American Revolution," a paper soon to be published by the Colonial Society of Massachusetts.
25. 2 July 1768.
26. 10 July 1768.
27. 10 December 1768.
28. The charges against Wigglesworth were that he had been engaged in business for ten years after graduation from college, had then taught school in Andover, had never been ordained, had been appointed a tutor at Harvard through the intercession of his father, who was his predecessor as Professor of Divinity, and then had succeeded to the professorship on the death of his father, almost as if it were an inheritance. The Phillipses must have known Wigglesworth during his tour of duty at Andover and may well have thought it strange that a small-town school teacher should be the Divinity Professor at Harvard. See *Sibley's Harvard Graduates*, XII, 507–517.
29. Sam Phillips to "Honoured Parents," Cambridge, 10 March 1768, Phillips Papers. Stephen Peabody mentions the Wigglesworth trouble in his diary entry for 2 March 1768. This diary is at the Massachusetts Historical Society.
30. For an extended account of the disorders of 1768, see Sheldon S. Cohen, "The Turkish Tyranny," *New England Quarterly*, 47 (1974), 564–583.
31. See the testimony of Sam Phillips and David Parsons, Depositions 37 and 3, in a folder entitled "Disorders of 1768," Harvard University Archives.
32. Squire Phillips to Sam Phillips, Andover, 17 March 1768. The Squire urged

that "Obedience and Submission is your Indispensable Duty" and hoped his son would "Shudder at the Thought of Rebellions."

33. 8 October 1768.
34. Cohen, "Harvard College on the Eve of the Revolution."
35. Park, "Earlier Annals," 58–59, says "The spirit of Liberty is now brought to Phillips' door. His journal contains less of religious experience . . . but it sparkles with observations upon debates and revolutionary proceedings." He speaks of Sam as writing of the political events of the day "with suppressed glee."
36. 1 October 1768.
37. 8 October 1768.
38. 26 March 1769.
39. 10 March 1770.
40. To be sure, during his undergraduate days Sam wrote a theme on liberty in which he said, "we cannot be happy without we are free. . . . Unborn generations will either bless us for our activity and magnanimity, or curse us for our sloth and pusillanimity . . ." and wrote of "the cruel usurpation of those rights and privileges, for the defence of which whole kingdoms are ready to sacrifice their lives and fortunes." Taylor, *Memoir*, 45–46. I believe that Sam's journal entries reflect his attitude more accurately than this set piece.
41. Journal Entry for 10 September 1768.
42. Ibid., 3 December 1768.
43. Sam Phillips to "Ever Honoured Parents," Cambridge, 1 December 1767, Phillips Papers. For William Brattle, see *Sibley's Harvard Graduates*, VII, 10–23.
44. Harvard Faculty Records, III, 55, 88, 116, 142, 187, Harvard University Archives.
45. Taylor, *Memoir*, 27.
46. Morison, *Three Centuries*, 138–141.
47. See Taylor, *Memoir*, 26, for two generally laudatory assessments of Sam's position as an undergraduate at Harvard. One is a quotation from Eliot's *Bigraphical Dictionary*, the other from the Reverend David Tappan's funeral sermon preached at the time of Sam's death.
48. Sam Phillips to Squire Phillips, Cambridge, 27 May 1771, quoted in Taylor, *Memoir*, 28–29. The original of this letter is no longer in the Phillips Papers.
49. For Francis Foxcroft, see *Sibley's Harvard Graduates*, V, 636–638.
50. Apparently Foxcrofts did visit in Andover. See Phoebe Foxcroft to Elizabeth Phillips, Cambridge, 10 May 1771, thanking her for a visit.
51. Taylor, *Memoir*, 31.
52. Phoebe Foxcroft to Mehitabel Foxcroft, undated, Phillips Papers.
53. Ibid., Boston, 28 February 1767.
54. Ibid., 7 November 1768.
55. Ibid., 28 February 1769.
56. Undated letter in the Phillips Papers.
57. Taylor, *Memoir*, 32–33.
58. Undated manuscript in the Phillips Papers.
59. Phoebe Phillips to Mehitabel Foxcroft, 28 July 1773.
60. Ibid., 23 February 1774.
61. Bailey, *Historical Sketches*, 306.
62. Phoebe Phillips to Samuel Phillips, undated, Phillips Papers.
63. Ibid.
64. Samuel Phillips to Phoebe Phillips, undated, Phillips Papers.

65. Taylor, *Memoir*, 105. There are a few documents in the Phillips Papers dealing with Sam's business activities with Samuel Abbot and with his Uncle William. For example, in July 1772 Sam addressed a business associate, asking him "to deliver the Bearer the Lemons my Father left at your Store, observing the Number of loose ones."

66. The material on Sam's service in the Provincial Congress is taken from Taylor, *Memoir*, 60-65. Another contribution of Sam's to the patriot cause was to have Thomas Paine's *Common Sense* reprinted. The title page reads at the bottom: "Philadelphia Printed: Newbury Port, Reprinted, for Samuel Phillips, jun. of Andover."

67. Samuel Phillips to Phoebe Phillips, undated, Phillips Papers.

68. Ibid.

69. The best secondary account of Sam's powder-making is in Bailey, *Historical Sketches*, 342-349. Unless otherwise noted, the following account has been taken from this source.

70. Washington to the President of Congress, Cambridge, 4 January 1776, in *Writings of Washington*, ed. Fitzpatrick, IV, 208.

71. Sam Phillips to Samuel Cunnabell, Watertown, 2 January 1776, Phillips Papers.

72. The General Court later authorized guards to fire on trespassers after they had been challenged three times. Bailey, *Historical Sketches*, 344.

73. Taylor, *Memoir*, 72.

74. All these documents are in the Pearson Papers, Phillips Academy Archives. See also E. A. Holyoke to Eliphalet Pearson, Salem, 22 December 1775, enclosing a document entitled "Process for Making Nitre." Park Family Papers, Sterling Memorial Library, Yale University.

75. Quoted in Charles H. Lyon, "Eliphalet Pearson: Puritan Educator," unpublished Senior Honors Thesis written in 1963 and now in Harvard University Archives.

76. Washington to Heath, Headquarters, Morris Town, 18 April 1777, in *Writings of Washington*, VII, 430. Miss Bailey, *Historical Sketches*, 346, gives the date of this letter as 8 April. This is one of the very few mistakes that I have found in her book.

77. Sam Phillips to Elbridge Gerry, Watertown, 11 September 1776, in Gerry Papers, Massachusetts Historical Society.

78. Lemuel Cox to Robert Treat Paine, Exeter, 8 October 1776, in Paine Papers, Massachusetts Historical Society.

79. Sam Phillips to Timothy Pickering, Boston, 24 December 1779, in Pickering Papers, Massachusetts Historical Society.

80. Ibid.

3. The Founding of Phillips Academy

1. Bailyn, *Education in the Forming of American Society*, 14.

2. Ibid., 21.

3. Ibid., 21-22.

4. Greven, *Four Generations*,

5. The undated letter is in the Phillips Papers. For the quotations from the School's Constitution, see the Appendix.

6. For a discussion of writers that may have influenced Sam, see Fuess, *An Old New England School*, 69-71; and Williams, *The Story of Phillips Exeter*, 24-25. Fuess says, "Much of this discussion of influences, however, is vain speculation, in which it is easy to exaggerate matters really of small sig-

nificance" (71). Williams says, "A careful reading of these works [Milton, Locke, etc.] must leave the reader unconvinced" (24).

7. For the following account of secondary education in colonial Massachusetts, I have depended primarily on Robert Middlekauff, *Ancients and Axioms: Secondary Education in Eighteenth-Century New England* (New Haven, Yale University Press, 1963); the appropriate chapters in Cremin, *American Education*; and the appropriate chapters in Samuel E. Morison, *The Puritan Pronaos: Studies in the Intellectual Life of New England in the Seventeenth Century* (New York, New York University Press, 1936).

8. This description of a typical New England grammar school is taken from Middle-kauff, 13–14.

9. The following material on schools in colonial Andover is taken from Bailey, *Historical Sketches of Andover*, 517–524.

10. Williams, in *The Story of Phillips Exeter*, says, "He [Sam Phillips] may have hoped to have a school . . . as little as possible like the one kept by Master Samuel Moody in South Byfield, which as a boy he had attended" (25). Fuess, *Old New England School*, speaks vaguely of the defects of Dummer School and later says, "It is clear that Phillips is inclined to disapprove of Dummer School as being too democratic" (54–55, 57).

11. For accounts of the early years of Dummer School, see Ragle, *Governor Dummer Academy History*, 3–27, and Nehemiah Cleaveland, *A History of Dummer Academy* (Newburyport, The Herald Press, 1914), 1–17.

12. For an account of Pearson, see the manuscript biographical sketch written by his son Henry in the Pearson Papers. See also Lyon, "Eliphalet Pearson: Puritan Educator."

13. William E. Park, "The Earlier Annals of Phillips Academy," (Centennial address, 1878), 67, believes that this document was "undoubtedly" later than the "Monday Morning at 5 o'clock" document printed below. I believe that he has the order reversed. In this first document Sam Phillips' ideas about secondary education range far and wide and have much less in common with the final Constitution of Phillips Academy than the second document. This first document contains a powerful attack on the classics and serious reservations about having "Charity Scholars" in the ideal school. Both of these positions have been abandoned in the second document, thus bringing the later plan much more in line with the Constitution. In addition, it is much more likely that Sam Phillips was discussing secondary education with Pearson in 1775 or 1776, when he was teaching school in Andover, than in 1777 when he was engaged in study, substitute preaching, and being inoculated for the smallpox (See Pearson's Diary for 1777, Pearson Papers). This is one of the very few places where I disagree with Park's scholarly account.

14. Sam Phillips to Timothy Pickering, Andover, 30 August 1794, Pickering Papers, Massachusetts Historical Society.

15. See 13 above for reasons why I believe this to be the later of the two long, undated documents in which Sam Phillips discusses his plans for a school. My guess is that it was written in late 1776 or early 1777.

16. This letter is in the Phillips Papers, Phillips Exeter Academy Archives.

17. Park, "Earlier Annals," 70.

18. For an account of these purchases, see Taylor, *Memoir*, 353–354.

19. In the Boston *Continental Journal and Weekly Advertiser* for 28 August 1777 the following advertisement appears: "The Public are hereby informed, That a free School will be opened at Andover, in a few Weeks, if a sufficient Number of Scholars apply, for the purpose of promoting Virtue and useful

Sciences, in which will be taught the English, Latin, and Greek Languages, Writing, Arithmetic, etc. etc." The identical ad appeared in the *Boston Gazette and Country Journal*, 8 September 1777. Vera M. Butler in her *Education as Revealed by New England Newspapers* (New York, Arno Press 1969, reprint), believes that this refers to a possible grammar school in the town of Andover (275). Yet the emphasis on "Virtue" and subjects to be taught closely parallel Phillips Academy's curriculum. It seems perfectly possible that some of those interested in founding Phillips Academy were testing the public to see what kind of support might attend a new school.

20. On the problem of deciding on Trustees, see Sam Phillips to John Phillips, Andover, 9 March 1778, 20 March 1778; and John Phillips to Sam Phillips, Exeter, 13 March 1778, all three in the Phillips Papers.

21. Sam Phillips to John Phillips, Andover, 9 March 1778, Phillips Papers.

22. The Constitution is printed in the Appendix.

23. Quoted in Gordon S. Wood, *The Creation of the American Republic, 1776–1787* (Chapel Hill, University of North Carolina Press, 1969), 124. Chapter III of this book, entitled "Moral Reformation" (91–124), is an admirable discussion of this whole subjeect of virtue. Samuel Adams hoped that the new nation would be a *"Christian* Sparta" (118).

24. For this gift see John Phillips' deed, dated Haverhill, 29 May 1777, Phillips Papers.

25. Jonathan French served in the army as a young man and then managed to go to Harvard, where he was a classmate of Sam Phillips'. When Parson Phillips died in 1771, Sam persuaded French to come to the South Parish, where, according to one authority, the two of them soon had the town "in a religious, economic, and social hammerlock." (*Sibley's Harvard Graduates*, Cambridge, Harvard University Press, 1975), XVII, 514–520. For more on French, see *Historical Manual of the South Church in Andover, Massachusetts* (Andover, 1859), 101–106. For some anecdotes about French, see Fuess, *Old New England School*, 73, note 1. For William Symmes, see Bailey, *Historical Sketches*, 447–452. For the other two clergymen, see *Biographical Catalogue of the Trustees, Teachers and Students of Phillips Academy, 1778–1830*, compiled by C. C. Carpenter (Andover, The Andover Press, 1903), 4–5. Josiah Stearns was an ancestor of Alfred E. Stearns, Headmaster of the Academy from 1903 to 1933. Oliver Wendell and John Lowell were both prominent in the government of Massachusetts; the former was the grandfather of Oliver Wendell Holmes, the latter of James Russell Lowell (4). Nemehiah Abbot, an Andover farmer, was elected the first treasurer of the School at the Trustees' first meeting.

26. This passage was not included in the earlier drafts of the Constitution. A draft of it is on a separate sheet of paper, filed with the earlier documents.

27. Fuess, *Old New England School*, 64.

28. John Phillips to Sam Phillips, Exeter, 1 January 1778, Phillips Papers.

29. *Sibley's Harvard Graduates*, IX, 568.

30. Pickering to Sam Phillips, Philadelphia, 29 May 1785, Pickering Papers, Massachusetts Historical Society.

31. Ibid., 18 June 1785.

32. For these actions by the Trustees, see Trustee Records, a manuscript volume containing the minutes of trustee meetings, 27–30.

33. Ibid., 19–20.

34. The Act of Incorporation is printed in *Acts and Laws of Massachusetts, 1780*, 327–329. It is reprinted in John L. Taylor, *A Memoir of His Honor Samuel*

Phillips, LL.D. (Boston, Congregation Board of Publication, 1856), 360–365.
35. Trustee Records, 31, 33.
36. I believe that Phillips Academy is the oldest incorporated *boarding* school in the country. Some day schools were incorporated earlier. For example, The William Penn Charter School in Philadelphia received a charter from William Penn in 1701.
37. Sam Phillips to John Phillips, Andover, 6 September 1780, quoted in Taylor, *Memoir*, 215. The original of this letter is no longer in the Phillips Papers.
38. Sam Phillips to John Phillips, Boston, 5 January 1781, Phillips Papers.
39. Trustee Records, 44–45.
40. See Claude M. Fuess, "Paul Revere and the Seal of Phillips Academy," *Phillips Bulletin* (April 1926), 8–9. See also Fuess, *Men of Andover* (New Haven, Yale University Press, 1928), 15–25.
41. See, for example, Martha Gandy Fales, *Early American Silver* (New York, Dutton, 1973), 220.
42. This letter is in the Phillips Papers.
43. Fuess, "Paul Revere," 11.
44. See Arthur S. Pease, "Finis Origine Pendet," *Phillips Bulletin* (January 1924), 15; and Myron Williams, *Story of Phillips Exeter*, 26.
45. Fuess, "Paul Revere," 11.

4. Eliphalet Pearson: Setting the Pattern

1. Park, "Earlier Annals," 70.
2. No copy of this sermon exists. The Trustees voted to have it printed, together with the Constitution and the Act of Incorporation, but apparently never had enough money to do so. See Trustee Records, 46.
3. For Pearson's early life see the biographical sketch by his son, Henry B. Pearson. There is a receipt for 17 pounds, one shilling, seven pence signed by David Pearson, dated Newbury, 20 October 1786, that acknowledges payment in full for collegiate education and clothing expenses from 19 July 1769 to that date. Both these documents are in the Pearson Papers.
4. The manuscript of Pearson's address is in the Pearson Papers. If this non-stop sentence is an example of prize-winning prose at Harvard during this period, one wonders how the poorer students wrote.
5. See above, 43–46.
6. See, for example, a letter to Pearson from his brother-in-law-to-be, Edward A. Holyoke, dated Andover, 6 October 1777, in which Holyoke writes that Pearson is "desired to preach at Boston New South Society." This letter is in the Park Family Papers, Yale University Library. See also a manuscript sermon preached on 3 November 1777, apparently on a text from Job; also in the Park Family Papers.
7. This was Samuel Kirkland, a missionary to the Indians. His son John entered Phillips Academy in 1784 and later became President of Harvard. See Fuess, *Men of Andover*, 79–91.
8. This diary is in the Pearson Papers.
9. From Henry B. Pearson's biographical sketch of his father p. 2; note 3 above.
10. Trustee Records, 27.
11. See above, 48.
12. Pearson Papers.
13. Phillips Papers. In a letter from John Smith, dated Hanover, New Hampshire, 10 May 1778, the following passage appears: "I think you are extremely

happy in your connexions, at Andover. Messrs. French and Phillips are most agreeable and excellent gentlemen."

14. This document, dated Andover, 17 April 1780, is in the Edwards Amasa Park Papers, Yale University Library. A fragment of the report is in the Pearson Papers. For an excellent summary of the material in the report, see Robert Middlekauff, *Ancients and Axioms: Secondary Education in Eighteenth-Century New England* (New Haven, Yale University Press, 1963) 155–157.

15. I am unable to discover what the "Fellowship" and "Practice" courses contained.

16. For material on Pearson's interest in music, see two letters to him from F. Colman dated Byfield, 5 January 1775, and Cambridge, 2 May [?] 1775. Colman writes about Handel's Oratorios, the *Harmonia Sacra*, the sale of his violincello for 4 guineas, and the "Bass of 3 fine Choruses" that he is sending to Pearson. Park Family Papers.

17. See, for example, Trustee Records, 53.

18. Ibid.

19. Ibid., 44, 48, 51.

20. There are two programs for Exhibitions in the Pearson Papers, one undated and one dated 15 April 1783.

21. Pickering to Sam Phillips, Philadelphia, 18 June 1783, Pickering Papers, Massachusetts Historical Society.

22. Edmund Quincy, *Life of Josiah Quincy* (Boston, 1868), 24–25.

23. Ibid., 26.

24. William E. Park, "The Earlier Annals of Phillips Academy" (Centennial address, 1878), 81.

25. For the account of Pearson's disciplinary system and the School's curriculum, see Quincy to Mr. Barnard, Boston, 1 December 1860, Manuscript File, 33–34.

26. Quincy to John L. Taylor, Boston, 13 December 1855, Manuscript File, 72–73.

27. Quincy, *Life of Josiah Quincy*, 23–24.

28. Park, "Earlier Annals," 81–82.

29. Ibid., 82. Fuess, *An Old New England School* (Boston, Houghton Mifflin, 1917), says that the students called Pearson "Elephant" as a pun on his name and a description of his bulk (86). I can find no documentation for this. Morison, *Three Centuries of Harvard*, says that Harvard students called Pearson "Elephant" for the same reasons (188). I think it much more likely that Harvard boys would be guilty of this *lèse-majesté* than Andover students.

30. Samuel Putnam to Pearson, Salem, 2 February 1826, copy made by Pearson's daughter in 1845, Park Family Papers.

31. This document, dated 17 August 1781 and signed by Jonathan French as Clerk of the Trustees, is in the Phillips Papers.

32. The material in the preceding paragraph has been taken from Carpenter, *Biographical Catalogue*, 25–33. For an example of an application for admission, see Nathaniel Sparhawk to Pearson, Haverhill, 26 July 1778, in which Sparhawk inquires about "entrance money," asks that his son be housed with Jonathan French, and promises to send his second son in the near future. Park Family Papers.

33. Middlekauff, *Ancients and Axioms*, 142.

34. Trustee Records, 42.

35. Ibid., 30.

36. Ibid., 36, 40.

37. Ibid., 37.

38. Ibid., 44, 54, 57. There is in the Phillips Papers the draft of a note to be signed by "Charity Scholars" in which the signer agreed to pay back the scholarship if he did not enter the ministry.
39. Ibid., 39.
40. Ibid., 45, 47, 51.
41. This contract, dated Andover, 26 May 1780, is in the Park Family Papers, Yale University Library.
42. Trustee Records, 56.
43. Ibid., 31, 33, 43, 51, 54, 57, 58.
44. Ibid., 52.
45. Ibid., 30, 32.
46. Ibid., 32, 34.
47. Ibid., 34, 35, 38, 44, 45.
48. Ibid., 58. See also two receipts in the Phillips Papers, dated Andover, 18 March 1779 and 18 April 1780, signed by Treasurer Nehemiah Abbot acknowledging the gift of Doddridge's *Family Expositor* and Montaine's *Essays* from Sam and Phoebe Phillips.
49. Trustee Records, 32.
50. This account, with several others of a similar nature, is in the Pearson Papers.
51. Sam Phillips to Jeremiah Smith, Andover, 22 July, 1783, Phillips Papers.
52. Trustee Records, 52.
53. Ibid., 53.
54. Mrs. Pearson was forty at the time of her marriage, twelve years older than her husband. She died in childbirth two years later. In a letter to his Uncle John dated Andover, 26 February 1781, Sam Phillips speaks of Mrs. Pearson's having had the fever for forty days. This letter is in the Phillips Papers. In 1785 Pearson married Sarah Bromfield, a very plain woman by whom he had four children and who survived him. Fuess, *Old New England School*, 88–89.
55. Sarah L. Bailey, *Historical Sketches of Andover* (Boston, Houghton Mifflin, 1880), 534, footnote 1. For a discussion of Sam Phillips' moves, see Leonard Woods to John L. Taylor, Brunswick, Maine, 4 February 1856, Phillips Papers.
56. Fuess, *Old New England School,* 32–33. He speaks of "tubs of punch provided by the thoughtful owner" for the workers.
57. For Samuel Phillips, Jr.'s later public career, see Taylor, *Memoir*, 76–103, and C. K. Shipton, *Sibley's Harvard Graduates* (Cambridge, Harvard University Press, 1975), XVII, 599–603. From now on Phillips was usually called "Judge."
58. Park, "Earlier Annals," 75–76.
59. See Joseph Willard to Pearson, Cambridge, 11 November 1785, Pearson Papers.
60. Trustee Records, 59.
61. Sam Phillips to Phoebe Phillips, Boston [?], 2 March 1786, Phillips Papers.

5. The Passing of the Phillipses

1. Trustee Records, 60.
2. Samuel Phillips to Phoebe Phillips, Boston [], 2 March 1786, Phillips Papers.
3. Ibid., 15 February 1786. It is difficult to determine who the other candidates were because Sam did not spell the names out.
4. John Abbot, 3d, was a graduate of Phillips Academy and Harvard who studied divinity but finally settled at Bowdoin College, where he was Professor of the Classics, Librarian, Trustee, and Treasurer. See Fuess, *Old New England*

School, 97, note 1.

5. The following account of Ebenezer Pemberton is based on *Sibley's Harvard Graduates*, XVI, 197–200; Park, "Earlier Annals," 85–87; and Fuess, *Old New England School*, 98–100.

6. Park, "Earlier Annals," 85.

7. Trustee Records, 53, 55.

8. Taylor, *Memoir*, 228. In a letter to his uncle John Phillips, dated Andover, 13 December 1793, Phillips Papers, Samuel Phillips gives the following dimensions for the new building: "Outside—64 feet, 8 inches by 33 feet, 4 inches. The length of the schoolroom inside was 36 feet. The height of the lower story was 12 feet, of the 'chamber' (second floor) 11 feet."

9. *The Diary of William Bentley* (Salem, The Essex Institute, 1905), I, 117. The members of the South Church were using the Academy building for Sunday services while they built a new church. See Trustee Records, 69.

10. Edmund Quincy, *Life of Josiah Quincy*, 28. See also a letter from Pemberton to John Locke, dated Andover, 2 September 1789, in which he encourages the former Phillips Academy student to do well on his entrance examinations for Dartmouth. The whole letter bespeaks the confidence that Pemberton has in his former pupil.

11. Park, "Earlier Annals," 86.

12. Ibid., 86, note 1.

13. Trustee Records, 86.

14. Robert Hallowell Gardiner, *Early Recollections* (privately printed, 1936), 32–33.

15. Samuel Phillips to John Phillips, Andover, 25 June 1787, Phillips Papers. See also another letter from Sam to his Uncle John, dated 26 July 1790, in which he expresses much the same sentiments. Phillips Papers.

16. Ibid., 18 January 1789.

17. Trustee Records, 62, 67, 69.

18. Ibid., 75.

19. Ibid., 82.

20. Ibid., 90.

21. Ibid., 83.

22. Ibid.

23. For Abbot, see Fuess, *Old New England School*, 110–111; for Kirkland, see Claude M. Fuess, *Men of Andover* (New Haven, Yale University Press, 1928), 79–91.

24. Trustee Records, 81. In the Phillips Academy Archives there is a sample bill for board in 1790. The cost was 7 shillings, 6 pence per week, or a total of 7 pounds 19 shillings, 6 pence for a twenty-one-and-a-third-week period. An additional 2 shillings, 6 pence was "To the making a pr. Breeches."

25. Trustee Records, 84.

26. See, for example, ibid., 80.

27. Samuel Phillips to his son John Phillips, Woburn, 3 July 1792, Phillips Papers.

28. Ibid., Andover, 4 July 1793.

29. These changes in the Board of Trustees can be followed in Trustee Records for the 1790's and early 1800's. They are printed in *Biographical Catalogue of the Trustees, Teachers, and Students of Phillips Academy, 1778–1830*, complied by C. C. Carpenter (Andover, The Andover Press, 1903), 4–7.

30. Trustee Records, 78. See also *Terms of Trusts*, printed for the use of the Trustees (Andover, 1932), 38–39.

31. Trustee Records, 92, See also *Terms of Trusts*, 39–40.

32. For this delightful contretemps, see Trustee Records, 96–97. Shortly after this the Exeter Trustees voted "to concur with the Trustees of Philips Academy

in the addition of another cow to the compensation to be made Mrs. Phillips."
33. *The Diaries of George Washington*, John C. Fitzpatrick, ed. (Boston, 1925),
    IV, 47–48.
34. Fuess, *Old New England School*, 107.
35. Douglas S. Freeman, *George Washington, A Biography* (New York, Scribner's,
    1954), VI, says, "For the greater part of the way he traveled in his carriage
    but for ceremonies he frequently mounted one of the horses" (241, note 5).
36. This story is given in Taylor, *Memoir*, 179. Apparently there is a similar glove-
    mending story told about George Washington's stop in Haverhill.
37. George Washington to William Augustine Washington, Philadelphia, 23
    November 1794, in *The Writings of George Washington*, John C. Fitzpatrick,
    ed. (Washington, D.C., Government Printing Office, 1934), XXXIV, 44–45.
38. Washington to William A. Washington, Philadelphia, 31 March 1795, *Writings
    of Washington*, 164–165.
39. Washington to Benjamin Lincoln, Mount Vernon, 21 April 1795, Phillips
    Academy Archives. This letter does not appear in *Writings of Washington*.
40. Cabot to Washington, Brookline, 9 May 1795, Phillips Academy Archives.
41. Charles Lee to Samuel Phillips, 10 May 1795, in Fuess, *Men of Andover*, 8–9.
    The place from which the letter was written is not given.
42. Carpenter, *Biographical Catalogue*, 41–42.
43. Hannah Washington to Samuel Phillips, Bushfield, Virginia, 5 October 1795,
    Phillips Papers.
44. William A. Washington to Samuel Phillips, Haywood, Virginia, 2 September
    1796, Phillips Papers.
45. See William A. Washington to George Washington, Haywood, 12 September
    1796, in which he speaks of the difficulty of exchanging notes of the
    Alexandria Bank for Bank Notes of the United States. See also two letters
    of George Washington's, both dated Mount Vernon, 28 September 1796. One
    was to William Washington, in which the President informed him that he
    had enough U.S. bank notes to effect the exchange: the other to Samuel
    Phillips, in which the President asked to be informed if his nephews' account
    was in arrears. In a letter dated 20 October 1796, the Judge wrote the
    President that he had received the money and that there were no arrears to
    speak of. All of these letters are in the Phillips Papers.
46. Samuel Phillips to John Phillips, Andover, 2 November 1796, Phillips Papers.
47. William Washington to Samuel Phillips, Haywood, 22 June 1797, Phillips
    Papers.
48. Samuel Phillips to William Washington, Andover, 20 July 1797, Phillips Papers.
49. Ibid., 3 September 1797. See also two letters from John Phillips to his father
    dated 14 and 20 July 1797, in which he speaks of making arrangements for
    "the young gentlemen" to go to Alexandria and then writes, "If the Wash-
    ingtons can be sent down tomorrow, they can have a safe and commodious
    passage on Saturday in the Lucy." Both these letters are in the Phillips
    Papers.
50. In 1787 the Trustees changed the name of the head of the School from
    "Preceptor" to "Principal," but it was some years before the new name stuck.
51. Trustee Records, 91.
52. See a long letter from Samuel Phillips to Eliphalet Pearson, dated Andover, 29
    October 1793, which reviews the whole problem occasioned by the Pember-
    ton resignation. This letter is in the Park Family Papers, Yale University
    Library.
53. Trustee Records, 91–92.
54. In the *Independent Chronicle*, 1 June 1795, the following advertisement appears:

712 : NOTES TO PAGES 97–102

"Mr. Pemberton, Late Principal of Phillips Academy in Andover, Having resigned his office, has removed to *Billerica*, where he will take charge of the education of young Gentlemen. Mr. P. has taken lodgings in the house of Capt. Josiah Bowers, near the *Meeting-House.*"

55. Fuess, *Old New England School*, 107–108.
56. John Phillips to Phoebe Phillips, Charlestown, 2 October 1796, Phillips Papers. In another letter to his Mother, John Phillips wrote the following puzzling statement: "Mr. Pemberton is this way, and we may soon expect to hear rumors. I think nobody appears to dispute his title. For my own part, I'm willing to give him a quit claim, and even to warrant and defend against the claims of all persons whatsoever." I have not been able to discover what John Phillips was referring to. This letter, dated 23 October 1796, is in the Phillips Papers. The only possible scandal that might be associated with Pemberton was the fact that he married Prudence Whitwell on 6 December 1796, and their first child was born on 16 December 1796. See *Sibley's Harvard Graduates*, XVI, 199. But these events took place almost three years after he left Andover.
57. See above, 69–70.
58. See Phoebe Phillips to John Phillips, Andover [?], 24 June 1795, Phillips Papers. See also an undated letter from Phoebe Phillips to Pemberton, certainly written after his marriage, in which she hopes to hear from Pemberton soon. This letter is in the Phillips Papers.
59. Shipton, *Sibley's Harvard Graduates*, XVI, 199.
60. On Newman's early life, see George Mooar, *Memorial of Deacon Mark Newman* (Andover, 1859), 1–16.
61. Mark Newman to John Phillips, Andover, 14 November 1793.
62. Ibid., 30 March 1793.
63. Ibid., 8 December 1794.
64. Claude M. Fuess, *An Old New England School* (Boston, Houghton Mifflin, 1917), 113.
65. Trustee Records, 91, 93, 95. On the other hand, Judge Phillips wrote his Uncle John that "Newman by no means flags in our estimation." This letter, dated Andover, 3 December 1793, is in the Phillips Papers.
66. William E. Park, "The Earlier Annals of Phillips Academy" (Centennial address, 1878), tells a story of Newman's triumph over some rebellious students in a town school where he was teaching (88). None of the other authorities mentions this. Since he came to Phillips Academy immediately upon graduation from Dartmouth, this episode would have to have taken place while he was still a Dartmouth undergraduate. In this case I think Park "bought" a family tradition.
67. See, for example, Trustee Records, 103, 110, 120.
68. For an extensive account of the activities of the Committee for the Sale of Eastern Lands, see my *William Bingham's Maine Lands, 1790–1820*, Publications of the Colonial Society of Massachusetts, (1954), 36, passim.
69. Harriet W. Marr, *The Old New England Academies* (New York, Comet Press, 1959), 19–22.
70. Ibid., 23.
71. Ibid., 23–25.
72. Trustee Records, 116, 128, 131–132.
73. Ibid., 133.
74. Ibid, 98, 100, 102.
75. Ibid., 98, 105.
76. Ibid., 128, 130, 134.

77. Ibid., 107, 108, 134.
78. Ibid., 98. Abiel Holbrook had been writing master at the Academy for some time. The first part of the Trustee Records are copied in his hand. In 1797 he resigned because of the "weakness of his eyes," and later became tutor for Colonel William A. Washington in Virginia. There is an interesting letter from him to Eliphalet Pearson, dated Westmoreland County, 16 December 1800, describing his impressions of Virginia. This letter is in the Park Family Papers, Yale University Library.
79. Trustee Records, 100, 118.
80. Ibid., 115, 116.
81. Ibid., 136–137.
82. Ibid., 106, 107, 127, 130. Apparently musical exercises under Ichabod Johnson were rowdy and tumultuous. See Fuess, *Old New England School*, 20.
83. Trustee Records, 109. I have been unable to discover with certainty what the "disorder" in Andover was. Since Judge Phillips's younger son Samuel died at this time, it was probably the same epidemic that led to his death.
84. Trustee Records, 116.
85. Ibid., 133. I believe this to have been a new dance. See Carlton Mabee, *The American Leonardo, A Life of Samuel F. B. Morse* (New York, Knopf, 1943), where he speaks of "the glorious whirls of the 'federal balloon,' the current fandango" (14).
86. Trustee Records, 121.
87. There is a puzzling letter from Sam Phillips to Dr. Morse, dated Andover, 14 October 1797, Phillips Papers. It reads in part: "It gives me pain to inform you, that the Trustees of Phillips Exeter Academy, at their annual meeting the present week, in considering what persons were qualified to receive the benefit of Doctor Phillips' donation for charitable purposes, found themselves under the disagreeable necessity of discontinuing young Morse from the number placed on that foundation. The Donor made 'a good moral character' one indispensable requisite in the objects of that charity. The information given the board obliged them to believe, that this person does not possess this qualification." Since Samuel F. B. Morse was not born until 27 April 1791, I cannot believe that it was he. He was, however, the eldest son, so it could not have been any of his brothers.
88. Mabee, *American Leonardo*, 12–14.
89. John L. Taylor, *A Memoir of His Honor Samuel Phillips, LL.D* (Boston, Congregation Board of Publication, 1856), 313.
90. On Judge Phillips's business affairs, see ibid., 104–109. There is also a copy of his Estate at the time of death in the Phillips Papers.
91. Samuel Phillips to General Keith, 7 February 1787, Heath Papers, Massachusetts Historical Society.
92. *Sibley's Harvard Graduates*, XVII, 599.
93. Ibid., 600.
94. Taylor, *Memoir*, 96–99.
95. Samuel Phillips to John Phillips, Andover, 3 August 1798, Phillips Papers.
96. Samuel Phillips to Timothy Pickering, Andover, 10 May 1799, Pickering Papers, Massachusetts Historical Society. I believe that this is the only account of a Jeffersonian in drag in the literature of the period.
97. Samuel Phillips to Jedidiah Morse, Andover, 22 December 1800, Manuscript Collection, Boston Public Library.
98. Samuel Phillips to Eliphalet Pearson, Andover, 4 May 1801, Park Family Papers, Yale University Library.
99. Samuel Phillips to John Phillips, Andover, 3 July 1801, Phillips Papers.

1. Taylor, *Memoir*, 107, See also Samuel Phillips to "Kind Madam," Medford, 30 April 1794, Phillips Papers, in which he thanks the lady for the care her daughter had given him. The "Kind Madam" was either Mrs. Brooks or Mrs. William Phillips, the mother of Sally.
2. Samuel Phillips to Phoebe Phillips, Boston, 11 February 1797, Phillips Papers.
3. Ibid., 22 January 1795.
4. Ibid., 13 February 1794, Phillips Papers. There are a substantial number of letters between the Judge and Phoebe in the Phillips Papers, some of which have been printed in Taylor, *Memoir*, 119–137.
5. Samuel Phillips to John Phillips, Andover, 17 October 1797, Park Family Papers, Yale University Library. This letter, which starts off "Finis Origine Pendet!" is printed in Taylor, *Memoir*, 278–284. For other correspondence involving John Phillips see Taylor, *Memoir*, 144–158.
6. Samuel Phillips to John Phillips, Andover, 1 January 1800 Phillips Papers; printed in Taylor, *Memoir*, 285–288.
7. Samuel Phillips to John Phillips, Andover, 4 January 1801, Phillips Papers, printed in Taylor, *Memoir*, 288–294.
8. Judge Phillips' endorsement on the last letter that his son Samuel wrote him, dated Andover, January 1796, Phillips Papers, printed in Taylor, *Memoir*, 165–166.
9. Samuel Phillips to Phoebe Phillips, Boston, 19 February 1796, printed in Taylor, *Memoir*, 168. The original of this letter is no longer in the Phillips Papers.
10. Jonathan French to Eliphalet Pearson, Andover, 25 May 1801, Park Family Papers, Yale University Library.
11. Ibid., 26 May 1801.
12. Ibid., 4 July 1801.
13. Eliphalet Pearson to John Phillips, Belchertown, 16 August 1801, Park Family Papers, Yale University Library.
14. The account of the funeral is taken from the Boston *Columbian Centinel*, 17 February 1801, as quoted in Taylor, *Memoir*, 318–319. See also Shipton, *Sibley's Harvard Graduates*, XVII, 604.
15. *The Diary of William Bentley* (Salem, The Essex Institute, 1905), II, 414.
16. *Terms of Trusts*, 45–50.
17. There is a sizable amount of material on the early administration of the two donations in the Phillips Academy Archives. The more modern part of the story, including the settlement of 1906, is in the files of the Treasurer's Office.
18. *Select Committee Record*, 1.
19. Ibid., 2.
20. Ibid., 3–4.
21. Ibid., 5.
22. Ibid., 7–8.
23. Ibid., 9–10.
24. Ibid., 19–20.
25. Ibid., 24.
26. Carpenter, *Biographical Catalogue*, 54–56.
27. Fuess, *Old New England School*, 134.
28. There is a folder of early admission applications in the Phillips Academy Archives.
29. See Trustee Records, 147, 154, 172, 184, 196. In 1803 Abner Johnson had his grant under the John Phillips foundation removed. Mark Newman was asked to explain to the father "the peculiar circumstances attending his case." Trustee Records, 163.

30. Henry Pearson to Eliphalet Pearson, Andover, 23 December 1804, Park Family Papers, Yale University Library.
31. Henry Pearson to parents, Andover, 3 January 1805, Park Family Papers.
32. Ibid., 11 January 1805.
33. Henry Pearson to E. Pearson, Andover, 19 March 1805, Park Family Papers.
34. Ibid., 28 April 1805.
35. Ibid., 13 June 1805.
36. Ibid., 2 July 1805.
37. Ibid., 3 August 1805.
38. Eliphalet Pearson to Henry Pearson, Cambridge, 4 August 1805, Park Family Papers.
39. Henry Pearson to E. Pearson, Andover, 7 August 1805, Park Family Papers.
40. Ibid., 28 Septemebr 1805.
41. Henry Pearson to parents, Andover, 20 October 1805, Park Family Papers.
42. Ibid., 12 December 1805.
43. Park Family Papers.
44. This document is in the Phillips Academy Archives. It is interesting to note that Miss Abigail French contributed "A Petrified Bone and A Singular Fly" to the collection, indicating that daughters in the community did occasionally participate in undergraduate activities.
45. Trustee Records, 140, 147, 161–162, 237, 283, 297, 206, 276.
46. Ibid., 154, 204, 150, 174, 198, 215, 208, 167, 165, 184.
47. Ibid., 267–270.
48. Ibid., 281, 289.
49. Ibid., 160.
50. Ibid., 284.
51. *Biographical Catalogue of the Trustees, Teachers and Students of Phillips Academy, 1778–1830*, compiled by C. C. Carpenter (Andover, The Andover Press, 1903), 60–61.
52. Mark Newman to the Trustees, Andover, 22 August 1809.
53. Trustee Records, 293–294.

6. The Andover Theological Seminary

1. I have not attempted original research for this chapter on the Seminary but have depended mainly on Leonard Woods, *History of the Andover Theological Seminary* (Boston, 1885); Henry K. Rowe, *History of the Andover Theological Seminary* (Newton, 1933); the appropriate chapters in Fuess, *Old New England School*; and some special articles by J. Earl Thompson, Jr., Professor of Church History at the Andover Newton Theological School, which will be cited in their appropriate places.
2. Quoted in Daniel D. Williams, *The Andover Liberals* (New York, King's Crown Press, 1941), 2.
3. The material on the changes at Harvard has been taken from Samuel E. Morison, *Three Centuries of Harvard, 1636–1936* (Cambridge, Harvard University Press, 1936), 187–191.
4. The material in the preceding paragraph has been taken from Sidney E. Ahlstrom, *A Religious History of the American People* (New Haven, Yale University Press, 1972), 390–393.
5. Theodore R. Sizer, *The Age of the Academies* (New York, Teachers College, Columbia University, 1964), 87. See also the Appendix.
6. *Terms of Trusts*, 49.

7. The material in the preceding paragraph has been taken from Woods, *History*, 17–26.
8. Jonathan French's letter, without specific date, is printed in Woods, *History*, 449–450.
9. See Appendix.
10. *Terms of Trust*, 40–41.
11. Trustee Records, 198.
12. Ahlstrom, *Religious History*, 394, believes that Morse was mainly responsible for the establishment of the Andover Seminary. He mentions neither the work of Pearson nor of Woods and speaks of the institution as "undoubtedly Morse's most enduring ecclesiastical memorial."
13. The material on Abbot is taken from Woods, *History*, 55–61.
14. Woods, *History*, 65.
15. For a discussion of the beliefs of the Hopkinsians, see Woods, *History*, 32–40. I have not been able to reduce them to any easily intelligible summary.
16. For the Newburyport group, see Woods, *History*, 65–69.
17. Woods, *History*, 86.
18. Trustee Records, 219–220. The act, passed 19 June 1807, authorized the Trustees to hold property the annual income of which should not exceed five thousand dollars. This was to be in addition to the authority in the original constitution.
19. Woods, *History*, 90.
20. Professor Edwards A. Park in an address given at the time of the Phillips Academy Centennial and printed in *Centennial History*, 170.
21. In the Act of Incorporation of Phillips Academy in 1780 there was the statement that "the Trustees aforesaid, and their *successors* . . . be the true *and sole Visitors, Trustees and Governors* of the said Phillips Academy," which would seem to rule out the Board of Visitors. In addition there was a clause that stated that "neither the Trustees nor their successors ever hereafter receive any grant or donation, the condition whereof shall require them . . . to act in any respect counter to the design of the first granters" which the acceptance of the donations of the Newburyport group might violate. The question remained moot, however. Like so many potentially dangerous legal issues, it was avoided because no one challenged the Seminary in the courts. See Woods, *History*, 109–114.
22. All these documents are printed in Woods, *History*, 232–269.
23. Rowe, *History*, 20.
24. Ibid., 23–25.
25. Ibid., 21.
26. Sarah Stuart Robbins, *Old Andover Days*, (Boston, The Pilgrim Press, 1908), 17–18.
27. There is a good account of these material changes in Claude M. Fuess, *An Old New England School* (Boston Houghton Mifflin, 1917), 153–156.
28. Ahlstrom, *Religious History*, 396.
29. Woods, *History*, 150–151.
30. Robbins, *Old Andover Days*, 170–171.
31. Oliver W. Holmes, *Pages from an Old Volume of Life* (New York, 1891), 249.
32. Most of the material in this paragraph has been taken from Scott H. Paradise, *A History of Printing in Andover*, (Andover, The Andover Press, 1931).
33. Rowe, *History*, 27–28.
34. Ibid., 29.
35. Ibid., 36–37, 2.
36. Robbins, *Old Andover Days*, 1–13.

37. Robbins, *Old Andover Days*, 29–55.
38. Ibid., 73–88.
39. Ibid., 90–106. See also accounts of Anniversary ceremonies in the New York *Observer*, 20 September 1834, 16 September 1837, and 15 September 1838, Phillips Academy Archives.
40. Unless otherwise noted, the material on the Murdock case has been taken from J. Earl Thompson, Jr. "Church History Comes to Andover: The Persecution of James Murdock," *Andover Newton Quarterly*, 15, 4 (March 1975), 213–227.
41. Rowe, *History*, 69.
42. This account of the Southern clergyman, signed simply "H", appeared in the Boston *Recorder*, May 1823. There is no more precise date on the clipping in the Phillips Academy Archives.
43. Unless otherwise noted, the material on the slavery question is taken from J. Earl Thompson, Jr. "Abolitionism and Theological Education at Andover," *New England Quarterly*, 47, 2 (June 1974), 238–261.
44. The reaction of the Phillips Academy students, however, was very different. See below, 184–186.
45. Unless otherwise noted, the material on the Seminary missionaries has been taken from Rowe, *History*, 111–135.
46. The material on Goodell has been taken from E. D. G. Prime, *Forty Years in the Turkish Empire; or, Memoirs of Rev. William Goodell, D.D.* (New York, 1875). See especially 22–31 and 43–45.
47. See Daniel Dana, *Remonstrance to the Trustees of Phillips Academy* (Boston, 1853), especially 23–24.
48. The material on Park has been taken from Rowe, *History*, 159–163.
49. Quoted in J. Earl Thompson, Jr., "The Andover Liberals as Theological Educators," *Andover Newton Quarterly*, 8, 4 (March 1968), footnote 11.
50. For a summary of liberal beliefs, see Ahlstrom, *Religious History*, 779–781.
51. The material on the Andover liberals has been taken from Daniel D. Williams, *The Andover Liberals*, Thompson, "The Andover Liberals as Theological Educators;" and Rowe, *History*, 176–178.
52. See, for example, Trustee Records, II, 101.
53. Horace E. Scudder, "A Group of Classical Schools," *Harper's New Monthly Magazine*, 55, (September 1877), 571.

7. The Days of Samuel Farrar

1. The best general account of Farrar is Claude M. Fuess, "The 'Immortal Squire,'" in the *Phillips Bulletin* (January 1917), 5–8.
2. This story is in M. H. Cornelius to "Cousin Edwards," Newton Center, 24 May 1878. I believe that Mrs. Cornelius was a step-granddaughter of Squire Farrar. The letter is in the Farrar Papers.
3. This story was told by Professor Edwards A. Park in a speech he gave to the graduating class at Abbot Academy in 1878. See Philena McKeen and Phebe F. McKeen, *A History of Abbot Academy* (Andover, 1880), 10.
4. The Cornelius to "Cousin Edwards" letter above, note 2.
5. There are two letters in the Farrar Papers written in 1801 by D. A. White addressed to Farrar as "Student at Law, Springfield."
6. *Terms of Trusts*, 49.
7. Trustee Records, 161.

718 : NOTES TO PAGES 150–158

8. Ibid., 167.

9. Ibid., 217. In 1809, at the Squire's suggestion, twelve dollars a year from this fund were to be devoted to prizes in Latin and Greek. But Principal John Adams vetoed the plan, presumably because he thought it was bribing the students to do better work. See Trustee Records, 285–286, 324.

10. E. R. H. Peck to William E. Park, Cincinnati, 23 May 1878, Farrar Papers.

11. Woods, *History*, 97.

12. Mrs. Peck, in the letter above, note 10, writes about Farrar's relationship with Madame Phillips as follows: " . . . there was every indication of his veneration for her character as a Christian, and as an intelligent and most dignified *Lady*. Their associations were those of intimate friendship and mutual confidence." And she remembers the Squire showing her a copy of "Dorney's Letters" that Madame Phillips had copied for him in her own hand.

13. There is a copy of this act in Trustee Records, 219–220.

14. This petition, dated Boston, 18 January 1814, and signed by Eliphalet Pearson, Jedidiah Morse, and Samuel H. Walley, is in the Massachusetts Archives.

15. The original of this act, dated 4 February 1814, is in the Massachusetts Archives.

16. This petition is in the Massachusetts Archives. It is undated.

17. See the *Columbian Centinel*, for 10 June 1815. See also the Journal of the Massachusetts House, 8 June 1815. The act to increase the power of the Trustees to hold property had a dangerous repercussion when the Town of Andover petitioned the legislature to be allowed to tax the School and Seminary. Fortunately, the petition was later withdrawn. The undated petition, signed by Thomas Kittridge and John Cornish, is in the Massachusetts Archives.

18. M. H. Cornelius to "Cousin Edwards," Newton Center, 24 May 1878.

19. This material has been taken from Fuess's article above note 1; from the Cornelius letter above note 18; and from E. R. H. Peck to W. E. Park, Cincinnati, 23 May 1878. For the founding of Abbot Academy, see the forthcoming volume by my colleague Susan M. Lloyd.

20. Committee circular, Salem, 28 March 1818, Farrar Papers.

21. Mills Day to Farrar, Yale College, 12 April 1811, Farrar Papers.

22. The material in the preceding paragraph has been taken from the Cornelius and Peck letters above, notes 18 and 19; and from Park, "Earlier Annals," 95, footnote 1.

23. The material in the preceding paragraph has been taken from M. E. and H. G. Brown, *The Story of John Adams, a New England Schoolmaster* (New York, Scribner's, 1900), 3–28.

24. Ibid., 59–60.

25. Ibid., 109–118.

26. Ibid., 178–186.

27. Ibid., 111–112.

28. Josiah Quincy to W. E. Park, Quincy, 27 May 1878.

29. William E. Park, "The Earlier Annals of Phillips Academy" (Centennial address, 1878), 90–91.

30. Trustee Records, 357.

31. Ibid., 349

32. Fuess, *Old New England School*, 168

33. Letter from Captain John Codman to the Editor of the *Christian Register*, 6 December 1894.

34. Quoted in Fuess, *Old New England School*, 169.

35. The Codman-*Christian Register* letter above, note 33.

36. Park, "Earlier Annals," 90, footnote 1.
37. Brown and Brown, *John Adams*, 60–62.
38. Jonathan F. Stearns to W. E. Park, Newark, New Jersey, 29 May 1878.
39. Park, "Earlier Annals," 91–92.
40. Ibid., 91, note 1.
41. Josiah Quincy, *Figures of the Past* (Boston, 1883), 11.
42. Trustee Records, 309, 337.
43. Ibid., 302, 319.
44. Ibid., 335–336.
45. Ibid., 321, 341.
46. Ibid., 335, 404.
47. Ibid., 302, 310, 349, 398.
48. Ibid., 332, 342.
49. Ibid., 397.
50. Ibid., 335.
51. Ibid., 386. As far as this writer can discover this vote has never been repealed.
52. Ibid., 312, 317–318.
53. This letter, dated Andover, 2 February 1818, is unsigned and addressed simply "Dear Parents." It is number 55 in a manuscript file volume, Phillips Academy Archives.
54. Trustee Records, 344–345.
55. See the printed copy of this appeal dated Andover, 27 March 1818.
56. Trustee Records, 348.
57. The material in the preceding paragraphs has been taken from Carpenter. *Biographical Catalogue* and from the individual catalogues printed after 1814. It is sometimes difficult to compare these two sources of information since Carpenter lists the students by year of entrance rather than by year of graduation.
58. Josiah Quincy, *Figures of the Past*, 4.
59. Ibid., 4–6. Brown, *John Adams*, 86–98. The latter source contains a substantial number of Person letters.
60. Account Book of Horace James, 1834–1836.
61. James Burrill, Jr. to John Adams, "last of May 1819" (copy).
62. James A. Burrill to his father, undated.
63. Ibid., Andover, 6 June 1819.
64. Ibid., 25 June 1819.
65. John Adams to James Burrill, Jr., Andover, 2 July 1819.
66. James A. Burrill to "Meus Care Pater," Andover, 22 November 1819.
67. James A. Burrill to his father, Andover, 15 December 1819.
68. Ibid., 21 December 1819.
69. Ibid., 30 January 1820.
70. Ibid., 21 December 1819.
71. Ibid., 7 March 1820.
72. Ibid., undated.
73. Ibid., Andover, 12 April 1820.
74. Edward J. Lowell to Mrs. R. R. Gardner, Andover, 11 September 1817.
75. "Thomas" to his mother, Andover, 15 November 1829.
76. Horace James to his father, Andover, 26 February 1835. It was said of John Adams that if he ever saw a boy smoking, he would strike the pipe from his mouth.
77. See the "Constitution of the Society for Promoting Good Morals" (Andover, 1814).

78. For the Social Fraternity, see its revised manuscript constitution dated 1829, and James Hardy Ropes, '85, later a Trustee, "The Social Fraternity in Phillips Academy" (manuscript).

79. See *Semi-Centennial of the Philomathean Society* (Hyde Park, Massachusetts, privately printed, 1875), 24–29. Principal Adams was death on "dangerous" books and did all he could to ban them from the School. When he heard that a student had some *plays*, he haled him into court and told him to turn in all books in his possession that were not connected with classical studies. When, at the end of the term, he returned the books to the boy, he discovered, to his rage, that the one on top was the Holy Bible. This was one of the few times that a student got the better of Principal Adams. See Brown and Brown, *John Adams*, 72–73.

80. Ray Palmer to W. E. Park, Newark, 27 May 1878.

81. *Semi-Centennial*, 27–28. See also Brown, *John Adams*, 70–72.

82. For an admirable account of one of these early experiments, see James McLachlan, *American Boarding Schools: A Historical Study* (New York, Scribner's, 1970), which describes the founding of Round Hill School outside Northampton, Massachusetts, by Joseph Cogswell and George Bancroft (19–101). On the other hand, in 1828, the Yale faculty adopted a very conservative report in which they restated their support for a primarily classical curriculum.

83. Park, "Earlier Annals," 94.

84. Ibid., 95, footnote.

85. Trustee Records, 387, 390.

86. Ibid., 393.

87. Fuess, *Old New England School*, 204.

88. Trustee Records, 398.

89. See Lydia A. H. Smith, *"Lectures on School-Keeping* by Samuel Read Hall (1829)," *Harvard Library Bulletin*, 20, 1 (January 1972). I am indebted to Headmaster Theodore R. Sizer for calling my attention to this article.

90. Trustee Records, 399.

91. This material has been taken from the catalogues of the Teachers' Seminary from 1831 to 1842.

92. Quoted in Claude M. Fuess, *An Old New England School* (Boston, Houghton Mifflin, 1917), 210–212.

93. See the manuscript copies of the *Literary Recorder*, 1837, 1838.

94. Davis Smith to "Mother," Andover, 30 August 1834.

95. See Trustee Records, 431, 436.

96. Ibid., 423, 429.

97. Ibid., 432. There is a copy of the circular and manuscript minutes of the meeting in the Teachers' Seminary Papers.

98. Trustee Records, 442.

99. There are several copies of this circular in the Teachers' Seminary Papers.

1. Trustee Records, 461.

2. Ibid., 466; Boston *Recorder*, 19 March 1841.

3. Ibid., 489. See also the report of a trustee committee, 19 April 1842, that recommended a complete overhaul of the program of the English School; and the report of a second trustee committee, 9 August 1842, that pointed out that the English school was losing about $1,000 a year and recommended uniting the School with Phillips Academy under the same Principal.

4. Quoted in Fuess, *Old New England School*, 217.

5. Trustee Records, 398. Fuess, *Old New England School*, says this motion was passed "at the instigation of the indefatigable Squire Farrar" (228). I be-

lieve this to be quite likely but have found nothing in the records to support it.

6. There is a good description of the Commons and life in them in Fuess, *Old New England School*, 229–232.

8. The Dictatorship of Samuel Harvey Taylor

1. See the undated report among the Trustee Papers. Samuel T. Worcester, in his letter to W. E. Park, dated Nashua, New Hampshire, 20 May 1878, speaks of Adams being "looked upon as somewhat antiquated in his ideas."
2. Brown and Brown, *John Adams*, 192.
3. Ibid., 195–200. This letter is also in Trustee Records, 410–414.
4. Brown and Brown, *John Adams*, 210–265.
5. Trustee Records, 415, 423.
6. L. J. Wright to W. E. Park, Boston, 25 May 1878. Mrs. Wright was Johnson's daughter.
7. Isaac P. Langworthy, quoted in Fuess, *Old New England School*, 223.
8. Horace Eaton to C. F. P. Bancroft, Palmyra, New York, 28 May 1878.
9. Park, "Earlier Annals," 97–98, footnote.
10. The Eaton-Bancroft letter above, note 8. In commenting further on the religious life of the School, Eaton writes: "The year 1834 was crowned by a genuine revival. The fruit remained. Sixty of our number were converted. Many became ministers. In a crisis of great solicitude lest the work should stop, in House No. 3, a prayer-meeting was continued during the entire night.
    At the dawn of the day, John P. Gulliver, an inmate of that house, came into the light of the Gospel."
11. Alexander H. Clapp to W. E. Park, New York, 24 May 1878.
12. The basic document for this affair is a long manifesto printed by the students entitled "A Statement of the Circumstances which induced Fifty Students of Phillips Academy, Andover, to ask a Dismission from that Institution," dated Andover, 5 August 1835. See also Park, "Earlier Annals," 99–101; and Fuess, *Old New England School*, 225–228. J. Earl Thompson, Jr. in his article "Abolition and Theological Education at Andover," 239, footnote 5, dismisses the Fuess account as "inaccurate." While some of Fuess' statements about the Theological Seminary professors may be in error, I believe the basic account of the *Academy's* part in this "rebellion" to be sound.
13. See Sherlock Bristol, *The Pioneer Preacher* (New York, F. H. Revell, 1887), 45–47.
14. See above, 137–139.
15. See Sherlock Bristol to C. F. P. Bancroft, Ventura, California, 6 December 1892.
16. This quotation appears in the manifesto, and also, with slightly different wording, in *Ephraim Adams' Sketch Book*, transcribed by James Douglas Adams (San Francisco, Sorg Printing Co., 1968), 7.
17. Park, "Earlier Annals," 100.
18. *Adams' Sketch Book*, 7–8.
19. Park, "Earlier Annals," 101..
20. This material on Johnson's last days is taken from the letter his daughter, Mrs. L. J. Wright wrote to W. E. Park, Boston, 25 May 1878.
21. Fuess, *Old New England School*, 235.
22. For Taylor's early life, see *A Memorial of Samuel Harvey Taylor*, (Andover, Warren F. Draper, 1871), 13–18.

23. See Horace E. Scudder, "A Group of Classical Schools," *Harper's New Monthly Magazine*, 55 (September 1877), 562–563. Also William A. Mowry, *Recollections of a New England Educator, 1838–1908* (New York, Silver, Burdett, 1908), 73.
24. G. H. Palmer to C. F. P. Bancroft, Cambridge, 5 February 1888.
25. Dr. Alexander McKenzie as quoted in Fuess, *Old New England School*, 238.
26. J. P. Gulliver to C. F. P. Bancroft, Binghamton, New York, 28 March 1878.
27. Published in Boston. Dr. Taylor published several other volumes including Kühner's Greek Grammar.
28. Ibid., 45.
29. Ibid., 51.
30. John Albee, *Three Memorials* (Portsmouth, L. W. Brewster, 1878), 12–14.
31. Undated and unaddressed letter by L. L. Paine, Class of 1855.
32. Ibid.
33. Albert Warren to C. M. Fuess, Hinckley, Minnesota, 6 August 1913.
34. A. Eugene Nolan to C. M. Fuess, Fitchburg, Massachusetts, 25 July 1913.
35. The Warren-Fuess letter above, note 33.
36. From an undated statement by Charles F. Thwing, President of Western Reserve University.
37. The Paine letter above, note 31.
38. The Thwing statement above, note 36.
39. Noah H. Swayne to C. M. Fuess, Toledo, Ohio, 10 June 1914. The undergraduates had written a poem with which to greet Uncle Sam on his return. One verse will suffice:

    Welcome! Welcome honoured teacher
    Home again from foreign lands,
    Glad we greet thine every feature
    While each joyful heart expands.

    See Simon McQuestion to "Friend," Andover, 17 September 1856, printed in the *Phillips Bulletin*, (January 1921), 24–25.
40. Ibid.
41. Ibid.
42. Ibid.
43. The Warren-Fuess letter above, note 33.
44. Dr. Alexander McKenzie quoted in Fuess, *Old New England School*, 257.
45. This account of the "Catalogue Rebellion" is based on S. P. Hadley to C. F. P. Bancroft, Lowell, Massachusetts, 22 May 1878; Wolds Coburn to W. E. Park, Dedham, Massachusetts, 25 May 1878; and an undated fragment of a letter by W. H. Wells.
46. The Hadley-Bancroft letter above, note 45.
47. There is a copy of this petition, dated Andover, 13 July 1846, in the Phillips Academy Archives.
48. The Hadley-Bancroft letter above, note 45.
49. Ibid. There is a copy of the bogus catalogue in the Phillips Academy Archives.
50. There is a copy of the *Phillipiad* in the Phillips Academy Archives. It is eight pages in length.
51. For the 1867 Rebellion, see Rufus A. Bullock to C. M. Fuess, Boston, undated; and William T. Carter to the *Phillips Bulletin*, Newark, New Jersey, 10 May 1915.
52. The Bullock-Fuess letter above, note 51.
53. Ibid.
54. J. W. Hird to C. M. Fuess, Interlaken, Massachusetts, 16 July 1913.
55. Trustee Records, 586.

56. Taylor's Report to the Trustees, 1868.
57. This petition, dated Andover, 12 July 1865, and signed by James S. Eaton, Isaac Bridgeman, A. C. Barrows, and Joseph Kimball, is in the Phillips Academy Archives. In 1852 Henry Saville reported to a friend: "The Faculty at Yale college have been endeavoring to stir up a breeze for some time past against the directors of Phillips Academy, alleging as reasons for the aforesaid 'enunciations,' what every one must admit as truth—namely, as you well know, 'that the graduates of *this* Academy, tho' above par excellence in their thoroughness in "lingua Latinorum,"—yet are withal so miserably poor in Mathematics as a general thing that they are *barely* able to pass a *hardly* decent examination at college: this taunt has proved effectual in inciting 'Uncle' to do his duty; for we poor 'victims' are now forced from the increased length and '*depth*' of our lessons to *study some*, if not more." Henry M. Saville, *A Schoolboy's Letters of Seventy-seven Years Ago* (Boston, R. G. Badger, 1930), 76.
58. The Bullock-Fuess letter above, note 51.
59. George H. Taylor to "Edwards," Kinderhook Academy, 22 May 1878.
60. The Bullock-Fuess letter above, note 51.
61. See the School Catalogue, 1857, 21–22.
62. See the report of James S. Eaton to the Trustees, 31 July 1849.
63. See undated letter from J. S. Eaton to S. H. Taylor.
64. See Eaton's report to the Trustees, 1852.
65. There are two diaries and a substantial number of letters about Taylor's trip to Europe in the Phillips Academy Archives.
66. Trustee Records, 580.
67. See, for example, the School Catalogue, 1868, 21–22.
68. This material has been taken from a folder containing the annual reports of Taylor to the Trustees.
69. Undated Report of the Examining Committee. Apparently it was presented at the end of Osgood Johnson's administration.
70. Report of the Examining Committee, 8 April 1843.
71. Report of the Examining Committee, 4 April 1845.
72. Reports of the Examining Committee, 3 August 1852, and 2 August 1853.
73. Report of Examining Committee, 24 July 1855.
74. Report of the Examining Committee, 2 July 1859.
75. Trustee Records, 505, 525, 541, 553.
76. Ibid., 598, 497, 504, 505.
77. Ibid., 570, 571, 573.
78. Ibid., 534, 594–595.
79. Ibid., 573.
80. This statistical material has been taken from the School Catalogues of the Taylor period.
81. Rufus A. Bullock to C. M. Fuess, Boston, undated.
82. This material on college choice and occupation has been taken from various class books, reunion publications, and the like of the classes concerned.
83. See the undated "Laws of the Academic Commons."
84. See an undated, unsigned document in the Phillips Academy Archives.
85. From an undated letter by Horace Deming to his mother, reprinted in the *Phillips Bulletin*, (April 1965), 3.
86. James M. Read to "Mother," Andover, 5 January 1849.
87. This material is taken from a folder of mock publications in the Phillips Academy Archives.
88. William R. Stevens to "Mother," Andover, December 1847.

89. S. R. Humphrey to J. P. Humphrey, Andover, 23 November 1849.
90. See Jesse L. Moss, "Recollections of Phillips Academy and Andover in the 1860's," a typescript in the Phillips Academy Archives.
91. E. H. Laws to "Parents," Andover, 1 July 1838.
92. Saville, *A School Boy's Letters*, 55, 71.
93. William R. Stevens to "Mother," Andover, December, 1847.
94. George H. Cross, "A Farm Boy at the Academy Fifty Years Ago," *Phillips Bulletin* (April 1926), 26–30.
95. W. D. Morse, "Some Reminiscences," *Phillips Bulletin* (October 1913), 19–21.
96. William R. Stevens to "Mother," Andover, 5 January 1849.
97. Saville, *A School Boy's Letters*, 44.
98. Ibid., 82–83.
99. J. Farrar to parents, Andover, 8 July 1841.
1. This account of the 1865 Exhibition has been taken from my article in the *Andover Bulletin* (April 1965), 6–7. The material is based on the letters of Horace Deming.
2. Saville, *A School Boy's Letters*, 24.
3. William E. Soule to John M. Kemper, Seymour, Connecticut, 17 April 1958.
4. From a letter dated Andover, 3 May 1861, from Dennis Beach to "Mother," printed in the *Phillips Bulletin* (January 1927), 22–23
5. Taylor Report to the Trustees, 1862.
6. A. Eugene Nolen to C. M. Fuess, 25 July 1913.
7. Susanna E. Jackson, *Reminiscences of Andover* (Andover, The Andover Press, 1914), 15–17.
8. On Smith, see Claude M. Fuess, *Men of Andover* (New Haven, Yale University Press, 1928), 45–50. The boarding house on Main Street in which Smith wrote the song was later acquired by the School and christened "America House."
9. For Webster's visit to Andover, see C. M. Fuess in the *Phillips Bulletin* (April 1929), 27–33.
10. This account of Uncle Sam's death is taken from the Memorial Address delivered at his funeral by Professor Edwards A. Park. See *A Memorial of Samuel Harvey Taylor*, 49–51.

9. Cecil Bancroft's Academic Reforms

1. There is almost nothing on Tilton in the Phillips Academy Archives. Unless otherwise stated, the account of his Principalship is taken from Claude M. Fuess, *Old New England School* (Boston, Houghton Mifflin, 1917), 323–330.
2. Trustee Records, 603.
3. Ibid., 605.
4. See School Catalogues, 1867 and 1873.
5. See School Catalogue, 1873.
6. Trustee Records, 610.
7. Ibid., 609, 611.
8. Undated fragment of a letter from Charles S. Bird to C. M. Fuess.
9. This mock program is in a file of such programs in the Archives.
10. Trustee Records, 608.
11. There is no satisfactory biographical account of Bancroft. Most of the material on his life is contained in eulogies given at the time of his death. The best account of his early life was written by the Reverend C. C. Carpenter in the *Andover Townsman*, 11 October 1901. See also George D. Pettee, "In

Memoriam, etc." in *The School Review*, 10, 4 (April 1902), 257–269. For Bancroft genealogy see John K. Allen, "Thomas Bancroft of Dedham and Reading, Massachusetts, and Some of his Descendants," *New England Historical and Genealogical Register*, 95 (July 1941), 276–285.

12. Reverend Charles Perry Mills in his tribute to Bancroft given at the Eighth Biennial Reunion of the Alumni of Phillips Academy, held at the Hotel Vendome in Boston, 19 February 1902. Except where otherwise noted, quotations in this and the following paragraph are from this tribute. Mills had been a pupil of Bancroft's at Lookout Mountain. Some idea of Reverend Mills's prose may be gained from his opening statement: "That you may know how freely I break the alabaster box of my heart with all its fragrance at the mention of his cherished name, etc."

13. Reverend C. C. Carpenter in the *Andover Townsman*, 11 October 1901. Carpenter was Superintendent (Business Manager) of the Lookout Mountain School while Bancroft was Principal.

14. Walter L. Wright, Jr., in the *Dictionary of American Biography*, XVI, 1. The "opposition," it seems clear, was directed against the concept of Yankees coming down South to try to reform Southerners rather than against Bancroft himself.

15. For a more extended account of the Lookout Mountain School, see Robert S. Walker, *Lookout: The Story of a Mountain* (Kingsport, Tennessee, Southern Publishers, 1941), 153–168.

16. Pettee, "In Memoriam," 261.

17. Bancroft to Seth Sweetser, Bad Wittekind bei Halle, 10 April 1873. On the same day, Bancroft wrote his friend C. C. Carpenter of his excitement at the prospect of becoming Principal. He was a little apprehensive about getting along with Uncle Sam Taylor's son George, but generally spoke of "glorious work taxing me to my utmost." And he asked Carpenter for a favor: "see if you can buy Tilton's carpets."

18. Bancroft to Sweetzer, Bad Wittekind, 19 May 1873.

19. Writing in the *Andover Townsman*, 11 October 1901, the Reverend C. C. Carpenter spoke of Bancroft's "long name, whose initials often proved a discomfort to correspondents and printers."

20. See the Principal's Report, 1873–1874.

21. Noah Porter to Bancroft, New Haven, 1 June 1875.

22. W. A. Stearns to Bancroft, Amherst, 20 May 1875, 1 June 1875.

23. A. Harkness to Bancroft, Providence, 22 May 1875; J. L. Lincoln to Bancroft, Providence, 25 May 1875.

24. Bancroft's address was published in the *Proceedings of the University Convocation held at Albany, N.Y. July 7th, 8th and 9th, 1874*, 165–173.

25. President Eliot wrote: "How extraordinary seems the complete neglect of the English language and literature as elements of education in England and the United States till within years still very recent." Quoted in Corwn F. Palmer, "Cecil F. P. Bancroft," in *Education* (January 1902), 265. Dr. Bancroft had correspondence with President Eliot on the subject of Phillips Academy religious services and the amount of time devoted to various subjects. See Bancroft to Eliot, Andover, 23 November 1883; Bancroft to Secretary Taussig, Andover, 12 November 1880. Taussig was acting for Eliot in this instance. These letters are in the Harvard Archives.

26. Bancroft's Report to the Trustees, 1875.

27. Ibid., 1876.

28. Ibid., 1880.

29. Ibid., 1885.

30. Ibid., 1893.
31. These curricula have been taken from the School Catalogues, 1873 and 1900 respectively.
32. Graves' Reports to the Trustees, 1887, 1888.
33. See School Catalogues, 1884, 1886.
34. Graves' Report to the Trustees, 1890.
35. See School Catalogue, 1894.
36. Graves' Report to the Trustees, 1883.
37. See, for example, Trustee Records, II, 40.
38. Graves to Bancroft, Paris, 13 November 1888. In the same letter Graves speaks of purchasing some physics apparatus that is of "first quality."
39. Graves' Report to the Trustees, 1886, 1887.
40. In his Report to the Trustees for that year.
41. Trustee Records, II, 34. The sum appropriated for the laboratory was $4,000.
42. Graves' Reports to the Trustees, 1892, 1893.
43. These sample questions have been taken from a manuscript volume of English Department Examinations, 1871–1875.
44. *Phillipian*, 21 May 1881, 29 September 1883.
45. Ibid., 24 November 1883.
46. Ibid., 8 December 1883.
47. Ibid., 31 January and 19 May 1888.
48. Ibid., 11 April 1891.
49. Ibid., 9 December 1891, 27 January 1894, 8 January 1896.
50. Ibid., 31 January 1894.
51. See C. W. Eliot to Bancroft, Cambridge, 21 November 1883; L. R. Briggs to Bancroft, Cambridge, 13 December 1898.
52. See Perkins to Bancroft, Exeter, 16 April 1883.
53. See fourteen letters from Carter to Bancroft from 1885 to 1898.
54. MacKenzie to Bancroft, Lawrenceville, 1 January 1895, 19 May 1892.
55. Jones to Bancroft, Philadelphia, 25 November 1892.
56. Bancroft's Report to the Trustees, 1879.
57. See "Should the Amount of Time given to Languages in our Secondary Schools (as they are) be Diminished in order to Make Room for a more extended Course in Physics, Botany, and Chemistry?" in *Addresses and Proceedings of the International Congress of Education* (New York, 1894), 196–198. In writing this section on curricular change under Bancroft I wish to acknowledge the help I have received from a paper on the Phillips Academy curriculum written by Susan Lambiris of the Class of 1975, a former student of mine.
58. See John M. Kemper, "Phillips Academy at Andover: A National Public School" (the Newcomen Society, 1957), 23.
59. This dinner was held on 24 March 1886.
60. See, for example, Bancroft's Reports to the Trustees, 1878, 1879.
61. Minutes of Meeting of 18 November 1892.
62. Ibid., 2 December 1892.
63. Ibid., 9 March 1894.
64. Ibid., 16 November 1894.
65. Ibid., 20 April 1895.
66. Ibid., 28 February 1896.
67. Ibid., 23 April 1900.
68. Ibid., 30 April 1900.
69. Ibid., 14 May 1900.
70. Ibid., 17 January 1898.

71. Ibid., 20 May 1892.
72. Ibid., 2 December 1892, 24 February 1893.
73. Ibid., 9 May 1898.
74. Ibid., 10 June 1895, 8 May 1896, 26 April 1897.
75. Ibid., 9 February 1897.
76. At the Phillips Exeter Academy the development of Faculty power followed a very different pattern. In November, 1857, the Exeter Trustees accepted the report of a committee "that it is expedient to constitute the Instructors a Faculty" and after that date the Faculty gradually took over more and more power until they were conducting virtually all the daily business of the school. Under the School Constitution, which is very similar to Andover's, the Headmaster is given all the power to run the institution, but Faculty control has never been directly challenged by any of Exeter's Headmasters. See Myron R. Williams, *The Story of Phillips Exeter*, (Exeter, New Hampshire, Phillips Exeter Academy, 1957), 44–45.
77. Meeting of 26 February 1892.
78. Ibid., 19 January 1894.
79. Ibid., 23 March 1894.
80. Ibid., 9 May, 1893.
81. Ibid., 26 October 1894. For a full treatment of Phillips Academy athletics during this period, see the forthcoming volume by my colleague Fred H. Harrison.
82. See Bancroft's Reports to the Trustees, 1881, 1882.
83. Minutes of Meeting of 21 December 1895.
84. Ibid., 2 June 1893, 2 November 1895, 17 April 1896.
85. See folder of applications dated mostly 1894 in the Bancroft Correspondence.
86. These departures can be determined from Bancroft's Reports to the Trustees and from the School Catalogues for the appropriate years.
87. These terms of service can be determined from the appropriate School Catalogues.
88. For a brief account of Coy's career, see Fuess, *Old New England School*, 344, footnote.
89. See the *Phillipian*, 24 February 1883.
90. Presumably at Dr. Bancroft's urging, the Trustees were fairly generous in the granting of sabbatical leaves during this period. Some of these were with full salary, some with the difference between full salary and the cost of the replacement.
91. See Bancroft's Report to the Trustees, 1877.
92. See Coy's Report to the Trustees, 13 July 1889.
93. J. C. MacKenzie to Bancroft, Lawrenceville, 19 May 1892.
94. See Joseph Fairbanks, "The Administration of David Y. Comstock, 1896–1906" in *An Historical Sketch of St. Johnsbury Academy 1842–1922* (privately printed, n.d.), 78. Comstock left Hotchkiss after four years to become Headmaster of St. Johnsbury Academy.
95. See *Phillips Bulletin* (April 1920), 28.
96. For Churchill, see Charles C. Morgan, *Biographic Sketch of Prof. John Wesley Churchill* (Boston, n.d.); and *John Wesley Churchill*, printed in the Necrology of the Andover Theological Seminary for June, 1900.
97. This address, dated Cambridge, 7 April 1894, is in manuscript and has no title. It apparently was a very long one, for Bancroft jokes about it at the start of his speech.
98. Charles H. Forbes to Bancroft, Providence, 4 September 1893.
99. George H. Palmer to Bancroft, Cambridge, 5 February 1888.

10. The Centennial

1. For these actions, See Trustee Records, I, 616–617. This chapter, in somewhat abbreviated form, was read as a paper before the April 1976 meeting of the Massachusetts Historical Society and later published in the Society's *Proceedings*, 88 (1976), 35–59.

2. See the original of the letter from Professor Taylor to Dr. Bancroft, dated 28 March 1876. A copy was transcribed into Trustee Records, I, 619–20. According to the latest Treasurer's Report (1974), the Taylor fund had grown to $8,456.41.

3. Trustee Records, I, 616.

4. See the copy of the Centennial Tree-Planting program in the Phillips Academy Archives. The ode, by W. W. Fay, started out:

   > O land of heroes dead,
   > Full ten decades are fled,
   > Yet thou art young; etc.

   My guess is that the ode was sung to the tune of "America."

5. For these actions, see Trustee Records, I, 625.

6. For the actions of the Town Meeting, see *Town Records*, 4 March 1878. These records have been microfilmed and are on file at the Memorial Hall Library, Andover.

7. For these activities, see a printed volume in the Phillips Academy Archives containing the record of the Centennial, 7–10. Apparently those in charge of the celebration hoped to publish a printed record, but they got only as far as page proof. As a result this page-proof volume is the only one in existence. See a letter from the Riverside Press in Cambridge to Professor John W. Churchill, 30 September 1881, which speaks of the "Centennial book" being "at a stand-still" and asking payment for the work done thus far. There were, it seems, insufficient funds to complete the publication. This unique volume will be referred to throughout the rest of this chapter as *Centennial History*. The lists of subscribers to the Town of Andover Centennial Fund are in the Centennial records of the Phillips Academy treasurer.

8. There are several copies of the program of this concert in the Archives. Phillips Academy musical events in those days had their moments. The Senior Class Concert in 1880 featured Miss Ella Chamberlain, Solo Whistler. Miss Chamberlain, according to the program, whistled Planquette's "Chimes of Normandy" and selections from Offenbach's "Geneviève." The program for this memorable event is in Dr. Bancroft's scrapbook.

9. See John K. Allen, "Thomas Bancroft of Dedham and Reading, Mass., and Some of His Descendants," *New England Historical and Genealogical Register*, 95 (July 1941), 283. The Phillips Academy undergraduates sent the "centennial baby" a bouquet.

10. See Horace Scudder, "A Group of Classical Schools," *Harper's New Monthly Magazine*, 55 (September 1877), 562–570.

11. Copies of these articles are in a scrapbook kept by the Reverend C. C. Carpenter.

12. There are several copies of this circular in the Archives. The plan to publish a centennial catalogue of officers and students was never realized, though the Reverend C. C. Carpenter did a lot of work on the project. The Committee chose the dates in June, rather than the exact date of April 21, "as the engagements of many would prevent their attendance on that day, and because it was deemed unadvisable to appoint an open-air celebration at such an uncertain season of the year." *Centennial History*, 3.

13. See *Centennial History*, 3–6.

14. There are several copies of this circular in the Archives.
15. Copies of the invitations are in the Archives. The list of special guests is in *Centennial History*, 10–11. The invitations to the Japanese and Chinese Ministers of Education are indicative of Phillips Academy's growing interest in Oriental students, several of whom had been enrolled in the School in the 1870's. Among the Centennial records is a letter from Yung Wing to Professor Churchill, dated Hartford, 29 May 1878, expressing his regret at being unable to attend the celebration but promising to send "a few of my Chinese students" to the School the following year.
16. Eliot to Churchill, Cambridge, 24 May and 4 June 1878.
17. Fox to Churchill, Boston, 1 June 1878.
18. Hardy to Churchill, Boston, 25 May 1878.
19. An unidentified clipping in Dr. Bancroft's scrapbook gives a report dated Washington, 2 March 1878, to the effect that the Honorable George B. Loring had tendered Dr. Bancroft's invitation to President Hayes and that the President "appeared to be favorably inclined to an acceptance of the invitation." Henry Wadsworth Longfellow apparently did not bother to reply, nor did the Honorable Benjamin Franklin ("Spoons") Butler of Lowell. Butler must have had some interest in the Academy, for he had proposed founding a scholarship there the year before (Trustee Records, 621). At the Exeter Centennial five years later, Butler was to tangle with Charles W. Eliot of Harvard. See Myron R. Williams, *The Story of Phillips Exeter*, 61.
20. Boston *Daily Advertiser*, 6 June 1878.
21. Lawrence *American*, 7 June 1878. For an account of the founding of the B & M in Andover, see *Centennial History*, 11.
22. This estimate has been arrived at by noting the opening and closing times of the various exercises as reported in the newspapers.
23. *Centennial History*, 19.
24. For the program, see *Centennial History*, 13–14. According to the Boston *Daily Advertiser*, 6 June 1878, the music for the occasion was "furnished acceptably" by the Hatton Quartette.
25. Boston *Daily Advertiser*, 6 June 1878.
26. From a typewritten report entitled "The Centennial at Andover" by "H.S.T." It apparently first appeared in the *Industrial School Advocate*, but no date is given.
27. The speeches that accompanied the presentation of the portraits are printed in *Centennial History*, 27–42. Only the Tilton portrait was painted from life. Since the subjects of the other six were all dead, their portraits were either copies or were done from drawings or photographs. Three were done by Emily A. Means of Andover.
28. For an account of the presentation of the banner, see *Centennial History*, 19–20, 43–44. Mention of the undergraduate cheering is in the account of the Boston *Daily Advertiser*, 6 June 1878. In the report of the Centennial in the *Congregationalist*, 12 June 1878, the reporter comments on the cheering: "It is very much to be doubted whether *this* art of speaking be consistent with the constitutional foundation of the academy. It is to be hoped that the trustees will, before another centennial, look into this matter with open ears." I cannot determine whether this comment was simply churlish or whether the author was trying to be funny.
29. This description is in *Centennial History*, 20. My guess is that it was written by Professor Churchill, who appears to have been the editor of the volume. The *Lawrence American and Andover Advertiser*, 7 June 1878, estimates

730 : NOTES TO PAGES 260–272

the crowd for this occasion as "over three thousand." The locomotive headlights were lent by the Boston & Maine.

30. *Lawrence American,* 7 June 1878.

31. I have studied most of the material that the Reverend Park used in the preparation of his address and have nothing but admiration for his scholarship. In
the few places where my interpretation differs from his, the variation is,
I believe, due more to the different times in which we wrote than anything
else. The Reverend Park did let himself go at the close. He wound up saying: " 'Phillips School,' of 1778, flowing out of the sanctuary like the waters
of Ezekiel's vision, fed by many a tributary stream, widening from a little
rill to a mighty river, sending her pupils on to all parts of the earth, giving
verdure, life, and beauty to the land through which she passes, each alumnus
and each friend helps to swell her current and assists her now to sweep with
stronger tide and deeper volume into a new century of life." Even with this
peroration, I find it difficult to agree with the reporter for the *Congregationalist,* 12 June 1878, who spoke of the speech as "spicily seasoned."

32. *The Congregationalist,* 12 June 1878.

33. For the full record of the Wednesday evening ceremonies, see *Centennial History,* 46–103.

34. Ibid., 10.

35. For an account of the formation of the Alumni Association, see *Centennial
History,* 20–22.

36. *The Congregationalist,* 12 June 1878. The reporter signed himself "Moccasin."

37. *Peabody Press,* 19 June 1878, in a letter to the editor signed "Ship Rock."

38. Ibid. See also the *Cambridge Tribune,* 13 June 1878.

39. Reverend McKenzie's oration is printed in full in *Centennial History,* 105–137.

40. Since I am not competent to deal with poetry, I asked my colleague, Dr. Donald
Goodyear, Phillips Academy English Department, to write me an analysis
of Dr. Holmes's Centennial Poem, "The Schoolboy." The following paragraphs on the poem are from his pen.

41. *The Congregationalist,* 26 June 1878, printed extracts from Holmes's poem
with identifications of the persons mentioned in it. According to this account,
the favorite master referred to was the Reverend Samuel H. Stearns, who
died in 1837.

42. The New York *Examiner & Chronicle,* 13 June 1878, said of the poem: "It was
good, as everything of his is, but not so good as one might have expected."
The paper then quoted the lines:
> Ask not the grandeurs of a labored song
> But let my easy couplets slide along
and added: "And they slid along almost too easily."

43. The entire text of "The Schoolboy" is printed in *Centennial History,* 138–147.

44. The best accounts of the procession are in the Boston *Daily Advertiser,* 7 June
1878, and the Boston *Journal* of the same date.

45. This story is from an unidentified clipping in Dr. Bancroft's scrapbook.

46. There is a sample press badge in the Reverend C. C. Carpenter's scrapbook.

47. Boston *Daily Advertiser,* 7 June 1878.

48. Unless otherwise noted, the following account of the afternoon speeches has
been taken from *Centennial History,* 147–238.

49. Boston *Daily Advertiser,* 7 June 1878. The reporter said, "His way of telling
the exploits of old academy days was well relished,—the printed sheet
enabling those who had it to see the queer mixture set before them."

50. A cynic might wonder if the attempts of the Parks, *père et fils,* to place more
emphasis on the role of Eliphalet Pearson, the founder of the Theological

Seminary, than on that of Samuel Phillips, the founder of the Academy, were not designed to elevate the importance of the former, over the latter, institution.

51. A small notebook in the Centennial records indicates that by sometime in 1879, the full sum had been contributed. Most of the balance was contributed to establish the "Peter Smith Byers Endowment Fund," $20,000 by Peter Smith of Andover, a Trustee of the Academy, $10,000 by his brother, John Smith of Andover, and $10,000 by John Byers of New York, their nephew. When the contributions totaled close to $97,000, Trustee Alpheus Hardy made up the balance.

52. An unidentified clipping in Dr. Bancroft's scrapbook records this resolution. It was read at the next Town Meeting.

53. Trustee Record, I, 626. It is interesting to note that Dr. Bancroft capitalized educators and clergymen, but not the other professions.

54. From an unidentified clipping in Dr. Bancroft's scrapbook.

11. The Bancroft Years: Administration and Students

1. George D. Pettee estimated that Dr. Bancroft averaged twenty to forty letters a day and commented on the care he took to answer completely all queries about the School or a student. See Pettee's article on Bancroft in *The School Review* (April 1902), 264.
2. Mrs. S. F. Abbott to Bancroft, Andover, 13 August 1883.
3. William B. Graves to Bancroft, Andover, 8 July 1892.
4. See, for example, Trustee Records, II, 89, 95.
5. E. K. Alden to Bancroft, Boston, 22 June 1876.
6. S. Sweetser to Bancroft, Worcester, 24 June 1876.
7. Trustee Records, II, 25, 55, 95.
8. This movement is explained in an article in the *Phillipian*, 27 September 1893.
9. Bancroft's Report to the Trustees, 1879.
10. Ibid., 1882.
11. Ibid., 1893.
12. Mrs. Abbey to Bancroft, Kingston, 9 June 1898.
13. This communication is dated Andover, 7 February 1889.
14. Sarah Abbott to Bancroft, Andover, 30 May (?).
15. W. B. Dwight to Bancroft, Martha's Vineyard, 19 August 1890.
16. Mrs. Davis to Bancroft, Andover, undated and 25 October 1882.
17. Mrs. John Smith to Bancroft, Andover, May 1883.
18. Mrs. R. A. Tilton to Bancroft, Andover, 13 July 1883.
19. Faculty Meeting Minutes, 17 June 1896.
20. E. P. Reed to A. E. Stearns, Andover, undated.
21. Laura Watson to Bancroft, Andover, 2 November 1894, 29 February [?].
22. Philena McKeen to Bancroft, Andover, 14 September 1885.
23. N. H. Taylor to Bancroft, Andover, 11 May 1892.
24. T. H. Brown to Bancroft, Sioux Falls, South Dakota, 12 October 1891, 19 February 1892.
25. A. E. Clark to Bancroft, Chicago, 4 January 1892.
26. H. T. Proctor to George Pettee, New York, 2 January 1899.
27. Azel Ames to Bancroft, Marshfield, Massachusetts, 16 August 1888.
28. Quoted in Claude M. Fuess, *Old New England School* (Boston, Houghton Mifflin, 1917), 366.
29. Bancroft's Report to the Trustees, 1885.

30. Fuess, *Old New England School*, 367-369.
31. See *Andover Townsman*, 8 May, 15 May, and 22 May 1891.
32. See the *Phillipian*, 16 April 1892.
33. Ibid., 22 October 1892, summarizes the progress made on the various cottages.
34. *Masque*, 100.
35. Ibid.
36. See School Catalogue, 1898.
37. D. C. Wells to Bancroft, Brunswick, Maine, 15 April 1893.
38. See, for example, School Catalogue, 1897.
39. Trustee Records, II, 104-105; The *Phillipian*, 12 October 1898.
40. For the progress of this project see The *Phillipian*, 24 September 1898; 19 February, 5 March, 8 March 1902.
41. Trustee Records, II, 113.
42. Ibid., 117-123. For an account of the work of the Archaeology Department see below, 353-355, 611-615.
43. These statistics have been taken from the School Catalogues during the Bancroft years.
44. The *Phillipian*, 3 October 1891.
45. See Bancroft's Report to the Trustees, 1891.
46. Frederick A. Peterson, "Black Students at Phillips Academy," a study prepared by the Office of Research and Evaluation, 1969.
47. P. E. Saffold to Bancroft, Tuskegee, Alabama, 26 January 1895.
48. The *Phillipian*, 17 May 1884, 21 January 1899, 21 February 1900.
49. C. C. Miller to George Pettee, Meridian, Mississippi, 25 March 1899.
50. E. G. Burgess to Bancroft, no place, 11 April 1901. For a fuller account of Black students at Andover, see below ooo-ooo.
51. Walter M. Whitehill, "Portrait of a Chinese Diplomat, Sir Chentung Liang Cheng" (Boston, Boston Athenaeum, 1974).
52. See Dr. Bancroft's scrapbook, which has many clippings about the beheading business.
53. See C. M. Folsom to Bancroft, Hampton, Virginia, 12 March 1895.
54. D. J. O'Mahoney to George Pettee, Andover, October 1898.
55. See School Catalogue, 1900.
56. This material has been taken from "Statistics of the Class of 'Eighty-Three in Phillips Academy." This particular class had an abnormally large number of Episcopalians.
57. The material on the Class of 1890 is taken from *A Class Report of the Class of Phillips Academy, Andover, Massachusetts, 1890* (Cambridge, 1920).
58. (Mayhew Publishing Company, Boston, 1908.)
59. Perrin, *My Three Years at Andover*, 115-116.
60. Henry L. Stimson, *On Active Service in Peace and War* (New York, Harper, 1947), xiii-xiv.
61. The *Phillipian*, 1 May 1880.
62. Ibid., 23 October 1880.
63. Ibid., 6 November 1880.
64. Ibid., 22 November 1884.
65. Ibid., 7 March 1885.
66. Ibid., 13 October, 15 November 1888.
67. Ibid., 27 February, 6 March 1889.
68. Ibid., 9 November 1892.
69. Ibid., 20 April, 27 April 1898.
70. Ibid., 2 February 1901.
71. Ibid., 13 March 1880.

72. Bancroft's Reports to the Trustees, 1874, 1880.
73. The *Phillipian*, 18 June 1881.
74. Ibid., 22 October 1881.
75. Ibid., 28 January 1882.
76. Ibid., 30 September 1882.
77. Ibid., 12 February 1890, 4 March 1893.
78. Ibid., 20 January 1894.
79. For a full discussion of the development of an athletic program during this period, see the forthcoming volume on Andover Athletics written by my colleague Fred H. Harrison.
80. The *Phillipian*, 8 February 1879.
81. Ibid., 10 March 1883.
82. Ibid., 22 October 1890.
83. Ibid., 4 March 1891.
84. For these organizations see *Pot Pourri* , 1895.
85. Ibid.
86. The material in this paragraph is taken from S. H. Dana, "Historical Reminscences of the Society of Inquiry" (1908), an address delivered at the seventy-fifth anniversary of the Society. See also Allan V. Heely, "A Hundred Years of 'Inquiry' " (Andover Press, 1933).
87. For an account of these proceedings see *Semi-Centennial of the Philomathean Society* (Hyde Park, Massachusetts, privately printed, 1875).
88. There are several mock trial programs in the School Archives.
89. The *Phillipian*, 13 September 1879, 10 February 1883.
90. See Dudley Fitts, "Editorial Reflections," *Mirror* (February 1961), 4–5.
91. The *Phillipian*, 24 May 1879, 25 October 1879.
92. Ibid., 17 April and 15 May 1880.
93. Ibid., 25 February 1882, 15 September 1883.
94. Ibid., 29 February 1888, 30 April 1892.
95. Ibid., 13 April 1895.
96. See, for example, ibid., 29 January 1881, 12 March 1881.
97. Ibid., 29 May 1880, 6 December 1879.
98. Ibid., 4 December 1880.
99. Ibid., 12 March 1881.
1. Ibid., 10 June 1882, 22 March 1887.
2. Ibid., 25 May 1889, 31 January 1880.
3. Ibid., 20 September 1886.
4. Ibid., 25 November 1882, 26 September 1888.
5. Ibid., 3 November and 20 June 1888.
6. See above, 293.
7. For the development of Greek-letter fraternities, see Frederick Rudolph, *The American College and University* (New York, Random House, 1962), 144–150.
8. See George W. Pierson, *Yale College, An Educational History, 1871–1921.* (New Haven, Yale University Press, 1952), 35–36.
9. The appearance of the various societies can be traced in the Faculty Meeting Minutes for this period. Two that did not survive were Sphinx Head and S.A.O.
10. See Faculty Meeting Minutes for this period. At nearly every meeting a boy was either approved or disapproved for membership in a society.
11. Quoted in Fuess, *Old New England School*, 379.
12. Quoted in ibid., 384.
13. Principal Bancroft was always going to bat for boys who got into trouble. When

he interceded for a boy who was guilty of two embezzlements, however, United State Attorney Sherman Hoar thought he was going too far. "You will pardon me I feel sure if I say that where a young man has confessed to two embezzlements, six months apart, in regard to one of which he has assumed a false name, neither embezzlement being occasioned by any poverty in his own family, and at times when he was posing before the community as the leader in Christian meetings, and as an example for the young people who surrounded him, I am far from considering that there's anything in his previous record which entitles him to much mercy." Hoar to Bancroft, Boston, 21 May 1895.

14. C. F. P. Bancroft, *The Guilt of Profanity* (Bellefonte, Pennsylvania, n.d.).
15. A. E. Stearns to Mabel Stearns, Andover, 9 March 1890. Fortunately for Al, he was living with his uncle, Principal Bancroft, and thus avoided having his room "stacked."
16. The preceding material comes from the manuscript of his speech to the undergraduates at the time of the "stacking" incident.
17. See the *Phillipian*, 19 March 1890.
18. Ibid., 8, 15 March 1890. One of the most tragic episodes of the Bancroft era took place in 1881, when twin boys who were students at Phillips Academy attempted to rob a house in North Andover. The owner shot one of them dead, and the other was arrested and jailed. See *Lawrence American and Andover Advertiser*, 15 April 1881.
19. E. W. Bucknell to Bancroft, New York, 19 February 1892.
20. B. H. Burt to Bancroft, Rutland, 1 September 1879.
21. S. R. Carter to Bancroft, East Orange, New Jersey, 11 September 1894.
22. G. H. Christian to Bancroft, Minneapolis, 9 June 1891.
23. W. H. Coleman to Bancroft, Brooklyn, 11 January, 15 February 1893.
24. W. H. Cornwell to Bancroft, Honolulu, 26 August 1892.
25. D. McKinnor to Bancroft, Eau Claire, Wisconsin, 29 October 1894.
26. E. H. Darling to Bancroft, Boston, 20 May 1881.
27. G. P. Davis to Bancroft, Hartford, 5 January 1895.
28. J. I. Dowsett to Bancroft, Honolulu, 12 January 1893.
29. Mrs. A. DuPont to Bancroft, Wilmington, Delaware, 17 August 1879.
30. L. W. Emerson to Bancroft, New York, 31 December 1889.
31. F. H. Pierce to Bancroft, undated.
32. A. B. Franklin to Bancroft, Boston, 2 April 1895.
33. J. H. Fry to Pettee, Detroit, Michigan, 18 March 1899.
34. B. M. Fullerton to Bancroft, Waltham, Massachusetts, 10 October 1882.
35. L. V. Garis to Bancroft, Cincinnati, Ohio, 12 February 1885.
36. Mrs. L. L. Haworth to Bancroft, Decatur, Illinois, 16 December 1882.
37. John N. Cole, "Dr. Bancroft—the Citizen," *Andover Townsman*, 11 October 1901.
38. C. F. P. Bancroft, "An Address at the First Commencement of Yankton College, June 8th 1887" (Yankton, Dakota).
39. N. T. Allen to Bancroft, West Newton, Massachusetts, 6 June 1882.
40. B. C. Auten to Bancroft, Cambridge, Massachusetts, 5 February 1896.
41. M. C. Jordan to Bancroft, Albany, 16 June 1890.
42. A. Comstock to Bancroft, New York, 17 October 1882.
43. F. A. Walker to Bancroft, Boston, 22 January 1895.
44. I. K. Funk to Bancroft, New York, 13 December 1895. Funk addressed the letter "Dear Madam—"
45. M. H. Williams to Bancroft, Philadelphia, 17 January, 5 October 1880.
46. G. H. Richter & Co. to Bancroft, Boston, 1 May 1897.

47. M. T. Stevens to Bancroft, Washington, D.C., 27 March 1893.
48. Anonymous letter, undated.
49. P. L. Horne to Bancroft, South Byfield, Massachusetts, 29 July 1898.
50. V. B. Caldwell to Pettee, Omaha, Nebraska, 4 June 1895.
51. E. Cutter to Bancroft, West Falmouth, Massachusetts, 7 September 1899.
52. Trustee Records, II, 104, 129.
53. For the funeral see *Andover Townsman*, 11 October 1901, and the *Phillipian*, 9 October 1901.
54. Perrin, *My There Years at Andover*, 114.
55. The *Phillipian*, 9 October 1901.
56. George T. Eaton, *Andover Townsman*, 11 October 1901.
57. Trustee Records, II, 132–133.

12. Alfred E. Stearns: A Strong Start

1. Trustee Records, II, 131, 133.
2. The judge's report is in the Ropes folder in the Andover Vertical File, Oliver Wendell Holmes Library.
3. This material on Ropes has been taken from an article in the *Andover Townsman*, 21 February 1902. See also the *Phillipian*, 15 February 1902.
4. A copy of the Ropes letter is in *Trustee Records*, II, 138–140.
5. Ibid., 142.
6. Ibid., 147, 179. For a letter on the subject of his election as Principal, see below, 324.
7. For Al Stearns's ancestry, see Claude M. Fuess, "Alfred Ernest Stearns," *Phillips Bulletin* (April 1933), 13. For the background of the move to Amherst, A. E. Stearns, *An Amherst Boyhood* (Amherst, Amherst College, 1946), 4–8.
8. Stearns, *An Amherst Boyhood*, 11–35.
9. Ibid., 46–54.
10. A. E. Stearns to Mabel Stearns, Andover, 21 November 1886.
11. Ibid., 15 May 1887.
12. Ibid., 2 October 1887.
13. John T. Brady in an article on Al Stearns that appeared in the Boston *Post*, 29 January 1933.
14. A. E. Stearns to Mabel Stearns, Andover, 23 March, 26 May 1890.
15. Ibid., 14 November 1886.
16. Ibid., 22 May 1887.
17. Ibid., 10 June 1888, 9 June 1889.
18. John T. Brady, Boston *Post*, 29 January 1933.
19. A. E. Stearns to Mabel Stearns, Andover, 1 June 1890.
20. Ibid., 16 January 1887.
21. Ibid., 30 January, 19 February 1887.
22. Ibid., 20 March 1887.
23. Ibid., 13 April 1890.
24. Ibid., 18 May 1890.
25. Ibid., 22 June 1890.
26. Ibid., 23 January 1887, 15 January 1888.
27. Ibid., 22 January 1888.
28. Ibid., 2 February 1890.
29. Ibid., 12 December 1886.
30. John T. Brady, Boston *Post*, 29 January 1933.

31. Ibid.
32. Stearns, *An Amherst Boyhood*, 79–80.
33. Ibid., 87–88.
34. For a charming account of Davis, ibid., 55–60.
35. Ibid., 104–106, 109–115.
36. Ibid., 141–154.
37. Ibid., 158–159.
38. Brady Boston *Post*, 5 February 1933.
39. M. F. Sweeney, *Mike Sweeney of the Hill* (New York, G. P. Putnam, 1940), 84–85.
40. Brady, Boston *Post*, 5 February 1933.
41. A. E. Stearns to Mary Stearns, Andover, 24 May 1903.
42. Ibid., 17 November 1903.
43. Ibid., 30 November, 5 December 1903. What action Al took is not recorded.
44. Ibid., 3 January 1904.
45. Ibid., 15 January 1904.
46. Ibid., 29 January 1904.
47. Ibid., 2 March 1904.
48. Ibid., 16 June 1904.
49. Ibid., 19 June 1904.
50. Ibid., 7 July 1904.
51. Ibid., 5, 29 September 1904.
52. Ibid., 8 September 1904.
53. Ibid., 25 September 1904.
54. Ibid., 10 October 1904.
55. Ibid., 21 October 1904.
56. Ibid., 16, 30 November 1904, 4 December 1904.
57. After his retirement Al Stearns wrote some twenty-odd short chapters about his experiences as a headmaster that were apparently intended for eventual publication. The book of reminiscences never did get published, however. This account of the "Princeton Cribbing Case" is based on one of these chapters, which will from now on be referred to as Manuscript Reminiscences. The School and I owe Al's daughter Marjorie Stearns a great debt of gratitude for giving this material to the Phillips Academy Archives.
58. Stearns, Manuscript Reminiscences, "Landlady Period," and "Boarding House Problems."
59. Ibid., "Pomp's Pond Parties."
60. Ibid., "Hazing Party."
61. Ibid., "Commons Glass Breaking."
62. Ibid., "Fire Alarm Case."
63. Ibid., "Boy Shot by Mate."
64. Ibid., "Mailbox Episode."
65. Ibid., "Pomp's Pond Parties."
66. A. E. Stearns, "Education—Old and New," *Phillips Bulletin* (October 1924), 8.
67. Boston *Herald*, 16 November 1949.
68. Olds to Stearns, Amherst, 23 March 1926.
69. Stearns to Olds, Andover, 26 March 1926. In presenting the material on the last three pages I have gained material assistance from a paper on Al Stearns written by Stephen Sullivan, '73, when he was a student in my seminar on the History of Phillips Academy.
70. Stearns to Headmaster William Mann Irvine of Mercersburg Academy, Andover, 30 September 1927.
71. Stearns, *The Challenge of Youth* (Boston, W. A. Wilde, 1923), 28. In the back

of the book the publishers advertised Frank H. Cheley's *The Job of Being a Dad*, and also included a one-hundred-point quiz by which the reader could rate himself on whether he was being a "Real Dad."

72. Ibid., 96.
73. Ibid., 128.
74. Ibid., 132.
75. Ibid., 180.
76. D. Brewer Eddy to Stearns, Boston, 24 September 1926.
77. Stearns to Brewer Eddy, Andover, 27 September 1926.
78. Stearns to Brewer Eddy, Andover, 20 October 1926.
79. Rupert Hughes to Stearns, Los Angeles, 20 June 1931.
80. I wish to acknowledge the help I have received from a paper on the Bernard Allen case written by Robert Emmet Kelly, '64, a student of mine in the American History course. I have also received a great deal of useful information from Allen's nephew, Philip K. Allen, '29.
81. Stearns to Allen, Andover, 12 April 1911.
82. For the 1919 Strike see Donald B. Cole, *Immigrant City, Lawrence, Massachusetts, 1845–1921* (Chapel Hill, University of North Carolina Press, 1963), 200–202.
83. Philip R. Allen to Claude M. Fuess, Boston, 31 October 1938.
84. Allen to Trustees of Phillips Academy, Cheshire, Connecticut, 27 October 1938.
85. The Lawrence *Eagle-Tribune*, 17 February 1919.
86. New York *Times*, 21 February 1919.
87. Frank R. Shipman to Stearns, Andover, 22 February 1919.
88. Macdonald to Stearns, Lawrence, 17 February 1919.
89. Stearns to Macdonald, Andover, 18 February 1919.
90. Bishop to Stearns, Newton Center, 21 February 1919.
91. Allen to Trustees of Phillips Academy, Cheshire, 27 October 1938.
92. Philip R. Allen to Claude M. Fuess, Walpole, 31 October 1938.
93. *Phillips Bulletin* (July 1919), 5–6.
94. Stearns to Allen, Andover, 21 March 1919.
95. Statement of E. H. Sturtevant, New Haven, 24 August 1938.
96. Allen to Trustees, Cheshire, 27 October 1938.
97. Trustees to Allen, Andover, 19 November 1938.
98. For this episode see Henry A. Yeomans, *Abbott Lawrence Lowell, 1856–1943* (Cambridge, Harvard University Press, 1948), 316–317.
99. Stearns to Drinkwater, Andover, 26 July 1928.
1. Alexander L. Jackson to Stearns, Chicago, 10 November 1927. See also Stearns to Jackson, Andover, 16 November 1927.
2. Emily A. Nichols to Stearns, Cambridge, 18 September 1930; Stearns to Nichols, Andover, 29 September 1930.
3. The material in this paragraph has been taken from A. E. Stearns, "Andover and China," *Phillips Bulletin* (October 1920), 6–7. See also Stearns, "Manuscript Reminiscences," "Chinese."
4. Robert E. Chandler to Edward H. Chandler, Tientsin, 1 July 1920. See also C. K. Sun to Stearns, Tientsin, 7 August 1920.
5. Stearns to Sun, Andover, 5 November 1920.
6. M. T. Liang to Stearns, Tientsin, 25 July 1920. Liang was an official at Tsing Hua College.
7. The reports were on subjects taken in the Chinese Department and the Western Department. The list of books read included other subjects as well as English.
8. Stearns to M. T. Liang, Andover, 13 December 1920.

9. Sun to Stearns, Tientsin, 26 December 1920.
10. Stearns to Liang, Andover, 8 February 1921.
11. Sun to Stearns, Tientsin, 7 February 1921.
12. Stearns to Liang, Andover, 24 June 1921.
13. Lin to Liang, Tientsin, 16 May 1921.
14. Sun to Stearns, Tientsin, 10 August 1921.
15. Sun to Stearns, Tientsin, 27 January 1922; Stearns to Sun, Andover, 19 April 1922.
16. Stearns to Sun, Andover, 14 April and 25 June 1923.
17. Sun to Stearns, Tientsin, 4 December 1923. Mary also took up the violin for a while.
18. Stearns to Sun, Andover, 10 January 1924.
19. Statistical material from *Who's Who in America*, the rest supplied by Marjorie Stearns.
20. The writer well remembers his first night in Andover Cottage when there was a rap on the door and there, to his amazement, was Al Stearns, making sure that he was getting settled all right.
21. John Batten, '31, to writer, Racine, Wisconsin, 4 August 1975.
22. Henry F. Howe, '22, to writer, Chicago, 21 July 1975.

13. Growth of the Plant

1. On Sawyer see Claude M. Fuess, *Phillips Bulletin* (October 1939), 12–13.
2. Trustee Records, II, 137.
3. Ibid., 146.
4. Ibid., 173.
5. Stearns, Manuscript Reminiscences, "Academy Building Unsafe."
6. Ibid., "1900 to 1912," 7–8.
7. Trustee Records, II, 117–121.
8. Ibid., 123.
9. See a copy of the dedication program in the Phillips Academy Archives. It is interesting to note that Professor Putnam was the man who had insulted Peabody earlier, thus causing him to change his plans for establishing an archaeological museum.
10. On the early history of the Department of Archaeology, see Warren K. Moorehead in the *Phillips Bulletin* (April 1938), 6–11; and John S. Barss, ibid. (April 1934), 13–15.
11. *General Catalogue of the Theological Seminary, Andover, Massachusetts, 1808–1908* (Boston, n.d), 497–504.
12. Henry K. Rowe, *History of the Andover Theological Seminary* (Newton, 1933), 187.
13. Trustee Records, II, 134, 141, 147.
14. Rowe, *History*, 188.
15. Trustee Records, II, 229–230. In the Eliot Papers, Harvard University Archives, there is a substantial amount of material on the negotiations leading to the merger.
16. Trustee Records, II, 235–236.
17. Ibid., 242–243.
18. Theodore R. Sizer, *The Age of the Academies* (New York, Teachers College, Columbia University, 1964), 88. See also Appendix.
19. Rowe, *History*, 188–192.

20. Stearns, Manuscript Reminiscences, "1900 to 1912," 9–10.
21. The Massachusetts Act is copied in Trustee Records, II, 262–263. The petition of the Trustees to the Legislature is also included.
22. Stearns, Manuscript Reminiscences, "1900 to 1912," 10.
23. Trustee Records, II, 266.
24. Ibid., 259, 266, 275, 277.
25. Ibid., 270, 277, 285–290.
26. The *Phillips Bulletin* (September 1908), 1; (January 1909), 1–2.
27. Ibid. (April 1909), 2.
28. Ibid. (September 1909), 10.
29. Stearns, Manuscript Reminiscences, "Piel and du Pont."
30. Stearns, Manuscript Reminiscences, "1900 to 1912," 5–7.
31. The *Phillips Bulletin* (September 1910), 11–12; (January 1911), 5.
32. Ibid. (April 1911), 5.
33. Ibid. (April 1912), 6; (April 1913), 18.
34. Trustee Records, II, 324, 333.
35. Stearns, Manuscript Reminiscences, "1900 to 1912," 4.
36. Frederic W. H. Stott, "How Andover Cares for its Younger Boys," the *Phillips Bulletin* (January 1936), 11–18.
37. Stearns, Manuscript Reminiscences, "1900 to 1912," 1–4.
38. On the pool see The *Phillips Bulletin* (April 1910), 8; (January 1911), 5; (July 1911), 13–14; (January 1912), 5. The last article includes a lengthy description of the pumps, filters, and other mechanical equipment that had been provided.
39. There is a harrowing description of a student dying in his dormitory in Herbert D. War, *The New Senior at Andover* (Boston, 1891), 166–182.
40. Stearns, Manuscript Reminiscences, "Sickness."
41. Trustee Records, II, 416, 447.
42. Ibid., II, 478, 482. See also the *Phillips Bulletin* (July 1921), 7–8.
43. This account of the drive is taken from Claude M. Fuess, *Independent Schoolmaster* (Boston, 1952), 138–144.
44. Trustee Records, II, 492, 500.
45. Stearns, Manuscript Reminiscences, "1900 to 1912," 11–13.
46. Trustee Records, II, 517–518.
47. Fuess, *Independent Schoolmaster*, 145.
48. See Sally Slade Warner, "The Andover Carillon," to appear in the *Bulletin* of the Guild of Carilloneurs of America. The carillon concerts were not always appreciated by the undergraduates. Dr. Carl F. Pfatteicher, the Musical Director, used to usher in Easter by playing the bells at dawn. One year a group of undergraduates, resentful of being roused from their slumber, managed to lock Pfatteicher in the tower so that he missed the Easter service in the chapel. Apparently this hurt his feelings so much that he seldom played the bells after that.
49. The *Phillips Bulletin* (January 1924), 2.
50. Ibid. (April 1922), 16–18.
51. Ibid. (October 1922), 16–17.
52. Ibid (July 1922), 35; (October 1924), 27.
53. There is a substantial amount of Cochran correspondence in the Phillips Academy Archives, mostly letters to his friend, Treasurer James Sawyer. There is also some straight biographical data. The best short account of the man is in Fuess, *Independent Schoolmaster*, 148–167. Two papers written by students in my seminar have also been useful: William H. Gifford, "Thomas

Cochran: A Great Vision" (1973); and Louis B. Harding, "Thomas Cochran as Progenitor of Phillips Academy, Andover."

54. Cochran to Bancroft, St. Paul, Minnesota, 6 July 1893.
55. Cochran to Stearns, New York, 21 November 1916.
56. Ibid., 24 November 1916.
57. "Contributions from Mr. Cochran," 1 May 1933.
58. Fuess, *Independent Schoolmaster*, 148–149.
59. Cochran later tried to have a building named for John Hancock, who had signed the School's Act of Incorporation, but was thwarted in this plan by Professor Ropes, who pointed out that Hancock had embezzled some of Harvard's funds and thus was not worthy of recognition. Fuess, *Independent Schoolmaster*, 153.
60. Quoted in Fuess, *Independent Schoolmaster*, 150–151.
61. Ibid., 160.
62. McCord to Sawyer, n.p., May [?] 1927.
63. Cochran to Sawyer, New York, 10 June 1927.
64. Cochran to Hopper, New York, 30 January 1930.
65. Cochran to Sawyer, New York, 31 January 1929.
66. Ibid., 15 April 1930.
67. Ibid., 25 October 1923.
68. Ibid., 18 July 1928.
69. Sawyer to Cochran, Andover, 26 March 1928; Cochran to Sawyer, New York, 29 March 1928.
70. Cochran to Sawyer, New York, 23 January 1928.
71. Ibid., 10 January 1927.
72. Cochran to Hopper, New York, 10 January 1928.
73. Cochran to Sawyer, New York, 16 July 1927.
74. Ibid., 20 July 1927.
75. Trustee Records, III, 77, 85, 135, 199–200.
76. Ibid., 56–57.
77. Ibid., 64–66.
78. Cochran to Sawyer, New York, 10 June 1927.
79. Trustee Records, III, 100.
80. Ibid., 69.
81. Ibid., 83–84. See also the correspondence among Alfred Ripley, James Sawyer, and James Harvey Ropes in January 1927, on this subject.
82. Though Samuel Phillips Hall was built before Cochran became really active in Andover affairs, he contributed to it as well. He wrote Jim Sawyer of a small colonial church on Long Island "in the steeple of which is a clock that faces four ways. The faces of this clock are blue. Behind these faces at night there shines a light and creates a beautiful pale blue effulgence so that those gazing at the clock see 'a pale blue moon.' . . . . The whole effect is quite romantic and alluring." Nothing would do but that Phillips Academy should have a similar clock. Originally it was thought that it would be in the new chapel, but the decision was finally made to put it in Sam Phillips Hall. See Cochran to Sawyer, Westbury, Long Island, dated only "Sunday."
83. Cochran to Sawyer, New York, 15 July 1927. For many years this model was housed in the Trustee Room.
84. Trustee Records, III, 92–93.
85. An attempt was made to get Justice Oliver Wendell Holmes, Jr., to attend the dedication of the library that was named for his father, but though he apparently took a drive through Andover the previous summer, the octogenarian jurist declined the invitation.

86. The writer participated in this exercise and found it a most exhilarating experience.
87. Fuess, *Independent Schoolmaster*, 152.
88. For Cochran's letter of gift, see Trustee Records, III, 243–249.
89. Cochran Memorandum, undated, but probably July 1929.
90. See Sawyer to Elias Bishop, Andover, 14 August 1929; Cochran to Sawyer, 30 July 1929.
91. The Cochran Memorandum above, note 89.
92. Cochran to Sawyer, New York, 30 July 1929.
93. Sawyer to Cochran, Andover, 1 February 1929.
94. Interview with Dick Hoyer, 7 March 1977. Unless otherwise noted, material on the early days of the Sanctuary was obtained from this interview.
95. Claude M. Fuess, "The Sanctuary," the *Phillips Bulletin* (October 1931), 7–8.
96. Trustee Records, III, 216.
97. The Academy continues to conduct a modest program in the breeding of quail.
98. The material in this paragraph has been taken from an editorial in the *Phillips Bulletin* (April 1930) entitled "The New Andover Cut-Off," 3–4; and from Fuess, *Independent Schoolmaster*, 154–155.
99. Trustee Records, III, 97–98.
1. Ibid., 133–134.
2. Ibid., 105.
3. Ibid., 197.
4. Fuess, *Independent Schoolmaster*, 166.
5. One reason for moving the armillary sphere was to get it further away from the center of undergraduate activity. The writer well remembers going to chapel just after the sphere had been installed and finding the figures in it decked out with derby hats, brassieres, Andover sweaters, and other disrespectful garments.
6. Trustee Records, III, 275. Cochran offered to contribute $600,000 for this building.
7. Stearns to Cochran, Andover, 22 October 1930.
8. Trustee Records, III, 332–333.
9. Ibid., 330–331. A hint of financial difficulties appears in a letter Cochran wrote Sawyer, 2 March 1931, in which he says he can send $20,000 for the Addison Gallery but does not wish to do so unless the money will actually be spent.
10. Fuess, *Independent Schoolmaster*, 165–167.
11. Cochran to Stevens, New York, 29 December 1927.
12. Sawyer to Cochran, Andover, 28 November 1927.

14. The Golden Twenties

1. The title of the head of the School was changed from "Principal" to "Headmaster" in 1926. I can find no record of the Trustee vote, however.
2. Trustee Records, II, 410.
3. Ibid., 418, 420. See also *Phillips Bulletin* (April 1916), 30.
4. The *Phillips Bulletin* (January 1915), 34; (October 1915), 30; (April 1916), 25–27.
5. Ibid. (April 1915), 22.
6. Ibid. (October 1915), 30.
7. Ibid. (July 1917), 3.
8. This account of the military training program has been taken from ibid. (January 1918), 10–11.
9. There will be no specific attribution for this and the following quotes from

alumni in this chapter. For a list of the alumni who have contributed to
this volume see above xx–xxii.

10. See Stearns, Manuscript Reminiscences, "Hearst."
11. Trustee Records, II, 476.
12. See A. E. Stearns, "The Trustees and the Principal," the *Phillips Bulletin*
   (April 1916), 9–10.
13. Trustee Records, II, 103.
14. Ibid., 136.
15. Ibid., 114.
16. Ibid., 266–267.
17. Testimony of Bartlett H. Hayes, Jr. to the writer.
18. Claude M. Fuess, "Going Out to the Forbes," *Phillips Bulletin* (October 1934),
   6. This whole article is a charming study of Charlie Forbes and his wife.
19. Ibid., 4–8.
20. Charles D. Brodhead, '25, "Forsan et Haec Olim Meminisse Iuvabit," *Andover
   Bulletin* (February 1968), 7.
21. Alston H. Chase in the *Phillips Bulletin* (July 1940), 8.
22. See the *Pot Pourri* (yearbook) for these years; a regular feature was a senior
   poll of the Faculty.
23. John U. Monro, '30, "Andover Personalities," in *In My Time*, ed. Claude M.
   Fuess (Andover, 1959), 74–75.
24. Ibid., 72–73.
25. Samuel C. Vail, '12, "Horace M. Poynter, '96," *Andover Bulletin* (Spring
   1975), 18.
26. See, for example, the School Catalogue for 1901, 26–39.
27. See *Phillipian*, 1 November 1924.
28. Interview with Roscoe E. Dake, 30 July 1975.
29. Ibid. See also interview with John S. Barss, 6 April 1975.
30. See School Catalogues for these years.
31. Most of this statistical material has been taken from the School Catalogues for
   the various years cited. The material on occupations has been taken from
   the Alumni Catalogue and from reunion records.
32. *The Blue Book* (rule book) for 1925–26, 19–21.
33. On the Bogart case I wish to acknowledge the help I received from a paper
   entitled "Bogart at Andover: The Facts and the Fiction" written by Arthur
   Winter, '73, a student in my seminar on Phillips Academy history.
34. Bogart to Stearns, New York, 30 January 1917, 9 February 1917.
35. Arthur Winter interview with Guy Forbush, French teacher, 20 May 1973.
36. A classmate, Charles Yardley Chittick, quoted in Joe Hyams, *Bogie* (New York,
   New American Library, 1966), 29.
37. Bogart to Stearns, New York, 18 February 1918.
38. For a fuller treatment of this riot, see my "A Documentary History of the
   Great May Day Riot of 1930," in Fuess, ed., *In My Time*, 76–83.
39. The material on these extra-curricular activities has been taken from *Pot
   Pourri*, 1928.
40. *Phillipian*, 25 May 1921.
41. Ibid., 28 September 1927.
42. Ibid., 21 January 1928.
43. Ibid., 26 October 1929.
44. Ibid., 1 October 1930.
45. Ibid., 13 May 1931.
46. Ibid., 4 February 1922.

47. Ibid., 9 February 1924.
48. Ibid., 15 October 1924.
49. Ibid., 11 February 1925.
50. Ibid., 5 February 1930.
51. The *Mirror*, December 1929.
52. The *Pot Pourri* (1928), 178–188.
53. See the manuscript volume "A Diary of George Washington Hall," which lists entertainment from 1926 to 1946.
54. See the chapter on Miss Bailey in Susan Lloyd's forthcoming history of Abbot.
55. The Glee Club used to have concerts, followed by dances, with both Bradford and Rogers Hall, but never with Abbot. An alumnus remembers a Glee Club dance at Rogers Hall where the boys and girls were paired off, more or less according to height, for the dance. His partner's opening gambit was, "The Headmistress told us this morning that we all had to wear brassieres to the dance but I haven't got one on." He is still trying to figure out the correct reply to that one.
56. Both Theodore Roosevelt and William Howard Taft visited the School in 1913, the former to speak at his son Archie's graduation, the latter to speak at Founder's Day, but neither was in office at the time. See the *Phillips Bulletin* (July 1913), 21–22; (January 1914), 29–31.
57. Trustee Records, III, 51.
58. Ibid., 88.
59. Ibid., 95.
60. For these Committees see the *Phillips Bulletin* (October 1928), 23–25.
61. Ibid., 10.
62. Stearns to Clark, Andover, 31 October 1927.
63. Stearns to Frank Stearns, Andover, 12 December 1927.
64. Cochran to Stearns, New York, 8 December 1927.
65. Stearns to Clark, Andover, 16 April 1928.
66. Clark to Stearns, Washington, 11 April 1928.
67. Stearns to Clark, Andover, 24 April 1928.
68. Clark to Stearns, Washington, 25 April, 16 May 1928.
69. Stearns to Clark, Andover, 4 May 1928.
70. Clark to Stearns, Washington, 17 May 1928.
71. P. S. Page to Harvard Coop, Andover, 11 April 1928.
72. Dugan to Cochran, New Haven, 11 May 1928.
73. Rines to Executive Committee, n.p., 2 May 1928.
74. Stearns to parents, Andover, 12 May 1928.
75. Stearns to Ford, Andover, 7 May 1928.
76. Stearns to Fred Walcott, Andover, 10 February 1928.
77. Eaton to Stearns, Sheffield, Massachusetts, 11 December 1927.
78. For a description of the start of the Sesquicentennial, see the *Phillips Bulletin* (October 1928), 10–11.
79. Stearns to Angell, Andover, 8 May 1928.
80. These speeches are all printed in the *Phillips Bulletin* (October 1928), 32–52.
81. Eaton's poem is ibid., 54–58.
82. This account was written by Donald B. Willard, but the clipping in one of the Sesquicentennial scrapbooks is otherwise unidentified.
83. This was Philip K. Allen, presently a Trustee of the Academy, who was representing Samuel Phillips.
84. According to another account, the coach also contained George W. Hinman, impersonating Eliphalet Pearson, while the boys were his first fifteen pupils.

85. Other accounts mention a float bearing a replica of the old carpenter shop in which the Phillips School was started in 1778, drawn by forty Boy Scouts; and a one hoss shay carrying Francis K. Murray and William B. Jacob of the Faculty, impersonating George Washington and Josiah Quincy. Behind rode Scott H. Paradise as Lafayette.

86. This account of Coolidge's arrival in Andover is taken from Fuess, *Independent Schoolmaster*, 161–162, and from the same author's taped interview with Frank W. Rounds, Jr., '34, a part of the Columbia University Oral History Project, 70–71.

87. The order of the procession is given in an undated memorandum in the Stearns correspondence.

88. Fuess, *Independent Schoolmaster*, 162–163.

89. Frank Stearns to Stearns, Washington, 21 May 1928.

90. The full text of the Coolidge address is printed in the *Phillips Bulletin* (October 1928), 27–32.

91. Frank Stearns to Stearns, Washington, 21 May 1928.

92. The *Phillips Bulletin* (October 1928), 15–16.

93. The speeches are all printed ibid., 59–89.

94. Fuess, *Independent Schoolmaster*, 164.

95. Trustee Records, III, 133–134.

96. Frank Stearns to Stearns, Washington, 21 May 1928.

97. J. E. Owsley to Lester E. Lynde, New Haven, 28 May 1928.

98. Davis to Stearns, Washington, 28 May 1928.

99. Interview with A. Graham Baldwin, 29 July 1975.

1. Dr. J. Dellinger Barney published an article about his operation on Al. See "Hemorrhagic Cyst of the Kidney," *Journal of Urology* (December 1936), 603–606. I am indebted to Marjorie Stearns for making this article available to me.

2. Stearns to Sawyer, Phillips House, Boston, 17 November 1931.

3. Barney, *Journal of Urology*, 606.

4. Sawyer to Stearns, Andover, 27 January 1932.

5. Stearns to Sawyer, Danvers, 4 February 1932.

6. Stearns to Sawyer, Danvers, 11 and 15 March 1932.

7. Ernest M. Hopkins to James H. Ropes, Hanover, 22 January 1932.

8. Ropes to Hopkins, Cambridge, 14 June 1932.

9. Interview with Roscoe E. Dake, 30 July 1975.

10. Interview with Marjorie Stearns, 14 October 1975.

11. Ropes to Hopkins, Cambridge, 16 July 1932.

12. Ibid. Al's friend Jim Sawyer attempted to raise funds to supplement the pension, but his attempt came in the depth of the Depression and many of the pledges could not be met. See a thick file of letters in the Sawyer Papers on what he called the "Alfred E. Stearns Club."

13. Hopkins to Ropes, Manset, Maine, 22 July 1932.

14. Ropes to Hopkins, Cotuit, Massachusetts, 13 and 15 August 1932.

15. Hopkins to Ropes, Manset, 3 August 1932.

16. Stearns to Ropes, Danvers, 27 July 1932.

17. Ropes to Hopkins, Cotuit, 13 August 1932.

18. Hopkins to Ropes, Manset, Maine, 17 August 1932.

19. Ropes to Hopkins, Cambridge, 14 June 1932; Hopkins to Ropes, Hanover, 8 June 1932, 5 October 1932.

20. Ropes to Hopkins, Cambridge, 6 October 1932.

21. The Stearns letter of resignation is in the minutes of the Trustee Meeting, 15

January 1933. It was also printed in the *Phillips Bulletin* (April 1933), 7.
22. Minutes of Trustee Meeting, 15 January 1933, Trustee Records, III, 345–346.

15. The Fuess Administration

1. Fuess, *Independent Schoolmaster*, 166–167.
2. Ibid., 170.
3. This list is in the Trustee Papers in the Archives. It is covered by a letter from Elias Bishop to James C. Sawyer, Newton Center, 15 April 1933.
4. James Sawyer to Elias Bishop, Andover, 29 May 1933.
5. The following account of Fuess's early career is based on *Independent Schoolmaster*, 3–117, and my own memoir of him in the *Proceedings of the Massachusetts Historical Society*, 76 (1964), 137–153.
6. Fuess, *Independent Schoolmaster*, 8–9.
7. Ibid., 32.
8. John U. Monro, in *In My Time: A Medley of Andover Reminiscences*, ed. Claude M. Fuess (Andover, 1959), 74.
9. Allis, *Proceedings of the Massachusetts Historical Society*, 76, 141–142.
10. The phrase is Alan R. Blackmer's, quoted in Robert Winer's paper, for my seminar, entitled "Andover in the 1940's: A Holding Operation."
11. Fuess, *Independent Schoolmaster*, 93.
12. Fuess to Bishop, Andover, 2 May 1933.
13. Fuess, *Independent Schoolmaster*, 173.
14. Minutes of Faculty Meeting, 23 March 1933.
15. Ibid., 9 May 1933.
16. For a good article see Lester E. Lynde, "The New Curriculum," the *Phillips Bulletin* (July 1933), 6–10.
17. Trustee Records, III, 317.
18. Ibid., 330.
19. Ibid., 337.
20. Ibid., 354.
21. See the relevant printed Treasurer's Reports for this period.
22. See the relevant School Catalogues for this period.
23. Trustee Records, III, 367.
24. Claude M. Fuess, "Peirson Sterling Page," the *Phillips Bulletin* (July 1939), 12.
25. J. Roswell Gallagher, "Can't Spell, Can't Read," *Atlantic Monthly* (June 1948), 35–39.
26. J. Roswell Gallagher, "There is No Average Boy," *Atlantic Monthly* (June 1949), 42–45.
27. On this program see Claude M. Fuess, "Andover's New Adolescent Study Project," the *Phillips Bulletin* (January 1941), 3–4; and J. Roswell Gallagher, "Physical Fitness," ibid., (January 1944), 1–6.
28. The material on the Andover Evening Study Program has been taken from Alan R. Blackmer, Jr.'s study of the subject made in 1963.
29. Lansing Reed, "History of the Teachers' Fund Campaign," the *Phillips Bulletin* (July 1937), 22–24.
30. See, for example, Trustee Records, IV, 71, in which a retirement allowance of $9 a week was voted to a retiring janitress. See also ibid., 199. For Dr. Fuess's campaign against the extension of Social Security, see a folder of about thirty letters from him to various officials offering to testify against the bill and generally opposing the whole idea. In the Fuess correspondence.

31. See Fuess, *Independent Schoolmaster*, chapter XV, for a detailed account Henry Stimson's relations with Andover.
32. Mr. Stimson's speech is printed in the *Phillips Bulletin* (July 1940), 3–4.
33. See Elting E. Morison, *Turmoil and Tradition* (Boston, Houghton, Mifflin, 1960), 481–482.
34. Fuess, *Independent Schoolmaster*, 249.
35. Robert Winer, '75, "Andover in the 1940's: A Holding Operation," a paper written for my seminar. This paper has been extremely useful in dealing with this decade.
36. Fuess, *Independent Schoolmaster*, 251.
37. Quoted in Winer, "Andover in the 1940's," 12.
38. See the *Phillips Bulletin* (January 1943), 5.
39. The *Phillipian*, 30 September 1942.
40. For an account of the first Summer Session, see Frederick S. Allis, Jr., "The First Andover Summer Session," the *Phillips Bulletin* (October 1942), 3–10.
41. For a good summary of the School's wartime activities in the early years, see Claude M. Fuess, "Andover at War," *Atlantic Monthly* (May 1942), 579–582.
42. Fuess, *Independent Schoolmaster*, 260–261.
43. Leonard F. James, *Phillips Academy in World War II* (Andover, 1948).
44. See an exchange of correspondence in 1942 between Dr. Fuess and various public officials, including Colonel Stimson, in the Fuess correspondence.
45. Harper Follansbee as quoted in Winer, "Andover in the 1940's," 16–17.
46. Fuess to Willet L. Eccles, Headmaster of St. George's, Andover, 13 February 1946.
47. See the Treasurer's printed reports for these years.
48. William T. Kelley, Jr. to the author, 11 October 1976.
49. See the *Phillips Bulletin* (Winter 1946), 17.
50. There is a copy of this constitution in the Archives.
51. For the drive see the *Phillips Bulletin* (Autumn 1947), "The Andover Fund," 5–6; (Spring 1948), "Andover Fund Progress Report," 14; (Summer 1949), "Alumni Luncheon," 14.
52. See "Andover: A Study in Independence," *Fortune* (May 1944), 167–168, 226–236; and Henry F. and Katharine Pringle, "America's Oldest Private School," *Saturday Evening Post* (27 September 1947), 32, 100–107.
53. I regret that I was responsible for spoiling Dick's straight-honor record.
54. I wish to express my appreciation to Dick Richardson for letting me use his splendid run of Andover letters.
55. For Roger Kiley and the Fitzpatrick story, see James D. Johnson, '72, "Fun and Games on Andover Hill," a paper done in my seminar and later printed. See also Tom Lawrence in the *Phillipian*, 11 March 1954. The leading authority is, of course, Mrs. N. Penrose Hallowell, Jr.
56. Johnson, *Fun and Games* (no page numbers in this printed pamphlet).
57. Tom Lawrence in the *Phillipian*, 11 March 1954.
58. Emory S. Basford, "I Arrive at Andover," in *In My Time*, ed. Fuess, 68.
59. Quoted in Winer, "Andover in the 1940's," 29.
60. Quoted ibid., 31.
61. The material in this paragraph is, for the most part, taken from my memoir of Dr. Fuess, *Proceedings of the Massachusetts Historical Society*, Vol. 76, p. 144.
62. See ibid., 146–151.
63. See Horace Poynter, "A Letter to Jack Fuess," the *Phillips Bulletin* (Summer 1948), 1–4.

16. The Secret Societies

1. In the text pages that follow are sketches of four of the eight Societies. To cover all eight would be repetitious, quite apart from the work of researching them. The four selected—K.O.A., A.U.V., A.G.C., and E.D.P.—were chosen because studies of them had already been made.
2. See Bancroft's Report to the Trustees, 1877.
3. These rules make up part of the Faculty Meeting Minutes, 16 October 1896. Apparently S.A.O. never got off the ground.
4. Claude M. Fuess, "Early Records of K.O.A." (privately printed, 1924). The material that follows is taken from this work.
5. For the material on A.U.V. I am indebted to Daniel Miner, '73, who wrote a paper for my seminar entitled "The History of the A.U.V. Society."
6. For the material on A.G.C. I have relied on a study entitled "A.G.C. The Brightest Years," by my colleague H. Schuyler Royce.
7. Hobson interview with Royce, 8 June 1974. See Royce, "A.G.C.," 25.
8. Memorandum of William Kirkland, '15, undated but sometime in 1974. See Royce, "A.G.C.," 26, 50–51.
9. These passages are taken from the "Key Book of Tradition," an undated mimeographed pamphlet in the Phillips Academy Archives.
10. Hobson interview, Royce, "A.G.C.," 33–34.
11. For the material on E.D.P. I have depended on a paper written by a student in my seminar, Randy Gross, '72, entitled "Eta Delta Phi: a Fraternity."
12. Dr. James H. Grew. See ibid., 12.
13. Ibid., 17–18.
14. Kemper to Southard Hay, Andover, 29 September 1949.
15. E.D.P. See Gross, "Eta Delta Phi," 16.
16. This story was told to me by Dr. Darling.
17. "The Reminiscences of Claude M. Fuess," a Columbia University Oral History Research Project, 1962, 97–99. Frank W. Rounds, Jr., interviewed Dr. Fuess for this Project. Hereafter it will be cited as Fuess, "Oral History."
18. On this point see the statement of Henry W. Hobson to a group that met to consider the Society problem on 10 June 1949, printed on page 7 of the Proceedings of that meeting.
19. Fuess, "Oral History," 94.
20. These passages are printed in the Report of the Society Alumni Committee of Inquiry, undated but clearly in the latter part of May 1943, 11–12.
21. Fuess, "Oral History," 99–100.
22. Trustee Records, IV, 248.
23. See statement on both Trustee and Faculty votes sent out by the School and dated 16 May 1943. The statement was signed by Dr. Fuess.
24. There is a copy of this appeal in the Phillips Academy Archives.
25. This exchange is printed in the Report of the Society Alumni's Committee of Inquiry, 3–4.
26. This letter is in the Phillips Academy Archives.
27. Dr. Fuess's statement is printed in the Report of the Society Alumni Committee of Inquiry, 14–20.
28. The Gardner statement is in an undated mimeographed collection of excerpts of letters: "Shall There Be Societies at Andover?", 1–2.
29. Fuess, "Oral History," 104–106.
30. Report of the Society Alumni Committee of Inquiry, 14.
31. Henry L. Stimson to Fuess, Washington, 31 May 1943.
32. See, for example, *Newsweek* (9 August 1943), 64.

33. Fuess, "Oral History," 102–103.
34. Ibid., 106–107.
35. Ibid., 107–108.
36. For a good account of how these discussions went, see the Minutes of the Meeting, 24 July 1943. The Society alumni also insisted that the School document its case against the Societies by providing statistical material to support its general statements. See a letter from James Gould, School Treasurer, to Morris Tyler, '20, Andover, 21 June 1943, in which Gould attempts to answer eighteen specific questions.
37. The School did not return to the old system. Instead all pledges were to be sent through the mails. This ensured much more privacy than had obtained when all pledging was done openly in the Commons.
38. For a full development of these points, see the Report of the Alumni Committee on Andover Societies, 7 October 1943.
39. See the undated report of the Committee of Faculty Guardians. It must have been written sometime in the spring of 1944.
40. See Report of the Annual Meeting of the Rogers Associates, Inc. (the A.G.C. Corporation), 6 June 1947.
41. This telegram is in the Phillips Academy Archives.
42. For the Kemper position see "The Headmaster's Views," an introductory statement to the Report on the Proceedings of the Meetings, 10 and 11 June 1943, 3.
43. Fuess, "Oral History," 109.
44. "The Headmaster's Views," 3–4.
45. Proceedings of the Meeting, 10 June 1949, 5–9.
46. Ibid., 11 June 1949, 9–11.
47. The assessed value of the Society houses, including P.L.S., which closed in 1940, was about $107,000. The insured value was $285,317. See financial statement dated 20 October 1949.
48. This letter is in the Phillips Academy Archives.

17. The Kemper Administration

1. For material on John Kemper's election as Headmaster, see James Phinney Baxter, III, "John Mason Kemper: The First Decade," the *Andover Bulletin* (February 1958), 1–2.
2. Henry W. Hobson, the *Andover Bulletin* (February 1972), 8.
3. On John Kemper's background see the taped interview with him conducted by Frank Rounds, '34, as part of the Columbia Oral History Research Project, referred to below as "Oral History." Unfortunately, it covers his career only through West Point.
4. Ibid., 8–10.
5. There is a convenient chronology of John Kemper's life in the *Andover Bulletin* (February 1972), 1–6. Grandmother Mason, who had presided at the birth, went in to check the baby shortly thereafter. She thought he looked very pale, pulled back the covers, and found that the knot on the umbilical cord had loosened and he was literally bleeding to death. It was a close call for everyone and particularly Phillips Academy. Kemper, "Oral History," 29.
6. For an account of the winning of the appointment, see "Oral History," 53–64.
7. For an account of the West Point years, see ibid., 64–113.
8. For his career from West Point to his appointment as Headmaster, see the chronology in the *Andover Bulletin* (February 1972), 1.

9. The material on the past few pages has come mostly from the recollections of the writer. There is a full account of the Inauguration ceremonies in the *Phillips Bulletin* (Autumn 1948), 3–20.
10. "Five Year Report" (November 1953), 1.
11. John M. Kemper, "Phillips Academy at Andover: A National Public School" (The Newcomen Society in North America, 1958), 23.
12. "Five Year Report," 1.
13. "Five Year Report," 7. Almost all the material in the preceding pages has been taken from this report. The remainder is from the recollections of the writer.
14. There is, unfortunately, no piece on Alan Blackmer worthy of the subject. There is an appreciation by John M. Kemper, on the occasion of Al's retirement, in the *Andover Bulletin* (August 1968), 6.
15. Interim Report of the Curriculum Committee to the Faculty, May 1950.
16. Report of the Curriculum Committee to the Alumni Committee and to the Faculty, 10 November 1950.
17. Quoted in *General Education in School and College: A Committee Report by Members of the Faculties of Andover, Exeter, Lawrenceville, Harvard, Princeton and Yale* (Cambridge, 1952), 24.
18. Ibid., 1–2.
19. Ibid., 13.
20. Ibid., 16.
21. Ibid., 10.
22. Ibid., 71.
23. For the early history of the Kenyon plan, see David A. Dudley, "The Beginnings of the Advanced Placement Program," 10–12.
24. Ibid., 13–25.
25. For the effects on the Advanced Placement program at Phillips Academy, see Susan Lambiris, "Events in the Rise of the Modern Curriculum at Phillips Academy, Andover," 51–61. This outstanding paper was written for my seminar in the history of Phillips Academy.
26. The following account of Hahn in general and Gordonstoun in particular is based on Joshua L. Miner, "My Most Unforgettable Character," *Readers Digest* (December 1975), 127–131.
27. The story of the introduction of Outward Bound concepts at Andover is based on an interview with Joshua L. Miner in July 1977.
28. See undated memorandum from John Kemper to the Trustees. There is also a copy of the agreement between Phillips Academy and the Instituto de Estudios Nordeamericanos dated 23 January 1964, together with other relevant material, in the same file.
29. See *Barcelona Bulletin*, 1, No. 2 (December 1964), 1–3.
30. For the itinerary of the spring trip, see ibid., 1, No. 5 (April 1965), 1.
31. The Harris-Thomas report, 30 April 1965, is in the Kemper Papers.
32. This undated evaluation, clearly made in the spring of 1965, is in the Kemper Papers.
33. Edmund E. Hammond to Richard Pieters, Barcelona, 11 November 1964.
34. Alston H. Chase, "What is Andover?," a paper delivered 23 November 1948.
35. "Quotations from Chairman Leonard," copyright 1969, by the students of Chairman Leonard.
36. David R. Slavitt, "A Master's Essay," an unpublished study of Fitts.
37. *Teacher in America* (Boston, Little, Brown, 1945), 55.
38. This is not quite correct. The School received the auto as part of the estate of Edward Houghton, '89. Though John Kemper drove it around the campus for a while, he never abandoned his original simplicity in taste when it

came to automobiles.

39. This is the poem about "the little lame balloonman" who "whistled far and   wee." (Spacing by cummings).

40. On the new gymnasium, see Edward J. Shea, "The War Memorial Gymnasium," in the *Phillips Bulletin* (Spring 1950), 1–5. Also ibid. (November 1952), 3–5.

41. On the progress of the Sumner Smith Hockey Rink, see the *Phillipian*, 8 May, 21 September, 29 November 1950; 14 February 1951.

42. On these changes, see the Revised Constitution, 28 May 1956; and a letter from David A. Dudley to the Andover Alumni Council, Marblehead, Massachusetts, 28 May 1956.

43. Quoted in the *Andover Bulletin* (Spring, 1959), 1.

44. Donald H. McLean, Jr., "The Story of the Campaign," supplement to the *Andover Bulletin* (Winter 1961), 4.

45. Ibid., 4.

46. "The Andover Program: What It Is," the *Andover Bulletin* (Spring, 1959), 2.

47. Ibid., 3.

48. This account of the campaign has been taken from McLean, "The Story of the Campaign," 4–10.

49. The final figures are in the *Andover Bulletin* (Spring, 1962), 8.

50. There is a box score on the progress of construction, together with some pictures, in the *Andover Bulletin* (Winter, 1962), 1–3.

51. For this article, see TIME (26 October 1962), 76–82.

18. Mid-Century Developments

1. Oliver Jensen, "Polling Alumni Opinion," the *Phillips Bulletin* (February 1956), 10.

2. On the explosion in the Arts generally, see Betsy Gootrad, '74, "Arts at Andover," a paper written for my seminar in Phillips Academy history.

3. See above, 378–380.

4. For the shows mounted by Charlie Sawyer, see the Reports of the Director and the individual catalogues in the files of the Addison Gallery.

5. Charles H. Sawyer, "Addison Gallery," the *Phillips Bulletin* (January 1931), 38.

6. On Bart Hayes's work, see Bartlett H. Hayes, Jr., "A Quarter of a Century for the Addison Gallery of American Art," ibid. (November, 1956), 15–17. Also the same author's "The Addison Gallery at Andover," ibid. (Spring 1945), 3–7. Also the Reports of the Director and the catalogues of various shows in the files of the Addison Gallery.

7. For Chris Cook's work, see Helen Eccles, "The Addison Gallery—Nothing Is Static except the Walls," the *Andover Bulletin* (December 1973), 3–7.

8. See Patrick Morgan, "Art in the Curriculum," *Phillips Bulletin* (Spring 1948), 5.

9. See Gordon G. Bensley, "Sight, Sound and Teaching," and "Art for the Man of Action," ibid. (April 1955), 1–4; (Winter 1960), 1–4.

10. These curricular changes can be followed in the School Catalogues for the 1960's.

11. The activities of the various dramatic clubs can be followed in issues of *Pot Pourri*, the School yearbook.

12. For the later production of *Many Happy Returns*, see the *Phillips Bulletin* (February 1955), 3–5.

13. N. P. Hallowell, Jr., "Dramatic Angles," ibid. (April 1952), 3–5.

14. The *Phillipian*, 6 October 1955.

15. See J. P. Christy, "Sixteen Years of P.A. Drama: The Phillips Academy Drama Workshop," 1–3. This paper was written for the seminar in the history of Phillips Academy.
16. Ibid., 3–9. See also Gootrad, "Arts at Andover," 34–38.
17. See Carl F. Pfatteicher, "Twenty-Five Years of Music at Phillips Academy," the *Phillips Bulletin* (April 1937), 15–18.
18. For music during the post-Pfatteicher period, see Harold H. Owen, Jr., "A Theme Developed," the *Andover Bulletin* (Spring 1959), 13–15.
19. See above 476–478.
20. R. I. W. Westgate, "The Second Andover Summer Session," the *Phillips Bulletin* (October 1943), 7–11.
21. "1945 Summer Session," ibid., 17–18.
22. Floyd T. Humphries, "The Andover Summer Session," an article prepared at the request of the Headmaster, now in the Phillips Academy Archives, dated 25 January 1949.
23. For changes in the Summer Session from 1960 on, see an admirable article "A Midsummer's Dream," by Harold H. Owen, Jr., and Frederick A. Peterson, the *Andover Bulletin* (October 1964), 3–7.
24. Douglas S. Byers, "The Peabody Foundation for Archaeology," the *Andover Bulletin* (Summer 1960), 11. Unless otherwise noted, the material for this section has been taken from this article; from Richard MacNeish, "Peabody's Past," *Archaeologica*, '70, 1 (published by the Peabody Foundation); from Daniel Wofsey, '70, "The R. S. Peabody Foundation: Its Founding, Development, and Early Work," a paper written for my seminar in the history of Phillips Academy; and from conversations with Douglas Byers and Richard MacNeish.
25. Trustee Records, II, 120.
26. I believe that this nickname, like so many others on Andover Hill, was the brainchild of Kilbrith J. (Count) Barrows.
27. Warren K. Moorehead to Charles Peabody, Andover, 15 June 1905.
28. Byers, "The Peabody Foundation," 12.
29. MacNeish, "Peabody's Past," 7.
30. C. M. Fuess to Miss Grace Swett, Headmistress of North Shore Country Day School, Beverly, Massachusetts, Andover, 25 April 1935. Miss Swett had written him on 22 April that Dean Lynde was not accepting any more "Hebrew" applications.
31. C. M. Fuess to Frederic B. Malim, Headmaster of Wellington (England), Andover, 8 April 1936.
32. Ibid., 1 May 1936.
33. C. M. Fuess to Winslow Ames, Andover, 21 January 1945.
34. J. R. Adriance, "On Getting Into Andover," the *Phillips Bulletin* (Winter 1948), 4–7.
35. For accounts of Admission policies under Bob Sides, see Donald H. McLean, Jr., "Admission to Andover," ibid. (November 1957), 2–7; and Robert W. Sides, "P. A. Admissions: Facts and Counsel," the *Andover Bulletin* (Summer 1959), 18–19.
36. On the program in the early 1950's, see F. S. Allis, Jr., "The Andover Scholarship Program," the *Phillips Bulletin* (April 1954), 1–5.
37. The material in the preceding paragraphs is based on the recollections of the writer.
38. The writer is indebted to Charles Dey, Head of Choate-Rosemary Hall, and to Joshua Miner, Andover's Director of Admissions, for materials on the early days of ABC.

39. These figures are taken from "Black Students at Phillips Academy," a study made by Frederick A. Peterson, then Director of the Office of Research and Evaluation.

40. Quoted in Helen Eccles, "The ABC Program," the *Andover Bulletin* (March 1974), 2. This article is an excellent summary of the program after ten years.

41. See the *Phillipian*, 24 February 1971.

42. D. Suisman, "Andover in American Society: A Sociological Study of Phillips Academy, 1920–1972," 48.

43. The colleges that Andover graduates went to are printed each year in the School Catalogue.

44. G. G. Benedict, "Gone is the Edwardian Era," the *Phillips Bulletin* (November 1953), 1–4.

45. G. G. Benedict, "Andover Graduates: To What Colleges—and Why," ibid. (July 1957), 1–2.

46. These figures may be found in the two Benedict articles cited above and in his "College-Going Patterns of Andover Boys," the *Andover Bulletin* (October 1965), 9–14.

47. See 92.

48. See 93.

49. See 108.

50. See 160.

51. See 213.

52. See 299–300.

53. See especially the following letters from Perkins to Bancroft, all from Exeter: 21 November 1877; 10 December 1877; 10 September 1878; 19 December 1878; 29 December 1881; 31 January 1882; 8 May 1882; 16 April 1883; 13 May 1885. These letters are in the Bancroft Papers, Phillips Academy Archives.

54. See Amen to Bancroft, all from Exeter: 8 October 1896; 12 October 1896; 11 November 1896; and 13 November 1896. These letters are also in the Bancroft Papers and all refer to the problems of Andover-Exeter athletic contests.

55. A detailed treatment of the early years of Andover-Exeter athletic competition will be seen in a forthcoming volume on Andover athletics by my colleague Fred H. Harrison.

56. I am indebted to my friend William G. Saltonstall, Principal Emeritus of the Phillips Exeter Academy, for this information on the Stearns-Perry relationship. He has just completed a biography of Lewis Perry, which should be published in the near future.

57. See 562–563.

58. See 561–562.

59. Myron R. Williams, *The Story of Phillips Exeter*, 113.

19. Revolution

1. "A Report on the Steering Committee," the *Andover Bulletin* (August 1967), 8.

2. Quoted in Douglas Billman, '72, "The Steering Committee: A Look Back at a Look Forward," a paper written for the seminar in the history of Phillips Academy, 1.

3. Ibid., 2.

4. "A Report on the Steering Committee," 9.

5. Billman, "The Steering Committee," 4–5.

6. Ibid., 5.
7. "A Report on the Steering Committee," 8–9.
8. Ibid., 10–11.
9. Billman, "The Steering Committee," 10–13.
10. "A Report on the Steering Committee," 11–12.
11. Billman, "The Steering Committee," 13–19.
12. John M. Kemper, "A Sense of Direction," the *Andover Bulletin* (July 1956), 2.
13. Billman, "The Steering Committee," 20–30.
14. See above, 626–628.
15. Quoted in Alan R. Blackmer, "An Inquiry into Student Unrest in Independent Secondary Schools," prepared for the National Association of Independent Schools (1970), 8.
16. Ibid., 9.
17. Ibid., 11.
18. Ibid., 12–16.
19. Ibid., 16.
20. Ibid., 23–51.
21. The *Phillipian*, 19 October 1960.
22. There is a picture of the protesters in the *Phillipian*, 10 May 1967.
23. See the *Phillipian*, 29 May 1968.
24. For two thoughtful articles on the conference, see William R. Torbert, "The Student Voice in School Affairs," and Mark A. Larner, '69, "Conference: The Forms of Communication," the *Andover Bulletin* (November 1968), 3–4, 5–6.
25. See the *Phillipian*, 3 June 1970, 23 September 1970.
26. Claude M. Fuess, *Independent Schoolmaster* (Boston, 1952), 171–172.
27. See the *Phillipian*, 15 January 1969.
28. J. R. Whyte, "One Year after Required Chapel," the *Andover Bulletin* (May 1972), 2.
29. For a clear, unemotional account of the Cambodian crisis at Phillips Academy see John H. Fenton, "The Restless Days in May," the *Andover Bulletin* (August 1970), 10–11.
30. See "Special Bullein No. 2," 7 May 1970, Kemper Papers.
31. See mimeographed sheet with results of this poll in the Kemper Papers.
32. See the *Phillipian*, 13 May 1970, for these plans.
33. The *Phillipian*, 19 May 1971.
34. Ibid., 11 June 1971.
35. *Pot Pourri* (1971), 40.
36. The *Phillipian*, 3 February 1971.
37. Hyde Memo to Faculty, 24 January 1972.
38. Harriet W. Marr, *The Old New England Academies* (New York, Comet Press, 1959), 99–100.
39. See the Summer School Handbook (1968), 4.
40. See above, 641.
41. Unless otherwise indicated, the remainder of this account of the coming of coeducation to Phillips Academy is based on "The Case for Coeducation," the admirable summary of all the steps prepared by Dean Simeon Hyde, Jr., for the Trustees, dated 28 October 1971. Dean Hyde included Trustee actions, Faculty actions, *Bulletin* articles, *Phillipian* articles, and any other relevant material.
42. Ibid., 5.
43. Ibid., 11.
44. Hart Leavitt in the *Andover Bulletin* (Summer 1975), 3.
45. The tabulation of these votes forms Appendix A in Dean Hyde's summary.

46. The tabulation of the Alumni votes is in Appendix B in the summary.
47. For a good account of Dr. Sizer's early career and a selection of his opinions on education, see Deckle McLean, "Sizer in Transition," the *Andover Bulletin* (May 1972), 6–12. This article first appeared in the magazine section of the Boston *Globe*, 21 November 1971, under a different title.
48. New York, 1964, and New Haven, 1964.
49. T. R. Sizer, "Speculations on Andover—I" (13–14 July 1972), 2. There is a copy of this document in the files in the Headmaster's Office.
50. "Specifications for a Possible Andover–Abbot Agreement," 20 July 1972.
51. Ibid., 1–3.
52. T. R. Sizer, "Speculations on Andover—II: the Issues of Coeducation" (11 September 1972), 1–22.
53. Quoted in the *Andover Bulletin* (November 1972), 1.
54. Minutes of the Trustee Meeting, 16 September 1972, in the files in the Headmaster's Office.
55. Minutes of the Trustee Meeting, 23 September 1972, in the files in the Headmaster's Office.
56. There is a brief account of the ceremony in the *Andover Bulletin* (May 1973), 7.
57. The *Andover Bulletin* (August, 1973), cover and inside front cover.

INDEX

In making the following index, we have concentrated mainly on material dealing directly with Phillips Academy; the indexing of background material has therefore not been done so fully. We have indexed almost no towns, since they are almost always included as ways of identifying people. Even with the Phillips Academy material, we have not always indexed names that appear only once and then of persons with minor roles in the history of the Academy. In identifying members of the Andover Faculty, we have used the title of their first positions at the School. We have not indexed source material, since this subject is covered in the Bibliographical Note. Subentries are arranged in logical order, not alphabetical or page order. Three abbreviations have been used: SPJr. is Samuel Phillips, Jr.; ATS is Andover Theological Seminary; and PA is Phillips Academy.

F.S.A., Jr.
B.H.H., Jr.

part in founding ATS, 124
Murdoch, James, Professor at ATS, controversy over, 135, 136
Museum of Curiosities, under Newman, 113, 114
Music: SPJr.'s interest in, at Dummer School, 20; in PA Constitution, 55; Pearson instructs students in, 70; Pearson's abilities in, 70; Watts's hymns and SPJr.'s enthusiasm for, 37, 70, 75; under Mark Newman, 102, 103; undergraduate activities in, under Bancroft, 298; student activities in, in *1920's*, 430; concert programs, 433; influence of Pfatteicher, 430, 605–608

Negroes: Salem Poor at Bunker Hill, xxxi; Parson Phillips' slaves, 9; Squire Phillips and the Negress Flora, 11, 12; Harvard servants, 25; Pearson-Parsons debate on slavery, 66; SPJr.'s politeness to, 107; interest in slavery issue at ATS, 137–139; Antislavery Rebellion at PA, 184, 185. *See also* Blacks
Newburyport, Mass.: proposed theological seminary at, 123, 124; merger with ATS, 125
Newman, Mark, third Principal of PA: character of, 98, 100; succeeds Pemberton, 96; Trustee supervision of, 97; resignation, *1809*, 115
Norris, John: supports Newburyport seminary, 124; donation to ATS, 127

Olivier, Daniel, Instructor in French, Assistant in School Year Abroad, 559
Olmsted, Frederick L., Landscape Architect, sites new cottages in *1890's*, 283
Oriental students: under Bancroft, 287, 288; under Stearns, 345–348
Outward Bound Program: initiated at PA, 556, 557; development in U.S., 557–559
Owen, Harold H., Jr., Instructor in English: Chairman of Committee on Performing Arts, 605; co-teacher of "Perception and Expression" course, 647

Page, Peirson S., Director of Athletics and School Doctor: appointed *1902*,

466; medical techniques, 466; helps with fund-raising for swimming pool, 362; description of, 391
Palmer, Reverend Ray F., participates in Centennial celebration, 260
Paradise, Scott H., Instructor in English: historian of PA, 481; as Alumni Secretary, 481
Park, Edwards A., Professor at ATS: importance of, at ATS, 144, 145; prayer at Philomathean Society celebration, 253; praises Pearson at Centennial, 272
Park, Reverend William E., address on PA history at Centennial, 262
Parmalee, Charles L. ("Liz"), Instructor in French: in classroom, 421, 422; in dormitory, 424
Peabody, Charles: Honorary Director of Peabody Foundation, 354; part in construction of Peabody House, 611
Peabody, George, philanthropist, gift of Foundation for mathematics and science, 200, 201
Peabody, Robert S.: establishes Archaeology Department, 286; spells out terms of gift, 353, 354; hope for student social center unrealized, 611
Pearson, Eliphalet, first Preceptor of PA: helps with gunpowder manufacture, 32; teaches at Andover grammar school, 41; letter on schools from SPJr. to, 43–46; member of first Board of Trustees, 53; first Preceptor, 58; on committee for PA seal, 61, 63; early career, 65–68; problems as Preceptor, 69, 70; Josiah Quincy's reminiscences about, 72–76; relations with Trustees, 78, 79; establishes pattern for PA in future, 83; role in establishment of ATS, 120, 122–124; versatility of, 82
Pearson, Henry (son of Eliphalet), account of student life, 112, 113
Pemberton, Ebenezer, second Preceptor of PA: early career, 85; Robert Gardiner's recollections of, 89; lack of interest in Exhibitions, 92; resignation, 96–98
Perry, Shaw and Hepburn, architectural firm: design for Bulfinch interior, 470; Faculty houses, 470
Peterson, Frederick A., Instructor in

Library of Congress Cataloging in Publication Data

Allis, Frederick Scouller, 1913–
    Youth from every quarter.

    Includes bibliographical references and index.
    1. Phillips Academy, Andover, Mass.—History.
I. Title.
LD7501.A5A85   373.744'5   78-56168
0-87451-157-7